ATLAS
For North-East India

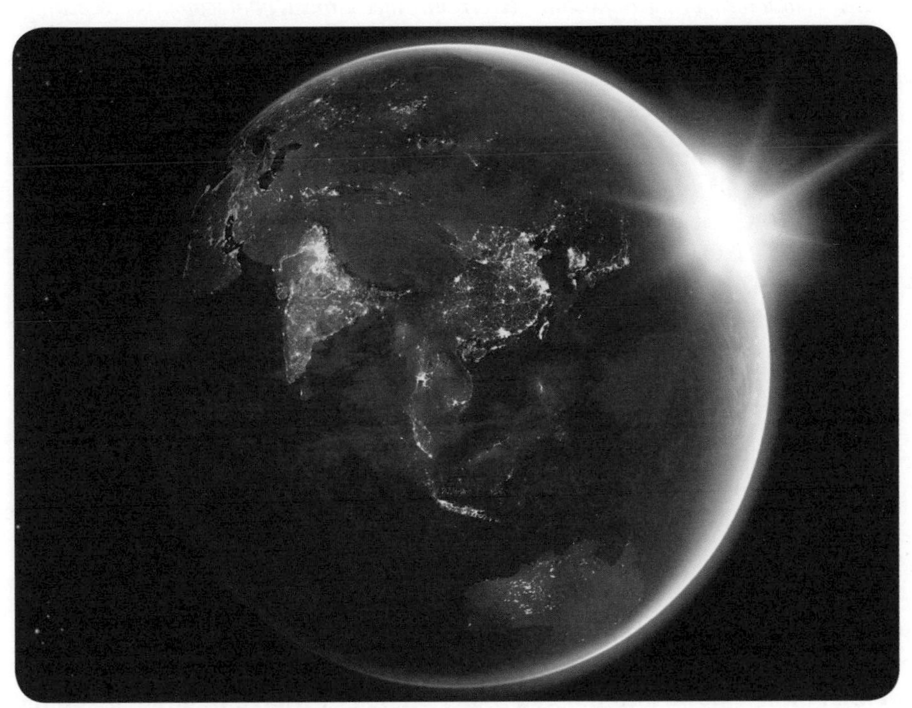

Regency Publications

A Unit of

Astral International Pvt Ltd.

New Delhi - 110002

P9-AGO-484

ISBN: 978-93-5222-145-5

Photo source: *http://districts.nic.in/*

Published & Cartographed by : **Regency Publications**
A Division of
Astral International Pvt. Ltd.
– ISO 9001:2015 Certified Company –
4736/23, Ansari Road, Darya Ganj,
New Delhi-110 002
Ph. 011-43549197, 23278134
E-mail: info@astralint.com
Website: www.astralint.com

Acknowledgment

- ***© Government of India, Copyright 2021***
- ***The responsibility for the correctness of internal details rests with the publisher.***
- ***The Territorial waters of India extend into the sea to a distance of twelve nautical miles measured from the appropriate base line.***
- ***The administrative headquarters of Chandigarh, Haryana and Punjab are at Chandigarh***
- ***The administrative headquarters of Telangana and Andhra Pradesh are at Hyderabad***
- ***The interstate boundaries amongst Arunachal Pradesh, Assam and Meghalaya shown on this map are interpreted from the "North-Eastern Areas (Reorganisation) Act. 1971," but have yet to be verified.***
- ***The external boundaries of India agree with the Record/Master copy certified by Survey of India, Dehradun vide their letter no. TB. 738/62-A-3/A dated: 11-06-2020 & TB. 218/62-A-3/A dated: 07-06-2021 & TB. 450/62-A-3/A dated: 24-11-2021***
- ***The state boundaries between Uttarakhand & Uttar Pradesh, Bihar & Jharkhand and Chattisgarh & Madhya Pradesh have not been verified by the Government concerned.***
- ***The spellings of names in this map, have been taken from various sources***

Contents

MEGHALAYA

MIZORAM

NAGALAND

SIKKIM

TRIPURA

WORLD

- The Greeks first introduced cartography by flattening the earth into a multitude of two-dimensional shapes that preserve specific traits of the earth. The study of cartography is the art and science of map making and can date back to clay tablets in 2300 B.C.

- The word cartography is derived from the Greek words "chartes", meaning sheet of papyrus, and "graphy", meaning writing. This phrase was composed in the 19th century although the Portuguese scholar Manuel Francisco de Barros e Sousa was in need of a new word that would describe maps, and in-turn, created cartography.

- By the end of the 19th century the meaning of cartography had changed to the word for map drawing. Dot maps of constellations have dated back from 12,000 B.C. where cave paintings and rock carvings used visual elements that aided in the recognition of physical features.

- Dating back to 25,000 B.C. a map-like representation of a mountain, river and routes, which are located in Pavlov, Czech Republic. Cartography is so old, in fact, that it predates written language as a form of communication.

- Modern cartography began with the advent of a variety of technological advancements. The invention of tools like the compass, telescope, the sextant, quadrant, and printing press all allowed for maps to be made more easily and accurately.

Cartography is the process of making maps by displaying a specific geographic area on a surface, usually a flat surface such as paper or a computer screen. Some common types of maps are general reference maps, nautical and aeronautical charts, and thematic maps

Cartography helps us understand our place in the world, analyze positional relationships, and reflect on geography's effect on our daily lives. It's important to note that cartography deals in representations of the world: representations shaped by the purpose of the map and intentions of the map maker.

- In the 20th century, the use of airplanes to take aerial photographs changed the types of data that could be used to create maps. Satellite imagery has since become a major source of data and is used to show large areas in great detail.

MAPS AND ATLASES

- A map is a visual representation or scale model of spatial concepts such as geographical regions, locations, and their attributes.

An atlas is a collection of various maps of the earth or a specific region of the earth,. The maps in atlases show geographic features, the topography of an area's landscape and political boundaries. They also show climatic, social, religious and economic statistics of an area.

- Maps may focus on a few selected characteristics of the region or give an overview of the region under consideration.

- They may project physical, biological, or cultural features of the region or depict correlation between several features of the region.

- Maps are made up of several components—symbols, title, legend, direction, map scale, source, and insets.

- An atlas is a compilation of maps presented in the form of a print publication or in a multimedia format.

- The purpose of an atlas is to help the user by providing additional information and analyses of maps.

- Atlases often contain social, religious, economic, and geopolitical information for a specific region.

- By definition all maps are scaled; that is, they are reduced from real-world dimensions to manageable proportions.

- Scale can be defined as the ratio of the distance between two points on the map and the same two points on the Earth's surface. Scale can be expressed as a ratio (e.g., 1:50,000), as a line or graphic with labeled distance gradations, or as a verbal statement (1 cm is equivalent to 0.5 km).

- A large-scale map is one that represents a small portion of the Earth's surface but shows a great amount of detail. Topographic maps and city street maps are examples of large-scale maps.

- Small scale maps, on the other hand, represent large portions of the Earth's surface but are not able to show much detail.

- Maps showing continents or the entire world are examples of small-scale maps. Maps showing a province or country could be considered intermediate scale maps.

The Universe

- The universe contains all of the star systems, galaxies, gas and dust, plus all the matter and energy that exists now, that existed in the past, and that will exist in the future. The universe includes all of space and time.

- Earth and the Moon are part of the universe, as are the other planets and their many dozens of moons. Along with asteroids and comets, the planets orbit the Sun.

- The Sun is one among hundreds of billions of stars in the Milky Way galaxy, and most of those stars have their own planets, known as exoplanets.

- The Milky Way is but one of billions of galaxies in the observable universe — all of them, including our own, are thought to have supermassive black holes at their centers.

- All the stars in all the galaxies and all the other stuff that astronomers can't even observe are all part of the universe. It is, simply, everything.

The Solar System

- The solar system is made up of the sun and everything that orbits around it, including planets, moons, asteroids, comets and meteoroids. It extends from the sun, called Sol by the ancient Romans, and goes past the four inner planets, through the Asteroid Belt to the four gas giants and on to the disk-shaped Kuiper Belt and far beyond to the teardrop-shaped heliopause.

- Scientists estimate that the edge of the solar system is about 9 billion miles (15 billion kilometers) from the sun. Beyond the heliopause lies the giant, spherical Oort Cloud, which is thought to surround the sol system.

- The solar system consists of the Sun and its eight ma planets, their satellites, asteroids, comets, meteors an other dwarf planets. The Sun is at the one of the tw "centers" of the Solar system and the planets revolvin around it in elliptical orbits.

Some Quick Facts about the Solar System:

- The closest planet to Sun is Mercury and the farthe is Neptune.

- Pluto is a dwarf planet – relegated from its status c the ninth planet.

- The eight planets of the solar system are Mercur Venus, Earth, Mars, Jupiter, Saturn, Uranus, Neptune.

The Sun

- The Sun is the primary source of energy for life o Earth. It is the closest star to the Earth, about 15 million kilometers from earth.

- The temperature of the Sun's visible surfac (photosphere) is about 6000 degree Celsius. Howeve the outer layer of Sun's atmosphere, known as th Corona, is, on an average, about 2 million degre Celsius. The core of the sun is the center, and is abou 15 million degree Celsius.

- The Sun is made up of 73% hydrogen and 25% helium. It also has trace amounts of oxygen, carbo iron and other elements. It is classified as a G-Typ Main Sequence Star.

- It is about 4.6 billion years old and will continue t shine for another 5 billion years. After that it will gro into a Red Giant and then finally end its life as a whit dwarf.

The Planets

There are a total eight planets in the solar system –

- The planets are divided in the two groups - Inne planets and Outer planets.

- Inner planets - Mercury, Venus, Earth, Mars. These ar also known as terrestrial planets or rocky planet These are denser and have a shorter periods o revolution.

- Outer planets - Jupiter, Saturn, Uranus, Neptune. These are also known as Gas Giants or Gaseous planets. They are big in size and have a longer periods of revolution.

- Jupiter is the biggest planet in the Solar System and Mercury is the smallest.

he Moon

- The Moon (or Luna) is the Earth's only natural satellite and was formed 4.6 billion years ago around some 30–50 million years after the formation of the solar system. The Moon is in synchronous rotation with Earth meaning the same side is always facing the Earth. The first uncrewed mission to the Moon was in 1959 by the Soviet Lunar Program with the first crewed landing being Apollo 11 in 1969.

acts about the Moon

- **The dark side of the moon is a myth:** In reality both sides of the Moon see the same amount of sunlight however only one face of the Moon is ever seen from Earth. This is because the Moon rotates around on its own axis in exactly the same time it takes to orbit the Earth, meaning the same side is always facing the Earth. The side facing away from Earth has only been seen by the human eye from spacecraft.

- **The rise and fall of the tides on Earth is caused by the Moon:** There are two bulges in the Earth due to the gravitational pull that the Moon exerts; one on the side facing the Moon, and the other on the opposite side that faces away from the Moon, The bulges move around the oceans as the Earth rotates, causing high and low tides around the globe.

- **The Moon is drifting away from the Earth:** The Moon is moving approximately 3.8 cm away from our planet every year. It is estimated that it will continue to do so for around 50 billion years. By the time that happens, the Moon will be taking around 47 days to orbit the Earth instead of the current 27.3 days.

- **A person would weigh much less on the Moon:** The Moon has much weaker gravity than Earth, due to its smaller mass, so you would weigh about one sixth (16.5%) of your weight on Earth. This is why the lunar astronauts could leap and bound so high in the air.

- **The Moon has only been walked on by 12 people; all American men:** The first man to set foot on the Moon in 1969 was Neil Armstrong on the Apollo 11 mission, while the last man to walk on the Moon in 1972 was Gene Cernan on the Apollo 17 mission. Since then the Moon has only be visited by unmanned vehicles.

- **The Moon has no atmosphere:** This means that the surface of the Moon is unprotected from cosmic rays, meteorites and solar winds, and has huge temperature variations. The lack of atmosphere means no sound can be heard on the Moon, and the sky always appears black.

- **The Moon has quakes:** These are caused by the gravitational pull of the Earth. Lunar astronauts used seismographs on their visits to the Moon, and found that small moonquakes occurred several kilometres beneath the surface, causing ruptures and cracks. Scientists think the Moon has a molten core, just like Earth.

- **The first spacecraft to reach the Moon was Luna 1 in 1959:** This was a Soviet craft, which was launched from the USSR. It passed within 5995 km of the surface of the Moon before going into orbit around the Sun.

- **The Moon is the fifth largest natural satellite in the Solar System:** At 3,475 km in diameter, the Moon is much smaller than the major moons of Jupiter and Saturn. Earth is about 80 times the volume than the Moon, but both are about the same age. A prevailing theory is that the Moon was once part of the Earth, and was formed from a chunk that broke away due to a huge object colliding with Earth when it was relatively young.

- **During the 1950's the USA considered detonating a nuclear bomb on the Moon:** The secret project was during the height cold war was known as "A Study of Lunar Research Flights" or "Project A119" and meant as a show of strength at a time they were lagging behind in the space race.

Realms of the Earth

The four realms of the earth : Lithosphere, Hydrosphere, Biosphere and Atmosphere.

- **Lithosphere:** The realm of land is called the lithosphere. The word lithosphere comes from a Greek word Lithos which means rock. It is the outer solid layer of earth which is composed of rocks and soils.

  - **The Earth structure:** The earth is made up of three different layers: the crust, the mantle and the core.

    - **The crust:** This is the outside layer of the earth and is made of solid rock, mostly basalt and granite. There are two types of crust; oceanic and continental. Oceanic crust is denser and thinner and mainly composed of basalt. Continental crust is less dense, thicker, and mainly composed of granite.

    - **Mantle:** The mantle lies below the crust and is up to 2900 km thick. It consists of hot, dense, iron and magnesium-rich solid rock. The crust and the upper part of the mantle make up the lithosphere, which is broken into plates, both large and small.

    - **The core:** The core is the centre of the ear and is made up of two parts: the liquid oute core and solid inner core. The outer cor is made of nickel, iron and molten roc Temperatures here can reach up to 50,000 C

- **Hydrosphere:** The realm of water is called th hydrosphere. This layer covers 71 per cent of th earth surface.

- **Biosphere:** The narrow zone where land, water an air meet is called the biosphere. It is the fourth real of the earth, and it supports life.

- **Atmosphere:** The atmosphere is the envelope of gase surrounding Earth that extends up to approximatel 10,000 km above Earth's surface. The bottor four layers of the atmosphere are tropospher stratosphere, mesosphere, and ionosphere.

CHINA
TIBET
NEPAL
BHUTAN
BANGLADESH
MYANMAR
AFGHANISTAN
PAKISTAN
SRI LANKA
INDIAN OCEAN
Arabian Sea
Bay of Bengal
K2(8611)
Nanga Parbat (8126)
Masherbrum (7821)
Gasherbrum (8068)
Karakoram Pass
Karakoram Range
Ladakh Range
Pir Panjal Range
Shiwalik Range
GREAT HIMALAYA
Shipiki La
Nanda Devi (7817)
Api (7132)
Kamet (7756)
Nanda Kot (6861)
Dhaulgiri (8172)
Mt. Everest (8848)
Kanchenjunga (8598)
Gauri Shankar (7145)
Nathula Pass
Bomdi-la Pass
Namcha Barwa (7756)
Mishmi Hills
Patkai Bom
Naga Hills
Assam Valley
Brahmaputra
R.Tsangpo
Mikir Hills
Khasi-Jaintia Hills
Garo Hills
Lusai Hills
Mizo Hills
Duars
Plain of the Indus
GREAT INDIAN DESERT (Thar Desert)
INDO GANGETIC PLAINS
Rohilkhand Plain
Avadh
Aravali Range
Rann of Kachchh
Kachchh Peninsula
Gulf of Kachchh
Kathiawar Peninsula
Gir Range
Diu
Gulf of Khambhat
Malwa Plateau
Bundelkhand
Baghelkhand
Hazaribagh Plateau
Vindhya Range
Satpura Range
Mahadeo Hills
Maikala Range
CHOTA NAGPUR PLATEAU
Rajmahal Hills
Garhjat Hills
Malayagiri (1187)
Ajanta Range
Satmala Hills
Kalsubai (1654)
Harishchandra Range
Balaghat Range
Bhor Ghat
Mahabaleshwar (1438)
Dandakaranya
Telangana Plateau
DECCAN
Northern Circars
Chilka Lake
Mahendragiri (1501)
EASTERN GHATS
WESTERN GHATS
Konkan
Malabar Coast
Nallamalai Hills
Velikonda Hills
Palkonda Range
Javadi Hills
Coromandel Coast
Doda Betta (2695)
Nilgiri Hills
Shevroy Hills
Cardamom Hills
Anaimalai Hills
Anaimudi (2695)
Palk Strait
Palk Bay
Adams Bridge
Gulf of Mannar
Cape Comorin
Sunderbans Delta
Mouths of the Ganga
Lakshadweep (INDIA)
Andaman & Nicobar Islands (INDIA)
Ten Degree Channel
Indus
Jhelum
Ravi
Sutlej
Yamuna
Ganga
Ghaghra
Kosi
Chambal
Luni
Betwa
Son
Sabarmati
Mahi
Narmada
Tapi
Mahanadi
Godawari
Krishna
Tungabhadra
Kaveri
REFERENCES
Heights in metres
Above 3000
1801 - 3000
1301 - 1800
901 - 1300
601 - 900
301 - 600
150 - 300
Sea Level - 150
Below Sea Level
N
S
E
W
Scale - 1:15.1 M approx.

C H I N A
PAKISTAN
NEPAL
TIBET
BHUTAN
BANGLADESH
MYANMAR
SRI LANKA
ISLAMABAD
KATHMANDU
THIMPHU
DHAKA
SRI JAYAWARDENEPURA KOTTE
JAMMU AND KASHMIR
LADAKH
HIMACHAL PRADESH
PUNJAB
HARYANA
UTTARAKHAND
DELHI
RAJASTHAN
UTTAR PRADESH
BIHAR
SIKKIM
ARUNACHAL PRADESH
ASSAM
NAGALAND
MEGHALAYA
MANIPUR
TRIPURA
MIZORAM
GUJARAT
MADHYA PRADESH
JHARKHAND
WEST BENGAL
CHHATTISGARH
ODISHA
MAHARASHTRA
TELANGANA
ANDHRA PRADESH
KARNATAKA
GOA
KERALA
TAMIL NADU
Lakshadweep (INDIA)
Andaman & Nicobar Islands (INDIA)
Arabian Sea
Bay of Bengal
INDIAN OCEAN
LEGEND
International Boundary
State Boundary
National Highway
Major Roads
Country Capital
State Capital
Other Town
N
S
E
W
Scale - 1:15.1 M approx.

Ishkuman
Yasin
Baltit
Nagir
Teru
Gupis
Gilgit
Indus
Rondu
Chilas
Astor
Skardu
Khapalu
Chung Tash
Haji Langar
Tolti
Siari
Dehra Compass
Kupwara
Bandipora
Muzaffarabad
Sonamarg
Kargil
LADAKH
Baramulla
1A
SRINAGAR
Iamayuru
Shyak
Pamzal
LEH
ISLAMABAD
Uri
Amarnath
Badgam
Pahalgam
Poonch
Pulwama
Anantnag
Abring
Rupshu
JAMMU AND KASHMIR
Padam
Kumdok
Rajouri
Kishtwar
Doda
Shar
Indus
Mirpur
Nowshera
Batot
Doda
Gian
Vaishno Devi
Akhnoor
Udhampur
Tisa
Nyoma
Killar
Udaipur
Jammu
Chumar
Demchok
Hanle
Chamba
1A
Kathua
Dalhousie
Keylang
HIMACHAL
Hansi
Dharamshala
Manali
21
Palampur
Dhankhar Gompa
20
Kullu
Dera Gopipur
Mandi
PRADESH
Hamirpur
Banjar
Namgia
PUNJAB
Una
Reckong Peo
Satluj
Bhakka
Rampur
22
Kalpa
Bilaspur
Narkanda
LEGEND
International Boundary
State Boundary
National Highway
Major Roads
Country Capital
State Capital
Other Town
SHIMLA
Solan
Kasumpti
1
UTTARAKHAND
Satluj
CHANDIGARH
N
Nahan
DEHRADUN
W
E
10
S

Scale - 1:4.3 M approx.

SHIMLA
CHANDIGARH
DEHRA DUN
UTTARAKHAND
CHINA
TIBET
NEPAL
DELHI
LUCKNOW
UTTAR PRADESH
BIHAR
JHARKHAND
Bandarpunch
Yamunotri
Gangotri
Uttarkashi
Badrinath
Joshimath
Gopeshwar
Mussoorie
Tehri
Kedarnath
Chamoli
Nanda Devi
Garbiang
Saharanpur
Narendra Ngr.
Pauri
Haridwar
Bagheshwar
Chaukhutia
Deoband
Rudrapur
Almora
Pithoragarh
Shamil
Muzaffarnagar
Corbett N.P.
Bijnor
Khatauli
Nagina
Naini Tal
Tanakpur
Baraut
Chandanpur
Kathgodam
Champawat
Haldwani
Meerut
Rudrapur
Amroha
Hapur
Baghpat
Rampur
Moradabad
Ghaziabad
Garhmukteshear
Pilibhit
Gauriphanta
Noida
Bulandshahr
Ahichhattra
Bareilly
Dudwa (National Park)
Khurja
Bisauli
Faridpur
Katarnighat
Mailari
Budaun
Aligarh
Kasganj
Miranpur Katra
Lakhimpur
Shahjahanpur
Kheri
Nanpara
Vrindavan
Hathras
Etah
Dhumri
Sitapur
Bahraich
Sravasti
Jarwa
Mathura
Sadabad
Sarai Aghat
Hardoi
Mainpuri
Biswan
Balrampur
Agra
Firozabad
Fatehgarh
Fatehpur Sikri
Shikohabad
Kishni
Kannauj
Fatehpur
Gonda
Naugarh
Maharajganj
Ramnagar
Etawah
Vidhuna
Barabanki
Khalilabad
Padrauna
Basti
Faizabad
Gorakhpur
Bhind
Auraiya
Unnao
Akbarpur
Deoria
Mihona
Sikandra
Jalaun
Kanpur
Rae Bareli
Amethi
Sultanpur
Shahganj
Ayodhya
Azamgarh
Orai
Kalpi
Hamirpur
Fatehpur
Khaga
Lalganj
Bela
Mau
Moth
Jaunpur
Ballia
Pratap Garh
Gursarai
Maudaha
Ghazipur
Buxar
Jhansi
Palhana
Banda
Prayagraj
Mau Ranipur
Mahoba
Chitrakoot
Kaushambi
Sarnath
Varanasi
Karwi
Bhadohi
Mirzapur
Chandauli
Manikpur
Kuraon
Lalitpur
Robertsganj
Gona
Bili
Dudhi
Renukoot
Satluj (Langchem Khabab)
Karnali
Naravani
Gandak
Ghaghara
Ganga
Yamuna
22
24
11
2
25
56
29
27
30
26
LEGEND
International Boundary
State Boundary
National Highway
Major Roads
Country Capital
State Capital
Other Town
N
S
E
W

Scale - 1:4.3 M approx.

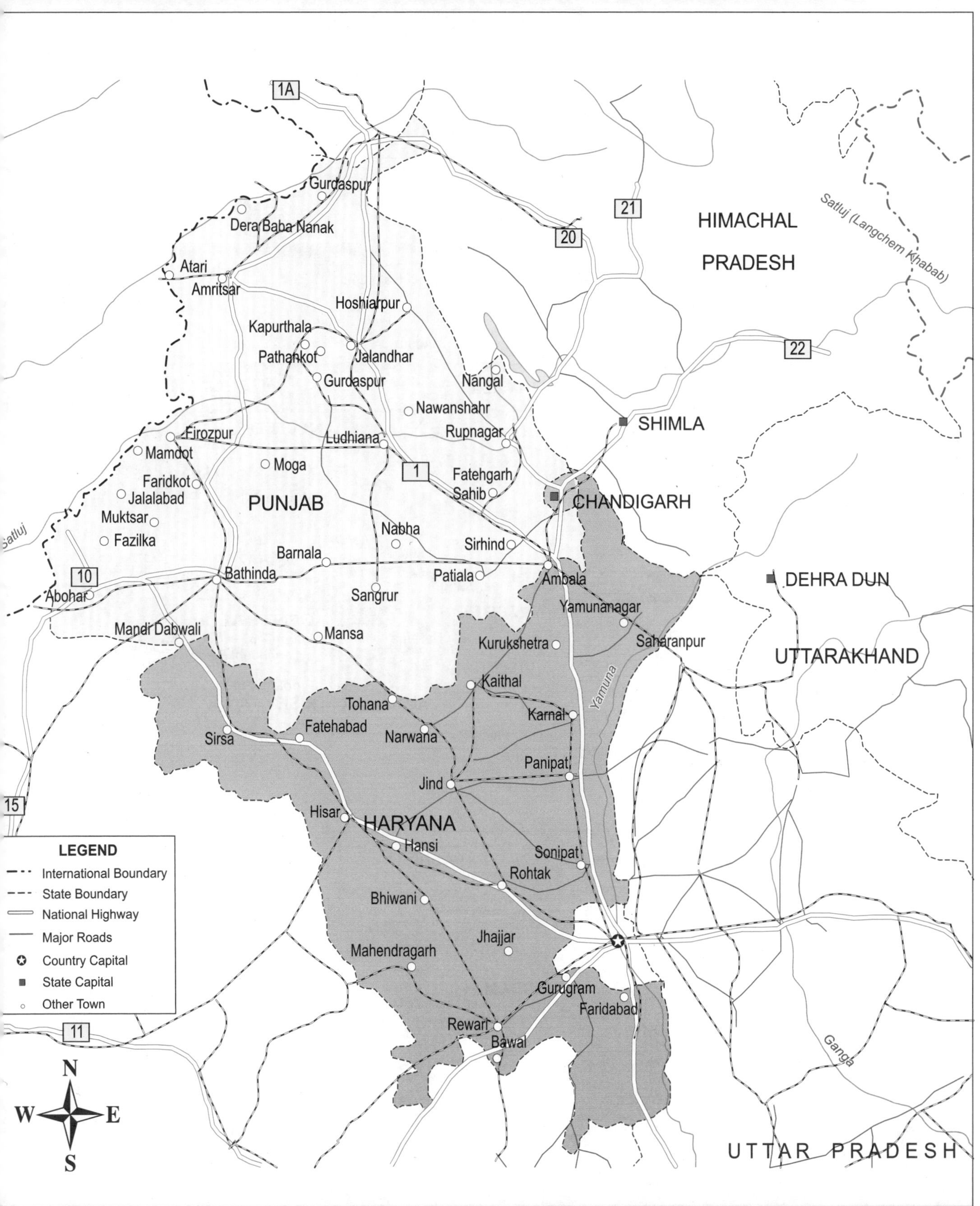

1A
Gurdaspur
Dera Baba Nanak
Atari
Amritsar
20
21
HIMACHAL
PRADESH
Satluj (Langchem Khabab)
Hoshiarpur
Kapurthala
Pathankot
Jalandhar
Gurdaspur
Nangal
22
Nawanshahr
SHIMLA
Firozpur
Ludhiana
Rupnagar
Mamdot
Moga
1
Fatehgarh
Sahib
Faridkot
Jalalabad
PUNJAB
CHANDIGARH
Muktsar
Satluj
Fazilka
Nabha
Sirhind
Barnala
10
Bathinda
Patiala
Ambala
DEHRA DUN
Abohar
Sangrur
Yamunanagar
Mandi Dabwali
Mansa
Kurukshetra
Saharanpur
UTTARAKHAND
Kaithal
Yamuna
Tohana
Karnal
Fatehabad
Sirsa
Narwana
Panipat
Jind
15
Hisar
HARYANA
Hansi
LEGEND
International Boundary
State Boundary
National Highway
Major Roads
Country Capital
State Capital
Other Town
Sonipat
Rohtak
Bhiwani
Jhajjar
Mahendragarh
Gurugram
Faridabad
11
Rewari
Bawal
Ganga
N
W
E
S
UTTAR PRADESH

Scale - 1:2.8 M approx.

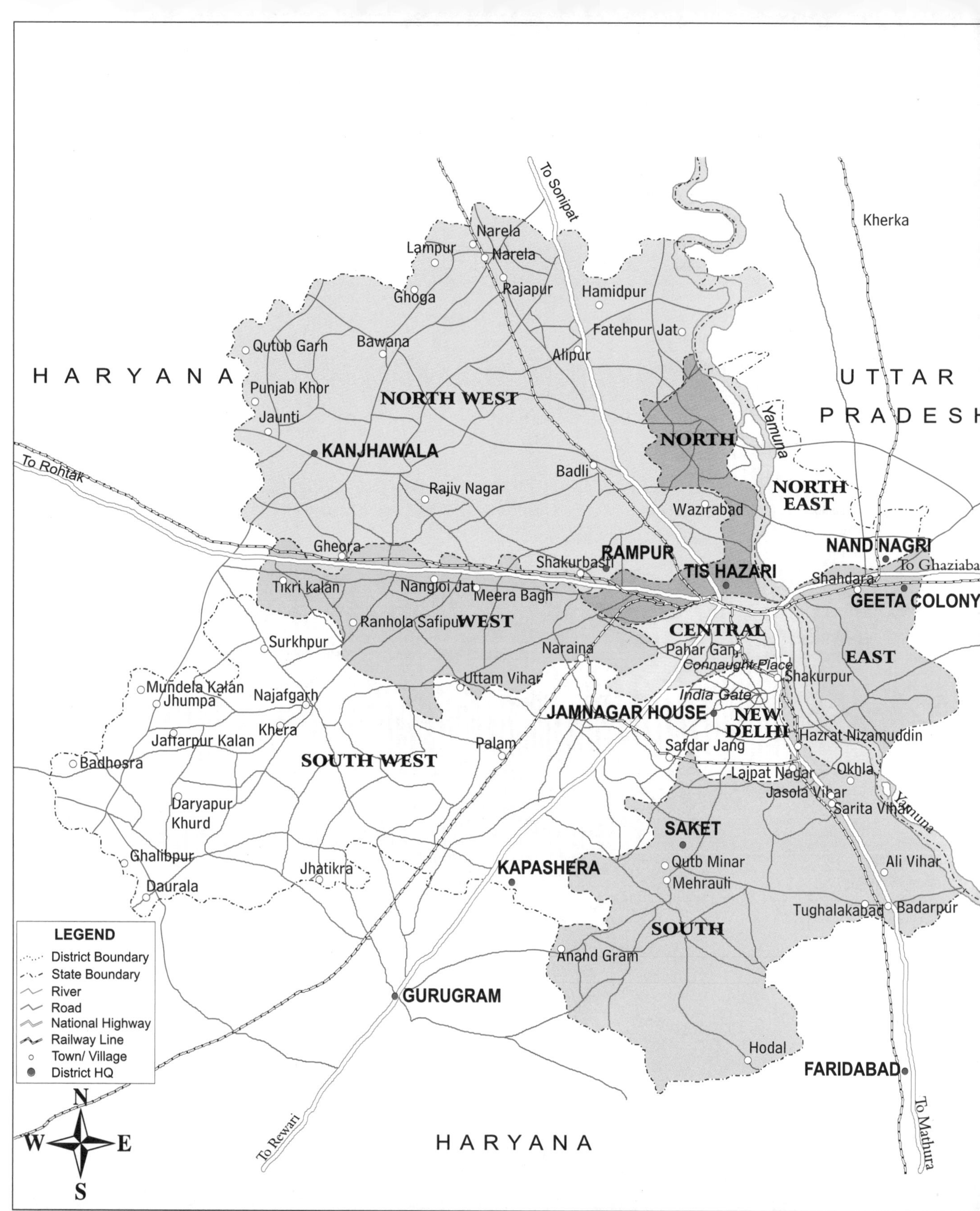
HARYANA
UTTAR PRADESH
HARYANA
To Sonipat
To Rohtak
To Ghaziabad
To Rewari
To Mathura
Kherka
Yamuna
NORTH WEST
NORTH
NORTH EAST
WEST
CENTRAL
EAST
NEW DELHI
SOUTH WEST
SOUTH
KANJHAWALA
RAMPUR
TIS HAZARI
NAND NAGRI
GEETA COLONY
JAMNAGAR HOUSE
SAKET
KAPASHERA
GURUGRAM
FARIDABAD
Narela
Lampur
Rajapur
Ghoga
Hamidpur
Fatehpur Jat
Alipur
Bawana
Qutub Garh
Punjab Khor
Jaunti
Badli
Rajiv Nagar
Wazirabad
Gheora
Shakurbasti
Shahdara
Tikri kalan
Nangloi Jat
Meera Bagh
Ranhola Safipur
Surkhpur
Naraina
Pahar Ganj
Connaught Place
Shakurpur
Mundela Kalan
Jhumpa
Najafgarh
Uttam Vihar
India Gate
Jaffarpur Kalan
Khera
Palam
Safdar Jang
Hazrat Nizamuddin
Badhosra
Lajpat Nagar
Okhla
Jasola Vihar
Sarita Vihar
Daryapur Khurd
Ghalibpur
Jhatikra
Qutb Minar
Mehrauli
Ali Vihar
Daurala
Tughalakabad
Badarpur
Anand Gram
Hodal
LEGEND
District Boundary
State Boundary
River
Road
National Highway
Railway Line
Town/ Village
District HQ
N
W
E
S
Projection: Lambert's Conical Orthomorphic
1000 0 1000 2000 km

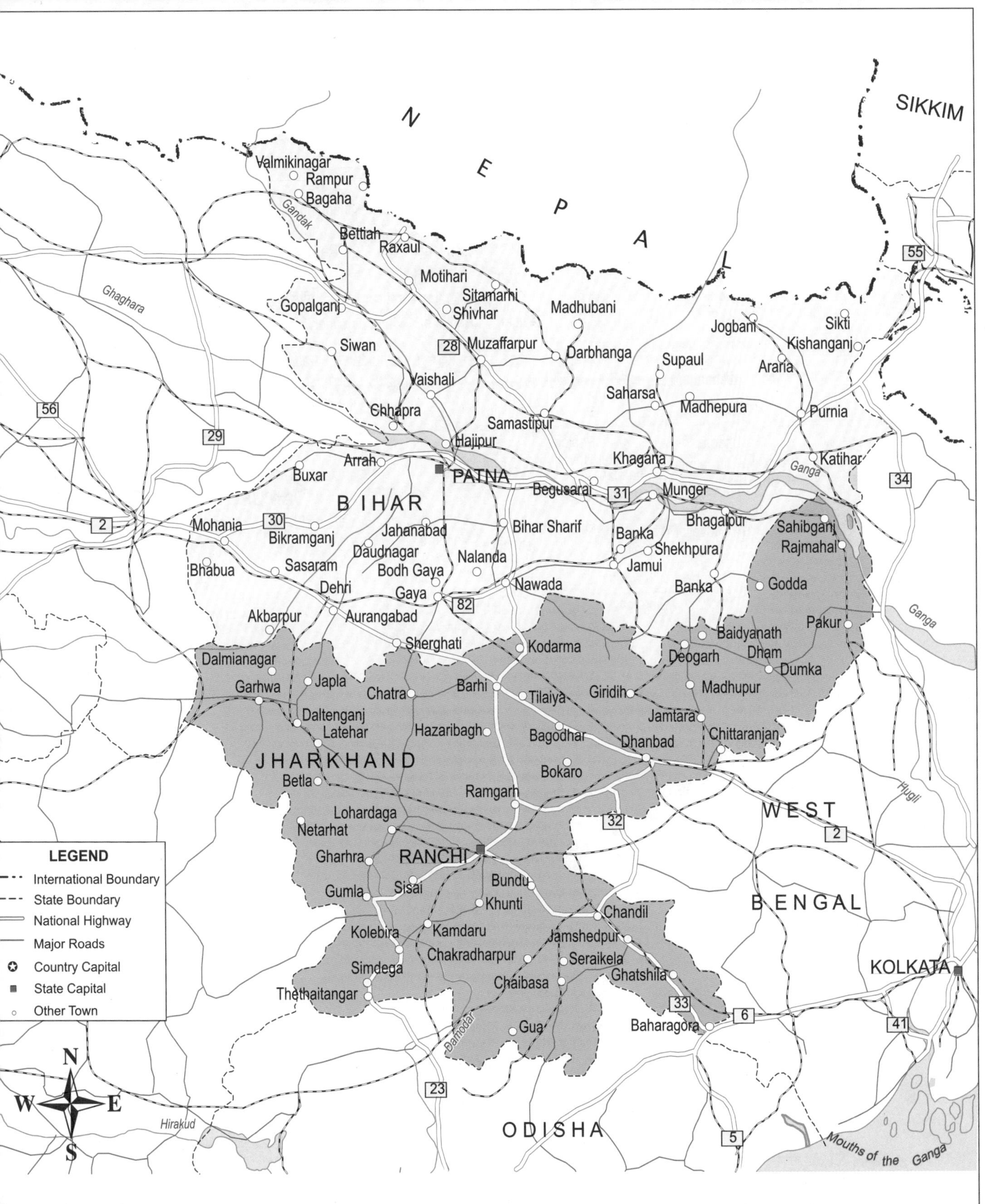

NEPAL
SIKKIM
BIHAR
JHARKHAND
WEST BENGAL
ODISHA
PATNA
RANCHI
KOLKATA
Valmikinagar
Rampur
Bagaha
Bettiah
Raxaul
Motihari
Sitamarhi
Shivhar
Madhubani
Gopalganj
Siwan
Muzaffarpur
Darbhanga
Supaul
Jogbani
Sikti
Kishanganj
Araria
Vaishali
Saharsa
Madhepura
Purnia
Chhapra
Samastipur
Hajipur
Arrah
Buxar
Khagaria
Katihar
Begusarai
Munger
Mohania
Bikramganj
Jahanabad
Bihar Sharif
Bhagalpur
Sahibganj
Rajmahal
Banka
Shekhpura
Daudnagar
Bodh Gaya
Nalanda
Jamui
Bhabua
Sasaram
Dehri
Gaya
Nawada
Godda
Akbarpur
Aurangabad
Sherghati
Kodarma
Baidyanath Dham
Pakur
Deogarh
Dumka
Dalmianagar
Japla
Garhwa
Chatra
Barhi
Tilaiya
Giridih
Madhupur
Jamtara
Daltenganj
Latehar
Hazaribagh
Bagodhar
Dhanbad
Chittaranjan
Bokaro
Betla
Ramgarh
Lohardaga
Netarhat
Gharhra
Sisai
Gumla
Bundu
Khunti
Chandil
Kolebira
Kamdaru
Jamshedpur
Chakradharpur
Seraikela
Simdega
Chaibasa
Ghatshila
Thethaitangar
Baharagora
Gua
Gandak
Ghaghara
Ganga
Hugli
Damodar
Hirakud
Mouths of the Ganga
55
28
56
29
2
30
31
34
82
32
2
6
33
41
23
5
LEGEND
International Boundary
State Boundary
National Highway
Major Roads
Country Capital
State Capital
Other Town
N
S
E
W

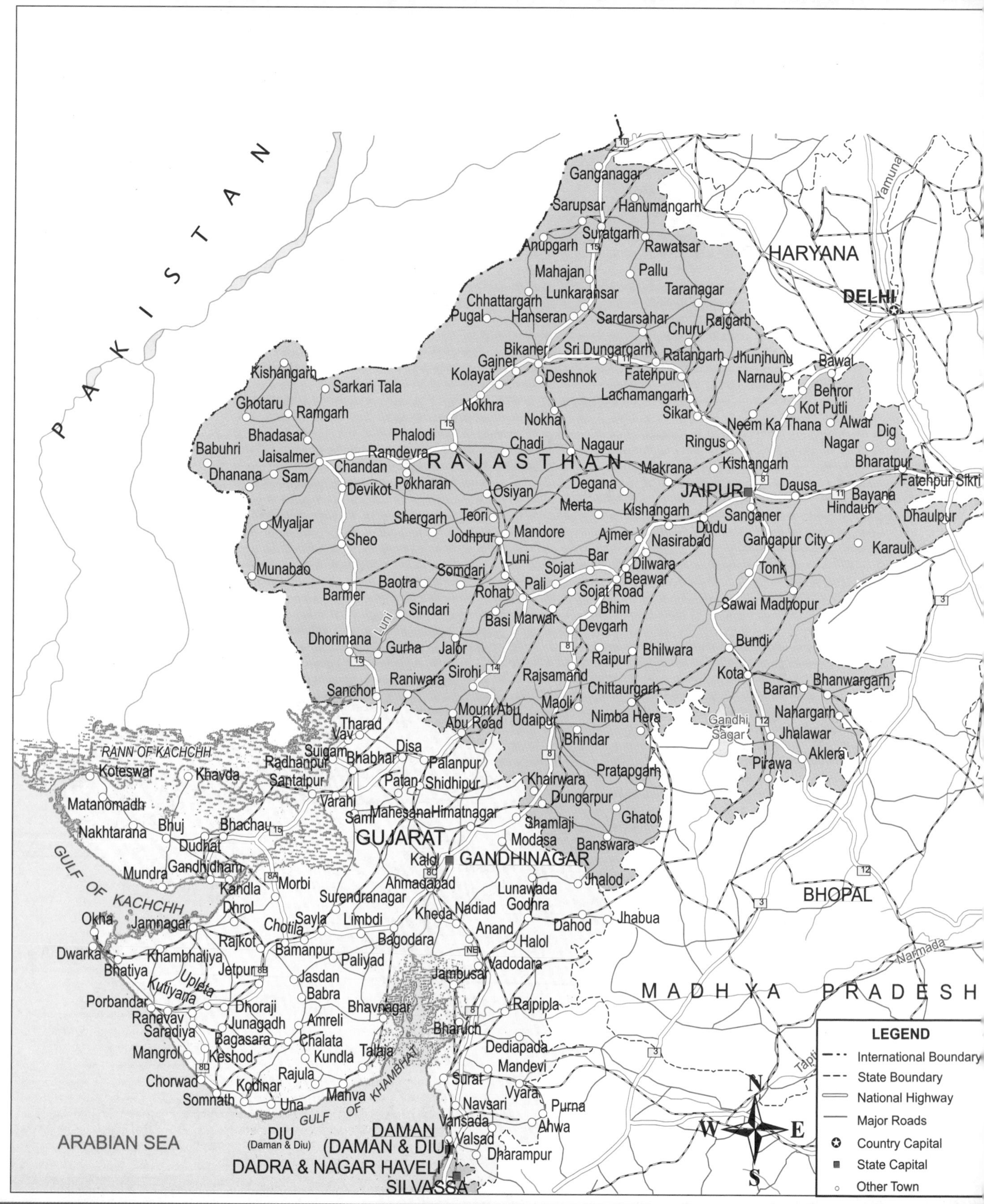
PAKISTAN
HARYANA
DELHI
RAJASTHAN
JAIPUR
GUJARAT
GANDHINAGAR
MADHYA PRADESH
BHOPAL
RANN OF KACHCHH
GULF OF KACHCHH
GULF OF KHAMBHAT
ARABIAN SEA
DIU (Daman & Diu)
DAMAN (DAMAN & DIU)
DADRA & NAGAR HAVELI
SILVASSA
LEGEND
International Boundary
State Boundary
National Highway
Major Roads
Country Capital
State Capital
Other Town

Scale - 1:5.5 M approx

RAJASTHAN
UTTAR PRADESH
JAIPUR
LUCKNOW
MADHYA PRADESH
MAHARASHTRA
CHHATTISGARH
ODISHA
RAIPUR
BHOPAL
Ambah
Mahgawn
Bhind
Morena
Gohad
Mihona
Jora
Shampur
Gwalior
Sabalgarh
Dabra
Sheopur
Pohri
Narwar
Datia
Goras
Karera
Jhansi
Shivpuri
Kolaras
Orchha
Lukwasa
Chittaurgarh
Miana
Isagarh
Guna
Chanderi
Lalitpur
Ashoknagar
Gona
Jawad
Gandhi Sagar
Nimach
Mandsaur
Sironj
Bina
Rajgarh
Maksundangarh
Khurai
Biaora
Sailana
Petlawad
Pachor
Shajapur
Sanchi
Vidisha
Sagar
Ratlam
Maksi
Sehore
Jaisinghnagr
Tarana
Ujjain
BHOPAL
Raisen
Badnawar
Dewas
Sonkach
Jhabua
Ashta
Goharganj
Bareli
Deori
Sardarpur
Indore
Hoshangabad
Dhar
Mhow
Mandu
Balri
Harda
Itarsi
Matkuli
Barwaha
Kukshi
Harsud
Pachmarhi
Sanawad
Barbani
Deshgaon
Julwana
Betul
Khandwa
Khargone
Multai
Sendhwa
Asirgarh
Nepu Nagar
Burhanpur
Tapti
Narmada
Jatara
Chhatarpur
Khajuraho
Sohagi
Tikamgarh
Chachai Falls
Mangawan
Guiganj
Panna
Satna
Mauganj
Kishangarh
Rewa
Hiranpur
Morwa
Amanganj
Sidhi
Banda
Waidhan
Beohari
Damoh
Katni
Rehli
Manpur
Jaisinghnagar
Deori Khas
Sihore
Bandhavgarh
Umaria
Patan
Sihagpur
Pali
Tendukheda
Shandol
Jabalpur
Shahpur
Dindori
Gadarwara
Narsimhapur
Mnadla Fort
Nainpur
Mandla
Manegaon
Supkhar
Seoni
Chhindwara
Kanha National Park
Balaghat
Damoh
Gondia
Ganga
Ghaghara
Godavari
Pranhita
24
8
11
2
25
56
27
2
26
12
3
12
7
12
3
3
6
7
43
LEGEND
International Boundary
State Boundary
National Highway
Major Roads
Country Capital
State Capital
Other Town
N
S
E
W
0
1000
2000 km.
Projection: Lambert's Conical Orthomorphic

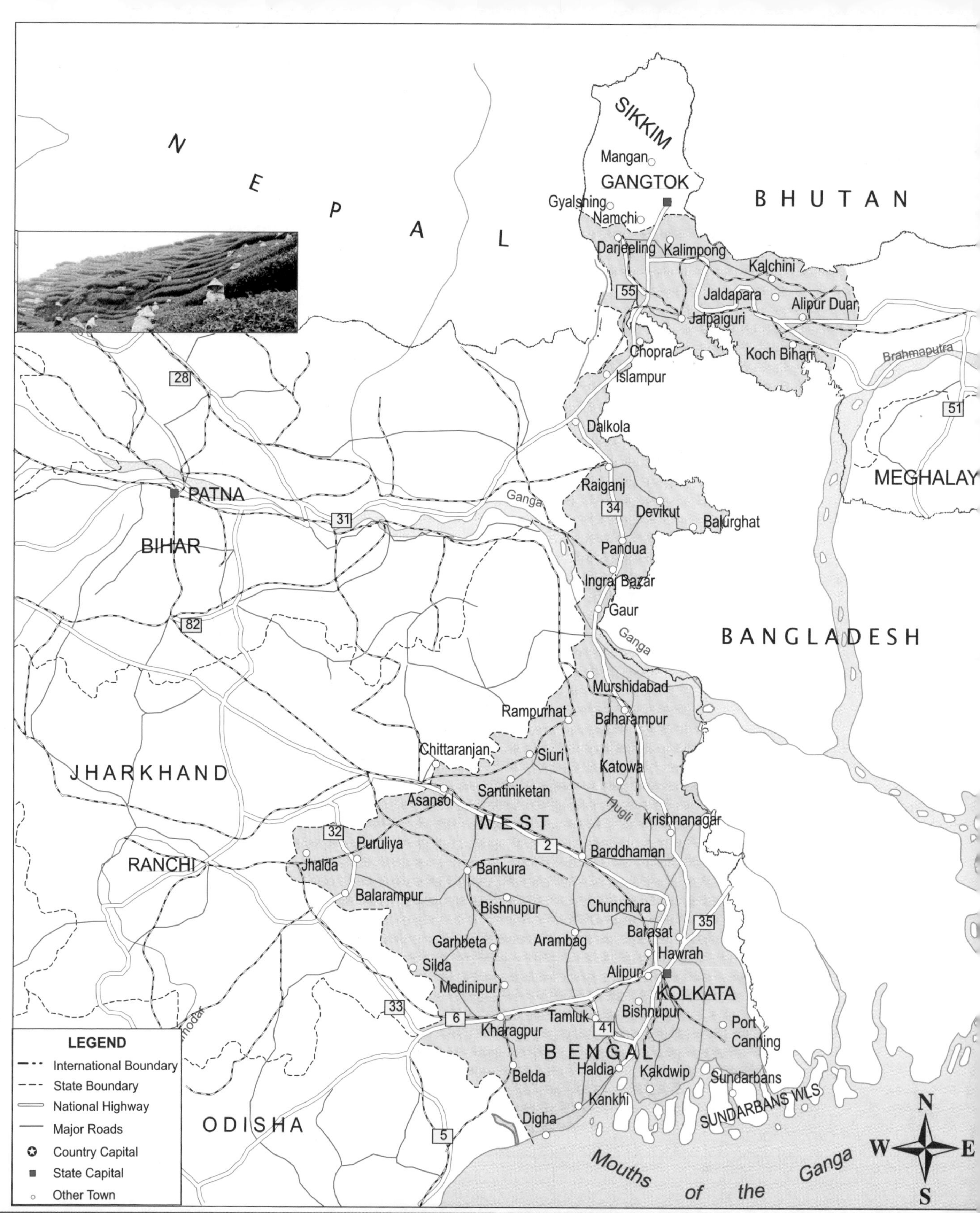
NEPAL
SIKKIM
Mangan
GANGTOK
Gyalshing
Namchi
BHUTAN
Darjeeling
Kalimpong
Kalchini
Jaldapara
Alipur Duar
Jalpaiguri
Koch Bihari
Chopra
Islampur
Brahmaputra
51
MEGHALAY
Dalkola
Raiganj
Devikut
Balurghat
34
55
28
PATNA
31
Ganga
BIHAR
Pandua
Ingraj Bazar
Gaur
82
BANGLADESH
Murshidabad
Rampurhat
Baharampur
Chittaranjan
Siuri
JHARKHAND
Katowa
Santiniketan
Asansol
Hugli
Krishnanagar
WEST
32
Puruliya
2
Barddhaman
RANCHI
Jhalda
Bankura
Balarampur
Bishnupur
Chunchura
35
Barasat
Garhbeta
Arambag
Hawrah
Silda
Alipur
KOLKATA
Medinipur
33
6
Tamluk
Bishnupur
Port
Canning
Kharagpur
41
BENGAL
Haldia
Kakdwip
Sundarbans
Belda
Kankhi
SUNDARBANS WLS
Digha
ODISHA
5
Mouths of the Ganga
N
W
E
S
LEGEND
International Boundary
State Boundary
National Highway
Major Roads
Country Capital
State Capital
Other Town

Scale - 1:3.5 M approx

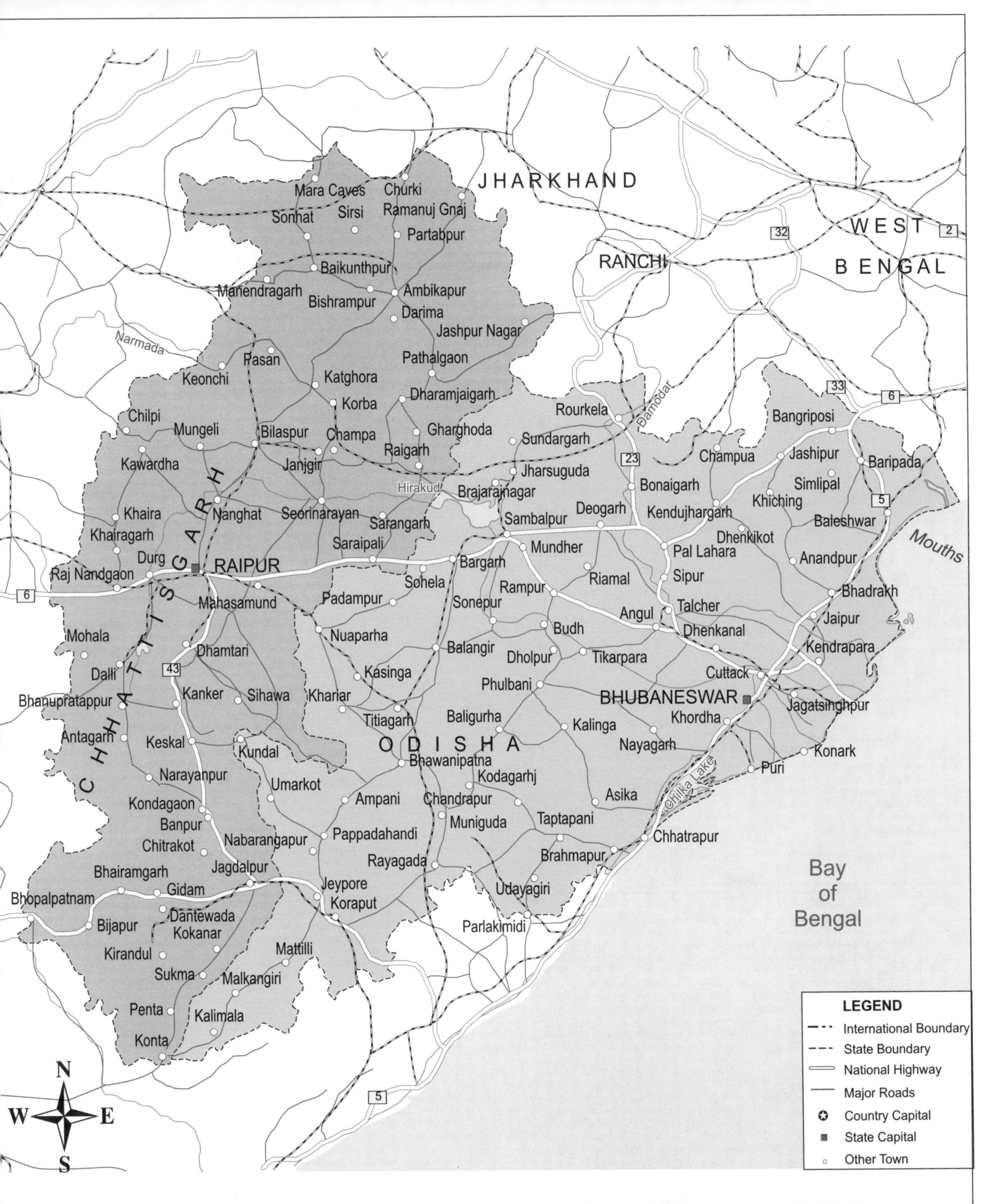
JHARKHAND
RANCHI
WEST BENGAL
CHHATTISGARH
RAIPUR
ODISHA
BHUBANESWAR
Bay of Bengal
Mouths
Narmada
Damodar
Hirakud
Chilika Lake
Mara Caves
Churki
Sonhat
Sirsi
Ramanuj Gnaj
Partabpur
Baikunthpur
Manendragarh
Bishrampur
Ambikapur
Darima
Jashpur Nagar
Pathalgaon
Pasan
Keonchi
Katghora
Korba
Dharamjaigarh
Chilpi
Mungeli
Bilaspur
Champa
Gharghoda
Raigarh
Kawardha
Janjgir
Khaira
Nanghat
Seorinarayan
Sarangarh
Khairagarh
Saraipali
Durg
Raj Nandgaon
Mahasamund
Padampur
Sohela
Bargarh
Mohala
Dhamtari
Nuaparha
Dalli
Kasinga
Bhanupratappur
Kanker
Sihawa
Khariar
Titiagarh
Antagarh
Keskal
Kundal
Narayanpur
Umarkot
Bhawanipatna
Kondagaon
Banpur
Ampani
Chitrakot
Nabarangapur
Pappadahandi
Bhairamgarh
Jagdalpur
Gidam
Bhopalpatnam
Jeypore
Koraput
Bijapur
Dantewada
Kokanar
Kirandul
Mattilli
Sukma
Malkangiri
Penta
Kalimala
Konta
Rourkela
Sundargarh
Jharsuguda
Brajarajnagar
Sambalpur
Mundher
Deogarh
Rampur
Riamal
Sonepur
Balangir
Dholpur
Budh
Tikarpara
Phulbani
Baligurha
Kalinga
Kodagarhj
Chandrapur
Muniguda
Rayagada
Taptapani
Brahmapur
Udayagiri
Parlakimidi
Asika
Chhatrapur
Nayagarh
Khordha
Puri
Konark
Jagatsinghpur
Cuttack
Kendrapara
Jaipur
Bhadrakh
Dhenkanal
Angul
Talcher
Sipur
Pal Lahara
Kendujhargarh
Bonaigarh
Champua
Bangriposi
Jashipur
Simlipal
Khiching
Baripada
Baleshwar
Dhenkikot
Anandpur
6
43
5
23
32
33
2
LEGEND
International Boundary
State Boundary
National Highway
Major Roads
Country Capital
State Capital
Other Town
N
S
E
W
Scale - 1:4 M approx

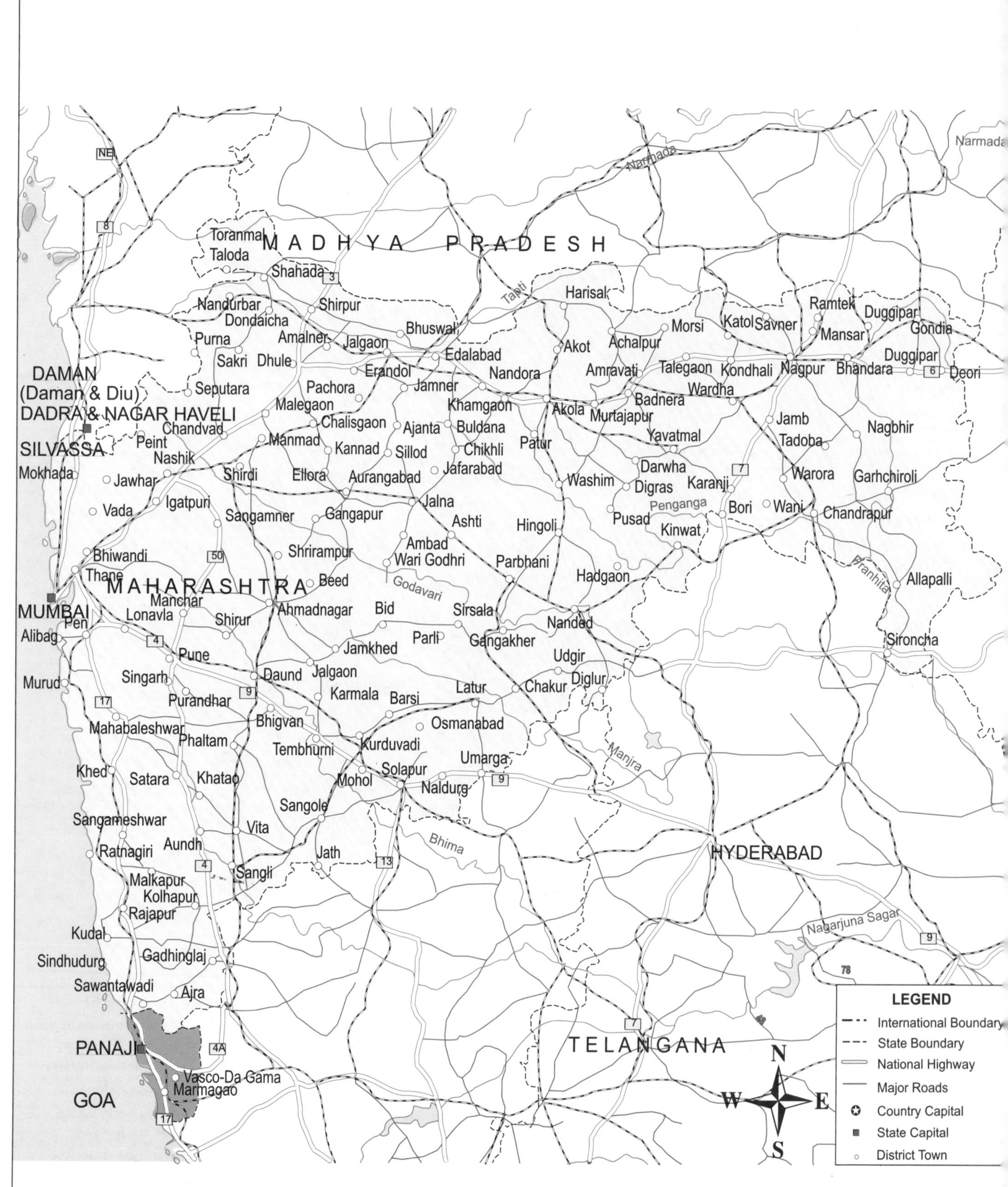
MADHYA PRADESH
MAHARASHTRA
TELANGANA
DAMAN
(Daman & Diu)
DADRA & NAGAR HAVELI
SILVASSA
MUMBAI
PANAJI
GOA
HYDERABAD
Narmada
Tapti
Godavari
Penganga
Pranhita
Manjra
Bhima
Nagarjuna Sagar
Toranmal
Taloda
Shahada
Shirpur
Nandurbar
Dondaicha
Purna
Amalner
Jalgaon
Bhuswal
Sakri
Dhule
Erandol
Edalabad
Nandora
Seputara
Pachora
Jamner
Malegaon
Chalisgaon
Ajanta
Buldana
Khamgaon
Chandvad
Peint
Nashik
Manmad
Kannad
Sillod
Chikhli
Jafarabad
Mokhada
Jawhar
Shirdi
Ellora
Aurangabad
Jalna
Igatpuri
Vada
Sangamner
Gangapur
Ashti
Bhiwandi
Thane
Shrirampur
Ambad
Wari Godhri
Parbhani
Beed
Manchar
Lonavla
Shirur
Ahmadnagar
Bid
Sirsala
Pen
Alibag
Jamkhed
Parli
Gangakher
Nanded
Pune
Daund
Jalgaon
Udgir
Murud
Singarh
Purandhar
Karmala
Barsi
Latur
Chakur
Diglur
Mahabaleshwar
Phaltam
Bhigvan
Osmanabad
Tembhurni
Kurduvadi
Umarga
Khed
Satara
Khatao
Mohol
Solapur
Naldurg
Sangole
Sangameshwar
Vita
Ratnagiri
Aundh
Jath
Sangli
Malkapur
Kolhapur
Rajapur
Kudal
Sindhudurg
Gadhinglaj
Sawantawadi
Ajra
Vasco-Da Gama
Marmagao
Harisal
Akot
Achalpur
Morsi
Katol
Savner
Ramtek
Mansar
Duggipar
Gondia
Amravati
Talegaon
Kondhali
Nagpur
Bhandara
Deori
Akola
Murtajapur
Badnera
Wardha
Patur
Yavatmal
Jamb
Tadoba
Nagbhir
Washim
Darwha
Digras
Karanji
Warora
Garhchiroli
Pusad
Bori
Wani
Chandrapur
Hingoli
Kinwat
Hadgaon
Allapalli
Sironcha
NE
8
3
6
7
50
4
9
17
13
4A
78
LEGEND
International Boundary
State Boundary
National Highway
Major Roads
Country Capital
State Capital
District Town
N
W
E
S

Scale - 1:4.6 M approx

KARNATAKA
ANDHRA PRADESH
GOA
PANAJI
HYDERABAD
BENGALURU
LAKSHADWEEP SEA
Aurad
Bhalki
Bidar
Manjra
Homnabad
Aland
Gulbarga
Chinchdi
Zalki
Bhima
Indi
Sedum
Wadi
Tikota
Athni
Bijapur
Sindgi
Andola
Yadgir
Jamkhandi
Khanapur
Chikodi
Mudhol
Talikota
Gokak
Aivali
Bagalkot
Raichur
Yargatti
Hungund
Sindhnur
Belgaum
Badami
Kushtagi
Tawargeri
Supa
Dharwad
Gangawati
Koppal
Gadag
Bellary
Dandeli
Hospet
Haveri
Sandur
Karwar
Harrpanahalli
Kumta
Sirsi
Harihar
Jagalur
Jog Falls
Davangere
Honavar
Talguppa
Challakere
Sagar
Holalkere
Chitradurga
Pavagade
Bhatkal
Shimoga
Bhadravati
Tunga
Kundapura
Sringeri
Bagepalli
Kadur
Huliyar
Koratagere
Udupi
Bhadra
Chikmagalur
Chintamani
Tumkur
Mulbagal
Mangalore
Beltangadi
Belur
Halebid
Kolar
Kunigal
Hassan
Bantval
Puttur
Madikeri
Shri Rangapattna
Kanakpura
Mandya
Hunsur
Mysore
Mogenkanal Falls
Chamrajnagar
Gundlupet
4
9
17
13
4A
7
46
48
78
N
W
E
S
LEGEND
International Boundary
State Boundary
National Highway
Major Roads
Country Capital
State Capital
Other Town

Scale - 1:4 M approx

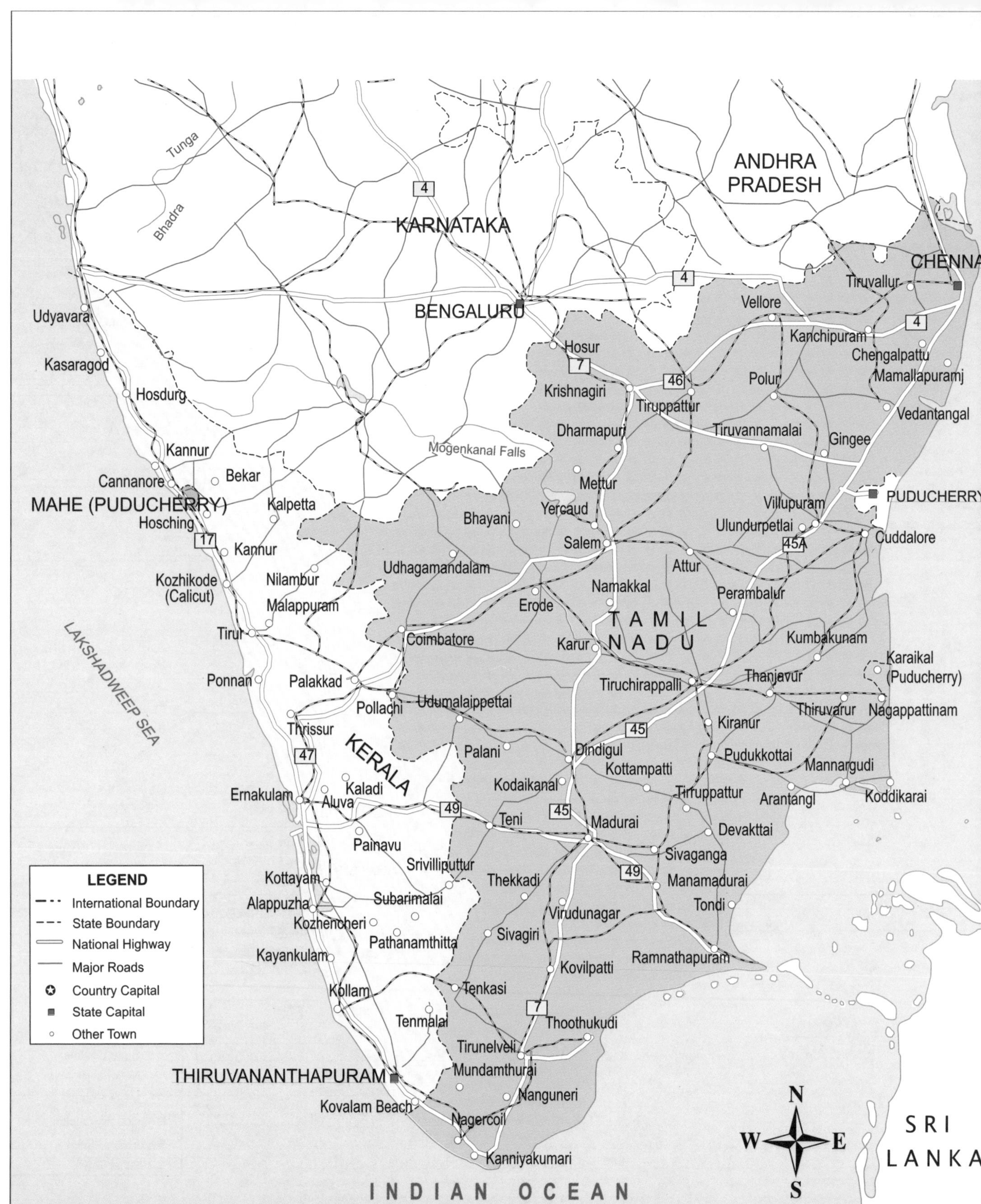
ANDHRA PRADESH
KARNATAKA
BENGALURU
CHENNA
TAMIL NADU
KERALA
PUDUCHERRY
MAHE (PUDUCHERRY)
THIRUVANANTHAPURAM
LAKSHADWEEP SEA
INDIAN OCEAN
SRI LANKA
Tunga
Bhadra
Mogenkanal Falls
Udyavara
Kasaragod
Hosdurg
Kannur
Cannanore
Bekar
Hosching
Kalpetta
Kannur
Kozhikode (Calicut)
Nilambur
Malappuram
Tirur
Ponnan
Palakkad
Thrissur
Pollachi
Udumalaippettai
Ernakulam
Aluva
Kaladi
Painavu
Kottayam
Alappuzha
Kozhencheri
Subarimalai
Pathanamthitta
Kayankulam
Kollam
Tenmalai
Kovalam Beach
Hosur
Krishnagiri
Tiruppattur
Dharmapuri
Mettur
Yercaud
Bhayani
Salem
Udhagamandalam
Attur
Namakkal
Erode
Coimbatore
Karur
Perambalur
Vellore
Tiruvallur
Kanchipuram
Chengalpattu
Mamallapuramj
Polur
Vedantangal
Tiruvannamalai
Gingee
Villupuram
Ulundurpetlai
Cuddalore
Kumbakunam
Karaikal (Puducherry)
Thanjavur
Tiruchirappalli
Thiruvarur
Nagappattinam
Kiranur
Pudukkottai
Mannargudi
Arantangl
Koddikarai
Dindigul
Kottampatti
Palani
Kodaikanal
Tirruppattur
Teni
Madurai
Devakttai
Sivaganga
Srivilliputtur
Thekkadi
Manamadurai
Tondi
Virudunagar
Sivagiri
Kovilpatti
Ramnathapuram
Tenkasi
Thoothukudi
Tirunelveli
Mundamthurai
Nanguneri
Nagercoil
Kanniyakumari
4
4
4
7
46
17
45A
45
47
49
45
49
7
N
W
E
S
LEGEND
International Boundary
State Boundary
National Highway
Major Roads
Country Capital
State Capital
Other Town

Scale - 1:3.4 M approx

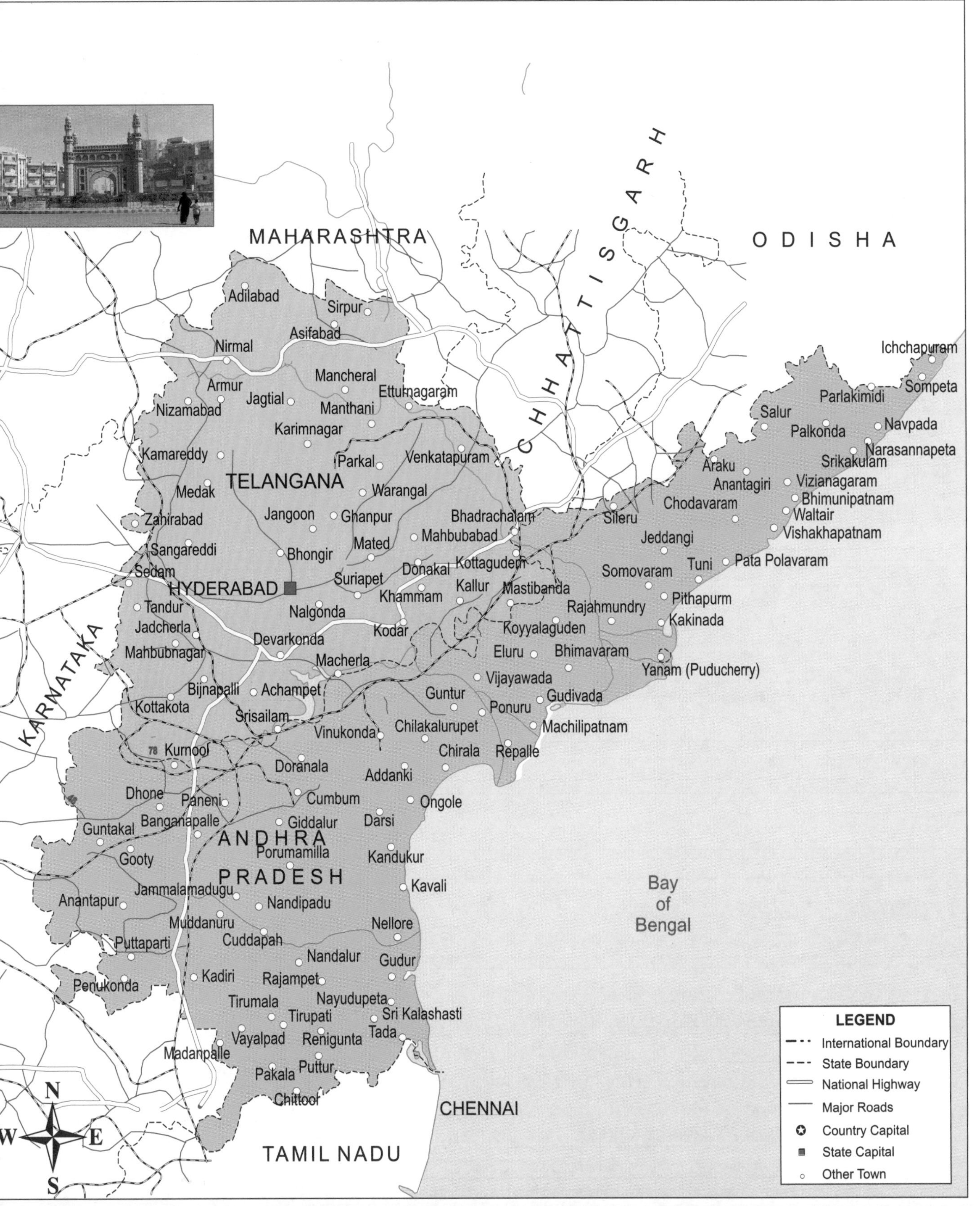
MAHARASHTRA
CHHATTISGARH
ODISHA
TELANGANA
HYDERABAD
ANDHRA PRADESH
KARNATAKA
TAMIL NADU
CHENNAI
Bay of Bengal
Adilabad
Sirpur
Asifabad
Nirmal
Mancheral
Armur
Jagtial
Ettumagaram
Manthani
Nizamabad
Karimnagar
Kamareddy
Parkal
Venkatapuram
Medak
Warangal
Jangoon
Ghanpur
Bhadrachalam
Zahirabad
Mahbubabad
Mated
Sangareddi
Bhongir
Kottagudem
Sedam
Donakal
Suriapet
Kallur
Mastibanda
Khammam
Tandur
Nalgonda
Koyyalaguden
Jadcherla
Kodar
Devarkonda
Mahbubnagar
Macherla
Eluru
Bhimavaram
Bijnapalli
Achampet
Vijayawada
Kottakota
Guntur
Gudivada
Srisailam
Ponuru
Vinukonda
Chilakalurupet
Machilipatnam
Kurnool
Chirala
Repalle
Doranala
Addanki
Dhone
Cumbum
Paneni
Ongole
Banganapalle
Darsi
Guntakal
Giddalur
Porumamilla
Gooty
Kandukur
Kavali
Jammalamadugu
Anantapur
Nandipadu
Muddanuru
Nellore
Cuddapah
Puttaparti
Nandalur
Gudur
Kadiri
Rajampet
Penukonda
Nayudupeta
Tirumala
Tirupati
Sri Kalashasti
Vayalpad
Renigunta
Tada
Madanpalle
Pakala
Puttur
Chittoor
Ichchapuram
Sompeta
Parlakimidi
Salur
Navpada
Palkonda
Narasannapeta
Srikakulam
Araku
Anantagiri
Vizianagaram
Sileru
Chodavaram
Bhimunipatnam
Waltair
Vishakhapatnam
Jeddangi
Tuni
Pata Polavaram
Somovaram
Pithapurm
Rajahmundry
Kakinada
Yanam (Puducherry)
LEGEND
International Boundary
State Boundary
National Highway
Major Roads
Country Capital
State Capital
Other Town
N
S
E
W

Scale - 1:4 M approx

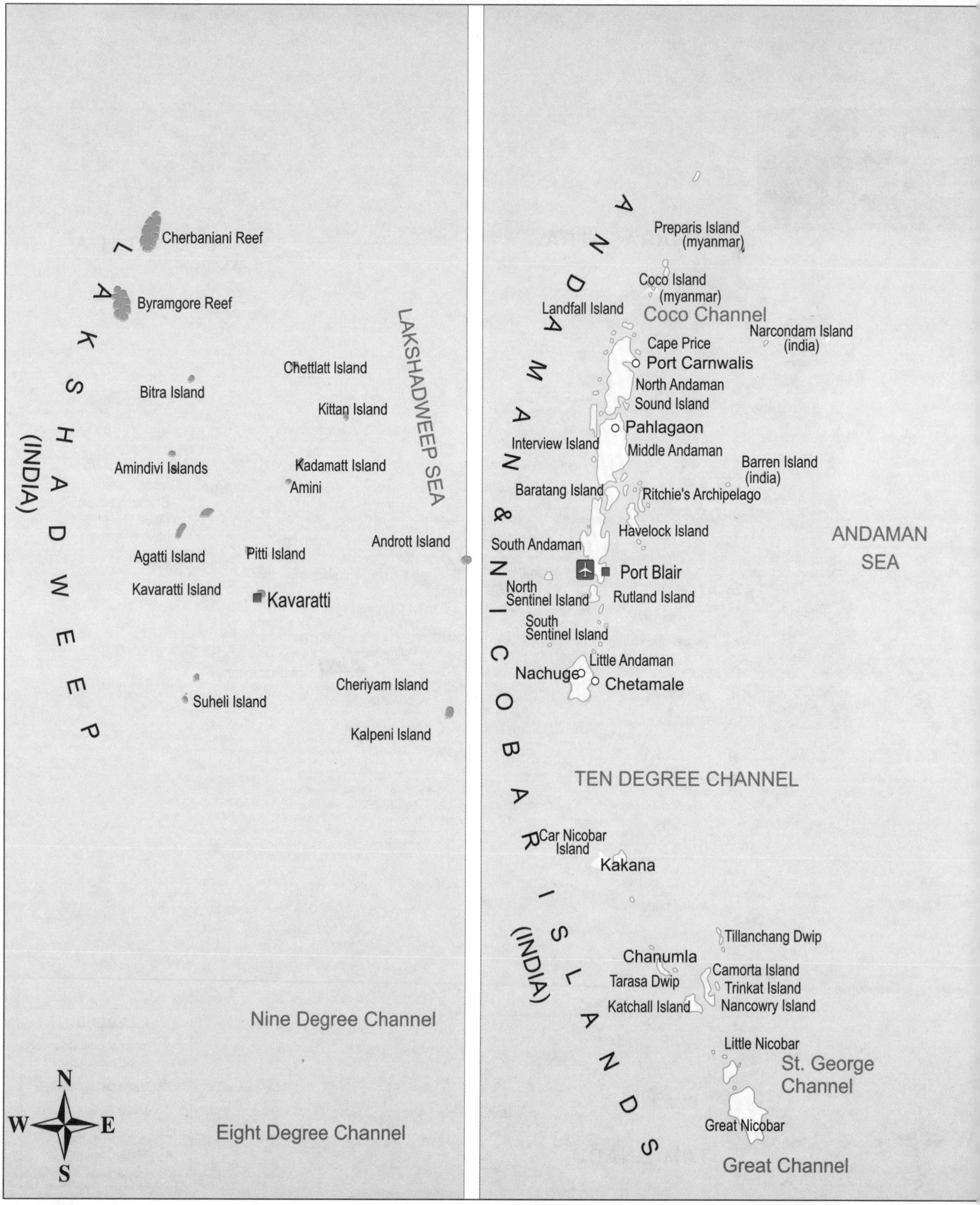

ANDAMAN-NICOBAR & LAKSHADWEEP

LAKSHADWEEP (INDIA)
Cherbaniani Reef
Byramgore Reef
Bitra Island
Chettlatt Island
Kittan Island
LAKSHADWEEP SEA
Amindivi Islands
Kadamatt Island
Amini
Agatti Island
Pitti Island
Andrott Island
Kavaratti Island
Kavaratti
Suheli Island
Cheriyam Island
Kalpeni Island
Nine Degree Channel
Eight Degree Channel
N
W
E
S

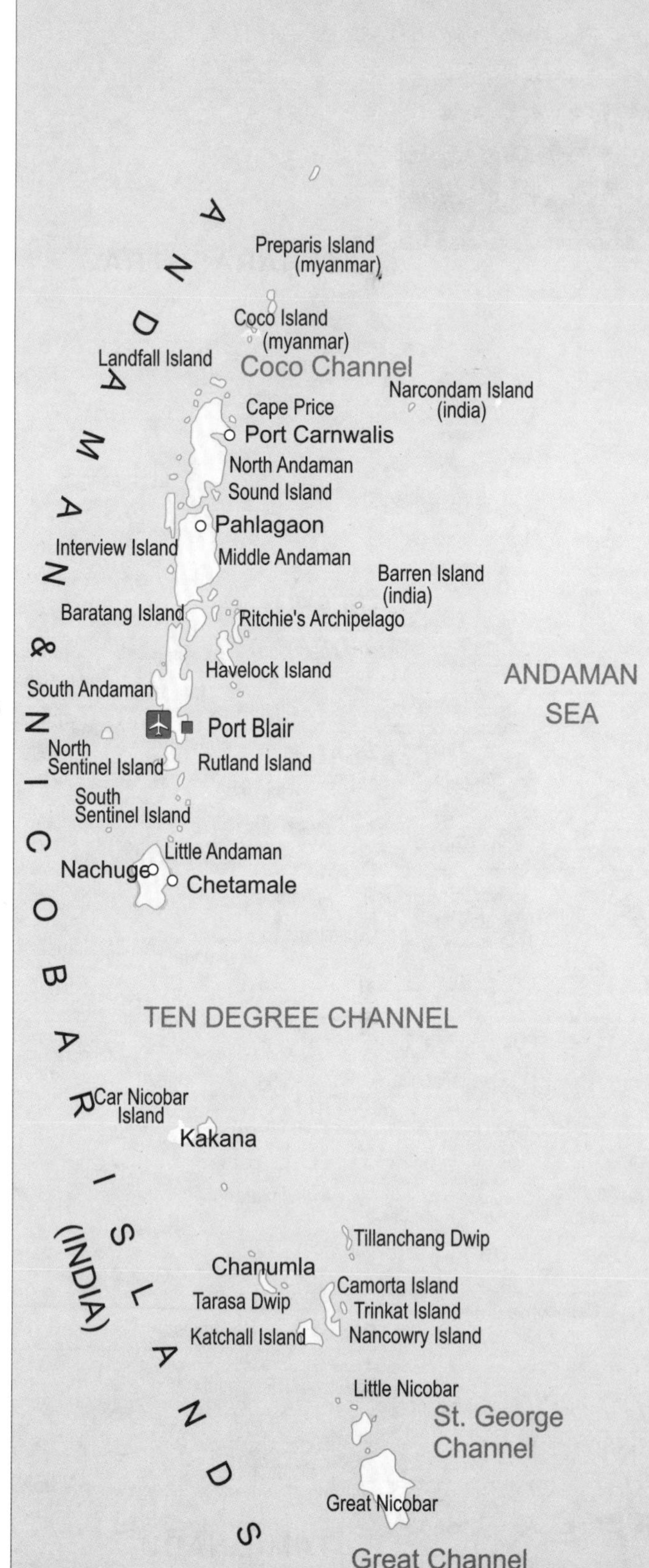
ANDAMAN & NICOBAR ISLANDS (INDIA)
Preparis Island (myanmar)
Coco Island (myanmar)
Landfall Island
Coco Channel
Narcondam Island (india)
Cape Price
Port Carnwalis
North Andaman
Sound Island
Pahlagaon
Interview Island
Middle Andaman
Barren Island (india)
Baratang Island
Ritchie's Archipelago
Havelock Island
South Andaman
ANDAMAN SEA
Port Blair
North Sentinel Island
Rutland Island
South Sentinel Island
Little Andaman
Nachuge
Chetamale
TEN DEGREE CHANNEL
Car Nicobar Island
Kakana
Tillanchang Dwip
Chanumla
Camorta Island
Tarasa Dwip
Trinkat Island
Katchall Island
Nancowry Island
Little Nicobar
St. George Channel
Great Nicobar
Great Channel

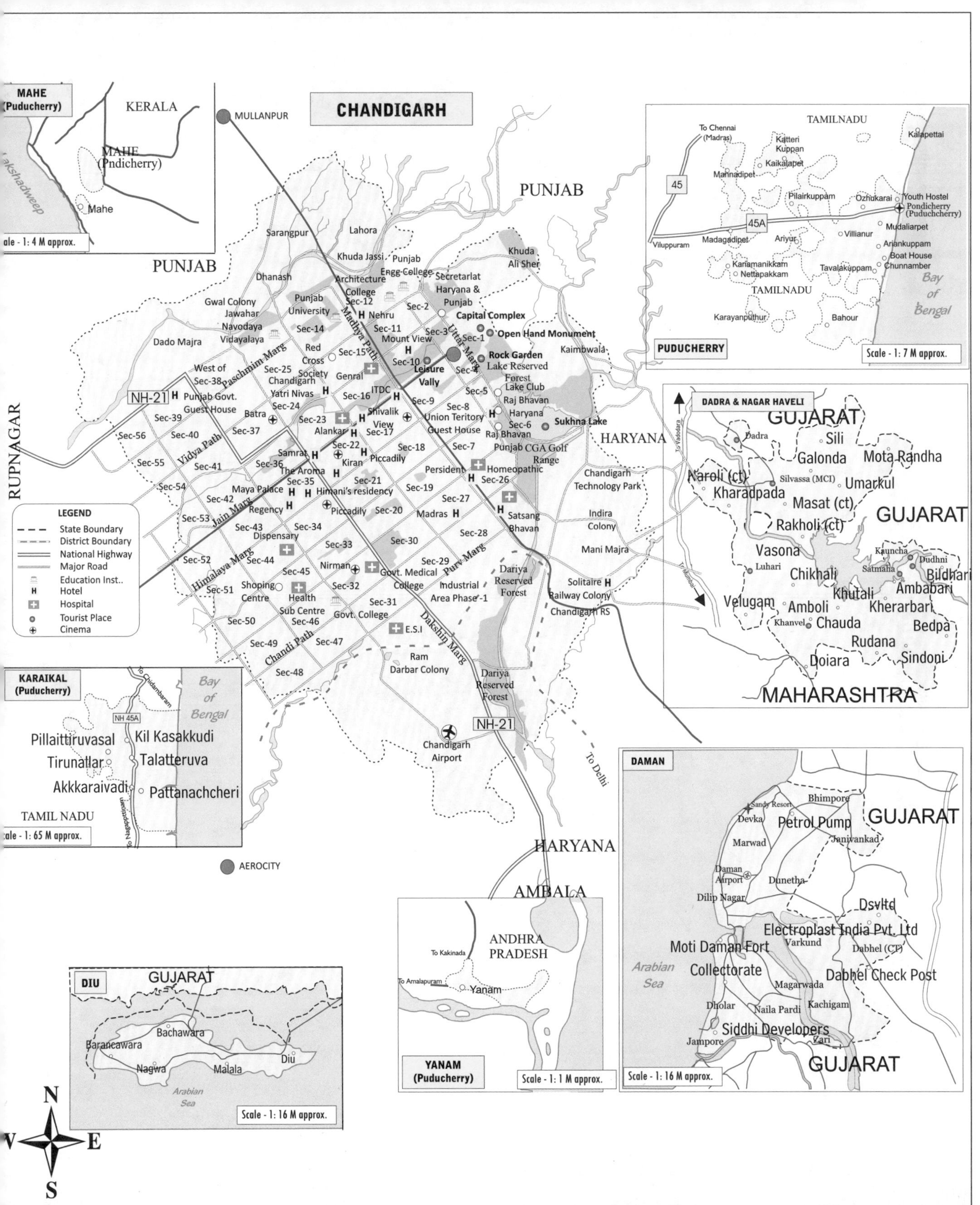

CHANDIGARH
MULLANPUR
PUNJAB
HARYANA
RUPNAGAR
AEROCITY
AMBALA
Sukhna Lake
Rock Garden
Capital Complex
Open Hand Monument
Chandigarh Airport
NH-21
To Delhi
LEGEND
State Boundary
District Boundary
National Highway
Major Road
Education Inst..
Hotel
Hospital
Tourist Place
Cinema
MAHE (Puducherry)
KERALA
Mahe
Scale - 1: 4 M approx.
PUDUCHERRY
TAMILNADU
Bay of Bengal
Scale - 1: 7 M approx.
DADRA & NAGAR HAVELI
GUJARAT
MAHARASHTRA
Silvassa (MCI)
KARAIKAL (Puducherry)
TAMIL NADU
Scale - 1: 65 M approx.
DAMAN
Arabian Sea
Scale - 1: 16 M approx.
DIU
Scale - 1: 16 M approx.
YANAM (Puducherry)
ANDHRA PRADESH
Yanam
Scale - 1: 1 M approx.
N
E
S

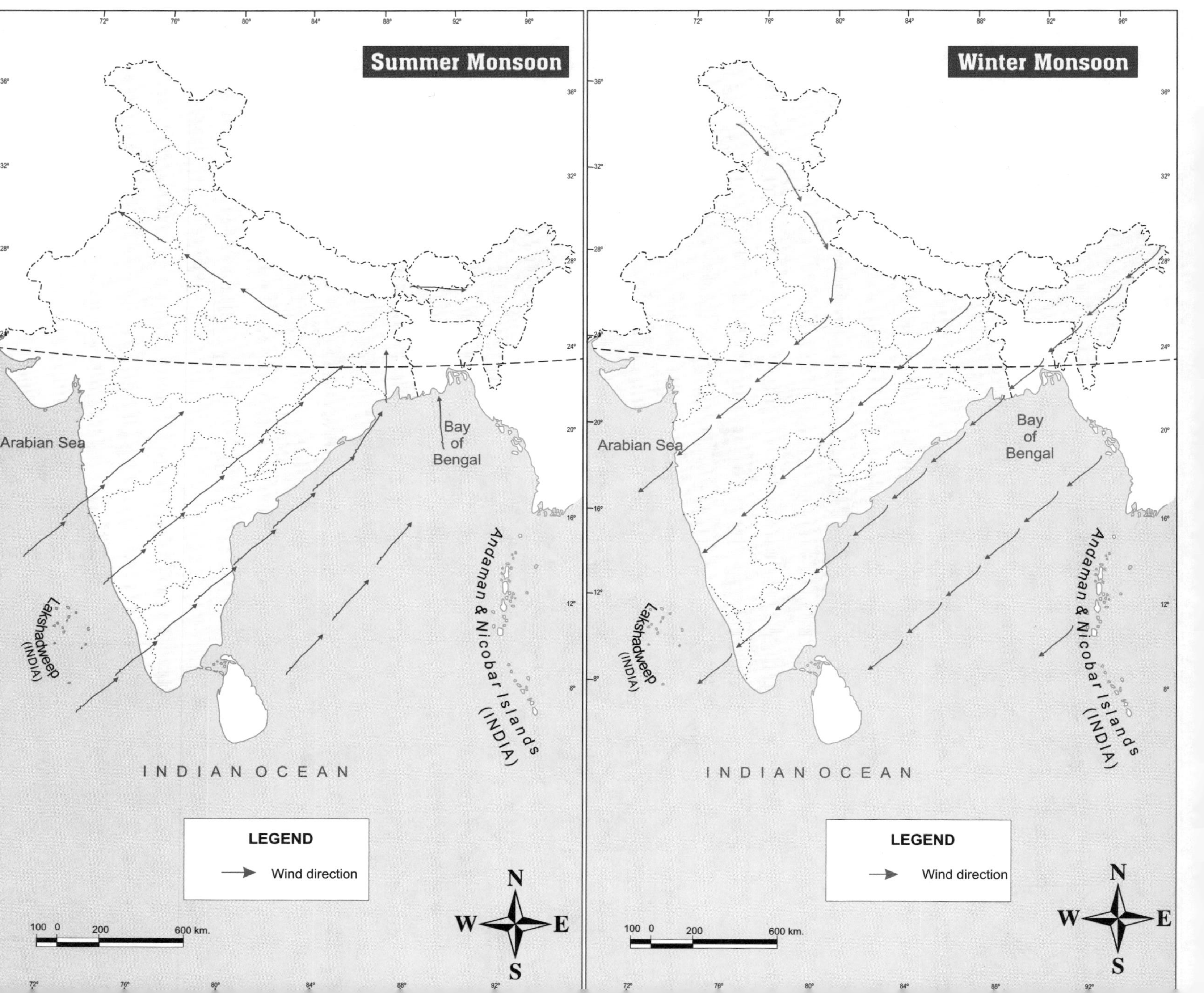

Summer Monsoon
Arabian Sea
Bay of Bengal
Lakshadweep (INDIA)
Andaman & Nicobar Islands (INDIA)
INDIAN OCEAN
LEGEND
Wind direction
100 0 200 600 km.
N
W
E
S
Winter Monsoon
Arabian Sea
Bay of Bengal
Lakshadweep (INDIA)
Andaman & Nicobar Islands (INDIA)
INDIAN OCEAN
LEGEND
Wind direction
100 0 200 600 km.
N
W
E
S

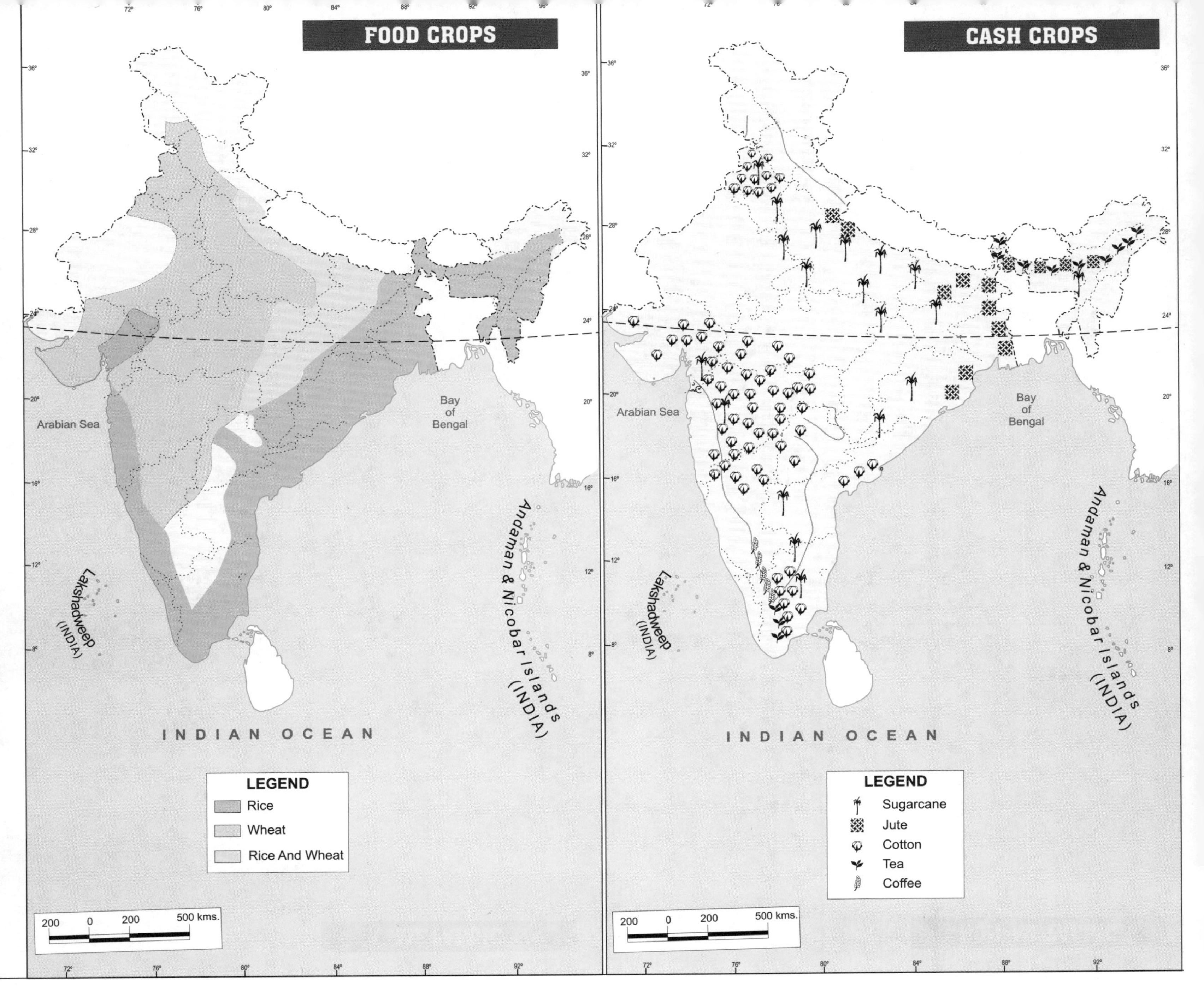
FOOD CROPS
Arabian Sea
Bay of Bengal
Lakshadweep (INDIA)
Andaman & Nicobar Islands (INDIA)
INDIAN OCEAN
LEGEND
Rice
Wheat
Rice And Wheat
200 0 200 500 kms.
CASH CROPS
Arabian Sea
Bay of Bengal
Lakshadweep (INDIA)
Andaman & Nicobar Islands (INDIA)
INDIAN OCEAN
LEGEND
Sugarcane
Jute
Cotton
Tea
Coffee
200 0 200 500 kms.

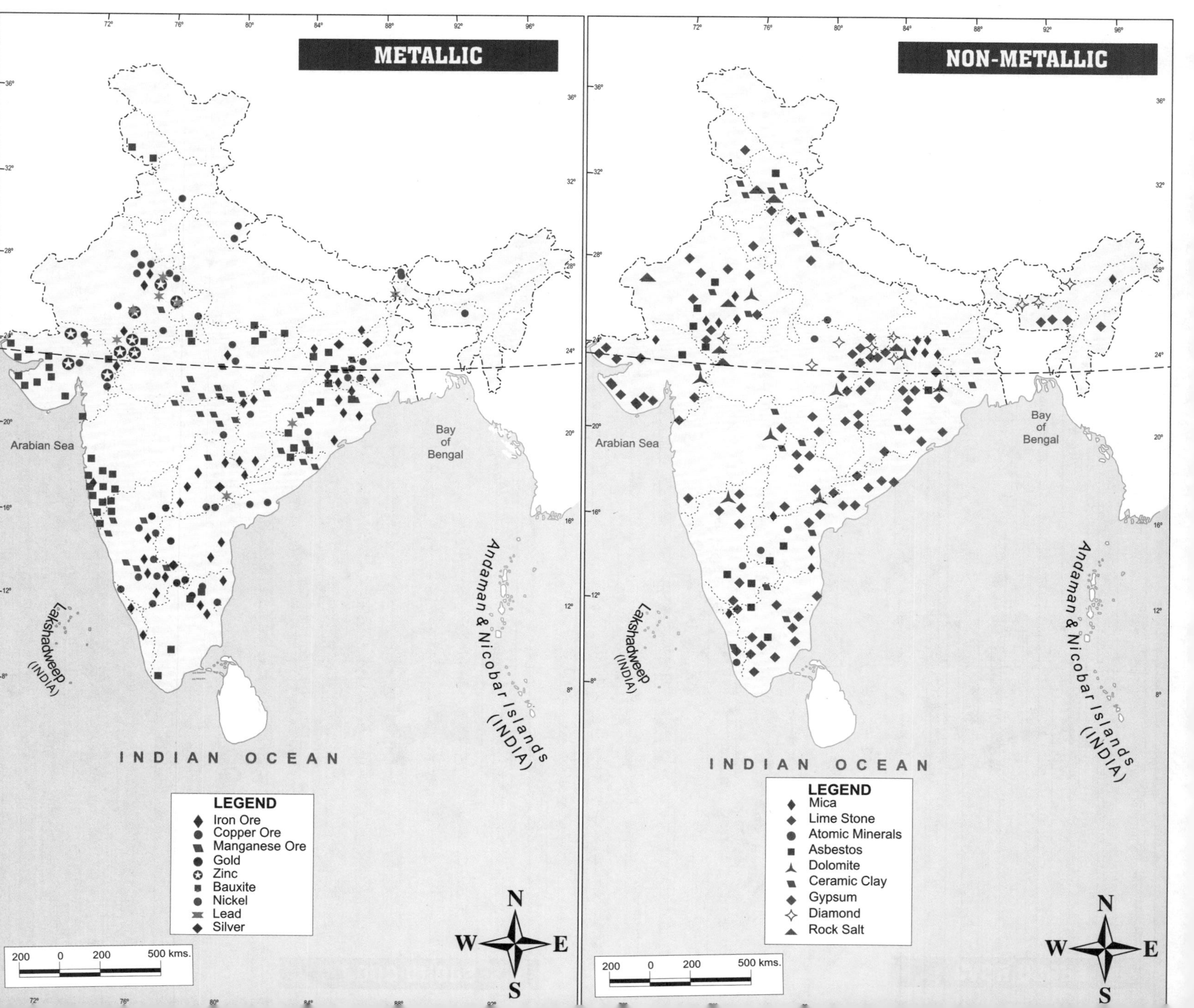
METALLIC
Arabian Sea
Bay of Bengal
Lakshadweep (INDIA)
Andaman & Nicobar Islands (INDIA)
INDIAN OCEAN
LEGEND
Iron Ore
Copper Ore
Manganese Ore
Gold
Zinc
Bauxite
Nickel
Lead
Silver
200 0 200 500 kms.
N
W
E
S
NON-METALLIC
Arabian Sea
Bay of Bengal
Lakshadweep (INDIA)
Andaman & Nicobar Islands (INDIA)
INDIAN OCEAN
LEGEND
Mica
Lime Stone
Atomic Minerals
Asbestos
Dolomite
Ceramic Clay
Gypsum
Diamond
Rock Salt
200 0 200 500 kms.
N
W
E
S

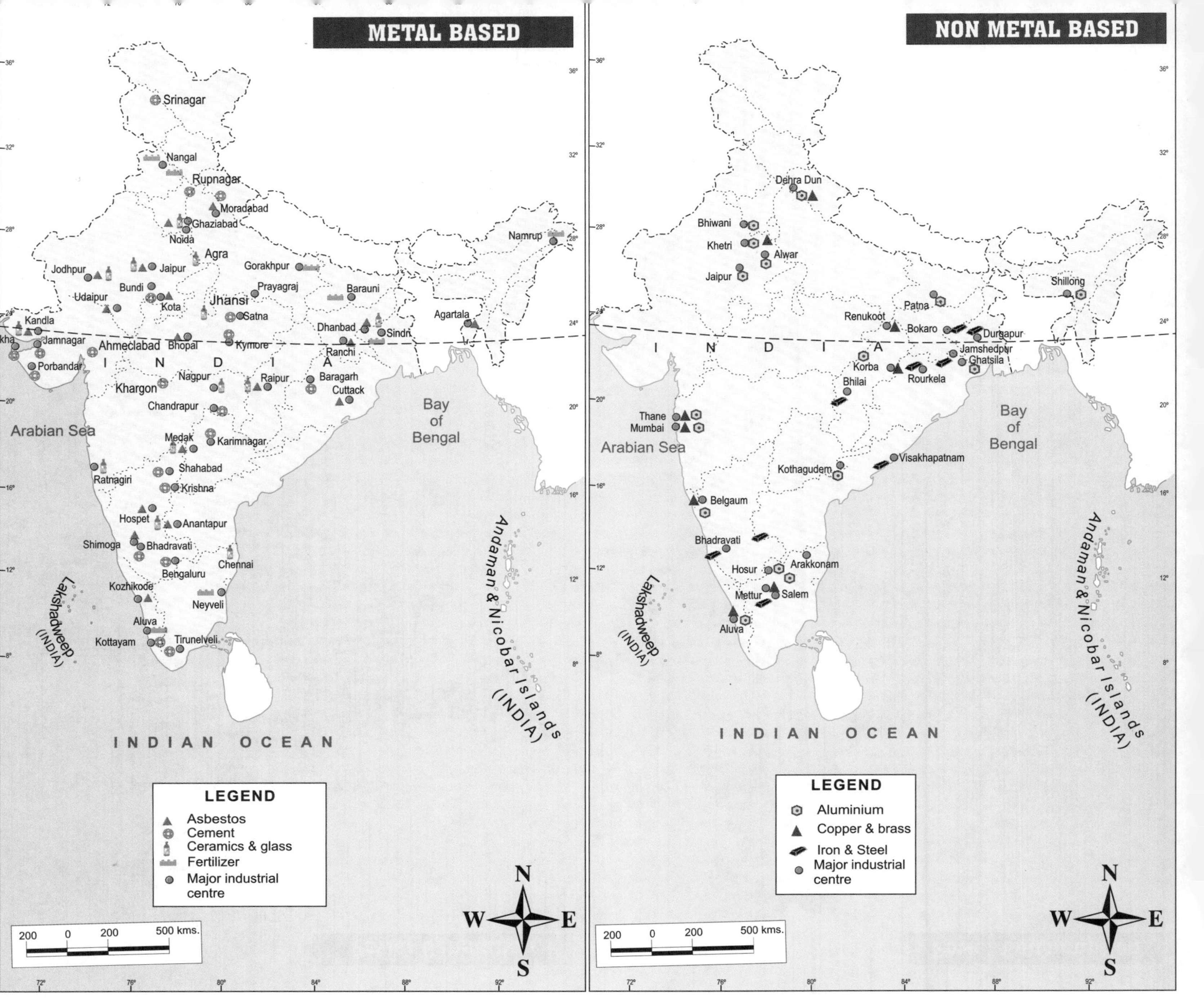

METAL BASED
Srinagar
Nangal
Rupnagar
Moradabad
Ghaziabad
Noida
Agra
Jodhpur
Jaipur
Gorakhpur
Prayagraj
Barauni
Namrup
Bundi
Udaipur
Kota
Jhansi
Satna
Agartala
Kandla
Okha
Jamnagar
Ahmedabad
Bhopal
Kymore
Dhanbad
Sindri
Ranchi
Porbandar
I N D I A
Khargon
Nagpur
Raipur
Baragarh
Cuttack
Chandrapur
Arabian Sea
Bay of Bengal
Medak
Karimnagar
Shahabad
Ratnagiri
Krishna
Hospet
Anantapur
Shimoga
Bhadravati
Chennai
Bengaluru
Lakshadweep (INDIA)
Kozhikode
Neyveli
Aluva
Kottayam
Tirunelveli
Andaman & Nicobar Islands (INDIA)
INDIAN OCEAN
LEGEND
Asbestos
Cement
Ceramics & glass
Fertilizer
Major industrial centre
200 0 200 500 kms.
N S E W
NON METAL BASED
Dehra Dun
Bhiwani
Khetri
Alwar
Jaipur
Shillong
Patna
Renukoot
Bokaro
Durgapur
Jamshedpur
Ghatsila
I N D I A
Korba
Rourkela
Bhilai
Thane
Mumbai
Arabian Sea
Bay of Bengal
Visakhapatnam
Kothagudem
Belgaum
Bhadravati
Arakkonam
Hosur
Mettur
Salem
Aluva
Lakshadweep (INDIA)
Andaman & Nicobar Islands (INDIA)
INDIAN OCEAN
LEGEND
Aluminium
Copper & brass
Iron & Steel
Major industrial centre
200 0 200 500 kms.
N S E W

Projection: Lambert's Conical Orthomorphic

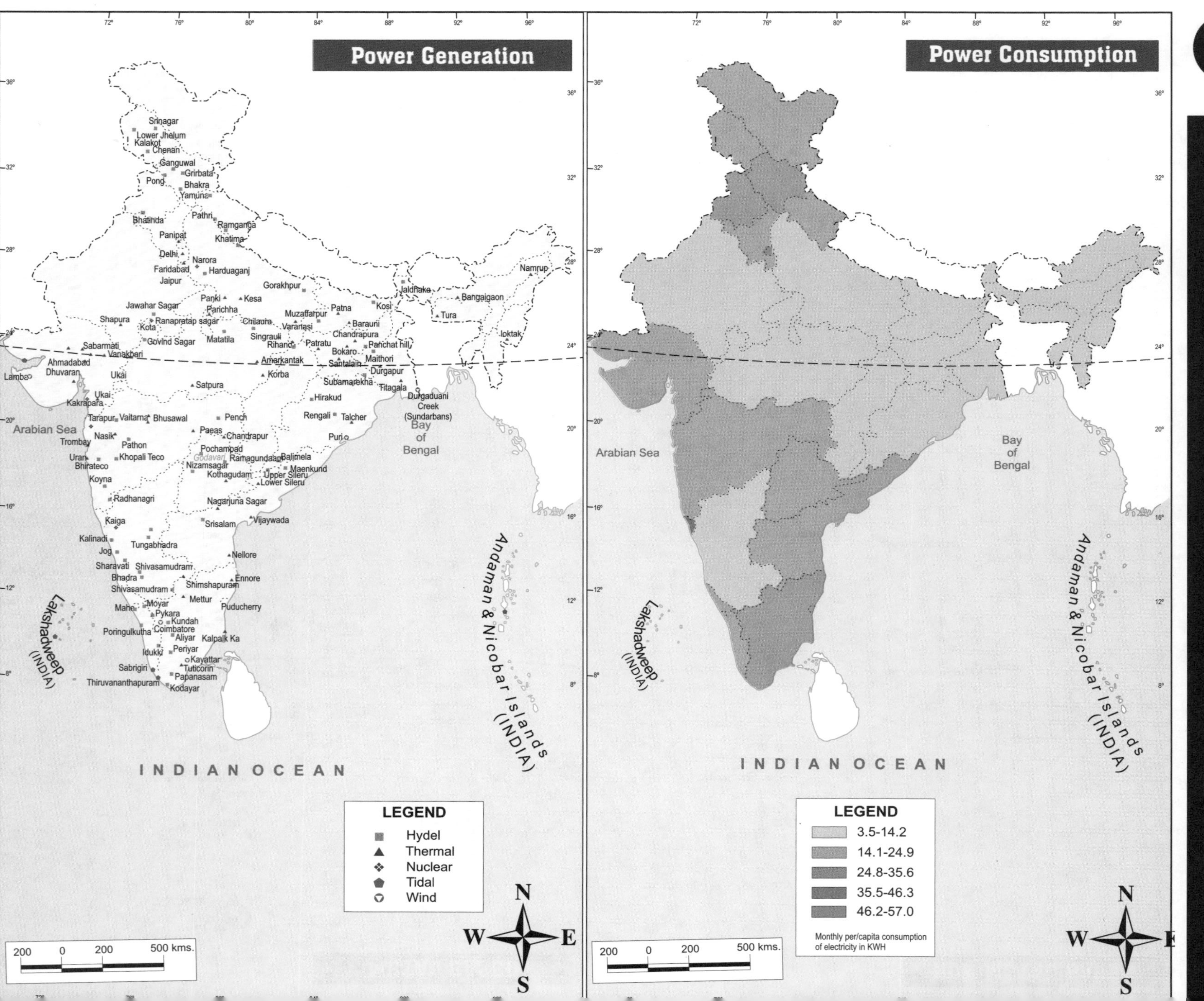
Power Generation
Srinagar
Lower Jhelum
Kalakot
Chenan
Ganguwal
Grirbata
Pong
Bhakra
Yamuna
Bhatinda
Pathri
Ramganga
Panipat
Khatima
Delhi
Narora
Faridabad
Harduaganj
Jaipur
Gorakhpur
Jaldhaka
Bangaigaon
Namrup
Jawahar Sagar
Panki
Kesa
Parichha
Patna
Kosi
Tura
Shapura
Kota
Ranapratap sagar
Chilaura
Muzaffarpur
Varanasi
Barauni
Loktak
Sabarmati
Govind Sagar
Matatila
Singrauli
Rihand
Patratu
Chandrapura
Panchat hill
Vanakbori
Ahmadabad
Amarkantak
Bokaro
Santalain
Maithori
Dhuvaran
Ukai
Korba
Durgapur
Lamba
Satpura
Subamarekha
Titagala
Ukai
Kakrapara
Hirakud
Durgaduani Creek (Sundarbans)
Tarapur
Vaitarna
Bhusawal
Pench
Rengali
Talcher
Arabian Sea
Nasik
Paeas
Chandrapur
Puri
Trombay
Pathon
Pochampad
Bay of Bengal
Uran
Khopali Teco
Godavari
Ramagundaaa
Balimela
Bhirateco
Nizamsagar
Maenkund
Kothagudam
Upper Sileru
Koyna
Lower Sileru
Radhanagri
Nagarjuna Sagar
Kaiga
Srisalam
Vijaywada
Kalinadi
Tungabhadra
Jog
Nellore
Sharavati
Shivasamudram
Bhadra
Ennore
Shimshapuram
Shivasamudram
Mettur
Mahe
Moyar
Puducherry
Pykara
Kundah
Poringulkutha
Coimbatore
Aliyar
Kalpak Ka
Idukki
Periyar
Kayattar
Sabrigiri
Tuticorin
Papanasam
Thiruvananthapuram
Kodayar
Lakshadweep (INDIA)
Andaman & Nicobar Islands (INDIA)
INDIAN OCEAN
LEGEND
Hydel
Thermal
Nuclear
Tidal
Wind
200 0 200 500 kms.
N
W
E
S
Power Consumption
Arabian Sea
Bay of Bengal
Lakshadweep (INDIA)
Andaman & Nicobar Islands (INDIA)
INDIAN OCEAN
LEGEND
3.5-14.2
14.1-24.9
24.8-35.6
35.5-46.3
46.2-57.0
Monthly per/capita consumption of electricity in KWH
200 0 200 500 kms.
N
W
E
S

Projection: Lambert's Conical Orthomorphi

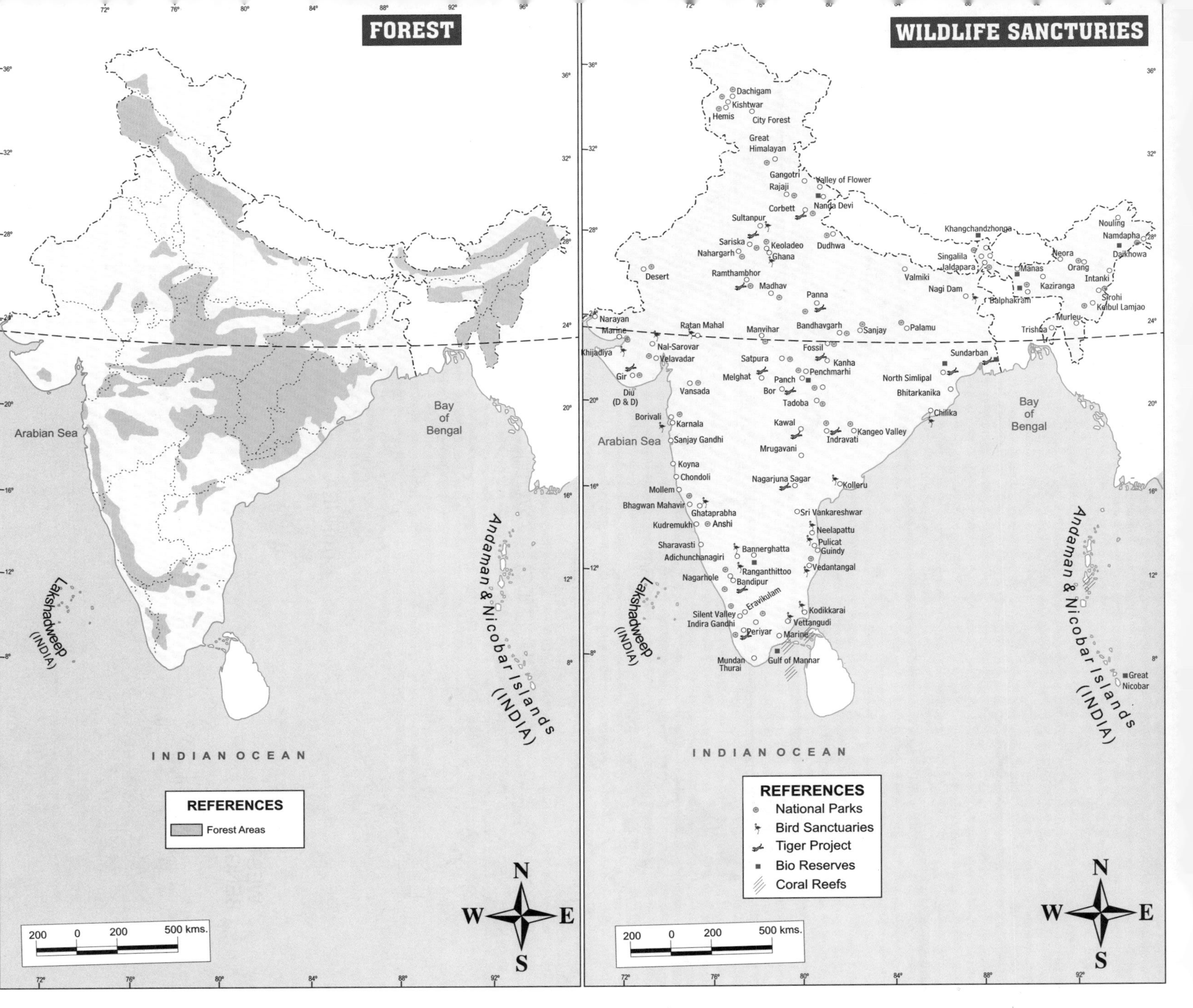

FOREST
Arabian Sea
Bay of Bengal
Lakshadweep (INDIA)
Andaman & Nicobar Islands (INDIA)
INDIAN OCEAN
REFERENCES
Forest Areas
200 0 200 500 kms.
N W E S
WILDLIFE SANCTURIES
Dachigam
Kishtwar
Hemis
City Forest
Great Himalayan
Gangotri
Valley of Flower
Rajaji
Nanda Devi
Corbett
Sultanpur
Sariska
Keoladeo
Dudhwa
Nahargarh
Ghana
Ramthambhor
Madhav
Desert
Panna
Valmiki
Nagi Dam
Khangchandzhonga
Singalila
Jaldapara
Manas
Balphakram
Neora
Orang
Kaziranga
Intanki
Nouling
Namdapha
Daikhowa
Sirohi
Keibul Lamjao
Murleu
Trishna
Narayan
Marine
Khijadiya
Ratan Mahal
Nal-Sarovar
Velavadar
Manvihar
Bandhavgarh
Sanjay
Palamu
Fossil
Kanha
Penchmarhi
Satpura
Melghat
Panch
Bor
Tadoba
Sundarban
North Simlipal
Bhitarkanika
Chilika
Gir
Diu (D & D)
Vansada
Borivali
Karnala
Arabian Sea
Sanjay Gandhi
Kawal
Indravati
Kangeo Valley
Mrugavani
Bay of Bengal
Koyna
Chondoli
Nagarjuna Sagar
Kolleru
Mollem
Bhagwan Mahavir
Ghataprabha
Kudremukh
Anshi
Sri Vankareshwar
Neelapattu
Pulicat
Guindy
Sharavasti
Adichunchanagiri
Bannerghatta
Vedantangal
Ranganthittoo
Nagarhole
Bandipur
Eravikulam
Silent Valley
Indira Gandhi
Periyar
Kodikkarai
Vettangudi
Marine
Mundan Thurai
Gulf of Mannar
Lakshadweep (INDIA)
Andaman & Nicobar Islands (INDIA)
Great Nicobar
INDIAN OCEAN
REFERENCES
National Parks
Bird Sanctuaries
Tiger Project
Bio Reserves
Coral Reefs
200 0 200 500 kms.
N W E S

Projection: Lambert's Conical Orthomorphic

NORTH EAST INDIA-PHYSICAL

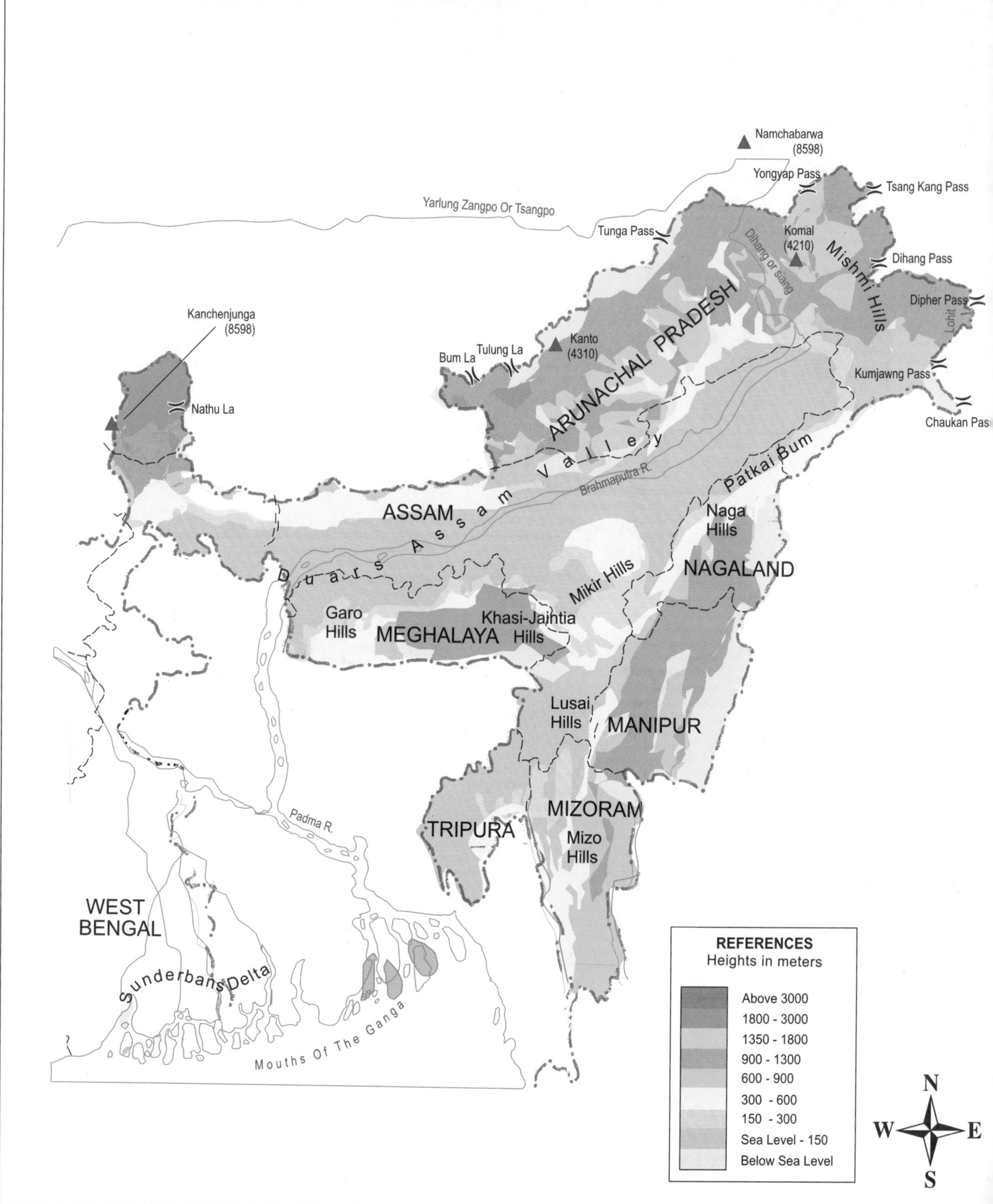
Namchabarwa
(8598)
Yongyap Pass
Tsang Kang Pass
Yarlung Zangpo Or Tsangpo
Tunga Pass
Komal
(4210)
Dihang or siang
Mishmi Hills
Dihang Pass
Dipher Pass
Lohit
Kanchenjunga
(8598)
Bum La
Tulung La
Kanto
(4310)
ARUNACHAL PRADESH
Kumjawng Pass
Nathu La
Chaukan Pass
Assam Valley
Brahmaputra R.
Patkai Bum
ASSAM
Naga
Hills
Duars
NAGALAND
Mikir Hills
Garo
Hills
MEGHALAYA
Khasi-Jaintia
Hills
Lusai
Hills
MANIPUR
Padma R.
MIZORAM
TRIPURA
Mizo
Hills
WEST
BENGAL
Sunderbans Delta
Mouths Of The Ganga
REFERENCES
Heights in meters
Above 3000
1800 - 3000
1350 - 1800
900 - 1300
600 - 900
300 - 600
150 - 300
Sea Level - 150
Below Sea Level
N
W
E
S

Scale - 1:5 M approx

CHINA
Yarlung Zangpo Or Tsangpo
ARUNACHAL PRADESH
Yingkiong
Bomda
Shimong
Anini
Riga
Dihang or siang
Lohitpur
Pangin
Lohit
Tezu
Along
Pasighat
Daporijo
Parshuram kund
Murkong Selek
Ziro
Dibrugarh
Tapun
Hawai
Lachen
Yunthang
THIMPHU
Lhuntsi Dz.
Tawang
Seppa
Dhemaji
Tinsukia
Mangan
Lilabari
Changlang
SIKKIM
Tashigang Dz
Bomdila
Lakhimpur
Tongsa Dz
ITANAGAR
Sivasagar
Khonsa
Gyalshing
GANGTOK
BHUTAN
Wakka
Darjeeling
Matiali
Subankhata
Sonai Rupa
Mon
Karseong
Brahmaputra R.
Jorhat
Chantongia
Nalbari
Tezpur
Bagdora
Alipurduar
Bongaigaon
ASSAM
Mangaldai
Golaghat
Mokokchung
Jalpaiguri
Koch Bihar
Barpeta
Bandari
Tuensang
Nagaon
Marigaon
Kiphire
Kokrajhar
Guwahati
Kamrup
Zunheboto
DISPUR
Wokha
Kishanganj
Dhuburi
Goalpara
NAGALAND
Dinhata
Nongpoh
Diphu
Phek
KOHIMA
Phulbari
Williamnagar
SHILLONG
Jowai
Paren
Chittaranjan
Nongstoin
Senapati
Raiganj
Tura
MEGHALAYA
Dauki
Hoflong
Ukhrul
Balurghat
Tamenglong
Silchar
IMPHAL
Ingraj Bazar
Karimganj
Bishnupur
Thoubal
Dharmanagar
MANIPUR
Hailakandi
BANGLADESH
Churachandpur
Palel
Kailashahar
Murshidabad
DHAKA
Chandel
Kamalpur
Seling
Suri
TRIPURA
Champhai
Baharampur
AGARTALA
AIZAWL
Demagiri
Padma R.
Bethuadahari
Sonamura
MIZORAM
Udaipur
Krishnanagar
Lungseri
MYANMAR
Sabrum
Bardhaman
Manu Bazar
Lunglei
Chunchura
Talabung
Lawngtlai
Mullianpui
Barasat
Howrah
Saiha
Tuipong
Alipur
Vahai
KOLKATA
Diamond Harbour
Mouths Of The Ganga
Haldia
Digha
LEGEND
International Boundary
State Boundary
National Highway
Major Roads
Country Capital
State Capital
Other towns
N
W
E
S

NORTH EAST INDIA- CLIMATE & VEGETATION

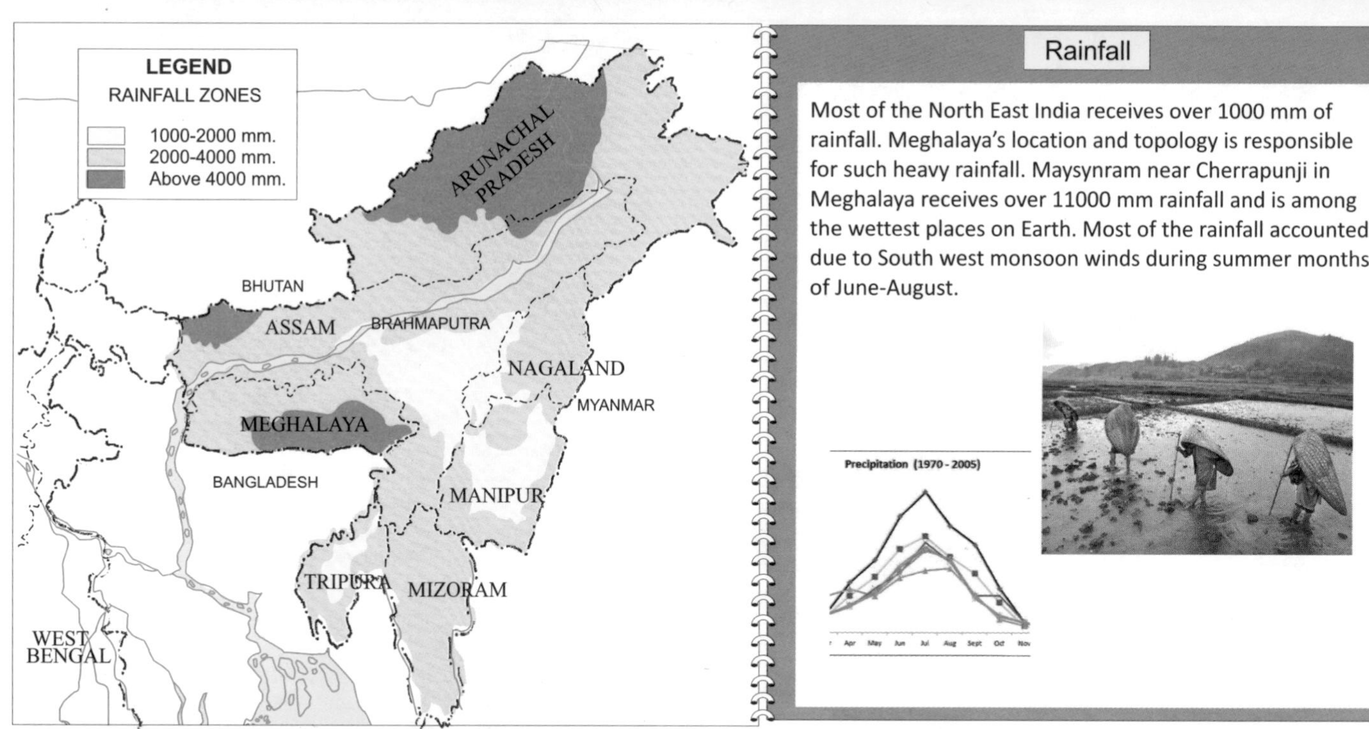
LEGEND
RAINFALL ZONES
1000-2000 mm.
2000-4000 mm.
Above 4000 mm.
ARUNACHAL PRADESH
BHUTAN
ASSAM
BRAHMAPUTRA
NAGALAND
MYANMAR
MEGHALAYA
BANGLADESH
MANIPUR
TRIPURA
MIZORAM
WEST BENGAL
Precipitation (1970 - 2005)
Apr May Jun Jul Aug Sept Oct Nov

Rainfall

Most of the North East India receives over 1000 mm of rainfall. Meghalaya's location and topology is responsible for such heavy rainfall. Maysynram near Cherrapunji in Meghalaya receives over 11000 mm rainfall and is among the wettest places on Earth. Most of the rainfall accounted due to South west monsoon winds during summer months of June-August.

Natural Vegetation

Natural Vegetation of North East India vary depending upon the altitute and geo-topological factors. While most of the Brahmaputra Valley is rich in evergreen forests, upper regions along Himalayan range are full of pine and scrubs vegetations. Wet areas of Meghalaya and other hilly areas are favourable for teak and sal forests. Hollong and Nahar of Assam valley are famous for rich source of timber in the region.

CHINA
ARUNACHAL PRADESH
BHUTAN
ASSAM
NAGALAND
MYANMAR
MEGHALAYA
BANGLADESH
MANIPUR
TRIPURA
MIZORAM
WEST BENGAL

LEGEND
Evergreen Forest
Deciduous Forest
Scrub/Degraded Fores
Grass

Projection: Lambert's Conical Orthomorphic 1000 0 1000 2000

LEGEND
Rice+Potato+Vegetable
Rice+Maize+Potato
Rice+Maize+Potato+Vegetable
Rice+Maize+Pulses
Rice+Maize+Oilseed+Pulses
Rice+Maize
Yarlung Zangpo Or Tsangpo
China
ARUNACHAL PRADESH
Dihang or siang
Lohit
Sikkim
Bhutan
Brahmaputra R.
ASSAM
NAGALAND
MEGHALAYA
Bangladesh
Myanmar
MANIPUR
Padma R.
TRIPURA
MIZORAM
WEST BENGAL
Mouths Of The Ganga

Crops

Agriculture is the main occupation of North East India. Arunachal Pradesh follows jhum type cultivation. It mainly produces Maize, Millets & Paddy besides many types of fruits. Assam is largely valley and mainly produces Rice & Maize as food crops and Tea as main cash crop. Many types of citrus & non-citrus fruits are also grown here throughout the year. Manipur mainly produces wheat & rice while Meghalaya has uneven terrain yet produces Millets & Paddy as major crops. It also produces many types of citrus fruits. Mizoram too produces Maize & Paddy. Tea and Coffee are also grown in some areas. Nagaland soil is good for Maize, Millets & Paddy besides tea, rubber and coffee. Tripura predominantly produces wheat besides paddy as maiin food crops and rubber & coconut as major cash crops.

Mineral

North East India is very rich in minerals resources. Yet to be tapped, untouched and unexplored vast natural resources is the key to development of the region in the next decade. Uneven terrain means different minerals in different parts of the region. Eg. Nagaland is rich in fossil fuels like Petroleum, Assam is rich in coal and petroleum both. Meghalaya has huge iron ore reserves besides granite and quartz. Manipur has reserves of Platinum & Uranium. Sikkim has copper and gold reserves. In the current government's NE region agenda lies economic growth driven by tapping and exploiting the natural resources and thus development of the the area is imminent.

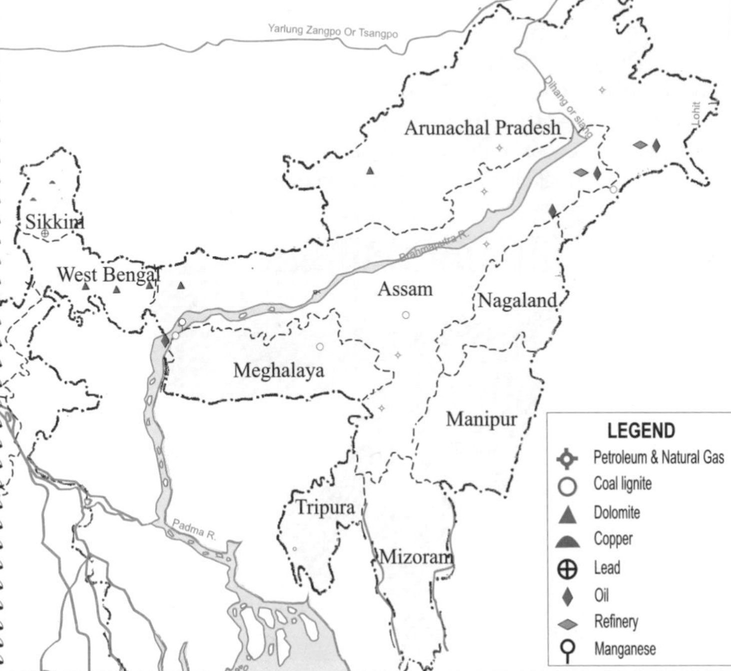
Yarlung Zangpo Or Tsangpo
Dihang or siang
Lohit
Arunachal Pradesh
Sikkim
West Bengal
Brahmaputra R.
Assam
Nagaland
Meghalaya
Manipur
Tripura
Mizoram
Padma R.
LEGEND
Petroleum & Natural Gas
Coal lignite
Dolomite
Copper
Lead
Oil
Refinery
Manganese

1000 0 1000 2000 km.

Projection: Lambert's Conical Orthomorphic

NORTH EAST INDIA-SOIL & POPULATION

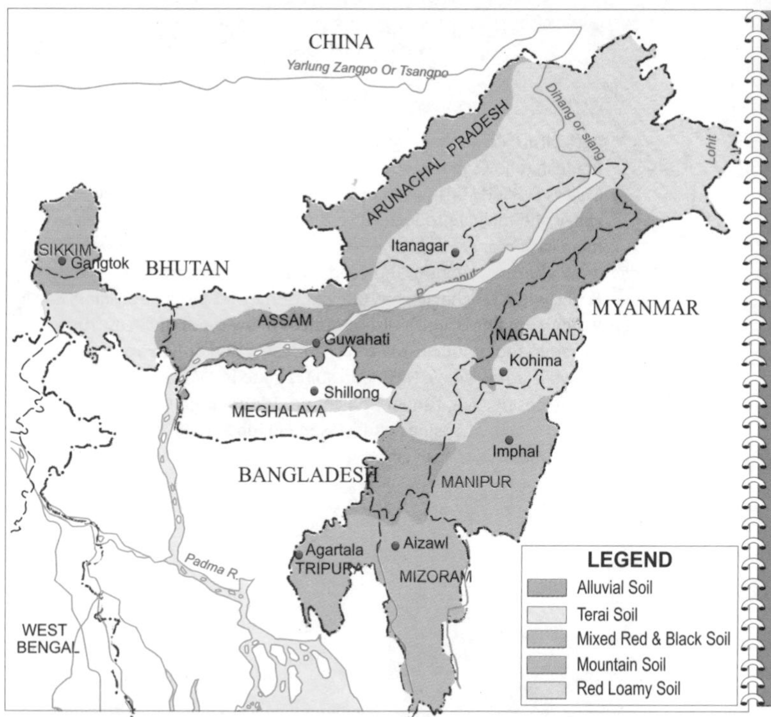
CHINA
Yarlung Zangpo Or Tsangpo
ARUNACHAL PRADESH
Dihang or siang
Lohit
SIKKIM
Gangtok
BHUTAN
Itanagar
ASSAM
Guwahati
MYANMAR
NAGALAND
Kohima
Shillong
MEGHALAYA
Imphal
BANGLADESH
MANIPUR
Agartala
TRIPURA
Aizawl
MIZORAM
Padma R.
WEST BENGAL
LEGEND
Alluvial Soil
Terai Soil
Mixed Red & Black Soil
Mountain Soil
Red Loamy Soil

SOIL

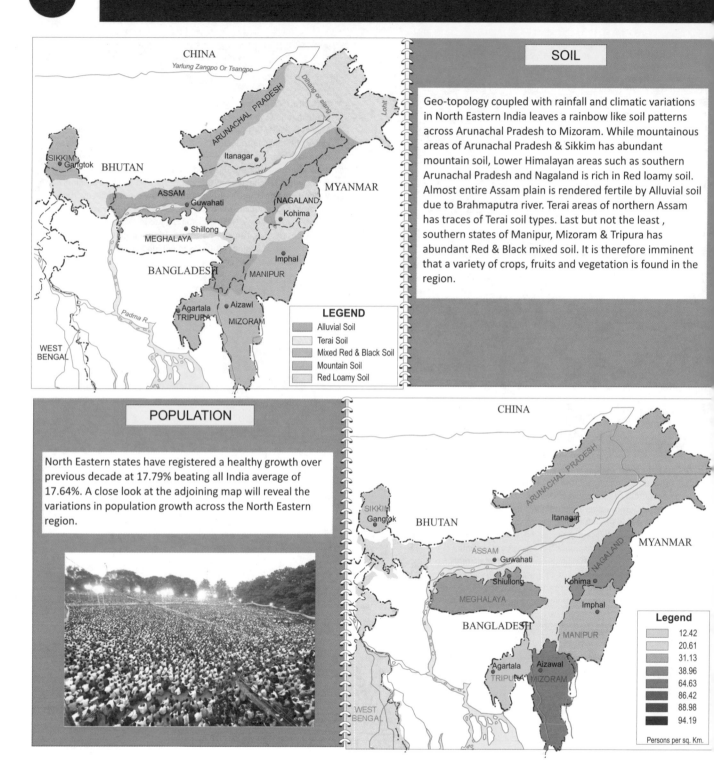

Geo-topology coupled with rainfall and climatic variations in North Eastern India leaves a rainbow like soil patterns across Arunachal Pradesh to Mizoram. While mountainous areas of Arunachal Pradesh & Sikkim has abundant mountain soil, Lower Himalayan areas such as southern Arunachal Pradesh and Nagaland is rich in Red loamy soil. Almost entire Assam plain is rendered fertile by Alluvial soil due to Brahmaputra river. Terai areas of northern Assam has traces of Terai soil types. Last but not the least , southern states of Manipur, Mizoram & Tripura has abundant Red & Black mixed soil. It is therefore imminent that a variety of crops, fruits and vegetation is found in the region.

POPULATION

North Eastern states have registered a healthy growth over previous decade at 17.79% beating all India average of 17.64%. A close look at the adjoining map will reveal the variations in population growth across the North Eastern region.

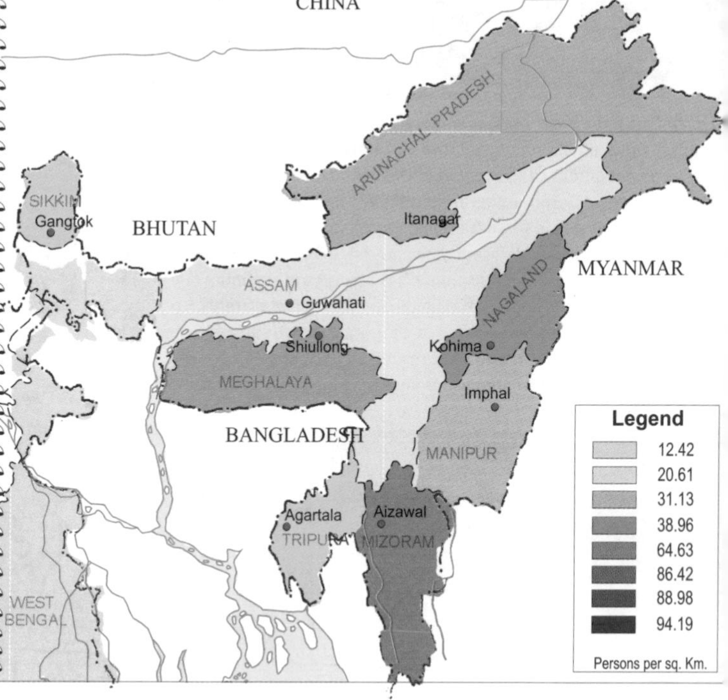
CHINA
ARUNACHAL PRADESH
SIKKIM
Gangtok
BHUTAN
Itanagar
MYANMAR
ASSAM
Guwahati
NAGALAND
Shiullong
Kohima
MEGHALAYA
Imphal
BANGLADESH
MANIPUR
Agartala
Aizawal
TRIPURA
MIZORAM
WEST BENGAL
Legend
12.42
20.61
31.13
38.96
64.63
86.42
88.98
94.19
Persons per sq. Km.

Projection: Lambert's Conical Orthomorphic

1000 0 1000 2000 km

NORTH EAST INDIA-FOREST & WILDLIFE

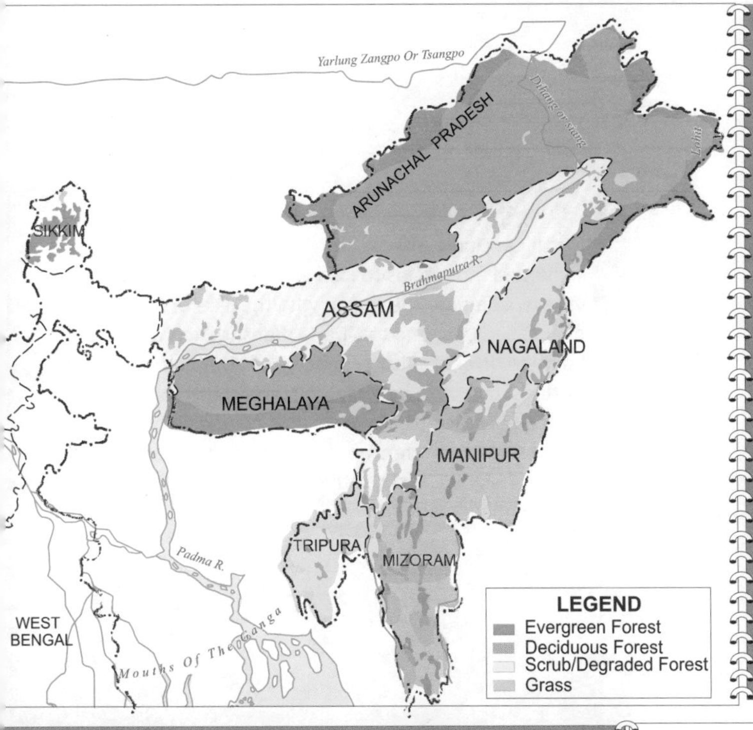

Yarlung Zangpo Or Tsangpo
ARUNACHAL PRADESH
SIKKIM
ASSAM
Brahmaputra R.
NAGALAND
MEGHALAYA
MANIPUR
TRIPURA
MIZORAM
Padma R.
WEST BENGAL
Mouths Of The Ganga
LEGEND
Evergreen Forest
Deciduous Forest
Scrub/Degraded Forest
Grass

Forest

North East India has most diverse forest cover. Temperate , Arctic and tropical climatic extents has rendered pine to decidous to wet evergreen forest cover across the length and breadth of the region. Due to its land cover, Arunachal Pradesh touches almost entire spectrum of forest variety. North East India has a forest cover of 1,63,814 km2 which is approximately one fourth of all India forest coverage. Of late there had been drastic reduction in the forest cover due to frequent clearing for shifting (Jhum) cultivation, urbanisation, timber, firewood, furniture and other human related activities.

Wildlife

Entire North East India is rich in flora and fauna due to diverse natural vegetation (as the region lies between temperate & tropical zone), vast physiographic & climatic region. This is home to various species of wildlife unique to this geography. One-horned rhinoceros, golden langurs, Tigers, Assam roofed turtles, pygmy hogs are notables. With numerous wildlife sanctuaries spread across North East India. Manas & Kaziranga, Nokrek National Park are UNESCO world heritage sites.

One-horned rhinoceros

Golden Langur

Tiger

Assam roofed turtle

Mehao
D'Ering
Namdapha
Hanagar
Barnadi
Pabha
Pakhul
Nameri
Holangapar
Barnadi
Sonai Rupai
Manas
Orang
Kaziranga
Garampani
Pobitara
Intanki
Intank
Nokrek
Siroy
Keibul Lamjao
Rowa
Sepahijila
Murlen
Dampa
Trishna
LEGEND
Wildlife Sanctuary
National Park

1000 0 1000 2000 km.
Projection: Lambert's Conical Orthomorphic

Yarlung Zangpo Or Tsangpo
ARUNACHAL PRADESH
Dihang or siang
Mehao
Lohit
Bomdila Monastery
Brahmaputra R.
Talatal Ghar
ASSAM
NAGALAND
Dimapur
Tryshi Falls
Shilloi Lake
MEGHALAYA
Kohima Zoo
Nawsmai Cave
Cherrapunji (Pool)
Shree Govindajee Temple
Bishnupur
MANIPUR
Unakoti Hills
Neermahal Palace
Ujjayanta Palace
Vantawang Falls
Padma R.
TRIPURA
MIZORAM
WEST BENGAL
Mouths Of The Ganga

Tourism

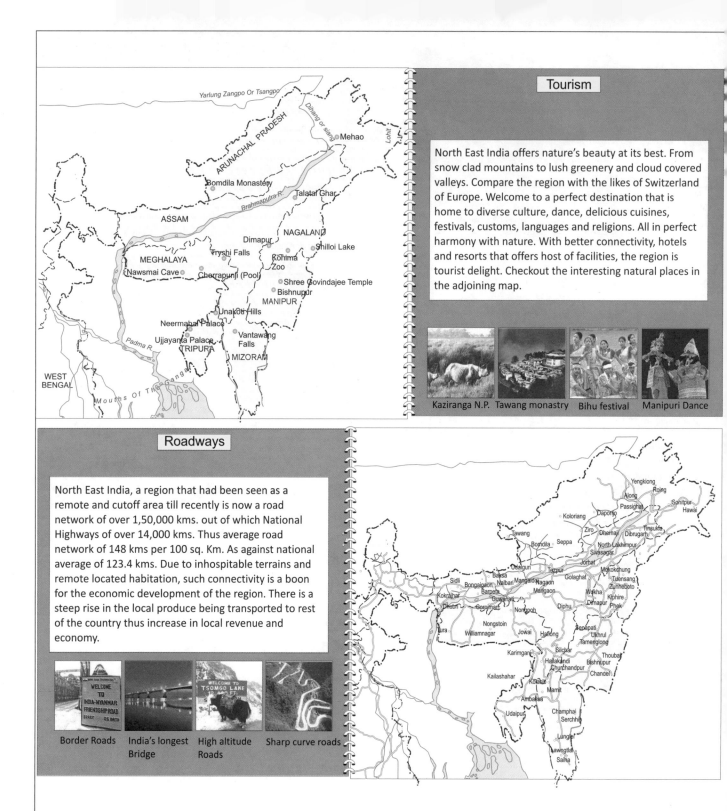

North East India offers nature's beauty at its best. From snow clad mountains to lush greenery and cloud covered valleys. Compare the region with the likes of Switzerland of Europe. Welcome to a perfect destination that is home to diverse culture, dance, delicious cuisines, festivals, customs, languages and religions. All in perfect harmony with nature. With better connectivity, hotels and resorts that offers host of facilities, the region is tourist delight. Checkout the interesting natural places in the adjoining map.

Kaziranga N.P.

Tawang monastry

Bihu festival

Manipuri Dance

Roadways

North East India, a region that had been seen as a remote and cutoff area till recently is now a road network of over 1,50,000 kms. out of which National Highways of over 14,000 kms. Thus average road network of 148 kms per 100 sq. Km. As against national average of 123.4 kms. Due to inhospitable terrains and remote located habitation, such connectivity is a boon for the economic development of the region. There is a steep rise in the local produce being transported to rest of the country thus increase in local revenue and economy.

WELCOME TO INDIA-MYANMAR FRIENDSHIP ROAD

Border Roads

India's longest Bridge

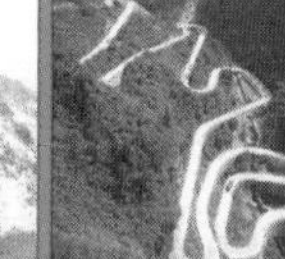

WELCOME TO TSOMGO LAKE

High altitude Roads

Sharp curve roads

Yengkiong
Roing
Along
Sonitpur
Hawai
Passighat
Koloriang
Daporijo
Tinsukia
Ziro
Dhemaji
Dibrugarh
Tawang
Bomdila
Seppa
North Lakhimpur
Sivasagar
Jorhat
Udalguri
Tezpur
Mokokchung
Golaghat
Tuensang
Sidli
Baksa
Bongaigaon
Nalbari
Mangaldoi
Nagaon
Zunheboto
Barpeta
Kokrajhar
Guwahati
Morigaon
Wokha
Kiphire
Dhubri
Goroimari
Nongpoh
Diphu
Dimapur
Phek
Nongstoin
Tura
Williamnagar
Jowai
Haflong
Senapati
Ukhrul
Tamenglong
Karimganj
Silchar
Thoubal
Hallakandi
Churchandpur
Bishnupur
Chandel
Kailashahar
Kolasib
Mamit
Ambassa
Udaipur
Champhai
Serchhip
Lunglei
Lawngtlai
Saiha

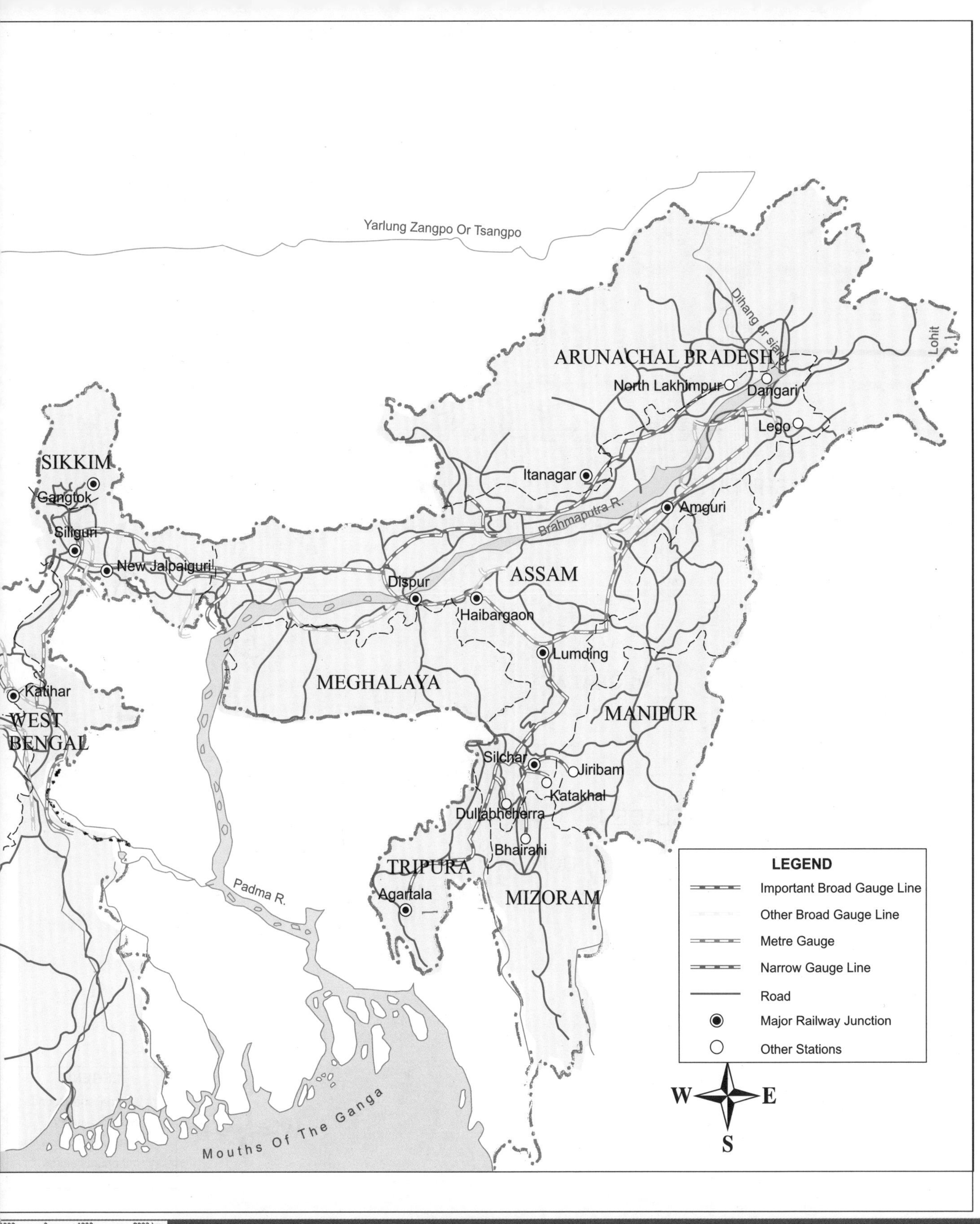

Yarlung Zangpo Or Tsangpo
Dihang or siang
Lohit
ARUNACHAL PRADESH
North Lakhimpur
Dangari
Lego
SIKKIM
Gangtok
Itanagar
Amguri
Brahmaputra R.
Siliguri
New Jalpaiguri
Dispur
ASSAM
Haibargaon
Lumding
Katihar
MEGHALAYA
MANIPUR
WEST
BENGAL
Silchar
Jiribam
Katakhal
Dullabhcherra
Bhairahi
TRIPURA
Agartala
MIZORAM
Padma R.
Mouths Of The Ganga
LEGEND
Important Broad Gauge Line
Other Broad Gauge Line
Metre Gauge
Narrow Gauge Line
Road
Major Railway Junction
Other Stations
W
E
S
1000
0
1000
2000 km.

Projection: Lambert's Conical Orthomorphic

NORTH EAST- NATIONAL WATERWAYS-II

Yarlung Zangpo Or Tsangpo
CHINA
ARUNACHAL PRADESH
Dihang or siang
Lohit
Sadiya
Saikhoa
Dibrugarh
Disangmukh
Neamati
Brahmaputra R.
Gamri Ghat
Dhansiri Mukh
Tezpur
SIKKIM
BHUTAN
WEST BENGAL
ASSAM
Guwahati
Jogi Ghopa
Pandu
Dhubri
NAGALAND
MYANMAR
MEGHALAYA
MANIPUR
BANGLADESH
TRIPURA
MIZORAM
Padma R.
Mouths Of The Ganga
N
W
E
S
LEGEND
International Boundary
State Boundary
National Waterways
Important centres

Scale - 1:5 M approx

ARUNACHAL PRADESH
Section

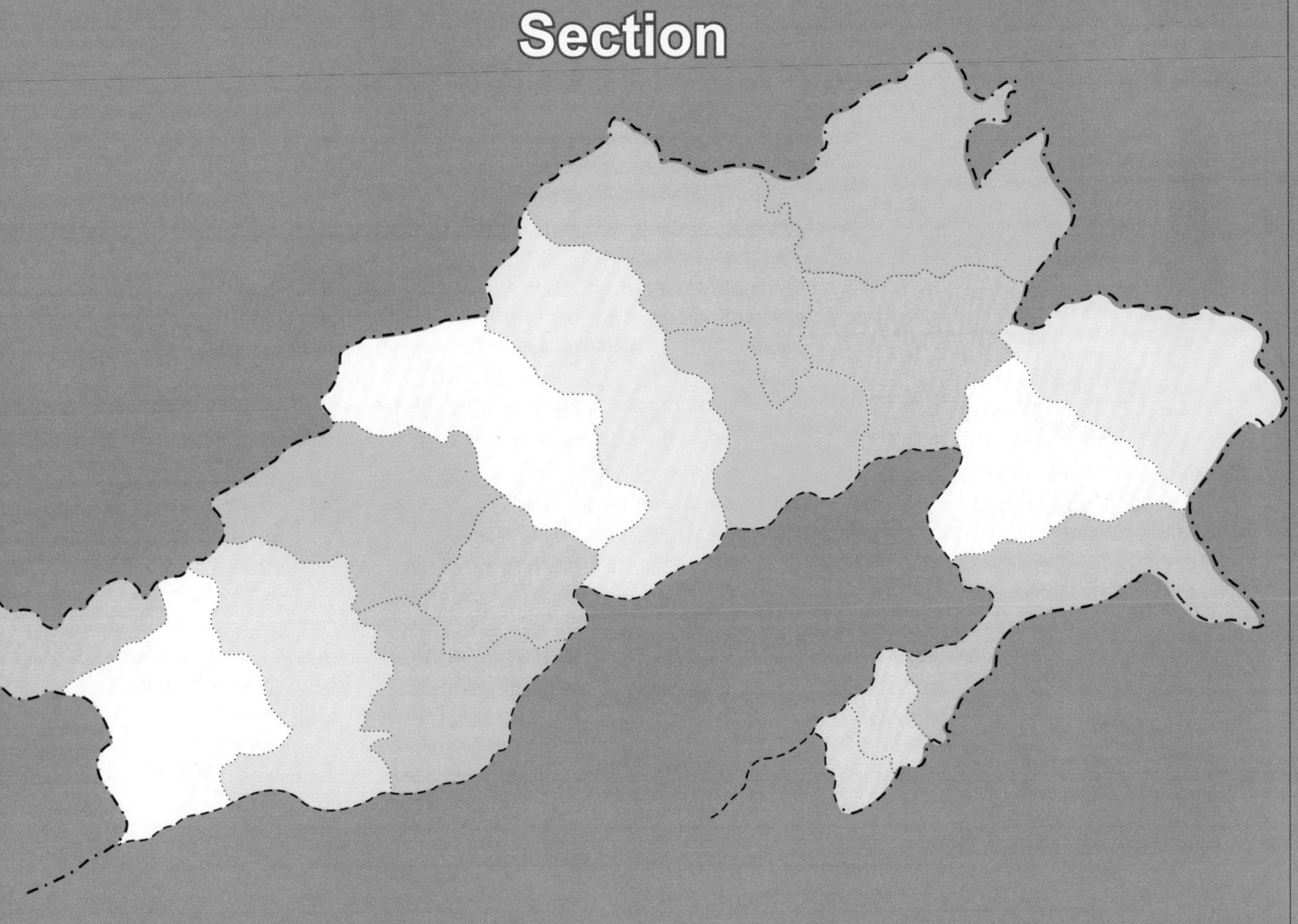

POPULATION:	***13,82,611***	**DISTRICTS:** ***25***
AREA:	***83,743 sq.km.***	**L.S. CONSTITUENCY:** ***2***
POP. DENSITY:	***16.5 persons / km^2***	**R.S. CONSTITUENCY:** ***1***
LITERACY:	***66.95 %***	**GRAM PANCHAYATS:** ***1,785***
SEX RATIO:	***920 females/1000 males***	**GSDP:** ***22,045***

Data and information pertaining to new districts eg. Kra Daadi, Kamle, Lepa Raada, etc. provided in the relevant pages reflect combined figures of mother districts. In some instances no authentic map sources were available hence indicative maps are provided. We will update these maps in subsequent editions as and when they are available .

ARUNACHAL PRADESH-PHYSICAL

VITAL STATISTICS

1.State Bird - Great Indian hornbill
2.State Animal - Gayal
3.State Flower - Foxtail Orchid
4.State Tree - Hollong
5.Languages - Monpa, Miji, Aka, sherdukpen, Apatani, Adi, Hill Miri.
6.Primary Rivers - Lohit, Kameng, Dikrong, Tirap, Dibang, subansiri, Noa-Dihing, Kamlang.
7.Neighbours - Assam, Nagaland
8.Forest and NPs - Dihang-Debang Biosphere Reserve, Namdapha Tiger Reserve, Mouling NP.
9.Tribes - Adi, Aka, Apatani, Galo Dafla, Galo, Khampti, Bugun, Mishmi, Momba, Naga, Sherdukpen, Singhpo.

Some of the important festivals of the state are Mopin and Solung of the Adis, Lossar of the Monpas, Boori-boot of the Hill Miris, Sherdukpens, Dree of the Apatanis, Si-Donyi of the Tagins, Reh of the Idu-Mishmis, Nyokum of the Nyishis, etc. Animal sacrifice is a common ritual in most festivels.

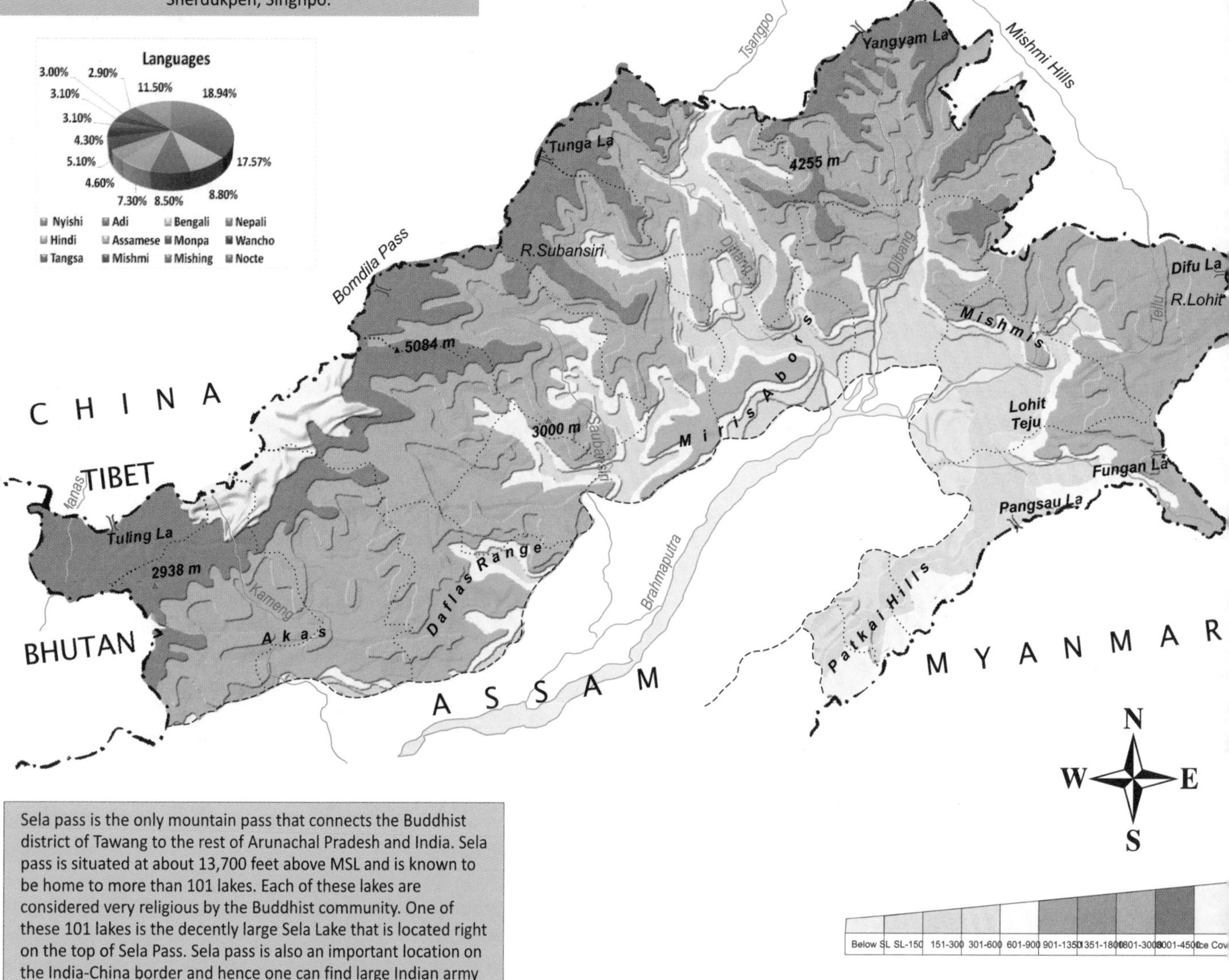

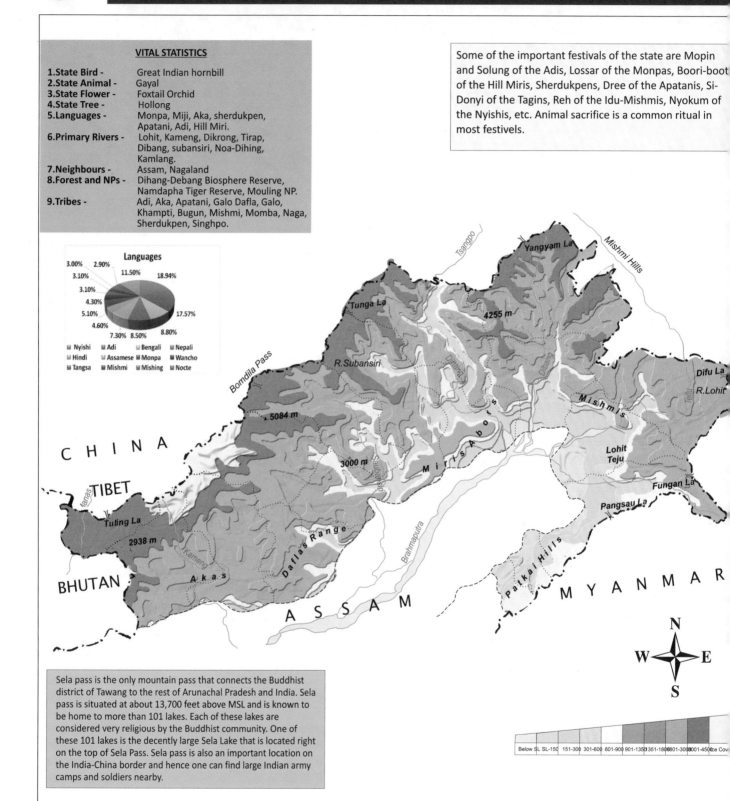

Languages
3.00%
2.90%
3.10%
11.50%
18.94%
3.10%
4.30%
5.10%
17.57%
4.60%
7.30%
8.50%
8.80%
Nyishi
Adi
Bengali
Nepali
Hindi
Assamese
Monpa
Wancho
Tangsa
Mishmi
Mishing
Nocte
Tsangpo
Yangyam La
Mishmi Hills
Tunga La
4255 m
R.Subansiri
Dibang
Difu La
R.Lohit
Tellu
Bomdila Pass
Mishmis
5084 m
Abors
CHINA
3000 m
Miris
Lohit
Teju
Subansiri
TIBET
Manas
Fungan La
Pangsau La
Tuling La
2938 m
Daflas Range
Brahmaputra
Kameng
Patkai Hills
BHUTAN
Akas
ASSAM
MYANMAR
N
W
E
S
Below SL
SL-150
151-300
301-600
601-900
901-1350
1351-1800
1801-3000
3001-4500
Ice Cov

Sela pass is the only mountain pass that connects the Buddhist district of Tawang to the rest of Arunachal Pradesh and India. Sela pass is situated at about 13,700 feet above MSL and is known to be home to more than 101 lakes. Each of these lakes are considered very religious by the Buddhist community. One of these 101 lakes is the decently large Sela Lake that is located right on the top of Sela Pass. Sela pass is also an important location on the India-China border and hence one can find large Indian army camps and soldiers nearby.

Scale - 1:3 M appro

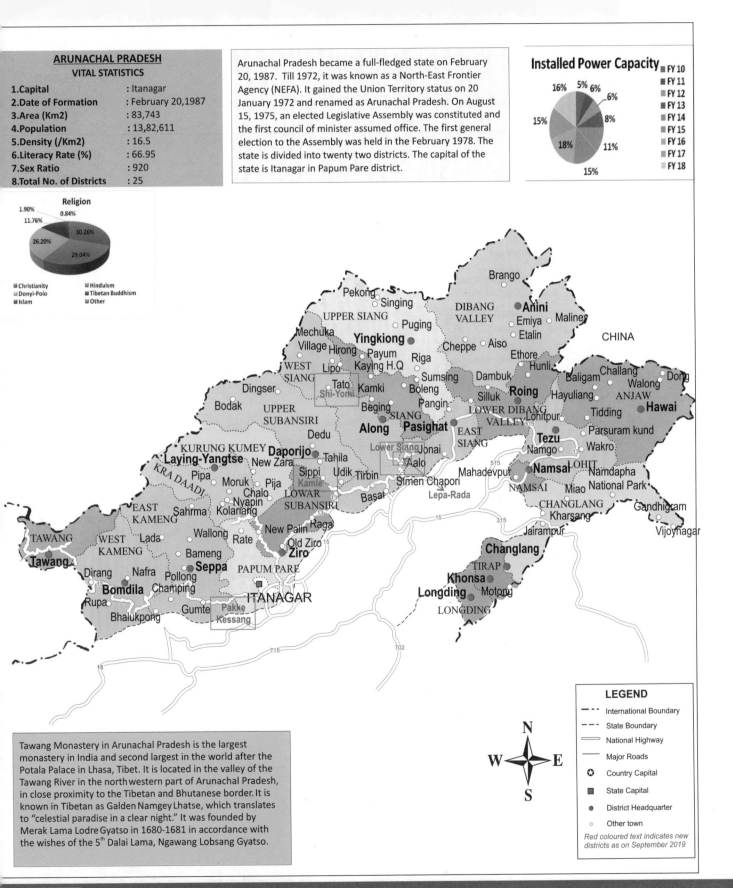

ARUNACHAL PRADESH
VITAL STATISTICS

1.Capital	: Itanagar
2.Date of Formation	: February 20,1987
3.Area (Km2)	: 83,743
4.Population	: 13,82,611
5.Density (/Km2)	: 16.5
6.Literacy Rate (%)	: 66.95
7.Sex Ratio	: 920
8.Total No. of Districts	: 25

Arunachal Pradesh became a full-fledged state on February 20, 1987. Till 1972, it was known as a North-East Frontier Agency (NEFA). It gained the Union Territory status on 20 January 1972 and renamed as Arunachal Pradesh. On August 15, 1975, an elected Legislative Assembly was constituted and the first council of minister assumed office. The first general election to the Assembly was held in the February 1978. The state is divided into twenty two districts. The capital of the state is Itanagar in Papum Pare district.

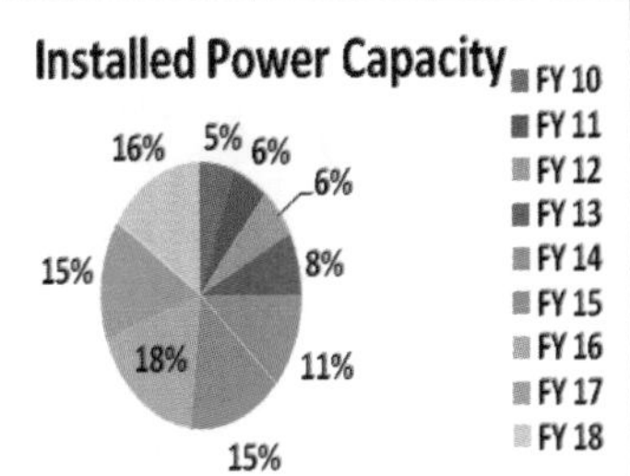

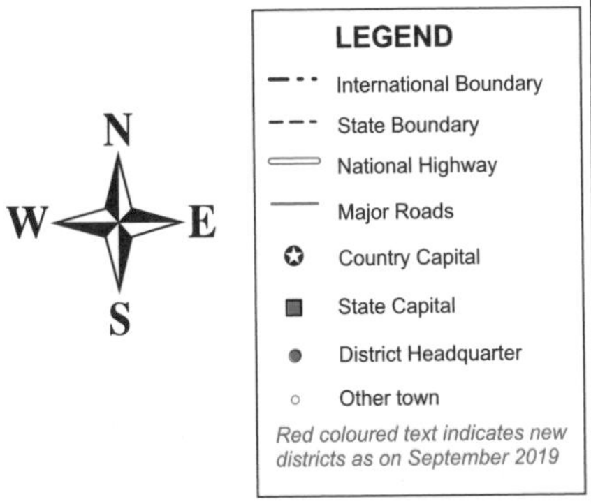

Installed Power Capacity
16%
5%
6%
6%
8%
11%
15%
18%
15%
FY 10
FY 11
FY 12
FY 13
FY 14
FY 15
FY 16
FY 17
FY 18

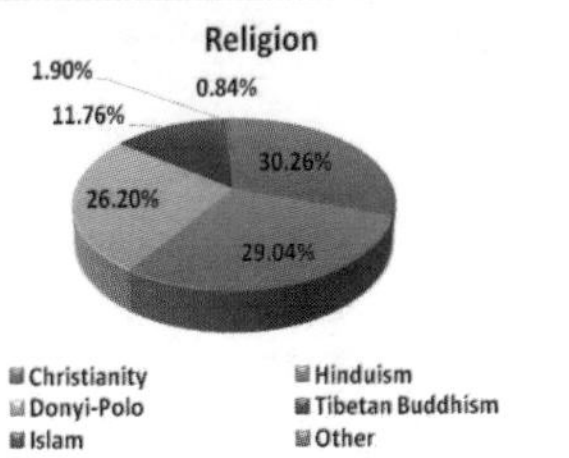

Religion

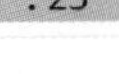

1.90% 0.84% 11.76% 30.26% 26.20% 29.04%

Christianity, Donyi-Polo, Islam, Hinduism, Tibetan Buddhism, Other

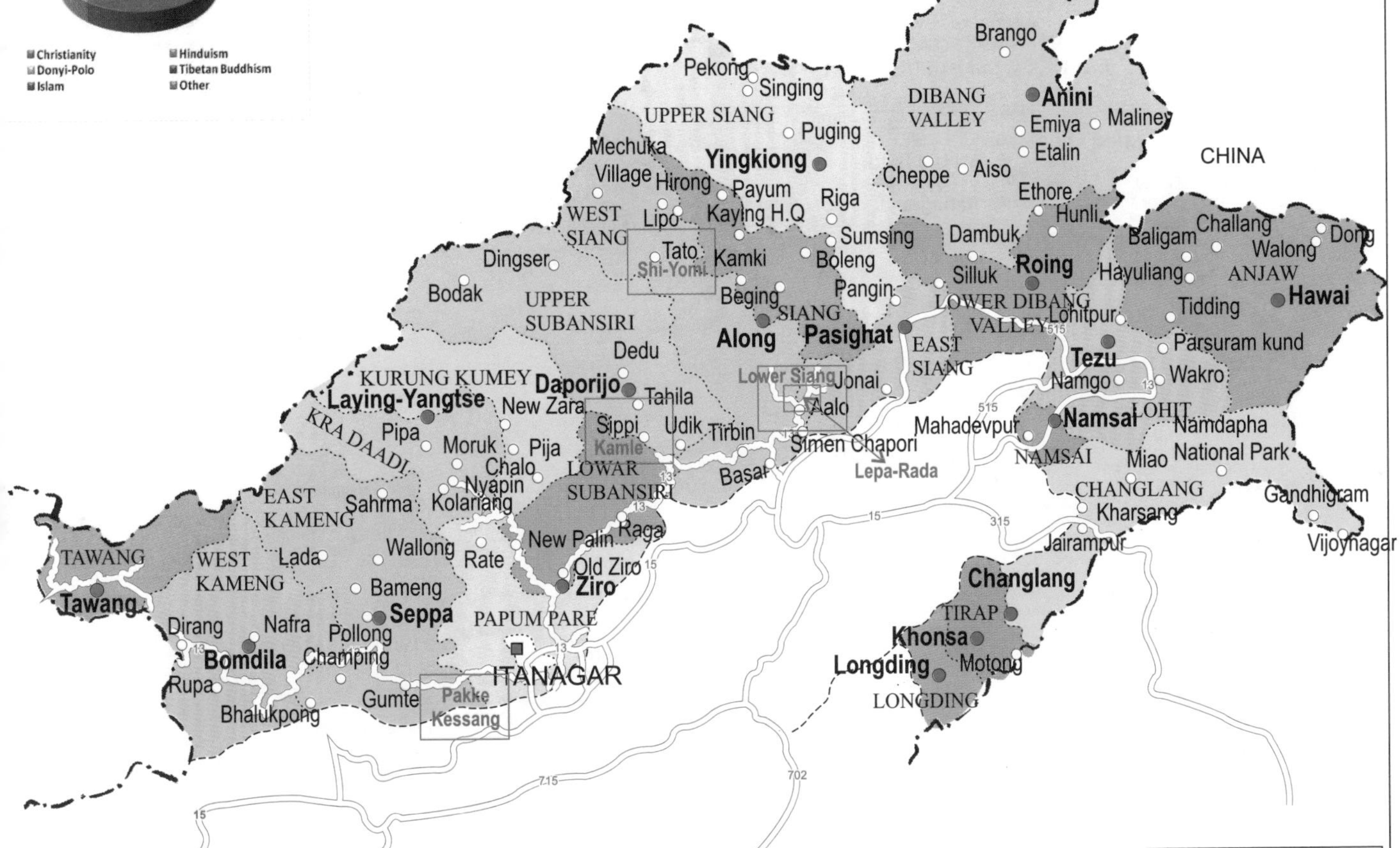

LEGEND

- International Boundary
- State Boundary
- National Highway
- Major Roads
- Country Capital
- State Capital
- District Headquarter
- Other town

Red coloured text indicates new districts as on September 2019

Tawang Monastery in Arunachal Pradesh is the largest monastery in India and second largest in the world after the Potala Palace in Lhasa, Tibet. It is located in the valley of the Tawang River in the northwestern part of Arunachal Pradesh, in close proximity to the Tibetan and Bhutanese border. It is known in Tibetan as Galden Namgey Lhatse, which translates to "celestial paradise in a clear night." It was founded by Merak Lama Lodre Gyatso in 1680-1681 in accordance with the wishes of the 5th Dalai Lama, Ngawang Lobsang Gyatso.

Scale - 1:3 M approx

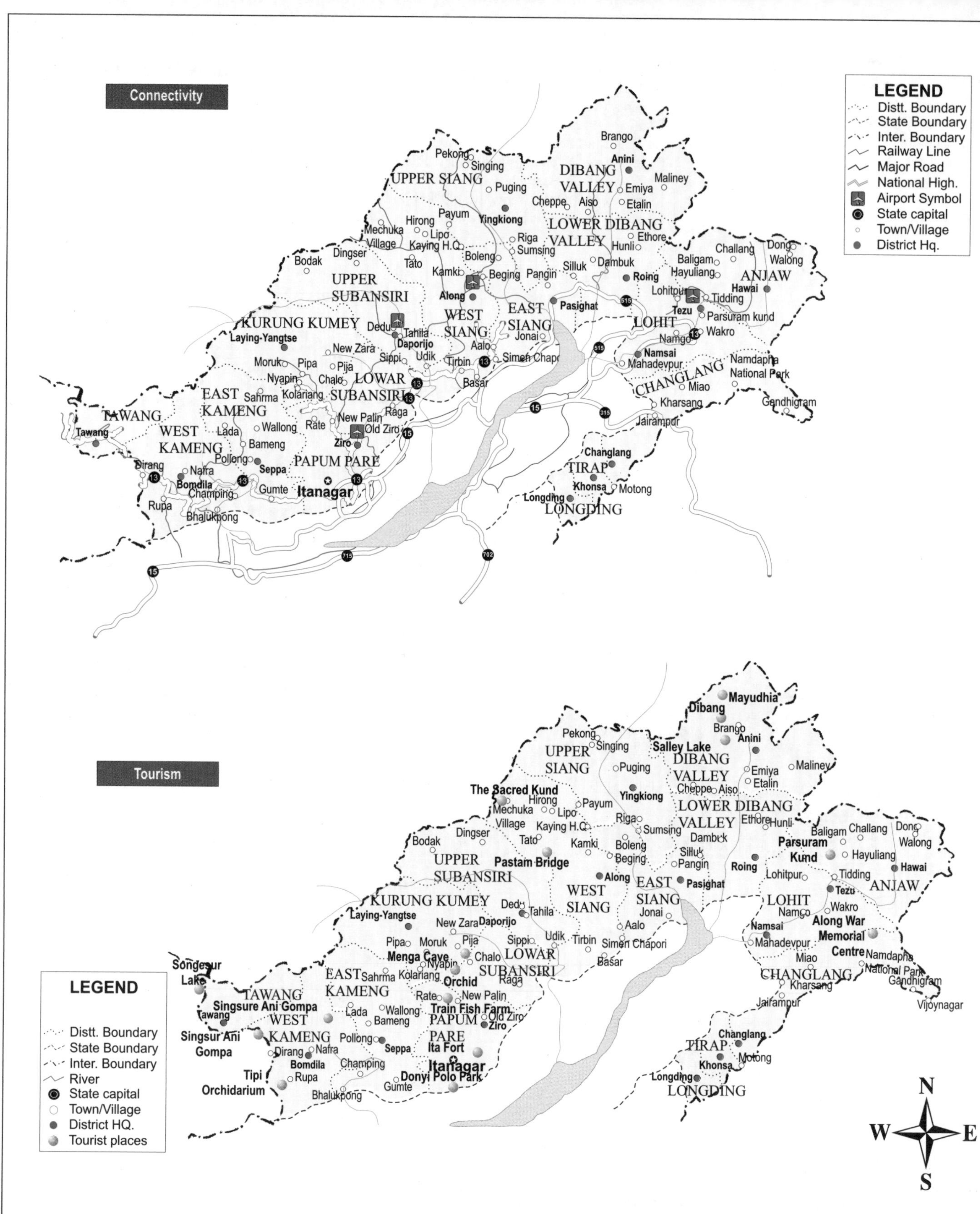

Connectivity
LEGEND
Distt. Boundary
State Boundary
Inter. Boundary
Railway Line
Major Road
National High.
Airport Symbol
State capital
Town/Village
District Hq.
UPPER SIANG
DIBANG VALLEY
LOWER DIBANG VALLEY
UPPER SUBANSIRI
KURUNG KUMEY
WEST SIANG
EAST SIANG
LOHIT
ANJAW
CHANGLANG
EAST KAMENG
LOWAR SUBANSIRI
TAWANG
WEST KAMENG
PAPUM PARE
TIRAP
LONGDING
Itanagar
Tourism
LEGEND
Distt. Boundary
State Boundary
Inter. Boundary
River
State capital
Town/Village
District HQ.
Tourist places
Mayudhia
Salley Lake
The Sacred Kund
Pastam Bridge
Parsuram Kund
Along War Memorial Centre
Songesur Lake
Singsure Ani Gompa
Singsur Ani Gompa
Tipi Orchidarium
Menga Cave
Orchid
Train Fish Farm
Ita Fort
Donyi Polo Park
N
W
E
S

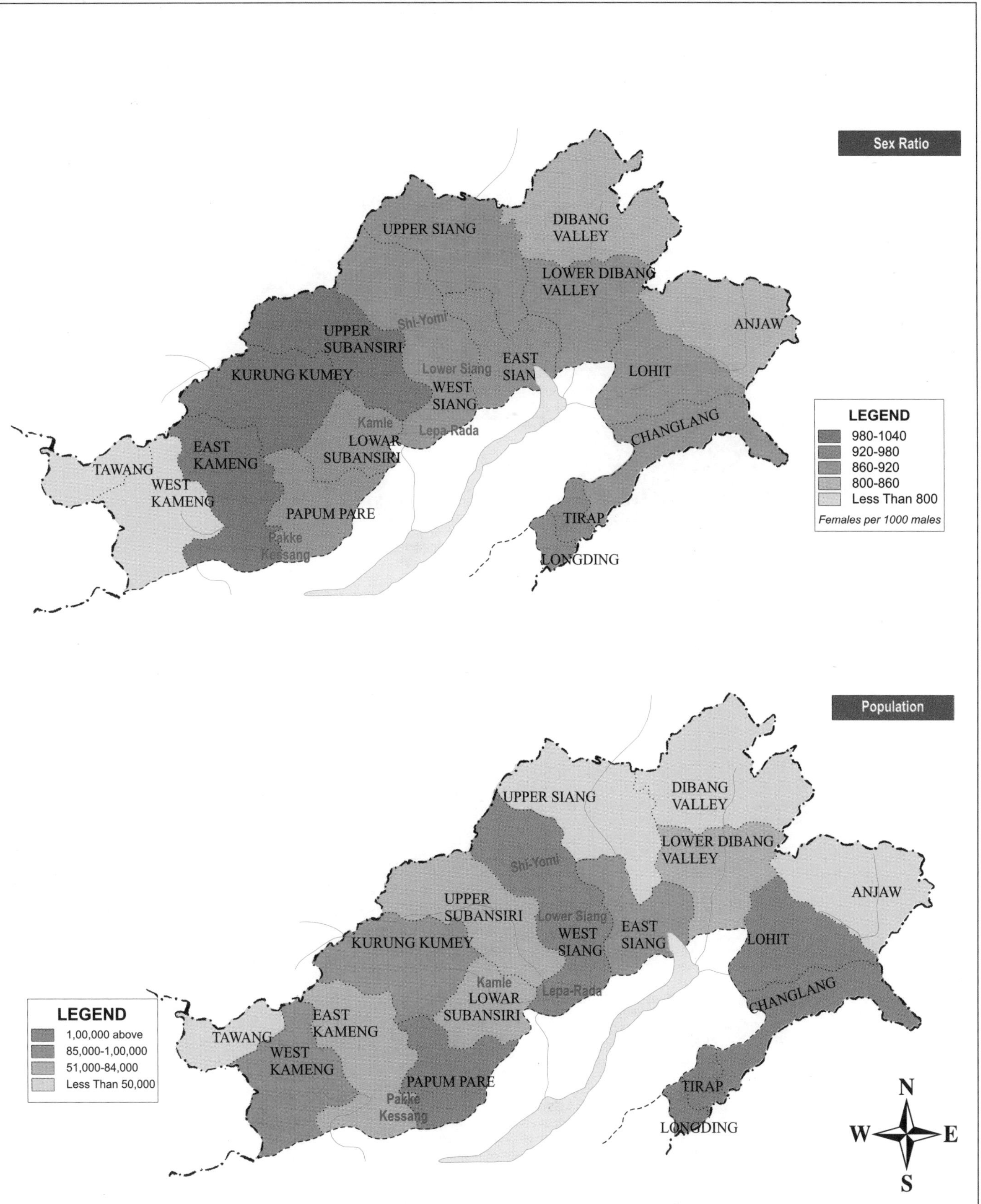
Sex Ratio
UPPER SIANG
DIBANG VALLEY
LOWER DIBANG VALLEY
ANJAW
Shi-Yomi
UPPER SUBANSIRI
KURUNG KUMEY
Lower Siang
EAST SIANG
WEST SIANG
LOHIT
CHANGLANG
Kamle
Lepa-Rada
LOWAR SUBANSIRI
EAST KAMENG
TAWANG
WEST KAMENG
PAPUM PARE
Pakke Kessang
TIRAP
LONGDING
LEGEND
980-1040
920-980
860-920
800-860
Less Than 800
Females per 1000 males
Population
UPPER SIANG
DIBANG VALLEY
LOWER DIBANG VALLEY
Shi-Yomi
ANJAW
UPPER SUBANSIRI
Lower Siang
WEST SIANG
EAST SIANG
LOHIT
KURUNG KUMEY
Kamle
LOWAR SUBANSIRI
Lepa-Rada
CHANGLANG
LEGEND
1,00,000 above
85,000-1,00,000
51,000-84,000
Less Than 50,000
EAST KAMENG
TAWANG
WEST KAMENG
PAPUM PARE
Pakke Kessang
TIRAP
LONGDING
N
W
E
S

Scale - 1:3.83 M approx

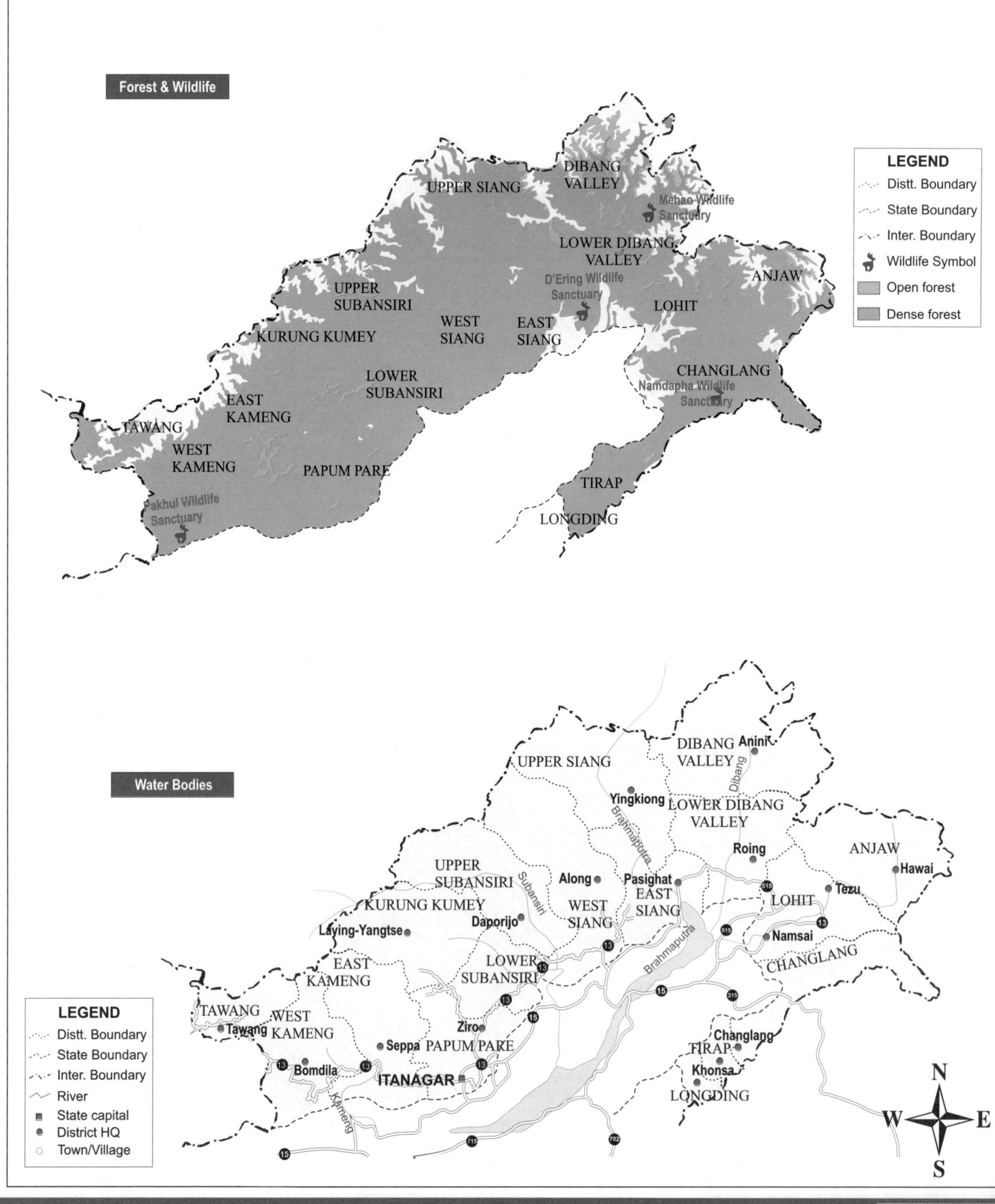
Forest & Wildlife
UPPER SIANG
DIBANG VALLEY
Mehao Wildlife Sanctuary
LOWER DIBANG VALLEY
ANJAW
D'Ering Wildlife Sanctuary
LOHIT
UPPER SUBANSIRI
KURUNG KUMEY
WEST SIANG
EAST SIANG
CHANGLANG
Namdapha Wildlife Sanctuary
LOWER SUBANSIRI
EAST KAMENG
TAWANG
WEST KAMENG
PAPUM PARE
TIRAP
LONGDING
Pakhui Wildlife Sanctuary
LEGEND
Distt. Boundary
State Boundary
Inter. Boundary
Wildlife Symbol
Open forest
Dense forest
Water Bodies
UPPER SIANG
DIBANG VALLEY
Anini
Dibang
Yingkiong
LOWER DIBANG VALLEY
Brahmaputra
Roing
ANJAW
Hawai
UPPER SUBANSIRI
Subansiri
Along
Pasighat
EAST SIANG
LOHIT
Tezu
KURUNG KUMEY
Daporijo
WEST SIANG
Namsai
Laying-Yangtse
EAST KAMENG
LOWER SUBANSIRI
CHANGLANG
TAWANG
Tawang
WEST KAMENG
Ziro
Seppa
PAPUM PARE
Changlang
TIRAP
Khonsa
LONGDING
Bomdila
ITANAGAR
Kameng
LEGEND
Distt. Boundary
State Boundary
Inter. Boundary
River
State capital
District HQ
Town/Village
N
W
E
S

TAWANG

VITAL STATISTICS

1. **District Headquarter:** Tawang
2. **Population:** 49,950
3. **Area:** 2,085sq. km2.
4. **Population Density:** 23 persons per sq. km.
5. **Literacy:** 60.60 %
6. **Sex Ratio:** 701 females per 1000 males

ECONOMIC PROFILES

1. **Agriculture:** Shifting cultivation, wet rice cultivation, terrace cultivation etc. Crops include paddy, wheat, sugarcane, millets, jowar etc. pineapple, guava, orange, etc.
2. **Industries:** Agro, Cotton textile, woolen, silk, jute, wooden, leather, chemical, Rubber, plastic and Petroleum.
3. **Minerals:** Limestone
4. **Tourism:** Sela pass, Tawang monastery, Taktsang Gompa, Gorichen peak, Shonga-tser lake, Nuranang waterfalls, Pankang Teng Tso Lake, Bumla pass, Bap Teng Kang etc.

Tawang district is inhabited by Monpa people. The sixth Dalai Lama, Tsangyang Gyatso, was born in Tawang. Tawang was historically part of Tibet. The 1914 Simla accord defined the McMahon line as the new boundary between British India and Tibet. During the Sino-Indian war of 1962, Tawang fell briefly under Chinese control, but China withdraw it's troops at the end of the war.

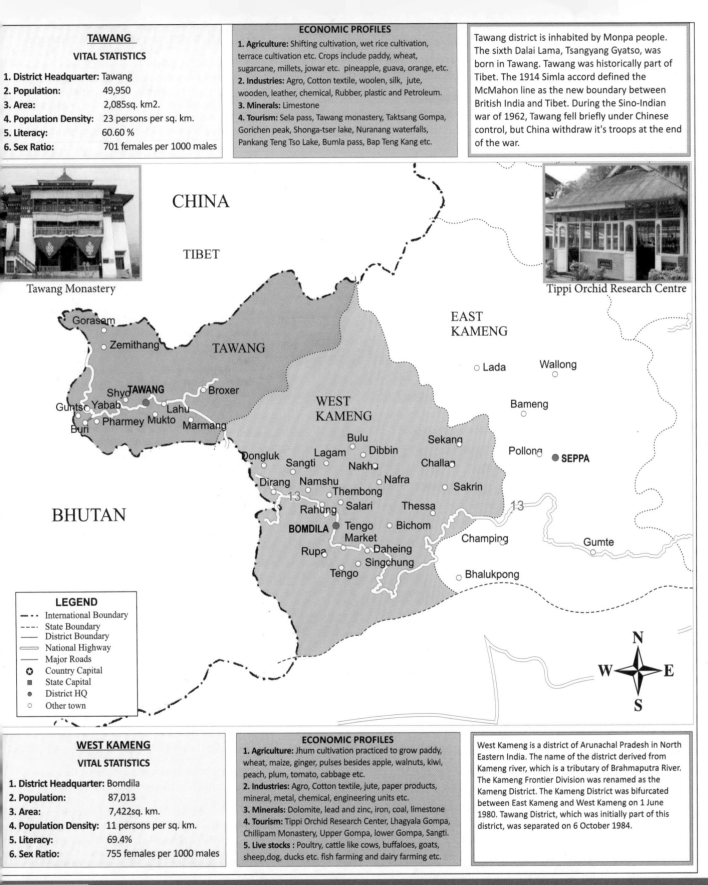

CHINA
TIBET
Tawang Monastery
Tippi Orchid Research Centre
EAST KAMENG
TAWANG
Gorasam
Zemithang
Shyo
TAWANG
Broxer
Guntso
Yabab
Lahu
Buri
Pharmey
Mukto
Marmang
WEST KAMENG
Lada
Wallong
Bameng
Pollong
SEPPA
Bulu
Lagam
Dibbin
Sekang
Dongluk
Sangti
Nakhu
Challan
Dirang
Namshu
Nafra
Thembong
Sakrin
13
Rahung
Salari
Thessa
BOMDILA
Tengo Market
Bichom
Champing
Gumte
Rupa
Daheing
Singchung
Tengo
Bhalukpong
BHUTAN
LEGEND
International Boundary
State Boundary
District Boundary
National Highway
Major Roads
Country Capital
State Capital
District HQ
Other town
N
W
E
S

WEST KAMENG

VITAL STATISTICS

1. **District Headquarter:** Bomdila
2. **Population:** 87,013
3. **Area:** 7,422sq. km.
4. **Population Density:** 11 persons per sq. km.
5. **Literacy:** 69.4%
6. **Sex Ratio:** 755 females per 1000 males

ECONOMIC PROFILES

1. **Agriculture:** Jhum cultivation practiced to grow paddy, wheat, maize, ginger, pulses besides apple, walnuts, kiwi, peach, plum, tomato, cabbage etc.
2. **Industries:** Agro, Cotton textile, jute, paper products, mineral, metal, chemical, engineering units etc.
3. **Minerals:** Dolomite, lead and zinc, iron, coal, limestone
4. **Tourism:** Tippi Orchid Research Center, Lhagyala Gompa, Chillipam Monastery, Upper Gompa, lower Gompa, Sangti.
5. **Live stocks :** Poultry, cattle like cows, buffaloes, goats, sheep,dog, ducks etc. fish farming and dairy farming etc.

West Kameng is a district of Arunachal Pradesh in North Eastern India. The name of the district derived from Kameng river, which is a tributary of Brahmaputra River. The Kameng Frontier Division was renamed as the Kameng District. The Kameng District was bifurcated between East Kameng and West Kameng on 1 June 1980. Tawang District, which was initially part of this district, was separated on 6 October 1984.

Scale - 1:1.1 M approx

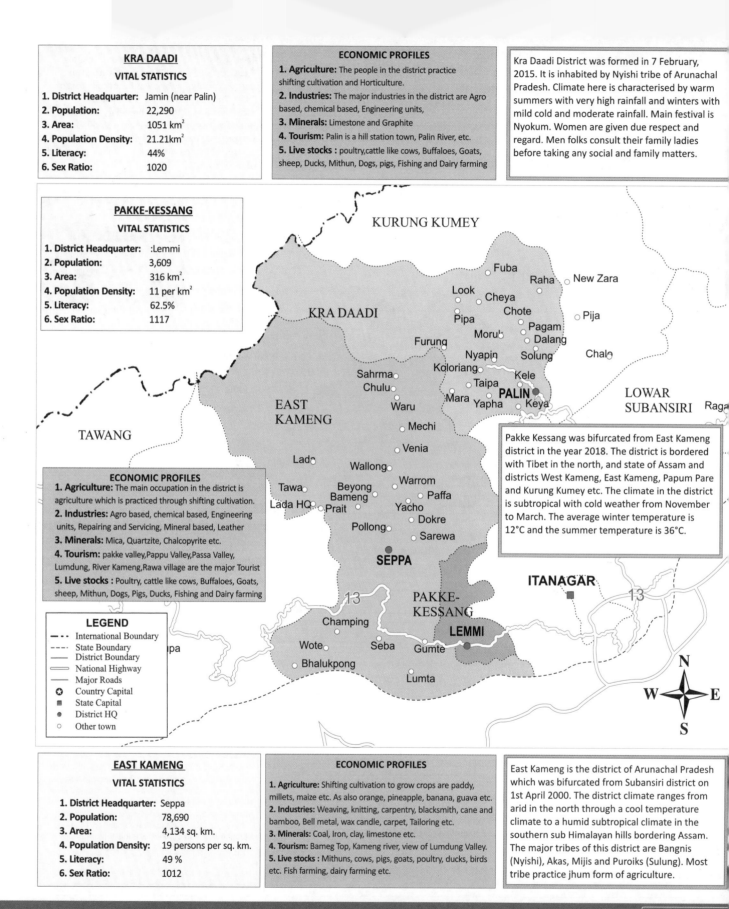

KRA DAADI

VITAL STATISTICS

1. **District Headquarter:** Jamin (near Palin)
2. **Population:** 22,290
3. **Area:** 1051 km^2
4. **Population Density:** 21.21km^2
5. **Literacy:** 44%
6. **Sex Ratio:** 1020

ECONOMIC PROFILES

1. **Agriculture:** The people in the district practice shifting cultivation and Horticulture.
2. **Industries:** The major industries in the district are Agro based, chemical based, Engineering units,
3. **Minerals:** Limestone and Graphite
4. **Tourism:** Palin is a hill station town, Palin River, etc.
5. **Live stocks :** poultry,cattle like cows, Buffaloes, Goats, sheep, Ducks, Mithun, Dogs, pigs, Fishing and Dairy farming

Kra Daadi District was formed in 7 February, 2015. It is inhabited by Nyishi tribe of Arunachal Pradesh. Climate here is characterised by warm summers with very high rainfall and winters with mild cold and moderate rainfall. Main festival is Nyokum. Women are given due respect and regard. Men folks consult their family ladies before taking any social and family matters.

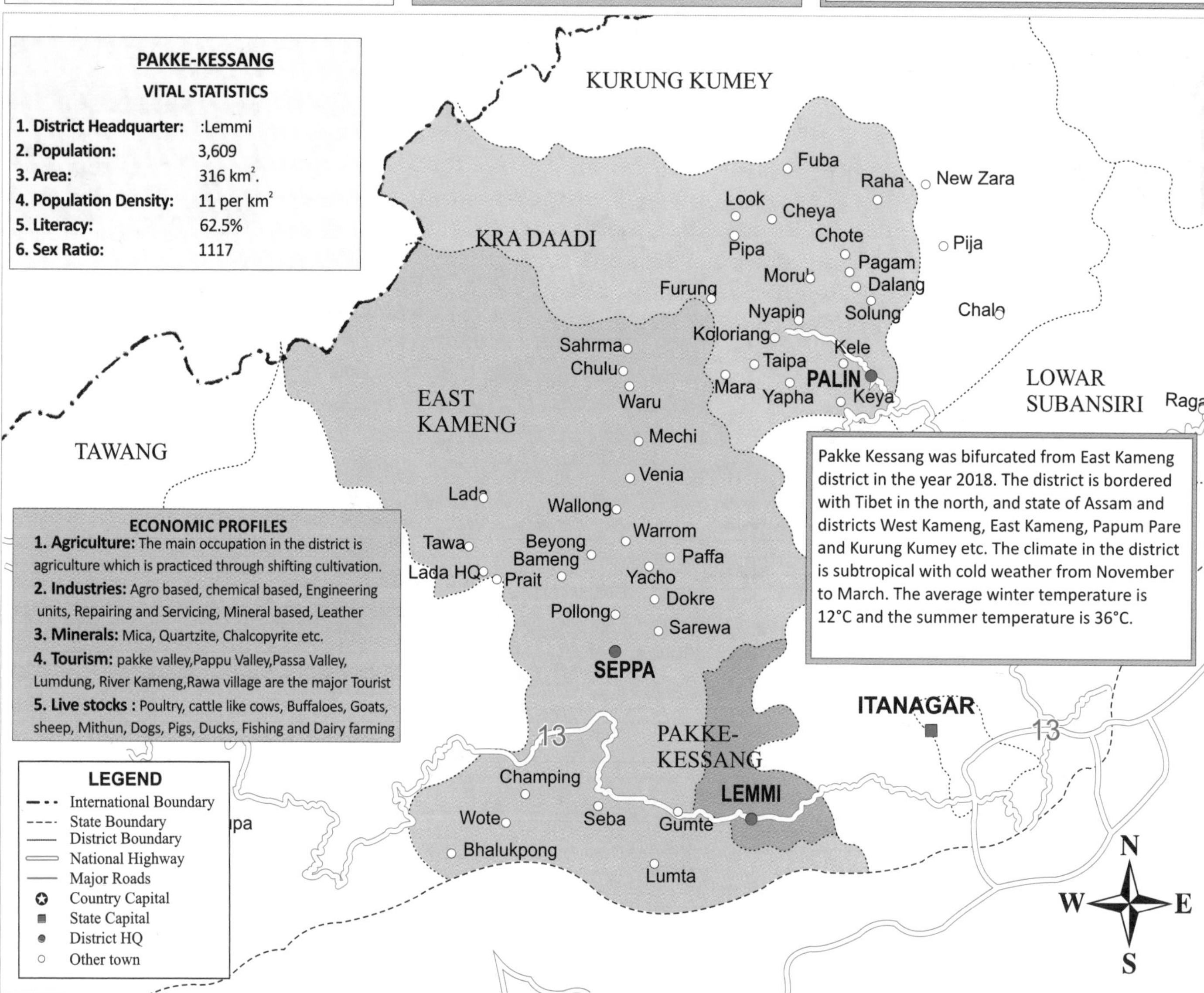

KURUNG KUMEY
KRA DAADI
Fuba
Raha
New Zara
Look
Cheya
Pipa
Chote
Pija
Pagam
Morub
Dalang
Furung
Nyapin
Solung
Chalo
Koloriang
Kele
Sahrma
Chulu
Taipa
PALIN
Mara
Yapha
Keya
LOWAR SUBANSIRI
Raga
EAST KAMENG
Waru
Mechi
TAWANG
Venia
Lada
Wallong
Warrom
Tawa
Beyong
Bameng
Paffa
Lada HQ
Prait
Yacho
Dokre
Pollong
Sarewa
SEPPA
ITANAGAR
13
PAKKE-KESSANG
Champing
LEMMI
Wote
Seba
Gumte
pa
Bhalukpong
Lumta
N
W
E
S
LEGEND
International Boundary
State Boundary
District Boundary
National Highway
Major Roads
Country Capital
State Capital
District HQ
Other town

PAKKE-KESSANG

VITAL STATISTICS

1. **District Headquarter:** :Lemmi
2. **Population:** 3,609
3. **Area:** 316 km^2.
4. **Population Density:** 11 per km^2
5. **Literacy:** 62.5%
6. **Sex Ratio:** 1117

Pakke Kessang was bifurcated from East Kameng district in the year 2018. The district is bordered with Tibet in the north, and state of Assam and districts West Kameng, East Kameng, Papum Pare and Kurung Kumey etc. The climate in the district is subtropical with cold weather from November to March. The average winter temperature is 12°C and the summer temperature is 36°C.

ECONOMIC PROFILES

1. **Agriculture:** The main occupation in the district is agriculture which is practiced through shifting cultivation.
2. **Industries:** Agro based, chemical based, Engineering units, Repairing and Servicing, Mineral based, Leather
3. **Minerals:** Mica, Quartzite, Chalcopyrite etc.
4. **Tourism:** pakke valley,Pappu Valley,Passa Valley, Lumdung, River Kameng,Rawa village are the major Tourist
5. **Live stocks :** Poultry, cattle like cows, Buffaloes, Goats, sheep, Mithun, Dogs, Pigs, Ducks, Fishing and Dairy farming

EAST KAMENG

VITAL STATISTICS

1. **District Headquarter:** Seppa
2. **Population:** 78,690
3. **Area:** 4,134 sq. km.
4. **Population Density:** 19 persons per sq. km.
5. **Literacy:** 49 %
6. **Sex Ratio:** 1012

ECONOMIC PROFILES

1. **Agriculture:** Shifting cultivation to grow crops are paddy, millets, maize etc. As also orange, pineapple, banana, guava etc.
2. **Industries:** Weaving, knitting, carpentry, blacksmith, cane and bamboo, Bell metal, wax candle, carpet, Tailoring etc.
3. **Minerals:** Coal, Iron, clay, limestone etc.
4. **Tourism:** Bameg Top, Kameng river, view of Lumdung Valley.
5. **Live stocks :** Mithuns, cows, pigs, goats, poultry, ducks, birds etc. Fish farming, dairy farming etc.

East Kameng is the district of Arunachal Pradesh which was bifurcated from Subansiri district on 1st April 2000. The district climate ranges from arid in the north through a cool temperature climate to a humid subtropical climate in the southern sub Himalayan hills bordering Assam. The major tribes of this district are Bangnis (Nyishi), Akas, Mijis and Puroiks (Sulung). Most tribe practice jhum form of agriculture.

Scale - 1:1.2 M appro

LOWER SUBANSIRI

VITAL STATISTICS

1. District Headquarter: Ziro
2. Population: 82,839
3. Area: 10,135 sq. km.
4. Population Density: 24 persons per sq. km.
5. Literacy: 76.3%
6. Sex Ratio: 975 females per 1000 males

ECONOMIC PROFILES

1. Agriculture: Rice, maize, millet, wheat, pulses, potato, ginger, oil seeds, spices, chilly, horticulture crops etc.
2. Industries: Agro, Cotton textile, chemical, engineering units, mineral, metal, paper, rubber, garments, leather etc.
3. Minerals: Clay, coal, Cobalt, Nickel, Copper, Graphite, Limestone, Mica, pyrite and pyrrhotite and iron ore etc.
4. Tourism: Shivalinga kardo, Tarin fish farm, Talley Valley wildlife sanctuary etc.
5. Live stocks : poultry, cattle like cows, buffaloes, Mithun, goats, pigs, ducks, dogs etc. Fishing and dairy farming etc.

Lower Subansiri District was formed when Subansiri District was bifurcated into Upper and Lower Subansiri Districts in 1987. It is bounded on the north by the upper Subansiri, on the south by Papum Pare and Assam, on the east by West Siang and some part of Upper Subansiri, on the west by East Kameng District. Yachuli and Languages used in the district include Apatani, Nyishi language.

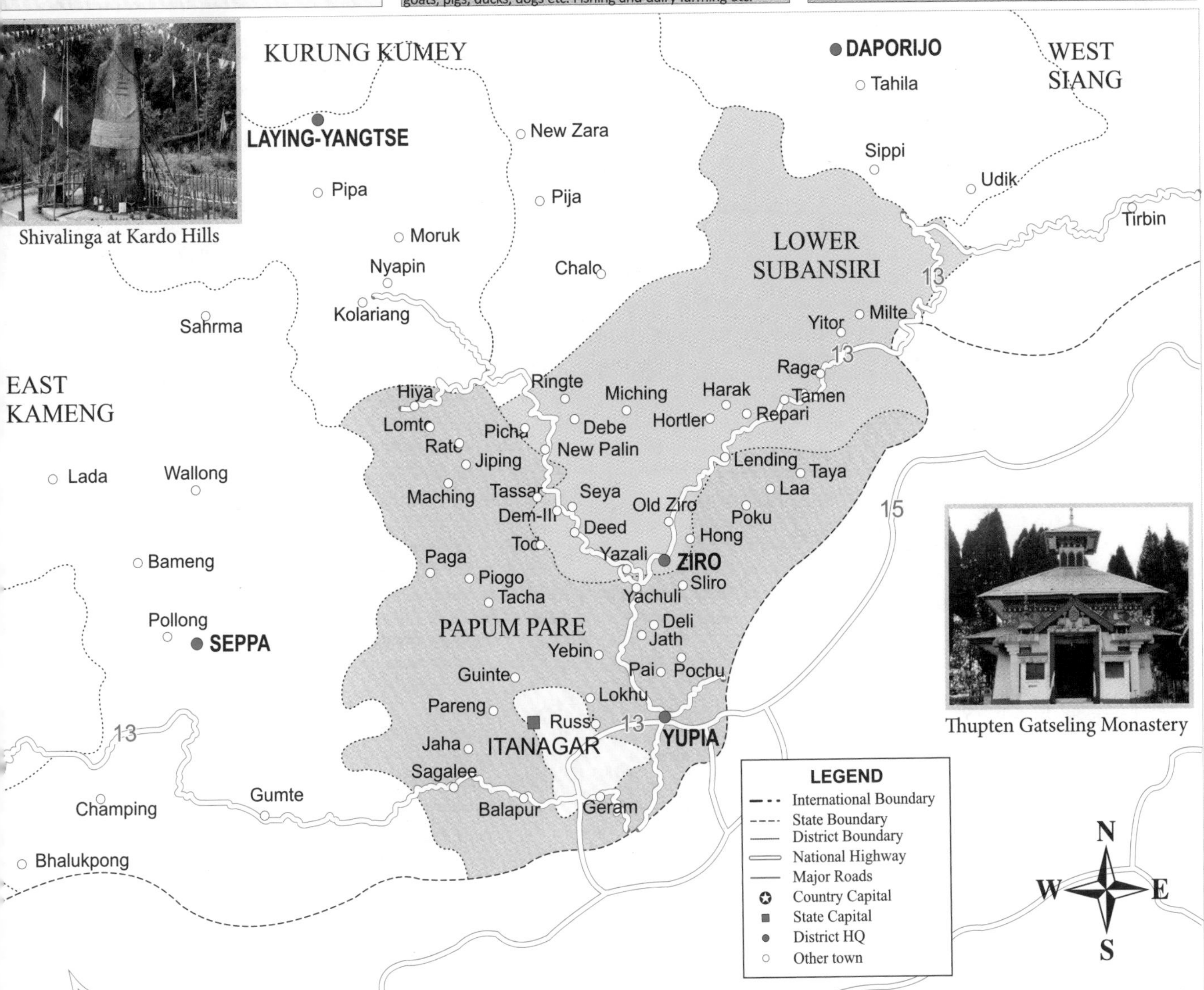
KURUNG KUMEY
LAYING-YANGTSE
Pipa
New Zara
Pija
Moruk
Nyapin
Chalo
Kolariang
Sahrma
DAPORIJO
Tahila
WEST SIANG
Sippi
Udik
Tirbin
LOWER SUBANSIRI
13
Yitor
Milte
Raga
Tamen
Harak
Repari
Hortler
Miching
Ringte
Hiya
Lomto
Rato
Picha
Debe
New Palin
Jiping
EAST KAMENG
Lada
Wallong
Maching
Tassar
Seya
Dem-III
Deed
Lending
Taya
Laa
Old Ziro
Poku
Hong
15
Toc
Yazali
ZIRO
Sliro
Yachuli
Paga
Piogo
Tacha
Bameng
Pollong
SEPPA
PAPUM PARE
Deli
Jath
Yebin
Guinte
Pai
Pochu
Lokhu
Pareng
Russ
ITANAGAR
YUPIA
Jaha
Sagalee
Gumte
Champing
Balapur
Geram
Bhalukpong
LEGEND
International Boundary
State Boundary
District Boundary
National Highway
Major Roads
Country Capital
State Capital
District HQ
Other town
N
W
E
S

Shivalinga at Kardo Hills

Thupten Gatseling Monastery

PAPUM PARE

VITAL STATISTICS

1. District Headquarter: Yupia
2. Population: 1,76,573
3. Area: 3,462 sq. km.
4. Population Density: 51 persons per sq. km.
5. Literacy: 68.55%
6. Sex Ratio: 950 females per 1000 males

ECONOMIC PROFILES

1. Agriculture: Shifting cultivation, rice cultivation, terrace cultivation etc. paddy, maize, millets. Crops like mango, orange, guava, pineapple, banana, lemon etc.
2. Industries: Agro, Cotton textile, jute, garments, wooden, paper, leather, chemical, engineering, rubber, mineral etc.
3. Minerals: Quaternary alluvium and terrace deposit like gravel, pebble, sand, silt, clay, phyllite, quartzite, Limestone.
4. Tourism: Thupten Gatseling Monastery, Theravada Buddhist temple, Ita fort, Geker sinying etc.
5. Live stocks : Poultry, ducks, goats, sheep, dogs fish farming.

Papum Pare district was formed in 1999 when it was split from Lower Subansiri district. There are 4 Arunachal Pradesh legislative Assembly constituencies located in this District: Itanagar, Naharlagun, Doimukh and Sagalee. Papum Pare is inhabited by Nyishis, who are traditionally followers of Donyi-polo. In 1978 Papum Pare District became home to the Itanagar wildlife sanctuary, which has an area of 140 sq. Km.

Scale - 1:1.1 M approx

UPPER SUBANSIRI

VITAL STATISTICS

1. **District Headquarter:** Daporijo
2. **Population:** 83,205
3. **Area:** 7,032 sq. km.
4. **Population Density:** 12 persons per sq. km.
5. **Literacy:** 64%
6. **Sex Ratio:** 982 females per 1000 males

ECONOMIC PROFILES

1. **Agriculture:** Shifting cultivation, Terrace rice cultivation etc. Paddy, wheat, Jowar, millets, sugarcane, etc. horticulture crops like pineapple, orange, jack fruits, banana etc.
2. **Industries:** Agro, Cotton textile, wooden, ready-made garments, leather, mineral, jute based, paper based etc.
3. **Minerals:** Biolite, Garnet, Sillimanite, Graphite, magnetite etc.
4. **Tourism:** Menga Mandir (Cave temple).
5. **Live stocks :** Poultry, cattle like cows, buffaloes, goats, sheep, Ducks, dogs and bitches etc. fish farming and dairy farming etc.

Upper Subansiri is an administrative district in the state of Arunachal Pradesh in India. The district was formed when Subansiri district was bifurcated into Upper and Lower Subansiri districts in 1987. It is the only district in Arunachal Pradesh currently receiving funds from the backward regions grant fund Programme. There are five Arunachal Pradesh legislative Assembly constituencies in this District.

KAMLE

VITAL STATISTICS

1. **District Headquarter:** Raga
2. **Population:** 22,256
3. **Area:** 200.9 sq. km.
4. **Population Density:** .11 persons per sq. km.
5. **Literacy:** 69%
6. **Sex Ratio:** females per 1000 males

ECONOMIC PROFILES

1. **Agriculture:** The Main crops grown in the district are rice, maize, wheat, cucumber, ginger, yams, etc.
2. **Industries:** Agro, chemical based, engineering units, leather, carpentry, blacksmith, mineral based.
3. **Minerals:** Limestone and graphite (in mother district-upper and lower Subansiri...)
4. **Tourism:** Not significant.
5. **Live stocks :** Poultry, like cows, buffaloes, goats, sheep, mithun, dogs, pigs, ducks, dairy farming and fishing etc.

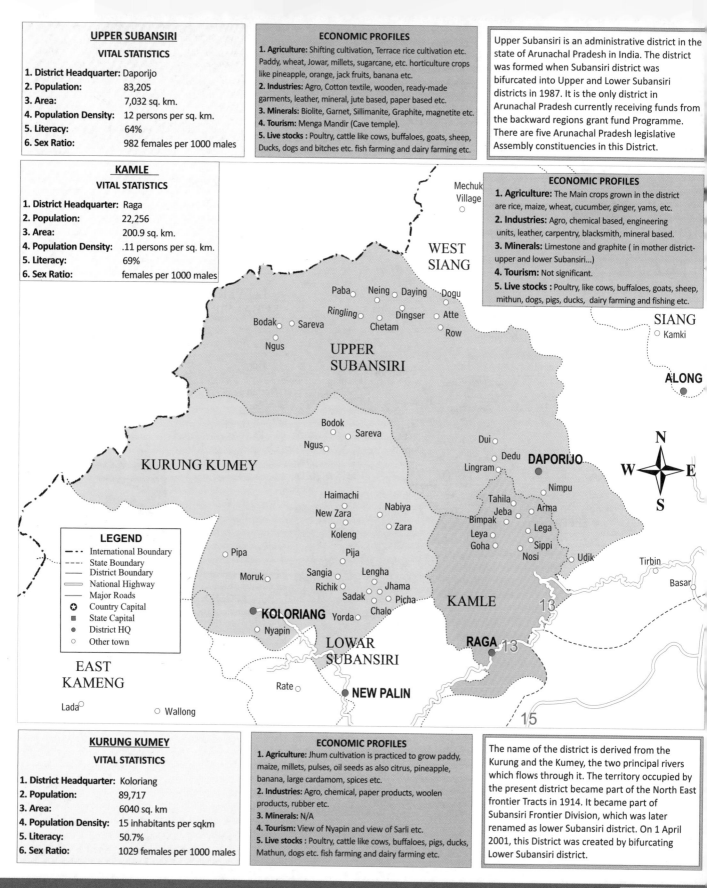

Mechuk Village
WEST SIANG
SIANG
Kamki
ALONG
Paba
Neing
Daying
Dogu
Ringling
Dingser
Atte
Chetam
Row
Bodak
Sareva
Ngus
UPPER SUBANSIRI
Bodok
Sareva
Ngus
Dui
Dedu
Lingram
DAPORIJO
KURUNG KUMEY
N
W
E
S
Nimpu
Tahila
Jeba
Arma
Bimpak
Lega
Leya
Goha
Sippi
Nosi
Udik
Haimachi
New Zara
Nabiya
Zara
Koleng
Pija
Pipa
Moruk
Sangia
Lengha
Richik
Jhama
Sadak
Picha
Chalo
Yorda
KOLORIANG
Nyapin
KAMLE
Tirbin
Basar
13
RAGA
13
LOWAR SUBANSIRI
NEW PALIN
Rate
EAST KAMENG
Lada
Wallong
15
LEGEND
International Boundary
State Boundary
District Boundary
National Highway
Major Roads
Country Capital
State Capital
District HQ
Other town

KURUNG KUMEY

VITAL STATISTICS

1. **District Headquarter:** Koloriang
2. **Population:** 89,717
3. **Area:** 6040 sq. km
4. **Population Density:** 15 inhabitants per sqkm
5. **Literacy:** 50.7%
6. **Sex Ratio:** 1029 females per 1000 males

ECONOMIC PROFILES

1. **Agriculture:** Jhum cultivation is practiced to grow paddy, maize, millets, pulses, oil seeds as also citrus, pineapple, banana, large cardamom, spices etc.
2. **Industries:** Agro, chemical, paper products, woolen products, rubber etc.
3. **Minerals:** N/A
4. **Tourism:** View of Nyapin and view of Sarli etc.
5. **Live stocks :** Poultry, cattle like cows, buffaloes, pigs, ducks, Mathun, dogs etc. fish farming and dairy farming etc.

The name of the district is derived from the Kurung and the Kumey, the two principal rivers which flows through it. The territory occupied by the present district became part of the North East frontier Tracts in 1914. It became part of Subansiri Frontier Division, which was later renamed as lower Subansiri district. On 1 April 2001, this District was created by bifurcating Lower Subansiri district.

Scale - 1:1.1 M approx

SIANG

VITAL STATISTICS

1. District Headquarter: Boleng
2. Population: 24,788
3. Area: 4,005 sq. km.
4. Population Density: 6.2 persons per sq. km.
5. Literacy: 56%
6. Sex Ratio: 916 females per 1000 males

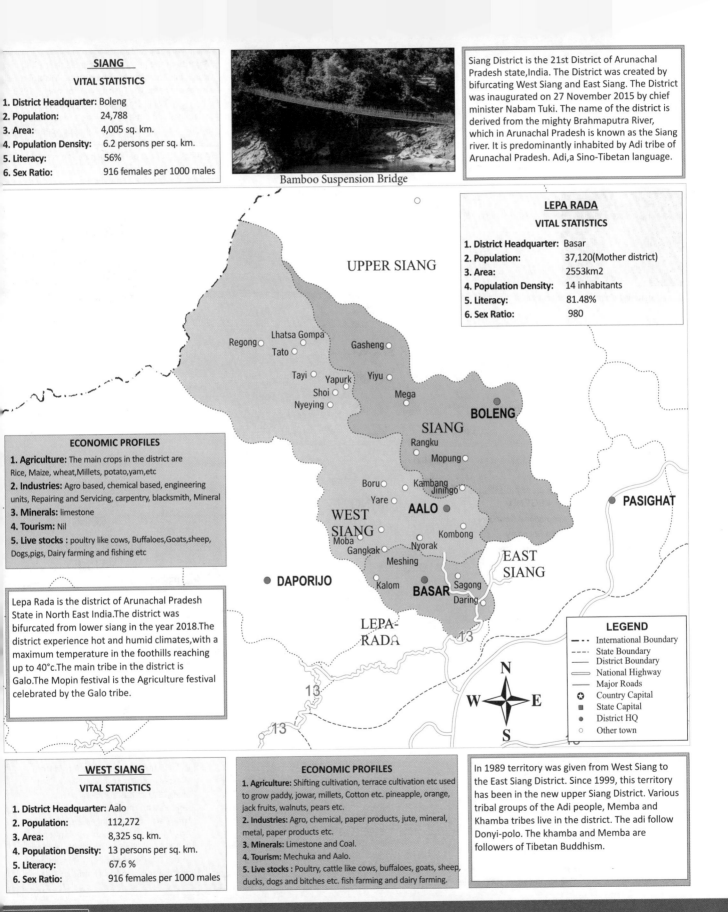

Bamboo Suspension Bridge

Siang District is the 21st District of Arunachal Pradesh state,India. The District was created by bifurcating West Siang and East Siang. The District was inaugurated on 27 November 2015 by chief minister Nabam Tuki. The name of the district is derived from the mighty Brahmaputra River, which in Arunachal Pradesh is known as the Siang river. It is predominantly inhabited by Adi tribe of Arunachal Pradesh. Adi,a Sino-Tibetan language.

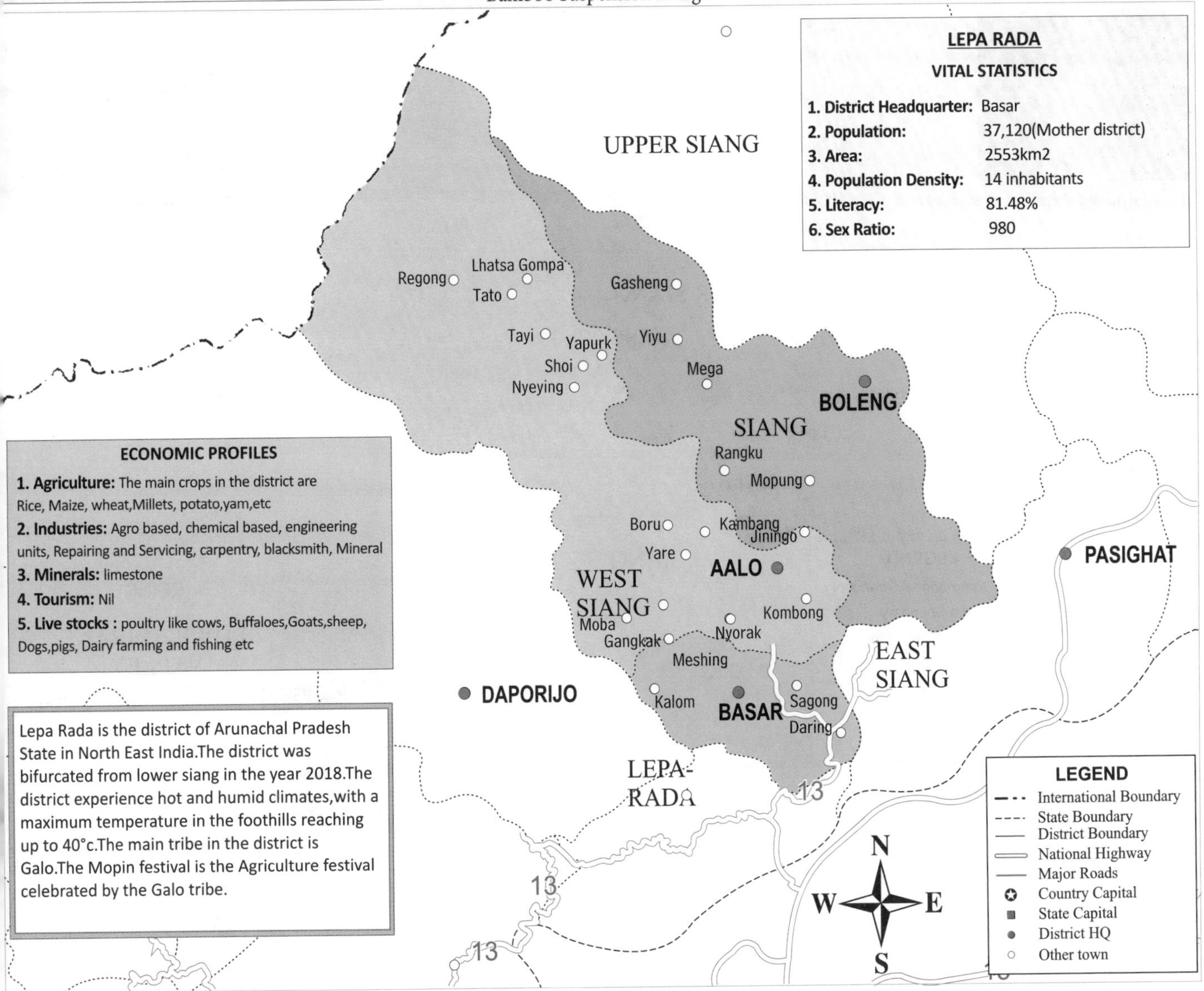

LEPA RADA

VITAL STATISTICS

1. District Headquarter: Basar
2. Population: 37,120(Mother district)
3. Area: 2553km2
4. Population Density: 14 inhabitants
5. Literacy: 81.48%
6. Sex Ratio: 980

UPPER SIANG
Regong
Lhatsa Gompa
Tato
Gasheng
Tayi
Yapurk
Yiyu
Shoi
Nyeying
Mega
BOLENG
SIANG
Rangku
Mopung
Boru
Kambang
Jiningo
Yare
AALO
PASIGHAT
WEST SIANG
Moba
Kombong
Gangkak
Nyorak
Meshing
EAST SIANG
DAPORIJO
Kalom
BASAR
Sagong
Daring
LEPA-RADA
13

ECONOMIC PROFILES

1. Agriculture: The main crops in the district are Rice, Maize, wheat,Millets, potato,yam,etc
2. Industries: Agro based, chemical based, engineering units, Repairing and Servicing, carpentry, blacksmith, Mineral
3. Minerals: limestone
4. Tourism: Nil
5. Live stocks : poultry like cows, Buffaloes,Goats,sheep, Dogs,pigs, Dairy farming and fishing etc

Lepa Rada is the district of Arunachal Pradesh State in North East India.The district was bifurcated from lower siang in the year 2018.The district experience hot and humid climates,with a maximum temperature in the foothills reaching up to 40°c.The main tribe in the district is Galo.The Mopin festival is the Agriculture festival celebrated by the Galo tribe.

LEGEND
International Boundary
State Boundary
District Boundary
National Highway
Major Roads
Country Capital
State Capital
District HQ
Other town

N
W
E
S

WEST SIANG

VITAL STATISTICS

1. District Headquarter: Aalo
2. Population: 112,272
3. Area: 8,325 sq. km.
4. Population Density: 13 persons per sq. km.
5. Literacy: 67.6 %
6. Sex Ratio: 916 females per 1000 males

ECONOMIC PROFILES

1. Agriculture: Shifting cultivation, terrace cultivation etc used to grow paddy, jowar, millets, Cotton etc. pineapple, orange, jack fruits, walnuts, pears etc.
2. Industries: Agro, chemical, paper products, jute, mineral, metal, paper products etc.
3. Minerals: Limestone and Coal.
4. Tourism: Mechuka and Aalo.
5. Live stocks : Poultry, cattle like cows, buffaloes, goats, sheep, ducks, dogs and bitches etc. fish farming and dairy farming.

In 1989 territory was given from West Siang to the East Siang District. Since 1999, this territory has been in the new upper Siang District. Various tribal groups of the Adi people, Memba and Khamba tribes live in the district. The adi follow Donyi-polo. The khamba and Memba are followers of Tibetan Buddhism.

Scale - 1:1.2 M approx

UPPER SIANG

VITAL STATISTICS

1. **District Headquarter:** Yingkiong
2. **Population:** 35,289
3. **Area:** 6,188 sq. km.
4. **Population Density:** 5 persons per sq. km.
5. **Literacy:** 60.0 %
6. **Sex Ratio:** 891 females per 1000 males

ECONOMIC PROFILES

1. **Agriculture:** Paddy, maize, millets, pulses, ginger, sugarcane, chilly, potato, oil seeds, Apple, pear, plum, peach, walnuts etc.
2. **Industries:** Agro, Cotton textile, jute, wooden, paper etc.
3. **Minerals:** Graphite and limestone, coal etc.
4. **Tourism:** Ekodumbing Riutala, Mouling National park, Gelling, Mariyang-Pekimodi etc.
5. **Live stocks :** poultry, cattle like cows, buffaloes, mithun, goats, pigs, ducks, dogs etc. fish farming and dairy farming.

Majority of the people in Upper Siang are Adi tribe while the Memba, Khamba Idu Mishmi tribe also exist there. The District was formed in 1999 when it was split from East Siang District. Languages spoken here are Adi, a Sino-Tibetan tongue with approximately 1,40,000 speakers. In 1986 Upper Siang district became home to Mouling National park, which has an area of 483km^2.

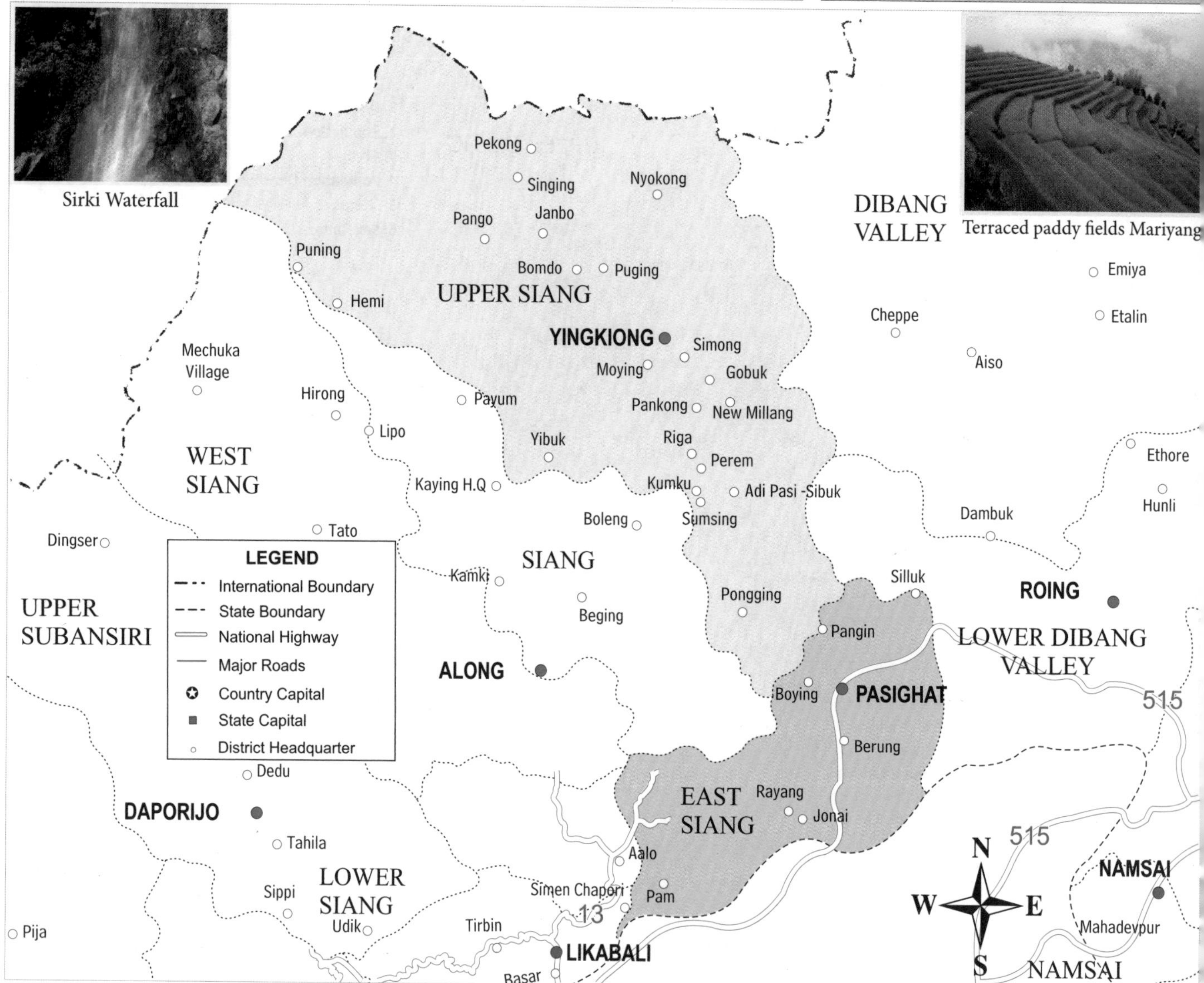

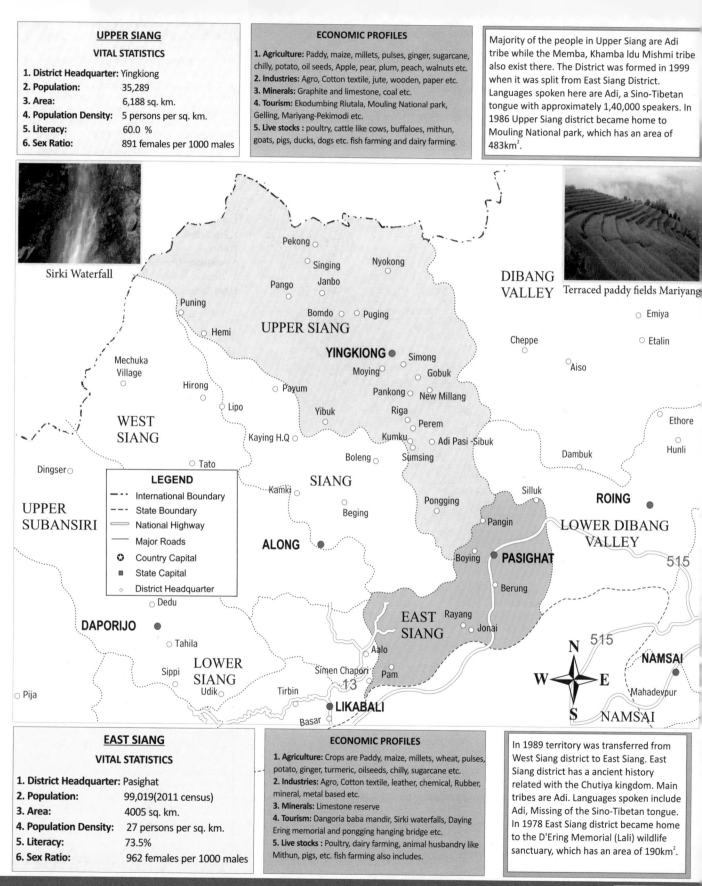

Pekong
Singing
Nyokong
Pango
Janbo
Puning
Bomdo
Puging
Hemi
UPPER SIANG
YINGKIONG
Simong
Moying
Gobuk
Mechuka Village
Hirong
Payum
Pankong
New Millang
Lipo
Yibuk
Riga
Perem
WEST SIANG
Kaying H.Q
Kumku
Adi Pasi -Sibuk
Boleng
Sumsing
Tato
Dingser
Kamki
SIANG
Pongging
Beging
UPPER SUBANSIRI
ALONG
LEGEND
International Boundary
State Boundary
National Highway
Major Roads
Country Capital
State Capital
District Headquarter
Dedu
DAPORIJO
Tahila
Sippi
LOWER SIANG
Udik
Pija
Tirbin
Simen Chapori
LIKABALI
Basar
13
Aalo
Pam
EAST SIANG
Rayang
Jonai
Berung
Boying
PASIGHAT
Pangin
Silluk
DIBANG VALLEY
Cheppe
Emiya
Etalin
Aiso
Ethore
Hunli
Dambuk
ROING
LOWER DIBANG VALLEY
515
N
W
E
S
NAMSAI
Mahadevpur

Sirki Waterfall

Terraced paddy fields Mariyang

EAST SIANG

VITAL STATISTICS

1. **District Headquarter:** Pasighat
2. **Population:** 99,019(2011 census)
3. **Area:** 4005 sq. km.
4. **Population Density:** 27 persons per sq. km.
5. **Literacy:** 73.5%
6. **Sex Ratio:** 962 females per 1000 males

ECONOMIC PROFILES

1. **Agriculture:** Crops are Paddy, maize, millets, wheat, pulses, potato, ginger, turmeric, oilseeds, chilly, sugarcane etc.
2. **Industries:** Agro, Cotton textile, leather, chemical, Rubber, mineral, metal based etc.
3. **Minerals:** Limestone reserve
4. **Tourism:** Dangoria baba mandir, Sirki waterfalls, Daying Ering memorial and pongging hanging bridge etc.
5. **Live stocks :** Poultry, dairy farming, animal husbandry like Mithun, pigs, etc. fish farming also includes.

In 1989 territory was transferred from West Siang district to East Siang. East Siang district has a ancient history related with the Chutiya kingdom. Main tribes are Adi. Languages spoken include Adi, Missing of the Sino-Tibetan tongue. In 1978 East Siang district became home to the D'Ering Memorial (Lali) wildlife sanctuary, which has an area of 190km^2.

Scale - 1:1.2 M approx

DIBANG VALLEY

VITAL STATISTICS

1. **District Headquarter:** Anini
2. **Population:** 8,004
3. **Area:** 9,129 km 2
4. **Population Density:** 0.87 inhabitants per square km
5. **Literacy:** 64.8%
6. **Sex Ratio:** 1125 females per 1000 males

ECONOMIC PROFILES

1. **Agriculture:** Crops like Paddy, maize, millets, wheat, potato, chilly, pulses, oil seeds, vegetable, ginger orange
2. **Industries:** Agro, Cotton textile, paper products, leather, chemical, rubber, mineral and metal based etc.
3. **Minerals:** Limestone and coarse grained marble etc.
4. **Tourism:** Anini, Mathun Valley, Dri valley, Athupopu- The sacred place of Idu Mishmis.
5. **Live stocks :** Animal husbandry, poultry, dairy farming, fish farming etc.

Dibang valley is a district of Arunachal Pradesh named after the Dibang river. It is the largest district in the state of Arunachal Pradesh. On 1, June 1980, Dibang valley district was created out of part of Lohit district. on 16 December 2001, Dibang valley district was bifurcated into upper Dibang Valley district and Lower Dibang Valley district. The Population of this district consists of Mishmi tribe.

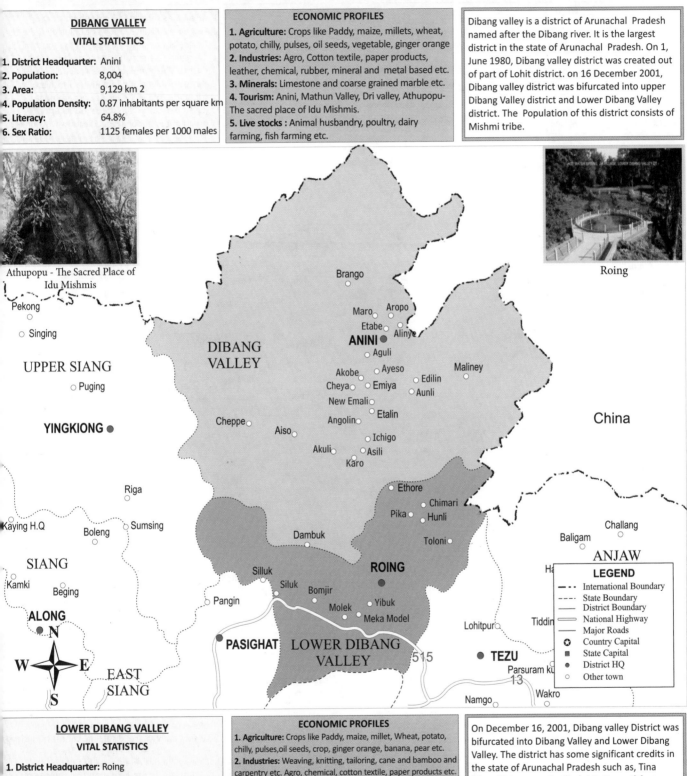

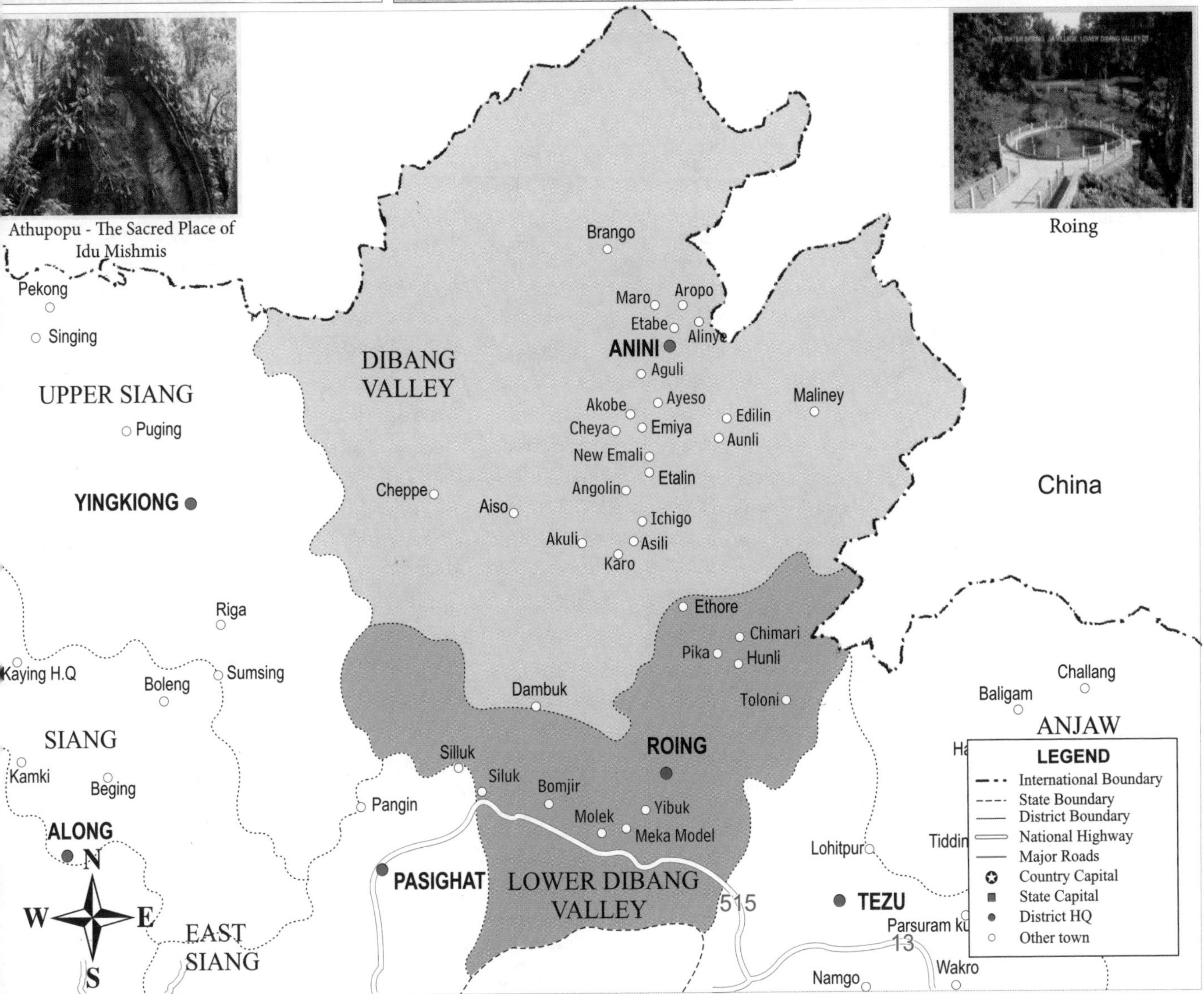
Athupopu - The Sacred Place of Idu Mishmis
Roing
Brango
Maro
Aropo
Etabe
Alinye
ANINI
Aguli
DIBANG VALLEY
Pekong
Singing
UPPER SIANG
Puging
Akobe
Ayeso
Cheya
Emiya
Edilin
Aunli
Maliney
New Emali
Etalin
Angolin
Cheppe
Aiso
YINGKIONG
Ichigo
Akuli
Asili
Karo
China
Riga
Ethore
Chimari
Pika
Hunli
Kaying H.Q
Boleng
Sumsing
Dambuk
Toloni
Challang
Baligam
ANJAW
SIANG
Silluk
ROING
Kamki
Siluk
Beging
Bomjir
Pangin
Yibuk
Molek
Meka Model
ALONG
Lohitpur
N
W
E
S
PASIGHAT
LOWER DIBANG VALLEY
515
TEZU
EAST SIANG
Parsuram ku
13
Namgo
Wakro
LEGEND
International Boundary
State Boundary
District Boundary
National Highway
Major Roads
Country Capital
State Capital
District HQ
Other town

LOWER DIBANG VALLEY

VITAL STATISTICS

1. **District Headquarter:** Roing
2. **Population:** 53,986
3. **Area:** 3900 sq. km.
4. **Population Density:** 14 persons per sq. km.
5. **Literacy:** 70.4 %
6. **Sex Ratio:** 919 females per 1000 males

ECONOMIC PROFILES

1. **Agriculture:** Crops like Paddy, maize, millet, Wheat, potato, chilly, pulses,oil seeds, crop, ginger orange, banana, pear etc.
2. **Industries:** Weaving, knitting, tailoring, cane and bamboo and carpentry etc. Agro, chemical, cotton textile, paper products etc.
3. **Minerals:** limestone and coarse grained marble.
4. **Tourism:** Mipi-pene, Roing, Sally and Mehao lake & Bhismaknagar etc.
5. **Live stocks :** Poultry, cattle like cows, buffaloes, pigs, goats, sheep, ducks, dogs and bitches etc. fish farming and dairy farming etc.

On December 16, 2001, Dibang valley District was bifurcated into Dibang Valley and Lower Dibang Valley. The district has some significant credits in the state of Arunachal Pradesh such as, Tina Mena (1st woman to climb Mt. Everest) from Arunachal Pradesh. Anayok James Tayeng, first IAS officer of 1964 batch. Dugyon Lego, first person to publish a book called PADAM KITAB in Roman script in the year 1935.

Scale - 1:1.25 M approx

ANJAW

VITAL STATISTICS

1. **District Headquarter:** Hawai
2. **Population:** 21,089(2011 census)
3. **Area:** 6190 sq. km.
4. **Population Density:** 3 persons per sq. km.
5. **Literacy:** 59.4 %
6. **Sex Ratio:** 805 females per 1000 males

ECONOMIC PROFILES

1. **Agriculture:** Crops like orange, large cardamom, medicinal seeds etc. maize, paddy, millets, wheat, potato and pulses.
2. **Industries:** Agro based, soda water, Cotton textile, woolen, silk and artificial clothes, jute, paper leather, chemical, mineral, Rubber, metal, engineering etc.
3. **Minerals:** Mica, limestone and coal etc.
4. **Tourism:** Kibithoo, Tezu, Hawaii and Hayuliang, Dong, walong, chaglogam etc.
5. **Live stocks :** Poultry, cattle like cows, buffaloes, Mithun, goats, pigs, duck, dogs and Bitches etc.

Anjaw was separated from Lohit district on February 2004. It is bound by China on the North, Myanmar in the east, on the south by Changlang district and on the west by Lohit district. The prominent rivers are Dalai, Dav, Hali,Lati, Kulung and Lam Rivers which are tributaries of Lohit river. The government developed cash crop, state food security programme, National Food Security Mission etc.

NAMSAI

VITAL STATISTICS

1. **District Headquarter:** Namsai
2. **Population:** 95,950
3. **Area:** 1,587 sq. km.
4. **Population Density:** 60 persons per sq. km.
5. **Literacy:** 76.61%
6. **Sex Ratio:** 984 females per 1000 males

Namsai was carved out of Lohit District in November 2014. The District is surrounded by Tinsukia district of Assam in the west and south west, Changlang district in the south and south east, Anjaw and Lohit in the east and Lohit in the north. It has pleasant climate and is a wonderful tourist destination with rich vegetation. Namsai is called the **"Land of golden pagoda"**. Dihang is a river located nearby which contributed a lot to the growth of Namsai. Majority of the population of Namsai follow Buddhist religion. This religion is being practised here since ages.

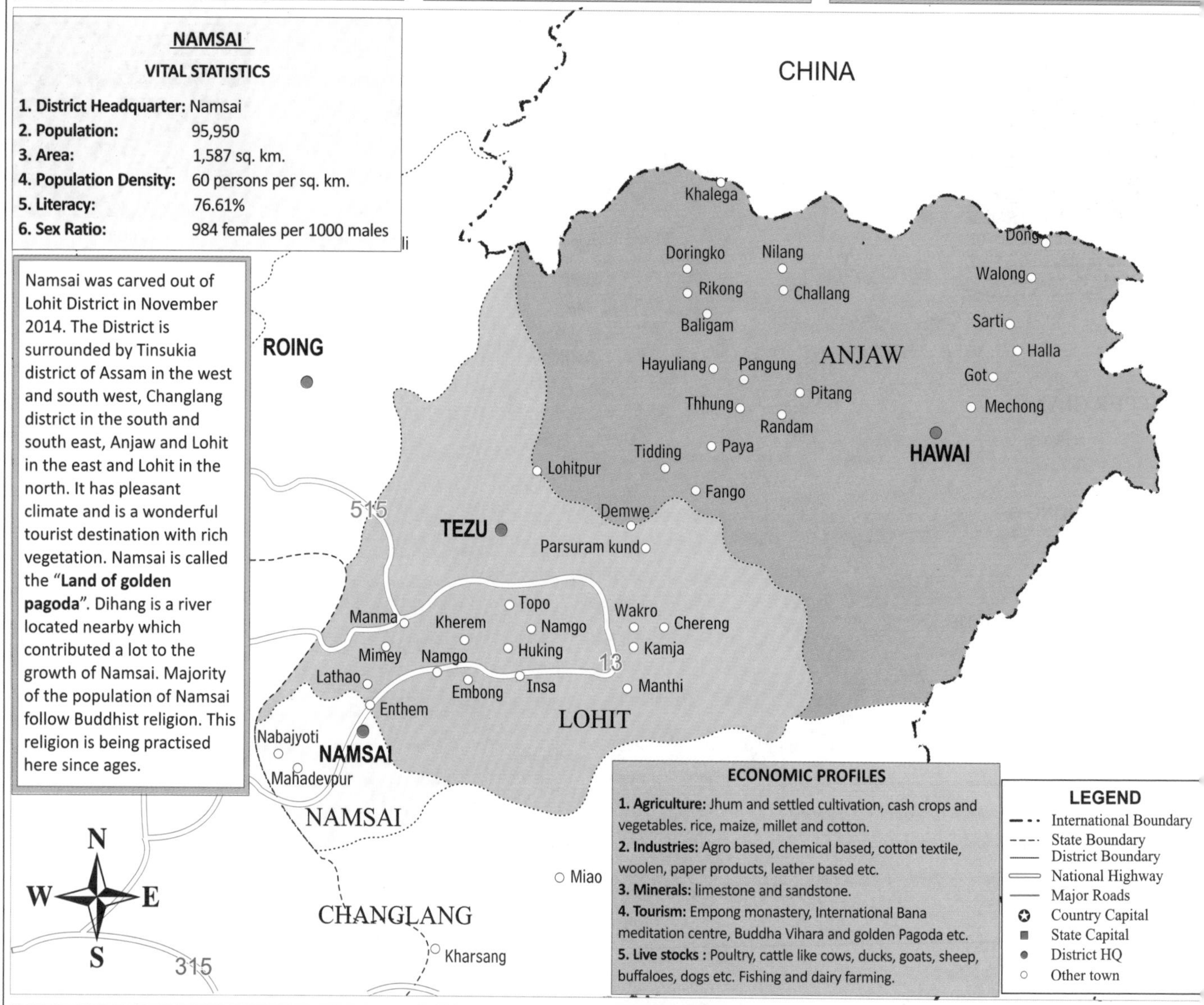

CHINA
ANJAW
Khalega
Doringko
Nilang
Dong
Walong
Rikong
Challang
Baligam
Sarti
Halla
ROING
Hayuliang
Pangung
Got
Pitang
Thhung
Mechong
Randam
HAWAI
Tidding
Paya
Lohitpur
Fango
515
Demwe
TEZU
Parsuram kund
Topo
Wakro
Chereng
Manma
Kherem
Namgo
Kamja
Mimey
Namgo
Huking
13
Lathao
Embong
Insa
Manthi
Enthem
LOHIT
Nabajyoti
NAMSAI
Mahadevpur
NAMSAI
N
W
E
S
Miao
CHANGLANG
Kharsang
315

ECONOMIC PROFILES

1. **Agriculture:** Jhum and settled cultivation, cash crops and vegetables. rice, maize, millet and cotton.
2. **Industries:** Agro based, chemical based, cotton textile, woolen, paper products, leather based etc.
3. **Minerals:** limestone and sandstone.
4. **Tourism:** Empong monastery, International Bana meditation centre, Buddha Vihara and golden Pagoda etc.
5. **Live stocks :** Poultry, cattle like cows, ducks, goats, sheep, buffaloes, dogs etc. Fishing and dairy farming.

LEGEND

- International Boundary
- State Boundary
- District Boundary
- National Highway
- Major Roads
- Country Capital
- State Capital
- District HQ
- Other town

LOHIT

VITAL STATISTICS

1. **District Headquarter:** Tezu
2. **Population:** 145,538(2011 census)
3. **Area:** 2,402 sq. km.
4. **Population Density:** 28 persons per sq. km.
5. **Literacy:** 69.9%
6. **Sex Ratio:** 901females per 1000 males

ECONOMIC PROFILES

1. **Agriculture:** Jhum cultivation, Terrace rice cultivation, horticulture crops etc.
2. **Industries:** weaving, carpentry, blacksmith, silversmith, carpet Making, wood carving, cane and bamboo,
3. **Minerals:** copper ore, Graphite, limestone, Mica, pyrite and pyrrhotite, etc.
4. **Tourism:** Viewpoint at Tohangam, Glaw lake, Parshuram kund etc.
5. **Live stocks :** Poultry, cattle like cows, goats, sheep, buffallo pigs, dogs etc. Fish farming and dairy farming etc.

Lohit is named after the Lohit River, from the Sanskrit louhitya (reddish), and consists of valleys and hills in the North and South. The area was ruled by Chutiya rulers in early 13th to 16th century and during 19th century it came into the hands of British control. Arunachal Pradesh Legislative Assemblies are: Tezu, Chowkham, Namsai, and Lekang. Lohit is the home of various tribals like Adi, Zekhring, Khampti, Singpho and Mishmi tribes.

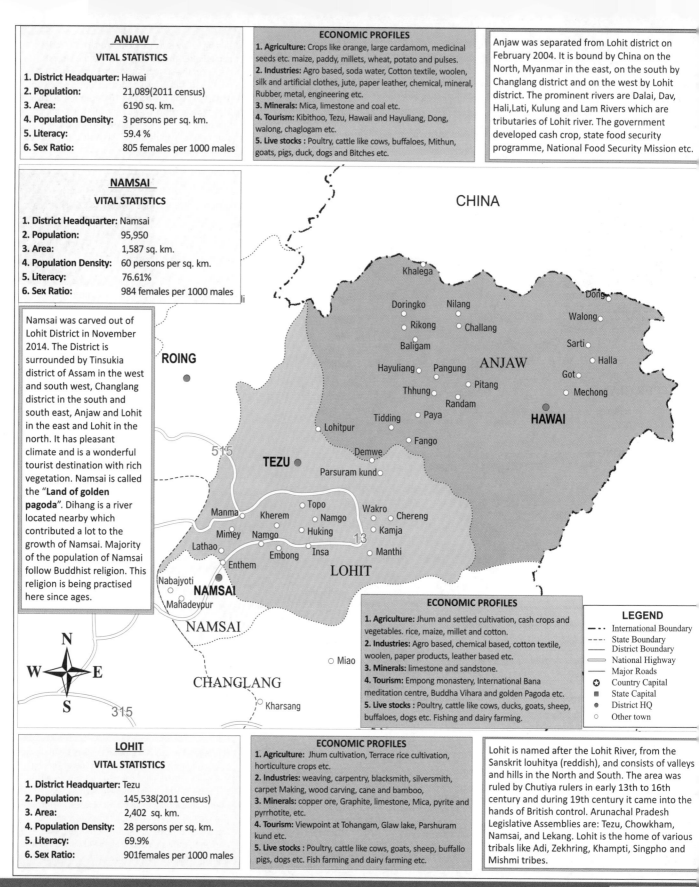

Scale - 1:1.1 M appro

CHANGLANG

VITAL STATISTICS

1. **District Headquarter:** Changlang
2. **Population:** 1,47,951(2011 census)
3. **Area:** 4662 sq. km.
4. **Population Density:** 27 persons per sq. km.
5. **Literacy:** 61.9 %
6. **Sex Ratio:** 914 females per 1000 males

ECONOMIC PROFILES

1. **Agriculture:** Rice, Oilseeds, pulses, jute, vegetables etc.
2. **Industries:** Cottage and small scale weaving centers etc.
3. **Minerals:** Oil and coal deposits.
4. **Tourism:** Miao, Namdapha NP and tiger reserve, Lake of No return, Tibetan camp, World War II, cemetery, stilwell road, Nampong, Ranglum, Kengkho, Jongpho-hate.
5. **Live stocks :** Poultry breeding farm, animal husbandry, cattle like buffaloes, pig, goat, sheep, Mithun, dog, horses and ponies.

Changlang was created on 14 November 1987, when it was split from Tirap district. The region is Rich in wildlife with variety of flora and fauna. Most of the plains are in the valley of river Dihing which is the main source of fishes for the local people. There are 5 Arunachal Pradesh legislative Assembly constituencies in this district. The various tribal groups in the district are Tangsa, Tutsa, Novte, Chakma, Gorkha etc. Languages spoken are of endangered Sino-Tibetan dialect.

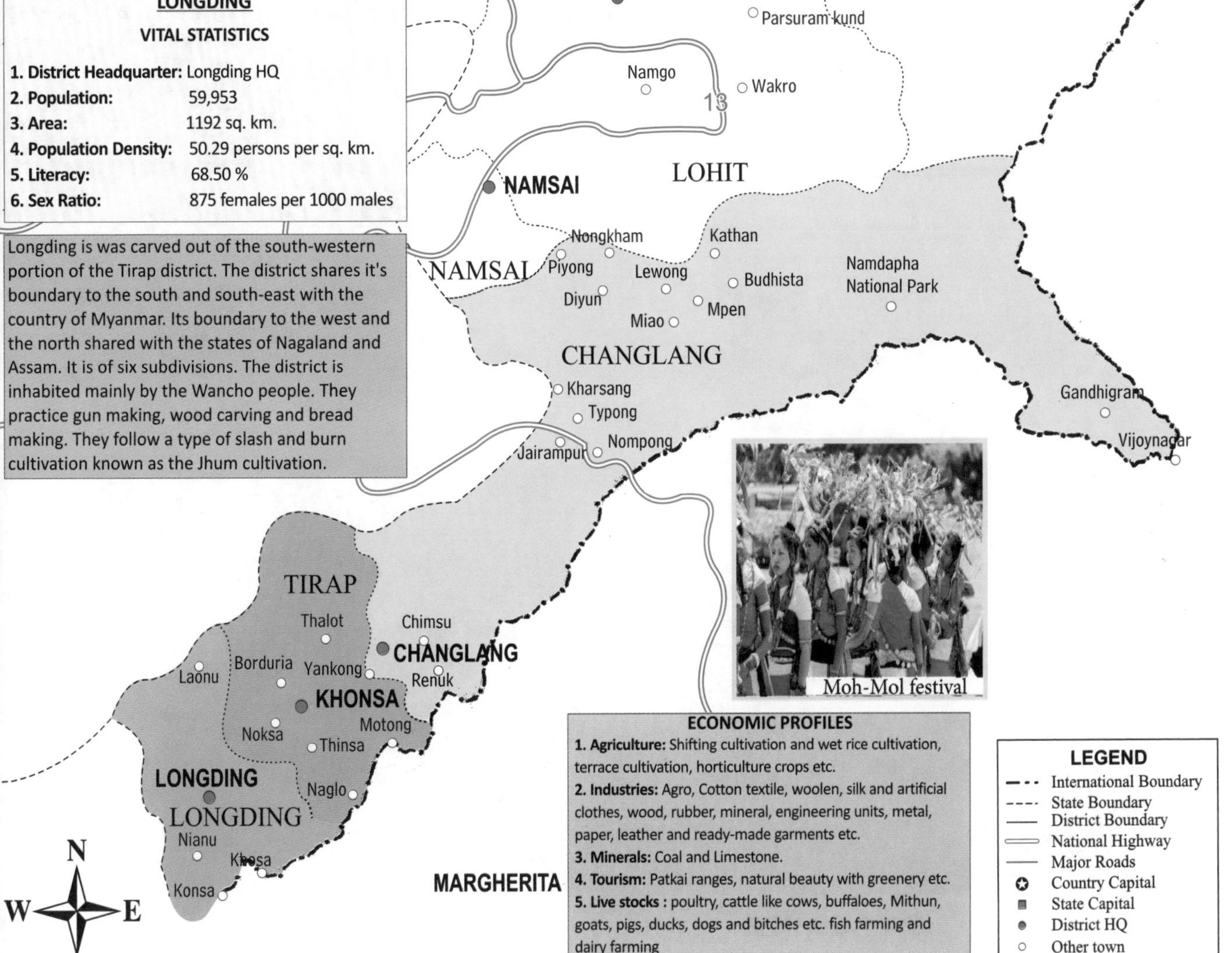
515
TEZU
Parsuram kund
Namgo
13
Wakro
LOHIT
NAMSAI
NAMSAI
Nongkham
Kathan
Piyong
Lewong
Budhista
Namdapha National Park
Diyun
Mpen
Miao
CHANGLANG
Kharsang
Typong
Jairampur
Nompong
Gandhigram
Vijoynagar
TIRAP
Thalot
Chimsu
CHANGLANG
Laonu
Borduria
Yankong
Renuk
KHONSA
Noksa
Motong
Thinsa
LONGDING
Naglo
LONGDING
Nianu
Khosa
Konsa
MARGHERITA
N
W
E
S
LEGEND
International Boundary
State Boundary
District Boundary
National Highway
Major Roads
Country Capital
State Capital
District HQ
Other town

Moh-Mol festival

LONGDING

VITAL STATISTICS

1. **District Headquarter:** Longding HQ
2. **Population:** 59,953
3. **Area:** 1192 sq. km.
4. **Population Density:** 50.29 persons per sq. km.
5. **Literacy:** 68.50 %
6. **Sex Ratio:** 875 females per 1000 males

Longding is was carved out of the south-western portion of the Tirap district. The district shares it's boundary to the south and south-east with the country of Myanmar. Its boundary to the west and the north shared with the states of Nagaland and Assam. It is of six subdivisions. The district is inhabited mainly by the Wancho people. They practice gun making, wood carving and bread making. They follow a type of slash and burn cultivation known as the Jhum cultivation.

ECONOMIC PROFILES

1. **Agriculture:** Shifting cultivation and wet rice cultivation, terrace cultivation, horticulture crops etc.
2. **Industries:** Agro, Cotton textile, woolen, silk and artificial clothes, wood, rubber, mineral, engineering units, metal, paper, leather and ready-made garments etc.
3. **Minerals:** Coal and Limestone.
4. **Tourism:** Patkai ranges, natural beauty with greenery etc.
5. **Live stocks :** poultry, cattle like cows, buffaloes, Mithun, goats, pigs, ducks, dogs and bitches etc. fish farming and dairy farming

TIRAP

VITAL STATISTICS

1. **District Headquarter:** Khonsa
2. **Population:** 111,997
3. **Area:** 2,362 sq. km.
4. **Population Density:** 47 persons per sq. km.
5. **Literacy:** 52.2%
6. **Sex Ratio:** 931 females per 1000 males

ECONOMIC PROFILES

1. **Agriculture:** Jhuming cultivation, permanent cultivation etc. Paddy, wheat, millets, maize, pulses, potato, ginger, chilly, vegetables, oil seeds Crops like orange, banana, pineapple, pears, jack fruits, black pepper, papaya, large cardamom etc.
2. **Industries:** Agro based, chemical based, paper products, leather based, mineral based, metal based, engineering units, Repairing and servicing etc.
3. **Minerals:** Coal, oil and gas reserve.
4. **Tourism:** Khonsa museum and Khonsa hill station etc.
5. **Live stocks :** Poultry, cattle like buffaloes, pigs, goats, birds,

The Tirap District is located in the southeastern part of the state. Tirap has been inhabited by ancestors of the indigenous tribes. Tribes such as Nocte came to settle in the area during the 16th century. On 14 November 1987, Tirap was bifurcated to create the new Changlang district. In 2013 Tirap was again split to create Longding district. Legislative assembly constituencies are Namsang, Khonsa East, Khonsa West and Borduria Bogapani.

Scale - 1:1.3 M approx

ASSAM

Section

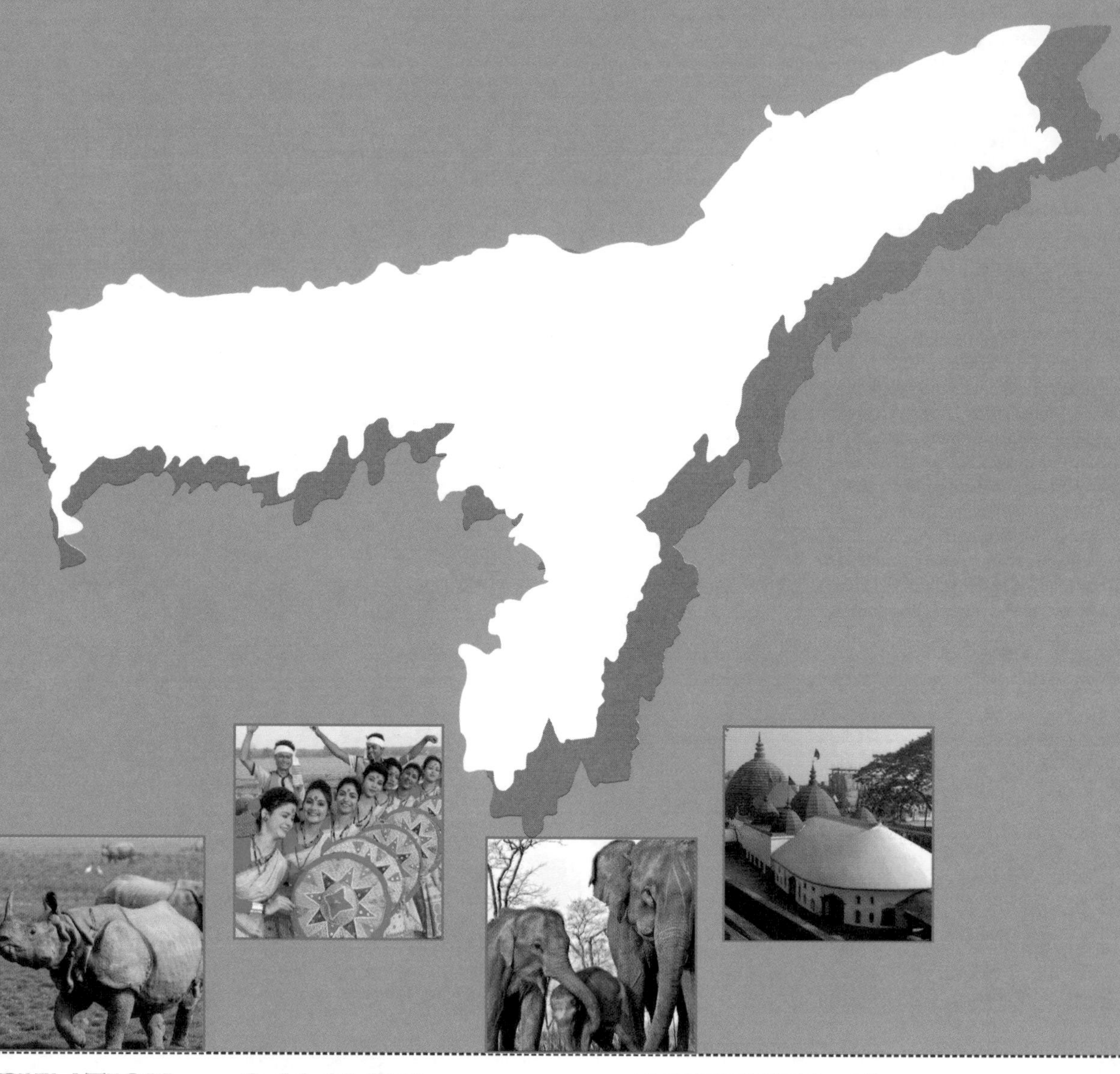

POPULATION:	***3,11,69,272***	**DISTRICTS:** ***33***
AREA:	***78,438 sq.km.***	**L.S. CONSTITUENCY:** ***14***
POP. DENSITY:	***397 persons/ Km^2***	**R.S. CONSTITUENCY:** ***7***
LITERACY:	***73.18%***	**GRAM PANCHAYATS:** ***2,199***
SEX RATIO:	***954 females/1000 males***	**GSDP:** ***2,88,494***

ASSAM - PHYSICAL

VITAL STATISTICS

State Bird - White-winged wood duck
State Animal - One-horned Rhinoceros
.State Flower - Kopou Phool (foxtail orchid)
.State Tree - Hollong
Languages - Assamese, Bodo, Karbi, Bengali
.Primary Rivers - Brahmaputra, Manas, Subansiri, Sonai, Barak
i.Neighbours - Meghalaya, Arunachal Pradesh, Nagaland, Manipur, Tripura, Mizoram, West Bengal
ii.Forest and NPs -Kaziranga NP, Manas NP, Orang NP, Sonai-Rupai WS.
.Tribes - Bodo, Kachari, Mishing, Deori, Rabha, Tiwa or Lalung, Khamti, Sonowal Kachari etc.

Assam covers an area of 78,438 sq. km, which represents 2.39 per cent of the total land area of the country. Assam-the gateway to the north-eastern states is surrounded by Bhutan and Arunachal Pradesh on the north, Manipur, Nagaland and Arunachal Pradesh on the east and Meghalaya, Tripura and Mizoram on the South.

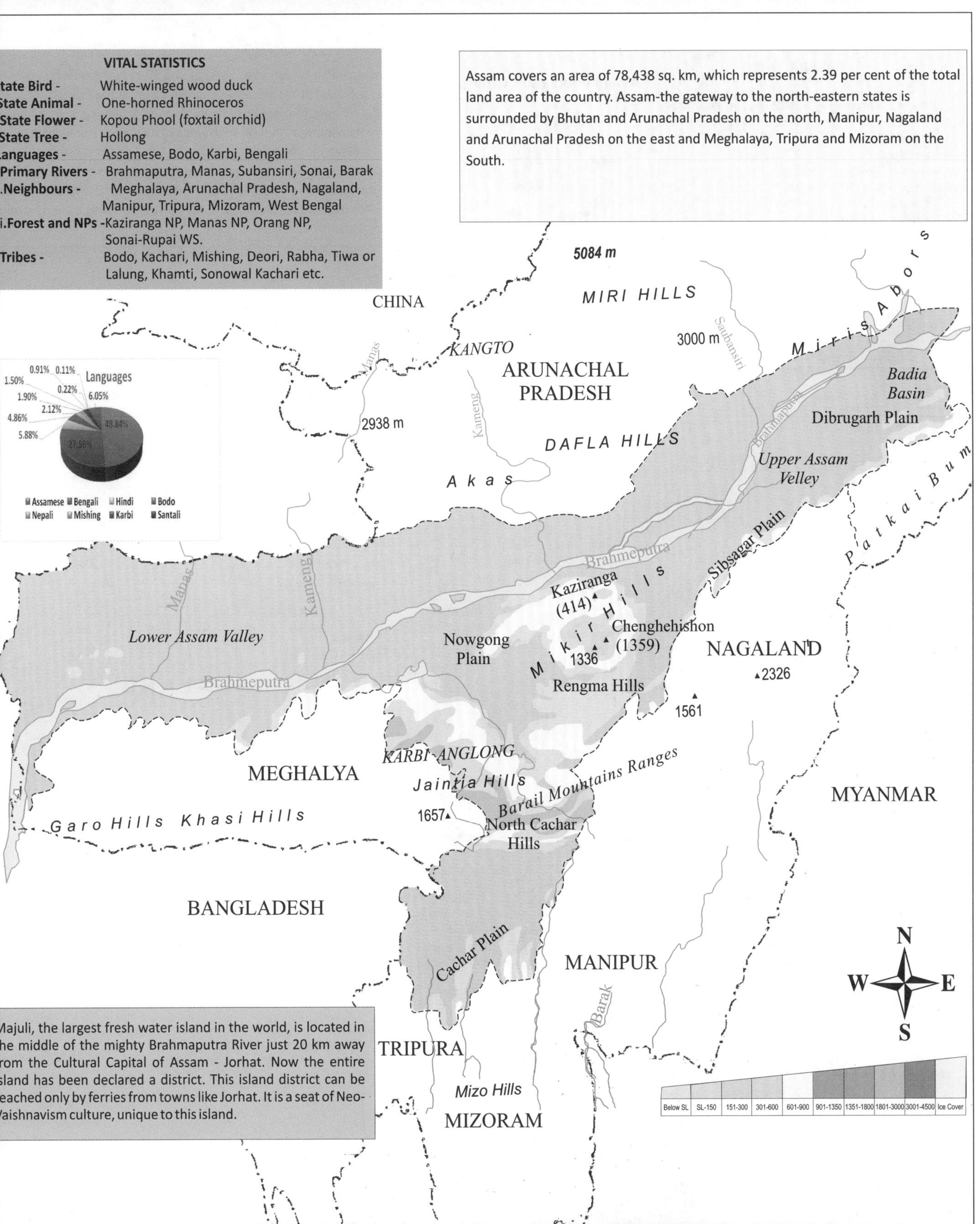
Languages
0.91%
0.11%
1.50%
0.22%
1.90%
6.05%
2.12%
4.86%
48.84%
5.88%
27.56%
Assamese
Bengali
Hindi
Bodo
Nepali
Mishing
Karbi
Santali
CHINA
5084 m
MIRI HILLS
Abors
Miris
KANGTO
3000 m
Manas
Subansiri
ARUNACHAL PRADESH
Badia Basin
Dibrugarh Plain
2938 m
Kameng
DAFLA HILLS
Brahmaputra
Upper Assam Velley
Akas
Patkai Bum
Sibsagar Plain
Brahmeputra
Kaziranga (414)
Mikir Hills
Chenghehishon (1359)
1336
Nowgong Plain
Lower Assam Valley
Kameng
Manas
Brahmeputra
NAGALAND
2326
Rengma Hills
1561
KARBI ANGLONG
MEGHALYA
Jaintia Hills
Barail Mountains Ranges
MYANMAR
1657
Garo Hills Khasi Hills
North Cachar Hills
BANGLADESH
Cachar Plain
MANIPUR
Barak
TRIPURA
Mizo Hills
MIZORAM
N
W
E
S
Below SL
SL-150
151-300
301-600
601-900
901-1350
1351-1800
1801-3000
3001-4500
Ice Cover

Majuli, the largest fresh water island in the world, is located in the middle of the mighty Brahmaputra River just 20 km away from the Cultural Capital of Assam - Jorhat. Now the entire island has been declared a district. This island district can be reached only by ferries from towns like Jorhat. It is a seat of Neo-Vaishnavism culture, unique to this island.

Scale - 1:1.7 M approx

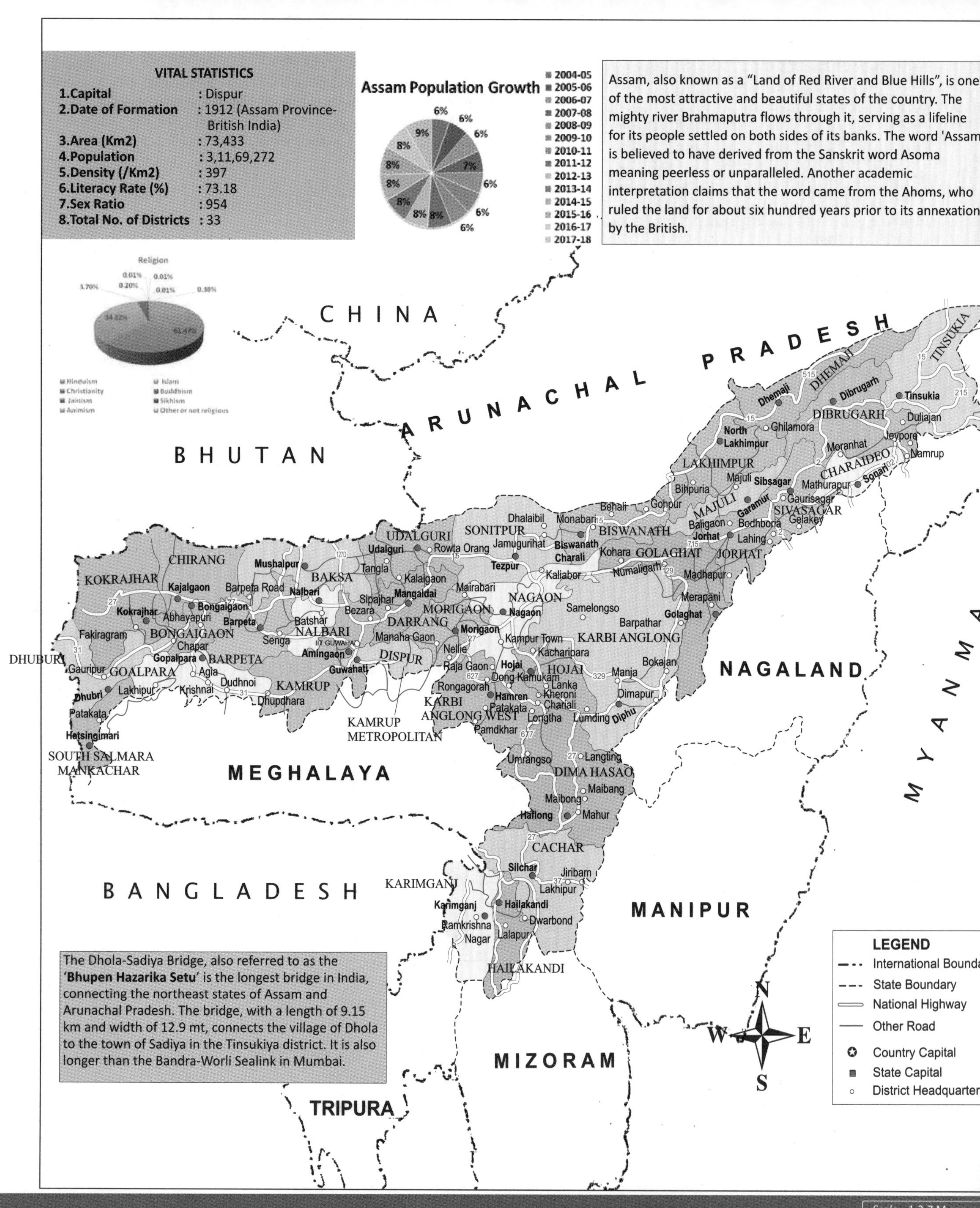
VITAL STATISTICS
1.Capital : Dispur
2.Date of Formation : 1912 (Assam Province-British India)
3.Area (Km2) : 73,433
4.Population : 3,11,69,272
5.Density (/Km2) : 397
6.Literacy Rate (%) : 73.18
7.Sex Ratio : 954
8.Total No. of Districts : 33
Assam Population Growth
2004-05
2005-06
2006-07
2007-08
2008-09
2009-10
2010-11
2011-12
2012-13
2013-14
2014-15
2015-16
2016-17
2017-18
Assam, also known as a "Land of Red River and Blue Hills", is one of the most attractive and beautiful states of the country. The mighty river Brahmaputra flows through it, serving as a lifeline for its people settled on both sides of its banks. The word 'Assam' is believed to have derived from the Sanskrit word Asoma meaning peerless or unparalleled. Another academic interpretation claims that the word came from the Ahoms, who ruled the land for about six hundred years prior to its annexation by the British.
Religion
Hinduism
Christianity
Jainism
Animism
Islam
Buddhism
Sikhism
Other or not religious
CHINA
ARUNACHAL PRADESH
BHUTAN
NAGALAND
MYANMAR
MEGHALAYA
BANGLADESH
MANIPUR
MIZORAM
TRIPURA
KOKRAJHAR
CHIRANG
BAKSA
UDALGURI
SONITPUR
BISWANATH
LAKHIMPUR
DHEMAJI
DIBRUGARH
TINSUKIA
CHARAIDEO
MAJULI
SIVASAGAR
JORHAT
GOLAGHAT
NAGAON
MORIGAON
DARRANG
NALBARI
BONGAIGAON
BARPETA
GOALPARA
DHUBRI
KAMRUP
DISPUR
KAMRUP METROPOLITAN
SOUTH SALMARA MANKACHAR
KARBI ANGLONG
KARBI ANGLONG WEST
HOJAI
DIMA HASAO
CACHAR
KARIMGANJ
HAILAKANDI
Dispur
Guwahati
Tezpur
Dibrugarh
Tinsukia
Jorhat
Silchar
Haflong
Diphu
Nagaon
The Dhola-Sadiya Bridge, also referred to as the 'Bhupen Hazarika Setu' is the longest bridge in India, connecting the northeast states of Assam and Arunachal Pradesh. The bridge, with a length of 9.15 km and width of 12.9 mt, connects the village of Dhola to the town of Sadiya in the Tinsukiya district. It is also longer than the Bandra-Worli Sealink in Mumbai.
LEGEND
International Bounda
State Boundary
National Highway
Other Road
Country Capital
State Capital
District Headquarter
N
W
E
S
Scale - 1:3.7 M approx

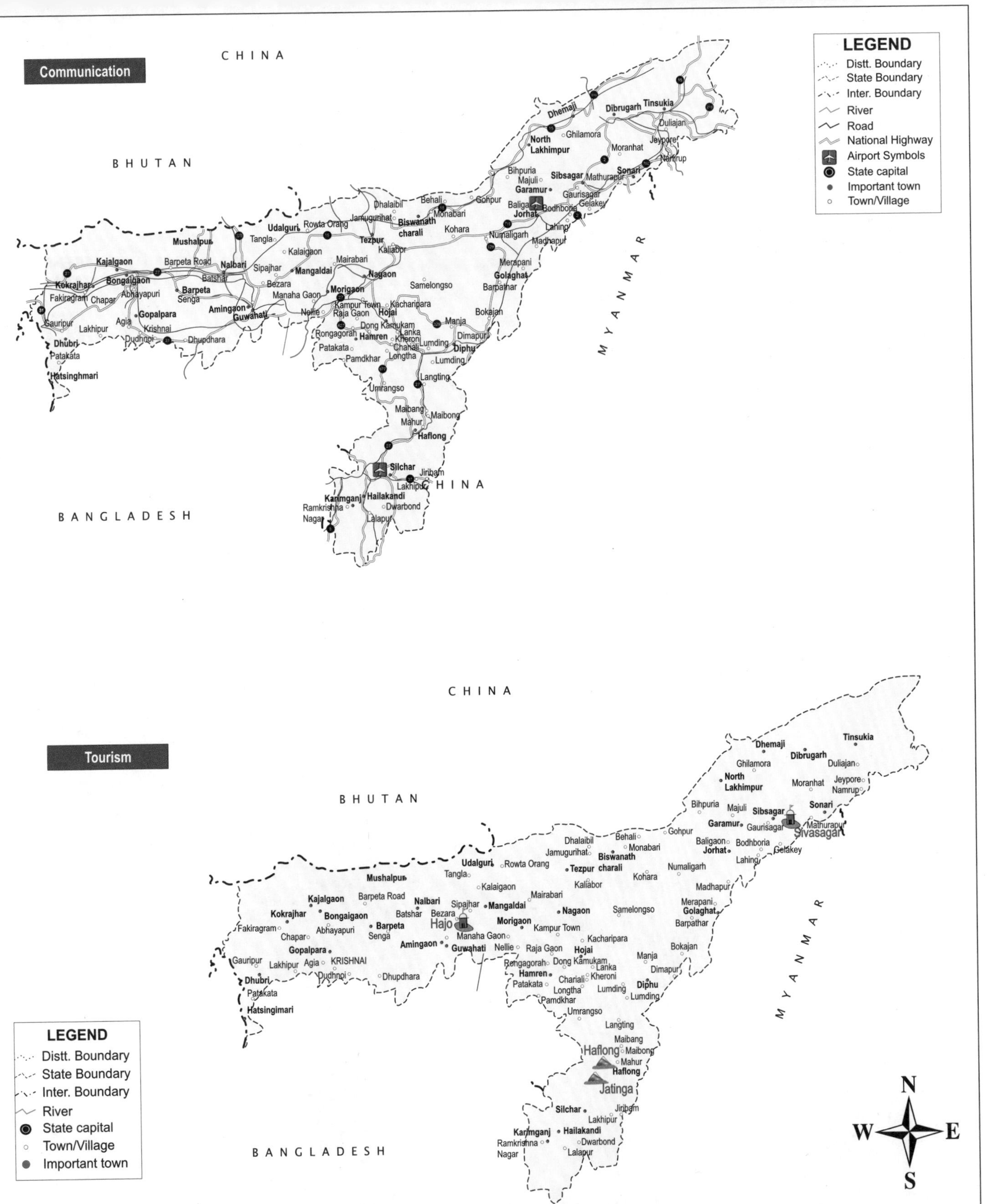

Communication
CHINA
BHUTAN
BANGLADESH
MYANMAR
LEGEND
Distt. Boundary
State Boundary
Inter. Boundary
River
Road
National Highway
Airport Symbols
State capital
Important town
Town/Village
Dhemaji
Dibrugarh
Tinsukia
Duliajan
North Lakhimpur
Ghilamora
Moranhat
Jeypore
Namrup
Bihpuria
Majuli
Sibsagar
Sonari
Garamur
Gaurisagar
Mathurapur
Baligaon
Jorhat
Bodhbori
Gelakey
Lahing
Gohpur
Dhalaibil
Behali
Monabari
Jamugurihat
Biswanath charali
Kohara
Numaligarh
Madhapur
Udalguri
Rowta Orang
Tezpur
Kaliabor
Mushalpur
Tangla
Kalaigaon
Merapani
Golaghat
Barpathar
Kajalgaon
Barpeta Road
Nalbari
Sipajhar
Mangaldai
Mairabari
Nagaon
Samelongso
Kokrajhar
Bongaigaon
Barpeta
Batshar
Bezara
Fakiragram
Chapar
Abhayapuri
Senga
Amingaon
Guwahati
Manaha Gaon
Morigaon
Kampur Town
Kacharipara
Nellie
Raja Gaon
Hojai
Gauripur
Lakhipur
Agia
Gopalpara
Krishnai
Dudhnoi
Dhupdhara
Dong Kamukam
Manja
Bokajan
Dhubri
Patakata
Hatsinghmari
Rongagorah
Hamren
Lanka
Kheroni
Chariali
Longtha
Lumding
Dimapur
Diphu
Pamdkhar
Langting
Umrangso
Maibang
Mahur
Haflong
Silchar
Jiribam
Lakhipur
Karimganj
Hailakandi
Ramkrishna Nagar
Dwarbond
Lalapur
Tourism
Hatsingimari
KRISHNAI
Hajo
Sivasagar
Jatinga
N
S
E
W

SEX RATIO & POPULATION

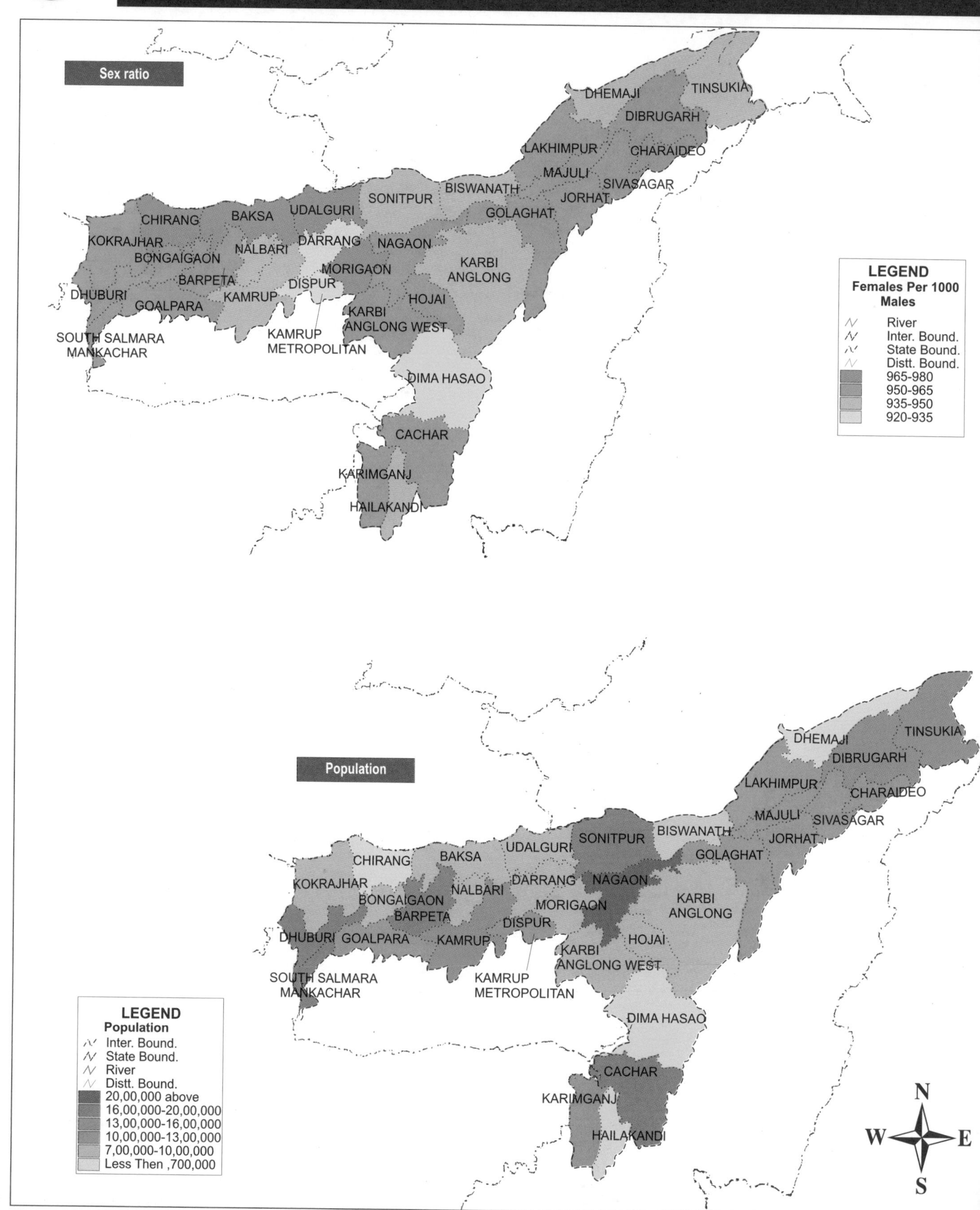
Sex ratio
DHEMAJI
TINSUKIA
DIBRUGARH
LAKHIMPUR
CHARAIDEO
MAJULI
SIVASAGAR
JORHAT
BISWANATH
SONITPUR
GOLAGHAT
UDALGURI
BAKSA
CHIRANG
KOKRAJHAR
DARRANG
NAGAON
NALBARI
BONGAIGAON
MORIGAON
KARBI ANGLONG
BARPETA
DISPUR
DHUBURI
KAMRUP
HOJAI
GOALPARA
KARBI ANGLONG WEST
SOUTH SALMARA MANKACHAR
KAMRUP METROPOLITAN
DIMA HASAO
CACHAR
KARIMGANJ
HAILAKANDI
LEGEND
Females Per 1000 Males
River
Inter. Bound.
State Bound.
Distt. Bound.
965-980
950-965
935-950
920-935
Population
DHEMAJI
TINSUKIA
DIBRUGARH
LAKHIMPUR
CHARAIDEO
MAJULI
SIVASAGAR
JORHAT
BISWANATH
SONITPUR
GOLAGHAT
UDALGURI
CHIRANG
BAKSA
DARRANG
NAGAON
KOKRAJHAR
NALBARI
KARBI ANGLONG
BONGAIGAON
MORIGAON
BARPETA
DISPUR
DHUBURI
GOALPARA
KAMRUP
HOJAI
KARBI ANGLONG WEST
SOUTH SALMARA MANKACHAR
KAMRUP METROPOLITAN
DIMA HASAO
CACHAR
KARIMGANJ
HAILAKANDI
LEGEND
Population
Inter. Bound.
State Bound.
River
Distt. Bound.
20,00,000 above
16,00,000-20,00,000
13,00,000-16,00,000
10,00,000-13,00,000
7,00,000-10,00,000
Less Then ,700,000
N
W
E
S

Scale - 1:5.5 M approx

FOREST/WILDLIFE & NATIONAL HIGHWAYS

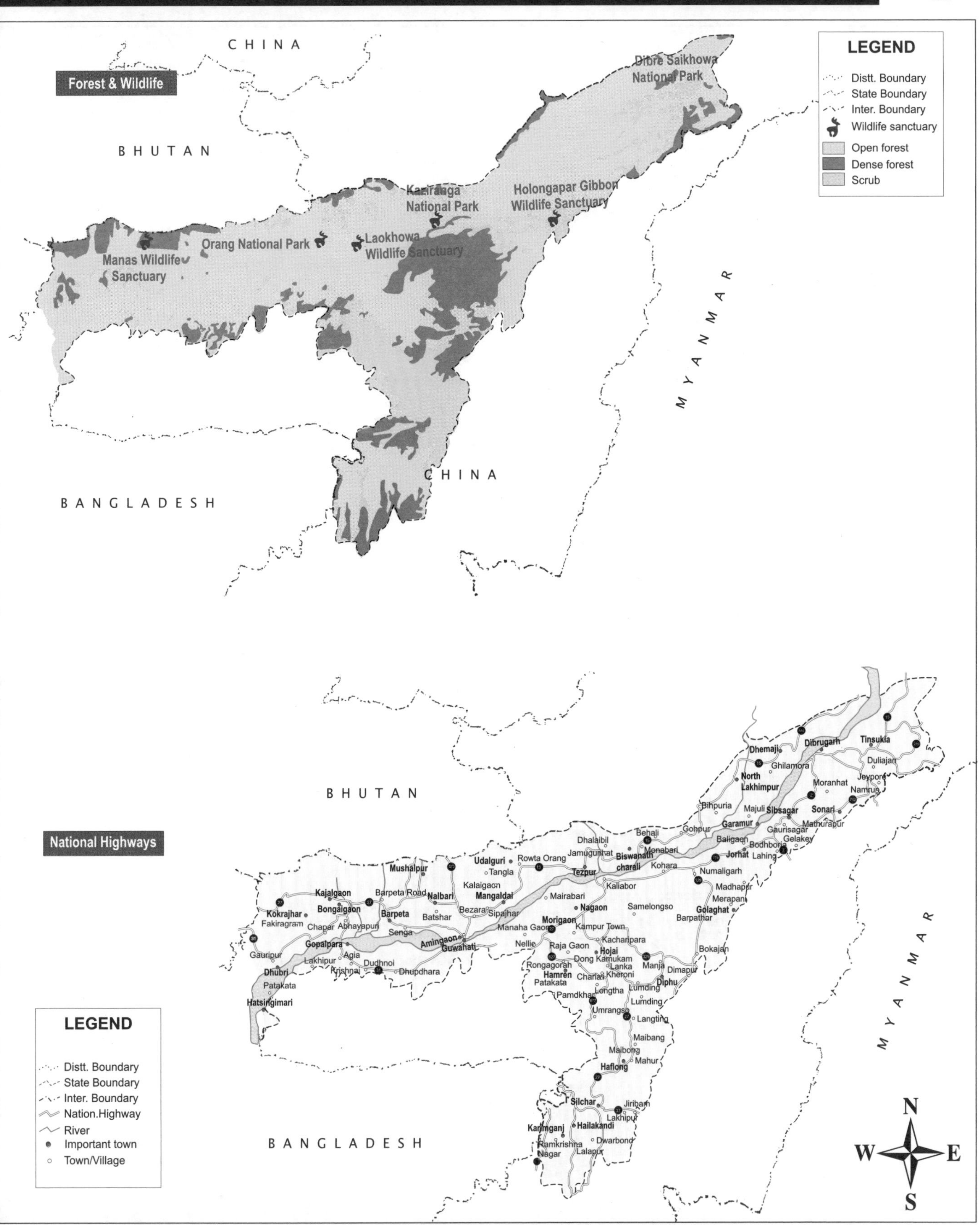

Forest & Wildlife
CHINA
BHUTAN
BANGLADESH
MYANMAR
Dibru Saikhowa National Park
Kaziranga National Park
Holongapar Gibbon Wildlife Sanctuary
Orang National Park
Laokhowa Wildlife Sanctuary
Manas Wildlife Sanctuary
LEGEND
Distt. Boundary
State Boundary
Inter. Boundary
Wildlife sanctuary
Open forest
Dense forest
Scrub
National Highways
Dhemaji
Dibrugarh
Tinsukia
Duliajan
North Lakhimpur
Ghilamora
Moranhat
Jeypore
Namrup
Bihpuria
Majuli
Sibsagar
Sonari
Garamur
Gohpur
Mathurapur
Gaurisagar
Baligaon
Gelakey
Bodhbora
Behali
Dhalaibil
Jamugurihat
Monabari
Biswanath charali
Kohara
Jorhat
Lahing
Udalguri
Rowta Orang
Tangla
Tezpur
Numaligarh
Mushalpur
Kalaigaon
Mangaldai
Kaliabor
Madhapur
Merapani
Kajalgaon
Barpeta Road
Nalbari
Mairabari
Nagaon
Samelongso
Golaghat
Barpathar
Kokrajhar
Bongaigaon
Barpeta
Batshar
Bezara
Sipajhar
Morigaon
Kampur Town
Fakiragram
Chapar
Abhayapuri
Senga
Manaha Gaon
Kacharipara
Bokajan
Gopalpara
Amingaon
Guwahati
Nellie
Raja Gaon
Hojai
Gauripur
Agia
Dudhnoi
Dong Kamukam
Lanka
Manja
Dimapur
Lakhipur
Rongagorah
Hamren
Charia
Kheroni
Diphu
Dhubri
Krishnai
Dhupdhara
Patakata
Pamdkhar
Longtha
Lumding
Hatsingimari
Umrangso
Langting
Maibang
Maibong
Mahur
Haflong
Silchar
Jiribam
Lakhipur
Karimganj
Hailakandi
Dwarbond
Ramkrishna Nagar
Lalapur
LEGEND
Distt. Boundary
State Boundary
Inter. Boundary
Nation.Highway
River
Important town
Town/Village
N
W
E
S

Scale - 1:5.5 M approx

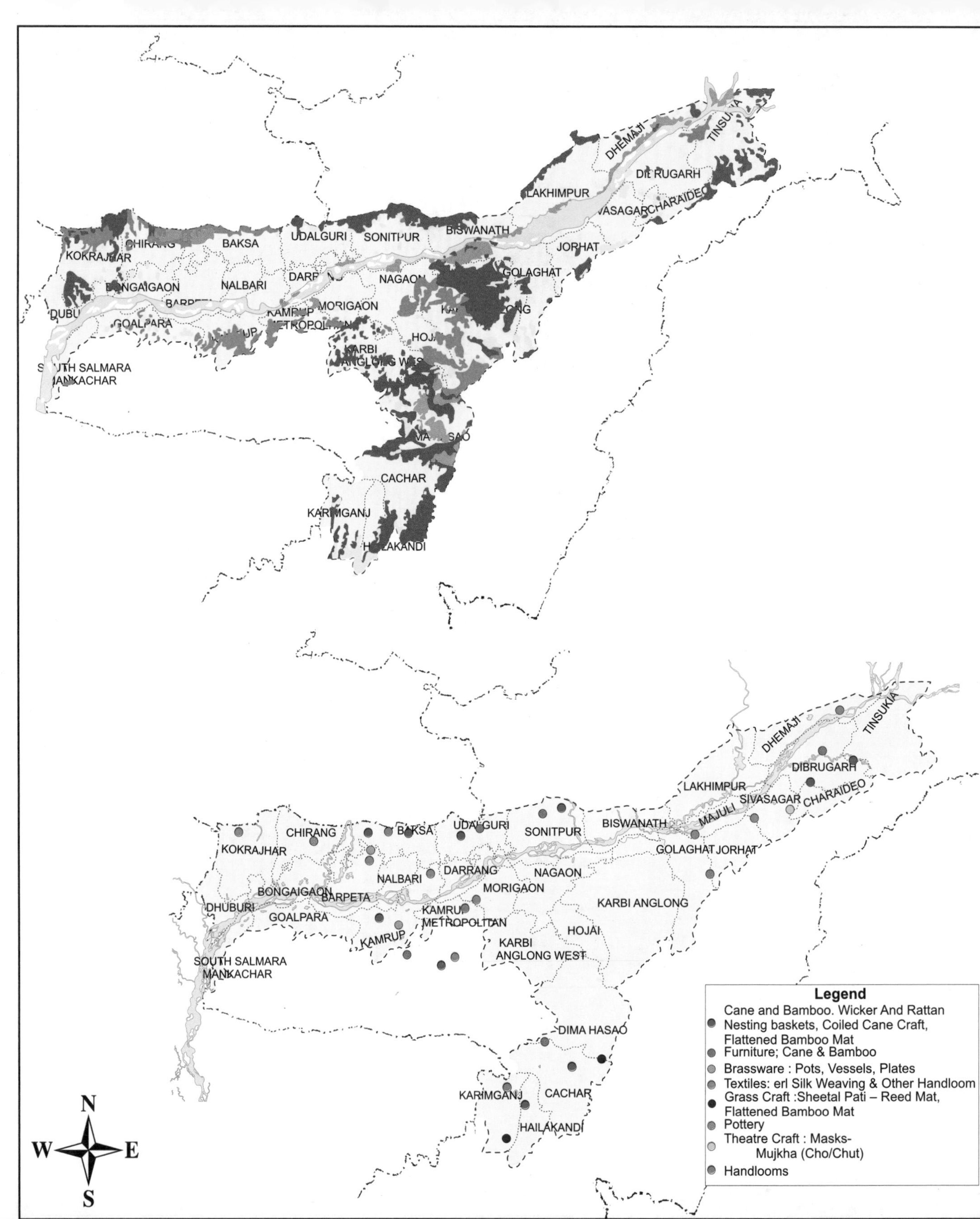
DHEMAJI
TINSUKIA
DIBRUGARH
LAKHIMPUR
CHARAIDEO
UDALGURI
SONITPUR
BISWANATH
BAKSA
CHIRANG
KOKRAJHAR
JORHAT
GOLAGHAT
NALBARI
NAGAON
MORIGAON
BONGAIGAON
GOALPARA
KAMRUP METROPOLITAN
KARBI ANGLONG WEST
SOUTH SALMARA MANKACHAR
CACHAR
KARIMGANJ
HAILAKANDI
SIVASAGAR
MAJULI
DARRANG
BARPETA
DHUBURI
KAMRUP
KARBI ANGLONG
HOJAI
DIMA HASAO
Legend
Cane and Bamboo. Wicker And Rattan
Nesting baskets, Coiled Cane Craft, Flattened Bamboo Mat
Furniture; Cane & Bamboo
Brassware : Pots, Vessels, Plates
Textiles: erl Silk Weaving & Other Handloom
Grass Craft :Sheetal Pati – Reed Mat, Flattened Bamboo Mat
Pottery
Theatre Craft : Masks- Mujkha (Cho/Chut)
Handlooms
N
S
E
W

Scale - 1:5 M approx

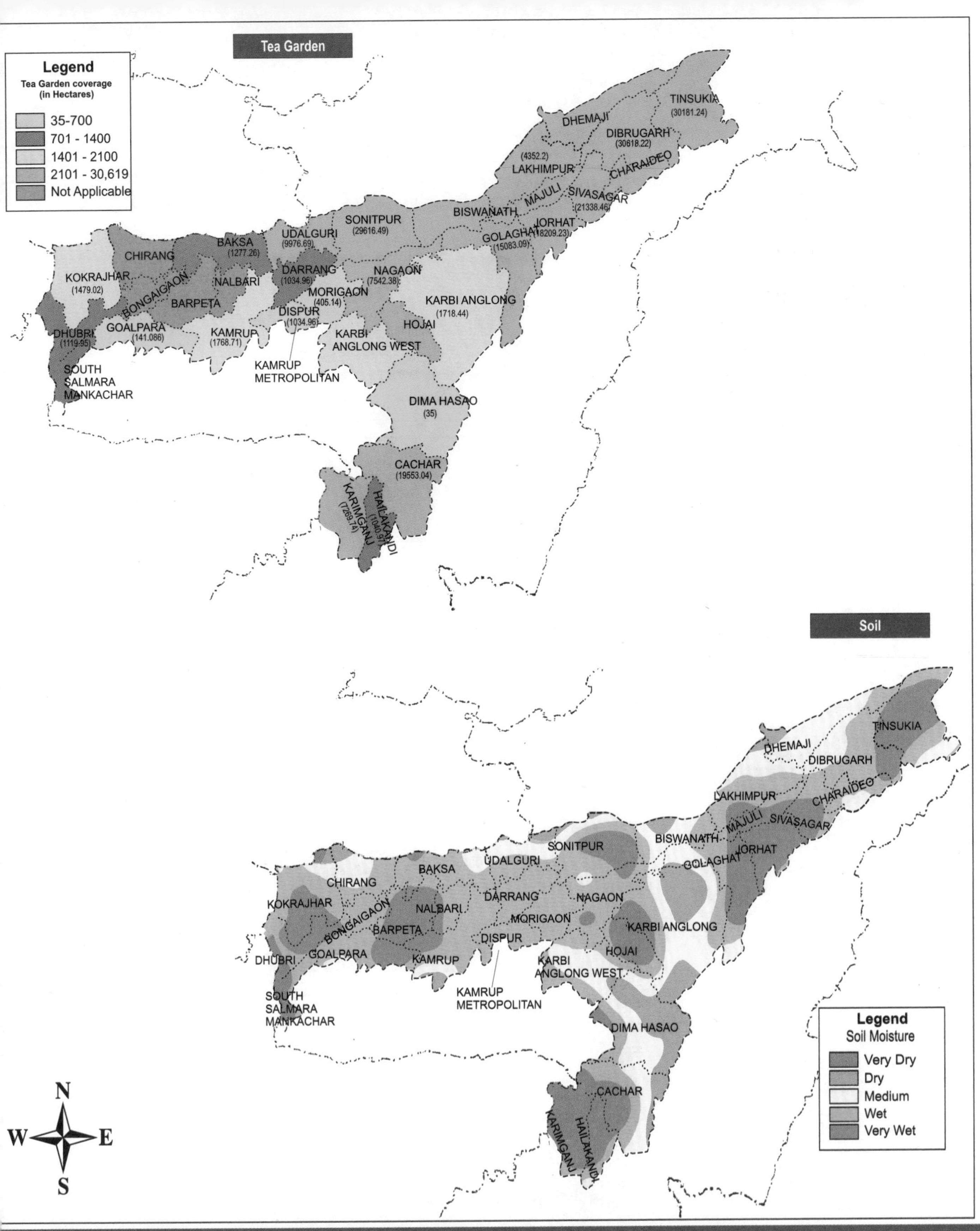

Tea Garden
Legend
Tea Garden coverage (in Hectares)
35-700
701 - 1400
1401 - 2100
2101 - 30,619
Not Applicable
TINSUKIA (30181.24)
DHEMAJI
DIBRUGARH (30618.22)
(4352.2) LAKHIMPUR
CHARAIDEO
MAJULI
SIVASAGAR (21338.46)
BISWANATH
JORHAT (18209.23)
GOLAGHAT (15083.09)
SONITPUR (29616.49)
UDALGURI (9976.69)
BAKSA (1277.26)
CHIRANG
KOKRAJHAR (1479.02)
BONGAIGAON
NALBARI
BARPETA
DARRANG (1034.96)
NAGAON (7542.38)
MORIGAON (405.14)
DISPUR (1034.96)
KARBI ANGLONG (1718.44)
HOJAI
KARBI ANGLONG WEST
DHUBRI (1119.95)
GOALPARA (141.086)
KAMRUP (1768.71)
KAMRUP METROPOLITAN
SOUTH SALMARA MANKACHAR
DIMA HASAO (35)
CACHAR (19553.04)
KARIMGANJ (7269.74)
HAILAKANDI (1040.97)
Soil
TINSUKIA
DHEMAJI
DIBRUGARH
LAKHIMPUR
CHARAIDEO
MAJULI
SIVASAGAR
BISWANATH
JORHAT
GOLAGHAT
SONITPUR
UDALGURI
BAKSA
CHIRANG
KOKRAJHAR
BONGAIGAON
NALBARI
BARPETA
DARRANG
NAGAON
MORIGAON
DISPUR
KARBI ANGLONG
HOJAI
KARBI ANGLONG WEST
DHUBRI
GOALPARA
KAMRUP
KAMRUP METROPOLITAN
SOUTH SALMARA MANKACHAR
DIMA HASAO
CACHAR
KARIMGANJ
HAILAKANDI
Legend
Soil Moisture
Very Dry
Dry
Medium
Wet
Very Wet
N
W
E
S

Scale - 1:5.5 M approx

KOKRAJHAR & CHIRANG

KOKRAJHAR

VITAL STATISTICS

1. **District Headquarter:** Kokrajhar
2. **Population:** 887,142
3. **Area:** 3,129 sq. km.
4. **Population Density:** 269 persons per sq. km.
5. **Literacy:** 65.22%
6. **Sex Ratio:** 959 females per 1000 males

ECONOMIC PROFILES

1. **Agriculture:** The main crops grown in the district are paddy, maize, wheat, sugarcane, cotton, pulses, cereals, jute etc.
2. **Industries:** Agro, chemical, engineering units, Cane and bamboo, carpentry, blacksmith, mineral, metal, Cotton textile etc.
3. **Minerals:** N/A
4. **Tourism:** Chakrashila wildlife sanctuary, Hanuman temple, Kali mandir, etc.
5. **Live stocks :** Poultry, cattle like cows, buffaloes, goat, sheep, pigs, dogs and bitches, mithun, fishing and dairy farming etc.

Kokrajhar is a district of the Assam state with its administrative headquarters located at Kokrajhar town. Originally, Kokrajhar was a significant part of the undivided Goalpara district. After sometime Kokrajhar was separated from the then Dhubri Sub-division of the Goalpara district and emerged as a Civil Sub-division in 1957. Prior to that, it was only a mere small town with a railway station. Later the place Kokrajhar was promoted into a district on 1st July, 1983.

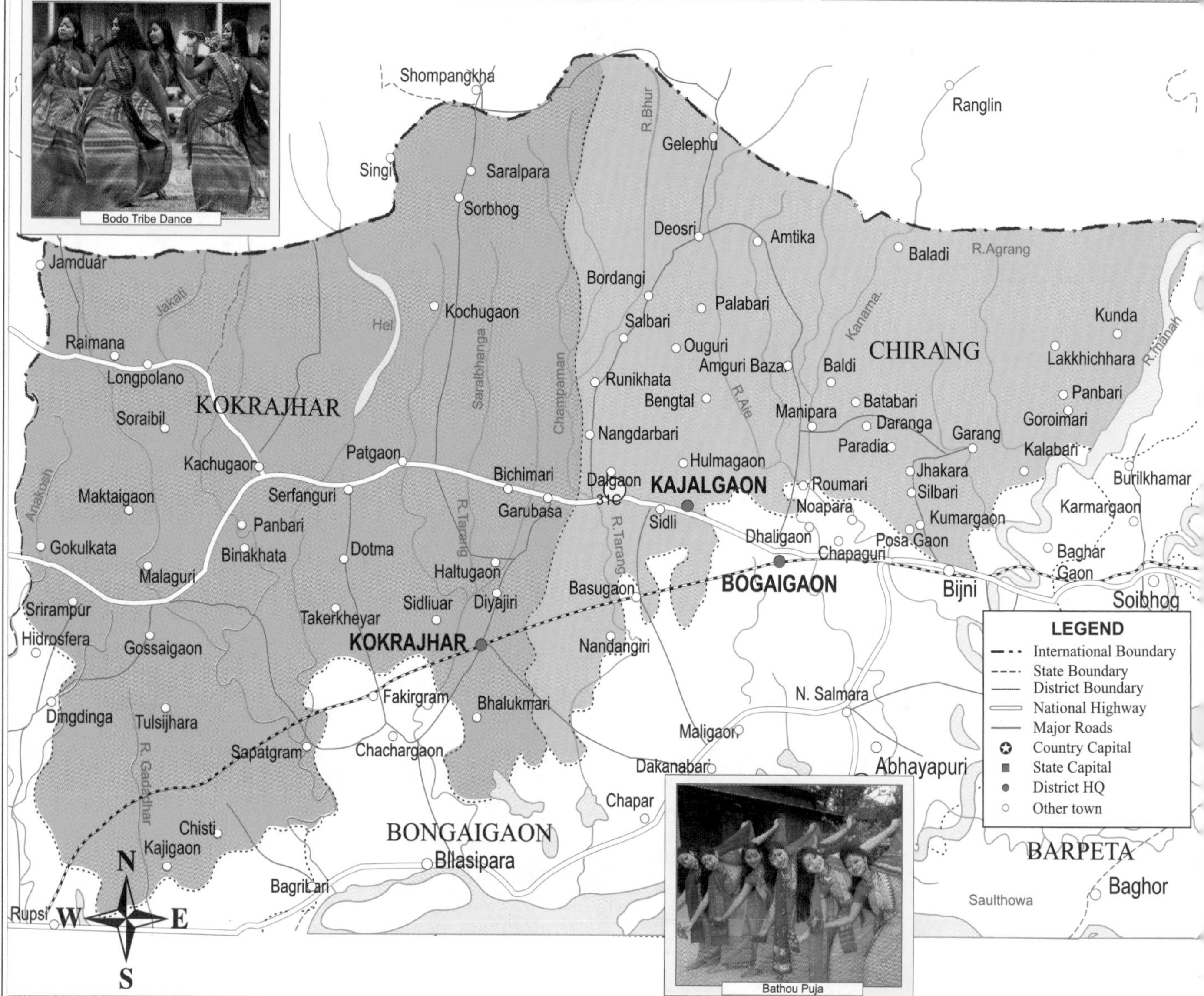

Shompangkha
Ranglin
Singi
Saralpara
Sorbhog
R.Bhur
Gelephu
Deosri
Amtika
Baladi
R.Agrang
Jamduar
Jakati
Hel
Kochugaon
Bordangi
Palabari
Salbari
Ouguri
Kanamai
CHIRANG
Kunda
Lakkhichhara
R.Manah
Raimana
Longpolano
KOKRAJHAR
Saralbhanga
Champaman
Runikhata
Amguri Bazar
Baldi
Bengtal
R.Aie
Manipara
Batabari
Daranga
Panbari
Goroimari
Soraibil
Nangdarbari
Garang
Paradia
Kalabari
Kachugaon
Patgaon
Hulmagaon
Bichimari
Anakosh
Maktaigaon
Serfanguri
Dalgaon
31C
KAJALGAON
Roumari
Jhakara
Burilkhamar
Silbari
Garubasa
Noapara
Karmargaon
Panbari
Sidli
Kumargaon
Dhaligaon
R.Tarang
Gokulkata
Binakhata
Dotma
Posa Gaon
Chapaguri
Baghar Gaon
Malaguri
Haltugaon
Basugaon
BOGAIGAON
Bijni
Soibhog
Srirampur
Sidliuar
Diyajiri
Hidrosfera
Takerkheyar
Gossaigaon
KOKRAJHAR
Nandangiri
Fakirgram
Bhalukmari
N. Salmara
Dingdinga
Tulsijhara
Maligaon
R. Gadadhar
Sapatgram
Chachargaon
Dakanabari
Abhayapuri
Chapar
Chisti
Kajigaon
BONGAIGAON
Bilasipara
BARPETA
Bagribari
Baghor
Saulthowa
Rupsi
N
W
E
S
LEGEND
International Boundary
State Boundary
District Boundary
National Highway
Major Roads
Country Capital
State Capital
District HQ
Other town

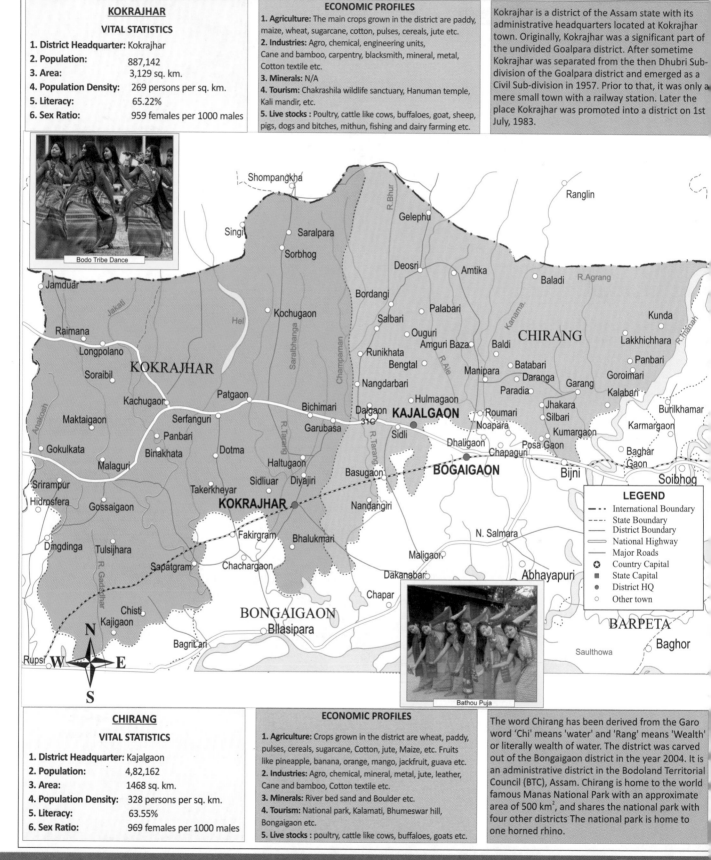

Bodo Tribe Dance

Bathou Puja

CHIRANG

VITAL STATISTICS

1. **District Headquarter:** Kajalgaon
2. **Population:** 4,82,162
3. **Area:** 1468 sq. km.
4. **Population Density:** 328 persons per sq. km.
5. **Literacy:** 63.55%
6. **Sex Ratio:** 969 females per 1000 males

ECONOMIC PROFILES

1. **Agriculture:** Crops grown in the district are wheat, paddy, pulses, cereals, sugarcane, Cotton, jute, Maize, etc. Fruits like pineapple, banana, orange, mango, jackfruit, guava etc.
2. **Industries:** Agro, chemical, mineral, metal, jute, leather, Cane and bamboo, Cotton textile etc.
3. **Minerals:** River bed sand and Boulder etc.
4. **Tourism:** National park, Kalamati, Bhumeswar hill, Bongaigaon etc.
5. **Live stocks :** poultry, cattle like cows, buffaloes, goats etc.

The word Chirang has been derived from the Garo word 'Chi' means 'water' and 'Rang' means 'Wealth' or literally wealth of water. The district was carved out of the Bongaigaon district in the year 2004. It is an administrative district in the Bodoland Territorial Council (BTC), Assam. Chirang is home to the world famous Manas National Park with an approximate area of 500 km^2, and shares the national park with four other districts The national park is home to one horned rhino.

Scale - 1:0.6 M approx

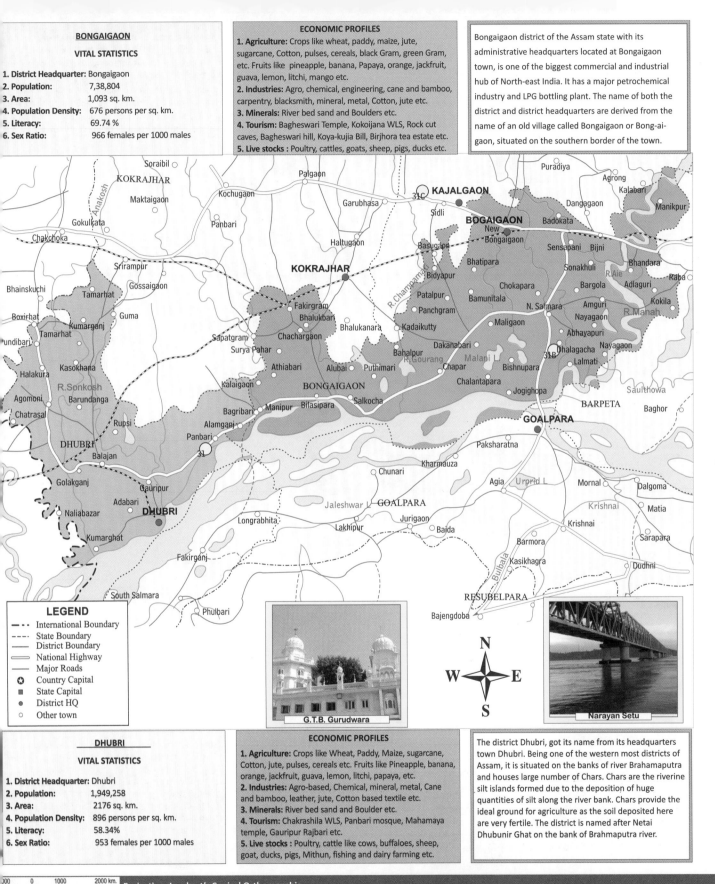

BONGAIGAON

VITAL STATISTICS

1. **District Headquarter:** Bongaigaon
2. **Population:** 7,38,804
3. **Area:** 1,093 sq. km.
4. **Population Density:** 676 persons per sq. km.
5. **Literacy:** 69.74 %
6. **Sex Ratio:** 966 females per 1000 males

ECONOMIC PROFILES

1. **Agriculture:** Crops like wheat, paddy, maize, jute, sugarcane, Cotton, pulses, cereals, black Gram, green Gram, etc. Fruits like pineapple, banana, Papaya, orange, jackfruit, guava, lemon, litchi, mango etc.
2. **Industries:** Agro, chemical, engineering, cane and bamboo, carpentry, blacksmith, mineral, metal, Cotton, jute etc.
3. **Minerals:** River bed sand and Boulders etc.
4. **Tourism:** Bagheswari Temple, Kokoijana WLS, Rock cut caves, Bagheswari hill, Koya-kujia Bill, Birjhora tea estate etc.
5. **Live stocks :** Poultry, cattles, goats, sheep, pigs, ducks etc.

Bongaigaon district of the Assam state with its administrative headquarters located at Bongaigaon town, is one of the biggest commercial and industrial hub of North-east India. It has a major petrochemical industry and LPG bottling plant. The name of both the district and district headquarters are derived from the name of an old village called Bongaigaon or Bong-ai-gaon, situated on the southern border of the town.

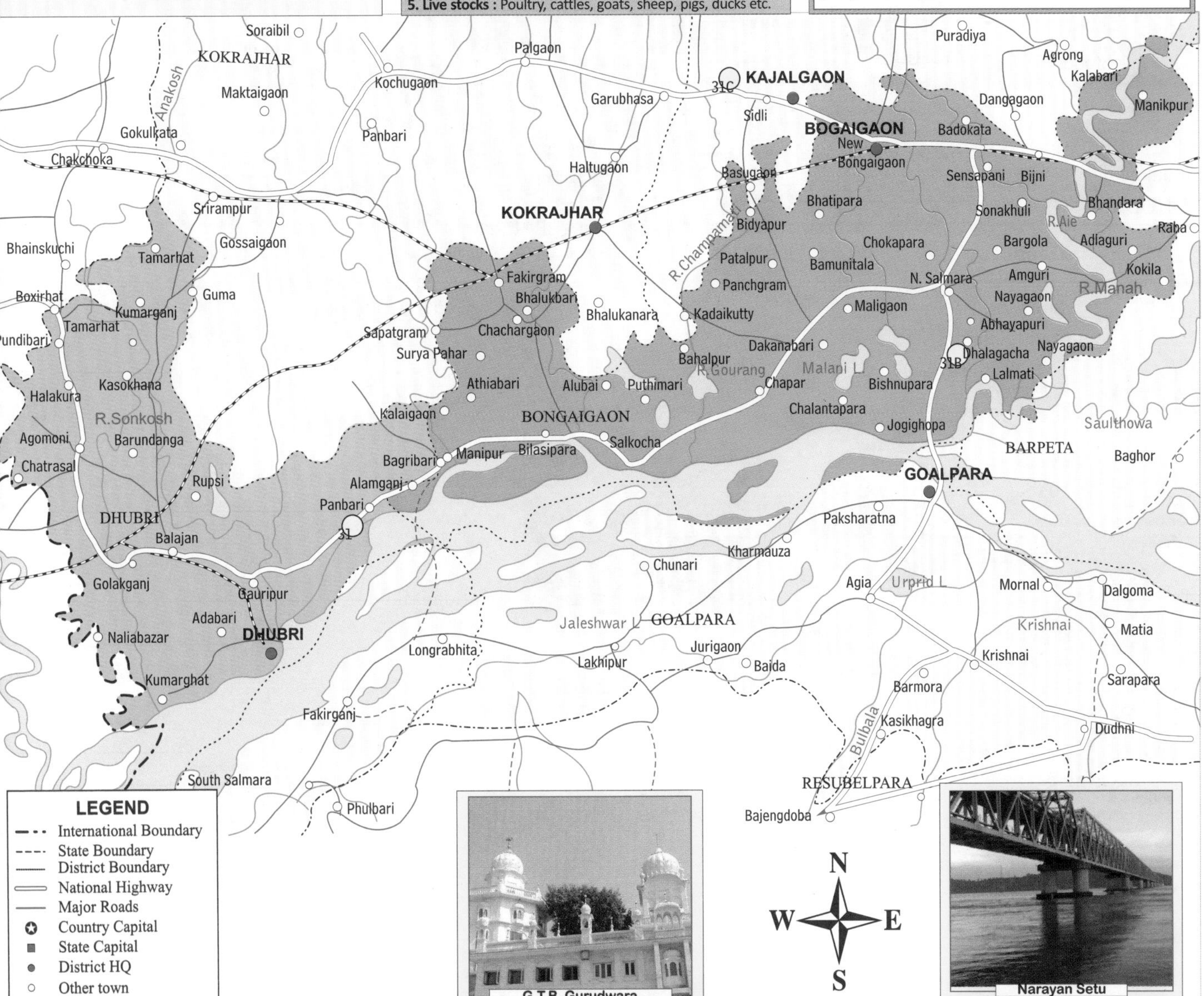

KOKRAJHAR
KAJALGAON
BOGAIGAON
New Bongaigaon
KOKRAJHAR
BONGAIGAON
GOALPARA
BARPETA
DHUBRI
GOALPARA
RESUBELPARA
Soraibil
Palgaon
Puradiya
Agrong
Kalabari
Manikpur
Kochugaon
Maktaigaon
Garubhasa
Sidli
Dangagaon
Badokata
Gokulkata
Panbari
Chakchoka
Haltugaon
Basugaon
Sensapani
Bijni
Srirampur
Bhatipara
Sonakhuli
Bhandara
Raha
Bidyapur
Chokapara
Bargola
Adlaguri
Bhainskuchi
Gossaigaon
Tamarhat
Patalpur
Bamunitala
Amguri
Kokila
Panchgram
N. Salmara
Fakirgram
Boxirhat
Guma
Bhalukbari
Nayagaon
R.Manah
Kumarganj
Bhalukanara
Kadaikutty
Maligaon
Abhayapuri
Tamarhat
Chachargaon
Sapatgram
Dakanabari
Dhalagacha
Nayagaon
Surya Pahar
Bahalpur
Lalmati
R.Gourang
Malani L.
Kasokhana
Athiabari
Alubai
Puthimari
Chapar
Bishnupara
Halakura
Chalantapara
Kalaigaon
R.Sonkosh
Jogighopa
Saulthowa
Agomoni
Barundanga
Salkocha
Bagribari
Manipur
Bilasipara
Baghor
Chatrasal
Alamganj
Rupsi
Panbari
Paksharatna
Balajan
Kharmauza
Chunari
Golakganj
Gauripur
Agia
Urprid L.
Mornal
Dalgoma
Adabari
Jaleshwar L.
Krishnai
Matia
Naliabazar
Longrabhita
Jurigaon
Krishnai
Lakhipur
Baida
Sarapara
Kumarghat
Barmora
Fakirganj
Kasikhagra
Dudhni
Bulbala
South Salmara
Phulbari
Bajengdoba
R.Champamati
Anakosh
R.Aie
31
31C
31B
LEGEND
International Boundary
State Boundary
District Boundary
National Highway
Major Roads
Country Capital
State Capital
District HQ
Other town
N
W
E
S

G.T.B. Gurudwara

Narayan Setu

DHUBRI

VITAL STATISTICS

1. **District Headquarter:** Dhubri
2. **Population:** 1,949,258
3. **Area:** 2176 sq. km.
4. **Population Density:** 896 persons per sq. km.
5. **Literacy:** 58.34%
6. **Sex Ratio:** 953 females per 1000 males

ECONOMIC PROFILES

1. **Agriculture:** Crops like Wheat, Paddy, Maize, sugarcane, Cotton, jute, pulses, cereals etc. Fruits like Pineapple, banana, orange, jackfruit, guava, lemon, litchi, papaya, etc.
2. **Industries:** Agro-based, Chemical, mineral, metal, Cane and bamboo, leather, jute, Cotton based textile etc.
3. **Minerals:** River bed sand and Boulder etc.
4. **Tourism:** Chakrashila WLS, Panbari mosque, Mahamaya temple, Gauripur Rajbari etc.
5. **Live stocks :** Poultry, cattle like cows, buffaloes, sheep, goat, ducks, pigs, Mithun, fishing and dairy farming etc.

The district Dhubri, got its name from its headquarters town Dhubri. Being one of the western most districts of Assam, it is situated on the banks of river Brahamaputra and houses large number of Chars. Chars are the riverine silt islands formed due to the deposition of huge quantities of silt along the river bank. Chars provide the ideal ground for agriculture as the soil deposited here are very fertile. The district is named after Netai Dhubunir Ghat on the bank of Brahmaputra river.

000 0 1000 2000 km.

Projection: Lambert's Conical Orthomorphic

GOALPARA & S.S. MANKACHAR

GOALPARA

VITAL STATISTICS

1. **District Headquarter:** Goalpara
2. **Population:** 1,008,183
3. **Area:** 1,824 sq. km.
4. **Population Density:** 553 persons per sq. km.
5. **Literacy:** 67.37 %
6. **Sex Ratio:** 964 females per 1000 males

ECONOMIC PROFILES

1. **Agriculture:** The crops include Wheat, paddy, sugarcane, jute, maize, pulses, cereals etc. Fruits like pineapple, banana, orange, Papaya, Jackfruit, mango, lemon, litchi etc.
2. **Industries:** Agro, chemical, mineral, metal, engineering, cane and bamboo, leather, carpentry, Blacksmith, jute,Cotton
3. **Minerals:** NIL
4. **Tourism:** Surya pahar, Manas N.P., Tukeswari, Kokrajhar, Nagaon, Joybhum kamakhya Temple, Chopta etc.
5. **Live stocks :** Poultry, cattle like cows, buffaloes, goats, Sheep, ducks, Mithun, fishing and dairy farming etc.

The district got its name from its HQ town, Goalpara. It is believed that the term Goalpara is originally derived from the word "Gwaltippika" or village of 'Gwala' meaning the village of the milk men. Earlier the place was under the rule of Rajbongsi Kings. In the year 1765 the British came to this place and started to rule over it. Goalpara is the mother district of Dhubri and Kokrajhar.

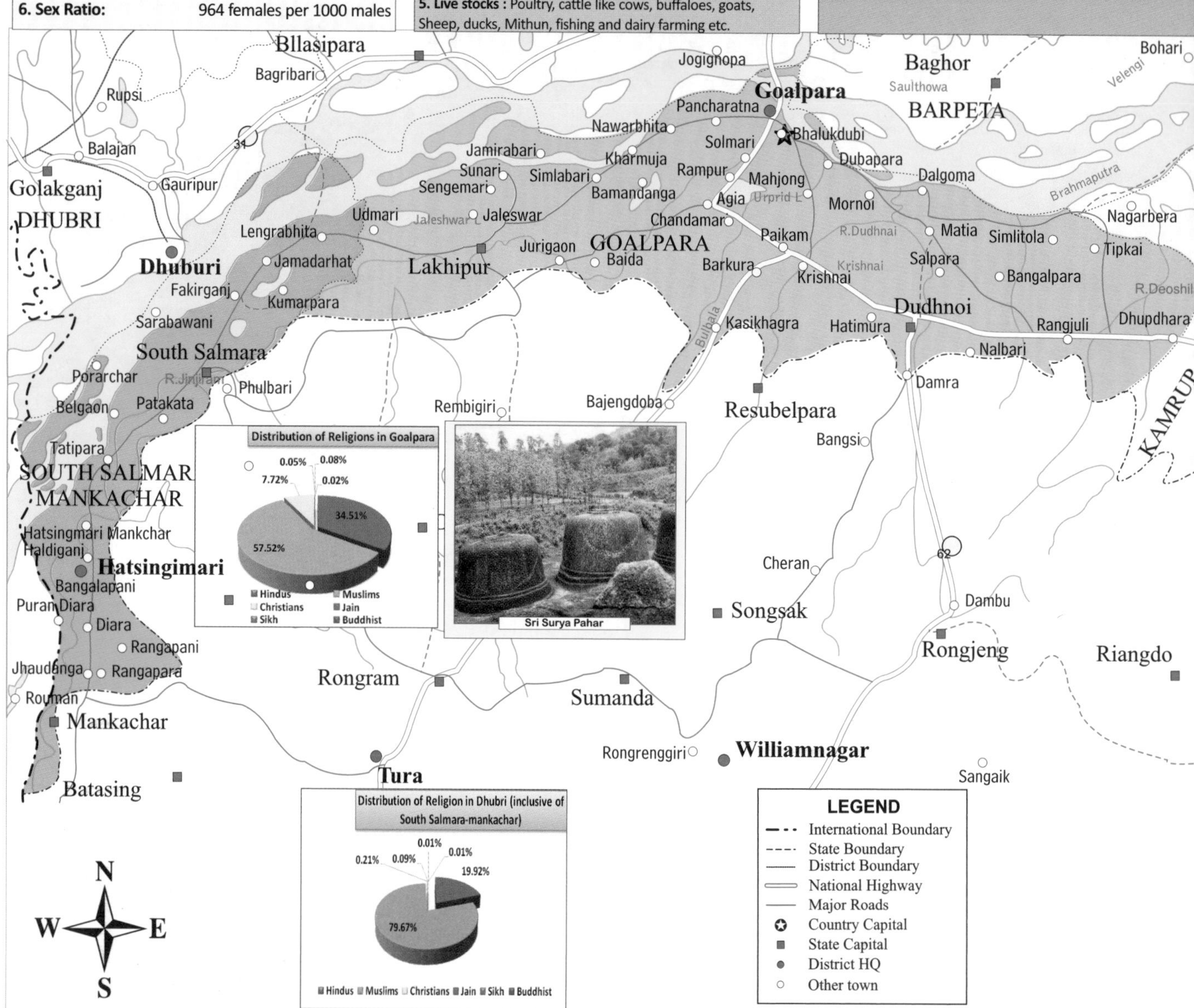

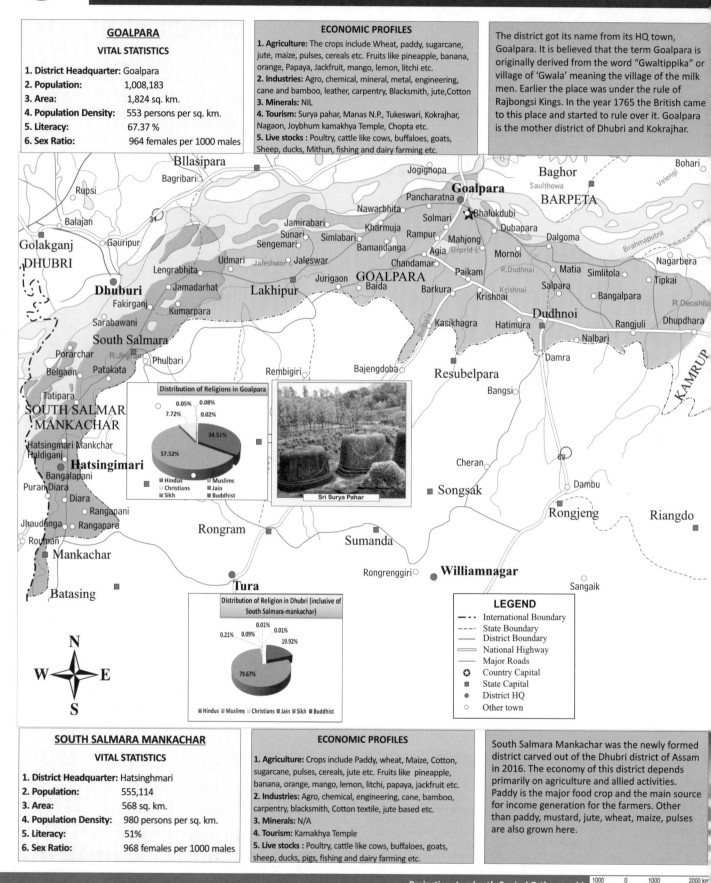

Bllasipara
Bagribari
Rupsi
Balajan
Golakganj
DHUBRI
Gauripur
Dhuburi
Fakirganj
Sarabawani
South Salmara
Porarchar
R.Jinjiram
Phulbari
Belgaon
Patakata
Tatipara
SOUTH SALMAR
MANKACHAR
Hatsingmari Mankchar
Haldiganj
Hatsingimari
Bangalapani
Puran Diara
Diara
Rangapani
Jhaudanga
Rangapara
Rouman
Mankachar
Batasing
Lengrabhita
Jamadarhat
Kumarpara
Udmari
Jaleshwar L
Jaleswar
Lakhipur
Jamirabari
Sunari
Sengemari
Simlabari
Nawarbhita
Kharmuja
Bamandanga
Jurigaon
GOALPARA
Baida
Jogighopa
Goalpara
Pancharatna
Solmari
Bhalukdubi
Rampur
Mahjong
Agia
Urpid L
Chandamari
Paikam
Barkura
Krishnai
Kasikhagra
Bullala
Dubapara
Mornoi
R.Dudhnai
Matia
Salpara
Hatimura
Dudhnoi
Baghor
Saulthowa
BARPETA
Dalgoma
Brahmaputra
Velengi
Bohari
Nagarbera
Simlitola
Tipkai
Bangalpara
R.Deoshila
Rangjuli
Dhupdhara
Nalbari
Damra
KAMRUP
Rembigiri
Bajengdoba
Resubelpara
Bangsi
Cheran
Songsak
Dambu
Rongjeng
Riangdo
Rongram
Sumanda
Tura
Rongrenggiri
Williamnagar
Sangaik
62
Distribution of Religions in Goalpara
0.05%
0.08%
7.72%
0.02%
34.51%
57.52%
Hindus
Muslims
Christians
Jain
Sikh
Buddhist
Sri Surya Pahar
Distribution of Religion in Dhubri (inclusive of South Salmara-mankachar)
0.01%
0.21%
0.09%
0.01%
19.92%
79.67%
Hindus
Muslims
Christians
Jain
Sikh
Buddhist
N
W
E
S
LEGEND
International Boundary
State Boundary
District Boundary
National Highway
Major Roads
Country Capital
State Capital
District HQ
Other town

SOUTH SALMARA MANKACHAR

VITAL STATISTICS

1. **District Headquarter:** Hatsinghmari
2. **Population:** 555,114
3. **Area:** 568 sq. km.
4. **Population Density:** 980 persons per sq. km.
5. **Literacy:** 51%
6. **Sex Ratio:** 968 females per 1000 males

ECONOMIC PROFILES

1. **Agriculture:** Crops include Paddy, wheat, Maize, Cotton, sugarcane, pulses, cereals, jute etc. Fruits like pineapple, banana, orange, mango, lemon, litchi, papaya, jackfruit etc.
2. **Industries:** Agro, chemical, engineering, cane, bamboo, carpentry, blacksmith, Cotton textile, jute based etc.
3. **Minerals:** N/A
4. **Tourism:** Kamakhya Temple
5. **Live stocks :** Poultry, cattle like cows, buffaloes, goats, sheep, ducks, pigs, fishing and dairy farming etc.

South Salmara Mankachar was the newly formed district carved out of the Dhubri district of Assam in 2016. The economy of this district depends primarily on agriculture and allied activities. Paddy is the major food crop and the main source for income generation for the farmers. Other than paddy, mustard, jute, wheat, maize, pulses are also grown here.

Projection: Lambert's Conical Orthomorphic

1000 0 1000 2000 km

BARPETA

VITAL STATISTICS

- District Headquarter: Barpeta
- Population: 1,693,622
- Area: 2,282 sq. km.
- Population Density: 742 persons per sq. km.
- Literacy: 63.81%
- Sex Ratio: 953 females per 1000 males

ECONOMIC PROFILES

1. Agriculture: Crops like Wheat, Paddy, Black Gram, green Gram, maize, pulses, cereals, sugarcane, jute, etc. Fruits like pineapple, banana, orange, guava, Jackfruit, mango etc.
2. Industries: Agro, chemical, mineral, metal, carpentry, blacksmith, Cane and bamboo, leather based, Cotton textile, engineering units, etc.
3. Minerals: Limestone
4. Tourism: Beki, Manas N.P., Brahmaputra,The Barpeta satra, Dargah of Syed shahnur Dewan, Sundariya satra.
5. Live stocks : Poultry, cattle like cows, buffaloes, goats,

Barpeta is a district of Assam state with its administrative HQ located at Barpeta town. Barpeta is a significant religious place and popularly known by various names likewise Tatikuchi, Porabhita, Mathura, Vrindavan, Chouk hutisthan, Nabaratna Sabha and many more. When the great saint Shrimanta Sankardeva came to Barpeta , he started numerous satras (religious places) in this region and because of these satras, the place was changed into a religious place.

CHIRANG
BAKSA
MUSHALPUR
NALBARI
BARPETA
KAMRUP METROPOLITAN
Kunda
Hajua
Vunchapara
Kumguri
Anchali
Uttar Nikashi
Kumarikhata
Adala
Tamulpur
Kamalabari
Baghamara
Hudakhata
Rehabari
Burilkhamar
Kalabari
Agrong
Karmargaon
Hastinapur
Patacharkuchi
Nijanaghati
Nathkuchi
Dhamdhama
Ranipukhuri
Barihar
Balitara
Barama
Namati
Sagarkuchi
Baniakuchi
Akana
Kachimpur
Tihu
Ghoghrapar
Barbhag
Bijni
Sorbhog
Barpeta Road
Bongaon
Haribhanga
Mathurapur
Kaithalkuchi
Amayapur
Raha
Howli
Kalijhar
Bhawanipur
Makhibaha
Chamata
Bangaon
Chankara
Dhanara
Tapa
Kalgachia
Marowa
Athgaon
Sarthebari
Ulubari
Rampur
Barnard
Chandakuchi
N. Salmara
Kayakuci
Belsor
Kulhati
Kamarkuchi
Sundaridia
Byaskuchi
Kakaya
Jagarasatra
Abhayapuri
Junia
Patbausi
Bijulighat
L.Gara Bil
Narowa
Jagara
Bhella
Chenga
Baihata
Mandia
Bortola
Mukalmua
Dagapara
Bohari
Doulasal
Tholabanka
Rampur
Haip
Tarabari
Phulara
Saulthowa
Baghbar
Balagaon
Sontali
Dalgoma
Kulsi
Mornai
Nagarbera
Matia
Simlitola
Tiplai
Peranga
Chayangaon
Krishnai
Sarapara
Samariasatra
Lakaduri
R. Beki
R. Palla
R. Pahumara
R. Kaldia
Calonrya
Tihu
Pagaladia
R. Buradia
R.Mora-pagladiya
R.Pagladia
R.Baralia
Mom Monas
Paraimarabil
R. Na-Khanda
R.Chaulkhowa
Velengi
Brahmaputra
Krishnai
Shirng
Bako
31
N
W
E
S
LEGEND
International Boundary
State Boundary
District Boundary
National Highway
Major Roads
Country Capital
State Capital
District HQ
Other town

NALBARI

VITAL STATISTICS

1. District Headquarter: Nalbari
2. Population: 771,639
3. Area: 1,052 sq. km.
4. Population Density: 773 persons per sq. km.
5. Literacy: 78.63 %
6. Sex Ratio: 949 females per 1000 males

ECONOMIC PROFILES

1. Agriculture: Crops like paddy, Wheat, Maize, pulses, cereals, Cotton, jute, sugarcane etc. The fruits like pineapple, banana, Orange, Jackfruit, mango, lemon, litchi, Papaya etc.
2. Industries: Agro, chemical, mineral, metal, Cotton textile, jute, leather, engineering units, Cane and bamboo etc.
3. Minerals: N/A
4. Tourism: Buddhist temple, Hari Mandir, Billeshwar Temple, Shripur Dewalay Mandir, Daulashal Temple, Ganga pukhari, Mahmara pukhari, Sonkuhira etc.
5. Live stocks : poultry, cattle like cows, buffaloes, goat, sheep,

Nalbari headquarter is located at Nalbari town. The district got its name from the word 'Nalbari' which means a place of reeds. In some 1890-91 A.D the present name was evolved. Earlier, the district was popularly known by various names such as Satra, Govindapur, Khata, etc. Moreover, in the ancient period of time this region was a part of the Kampitha, Pagarjotic, Pragjyotisha, Kamarupa, Kangoor, Rumi, Vaisali, etc.

000 0 1000 2000 km.
Projection: Lambert's Conical Orthomorphic

BAKSA

VITAL STATISTICS

1. **District Headquarter:** Mushalpur
2. **Population:** 950,075
3. **Area:** 2,457 sq. km.
4. **Population Density:** 387 persons per sq. km.
5. **Literacy:** 69.25%
6. **Sex Ratio:** 974 females per 1000 males

ECONOMIC PROFILES

1. **Agriculture:** Crops like paddy, sugarcane, jute, maize, etc. Fruits like pineapple, Banana, Jackfruit, orange, guava, etc.
2. **Industries:** Agro-based, chemical based, mineral based, metal based, cotton textile, carpentry, blacksmith, cane and bamboo, etc.
3. **Minerals:** NIL
4. **Tourism:** Manas National Park, Pagladia River, Bogamati River, Manas Soushi Khongkhor, Moina Pukhuri etc.
5. **Live stocks :** Poultry, Cattle like cows, buffaloes, goats, Mithun, etc.

Baksa is a district of the Assam state with its administrative headquarters located at Mushalpur town. It was formed by comprising a part of the Nalbari district, Barpeta district, Kamrup district and small portion of the Darrang district. Due to the BTC (Bodoland Territorial Council) accord signed on 10th February, 2003 formed BTAD (Bodo land Territorial Autonomous District) with four districts namely Kokrajhar , Chirang, Baksa and Udalguri. Baksa district was declared as a separate district on 1 st June, 2004.

Phankhai, Pakpabhi, Kerom, Risinghjor, Lablagompa, Naitola, Simsim, Thunsing, Yarphu, Marsala, Nortala, Dighlai, Chennari, R. Baralia, R. Forest, R. Pahumara, R. Mora-Manah, R. Manah, Kunda, Fatemabad, Bhatipara, Hajua, Doomni, Batabari, Chaulkara, Subankhata, Darranga, Nagrijuli Bagichat, Uttar Nikashi, Kumarikata, Goibari, Pagladia, Kadamtala, Nagrijuli, Atharikhat, BAKSA, Bhalukmari, Adala, Bhetagaon, Latibari, R. Puthimari, Naokata, Safakhamar, Kumguri, Moh Monas, Hatimura, Anchali, Jalah, Mushalpur, Ghoramara, Kataligaon, Hudakhata, Baghamara, Majadia, Tamulpur, Nimota, Gameriguri, Rihabari, Bamunpara, Tihu, Calonrya, Deochara, Simaluguri, Burilkhamar, Nijanaghati, Dhamdhama, Tinpukhuriya, Karmargaon, Patacharkuchi, Barama, Sagarkuchi, Goreswar, Barpeta Road, Tihu, Khandikar, Soibhog, Bhawanipur, Ghoghrapar, Kaithalkuchi, Raha, Howli, 31, Nalbari, Rangla, Lochh, Paraimarabil, Kendukara, Sarthobari, Bangaon, Chandakuchi, Karara, Barpeta, Byaskuchi, NALBARI, Bijlighat, Baihata, Kamalpur, Patbausi, Chenga, N, W, E, S

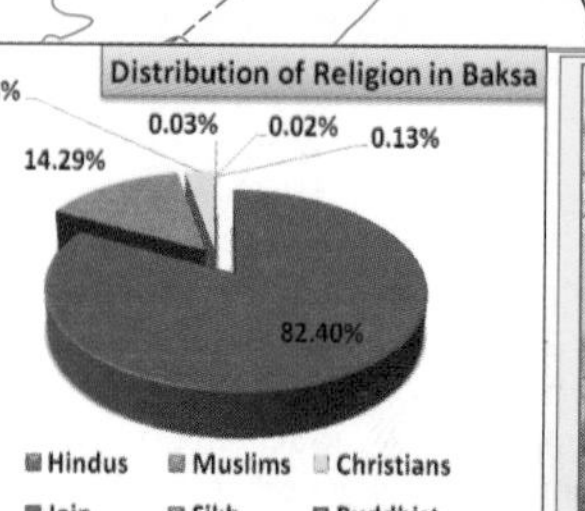

Distribution of Religion in Baksa
2.85%
0.03%
0.02%
0.13%
14.29%
82.40%
Hindus
Muslims
Christians
Jain
Sikh
Buddhist

Manas National Park

LEGEND

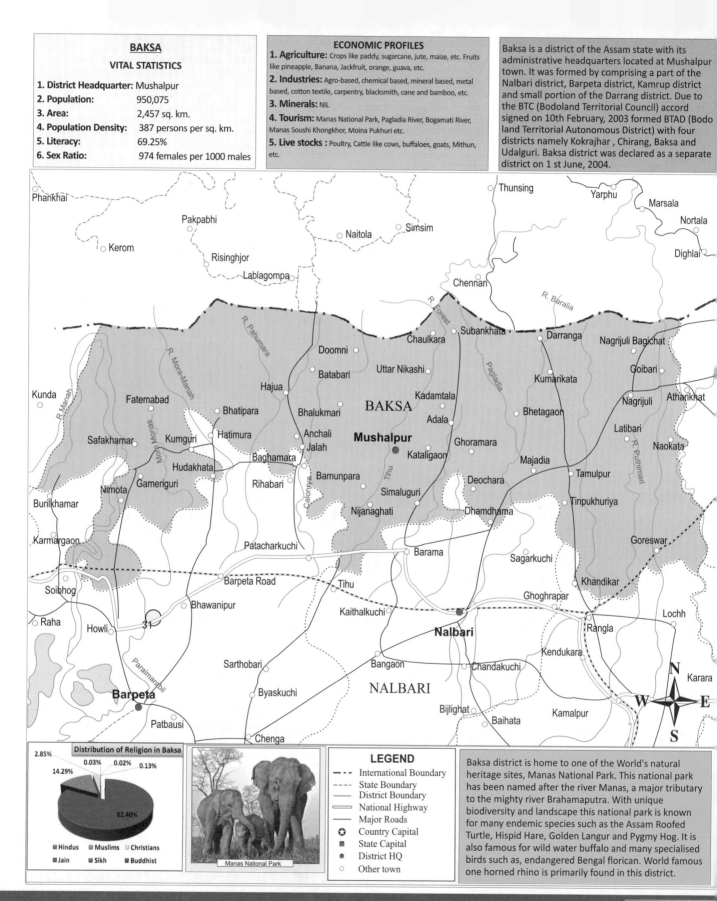

- International Boundary
- State Boundary
- District Boundary
- National Highway
- Major Roads
- Country Capital
- State Capital
- District HQ
- Other town

Baksa district is home to one of the World's natural heritage sites, Manas National Park. This national park has been named after the river Manas, a major tributary to the mighty river Brahamaputra. With unique biodiversity and landscape this national park is known for many endemic species such as the Assam Roofed Turtle, Hispid Hare, Golden Langur and Pygmy Hog. It is also famous for wild water buffalo and many specialised birds such as, endangered Bengal florican. World famous one horned rhino is primarily found in this district.

Scale - 1:0.5 M approx

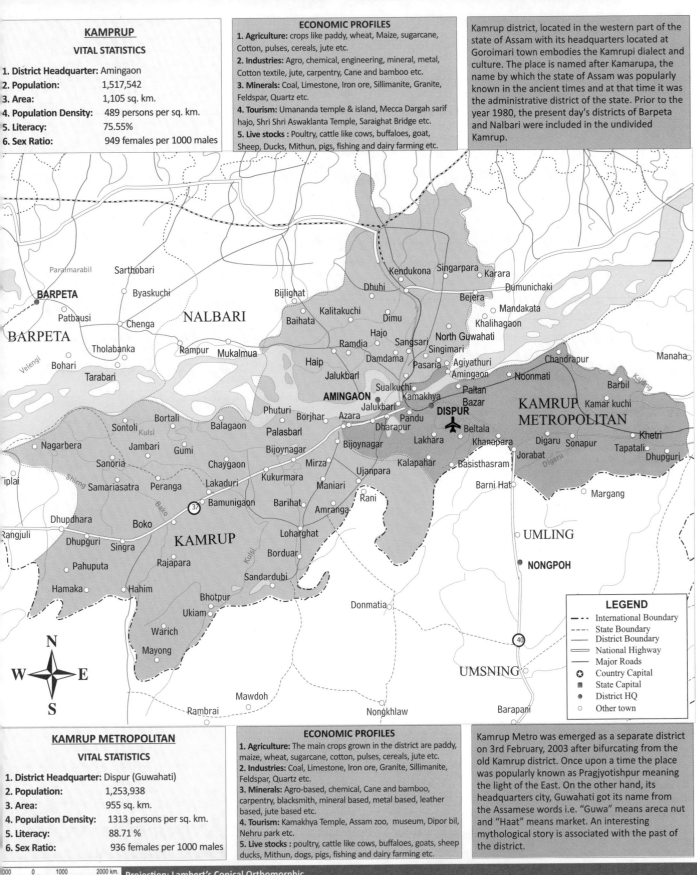

KAMPRUP

VITAL STATISTICS

1. **District Headquarter:** Amingaon
2. **Population:** 1,517,542
3. **Area:** 1,105 sq. km.
4. **Population Density:** 489 persons per sq. km.
5. **Literacy:** 75.55%
6. **Sex Ratio:** 949 females per 1000 males

ECONOMIC PROFILES

1. **Agriculture:** crops like paddy, wheat, Maize, sugarcane, Cotton, pulses, cereals, jute etc.
2. **Industries:** Agro, chemical, engineering, mineral, metal, Cotton textile, jute, carpentry, Cane and bamboo etc.
3. **Minerals:** Coal, Limestone, Iron ore, Sillimanite, Granite, Feldspar, Quartz etc.
4. **Tourism:** Umananda temple & island, Mecca Dargah sarif hajo, Shri Shri Aswaklanta Temple, Saraighat Bridge etc.
5. **Live stocks :** Poultry, cattle like cows, buffaloes, goat, Sheep, Ducks, Mithun, pigs, fishing and dairy farming etc.

Kamrup district, located in the western part of the state of Assam with its headquarters located at Goroimari town embodies the Kamrupi dialect and culture. The place is named after Kamarupa, the name by which the state of Assam was popularly known in the ancient times and at that time it was the administrative district of the state. Prior to the year 1980, the present day's districts of Barpeta and Nalbari were included in the undivided Kamrup.

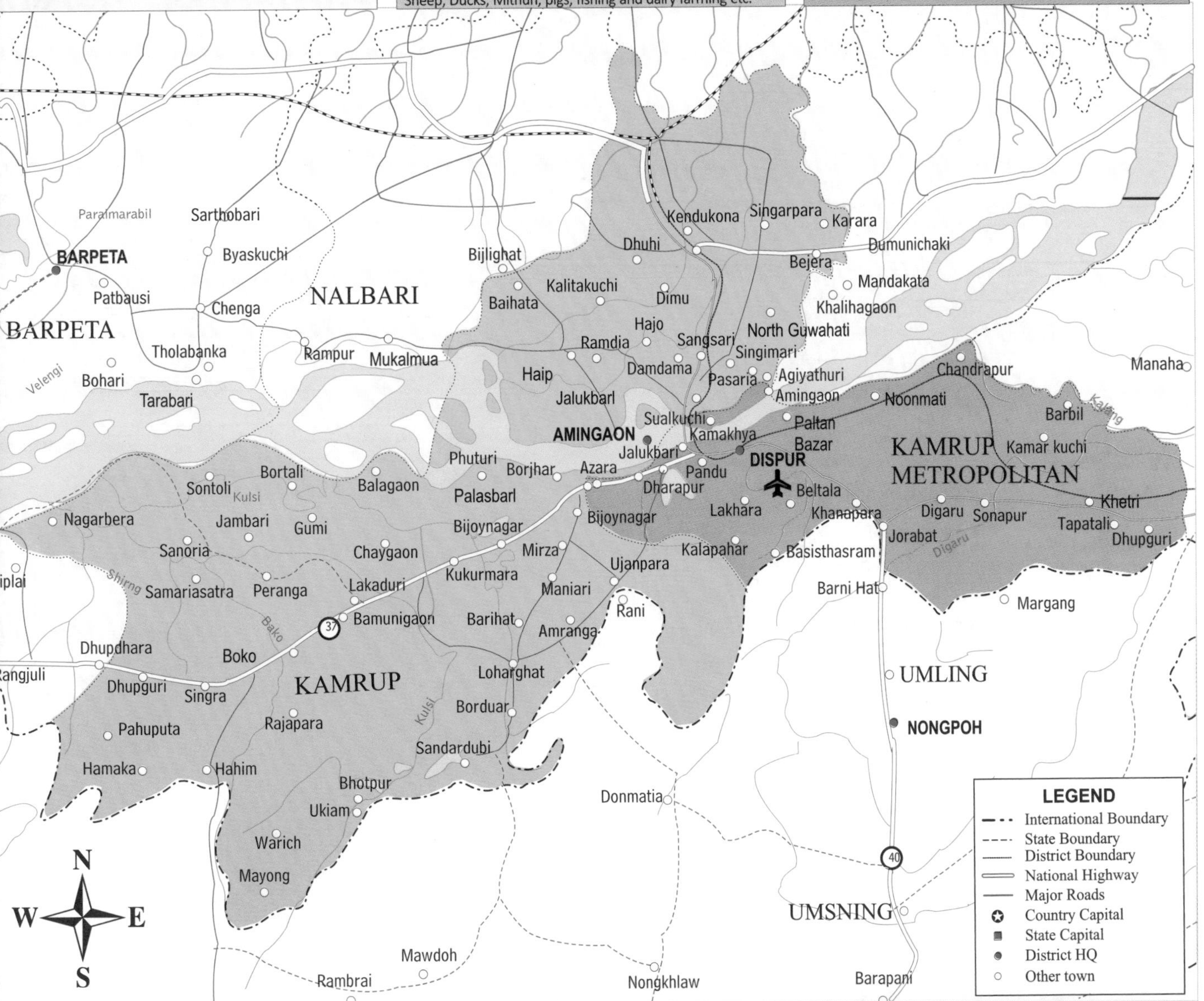

BARPETA
NALBARI
KAMRUP
KAMRUP METROPOLITAN
AMINGAON
DISPUR
UMLING
NONGPOH
UMSNING
Paraimarabil
Sarthobari
Byaskuchi
Patbausi
Chenga
Tholabanka
Rampur
Mukalmua
Bohari
Tarabari
Velengi
Bijlighat
Baihata
Kalitakuchi
Dhuhi
Dimu
Kendukona
Singarpara
Karara
Dumunichaki
Bejera
Mandakata
Khalihagaon
Hajo
Ramdia
Sangsari
North Guwahati
Singimari
Haip
Damdama
Pasaria
Agiyathuri
Amingaon
Noonmati
Chandrapur
Manaha
Jalukbari
Sualkuchi
Paltan Bazar
Kamakhya
Barbil
Kalang
Kamar kuchi
Phuturi
Borjhar
Azara
Pandu
Dharapur
Beltala
Khetri
Bortali
Sontoli
Kulsi
Balagaon
Palasbari
Lakhara
Khanapara
Digaru
Sonapur
Tapatali
Dhupguri
Nagarbera
Jambari
Gumi
Bijoynagar
Jorabat
Sanoria
Chaygaon
Mirza
Kalapahar
Basisthasram
Tiplai
Shirng
Samariasatra
Peranga
Lakaduri
Kukurmara
Maniari
Ujanpara
Barni Hat
Margang
Bako
Bamunigaon
Barihat
Rani
Amranga
Dhupdhara
Boko
Rangjuli
Dhupguri
Singra
Loharghat
Pahuputa
Rajapara
Borduar
Hamaka
Hahim
Sandardubi
Bhotpur
Ukiam
Donmatia
Warich
Mayong
Mawdoh
Rambrai
Nongkhlaw
Barapani
N
W
E
S
LEGEND
International Boundary
State Boundary
District Boundary
National Highway
Major Roads
Country Capital
State Capital
District HQ
Other town
37
40

KAMRUP METROPOLITAN

VITAL STATISTICS

1. **District Headquarter:** Dispur (Guwahati)
2. **Population:** 1,253,938
3. **Area:** 955 sq. km.
4. **Population Density:** 1313 persons per sq. km.
5. **Literacy:** 88.71 %
6. **Sex Ratio:** 936 females per 1000 males

ECONOMIC PROFILES

1. **Agriculture:** The main crops grown in the district are paddy, maize, wheat, sugarcane, cotton, pulses, cereals, jute etc.
2. **Industries:** Coal, Limestone, Iron ore, Granite, Sillimanite, Feldspar, Quartz etc.
3. **Minerals:** Agro-based, chemical, Cane and bamboo, carpentry, blacksmith, mineral based, metal based, leather based, jute based etc.
4. **Tourism:** Kamakhya Temple, Assam zoo, museum, Dipor bil, Nehru park etc.
5. **Live stocks :** poultry, cattle like cows, buffaloes, goats, sheep ducks, Mithun, dogs, pigs, fishing and dairy farming etc.

Kamrup Metro was emerged as a separate district on 3rd February, 2003 after bifurcating from the old Kamrup district. Once upon a time the place was popularly known as Pragjyotishpur meaning the light of the East. On the other hand, its headquarters city, Guwahati got its name from the Assamese words i.e. "Guwa" means areca nut and "Haat" means market. An interesting mythological story is associated with the past of the district.

1000 0 1000 2000 km.

Projection: Lambert's Conical Orthomorphic

UDALGURI & DARRANG

UDALGURI

VITAL STATISTICS

1. District Headquarter:	Udalguri
2. Population:	831,668
3. Area:	1,676 sq. km.
4. Population Density:	497 persons per sq. km.
5. Literacy:	65.41%
6. Sex Ratio:	973 females per 1000 males

ECONOMIC PROFILES

1. Agriculture: Crops like Paddy, Maize, wheat, jute, Cotton, sugarcane, pulses, cereals etc. Fruits like pineapple, banana, orange, Jackfruit, mango, lemon, litchi, papaya, cauliflower, cabbage etc.
2. Industries: Agro, chemical, mineral, metal, Cotton textile, jute, carpentry, blacksmith, cane and bamboo etc.
3. Minerals: NIL
4. Tourism: Manas National Park, Bhairabhkunda etc.
5. Live stocks : Poultry, cattle like cows, buffaloes, goats, sheep, Ducks, pigs, Mithun, fishing and dairy farming etc.

Udalguri is a district of the Assam state with its administrative headquarters located at Udalguri town. The district got its name from its headquarters town, Udalguri. There are three different point of views in context of the etymology of Udalguri. Some of its natives believe that the name is taken from the term Odal means a tree and Guri means the roots or surrounding of the tree since it was originally developed around an Odal tree.

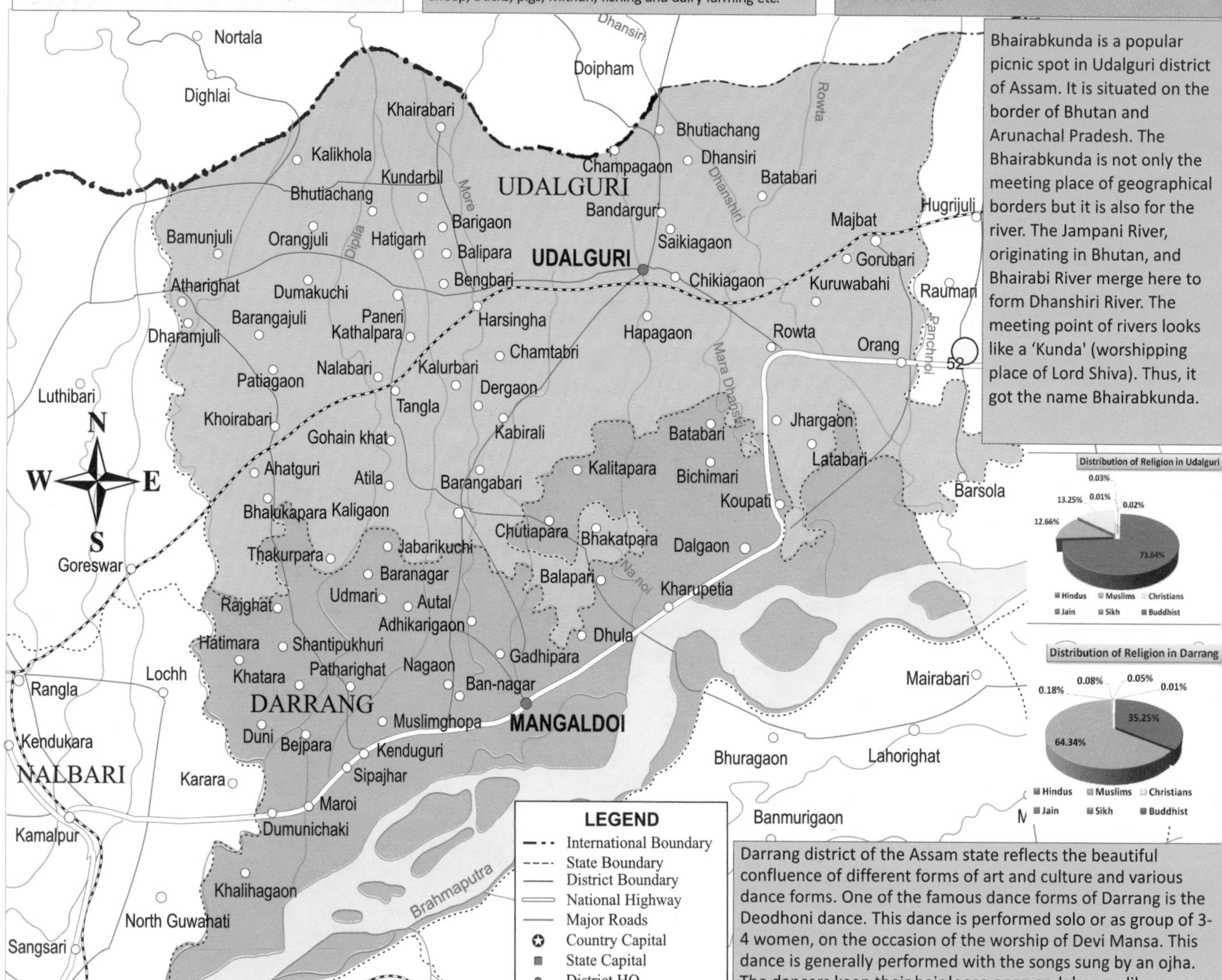

Nortala
Dighlai
Dhansiri
Doipham
Rowta
Khairabari
Kalikhola
Kundarbil
Bhutiachang
UDALGURI
Champagaon
Dhansiri
Batabari
Bandarguri
Bamunjuli
Orangjuli
Hatigarh
Barigaon
Balipara
Saikiagaon
Majbat
Hugrijuli
Gorubari
UDALGURI
Bengbari
Chikiagaon
Kuruwabahi
Raumari
Atharighat
Dumakuchi
Barangajuli
Paneri
Kathalpara
Harsingha
Hapagaon
Rowta
Orang
Dharamjuli
Chamtabri
52
Patiagaon
Nalabari
Kalurbari
Dergaon
Luthibari
Tangla
Khoirabari
Gohain khat
Kabirali
Batabari
Jhargaon
Latabari
Ahatguri
Atila
Barangabari
Kalitapara
Bichimari
Koupati
Barsola
Bhalukapara
Kaligaon
Chutiapara
Bhakatpara
Dalgaon
Thakurpara
Jabarikuchi
Goreswar
Baranagar
Balapari
Nanoi
Rajghat
Udmari
Autal
Kharupetia
Adhikarigaon
Hatimara
Shantipukhuri
Dhula
Gadhipara
Lochh
Khatara
Patharighat
Nagaon
Rangla
Ban-nagar
Mairabari
DARRANG
Muslimghopa
MANGALDOI
Kendukara
Duni
Bejpara
Kenduguri
Bhuragaon
Lahorighat
NALBARI
Sipajhar
Karara
Maroi
Banmurigaon
Kamalpur
Dumunichaki
Brahmaputra
Khalihagaon
North Guwahati
Sangsari
Jalukbari
Noonmati
N
W
E
S
LEGEND
International Boundary
State Boundary
District Boundary
National Highway
Major Roads
Country Capital
State Capital
District HQ
Other town
Distribution of Religion in Udalguri
0.03%
13.25%
0.01%
0.02%
12.66%
73.64%
Hindus
Muslims
Christians
Jain
Sikh
Buddhist
Distribution of Religion in Darrang
0.18%
0.08%
0.05%
0.01%
35.25%
64.34%
Hindus
Muslims
Christians
Jain
Sikh
Buddhist

Bhairabkunda is a popular picnic spot in Udalguri district of Assam. It is situated on the border of Bhutan and Arunachal Pradesh. The Bhairabkunda is not only the meeting place of geographical borders but it is also for the river. The Jampani River, originating in Bhutan, and Bhairabi River merge here to form Dhanshiri River. The meeting point of rivers looks like a 'Kunda' (worshipping place of Lord Shiva). Thus, it got the name Bhairabkunda.

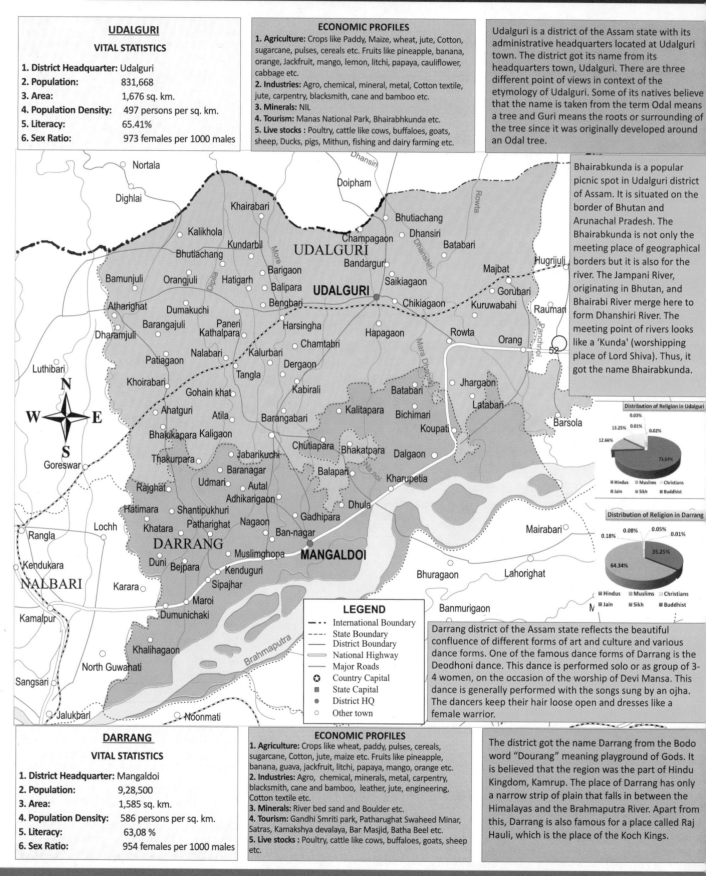

Darrang district of the Assam state reflects the beautiful confluence of different forms of art and culture and various dance forms. One of the famous dance forms of Darrang is the Deodhoni dance. This dance is performed solo or as group of 3-4 women, on the occasion of the worship of Devi Mansa. This dance is generally performed with the songs sung by an ojha. The dancers keep their hair loose open and dresses like a female warrior.

DARRANG

VITAL STATISTICS

1. District Headquarter:	Mangaldoi
2. Population:	9,28,500
3. Area:	1,585 sq. km.
4. Population Density:	586 persons per sq. km.
5. Literacy:	63,08 %
6. Sex Ratio:	954 females per 1000 males

ECONOMIC PROFILES

1. Agriculture: Crops like wheat, paddy, pulses, cereals, sugarcane, Cotton, jute, maize etc. Fruits like pineapple, banana, guava, jackfruit, litchi, papaya, mango, orange etc.
2. Industries: Agro, chemical, minerals, metal, carpentry, blacksmith, cane and bamboo, leather, jute, engineering, Cotton textile etc.
3. Minerals: River bed sand and Boulder etc.
4. Tourism: Gandhi Smriti park, Patharughat Swaheed Minar, Satras, Kamakshya devalaya, Bar Masjid, Batha Beel etc.
5. Live stocks : Poultry, cattle like cows, buffaloes, goats, sheep etc.

The district got the name Darrang from the Bodo word "Dourang" meaning playground of Gods. It is believed that the region was the part of Hindu Kingdom, Kamrup. The place of Darrang has only a narrow strip of plain that falls in between the Himalayas and the Brahmaputra River. Apart from this, Darrang is also famous for a place called Raj Hauli, which is the place of the Koch Kings.

Scale - 1:0.5 M approx

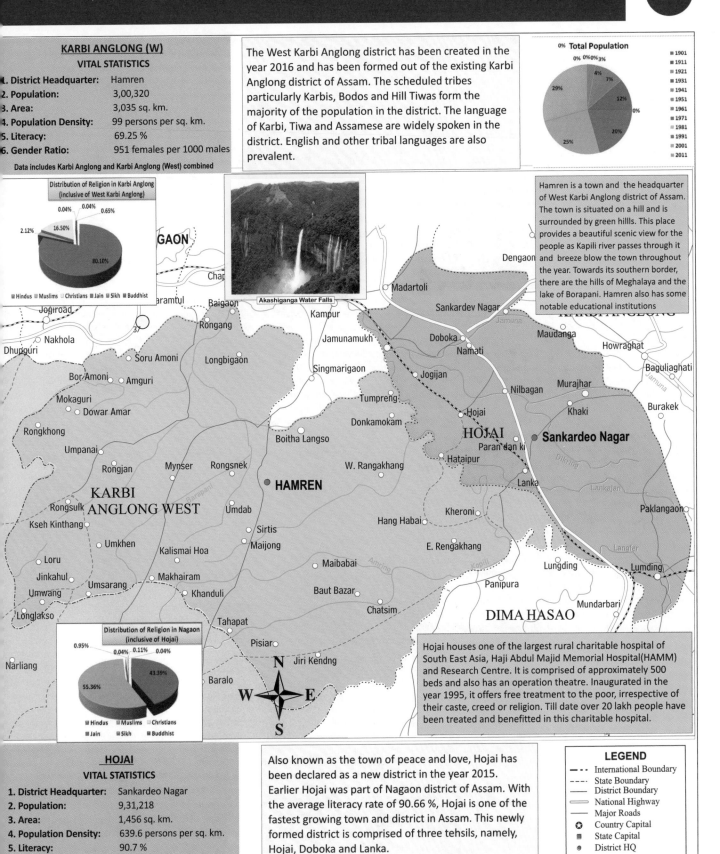

KARBI ANGLONG WEST & HOJAI

KARBI ANGLONG (W)

VITAL STATISTICS

1. District Headquarter:	Hamren
2. Population:	3,00,320
3. Area:	3,035 sq. km.
4. Population Density:	99 persons per sq. km.
5. Literacy:	69.25 %
6. Gender Ratio:	951 females per 1000 males

Data includes Karbi Anglong and Karbi Anglong (West) combined

The West Karbi Anglong district has been created in the year 2016 and has been formed out of the existing Karbi Anglong district of Assam. The scheduled tribes particularly Karbis, Bodos and Hill Tiwas form the majority of the population in the district. The language of Karbi, Tiwa and Assamese are widely spoken in the district. English and other tribal languages are also prevalent.

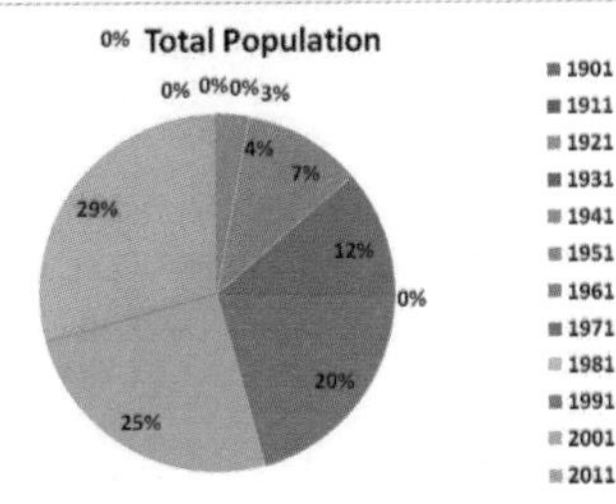
0% Total Population
0% 0%0%3%
4%
7%
29%
12%
0%
20%
25%
1901
1911
1921
1931
1941
1951
1961
1971
1981
1991
2001
2011

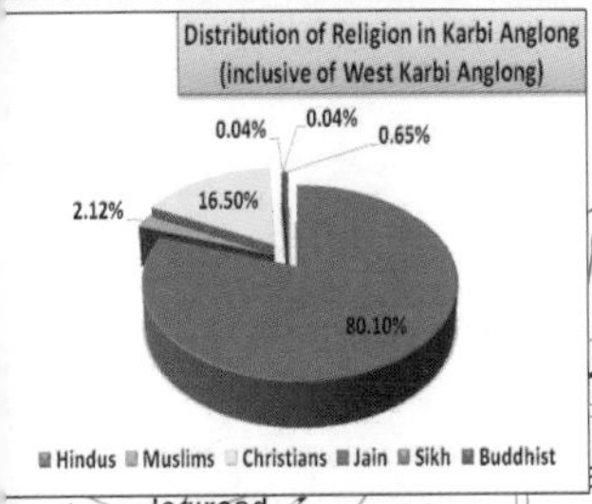

Distribution of Religion in Karbi Anglong (inclusive of West Karbi Anglong)

0.04% 0.04% 0.65% 2.12% 16.50% 80.10%

Hindus, Muslims, Christians, Jain, Sikh, Buddhist

Akashiganga Water Falls

Hamren is a town and the headquarter of West Karbi Anglong district of Assam. The town is situated on a hill and is surrounded by green hillls. This place provides a beautiful scenic view for the people as Kapili river passes through it and breeze blow the town throughout the year. Towards its southern border, there are the hills of Meghalaya and the lake of Borapani. Hamren also has some notable educational institutions

Hojai houses one of the largest rural charitable hospital of South East Asia, Haji Abdul Majid Memorial Hospital(HAMM) and Research Centre. It is comprised of approximately 500 beds and also has an operation theatre. Inaugurated in the year 1995, it offers free treatment to the poor, irrespective of their caste, creed or religion. Till date over 20 lakh people have been treated and benefitted in this charitable hospital.

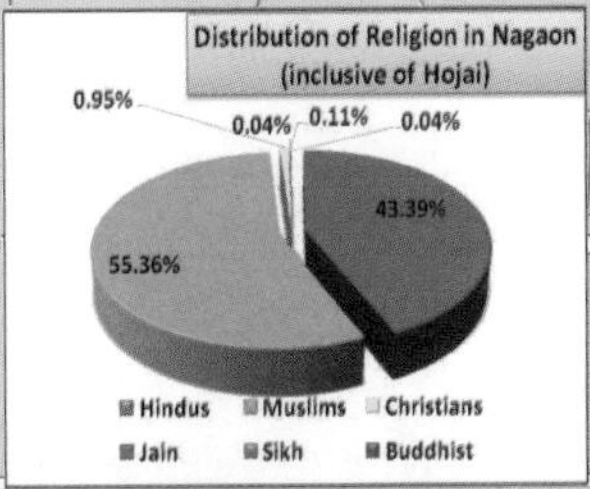

Distribution of Religion in Nagaon (inclusive of Hojai)

0.95% 0.04% 0.11% 0.04% 43.39% 55.36%

Hindus, Muslims, Christians, Jain, Sikh, Buddhist

HOJAI

VITAL STATISTICS

1. District Headquarter:	Sankardeo Nagar
2. Population:	9,31,218
3. Area:	1,456 sq. km.
4. Population Density:	639.6 persons per sq. km.
5. Literacy:	90.7 %
6. Gender Ratio:	956 females per 1000 males

Data includes Hojai and Nagaon combined

Also known as the town of peace and love, Hojai has been declared as a new district in the year 2015. Earlier Hojai was part of Nagaon district of Assam. With the average literacy rate of 90.66 %, Hojai is one of the fastest growing town and district in Assam. This newly formed district is comprised of three tehsils, namely, Hojai, Doboka and Lanka.

LEGEND

- International Boundary
- State Boundary
- District Boundary
- National Highway
- Major Roads
- Country Capital
- State Capital
- District HQ
- Other town

1000 0 1000 2000 km.

Projection: Lambert's Conical Orthomorphic

MORIGAON & NAGAON

MORIGAON

VITAL STATISTICS

1. **District Headquarter:** Morigaon
2. **Population:** 957,423
3. **Area:** 1,551 sq. km.
4. **Population Density:** 617 persons per sq. km.
5. **Literacy:** 68.03%
6. **Sex Ratio:** 967 females per 1000 males

ECONOMIC PROFILES

1. **Agriculture:** Crops like paddy, wheat, Maize, pulses, cereals, sugarcane, Cotton, jute etc. Fruits like pineapple, banana, orange, guava, litchi, Papaya etc.
2. **Industries:** Agro, chemical, mineral, metal, carpentry, blacksmith, Cane and bamboo, jute , Cotton textile, etc.
3. **Minerals:** River bed, stone, sand etc.
4. **Tourism:** Sitajakhala, Sivakunda, Kachasila hill, Mayong, Deosal Siva temple.
5. **Live stocks :** Poultry, cattle like cows, buffaloes, goats, sheep ducks, pigs, Mithun, dogs, fishing and dairy farming etc.

Morigaon is headquartered at Morigaon town. The history of the Morigaon district is not very clear. The history revolves around Arimatta, a famous traditional ruler of the region. When Arimatta died, his son named Jongalbalahu became the next ruler. But after some time Jongalbalahu was killed by the Kacharis (a tribe) with a bamboo spear near Kajalimukh.

Hornbill Park
Ankia Bhauna Nat
SONITPUR
TEZPUR
DARRANG
MANGALDAI
MORIGAON
MARIGAON
NAGAON
KARBI ANGLONG
DISPUR
Brahmaputra
Arabari
Bihuguri
Gabharupara
Amguri
Dekargaon
Biswanath Chariali
Teliagaon
Kobirali
Bichimari
Batabari
Kalajgaon
Dalgaon
Kharupatia
Orang Sanctuary
Bannagar
Khatanipara
Garakhia Gaon
Nowagaon
Moirabari
Dhing
Dumdumia
Laharighat
Barchala
Rarat
Kadamani
Juria
Arabari
Tarabari
Bhuragaon
Barangabari
Bar Dhowa
Akarabari
Rupohi
Samaguri
Parjari
Mikirbheta
Lonmati
Banhuriagaon
Garmarigaon
Kajali
Garjan
Oujari
Jaluguti
Rebejia
Senchoa
Puranigudam
Chapanatla
Raja-mayong
Manaha
Baghmara
Aujari
Barapujia
Raha
Fulguri
Na-go saikhat
Mikirgaon
Jagibhakatgaon
Ahatguri
Chaparmukh
Laopani
Kathiatali
Khetri
Dharamtul
Jogiroad
Neli
Silsang
Kampur
Rajagaon
Sonapur
Dhupguri
Nakhola
Amguri
Jamunamukh
Singmarigaon
Dabaka
Latumai
Jogijan
Rangagora
Donkamokam
Baritha Langso
Naltali
Silghat
Amguri
Khutri
Kunwaritol
Hatbar
Chekoni
Kaliaboy
Ambagan
Chekani
Missa
Doar Chalna
Lengteng
Amalakhi
Doar Dikharu
Doar
Sonai
Pakaria
Kalang
Kopili
Killing
Kallong
Baharali
LEGEND
International Boundary
State Boundary
District Boundary
National Highway
Major Roads
Country Capital
State Capital
District HQ
Other town
N
S
E
W

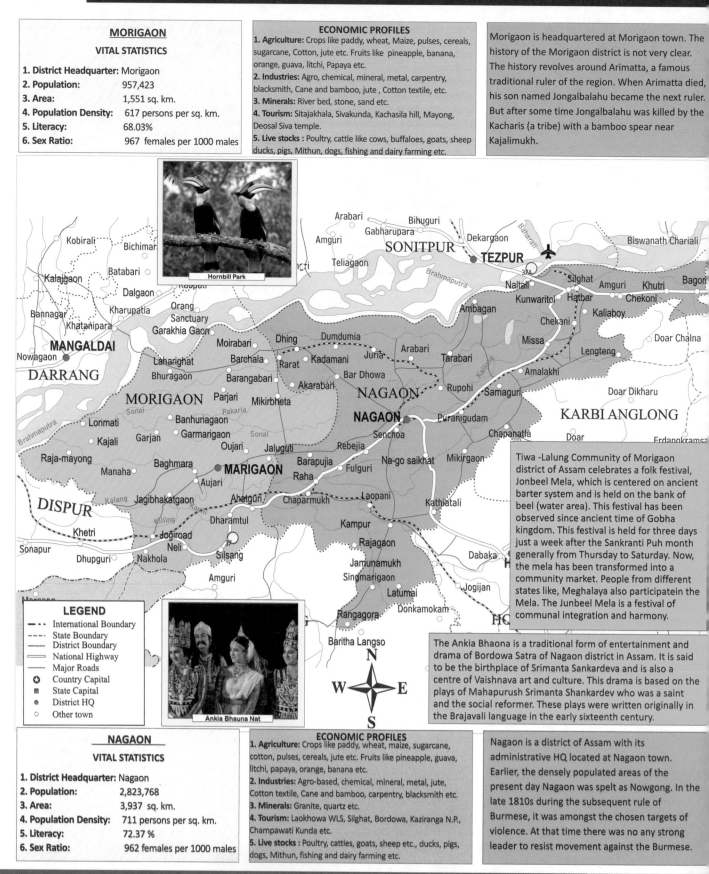

Tiwa -Lalung Community of Morigaon district of Assam celebrates a folk festival, Jonbeel Mela, which is centered on ancient barter system and is held on the bank of beel (water area). This festival has been observed since ancient time of Gobha kingdom. This festival is held for three days just a week after the Sankranti Puh month generally from Thursday to Saturday. Now, the mela has been transformed into a community market. People from different states like, Meghalaya also participatein the Mela. The Junbeel Mela is a festival of communal integration and harmony.

The Ankia Bhaona is a traditional form of entertainment and drama of Bordowa Satra of Nagaon district in Assam. It is said to be the birthplace of Srimanta Sankardeva and is also a centre of Vaishnava art and culture. This drama is based on the plays of Mahapurush Srimanta Shankardev who was a saint and the social reformer. These plays were written originally in the Brajavali language in the early sixteenth century.

NAGAON

VITAL STATISTICS

1. **District Headquarter:** Nagaon
2. **Population:** 2,823,768
3. **Area:** 3,937 sq. km.
4. **Population Density:** 711 persons per sq. km.
5. **Literacy:** 72.37 %
6. **Sex Ratio:** 962 females per 1000 males

ECONOMIC PROFILES

1. **Agriculture:** Crops like paddy, wheat, maize, sugarcane, cotton, pulses, cereals, jute etc. Fruits like pineapple, guava, litchi, papaya, orange, banana etc.
2. **Industries:** Agro-based, chemical, mineral, metal, jute, Cotton textile, Cane and bamboo, carpentry, blacksmith etc.
3. **Minerals:** Granite, quartz etc.
4. **Tourism:** Laokhowa WLS, Silghat, Bordowa, Kaziranga N.P., Champawati Kunda etc.
5. **Live stocks :** Poultry, cattles, goats, sheep etc., ducks, pigs, dogs, Mithun, fishing and dairy farming etc.

Nagaon is a district of Assam with its administrative HQ located at Nagaon town. Earlier, the densely populated areas of the present day Nagaon was spelt as Nowgong. In the late 1810s during the subsequent rule of Burmese, it was amongst the chosen targets of violence. At that time there was no any strong leader to resist movement against the Burmese.

Projection: Lambert's Conical Orthomorphic

1000 0 1000 2000 km

DIMA HASAO

DIMA HASAO

VITAL STATISTICS

1. **District Headquarter:** Haflong
2. **Population:** 214,102
3. **Area:** 4,888 sq. km.
4. **Population Density:** 44 persons per sq. km.
5. **Literacy:** 77.54%
6. **Sex Ratio:** 932 females per 1000 males

ECONOMIC PROFILES

1. Agriculture: crops like wheat, paddy, Maize, sugarcane, jute, pulses, cereals etc. Fruits like pineapple, banana, papaya, orange, Jackfruit, Mango, litchi etc.

2. Industries: Agro, chemical, mineral, metal based, cane and bamboo, carpentry, Cotton textile, jute, leather based, et.

3. Minerals: Coal and limestone.

4. Tourism: Haflong lake, Panimur waterfalls, Barail Range, Sampadisa village, Jatinga bird watching centre etc.

5. Live stocks : Poultry, cattle like cows, buffaloes, goats, sheep, ducks, pigs, Mithun, fishing and dairy farming etc.

Dima Hasao is a district of the Assam state with its administrative headquarters located at Haflong town. Prior to the year 1832 Dima Hasao district was a part of the Dimasa Kachari Kingdom. At that time the kingdom was spreaded from Jamuna in the North to the foot-hills of Lushai Hills in the south and from the Kopili in the west to the Angami and Katcha Naga hills beyond the Dhansiri in the east.

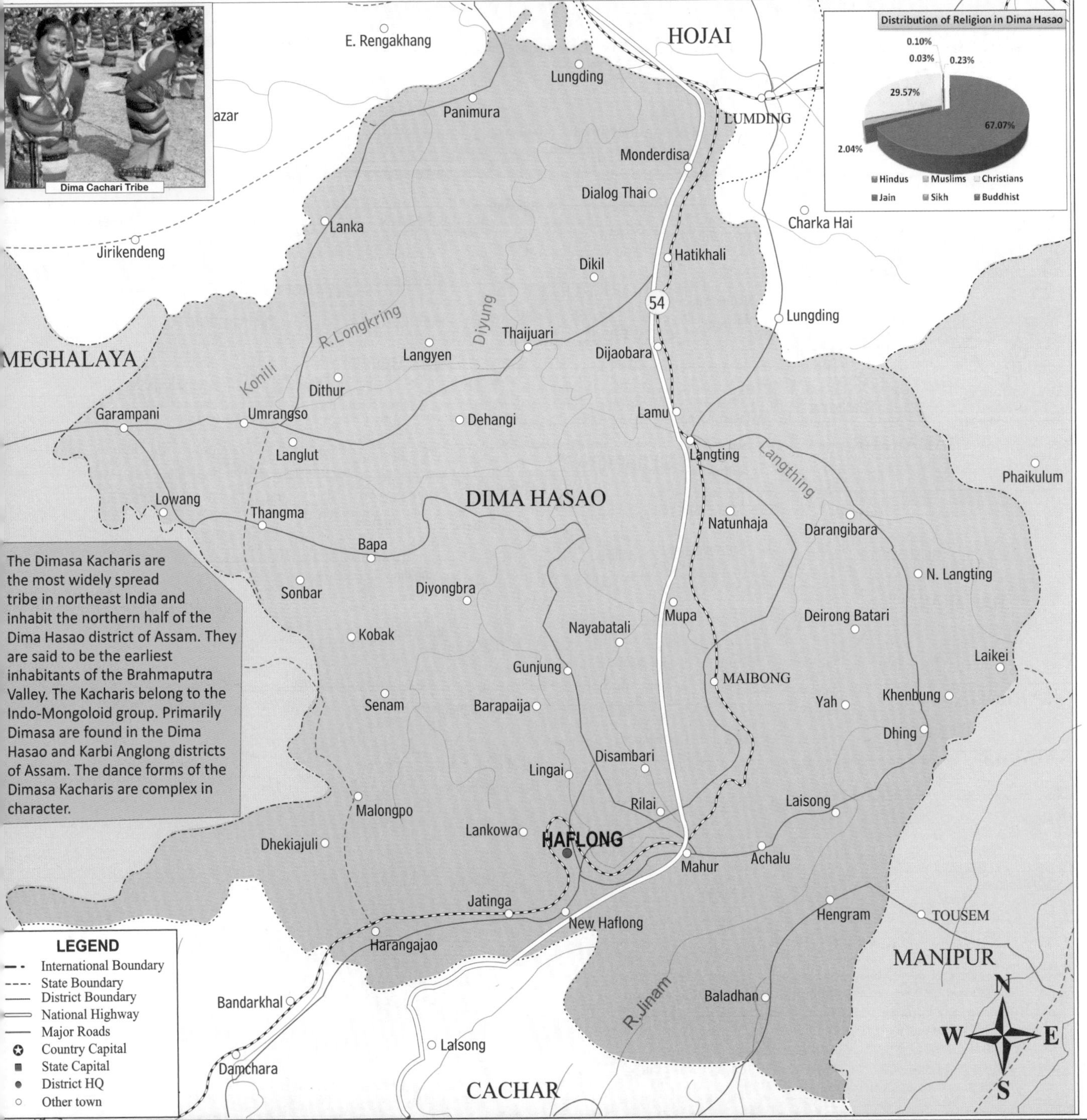
Dima Cachari Tribe
Distribution of Religion in Dima Hasao
0.10%
0.03%
0.23%
29.57%
67.07%
2.04%
Hindus
Muslims
Christians
Jain
Sikh
Buddhist
HOJAI
E. Rengakhang
Lungding
Panimura
LUMDING
Monderdisa
Dialog Thai
Charka Hai
Lanka
Jirikendeng
Hatikhali
Dikil
54
Lungding
R. Longkring
Diyung
Thaijuari
Langyen
Dijaobara
MEGHALAYA
Konili
Dithur
Garampani
Umrangso
Dehangi
Lamu
Langlut
Langting
Langthing
Phaikulum
Lowang
DIMA HASAO
Thangma
Natunhaja
Darangibara
Bapa
N. Langting
Sonbar
Diyongbra
Mupa
Deirong Batari
Kobak
Nayabatali
Laikei
Gunjung
MAIBONG
Senam
Barapaija
Yah
Khenbung
Dhing
Disambari
Lingai
Rilai
Laisong
Malongpo
Lankowa
HAFLONG
Dhekiajuli
Mahur
Achalu
Jatinga
New Haflong
Hengram
TOUSEM
Harangajao
MANIPUR
Bandarkhal
R.Jinam
Baladhan
Lalsong
Damchara
CACHAR
N
W
E
S
LEGEND
International Boundary
State Boundary
District Boundary
National Highway
Major Roads
Country Capital
State Capital
District HQ
Other town

The Dimasa Kacharis are the most widely spread tribe in northeast India and inhabit the northern half of the Dima Hasao district of Assam. They are said to be the earliest inhabitants of the Brahmaputra Valley. The Kacharis belong to the Indo-Mongoloid group. Primarily Dimasa are found in the Dima Hasao and Karbi Anglong districts of Assam. The dance forms of the Dimasa Kacharis are complex in character.

CACHAR

VITAL STATISTICS

1. **District Headquarter:** Silchar
2. **Population:** 17,36,617
3. **Area:** 3,786 sq. km.
4. **Population Density:** 459 persons per sq. km.
5. **Literacy:** 79.34%
6. **Sex Ratio:** 959 females per 1000 males

ECONOMIC PROFILES

1. **Agriculture:** Crops like Wheat, paddy, pulses, cereals, sugarcane, Cotton, jute, ginger etc. Fruits like Pineapple, banana, orange, mango, Jackfruit, guava, lemon, papaya etc.
2. **Industries:** Agro-based, chemical, cane and bamboo, carpentry, blacksmith, jute based, Cotton textile etc.
3. **Minerals:** Nil
4. **Tourism:** Sri Kancha Kanti Devi Mandir, Kachari Fort, Bhubeneshwar Temple, Gandhi bagh etc.
5. **Live stocks :** Poultry, cattle like cows, buffaloes, goats, sheep, Ducks, pigs, Mithun, fishing and dairy farming etc.

The name Cachar is believed to have derived from Sanskrit word "Khachar", which means a broad region near mountain or water. Though many historians argue this vary fact and gives credit to the Khachari Kings might have named the place after their name. The district is house to the famous Kanchakanti Kali Temple which is a union of goddess Durga and goddess Kali. The temple is a major tourist attraction of the place.

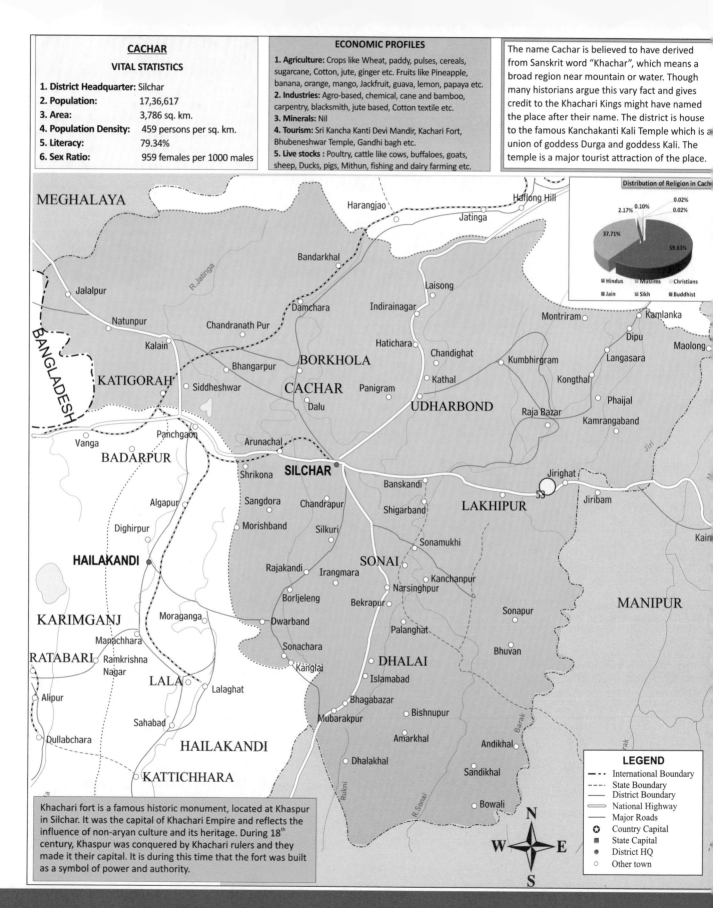

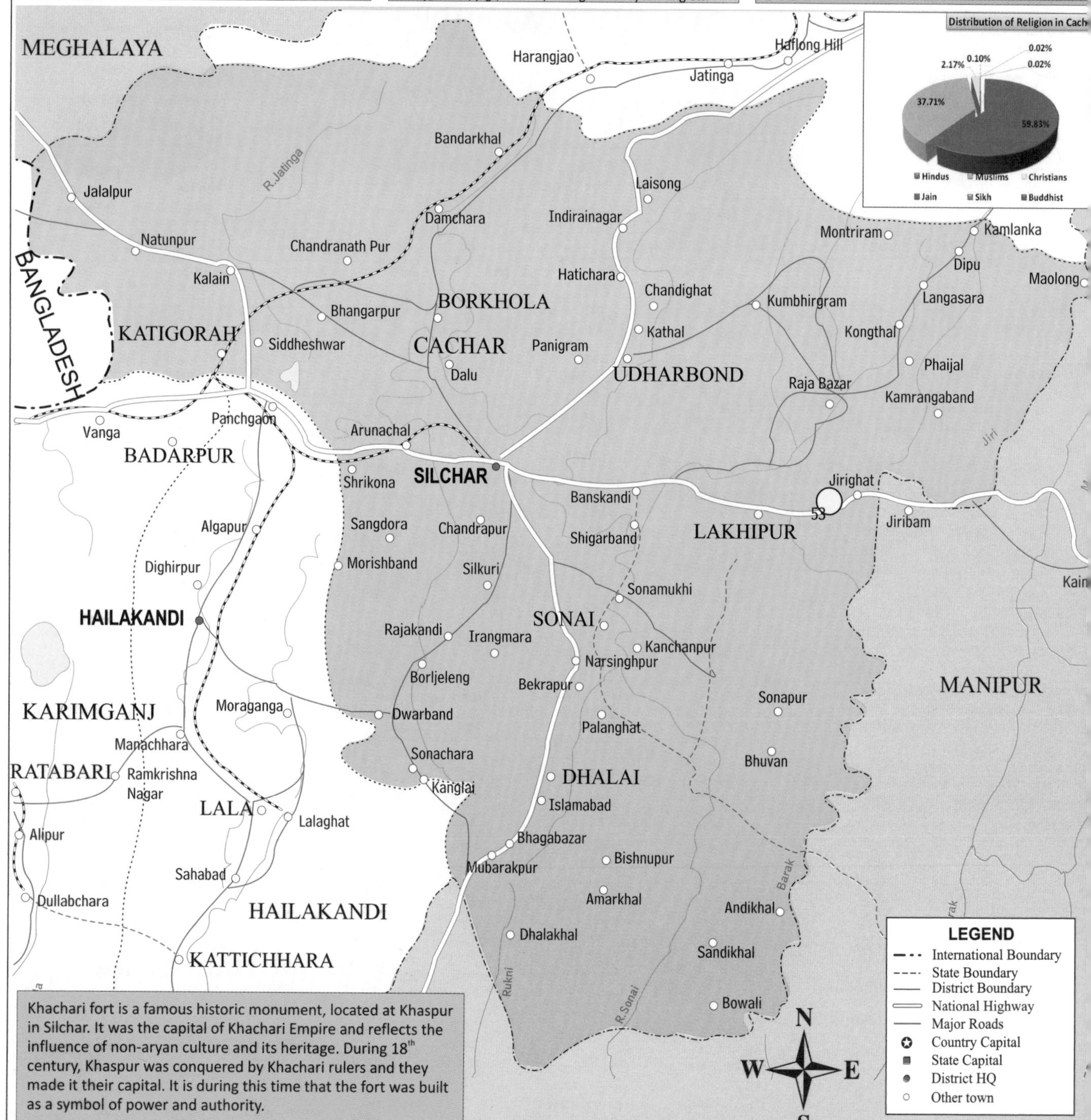
MEGHALAYA
BANGLADESH
MANIPUR
KATIGORAH
BORKHOLA
CACHAR
UDHARBOND
SILCHAR
LAKHIPUR
SONAI
DHALAI
BADARPUR
HAILAKANDI
KARIMGANJ
RATABARI
LALA
KATTICHHARA
Harangjao
Haflong Hill
Jatinga
Bandarkhal
Jalalpur
Laisong
Damchara
Indirainagar
Natunpur
Chandranath Pur
Kalain
Hatichara
Chandighat
Kumbhirgram
Bhangarpur
Siddheshwar
Kathal
Panigram
Dalu
Montriram
Kamlanka
Dipu
Maolong
Langasara
Kongthal
Phaijal
Raja Bazar
Kamrangaband
Panchgaon
Vanga
Arunachal
Shrikona
Banskandi
Jirighat
Jiribam
Sangdora
Chandrapur
Shigarband
Algapur
Morishband
Dighirpur
Silkuri
Sonamukhi
Rajakandi
Irangmara
Kanchanpur
Narsinghpur
Borljeleng
Bekrapur
Moraganga
Dwarband
Sonapur
Palanghat
Manachhara
Sonachara
Bhuvan
Ramkrishna Nagar
Kanglai
Islamabad
Lalaghat
Alipur
Bhagabazar
Bishnupur
Mubarakpur
Sahabad
Amarkhal
Dullabchara
Andikhal
Dhalakhal
Sandikhal
Bowali
R.Jatinga
Jiri
Barak
Rukni
R.Sonai
53
Distribution of Religion in Cachar
2.17%
0.10%
0.02%
0.02%
37.71%
59.83%
Hindus
Muslims
Christians
Jain
Sikh
Buddhist
LEGEND
International Boundary
State Boundary
District Boundary
National Highway
Major Roads
Country Capital
State Capital
District HQ
Other town
N
W
E
S

Khachari fort is a famous historic monument, located at Khaspur in Silchar. It was the capital of Khachari Empire and reflects the influence of non-aryan culture and its heritage. During 18th century, Khaspur was conquered by Khachari rulers and they made it their capital. It is during this time that the fort was built as a symbol of power and authority.

KARIMGANJ
VITAL STATISTICS

District Headquarter:	Karimganj
Population:	1,228,686
Area:	1,809 sq. km.
Population Density:	679 persons per sq. km.
Literacy:	78.22 %
Gender Ratio:	963 females per 1000 males

Karimganj is a district of the state of Assam with its administrative headquarters located at Karimganj town. For the better understanding of the history of the district, it is divided into four specific periods i.e. early period, middle age, British Era and the country's partition period. But the very early history of the district is quite vague. Moreover, there is no any clear evidence of that period. In the 7th Century AD, the Samatata Kingdom of the East Bengal captured the Karimganj region along with the foothills of North Cachar Hills.

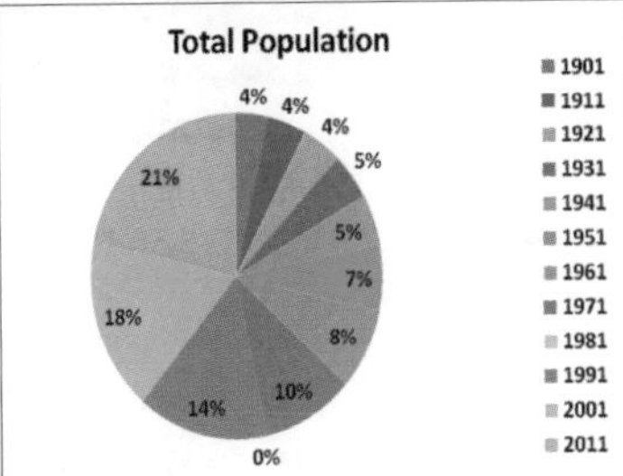

Total Population
4%
4%
4%
5%
5%
7%
8%
10%
0%
14%
18%
21%
1901
1911
1921
1931
1941
1951
1961
1971
1981
1991
2001
2011

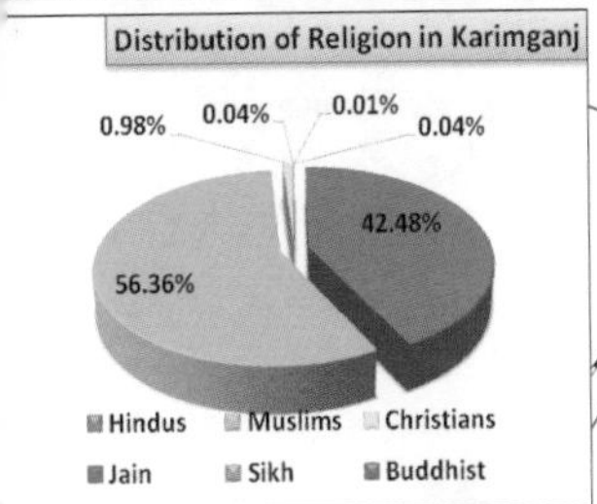

Distribution of Religion in Karimganj

0.98% 0.04% 0.01% 0.04% 42.48% 56.36%

Hindus, Muslims, Christians, Jain, Sikh, Buddhist

Magnificent Kushiara River

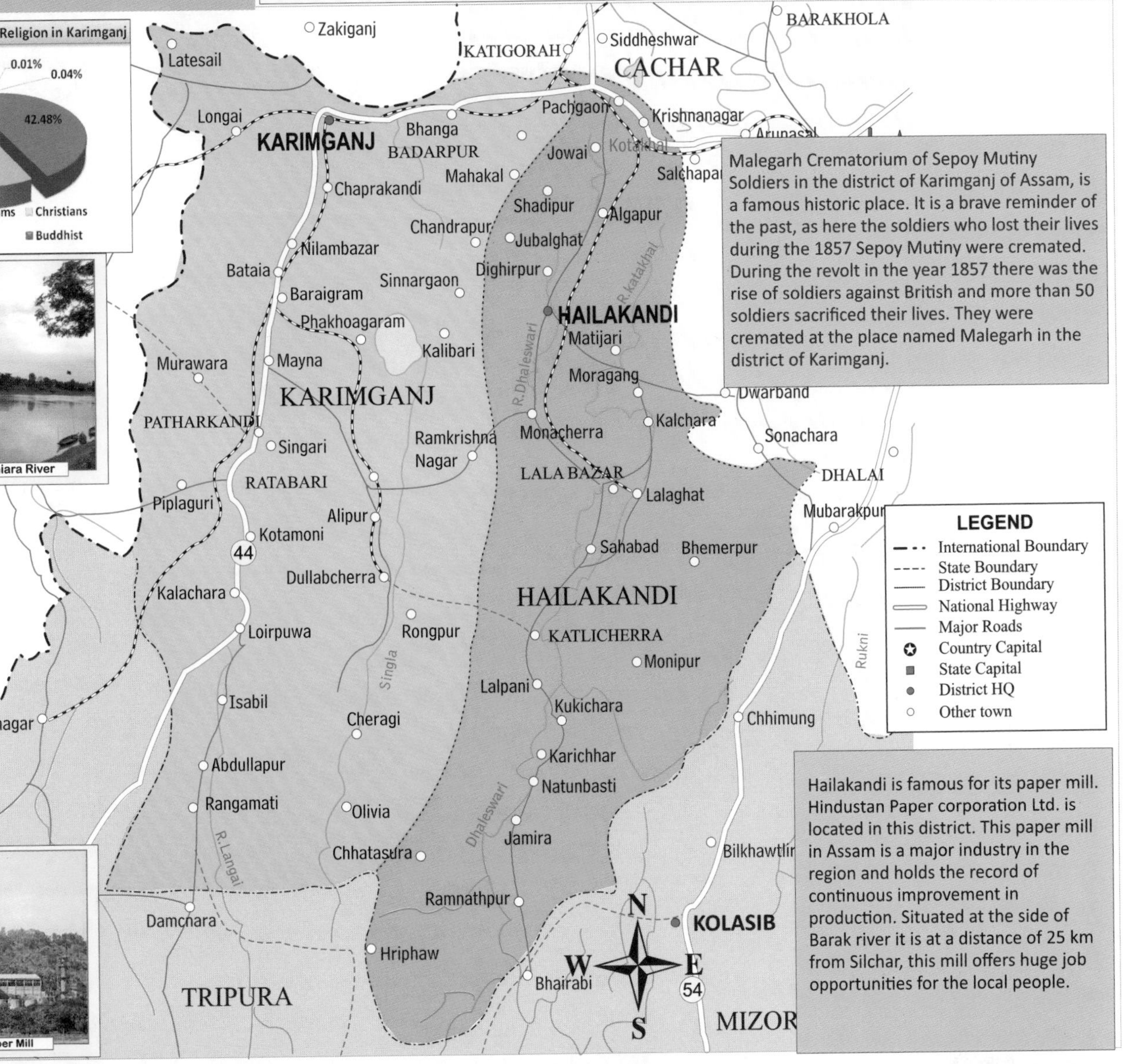

Malegarh Crematorium of Sepoy Mutiny Soldiers in the district of Karimganj of Assam, is a famous historic place. It is a brave reminder of the past, as here the soldiers who lost their lives during the 1857 Sepoy Mutiny were cremated. During the revolt in the year 1857 there was the rise of soldiers against British and more than 50 soldiers sacrificed their lives. They were cremated at the place named Malegarh in the district of Karimganj.

LEGEND

- International Boundary
- State Boundary
- District Boundary
- National Highway
- Major Roads
- Country Capital
- State Capital
- District HQ
- Other town

Hindustan Paper Mill

Hailakandi is famous for its paper mill. Hindustan Paper corporation Ltd. is located in this district. This paper mill in Assam is a major industry in the region and holds the record of continuous improvement in production. Situated at the side of Barak river it is at a distance of 25 km from Silchar, this mill offers huge job opportunities for the local people.

HAILAKANDI
VITAL STATISTICS

1. District Headquarter:	Hailakandi
2. Population:	6,59,260
3. Area:	1,326 sq. km.
4. Population Density:	497 persons per sq. km.
5. Literacy:	65.22 %
6. Gender Ratio:	946 females per 1000 males

Hailakandi is a district of the Assam state with its administrative headquarters located at Hailakandi town. Hailakandi was declared as the sub-divisions of Assam on 1st June, 1869. Then Hailakandi was announced as a civil sub-division under the Cachar district. Though the place of Hailakandi has adopted the modern way of life yet it is rich in cultural heritage and tradition.

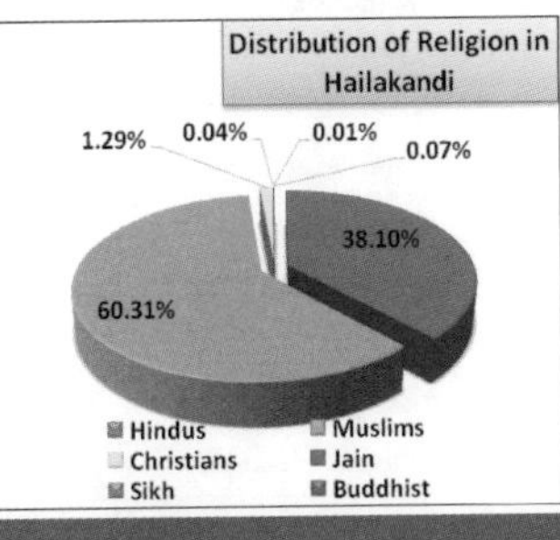

Distribution of Religion in Hailakandi
1.29%
0.04%
0.01%
0.07%
38.10%
60.31%
Hindus
Muslims
Christians
Jain
Sikh
Buddhist

1000 0 1000 2000 km.

Projection: Lambert's Conical Orthomorphic

KARBI ANGLONG

KARBI ANGLONG
VITAL STATISTICS

1. District Headquarter:	Diphu
2. Population:	9,56,313
3. Area:	10,434 sq. km.
4. Population Density:	93 persons per sq. km.
5. Literacy:	65.22 %
6. Gender Ratio:	922 females per 1000 males

Karbi Anglong is a district of the Assam state with its administrative headquarters located at Diphu town. The name of the district is a blend of two words such as Karbi and Anglong. Karbi is a very famous tribe commonly found in most of the regions in the state of Assam. On the other hand, Anglong is a Karbi term which means Hills. Both the terms Karbi Anglong together means the Hills of Karbi people.

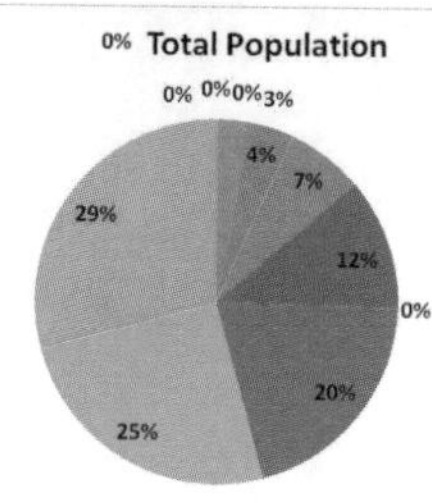
Total Population
0%
0% 0%0%3%
4%
7%
12%
0%
20%
25%
29%

TEZPUR, GOLAGHAT, Kaziranga, Bokakhat, Hatikhuli, Silghat, Amguri, Bagari, Kulhari, Terangaon, Amgaon, Khumtai, Shaotani, Letekujan, Shatamari, Amabagan, Kaliaboy, Chekani, Dwar Bagari, Fanshogaon, Phangehogaon, Parajen, Misa, Lengteng, Doar Chalna, NAGAON, Amalakhi, Shared, Deihar, Kaliani, Baigro, Rupohi, Ingdigaon, Doar Dikharu, Hot Spring, Dikrotgaon, Jengpata, Arlangbati, Kalyani, Garampani, Chapanatla, Doar, Erdangkramsa, R.Daigurung, Barpathar, Namabar, Mikirgaon, Dokmoka, R.Digaru, Dentagaon, Sarupathar (dhansiri), Dengaon, KARBI ANGLONG, Dili Terang, Langhin, Dokmoka, Tumpreng, Longkamgaon, Phuloni, Tarabacha, Rengma Pathar, Naojan, Maudanga, R.Dighalpani, Dabaka, HOJAI, Howraghat, Naojan, Baguliaghat, Bar Dambuk, Kalaigaon, Sungajan, Murajhar, Sarihajan, HOJAI, Jamuna, Dichabai, Silhueta, Hojai, Khaki, Burakek, Mahandijua, Hidipi, Bokajan, Hataipur, Shankardeo Nagar, Howang, Amlakhi, Dilai, Manjaghat, Manja, Kheroni, DIMA, Paklangaon, DIPHU, Mohangaon, Lamchakhang, Daldali, Dhansiri, Nichuguard, Lumding, Nailalung, Langcholiate, Mundarbari, Charka Hai, R.Lending, Hatikhali, Lungding, Dijaobara, NAGALAND, N, E, S, W

LEGEND
- International Boundary
- State Boundary
- District Boundary
- National Highway
- Major Roads
- Country Capital
- State Capital
- District HQ
- Other town

Karbi Dance

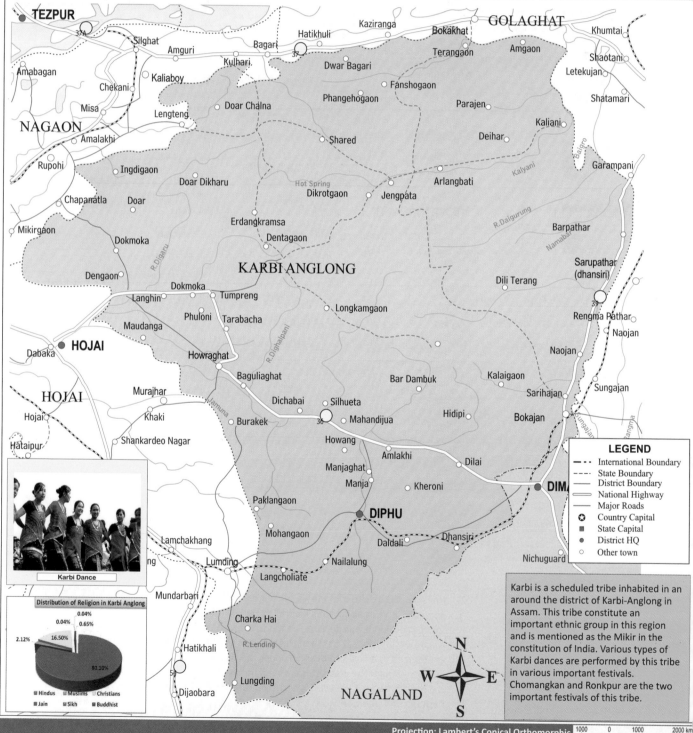

Distribution of Religion in Karbi Anglong

0.04%, 0.04%, 0.65%, 2.12%, 16.50%, 80.10%

Hindus, Muslims, Christians, Jain, Sikh, Buddhist

Karbi is a scheduled tribe inhabited in an around the district of Karbi-Anglong in Assam. This tribe constitute an important ethnic group in this region and is mentioned as the Mikir in the constitution of India. Various types of Karbi dances are performed by this tribe in various important festivals. Chomangkan and Ronkpur are the two important festivals of this tribe.

Projection: Lambert's Conical Orthomorphic

1000 0 1000 2000 km

SONITPUR & BISWANATH

SONITPUR

VITAL STATISTICS

1. **District Headquarter:** Tezpur
2. **Population:** 1,924,110
3. **Area:** 5,204 sq. km.
4. **Population Density:** 370 persons per sq. km.
5. **Literacy:** 67.34%
6. **Sex Ratio:** 956 females per 1000 males

ECONOMIC PROFILES

1. **Agriculture:** crops like paddy, wheat, Maize, sugarcane, Cotton, jute, pulses, cereals, etc. Fruits like pineapple,banana, orange, guava, Jackfruit, mango, litchi, papaya, ginger et.
2. **Industries:** Agro-based, chemical, mineral, leather based, jute, engineering units, carpentry, Cane and bamboo etc.
3. **Minerals:** N/A
4. **Tourism:** Kaziranga N.P., Orang N.P., Agnigarh, Chitralekha Udyan, Kolia Bhomora setu, Bhairabi Temple etc.
5. **Live stocks :** Poultry, cattle like cows, buffaloes, goats, pigs, fishing and dairy farming etc.

Sonitpur is a district of Assam with its admin. headquarters located at Tezpur town. The administrative headquarters of the district, Tezpur got its name from the two Sanskrit terms likewise 'Teza' meaning blood and 'Pura' meaning town or city. Legends believe that the original name of the Tezpur town was 'Sonitpur' since the word "sonit" in Sanskrit also means blood.

Kaliabhomora Bridge

The Kaliabhomora Setu is a three km long concrete bridge connecting the Sonitpur to the north bank of Nagaon district of Assam. It is the second major bridge ever constructed over the mighty river Brahamaputra. This bridge is named after the king Kalia Bhumora Phukan and the construction took place from 1981 to 1987. This bridge has a tremendous significance in improving the transport and communication in Assam and is a point of attraction of Sonitpur district.

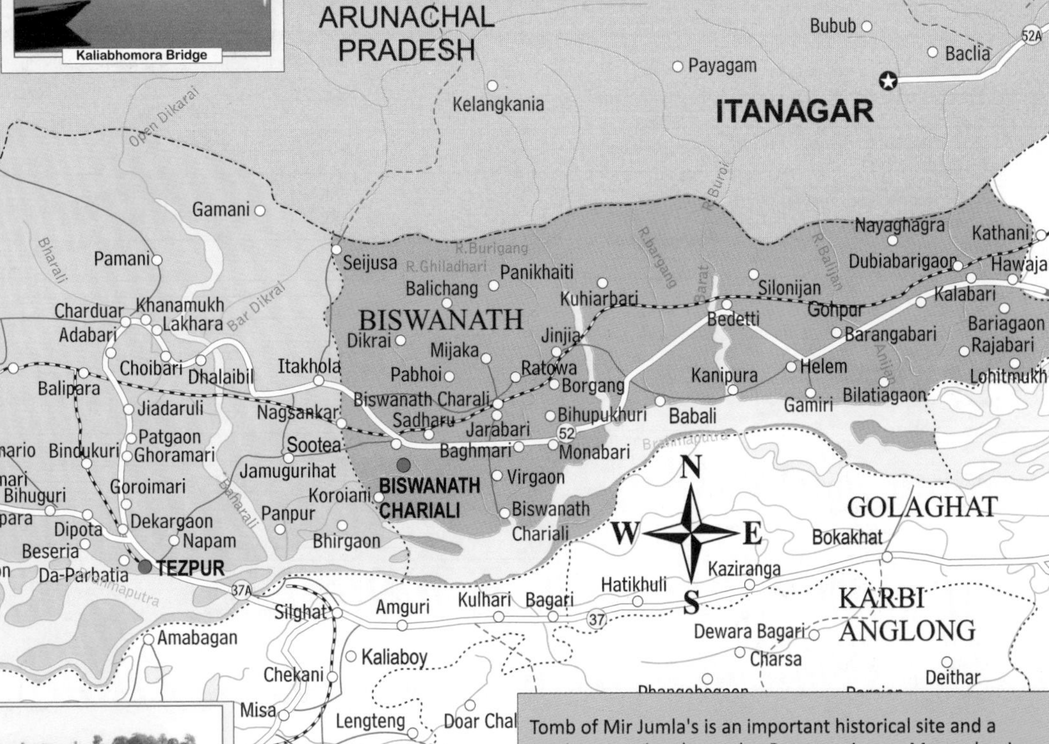

ARUNACHAL PRADESH
ITANAGAR
Rupa
Jamiri
Chakoo
Bubub
Baclia
Payagam
Kelangkania
Doimara
Bhalukpong
Foot Hills
Sonai Rupai
Gamani
Pamani
Seijusa
Panikhaiti
Balichang
Kuhiarbari
BISWANATH
Nayaghagra
Kathani
Dubiabarigaon
Hawajan
Silonijan
Kalabari
Gohpur
Bariagaon
Rajabari
Barangabari
Lohitmukh
Bedetti
Helem
Kanipura
Gamiri
Bilatiagaon
Babali
Jinjia
Ratowa
Borgang
Mijaka
Dikrai
Pabhoi
Biswanath Charali
Sadharu
Jarabari
Bihupukhuri
Baghmari
Monabari
Virgaon
Biswanath Chariali
BISWANATH CHARIALI
Charduar
Khanamukh
Lakhara
Adabari
Dhekiajuli Rd.
Rangapara
Hugrijuli
Kalagachi
Balipara
Choibari
Dhalaibil
Itakhola
Jiadaruli
Nagsankar
SONITPUR
Raumari
Bandarmario
Bindukuri
Patgaon
Ghoramari
Sootea
Jamugurihat
Dhekiajuli
Thelamara
Kawaimari
Bihuguri
Goroimari
Koroiani
Chirajuli
Arabari
Gabharupara
Amguri
Dipota
Dekargaon
Napam
Panpur
Bhirgaon
Beseria
Teliagaon
Da-Parbatia
TEZPUR
Borkhola
Singri
Silghat
Amguri
Kulhari
Bagari
Hatikhuli
Kaziranga
Bokakhat
GOLAGHAT
KARBI ANGLONG
Dewara Bagari
Charsa
Deithar
Amabagan
Kaliaboy
Chekani
Misa
Lengteng
Doar Chal
Amalakhi
Doar Dikh
R.Jia-Gabharu
Bharali
Belsiri
Open Dikarai
Bar Dikrai
R.Burigang
R.Ghiladhari
R.Buroi
Brahmaputra
N
S
E
W

LEGEND

- International Boundary
- State Boundary
- District Boundary
- National Highway
- Major Roads
- Country Capital
- State Capital
- District HQ
- Other town

Biswanath Ghat

Tomb of Mir Jumla's is an important historical site and a tourist attraction, located at Rangapani, near Mancachar in Garo Hills of Assam. The tomb is situated over a small hillock and has been maintained by the local Muslim associations for over centuries. Mir Jumla was a Mughal General, and was appointed as the Governor of Bengal by Emperor Aurangzeb. Mir Jumla led an attack on Assam as the head of a huge army, to conquer one of the local rulers. Soon after his long battle he suffered from malaria which led to his ultimate demise.

BISWANATH

VITAL STATISTICS

1. **District Headquarter:** Biswanath Chariali
2. **Population:** 6,12,000
3. **Area:** 1,100 sq. km.
4. **Population Density:** 556 persons per sq. km.
5. **Literacy:** 67.34 %
6. **Sex Ratio:** 956 females per 1000 males

ECONOMIC PROFILES

1. **Agriculture:** crops like wheat, Paddy, Maize, sugarcane, pulses, cereals, jute, Black Gram, green Gram etc. Fruits like pineapple, banana, guava, orange, jackfruit, litchi, Papaya etc.
2. **Industries:** Agro, chemical, mineral, carpentry, blacksmith, Cane and bamboo, leather, jute based, Cotton textile etc.
3. **Minerals:** N/A
4. **Tourism:** Biswanath temple, Umatumi island, Biswanath ghat (Gupta Kashi).
5. **Live stocks :** poultry, cattles, goats, Sheep, ducks, pigs, etc. Mithun, fishing and dairy farming etc.

The Biswanath district was formed in the year 2015, earlier it was part of Sonitpur district of Assam. The district derives its name from Biswanath Ghat and holds the first "Clock Tower" of Assam.

000 0 1000 2000 km.

Projection: Lambert's Conical Orthomorphic

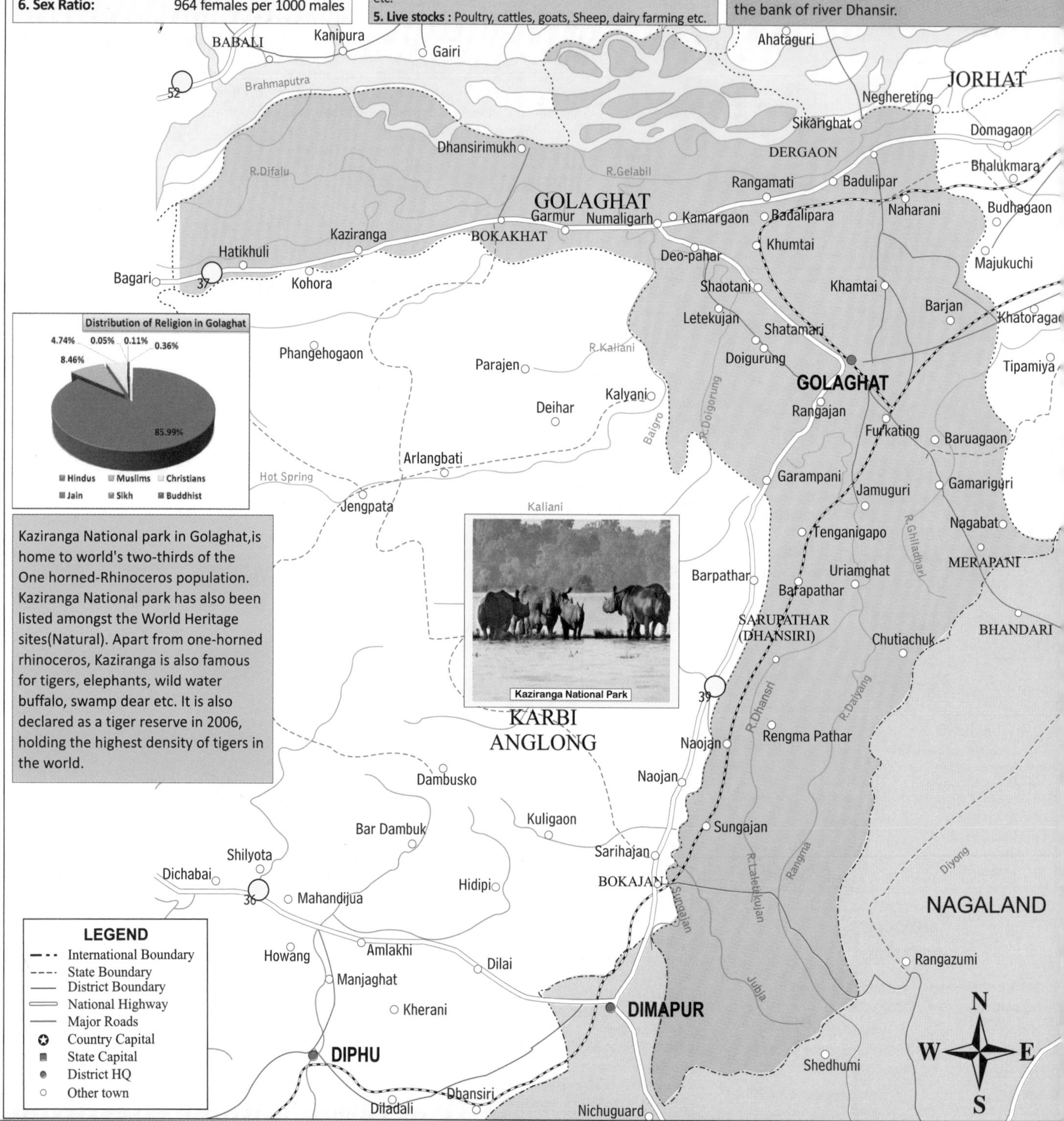

Distribution of Religion in Golaghat
85.99%
8.46%
4.74%
0.05%
0.11%
0.36%
Hindus
Muslims
Christians
Jain
Sikh
Buddhist
Kaziranga National Park
BABALI
Kanipura
Gairi
Ahataguri
JORHAT
Brahmaputra
52
Neghereting
Sikarighat
Domagaon
Dhansirimukh
DERGAON
Bhalukmara
R.Difalu
R.Gelabil
Rangamati
Badulipar
GOLAGHAT
Garmur
Numaligarh
Kamargaon
Badalipara
Naharani
Budhagaon
Kaziranga
BOKAKHAT
Khumtai
Hatikhuli
Deo-pahar
Majukuchi
Bagari
37
Kohora
Shaotani
Khamtai
Barjan
Letekujan
Shatamari
Khatoragaon
Phangehogaon
R.Kaliani
Parajen
Doigurung
Tipamiya
GOLAGHAT
Kalyani
Deihar
Rangajan
R.Doigorung
Baigro
Furkating
Baruagaon
Arlangbati
Hot Spring
Garampani
Gamariguri
Jamuguri
Jengpata
Kaliani
Tenganigapo
Nagabat
R.Ghiladhari
Uriamghat
MERAPANI
Barpathar
Barapathar
SARUPATHAR
(DHANSIRI)
Chutiachuk
BHANDARI
39
R.Dhansri
R.Daiyang
KARBI
ANGLONG
Naojan
Rengma Pathar
Dambusko
Naojan
Kuligaon
Sungajan
Bar Dambuk
Shilyota
Sarihajan
Rangma
Diyong
Dichabai
Hidipi
BOKAJAN
36
Mahandijua
Sungajan
R.Laletekujan
NAGALAND
Howang
Amlakhi
Dilai
Jubla
Rangazumi
Manjaghat
Kherani
DIMAPUR
N
W
E
S
DIPHU
Shedhumi
Dhansiri
Diladali
Nichuguard
LEGEND
International Boundary
State Boundary
District Boundary
National Highway
Major Roads
Country Capital
State Capital
District HQ
Other town
1000
0
1000
2000 km

GOLAGHAT

VITAL STATISTICS

1. **District Headquarter:** Golaghat
2. **Population:** 1,066,888
3. **Area:** 3,502 sq. km.
4. **Population Density:** 305 persons per sq. km.
5. **Literacy:** 77.43%
6. **Sex Ratio:** 964 females per 1000 males

ECONOMIC PROFILES

1. **Agriculture:** crops like wheat, paddy, maize, sugarcane, jute, pulses, cereals etc. Fruits like pineapple, banana, orange, Jackfruit, mango, lemon, litchi, papaya etc.
2. **Industries:** Agro, chemical, carpentry, blacksmith, cane and bamboo etc.
3. **Minerals:** Clay Soil, sand, murom, bolder etc.
4. **Tourism:** Garampani WLS, Negheriting Shiva doul, Deopahar, Golaghat Baptist Church, Kaziranga National Park etc.
5. **Live stocks :** Poultry, cattles, goats, Sheep, dairy farming etc.

Golaghat was elevated to a full-fledged district of Assam on 14th August 1987. Earlier it was a sub division of Sibsagar district. The district got its name from the two Assamese words, one "gola" means shop and "ghat" means the landing point of river ferry. There is a story associated with the name of the place Golaghat which is originated from the shops established by Marwari businessmen during the mid of 20th century AD at the bank of river Dhansir.

Kaziranga National park in Golaghat,is home to world's two-thirds of the One horned-Rhinoceros population. Kaziranga National park has also been listed amongst the World Heritage sites(Natural). Apart from one-horned rhinoceros, Kaziranga is also famous for tigers, elephants, wild water buffalo, swamp dear etc. It is also declared as a tiger reserve in 2006, holding the highest density of tigers in the world.

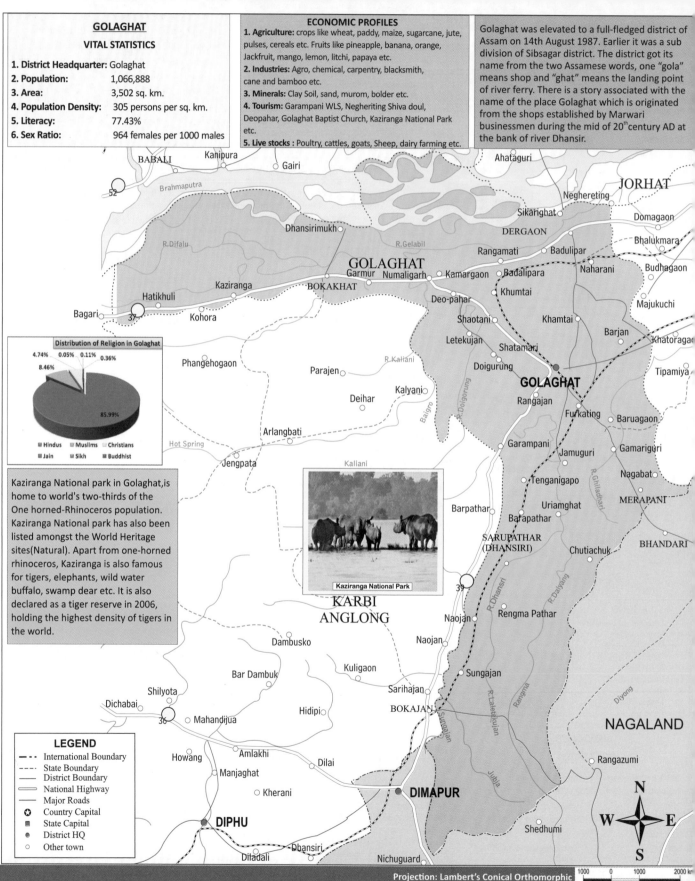

Projection: Lambert's Conical Orthomorphic

JORHAT

VITAL STATISTICS

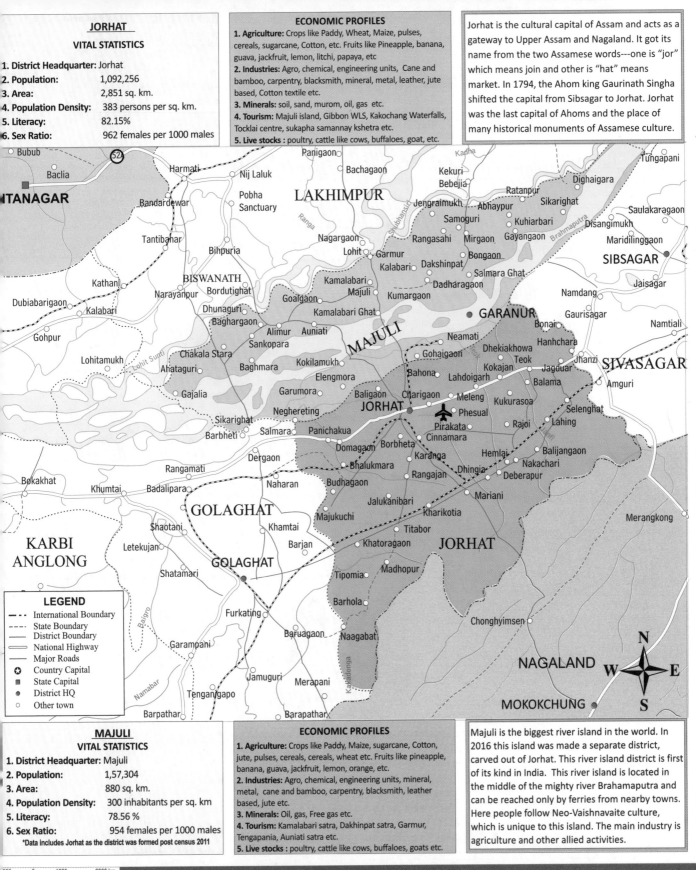

1. **District Headquarter:** Jorhat
2. **Population:** 1,092,256
3. **Area:** 2,851 sq. km.
4. **Population Density:** 383 persons per sq. km.
5. **Literacy:** 82.15%
6. **Sex Ratio:** 962 females per 1000 males

ECONOMIC PROFILES

1. **Agriculture:** Crops like Paddy, Wheat, Maize, pulses, cereals, sugarcane, Cotton, etc. Fruits like Pineapple, banana, guava, jackfruit, lemon, litchi, papaya, etc
2. **Industries:** Agro, chemical, engineering units, Cane and bamboo, carpentry, blacksmith, mineral, metal, leather, jute based, Cotton textile etc.
3. **Minerals:** soil, sand, murom, oil, gas etc.
4. **Tourism:** Majuli island, Gibbon WLS, Kakochang Waterfalls, Tocklai centre, sukapha samannay kshetra etc.
5. **Live stocks :** poultry, cattle like cows, buffaloes, goat, etc.

Jorhat is the cultural capital of Assam and acts as a gateway to Upper Assam and Nagaland. It got its name from the two Assamese words---one is "jor" which means join and other is "hat" means market. In 1794, the Ahom king Gaurinath Singha shifted the capital from Sibsagar to Jorhat. Jorhat was the last capital of Ahoms and the place of many historical monuments of Assamese culture.

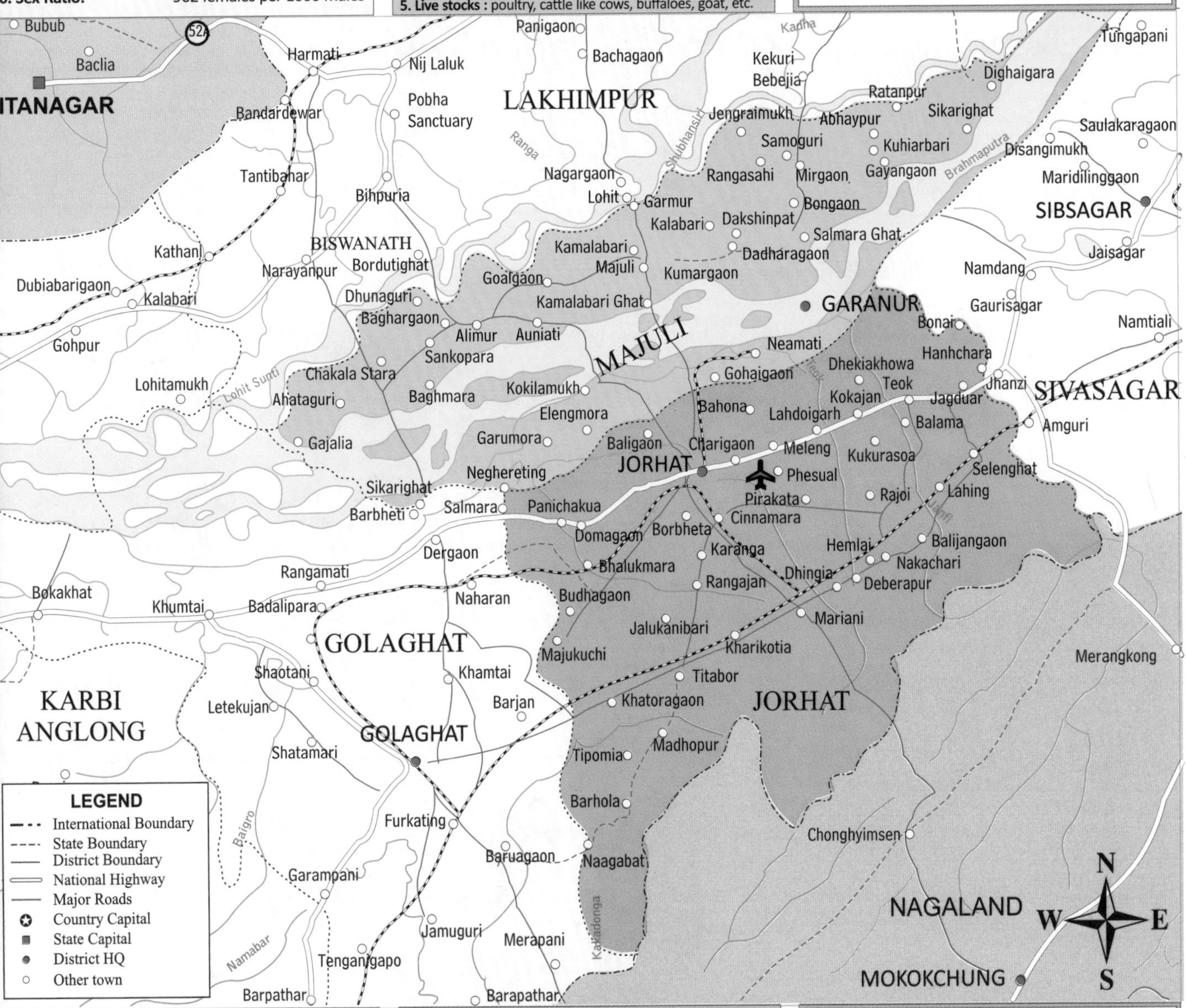

LAKHIMPUR
MAJULI
JORHAT
GOLAGHAT
KARBI ANGLONG
NAGALAND
SIBSAGAR
SIVASAGAR
BISWANATH
ITANAGAR
GARANUR
MOKOKCHUNG
LEGEND
International Boundary
State Boundary
District Boundary
National Highway
Major Roads
Country Capital
State Capital
District HQ
Other town
N
S
E
W

MAJULI

VITAL STATISTICS

1. **District Headquarter:** Majuli
2. **Population:** 1,57,304
3. **Area:** 880 sq. km.
4. **Population Density:** 300 inhabitants per sq. km
5. **Literacy:** 78.56 %
6. **Sex Ratio:** 954 females per 1000 males

*Data includes Jorhat as the district was formed post census 2011

ECONOMIC PROFILES

1. **Agriculture:** Crops like Paddy, Maize, sugarcane, Cotton, jute, pulses, cereals, cereals, wheat etc. Fruits like pineapple, banana, guava, jackfruit, lemon, orange, etc.
2. **Industries:** Agro, chemical, engineering units, mineral, metal, cane and bamboo, carpentry, blacksmith, leather based, jute etc.
3. **Minerals:** Oil, gas, Free gas etc.
4. **Tourism:** Kamalabari satra, Dakhinpat satra, Garmur, Tengapania, Auniati satra etc.
5. **Live stocks :** poultry, cattle like cows, buffaloes, goats etc.

Majuli is the biggest river island in the world. In 2016 this island was made a separate district, carved out of Jorhat. This river island district is first of its kind in India. This river island is located in the middle of the mighty river Brahamaputra and can be reached only by ferries from nearby towns. Here people follow Neo-Vaishnavaite culture, which is unique to this island. The main industry is agriculture and other allied activities.

000 0 1000 2000 km.

Projection: Lambert's Conical Orthomorphic

SIVASAGAR & CHARAIDEO

SIVASAGAR
VITAL STATISTICS

1. District Headquarter:	Sivasagar
2. Population:	1,151,050
3. Area:	2,668 sq. km.
4. Population Density:	431 persons per sq. km.
5. Literacy:	80.41 %
6. Gender Ratio:	954 females per 1000 males

Sivasagar, the historical city of Assam, was the capital of Ahoms who ruled over Assam for more than 600 years. During the time of Ahoms, Sivasagar was known as "Rangpur". However, when Ahom Dynasty was over, it was renamed as Sivasagar, "The Ocean of Lord Shiva". There is an interesting story associated with the name of the place Sibsagar. Siba Singha, a veteran Ahom king, and his wife Ambika were great worshiper of Lord Shiva.

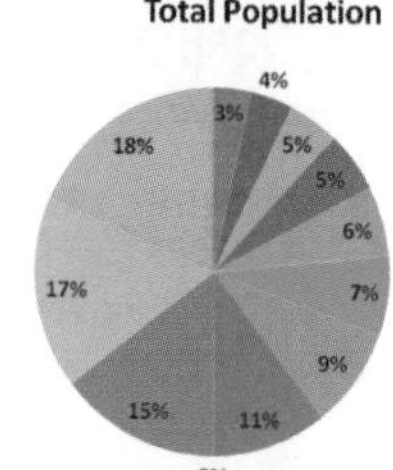

Total Population
3%
4%
5%
5%
6%
7%
9%
11%
15%
17%
18%
0%
1901
1911
1921
1931
1941
1951
1961
1971
1981
1991
2001
2011

Shiva Dole

Rang Ghar is one of the oldest surviving amphitheater of Asia and is located near Rangpur Palace, 3 km from Sivasagar town of Assam. It is often referred to as the 'Colosseum of the East. This entertainment building belongs to the Ahoms and dates back to 1746 A.D. This monument is an important example of the architectural precision and grandeur of that time. Originally it was built by Swagadeo Rudra Singh with bamboo and wood but later it was modified by Swagadeo Pramatta Singha with brick.

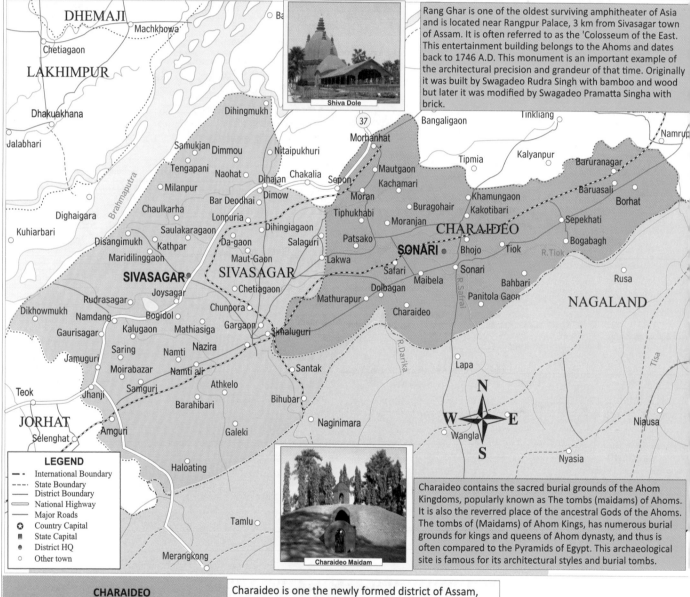

LEGEND
- International Boundary
- State Boundary
- District Boundary
- National Highway
- Major Roads
- Country Capital
- State Capital
- District HQ
- Other town

Charaideo Maidam

Charaideo contains the sacred burial grounds of the Ahom Kingdoms, popularly known as The tombs (maidams) of Ahoms. It is also the reverred place of the ancestral Gods of the Ahoms. The tombs of (Maidams) of Ahom Kings, has numerous burial grounds for kings and queens of Ahom dynasty, and thus is often compared to the Pyramids of Egypt. This archaeological site is famous for its architectural styles and burial tombs.

CHARAIDEO
VITAL STATISTICS

1. District Headquarter:	Sonari
2. Population:	3,30,000
3. Area:	2,668 sq. km.
4. Population Density:	430 inhabitants per sq km
5. Literacy:	81.36 %
6. Gender Ratio:	951 females per 1000 males

Data above includes Sivasagar and Charideo combined

Charaideo is one the newly formed district of Assam, carved out of Sivasagar district in 2015. The literal meaning of the word Charaideo is "a prominent city in the hill top". 30 km of the town of Sivasagar, Assam. Charaideo is located at the foothills of Nagaland. Charaideo was the first capital of Ahom Kingdom in 1228. Though the capital of Ahom kingdom shifted many times, but this place remained at the centre of the kingdom.

Projection: Lambert's Conical Orthomorphic

1000 0 1000 2000 km

LAKHIMPUR

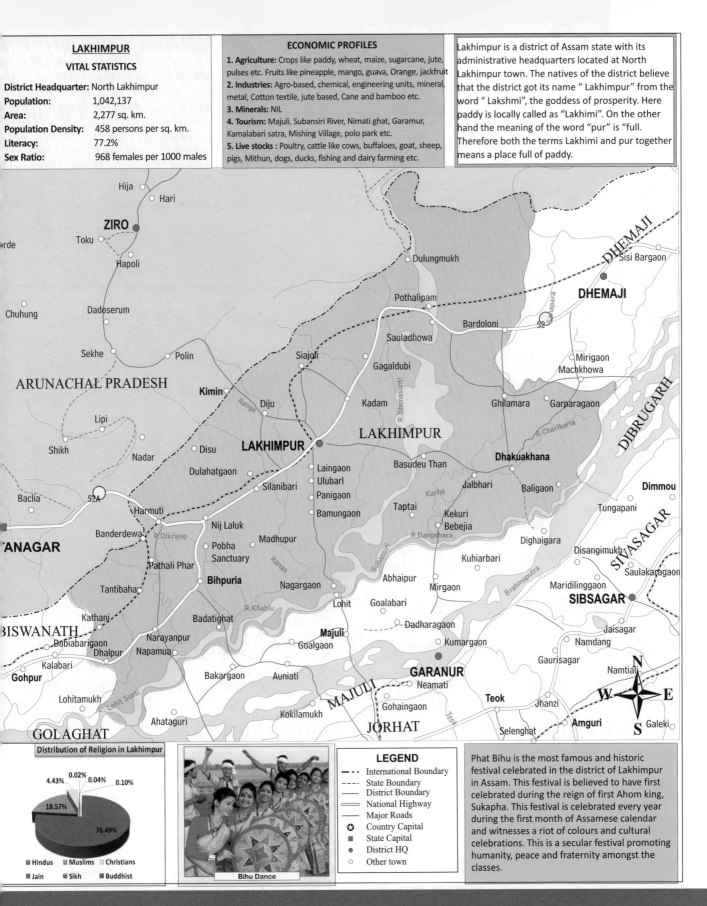

VITAL STATISTICS

District Headquarter:	North Lakhimpur
Population:	1,042,137
Area:	2,277 sq. km.
Population Density:	458 persons per sq. km.
Literacy:	77.2%
Sex Ratio:	968 females per 1000 males

ECONOMIC PROFILES

1. **Agriculture:** Crops like paddy, wheat, maize, sugarcane, jute, pulses etc. Fruits like pineapple, mango, guava, Orange, jackfruit
2. **Industries:** Agro-based, chemical, engineering units, mineral, metal, Cotton textile, jute based, Cane and bamboo etc.
3. **Minerals:** NIL
4. **Tourism:** Majuli, Subansiri River, Nimati ghat, Garamur, Kamalabari satra, Mishing Village, polo park etc.
5. **Live stocks :** Poultry, cattle like cows, buffaloes, goat, sheep, pigs, Mithun, dogs, ducks, fishing and dairy farming etc.

Lakhimpur is a district of Assam state with its administrative headquarters located at North Lakhimpur town. The natives of the district believe that the district got its name " Lakhimpur" from the word " Lakshmi", the goddess of prosperity. Here paddy is locally called as "Lakhimi". On the other hand the meaning of the word "pur" is "full. Therefore both the terms Lakhimi and pur together means a place full of paddy.

Hija, Hari, ZIRO, Toku, Hapoli, Chuhung, Dadoserum, Sekhe, Polin, ARUNACHAL PRADESH, Kimin, Lipi, Shikh, Nadar, Disu, Baclia, 52A, Harmuti, Banderdewa, ANAGAR, Pathali Phar, Tantibaha, Kathani, BISWANATH, Dubiabarigaon, Dhalpur, Kalabari, Gohpur, Lohitamukh, Lohit Sunti, Ahataguri, GOLAGHAT, Dulungmukh, Pothalipam, Sauladhowa, Siajuli, Gagaldubi, Diju, Ranga, Kadam, R. Dhunasunti, LAKHIMPUR, Laingaon, Ulubarl, Panigaon, Bamungaon, Dulahatgaon, Silanibari, Nij Laluk, R. Dikrung, Pobha Sanctuary, Madhupur, Bihpuria, Nagargaon, R. Khablu, Badatighat, Narayanpur, Napamua, Bakargaon, Auniati, Majuli, Goalgaon, Lohit, Goalabari, Kokilamukh, MAJULI, Gohaingaon, JORHAT, Neamati, GARANUR, Kumargaon, Dadharagaon, Abhaipur, Mirgaon, Subansiri, Taptai, Karha, Basudeu Than, Kekuri, Bebejia, R. Dangdhara, Jalbhari, Dhakuakhana, Baligaon, Kuhiarbari, Brahmaputra, Bardoloni, 52, Sanapara, DHEMAJI, Sisi Bargaon, Mirigaon, Machkhowa, Ghilamara, Garparagaon, R. Charikaria, DIBRUGARH, Dimmou, Tungapani, Dighaigara, Disangimukh, SIVASAGAR, Saulakaragaon, Maridilinggaon, SIBSAGAR, Jaisagar, Namdang, Gaurisagar, Namtiali, Teok, Jhanzi, Amguri, Selenghat, Galeki, N, W, E, S

Distribution of Religion in Lakhimpur

- 76.49%
- 18.57%
- 4.43%
- 0.02%
- 0.04%
- 0.10%

Hindus, Muslims, Christians, Jain, Sikh, Buddhist

Bihu Dance

LEGEND

- International Boundary
- State Boundary
- District Boundary
- National Highway
- Major Roads
- Country Capital
- State Capital
- District HQ
- Other town

Phat Bihu is the most famous and historic festival celebrated in the district of Lakhimpur in Assam. This festival is believed to have first celebrated during the reign of first Ahom king, Sukapha. This festival is celebrated every year during the first month of Assamese calendar and witnesses a riot of colours and cultural celebrations. This is a secular festival promoting humanity, peace and fraternity amongst the classes.

DHEMAJI

VITAL STATISTICS

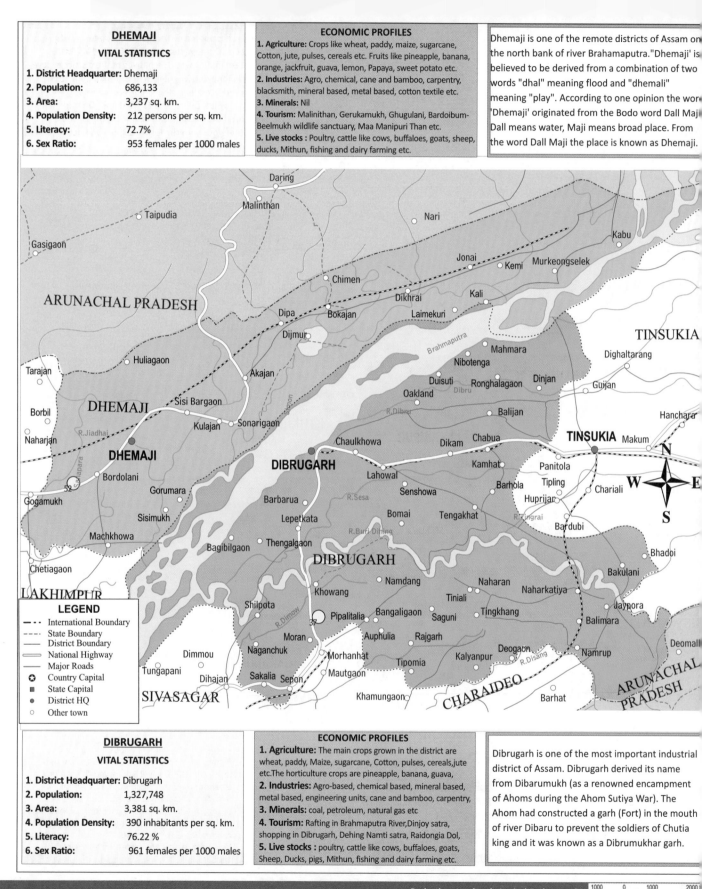

1. **District Headquarter:** Dhemaji
2. **Population:** 686,133
3. **Area:** 3,237 sq. km.
4. **Population Density:** 212 persons per sq. km.
5. **Literacy:** 72.7%
6. **Sex Ratio:** 953 females per 1000 males

ECONOMIC PROFILES

1. **Agriculture:** Crops like wheat, paddy, maize, sugarcane, Cotton, jute, pulses, cereals etc. Fruits like pineapple, banana, orange, jackfruit, guava, lemon, Papaya, sweet potato etc.
2. **Industries:** Agro, chemical, cane and bamboo, carpentry, blacksmith, mineral based, metal based, cotton textile etc.
3. **Minerals:** Nil
4. **Tourism:** Malinithan, Gerukamukh, Ghugulani, Bardoibum-Beelmukh wildlife sanctuary, Maa Manipuri Than etc.
5. **Live stocks :** Poultry, cattle like cows, buffaloes, goats, sheep, ducks, Mithun, fishing and dairy farming etc.

Dhemaji is one of the remote districts of Assam on the north bank of river Brahamaputra."Dhemaji' is believed to be derived from a combination of two words "dhal" meaning flood and "dhemali" meaning "play". According to one opinion the word 'Dhemaji' originated from the Bodo word Dall Maji. Dall means water, Maji means broad place. From the word Dall Maji the place is known as Dhemaji.

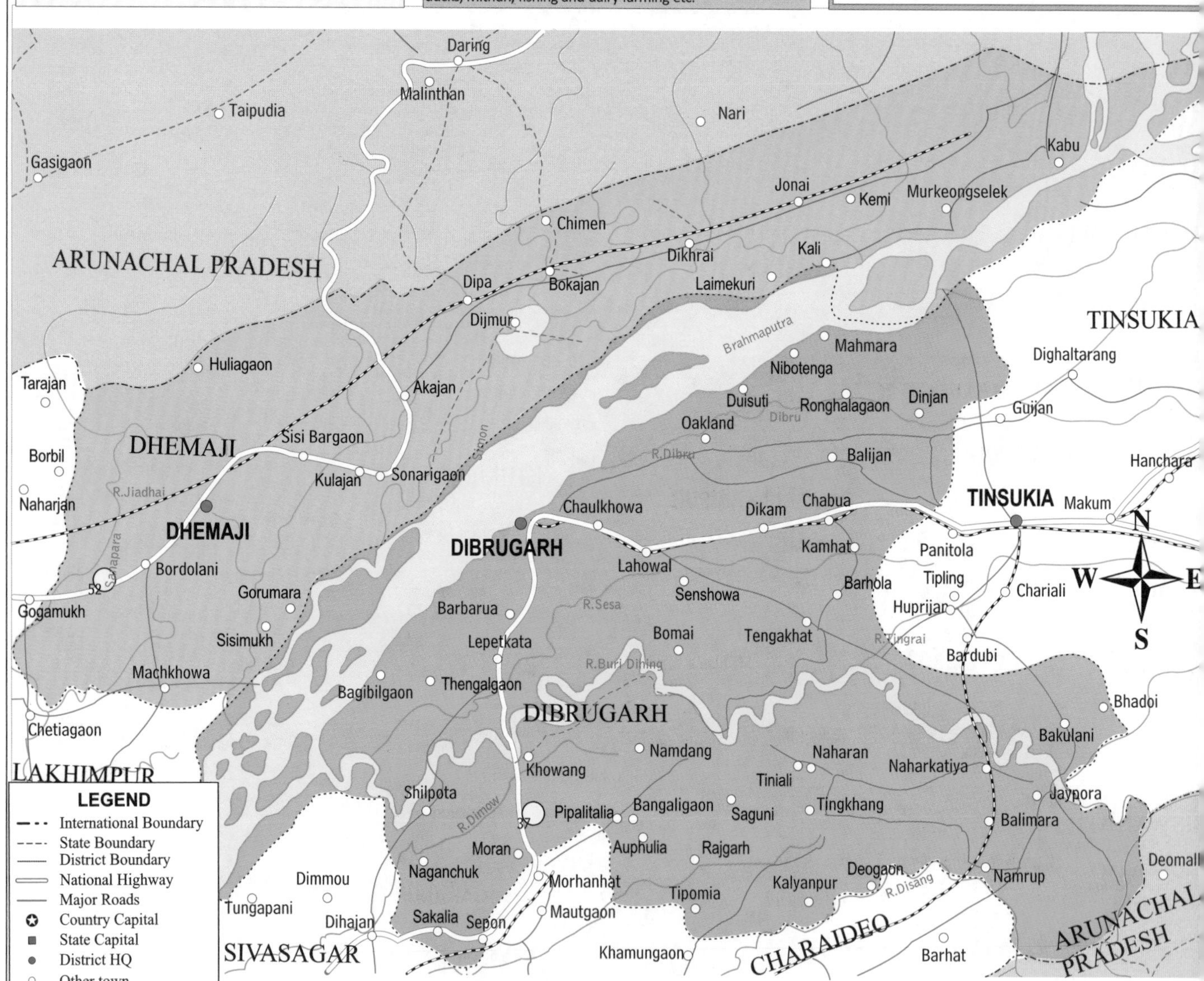

Daring
Malinthan
Taipudia
Nari
Gasigaon
Kabu
Jonai
Kemi
Murkeongselek
Chimen
Kali
Dikhrai
ARUNACHAL PRADESH
Dipa
Bokajan
Laimekuri
Dijmur
Brahmaputra
TINSUKIA
Mahmara
Dighaltarang
Huliagaon
Nibotenga
Tarajan
Akajan
Duisuti
Ronghalagaon
Dinjan
Guijan
Dibru
Oakland
Sisi Bargaon
DHEMAJI
Simon
R.Dibru
Balijan
Borbil
Hanchara
Kulajan
Sonarigaon
Naharjan
R.Jiadhai
Chaulkhowa
Dikam
Chabua
TINSUKIA
Makum
N
DHEMAJI
DIBRUGARH
Kamhat
Panitola
Lahowal
Bordolani
Tipling
Gorumara
Senshowa
Barhola
Chariali
W
E
Gogamukh
Huprijan
Barbarua
R.Sesa
Bomai
Tengakhat
R.Tingrai
Sisimukh
Lepetkata
S
Bardubi
R.Buri Dihing
Machkhowa
Bagibilgaon
Thengalgaon
Bhadoi
DIBRUGARH
Chetiagaon
Bakulani
Namdang
Naharan
LAKHIMPUR
Khowang
Tiniali
Naharkatiya
Shilpota
Jaypora
Pipalitalia
Bangaligaon
Saguni
Tingkhang
Balimara
R.Dimow
Moran
Auphulia
Rajgarh
Deomali
Naganchuk
Dimmou
Morhanhat
Deogaon
Namrup
Tipomia
Kalyanpur
R.Disang
Tungapani
Mautgaon
Dihajan
Sakalia
Sepon
CHARAIDEO
ARUNACHAL PRADESH
SIVASAGAR
Khamungaon
Barhat
LEGEND
International Boundary
State Boundary
District Boundary
National Highway
Major Roads
Country Capital
State Capital
District HQ
Other town

DIBRUGARH

VITAL STATISTICS

1. **District Headquarter:** Dibrugarh
2. **Population:** 1,327,748
3. **Area:** 3,381 sq. km.
4. **Population Density:** 390 inhabitants per sq. km.
5. **Literacy:** 76.22 %
6. **Sex Ratio:** 961 females per 1000 males

ECONOMIC PROFILES

1. **Agriculture:** The main crops grown in the district are wheat, paddy, Maize, sugarcane, Cotton, pulses, cereals,jute etc.The horticulture crops are pineapple, banana, guava,
2. **Industries:** Agro-based, chemical based, mineral based, metal based, engineering units, cane and bamboo, carpentry,
3. **Minerals:** coal, petroleum, natural gas etc
4. **Tourism:** Rafting in Brahmaputra River,Dinjoy satra, shopping in Dibrugarh, Dehing Namti satra, Raidongia Dol,
5. **Live stocks :** poultry, cattle like cows, buffaloes, goats, Sheep, Ducks, pigs, Mithun, fishing and dairy farming etc.

Dibrugarh is one of the most important industrial district of Assam. Dibrugarh derived its name from Dibarumukh (as a renowned encampment of Ahoms during the Ahom Sutiya War). The Ahom had constructed a garh (Fort) in the mouth of river Dibaru to prevent the soldiers of Chutia king and it was known as a Dibrumukhar garh.

Projection: Lambert's Conical Orthomorphic

1000 0 1000 2000

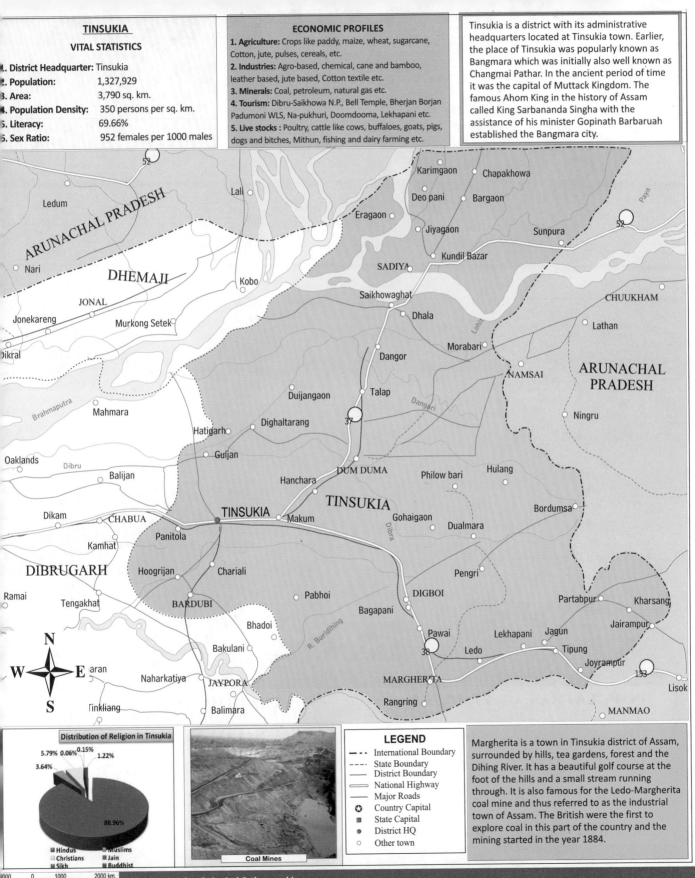

TINSUKIA

VITAL STATISTICS

1. **District Headquarter:** Tinsukia
2. **Population:** 1,327,929
3. **Area:** 3,790 sq. km.
4. **Population Density:** 350 persons per sq. km.
5. **Literacy:** 69.66%
6. **Sex Ratio:** 952 females per 1000 males

ECONOMIC PROFILES

1. **Agriculture:** Crops like paddy, maize, wheat, sugarcane, Cotton, jute, pulses, cereals, etc.
2. **Industries:** Agro-based, chemical, cane and bamboo, leather based, jute based, Cotton textile etc.
3. **Minerals:** Coal, petroleum, natural gas etc.
4. **Tourism:** Dibru-Saikhowa N.P., Bell Temple, Bherjan Borjan Padumoni WLS, Na-pukhuri, Doomdooma, Lekhapani etc.
5. **Live stocks :** Poultry, cattle like cows, buffaloes, goats, pigs, dogs and bitches, Mithun, fishing and dairy farming etc.

Tinsukia is a district with its administrative headquarters located at Tinsukia town. Earlier, the place of Tinsukia was popularly known as Bangmara which was initially also well known as Changmai Pathar. In the ancient period of time it was the capital of Muttack Kingdom. The famous Ahom King in the history of Assam called King Sarbananda Singha with the assistance of his minister Gopinath Barbaruah established the Bangmara city.

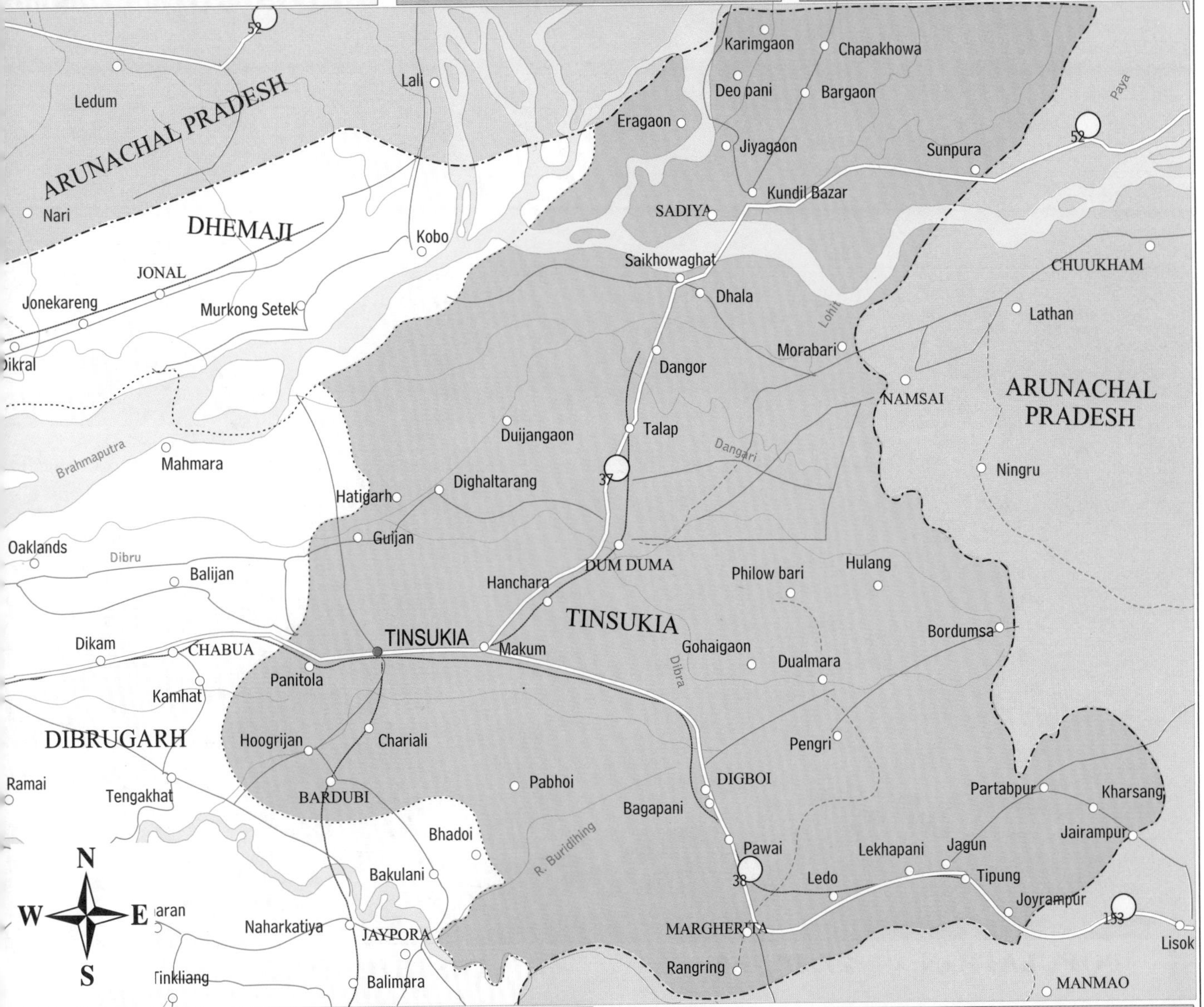

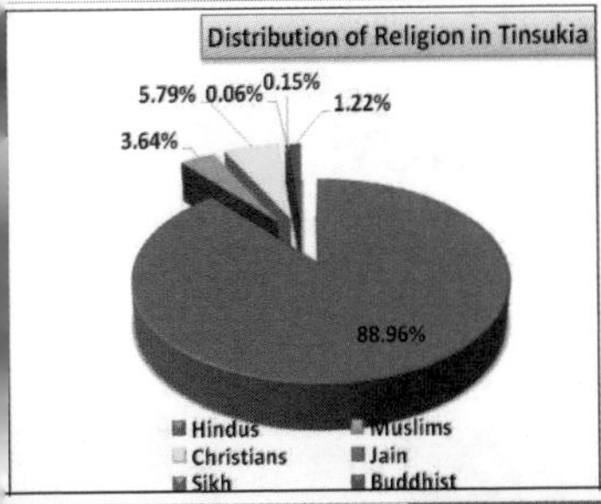

Distribution of Religion in Tinsukia

88.96%, 5.79%, 3.64%, 0.06%, 0.15%, 1.22%

Hindus, Muslims, Christians, Jain, Sikh, Buddhist

Coal Mines

LEGEND

- International Boundary
- State Boundary
- District Boundary
- National Highway
- Major Roads
- Country Capital
- State Capital
- District HQ
- Other town

Margherita is a town in Tinsukia district of Assam, surrounded by hills, tea gardens, forest and the Dihing River. It has a beautiful golf course at the foot of the hills and a small stream running through. It is also famous for the Ledo-Margherita coal mine and thus referred to as the industrial town of Assam. The British were the first to explore coal in this part of the country and the mining started in the year 1884.

1000 0 1000 2000 km.

Projection: Lambert's Conical Orthomorphic

MANIPUR

Section

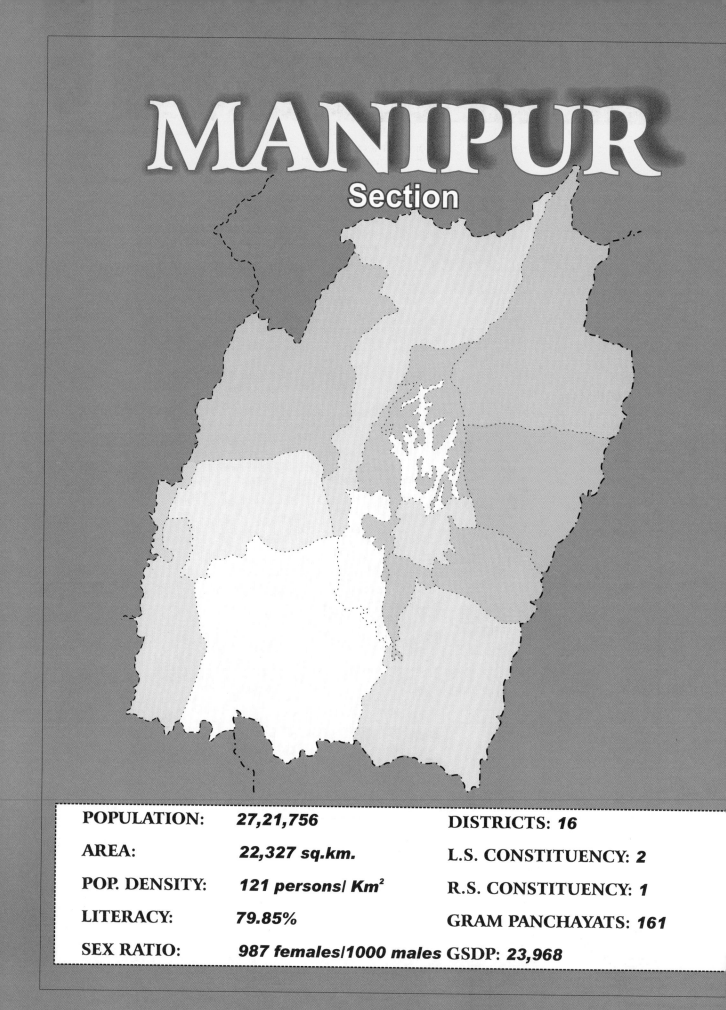

POPULATION:	***27,21,756***	**DISTRICTS:** ***16***
AREA:	***22,327 sq.km.***	**L.S. CONSTITUENCY:** ***2***
POP. DENSITY:	***121 persons/ Km^2***	**R.S. CONSTITUENCY:** ***1***
LITERACY:	***79.85%***	**GRAM PANCHAYATS:** ***161***
SEX RATIO:	***987 females/1000 males***	**GSDP:** ***23,968***

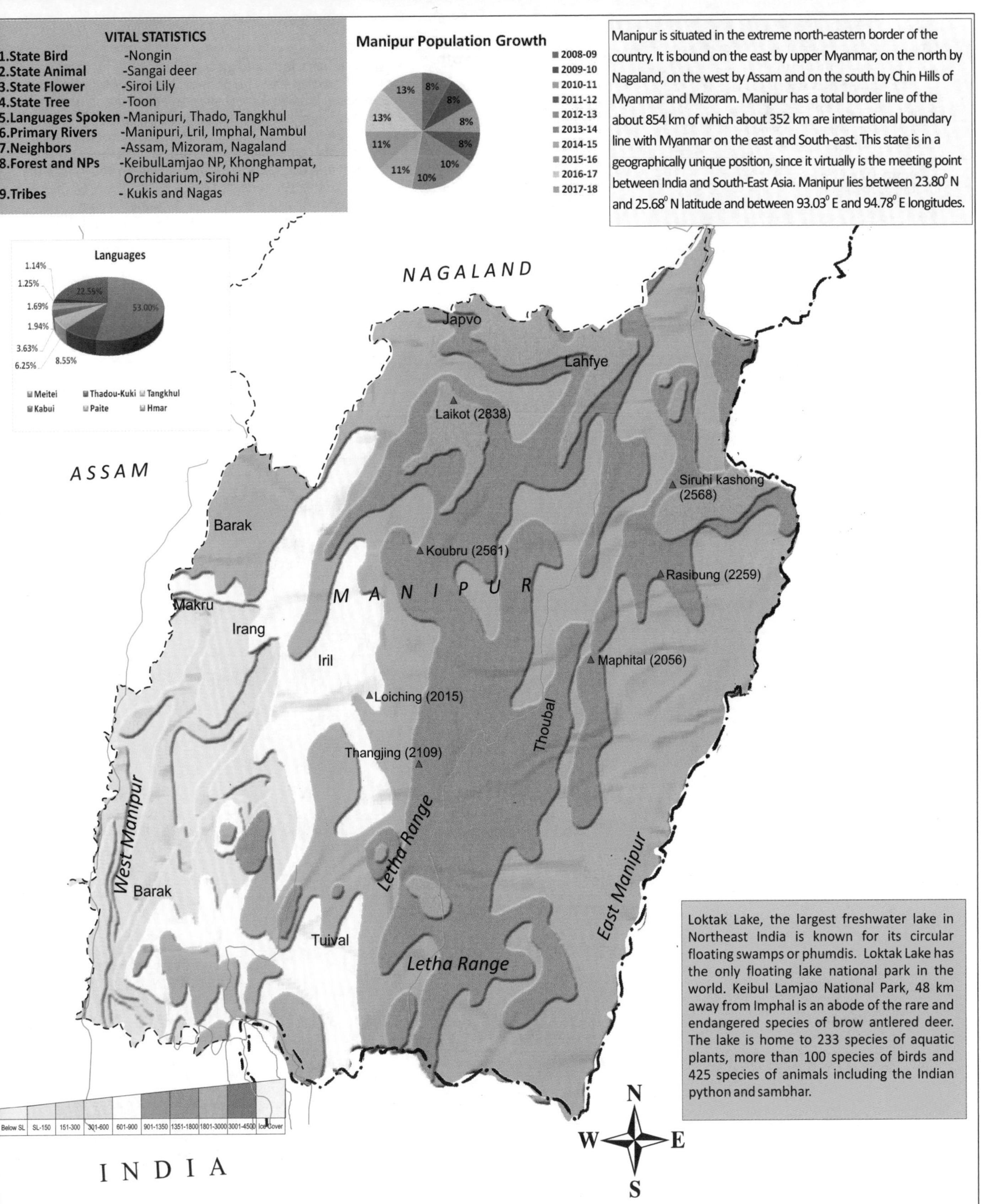

VITAL STATISTICS
1.State Bird -Nongin
2.State Animal -Sangai deer
3.State Flower -Siroi Lily
4.State Tree -Toon
5.Languages Spoken -Manipuri, Thado, Tangkhul
6.Primary Rivers -Manipuri, Lril, Imphal, Nambul
7.Neighbors -Assam, Mizoram, Nagaland
8.Forest and NPs -KeibulLamjao NP, Khonghampat, Orchidarium, Sirohi NP
9.Tribes - Kukis and Nagas
Manipur Population Growth
2008-09
2009-10
2010-11
2011-12
2012-13
2013-14
2014-15
2015-16
2016-17
2017-18
8%
8%
8%
8%
10%
10%
11%
11%
13%
13%
Manipur is situated in the extreme north-eastern border of the country. It is bound on the east by upper Myanmar, on the north by Nagaland, on the west by Assam and on the south by Chin Hills of Myanmar and Mizoram. Manipur has a total border line of the about 854 km of which about 352 km are international boundary line with Myanmar on the east and South-east. This state is in a geographically unique position, since it virtually is the meeting point between India and South-East Asia. Manipur lies between 23.80° N and 25.68° N latitude and between 93.03° E and 94.78° E longitudes.
Languages
1.14%
1.25%
1.69%
1.94%
3.63%
6.25%
8.55%
22.55%
53.00%
Meitei
Thadou-Kuki
Tangkhul
Kabui
Paite
Hmar
NAGALAND
ASSAM
Japvo
Lahfye
Laikot (2838)
Siruhi kashong (2568)
Barak
Koubru (2561)
Rasibung (2259)
M A N I P U R
Makru
Irang
Iril
Maphital (2056)
Loiching (2015)
Thoubal
Thangjing (2109)
Letha Range
West Manipur
Barak
East Manipur
Tuival
Letha Range
Loktak Lake, the largest freshwater lake in Northeast India is known for its circular floating swamps or phumdis. Loktak Lake has the only floating lake national park in the world. Keibul Lamjao National Park, 48 km away from Imphal is an abode of the rare and endangered species of brow antlered deer. The lake is home to 233 species of aquatic plants, more than 100 species of birds and 425 species of animals including the Indian python and sambhar.
Below SL
SL-150
151-300
301-600
601-900
901-1350
1351-1800
1801-3000
3001-4500
Ice Cover
N
W
E
S
INDIA

Scale - 1:1.26 M approx

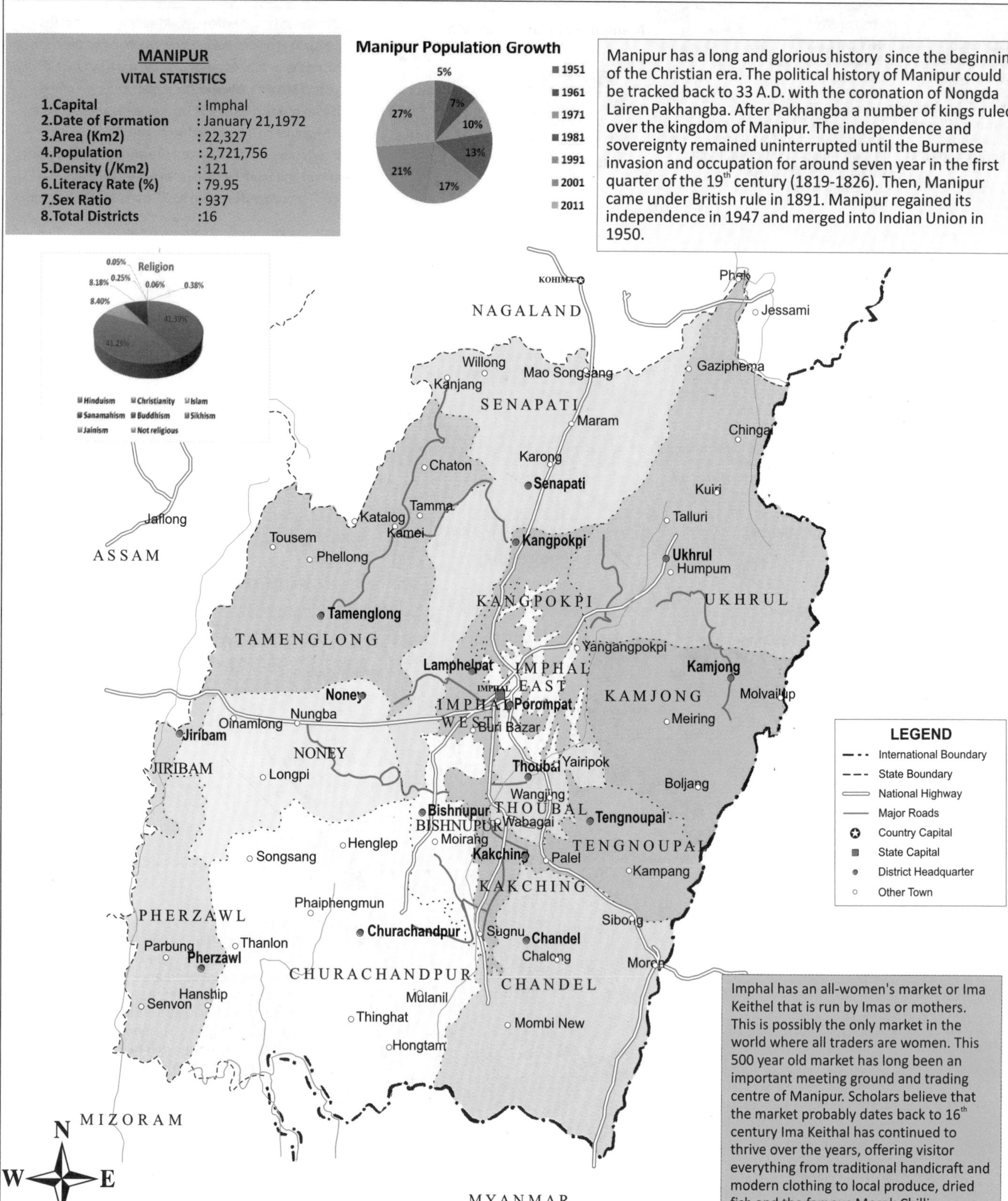
MANIPUR
VITAL STATISTICS
1.Capital : Imphal
2.Date of Formation : January 21,1972
3.Area (Km2) : 22,327
4.Population : 2,721,756
5.Density (/Km2) : 121
6.Literacy Rate (%) : 79.95
7.Sex Ratio : 937
8.Total Districts :16
Manipur Population Growth
5%
7%
10%
13%
17%
21%
27%
1951
1961
1971
1981
1991
2001
2011
Manipur has a long and glorious history since the beginning of the Christian era. The political history of Manipur could be tracked back to 33 A.D. with the coronation of Nongda Lairen Pakhangba. After Pakhangba a number of kings ruled over the kingdom of Manipur. The independence and sovereignty remained uninterrupted until the Burmese invasion and occupation for around seven year in the first quarter of the 19th century (1819-1826). Then, Manipur came under British rule in 1891. Manipur regained its independence in 1947 and merged into Indian Union in 1950.
Religion
0.05%
8.18%
0.25%
0.06%
0.38%
8.40%
41.39%
41.29%
Hinduism
Christianity
Islam
Sanamahism
Buddhism
Sikhism
Jainism
Not religious
KOHIMA
NAGALAND
Phek
Jessami
Willong
Mao Songsang
Kanjang
Gaziphema
SENAPATI
Maram
Chinga
Chaton
Karong
Senapati
Kuiri
Tamma
Katalog
Talluri
Jaflong
Kamei
Tousem
Phellong
Kangpokpi
Ukhrul
Humpum
ASSAM
KANGPOKPI
UKHRUL
Tamenglong
TAMENGLONG
Yangangpokpi
Lamphelpat
IMPHAL EAST
Kamjong
IMPHAL
Noney
Porompat
KAMJONG
Molvailup
IMPHAL WEST
Nungba
Oinamlong
Buri Bazar
Meiring
Jiribam
NONEY
Yairipok
JIRIBAM
Longpi
Thoubal
Boljang
Wangjing
Bishnupur
THOUBAL
BISHNUPUR
Wabagai
Tengnoupal
Moirang
Henglep
TENGNOUPAL
Songsang
Kakching
Palel
Kampang
KAKCHING
Phaiphengmun
PHERZAWL
Sibong
Churachandpur
Sugnu
Chandel
Parbung
Thanlon
Pherzawl
Chalong
CHURACHANDPUR
Moreh
Hanship
CHANDEL
Senvon
Mulanil
Thinghat
Mombi New
Hongtam
MIZORAM
MYANMAR
N
W
E
S
LEGEND
International Boundary
State Boundary
National Highway
Major Roads
Country Capital
State Capital
District Headquarter
Other Town
Imphal has an all-women's market or Ima Keithel that is run by Imas or mothers. This is possibly the only market in the world where all traders are women. This 500 year old market has long been an important meeting ground and trading centre of Manipur. Scholars believe that the market probably dates back to 16th century Ima Keithal has continued to thrive over the years, offering visitor everything from traditional handicraft and modern clothing to local produce, dried fish and the famous Morok Chilli.

Scale - 1:1.31 M approx

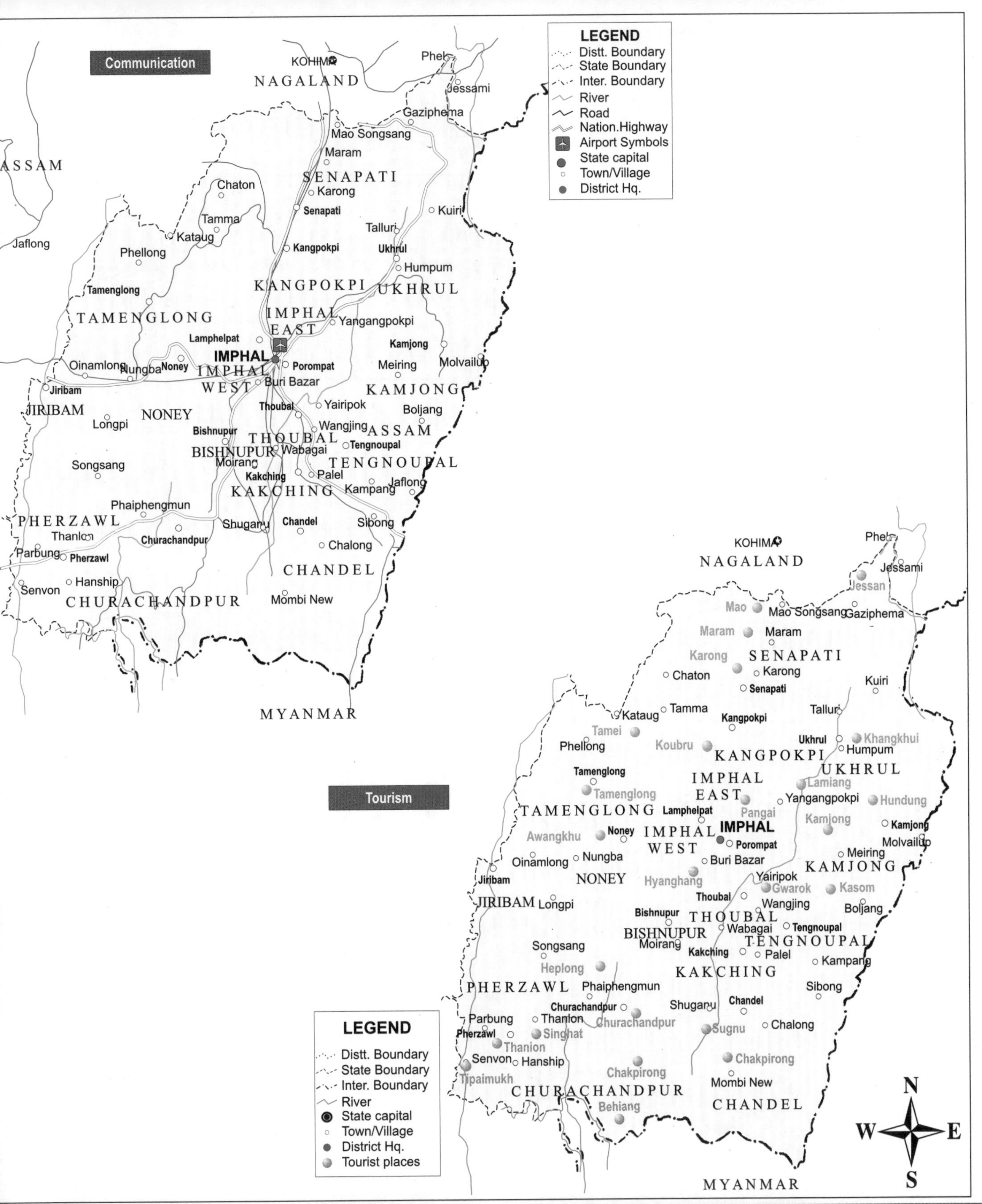
Communication
LEGEND
Distt. Boundary
State Boundary
Inter. Boundary
River
Road
Nation.Highway
Airport Symbols
State capital
Town/Village
District Hq.
NAGALAND
ASSAM
SENAPATI
KANGPOKPI
UKHRUL
TAMENGLONG
IMPHAL EAST
IMPHAL WEST
IMPHAL
JIRIBAM
NONEY
KAMJONG
THOUBAL
BISHNUPUR
TENGNOUPAL
KAKCHING
PHERZAWL
CHANDEL
CHURACHANDPUR
MYANMAR
Tourism
LEGEND
Distt. Boundary
State Boundary
Inter. Boundary
River
State capital
Town/Village
District Hq.
Tourist places
N
W
E
S

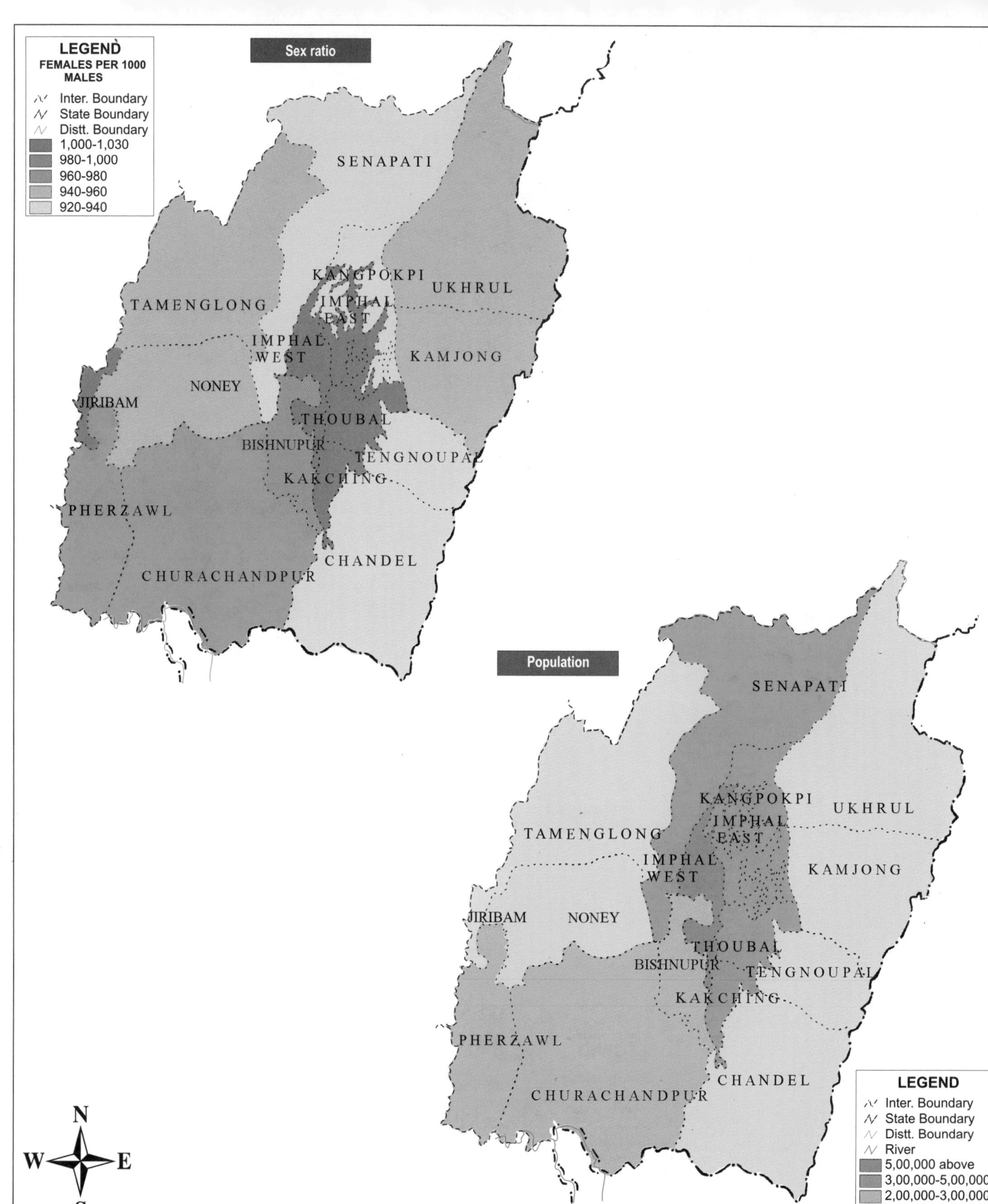

Sex ratio
LEGEND
FEMALES PER 1000 MALES
Inter. Boundary
State Boundary
Distt. Boundary
1,000-1,030
980-1,000
960-980
940-960
920-940
SENAPATI
KANGPOKPI
UKHRUL
TAMENGLONG
IMPHAL EAST
IMPHAL WEST
KAMJONG
NONEY
JIRIBAM
THOUBAL
BISHNUPUR
TENGNOUPAL
KAKCHING
PHERZAWL
CHANDEL
CHURACHANDPUR
Population
SENAPATI
KANGPOKPI
UKHRUL
TAMENGLONG
IMPHAL EAST
IMPHAL WEST
KAMJONG
JIRIBAM
NONEY
THOUBAL
BISHNUPUR
TENGNOUPAL
KAKCHING
PHERZAWL
CHANDEL
CHURACHANDPUR
LEGEND
Inter. Boundary
State Boundary
Distt. Boundary
River
5,00,000 above
3,00,000-5,00,000
2,00,000-3,00,000
Less Than 2,00,000
N
W
E
S

Scale - 1:1.73 M approx

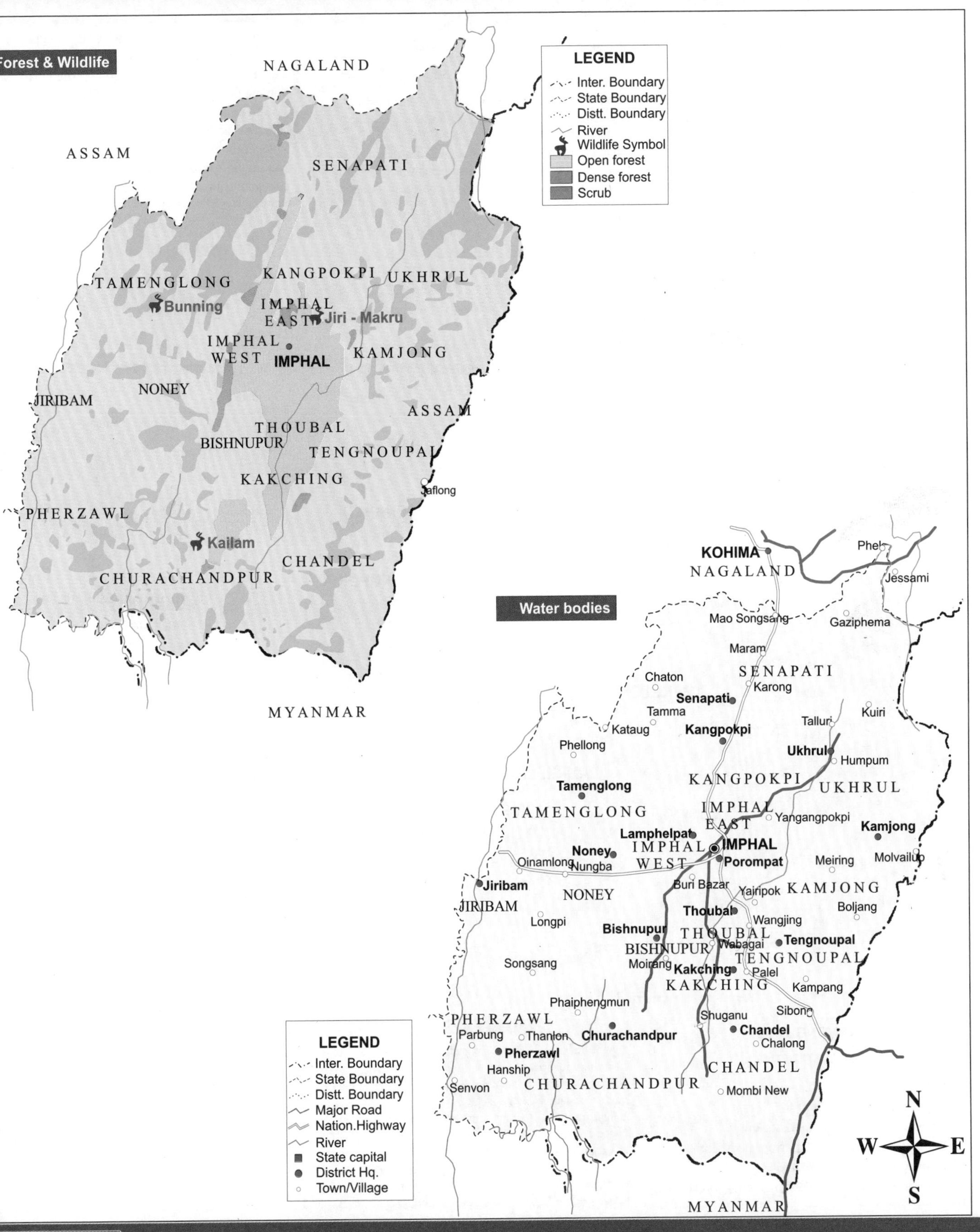

Forest & Wildlife
NAGALAND
ASSAM
SENAPATI
LEGEND
Inter. Boundary
State Boundary
Distt. Boundary
River
Wildlife Symbol
Open forest
Dense forest
Scrub
TAMENGLONG
KANGPOKPI
UKHRUL
Bunning
IMPHAL EAST
Jiri - Makru
IMPHAL WEST
IMPHAL
KAMJONG
NONEY
JIRIBAM
ASSAM
THOUBAL
BISHNUPUR
TENGNOUPAL
KAKCHING
Jaflong
PHERZAWL
Kailam
CHANDEL
CHURACHANDPUR
MYANMAR
Water bodies
KOHIMA
NAGALAND
Phek
Jessami
Mao Songsang
Gaziphema
Maram
SENAPATI
Chaton
Karong
Senapati
Tamma
Kuiri
Kataug
Kangpokpi
Tallui
Phellong
Ukhrul
Humpum
Tamenglong
KANGPOKPI
UKHRUL
TAMENGLONG
IMPHAL EAST
Yangangpokpi
Lamphelpat
Kamjong
Noney
IMPHAL WEST
IMPHAL
Oinamlong
Nungba
Porompat
Meiring
Molvailup
Jiribam
Buri Bazar
Yairipok
KAMJONG
JIRIBAM
NONEY
Thoubal
Boljang
Longpi
Wangjing
Bishnupur
THOUBAL
Tengnoupal
BISHNUPUR
Wabagai
TENGNOUPAL
Songsang
Moirang
Kakching
Palel
KAKCHING
Kampang
Phaiphengmun
Sibong
PHERZAWL
Shuganu
Parbung
Thanlon
Churachandpur
Chandel
Chalong
Pherzawl
Hanship
CHANDEL
Senvon
CHURACHANDPUR
Mombi New
LEGEND
Inter. Boundary
State Boundary
Distt. Boundary
Major Road
Nation.Highway
River
State capital
District Hq.
Town/Village
N
W
E
S
MYANMAR

Scale - 1:1.73 M approx

SENAPATI

VITAL STATISTICS

1. **District Headquarter:** Senapati
2. **Population:** 479,148
3. **Area:** 3,271 sq. km.
4. **Population Density:** 109 persons per sq. km.
5. **Literacy:** 74.13%
6. **Sex Ratio:** 959 females per 1000 males

ECONOMIC PROFILES

1. **Agriculture:** Terrace cultivation, paddy, maize, cabbage, potato, cereals etc.
2. **Industries:** Agro, Cotton textile, woollen, silk and artificial threads based clothes, wooden, Paper products, chemical, Rubber, engineering units, mineral, metal etc.
3. **Minerals:** Limestone and sandstone etc.
4. **Tourism:** Mao (gateway to manipur), Yangkhullen (landscape), Liyai, Makhel, purul (rich traditional place).
5. **Live stocks :** poultry, cattle like cows, buffaloes, goats, pigs ,

Senapati is bounded on the south by Kangpokpi district, on the east by Ukhrul district, on the west by Tamenglong district and on the north by Kohima district and Phek district of Nagaland state. The district is under humid subtropical climate. The major languages spoken here are Mao, Poumai, Rongmei, Zeme, and lianglad etc. The major festivals are Chaga Ngee celebrated by Liangmai tribe on 30 October every year.

NAGALAND
Jessami
Willong
Mao Songsang
Kanjang
Khullen
Gaziphema
Laii
Liyai Khullen
Paomata
SENAPATI
Maram
Phyabu
Tepun
Keiye
Chingai
Chaton
Karong
Nriangluang
Kotlen
Vakho
Kachai
Kuiri
Gelnel
SENAPATI
Konphung
Tamah
Ngam
Joupi
Talluri
Tamei
Chanjang
Haipi
KANGPOKPI
Tousem
Langmei
Makui
Daili
UKHRUL
Phellong
Kalapahar
Humpum
Mandu
Keithelmanbi
Namtiram
Tharon
Bongmoul
Dailong
Pumram
KANGPOKPI
UKHRUL
Aben
TAMENGLONG
Leimakhong
TAMENGLONG
Samuk
Yangangpokpi
LAMPHELPAT
IMPHAL EAST
KAMJONG
NONEY
IMPHAL
Molvailup
IMPHAL WEST
POROMPAT
KAMJONG
JIRIBAM
Nungba
Meiring
Oinamlong
Kotlen
Buri Bazar
JIRIBAM
NONEY
THOUBAL
Yairipok
N
W
E
S
Varok
Wangjing
BISHNUPUR
THOUBAL
LEGEND
International Boundary
State Boundary
District Boundary
National Highway
Major Roads
Country Capital
State Capital
District HQ
Other town

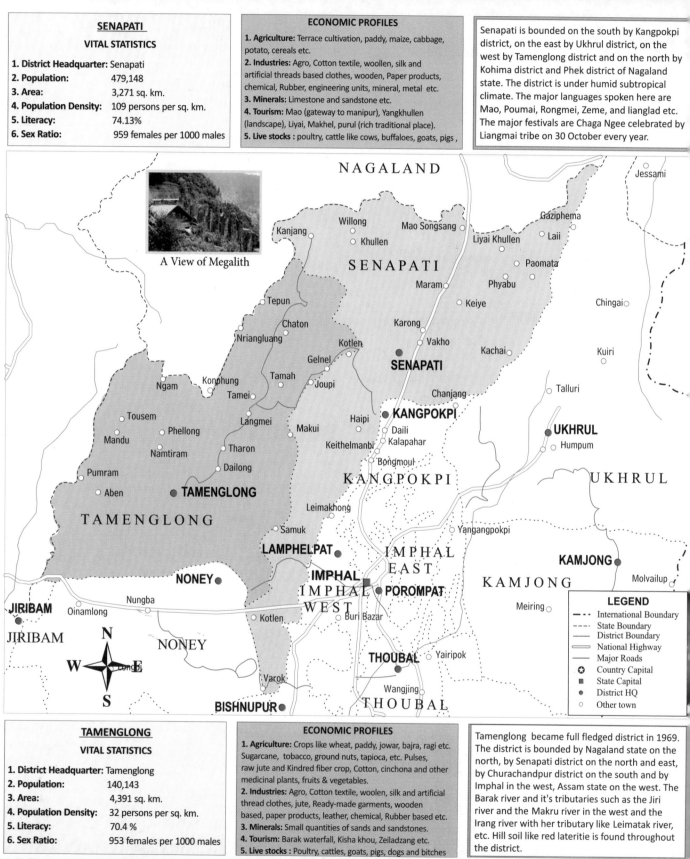

A View of Megalith

TAMENGLONG

VITAL STATISTICS

1. **District Headquarter:** Tamenglong
2. **Population:** 140,143
3. **Area:** 4,391 sq. km.
4. **Population Density:** 32 persons per sq. km.
5. **Literacy:** 70.4 %
6. **Sex Ratio:** 953 females per 1000 males

ECONOMIC PROFILES

1. **Agriculture:** Crops like wheat, paddy, jowar, bajra, ragi etc. Sugarcane, tobacco, ground nuts, tapioca, etc. Pulses, raw jute and Kindred fiber crop, Cotton, cinchona and other medicinal plants, fruits & vegetables.
2. **Industries:** Agro, Cotton textile, woolen, silk and artificial thread clothes, jute, Ready-made garments, wooden based, paper products, leather, chemical, Rubber based etc.
3. **Minerals:** Small quantities of sands and sandstones.
4. **Tourism:** Barak waterfall, Kisha khou, Zeiladzang etc.
5. **Live stocks :** Poultry, cattles, goats, pigs, dogs and bitches

Tamenglong became full fledged district in 1969. The district is bounded by Nagaland state on the north, by Senapati district on the north and east, by Churachandpur district on the south and by Imphal in the west, Assam state on the west. The Barak river and it's tributaries such as the Jiri river and the Makru river in the west and the Irang river with her tributary like Leimatak river, etc. Hill soil like red lateritie is found throughout the district.

Projection: Lambert's Conical Orthomorphic

1000 0 1000 2000 km

JIRIBAM

VITAL STATISTICS

1. **District Headquarter:** Jiribam
2. **Population:** 43,818
3. **Area:** 232 sq. km.
4. **Population Density:** 190 persons per sq. km.
5. **Literacy:** 73 %
6. **Sex Ratio:** 920 females per 1000 males

ECONOMIC PROFILES

1. **Agriculture:** Rice, paddy, etc. Tea, rubber etc.
2. **Industries:** Tailoring, watch repairing, automobile workshop, embroidery and knitting, jewellery works, bamboo and cane work, Rice milling, carpentry works etc.
3. **Minerals:** N/A
4. **Tourism:** Manipur zoo, Manipur state museum, saheed Minar, Mankhan pinic spot, Matai garden etc.
5. **Live stocks :** Poultry, dairy farming, cattles like cows, buffaloes etc. goats, sheep, dogs and bitches, pigs etc.

Jiribam is inhabitated by various tribal communities, such as the Meiteis, Pangals, Nagas, Thado U-kuki, Kabui, bengalis, and hmars. The majority of the people in jiribam are Meiteis. At the beginning of the 19th century, several tribes and religious groups began to migrate to the area along the jiri river. During this era Jiribam was a major trade center. Short Winters and long summers with heavy rainfall.

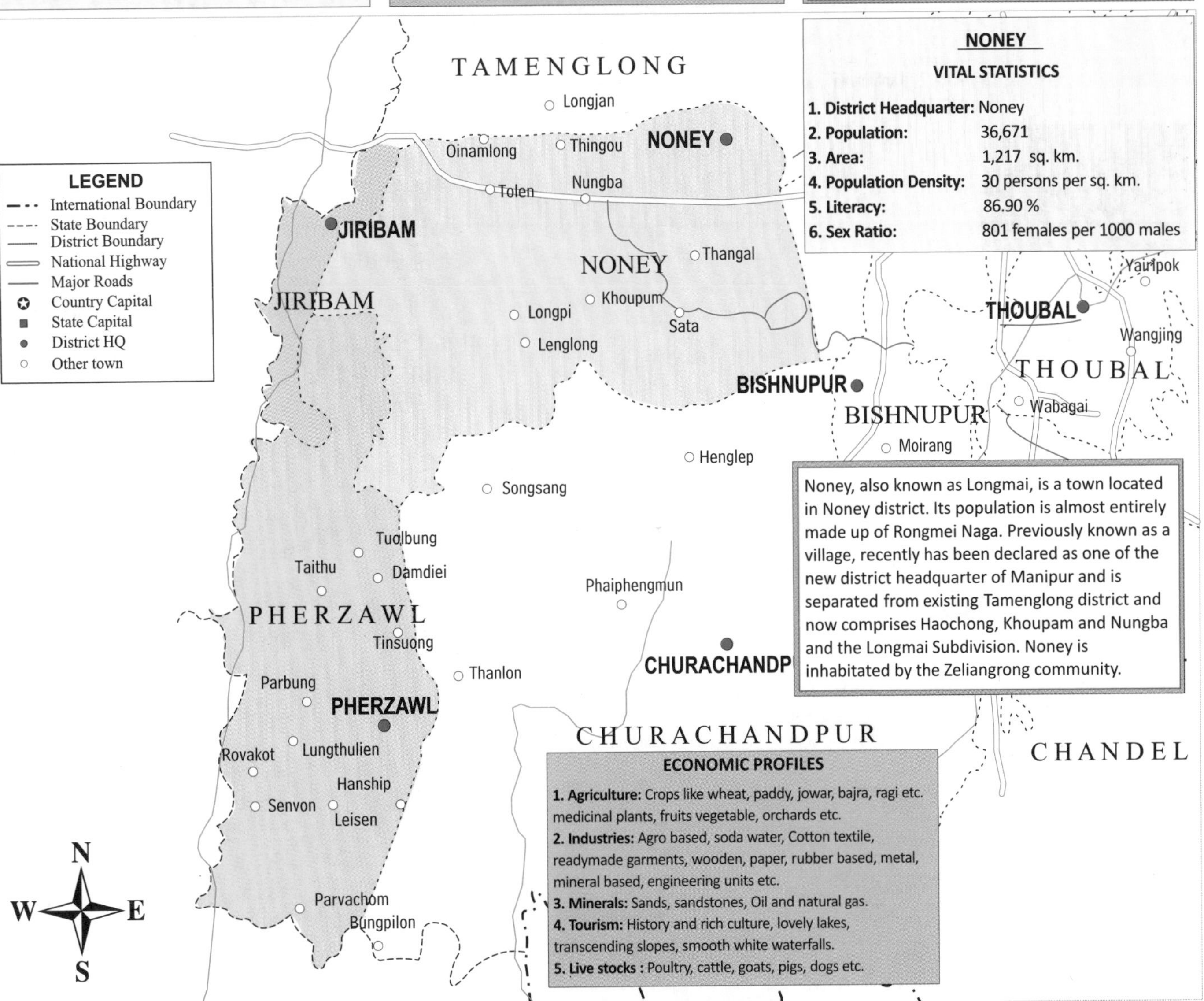

TAMENGLONG
Longjan
Oinamlong
Thingou
NONEY
Tolen
Nungba
JIRIBAM
NONEY
Thangal
Khoupum
Sata
Longpi
Lenglong
JIRIBAM
BISHNUPUR
BISHNUPUR
Moirang
Henglep
Songsang
THOUBAL
Yairipok
Wangjing
THOUBAL
Wabagai
LEGEND
International Boundary
State Boundary
District Boundary
National Highway
Major Roads
Country Capital
State Capital
District HQ
Other town
Tuolbung
Taithu
Damdiei
PHERZAWL
Tinsuong
Phaiphengmun
Parbung
Thanlon
PHERZAWL
CHURACHANDPUR
CHURACHANDPUR
CHANDEL
Rovakot
Lungthulien
Hanship
Senvon
Leisen
Parvachom
Bungpilon
N
W
E
S

NONEY

VITAL STATISTICS

1. **District Headquarter:** Noney
2. **Population:** 36,671
3. **Area:** 1,217 sq. km.
4. **Population Density:** 30 persons per sq. km.
5. **Literacy:** 86.90 %
6. **Sex Ratio:** 801 females per 1000 males

Noney, also known as Longmai, is a town located in Noney district. Its population is almost entirely made up of Rongmei Naga. Previously known as a village, recently has been declared as one of the new district headquarter of Manipur and is separated from existing Tamenglong district and now comprises Haochong, Khoupam and Nungba and the Longmai Subdivision. Noney is inhabitated by the Zeliangrong community.

ECONOMIC PROFILES

1. **Agriculture:** Crops like wheat, paddy, jowar, bajra, ragi etc. medicinal plants, fruits vegetable, orchards etc.
2. **Industries:** Agro based, soda water, Cotton textile, readymade garments, wooden, paper, rubber based, metal, mineral based, engineering units etc.
3. **Minerals:** Sands, sandstones, Oil and natural gas.
4. **Tourism:** History and rich culture, lovely lakes, transcending slopes, smooth white waterfalls.
5. **Live stocks :** Poultry, cattle, goats, pigs, dogs etc.

PHERZAWL

VITAL STATISTICS

1. **District Headquarter:** Pherzawl
2. **Population:** 47,250
3. **Area:** 2,285 sq. km.
4. **Population Density:** 20.68 persons per sq. km.
5. **Literacy:** 79 %
6. **Sex Ratio:** 947 females per 1000 males

ECONOMIC PROFILES

1. **Agriculture:** Crops like Rice, Maize and Ginger etc.Jhum cultivation is practiced.
2. **Industries:** Agro based, Cotton textile, jute based, ready-made garments, leather based, repairing and servicing etc.
3. **Minerals:** N/A
4. **Tourism:** Village Greenery locations.
5. **Live stocks :** Poultry, cattle like cows, buffaloes, goats, sheep, dogs and bitches and pigs etc.

Pherzawl is a District of Manipur state in India. It is bounded on the east by Churachandpur District, on the North by Tamenglong District, on the west by the Cachar District of Assam and on the South by Sinlung hills, Mizoram. Pherzawl District came into existence on 8 December 2016. The soil is moderately fertile with clay loam soil. About 80% of the land area is covered by forest while the remaining 20% is utilized for cultivation.

Scale - 1:1.73 M approx

BISHNUPUR & CHURACHANDPUR

BISHNUPUR

VITAL STATISTICS

1. District Headquarter:	Bishnupur
2. Population:	240,363
3. Area:	496 sq. km.
4. Population Density:	485 persons per sq. km.
5. Literacy:	76.35 %
6. Sex Ratio:	1000 females per 1000 males

ECONOMIC PROFILES

1. **Agriculture:** Crops like Rice, potato, cabbage, Brinjal and tomato etc.
2. **Industries:** Agro-based, Forest based, Sericulture, Textile, Engineering etc.
3. **Minerals:** Stone deposit and quarries Found.
4. **Tourism:** Rasmancha, Lalji temple, Susunia hill, Jorebangla temple, Biharinath hill, Joyrambati etc.
5. **Live stocks :** Poultry, hatchery and processing, Dairy farming, milk products.

Bishnupur name is derived from a Vishnu temple located at Lomangdong. Primary language spoken is Meiteilon. Other languages spoken include Bishnupriya Manipuri, Aimol a sino-Tibetan tongue with less than 3000 speakers. Keibul Lamjao N.P. has an area of 40km^2. The District is divided into 3 subdivisions: Bishnupur, Nambol, Moirang. The district enjoys monsoon type climate here with pleasant climate throughout the year.

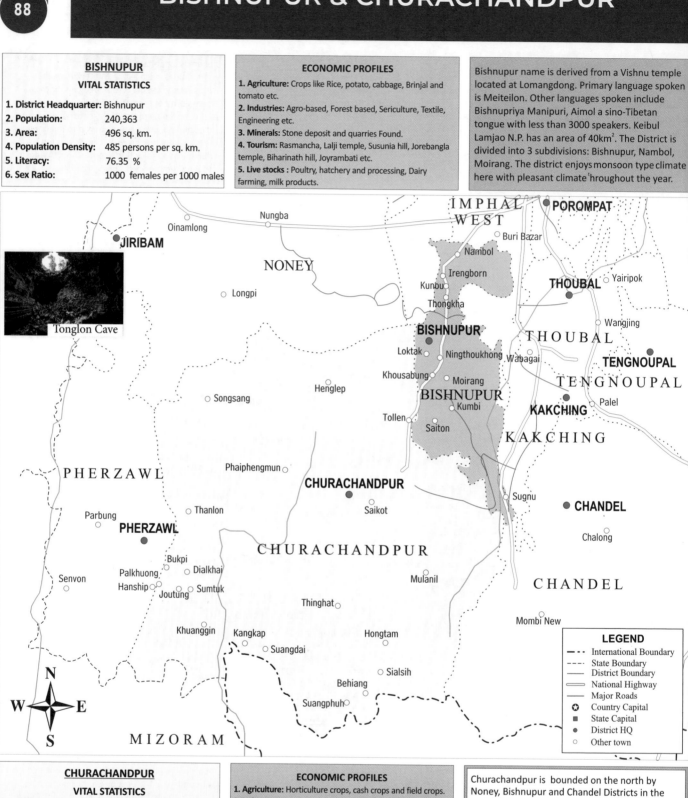

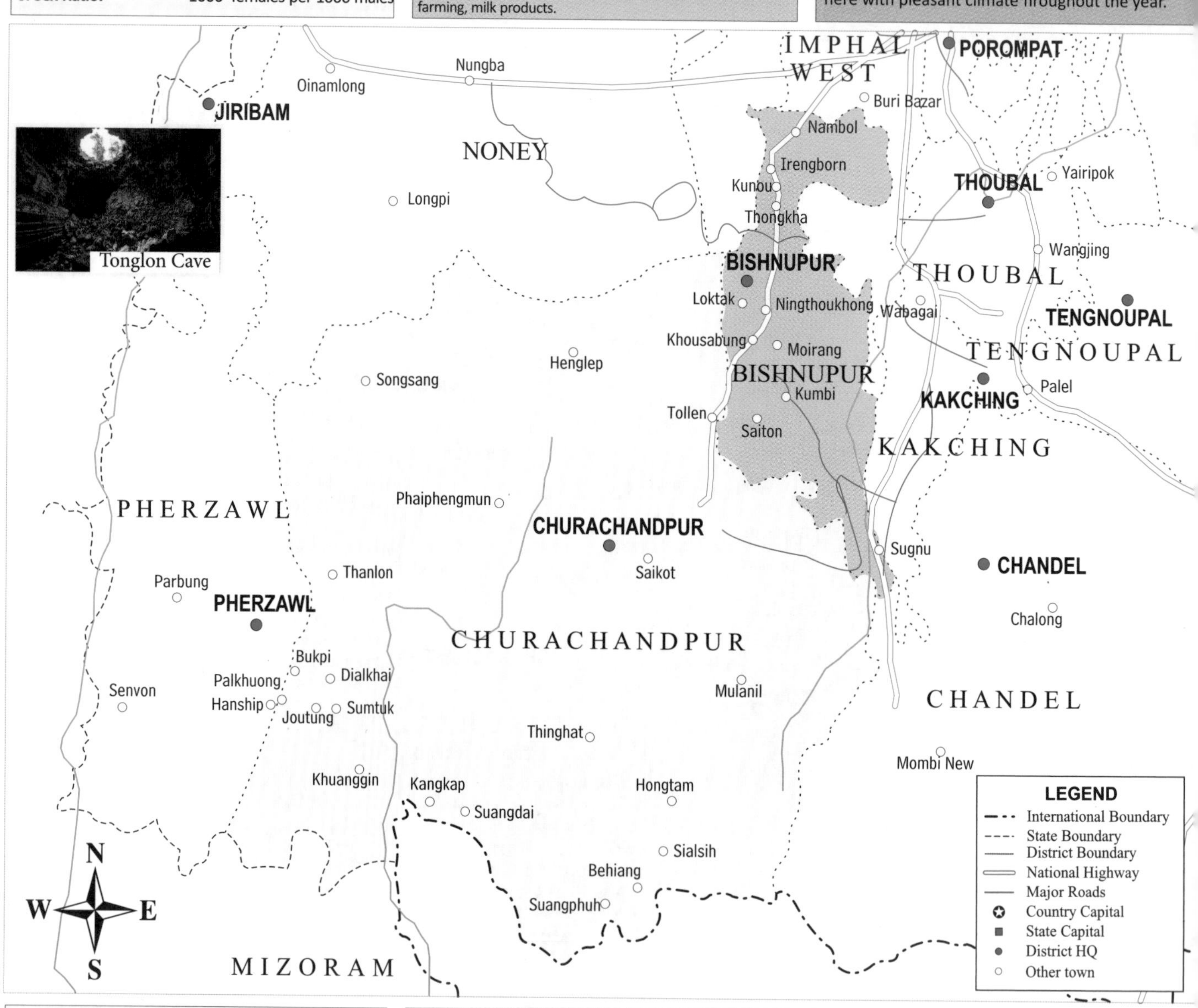
IMPHAL WEST
POROMPAT
Nungba
Oinamlong
JIRIBAM
Buri Bazar
Nambol
NONEY
Irengborn
Kunou
THOUBAL
Yairipok
Longpi
Thongkha
Tonglon Cave
Wangjing
BISHNUPUR
THOUBAL
Loktak
Ningthoukhong
Wabagai
TENGNOUPAL
Khousabung
Moirang
TENGNOUPAL
Henglep
Songsang
BISHNUPUR
Kumbi
Palel
KAKCHING
Tollen
Saiton
KAKCHING
Phaiphengmun
PHERZAWL
CHURACHANDPUR
Sugnu
Saikot
CHANDEL
Thanlon
Parbung
PHERZAWL
Chalong
CHURACHANDPUR
Bukpi
Palkhuong
Dialkhai
Senvon
Hanship
Sumtuk
Joutung
Mulanil
CHANDEL
Thinghat
Mombi New
Khuanggin
Kangkap
Hongtam
Suangdai
Sialsih
Behiang
Suangphuh
MIZORAM
N
W
E
S
LEGEND
International Boundary
State Boundary
District Boundary
National Highway
Major Roads
Country Capital
State Capital
District HQ
Other town

CHURACHANDPUR

VITAL STATISTICS

1. District Headquarter:	Churachandpur
2. Population:	271,274
3. Area:	4,570 sq. km.
4. Population Density:	59 persons per sq. km.
5. Literacy:	84.29 %
6. Sex Ratio:	969 females per 1000 males

ECONOMIC PROFILES

1. **Agriculture:** Horticulture crops, cash crops and field crops.
2. **Industries:** Agro based, soda water, paper products, Rubber based, mineral based, metal based etc.
3. **Minerals:** Deposits of lignite.
4. **Tourism:** Khuga dam, Ngaloi, Tipaimukh, Tribal museum and Tonglon caves etc.
5. **Live stocks :** Poultry, cows, buffaloes, goats, pigs, Dogs and bitches etc. Dairy farming and milk products etc.

Churachandpur is bounded on the north by Noney, Bishnupur and Chandel Districts in the east, Mizoram state in the south, Pherzawl in the west. The District is divided into 3 hilly regions: western hilly region, Eastern hilly region, and southern hilly region based on geology, soils, topography, climate, and natural vegetation. The District is drained by two rivers system: The barak and the Manipur river system.

Scale - 1:68 M approx

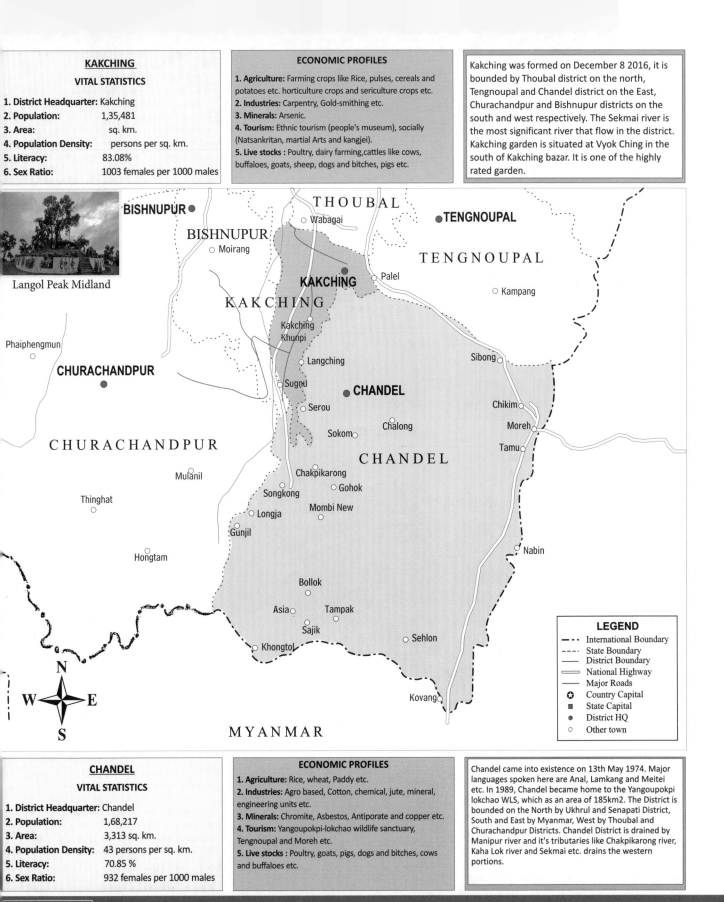

KAKCHING

VITAL STATISTICS

1. **District Headquarter:** Kakching
2. **Population:** 1,35,481
3. **Area:** sq. km.
4. **Population Density:** persons per sq. km.
5. **Literacy:** 83.08%
6. **Sex Ratio:** 1003 females per 1000 males

ECONOMIC PROFILES

1. **Agriculture:** Farming crops like Rice, pulses, cereals and potatoes etc. horticulture crops and sericulture crops etc.
2. **Industries:** Carpentry, Gold-smithing etc.
3. **Minerals:** Arsenic.
4. **Tourism:** Ethnic tourism (people's museum), socially (Natsankritan, martial Arts and kangjei).
5. **Live stocks :** Poultry, dairy farming,cattles like cows, buffaloes, goats, sheep, dogs and bitches, pigs etc.

Kakching was formed on December 8 2016, it is bounded by Thoubal district on the north, Tengnoupal and Chandel district on the East, Churachandpur and Bishnupur districts on the south and west respectively. The Sekmai river is the most significant river that flow in the district. Kakching garden is situated at Vyok Ching in the south of Kakching bazar. It is one of the highly rated garden.

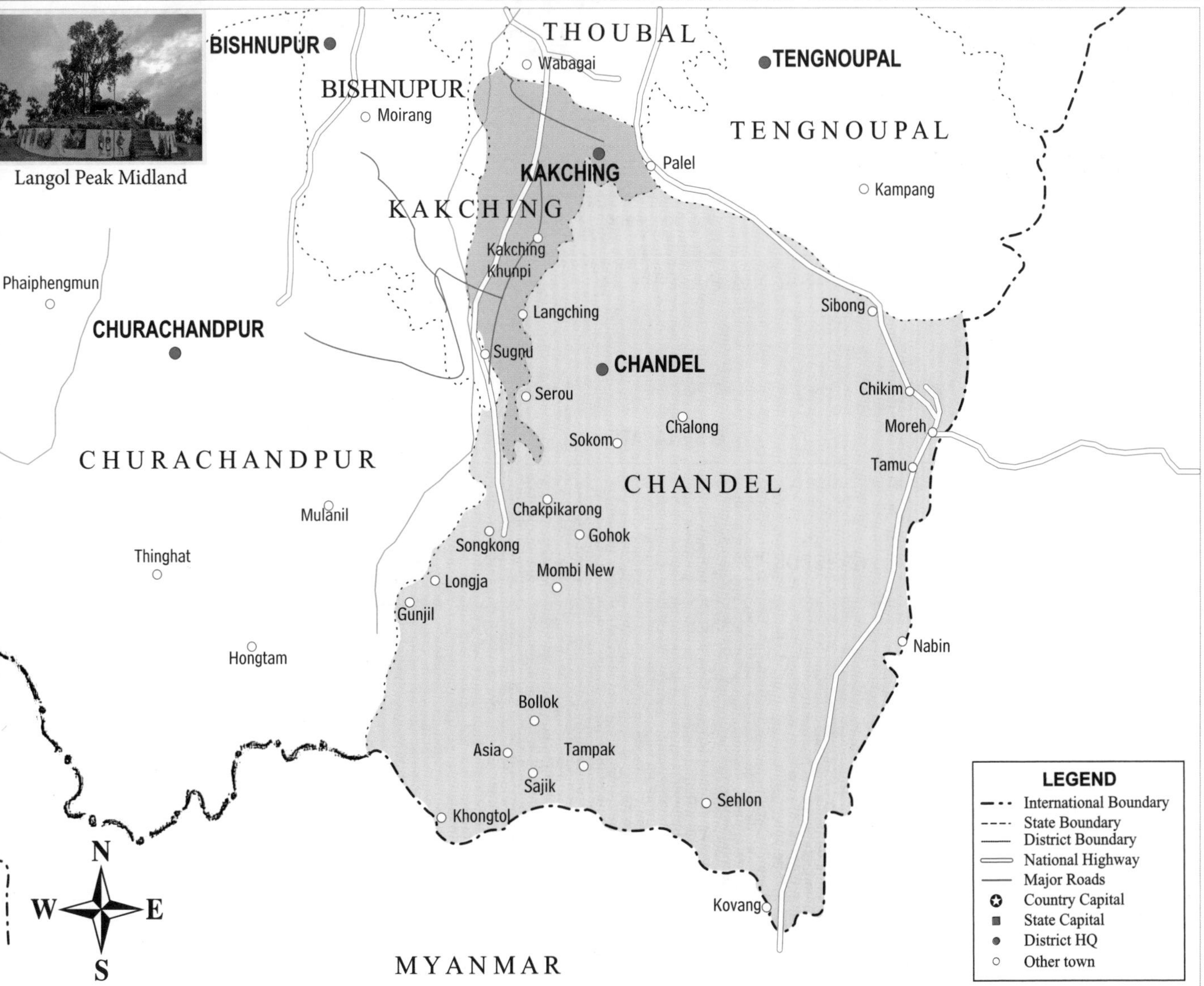

Langol Peak Midland
BISHNUPUR
THOUBAL
TENGNOUPAL
Wabagai
BISHNUPUR
Moirang
TENGNOUPAL
KAKCHING
Palel
Kampang
KAKCHING
Kakching Khunpi
Phaiphengmun
Langching
Sibong
CHURACHANDPUR
Sugnu
CHANDEL
Serou
Chikim
Chalong
Moreh
Sokom
Tamu
CHURACHANDPUR
CHANDEL
Mulanil
Chakpikarong
Gohok
Songkong
Thinghat
Mombi New
Longja
Gunjil
Nabin
Hongtam
Bollok
Asia
Tampak
Sajik
Sehlon
Khongtol
N
W
E
S
Kovang
MYANMAR
LEGEND
International Boundary
State Boundary
District Boundary
National Highway
Major Roads
Country Capital
State Capital
District HQ
Other town

CHANDEL

VITAL STATISTICS

1. **District Headquarter:** Chandel
2. **Population:** 1,68,217
3. **Area:** 3,313 sq. km.
4. **Population Density:** 43 persons per sq. km.
5. **Literacy:** 70.85 %
6. **Sex Ratio:** 932 females per 1000 males

ECONOMIC PROFILES

1. **Agriculture:** Rice, wheat, Paddy etc.
2. **Industries:** Agro based, Cotton, chemical, jute, mineral, engineering units etc.
3. **Minerals:** Chromite, Asbestos, Antiporate and copper etc.
4. **Tourism:** Yangoupokpi-lokchao wildlife sanctuary, Tengnoupal and Moreh etc.
5. **Live stocks :** Poultry, goats, pigs, dogs and bitches, cows and buffaloes etc.

Chandel came into existence on 13th May 1974. Major languages spoken here are Anal, Lamkang and Meitei etc. In 1989, Chandel became home to the Yangoupokpi lokchao WLS, which as an area of 185km2. The District is bounded on the North by Ukhrul and Senapati District, South and East by Myanmar, West by Thoubal and Churachandpur Districts. Chandel District is drained by Manipur river and it's tributaries like Chakpikarong river, Kaha Lok river and Sekmai etc. drains the western portions.

Scale - 1:0.62 M approx

KANGPOKPI

VITAL STATISTICS

1. **District Headquarter:** Kangpokpi
2. **Population:** 1,93,744 km.
3. **Area:** 1,698 sq. km.
4. **Population Density:** 114 inhabitants per sq. km.
5. **Literacy:** 83 %
6. **Sex Ratio:** 989 females per 1000 males

ECONOMIC PROFILES

1. **Agriculture:** terrace cultivation and Jhum cultivation is is practiced.The Major crops are paddy, maize, Cotton,jute,
2. **Industries:**Agro based, chemical based,mineral based,metal based, Cotton textile, carpentry, blacksmith,
3. **Minerals:**Limestone and Sandstone etc.
4. **Tourism:** Dzuko Valley and Dzuko Lilly etc.
5. **Live stocks :**poultry, cattle like cows, buffaloes, ducks, pigs, dogs and bitches, goats etc.fish and dairy farming.

Kangpokpi District is a district in the Indian state of Manipur created in December 2016 by bifurcating the former Senapati district in the Sadar hills region.The district bounded on the north by Senapati district, south by Imphal east, east by Kamjong and on the west by Lamphelpat etc. In Kangpokpi district, the climate is warm and temparate. In winter, there is much less rainfall in Kangpokpi than in summer.

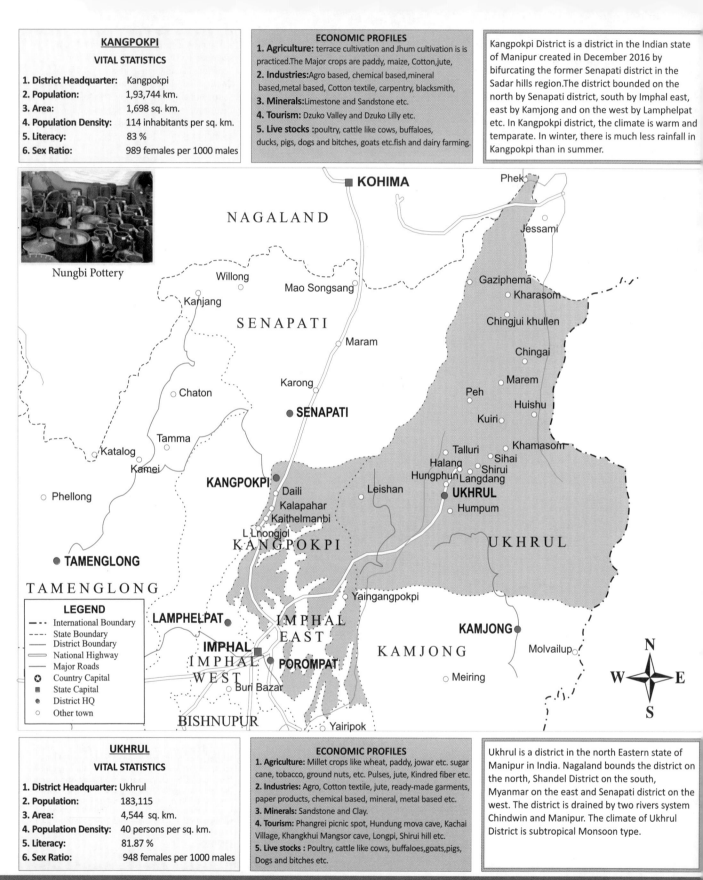

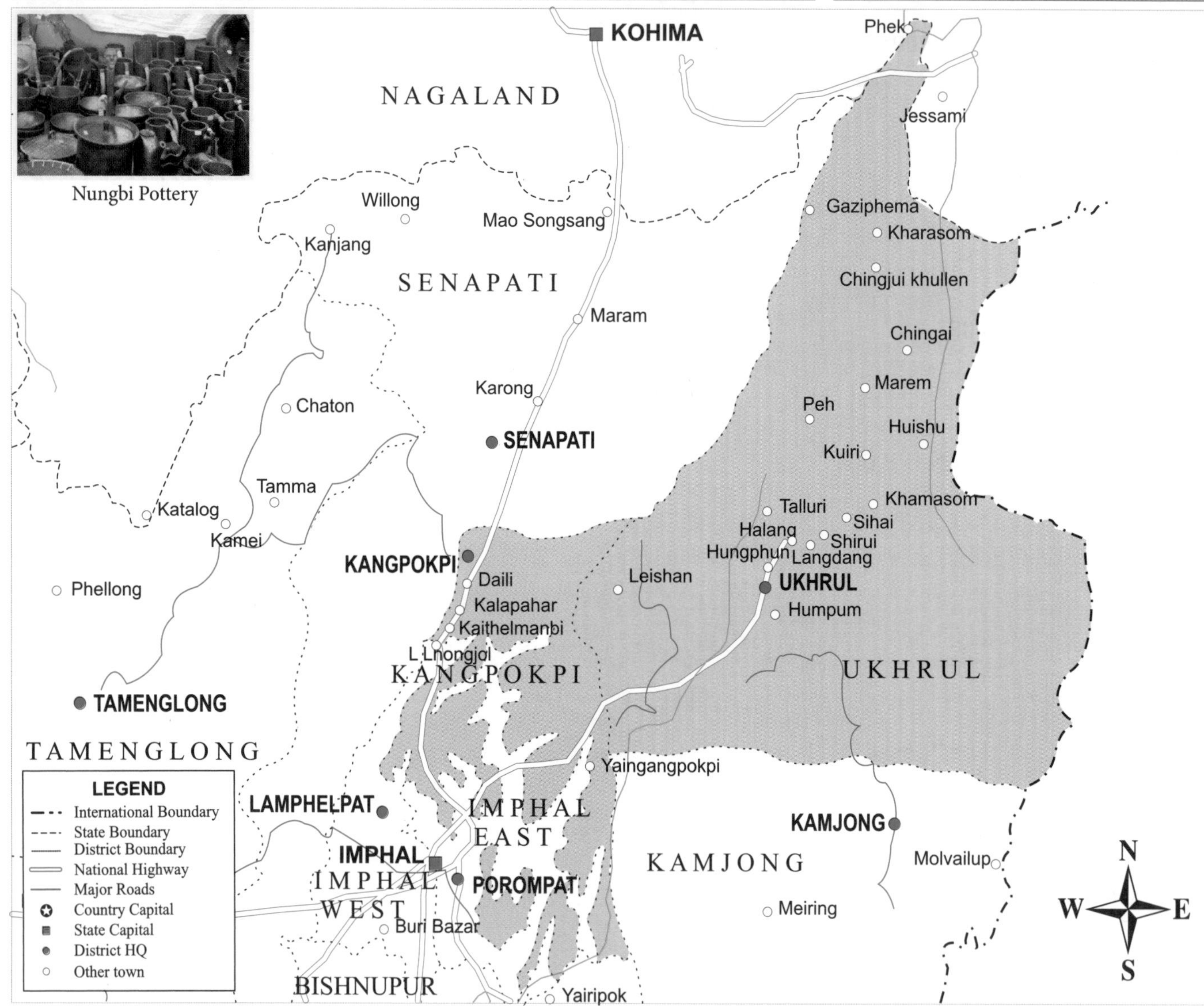
Nungbi Pottery
KOHIMA
Phek
NAGALAND
Jessami
Willong
Mao Songsang
Kanjang
Gaziphema
Kharasom
SENAPATI
Chingjui khullen
Maram
Chingai
Marem
Karong
Peh
Chaton
Huishu
SENAPATI
Kuiri
Tamma
Talluri
Khamasom
Katalog
Halang
Sihai
Kamei
Shirui
Hungphun
Langdang
KANGPOKPI
Daili
Leishan
UKHRUL
Phellong
Kalapahar
Humpum
Kaithelmanbi
L Lhongjol
KANGPOKPI
UKHRUL
TAMENGLONG
TAMENGLONG
Yaingangpokpi
LEGEND
International Boundary
State Boundary
District Boundary
National Highway
Major Roads
Country Capital
State Capital
District HQ
Other town
LAMPHELPAT
IMPHAL EAST
KAMJONG
IMPHAL
Molvailup
KAMJONG
IMPHAL WEST
POROMPAT
Meiring
Buri Bazar
BISHNUPUR
Yairipok
N
W
E
S

UKHRUL

VITAL STATISTICS

1. **District Headquarter:** Ukhrul
2. **Population:** 183,115
3. **Area:** 4,544 sq. km.
4. **Population Density:** 40 persons per sq. km.
5. **Literacy:** 81.87 %
6. **Sex Ratio:** 948 females per 1000 males

ECONOMIC PROFILES

1. **Agriculture:** Millet crops like wheat, paddy, jowar etc. sugar cane, tobacco, ground nuts, etc. Pulses, jute, Kindred fiber etc.
2. **Industries:** Agro, Cotton textile, jute, ready-made garments, paper products, chemical based, mineral, metal based etc.
3. **Minerals:** Sandstone and Clay.
4. **Tourism:** Phangrei picnic spot, Hundung mova cave, Kachai Village, Khangkhui Mangsor cave, Longpi, Shirui hill etc.
5. **Live stocks :** Poultry, cattle like cows, buffaloes,goats,pigs, Dogs and bitches etc.

Ukhrul is a district in the north Eastern state of Manipur in India. Nagaland bounds the district on the north, Shandel District on the south, Myanmar on the east and Senapati district on the west. The district is drained by two rivers system Chindwin and Manipur. The climate of Ukhrul District is subtropical Monsoon type.

Scale - 1:0.8 M approx

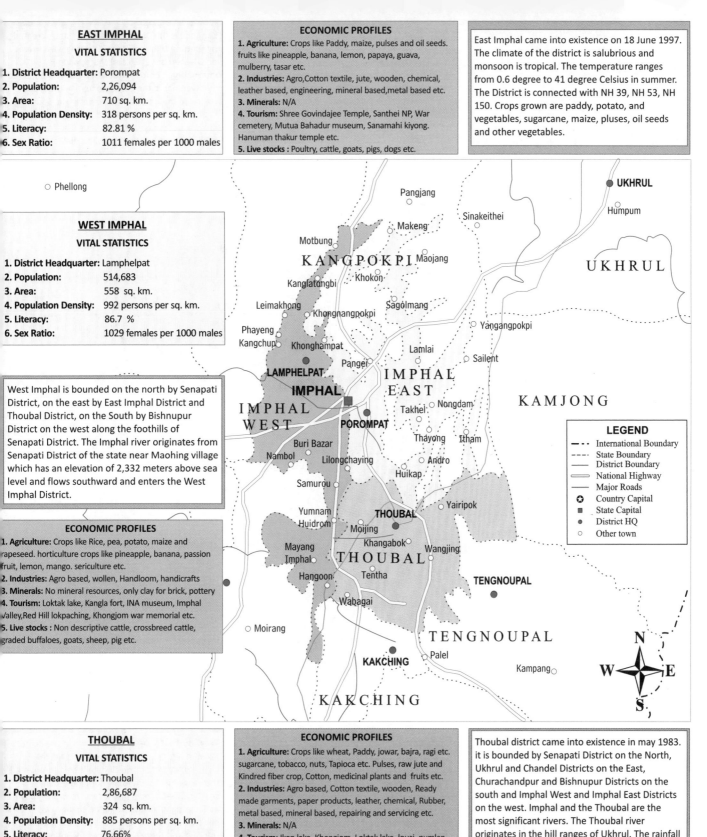

EAST IMPHAL

VITAL STATISTICS

1. **District Headquarter:** Porompat
2. **Population:** 2,26,094
3. **Area:** 710 sq. km.
4. **Population Density:** 318 persons per sq. km.
5. **Literacy:** 82.81 %
6. **Sex Ratio:** 1011 females per 1000 males

ECONOMIC PROFILES

1. **Agriculture:** Crops like Paddy, maize, pulses and oil seeds. fruits like pineapple, banana, lemon, papaya, guava, mulberry, tasar etc.
2. **Industries:** Agro,Cotton textile, jute, wooden, chemical, leather based, engineering, mineral based,metal based etc.
3. **Minerals:** N/A
4. **Tourism:** Shree Govindajee Temple, Santhei NP, War cemetery, Mutua Bahadur museum, Sanamahi kiyong. Hanuman thakur temple etc.
5. **Live stocks :** Poultry, cattle, goats, pigs, dogs etc.

East Imphal came into existence on 18 June 1997. The climate of the district is salubrious and monsoon is tropical. The temperature ranges from 0.6 degree to 41 degree Celsius in summer. The District is connected with NH 39, NH 53, NH 150. Crops grown are paddy, potato, and vegetables, sugarcane, maize, pluses, oil seeds and other vegetables.

WEST IMPHAL

VITAL STATISTICS

1. **District Headquarter:** Lamphelpat
2. **Population:** 514,683
3. **Area:** 558 sq. km.
4. **Population Density:** 992 persons per sq. km.
5. **Literacy:** 86.7 %
6. **Sex Ratio:** 1029 females per 1000 males

West Imphal is bounded on the north by Senapati District, on the east by East Imphal District and Thoubal District, on the South by Bishnupur District on the west along the foothills of Senapati District. The Imphal river originates from Senapati District of the state near Maohing village which has an elevation of 2,332 meters above sea level and flows southward and enters the West Imphal District.

ECONOMIC PROFILES

1. **Agriculture:** Crops like Rice, pea, potato, maize and rapeseed. horticulture crops like pineapple, banana, passion fruit, lemon, mango. sericulture etc.
2. **Industries:** Agro based, wollen, Handloom, handicrafts
3. **Minerals:** No mineral resources, only clay for brick, pottery
4. **Tourism:** Loktak lake, Kangla fort, INA museum, Imphal Valley,Red Hill lokpaching, Khongjom war memorial etc.
5. **Live stocks :** Non descriptive cattle, crossbreed cattle, graded buffaloes, goats, sheep, pig etc.

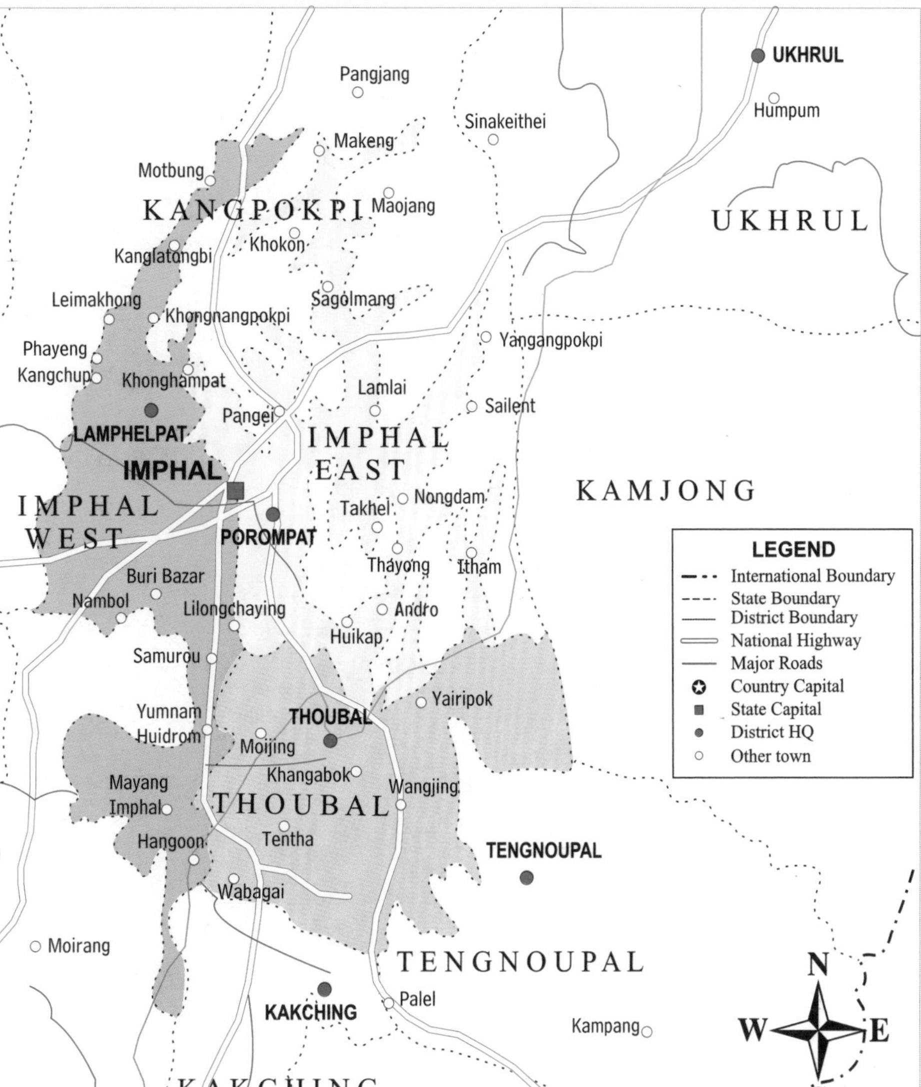

Phellong
Pangjang
UKHRUL
Humpum
Sinakeithei
Makeng
Motbung
KANGPOKPI
Maojang
UKHRUL
Kanglatongbi
Khokon
Sagolmang
Leimakhong
Khongnangpokpi
Yangangpokpi
Phayeng
Kangchup
Khonghampat
Lamlai
Sailent
LAMPHELPAT
Pangei
IMPHAL EAST
IMPHAL
IMPHAL WEST
KAMJONG
Takhel
Nongdam
POROMPAT
Thayong
Itham
Buri Bazar
Nambol
Lilongchaying
Andro
Huikap
Samurou
Yairipok
Yumnam Huidrom
THOUBAL
Moijing
Khangabok
Mayang Imphal
Wangjing
THOUBAL
Hangoon
Tentha
TENGNOUPAL
Wabagai
Moirang
TENGNOUPAL
KAKCHING
Palel
Kampang
KAKCHING
LEGEND
International Boundary
State Boundary
District Boundary
National Highway
Major Roads
Country Capital
State Capital
District HQ
Other town
N
W
E
S

THOUBAL

VITAL STATISTICS

1. **District Headquarter:** Thoubal
2. **Population:** 2,86,687
3. **Area:** 324 sq. km.
4. **Population Density:** 885 persons per sq. km.
5. **Literacy:** 76.66%
6. **Sex Ratio:** 1002 females per 1000 males

ECONOMIC PROFILES

1. **Agriculture:** Crops like wheat, Paddy, jowar, bajra, ragi etc. sugarcane, tobacco, nuts, Tapioca etc. Pulses, raw jute and Kindred fiber crop, Cotton, medicinal plants and fruits etc.
2. **Industries:** Agro based, Cotton textile, wooden, Ready made garments, paper products, leather, chemical, Rubber, metal based, mineral based, repairing and servicing etc.
3. **Minerals:** N/A
4. **Tourism:** Ikop lake, Khongjom, Loktak lake, lousi, pumlen.
5. **Live stocks :** Poultry, cattle like cows, buffaloes, goats etc.

Thoubal district came into existence in may 1983. it is bounded by Senapati District on the North, Ukhrul and Chandel Districts on the East, Churachandpur and Bishnupur Districts on the south and Imphal West and Imphal East Districts on the west. Imphal and the Thoubal are the most significant rivers. The Thoubal river originates in the hill ranges of Ukhrul. The rainfall here starts in June and continue till September.

00 0 1000 2000 km.

Projection: Lambert's Conical Orthomorphic

KAMJONG

VITAL STATISTICS

1. **District Headquarter:** Kamjong
2. **Population:** 45,616
3. **Area:** 2000 sq. km.
4. **Population Density:** 23 persons per sq. km.
5. **Literacy:** 71.96 %
6. **Sex Ratio:** 903 females per 1000 males

ECONOMIC PROFILES

1. **Agriculture:** Crops like wheat, paddy, jowar, bajra ragi etc. medicinal herbs, fruits and vegetables etc.
2. **Industries:** Agro based, soda water, Cotton textile, woolen, silk products, paper products, leather based, chemical based, mineral based, metal based, engineering units, repairing and servicing etc.
3. **Minerals:** Limestone, chromite and sandstone etc.
4. **Tourism:** Ethnic and historical places.
5. **Live stocks :** Poultry, cattle like cows and buffaloes, goats, pigs, dogs and bitches etc.

Kamjong is the District in Manipur state, created by splitting Ukhrul district. Kamjong was created on 8 December 2016 and shares a long international border with Myanmar. It is bounded by Myanmar in the east, Senapati in the west, Ukhrul in the north and Chandel in the South. Kamjong District is inhabited by Tangkhul and Kukis tribes which are minorities. The Tangkhul tribe speaks more than hundred dialects.

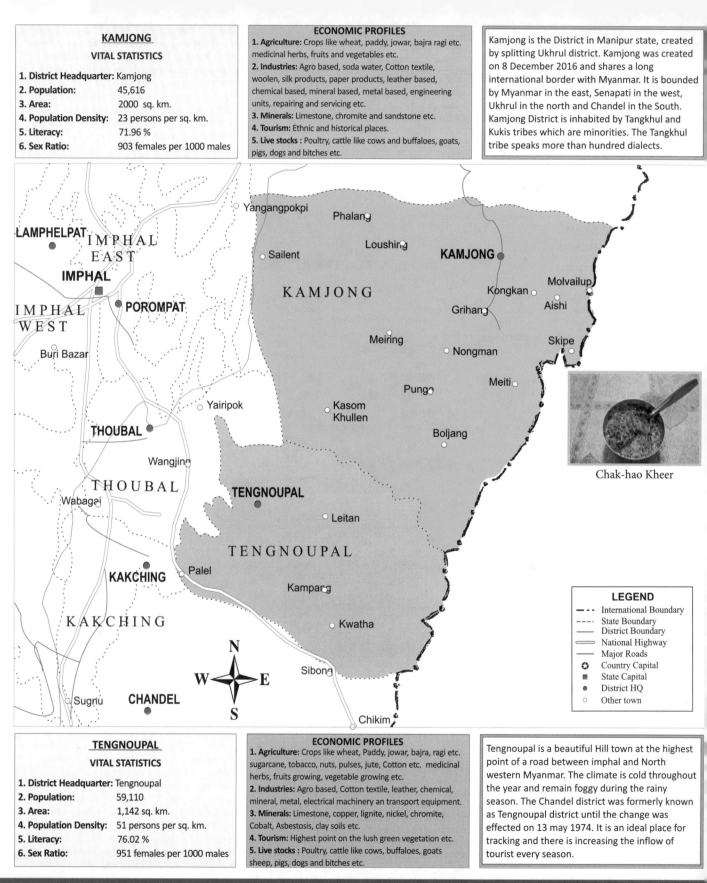

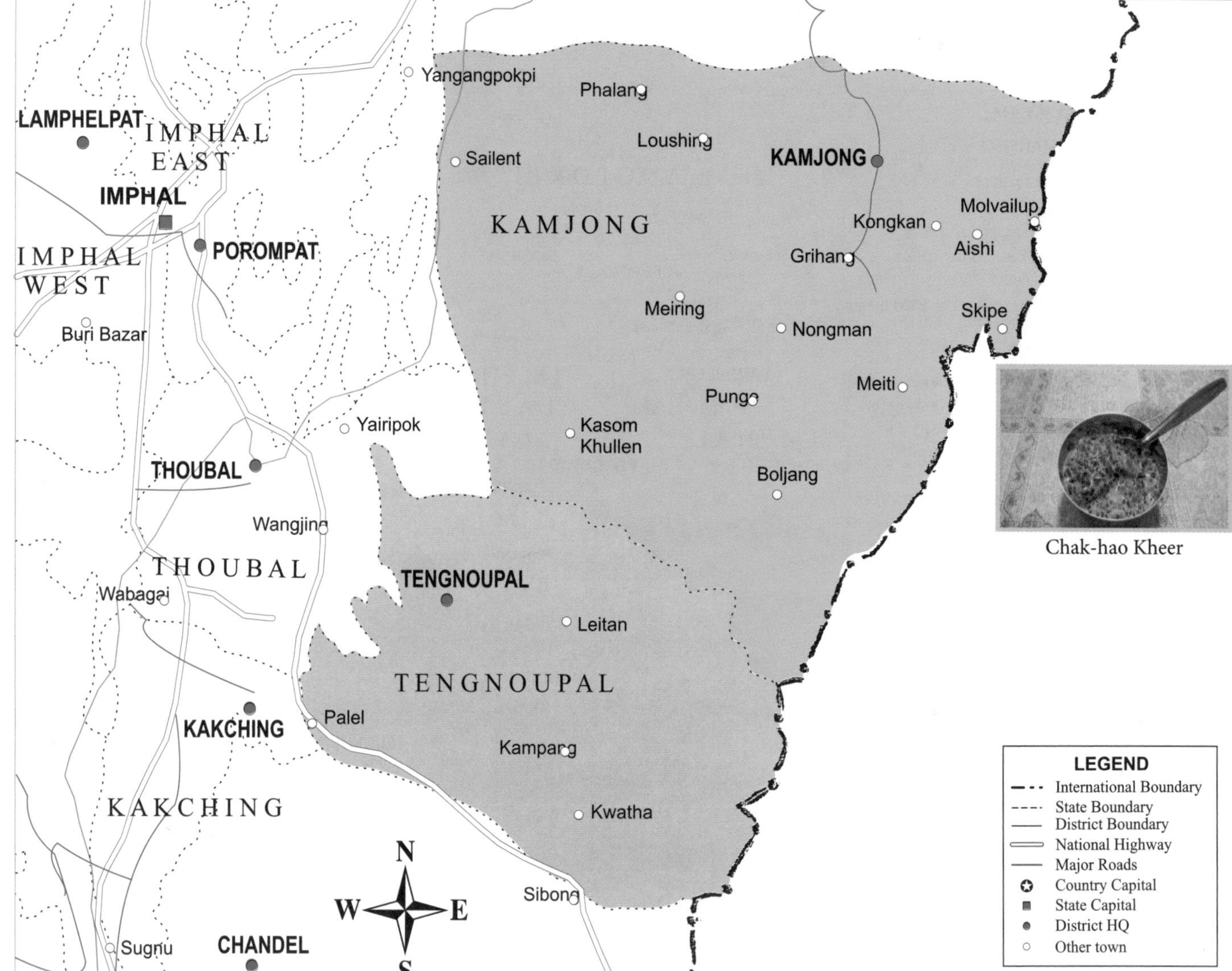
Yangangpokpi
Phalang
LAMPHELPAT
IMPHAL EAST
Loushing
Sailent
KAMJONG
IMPHAL
KAMJONG
Molvailup
Kongkan
IMPHAL WEST
POROMPAT
Grihang
Aishi
Meiring
Skipe
Buri Bazar
Nongman
Meiti
Pungo
Yairipok
Kasom Khullen
THOUBAL
Boljang
Wangjing
THOUBAL
TENGNOUPAL
Wabagai
Leitan
TENGNOUPAL
KAKCHING
Palel
Kampang
KAKCHING
Kwatha
N
W
E
S
Sibong
Sugnu
CHANDEL
Chikim
LEGEND
International Boundary
State Boundary
District Boundary
National Highway
Major Roads
Country Capital
State Capital
District HQ
Other town

Chak-hao Kheer

TENGNOUPAL

VITAL STATISTICS

1. **District Headquarter:** Tengnoupal
2. **Population:** 59,110
3. **Area:** 1,142 sq. km.
4. **Population Density:** 51 persons per sq. km.
5. **Literacy:** 76.02 %
6. **Sex Ratio:** 951 females per 1000 males

ECONOMIC PROFILES

1. **Agriculture:** Crops like wheat, Paddy, jowar, bajra, ragi etc. sugarcane, tobacco, nuts, pulses, jute, Cotton etc. medicinal herbs, fruits growing, vegetable growing etc.
2. **Industries:** Agro based, Cotton textile, leather, chemical, mineral, metal, electrical machinery an transport equipment.
3. **Minerals:** Limestone, copper, lignite, nickel, chromite, Cobalt, Asbestosis, clay soils etc.
4. **Tourism:** Highest point on the lush green vegetation etc.
5. **Live stocks :** Poultry, cattle like cows, buffaloes, goats sheep, pigs, dogs and bitches etc.

Tengnoupal is a beautiful Hill town at the highest point of a road between imphal and North western Myanmar. The climate is cold throughout the year and remain foggy during the rainy season. The Chandel district was formerly known as Tengnoupal district until the change was effected on 13 may 1974. It is an ideal place for tracking and there is increasing the inflow of tourist every season.

Scale - 1:0.53 M approx

MEGHALAYA

Section

POPULATION:	***29,64,007***	DISTRICTS: 8
AREA:	***22429 sq.km.***	L.S. CONSTITUENCY: ***2***
POP. DENSITY:	***132 persons/ Km^2***	R.S. CONSTITUENCY: ***1***
LITERACY:	***75.48%***	GRAM PANCHAYATS: ***N.A***
SEX RATIO:	***986 females/1000 males***	GSDP: ***30,790***

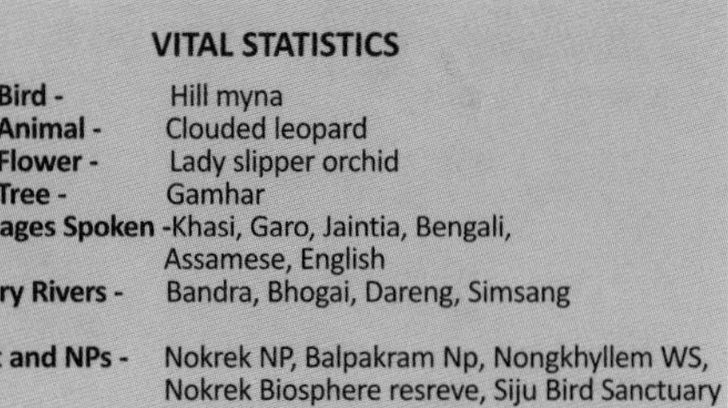

VITAL STATISTICS

1.State Bird - Hill myna
2.State Animal - Clouded leopard
3.State Flower - Lady slipper orchid
4.State Tree - Gamhar
5.Languages Spoken - Khasi, Garo, Jaintia, Bengali, Assamese, English
6.Primary Rivers - Bandra, Bhogai, Dareng, Simsang
7.Forest and NPs - Nokrek NP, Balpakram Np, Nongkhyllem WS, Nokrek Biosphere resreve, Siju Bird Sanctuary
8.Tribes - Khasis, Garos, Jaintias,hill tribes, Biates, Koch, Boro, Hajong, Dimasa, Kuki, Tiwa, Karbi etc.

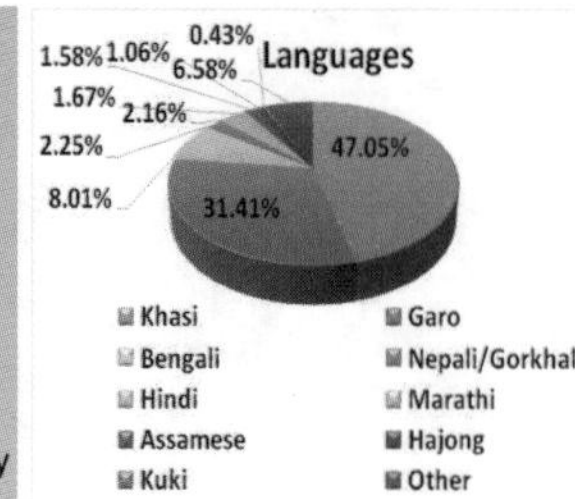
Languages
1.58%
1.06%
0.43%
6.58%
1.67%
2.16%
2.25%
8.01%
31.41%
47.05%
Khasi
Garo
Bengali
Nepali/Gorkhali
Hindi
Marathi
Assamese
Hajong
Kuki
Other

Meghalaya literally means the 'Abode of Clouds' and is essentially a hilly state. It is predominately inhabited by the tribal Khasis, Jaintias and Garos population. The Khas Hills and Jaintia Hills which from the central and eastern part of the state form an imposing plateau with rolling grassland, Hills and River Valleys. The Southern face of th plateau is marked by deep gorges and abrupt slopes, at the foot of which, a narrow strip of plain runs along the international border with Bangladesh.

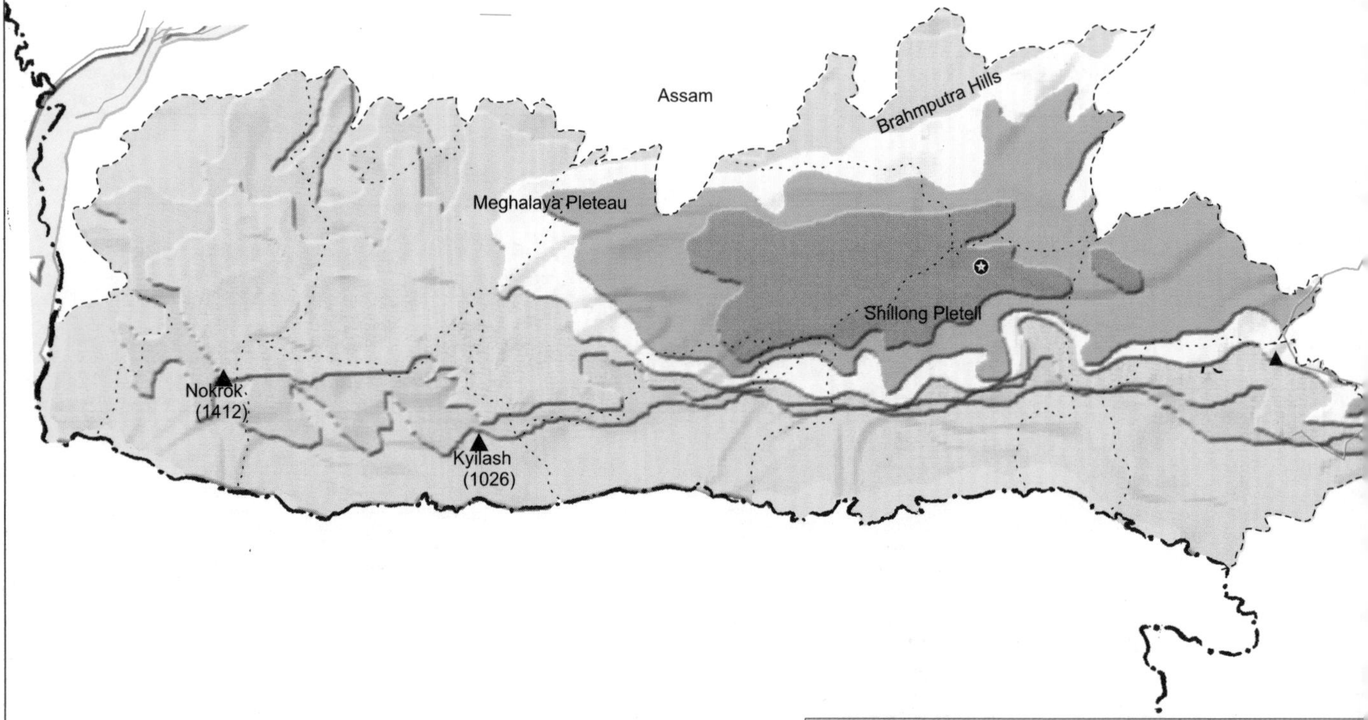

Assam
Brahmputra Hills
Meghalaya Pleteau
Shillong Pletell
Nokrok (1412)
Kyilash (1026)

Living root bridges in Meghalaya is a natural wonder of the world. These Bridges are made from rubber tree roots also known as Ficuselastica tree. Long ago, War-Khasis, a tribe of Meghalaya, used this tree to cross rivers. The villagers have created a root-guiding system that forces the tender roots of the rubber tree to grow straight. Such roots make a strong, living bridge in about 10-15 years.

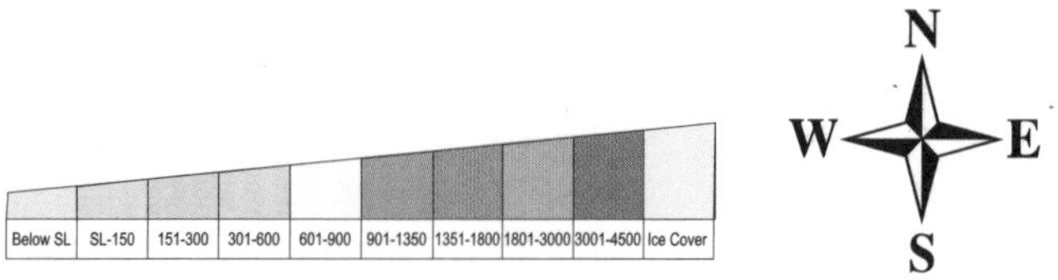

Below SL	SL-150	151-300	301-600	601-900	901-1350	1351-1800	1801-3000	3001-4500	Ice Cover

N
W
E
S

Scale - 1:1.62 M appr

VITAL STATISTICS

1.Capital	: Shillong
2.Date of Formation	: January 21,1972
3.Area (Km2)	: 22,429
4.Population	: 29,64,007
5.Density (/Km2)	: 132
6.Literacy Rate (%)	: 75.48
7.Sex Ratio	: 986
8.Total No. of Districts	: 11

Meghalaya was created as an autonomous state within the state of Assam in 1970. The full-fledged state of Meghalaya came into existence in 1972. It is bound on the north and east by Assam and on the south and west Bangladesh. Meghalaya is spread over an area of 22,429 square kilometers, and lies between 24°57' and 26°10 north latitude and 89°46' and 92°53' east longitude.

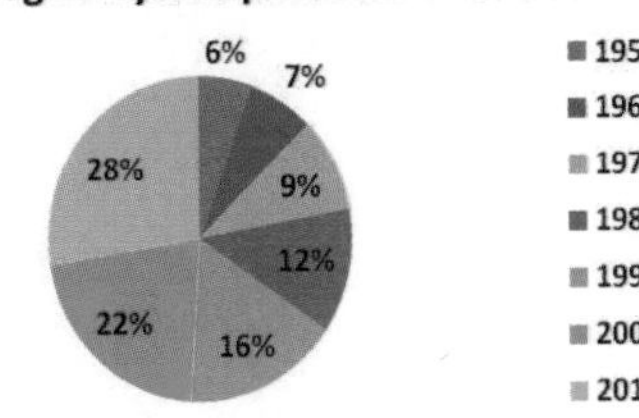

Meghalaya Population Growth
6%
7%
9%
12%
16%
22%
28%
1951
1961
1971
1981
1991
2001
2011

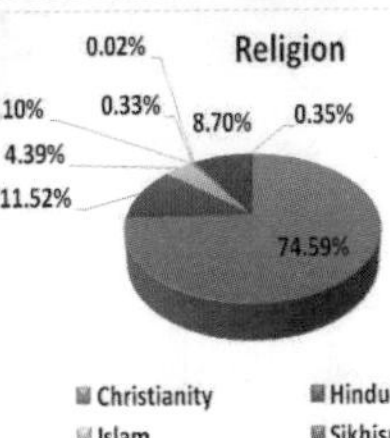

Religion
0.02%
0.33%
10%
4.39%
11.52%
8.70%
0.35%
74.59%
Christianity
Islam
Buddhism
Hinduism
Sikhism
Jainism

Dhubri
ASSAM
NORTH GARO HILLS
Phulbari Tikrikila Paham Rembigiri Balengdoba Resubelpara Dainadubi Bangsi
Rongmachokgiri Rongohugiri
WEST GARO HILLS
Garobadha Rongram Tura Songsak Cheran Dambu
EAST GARO HILLS
Rongrenggiri William Nagar
Ampati
SOUTH WEST GARO HILLS
Kherapara Ringkhap Songmong Chokpot Burengapara
SOUTH GARO HILLS
Baghmara Panikunda
Shallang Langpih Rambrai
WEST KHASI HILLS
Nongstoin Pambriew Mawkyrwat Jarem Phlangdiloin
SOUTH WEST KHASI HILLS
Barni Hat Margang
RI-BHOI
Nongpoh Donmatia Ksehkima Bazar Mawhati Umsning
Nongkhlaw Mairang Barapani SHILLONG Nongkrem
Mawphlang Laitlyngkoi Serrarim
EAST KHASI HILLS
Pynurela Mawsynram Cherrapunji Shella
ASSAM
Pamdkhar
WEST JAINTIA HILLS
Barato Jowai Shangpung Sohkyamphor Khliehriat Jarain Mopad
EAST JAINTIA HILLS
BANGLADESH

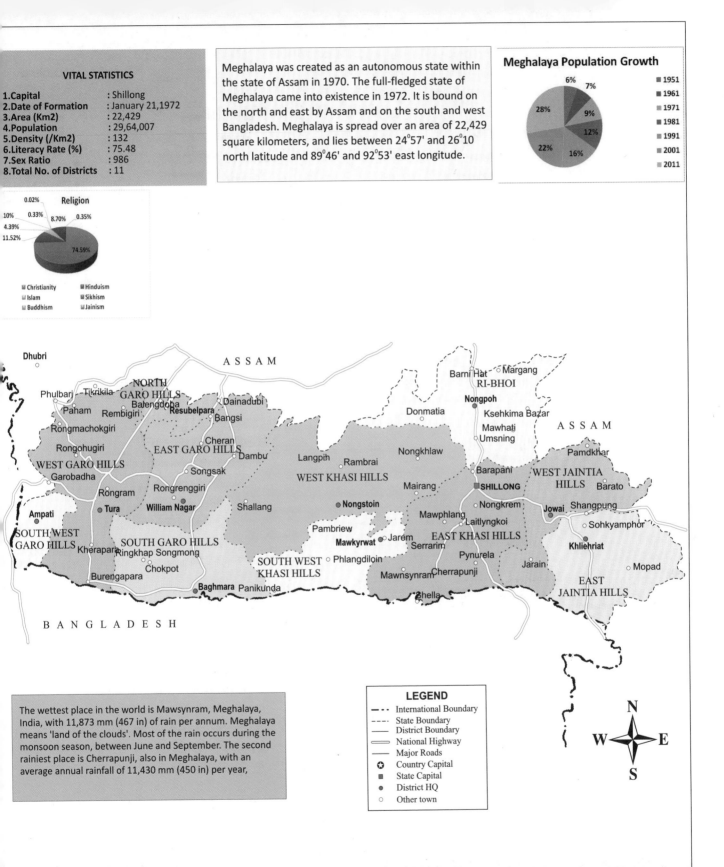

The wettest place in the world is Mawsynram, Meghalaya, India, with 11,873 mm (467 in) of rain per annum. Meghalaya means 'land of the clouds'. Most of the rain occurs during the monsoon season, between June and September. The second rainiest place is Cherrapunji, also in Meghalaya, with an average annual rainfall of 11,430 mm (450 in) per year,

LEGEND

- International Boundary
- State Boundary
- District Boundary
- National Highway
- Major Roads
- Country Capital
- State Capital
- District HQ
- Other town

N
W E
S

Scale - 1:1.62 M approx

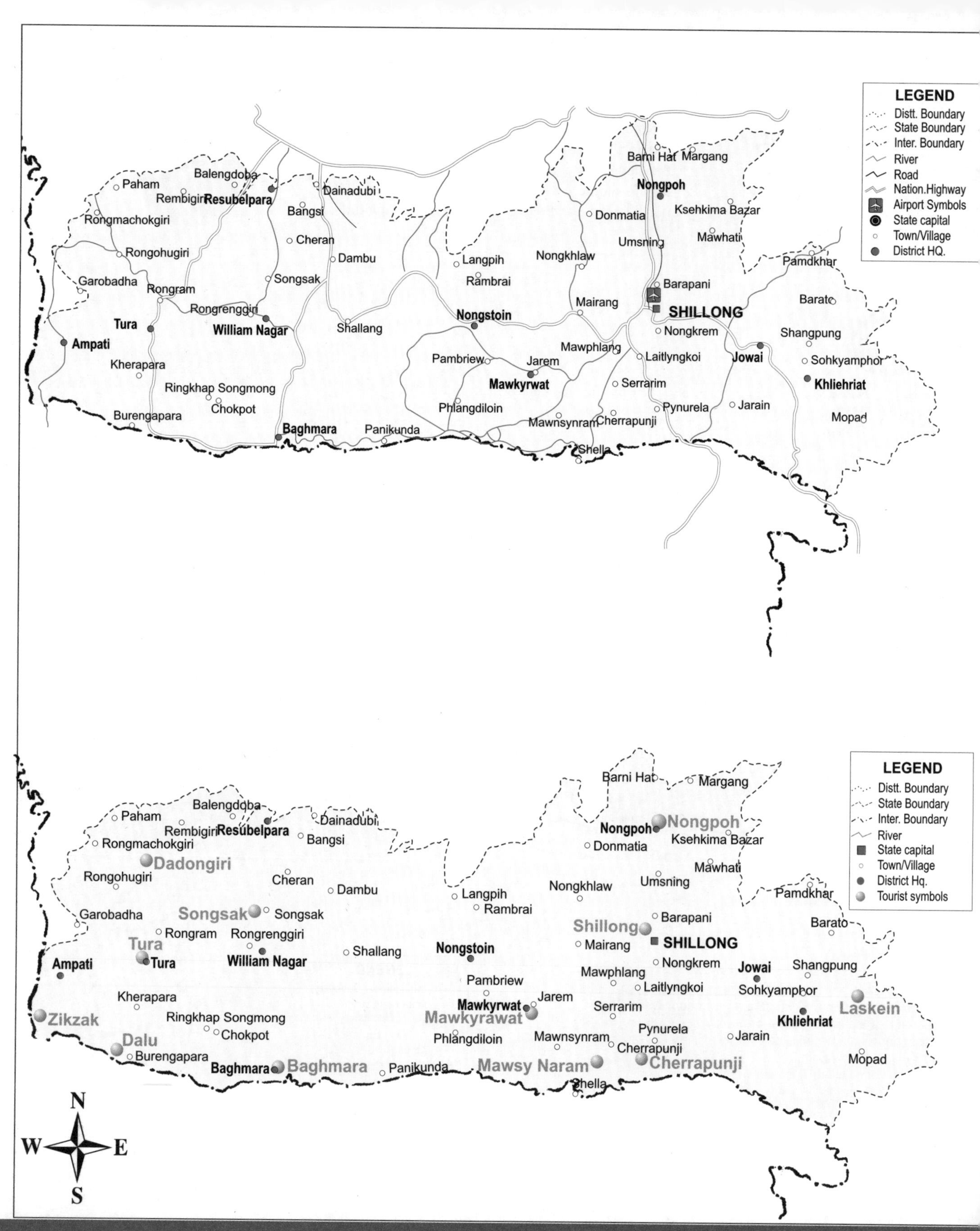
LEGEND
Distt. Boundary
State Boundary
Inter. Boundary
River
Road
Nation.Highway
Airport Symbols
State capital
Town/Village
District HQ.
Paham
Balengdoba
Rembigiri
Resubelpara
Dainadubi
Bangsi
Rongmachokgiri
Cheran
Dambu
Rongohugiri
Songsak
Garobadha
Rongram
Rongrenggiri
Tura
William Nagar
Shallang
Ampati
Kherapara
Ringkhap Songmong
Chokpot
Burengapara
Baghmara
Panikunda
Barni Hat
Margang
Nongpoh
Ksehkima Bazar
Donmatia
Umsning
Mawhati
Langpih
Nongkhlaw
Rambrai
Pamdkhar
Barapani
Mairang
Nongstoin
SHILLONG
Barato
Nongkrem
Shangpung
Mawphlang
Pambriew
Jarem
Laitlyngkoi
Jowai
Sohkyamphor
Mawkyrwat
Serrarim
Khliehriat
Phlangdiloin
Pynurela
Jarain
Mawsynram
Cherrapunji
Mopad
Shella
LEGEND
Distt. Boundary
State Boundary
Inter. Boundary
River
State capital
Town/Village
District Hq.
Tourist symbols
Dadongiri
Songsak
Tura
Zikzak
Dalu
Baghmara
Mawkyrawat
Mawsy Naram
Cherrapunji
Shillong
Nongpoh
Laskein
N
W
E
S

Scale - 1:1.69 M approx

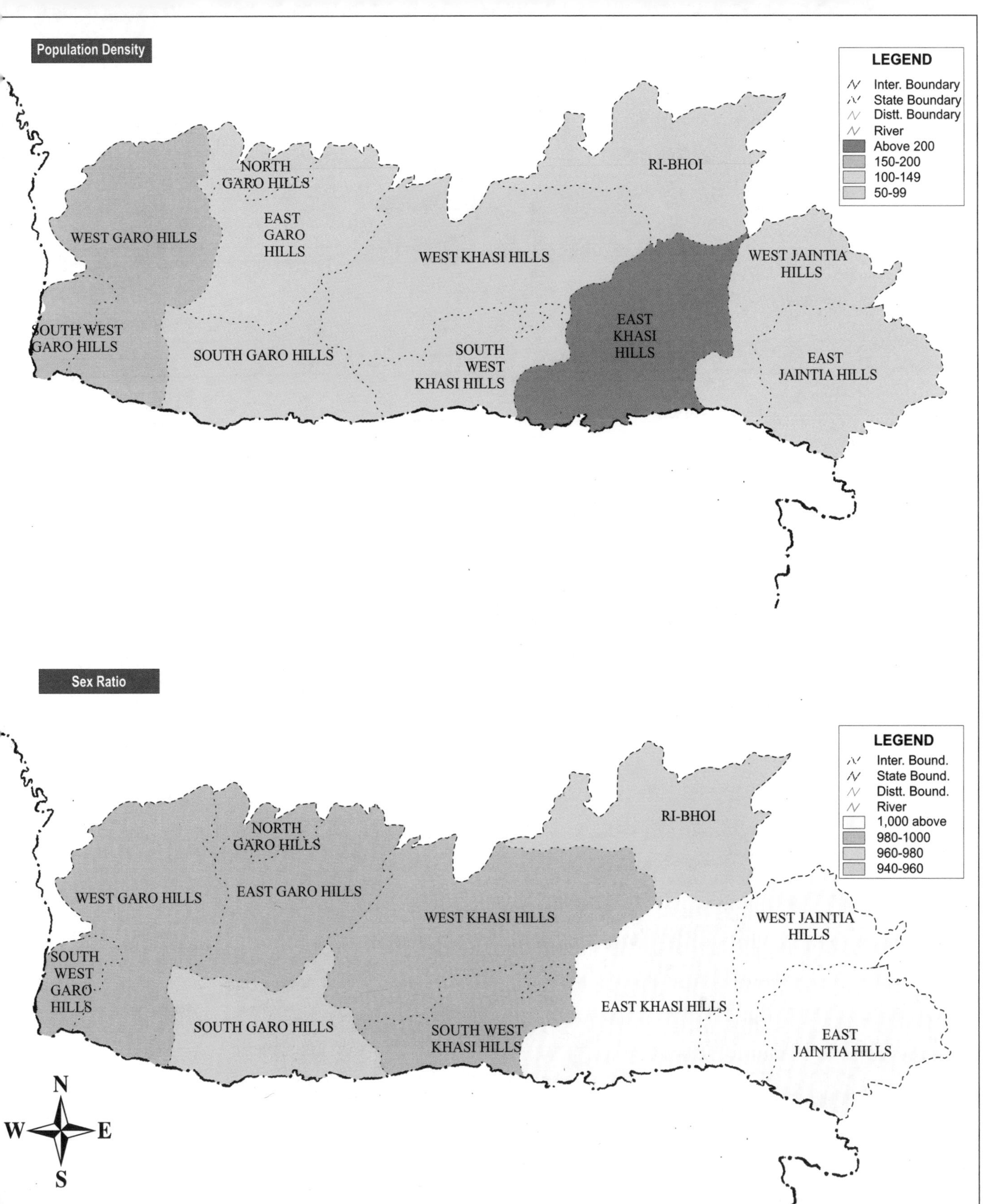

Population Density
LEGEND
Inter. Boundary
State Boundary
Distt. Boundary
River
Above 200
150-200
100-149
50-99
NORTH GARO HILLS
WEST GARO HILLS
EAST GARO HILLS
SOUTH WEST GARO HILLS
SOUTH GARO HILLS
WEST KHASI HILLS
SOUTH WEST KHASI HILLS
EAST KHASI HILLS
RI-BHOI
WEST JAINTIA HILLS
EAST JAINTIA HILLS
Sex Ratio
LEGEND
Inter. Bound.
State Bound.
Distt. Bound.
River
1,000 above
980-1000
960-980
940-960
NORTH GARO HILLS
WEST GARO HILLS
EAST GARO HILLS
SOUTH WEST GARO HILLS
SOUTH GARO HILLS
WEST KHASI HILLS
SOUTH WEST KHASI HILLS
EAST KHASI HILLS
RI-BHOI
WEST JAINTIA HILLS
EAST JAINTIA HILLS
N
W
E
S

Scale - 1:1.69 M approx

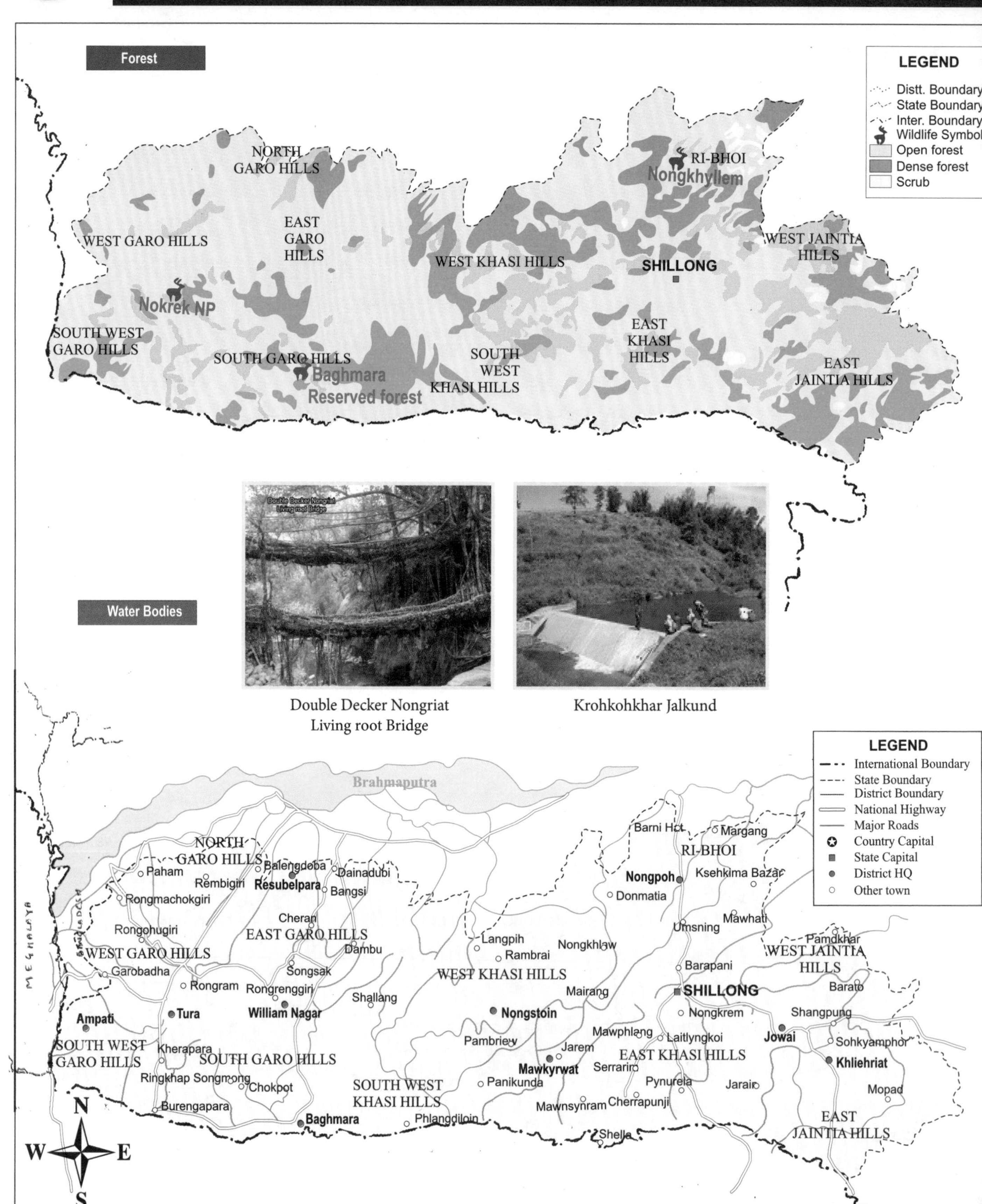
Forest
LEGEND
Distt. Boundary
State Boundary
Inter. Boundary
Wildlife Symbol
Open forest
Dense forest
Scrub
NORTH GARO HILLS
RI-BHOI
Nongkhyllem
WEST GARO HILLS
EAST GARO HILLS
WEST KHASI HILLS
SHILLONG
WEST JAINTIA HILLS
Nokrek NP
SOUTH WEST GARO HILLS
SOUTH GARO HILLS
Baghmara Reserved forest
SOUTH WEST KHASI HILLS
EAST KHASI HILLS
EAST JAINTIA HILLS
Water Bodies
Brahmaputra
LEGEND
International Boundary
State Boundary
District Boundary
National Highway
Major Roads
Country Capital
State Capital
District HQ
Other town
Paham
Rembigiri
Resubelpara
Balengdoba
Dainadubi
Bangsi
Rongmachokgiri
Rongohugiri
Cheran
Dambu
Garobadha
Songsak
Rongram
Rongrenggiri
Shallang
Ampati
Tura
William Nagar
Kherapara
Ringkhap
Songmong
Chokpot
Burengapara
Baghmara
Barni Hat
Margang
Nongpoh
Ksehkima Bazar
Donmatia
Umsning
Mawhati
Langpih
Rambrai
Nongkhlaw
Barapani
Pamdkhar
Mairang
Nongkrem
Barato
Nongstoin
Shangpung
Mawphlang
Laitlyngkoi
Jowai
Pambriew
Jarem
Sohkyamphor
Mawkyrwat
Serrariro
Khliehriat
Panikunda
Pynurela
Jarain
Mopad
Mawnsynram
Cherrapunji
Phlangdiloin
Shella
N
W
E
S

Double Decker Nongriat Living root Bridge

Krohkohkhar Jalkund

Scale - 1:1.69 M approx

EAST JAINTIA HILLS

VITAL STATISTICS

1. **District Headquarter:** Khliehriat
2. **Population:** 1,22,436
3. **Area:** 2,115 sq. km.
4. **Population Density:** 60 persons per sq. km.
5. **Literacy:** 58.27%
6. **Sex Ratio:** 1008 females per 1000 males

ECONOMIC PROFILES

1. **Agriculture:** Crops like Rice, maize, pulses, cowpeas, oil seeds, sesame, sugarcane, rape and mustard seeds etc. Fruits like citrus, Papaya, sweet potato, spices, black pepper etc.
2. **Industries:** Agro based, chemical, paper products, mineral, metal, engineering, rubber, jute, woolen based etc.
3. **Minerals:** Coal, limestone, kaolin, granite, glass, uranium
4. **Tourism:** Moopun waterfalls, umhang lake, Borghat temple etc.
5. **Live stocks :** Cattle, cross Breed, buffaloes, goats, pigs, poultry, ducks etc. Fisheries.

East Jaintia Hills was carved out of erstwhile Jaintia Hills district on 31 July 2012. The main inhabitants of the district are Pnars, Khynriam and Biates. The major rivers of the district are The Mynngot, The Myntdu, The Orange, The Lukha and The Simlieng, etc. The average temperature ranges from 20.47°C to 18.59°C. June to August are hottest months and December to February, coldest. Forest play a vital role in the economy and provide large quantities of timber for construction of building etc.

Umsning
Chirr
Pamdkhar
Saitsama
Tamu
Barapani
WEST JAINTIA HILLS
Barato
SHILLONG
Thadlaskein
Nartiang
Mynso
Mulum
Saitthad
Ummulong
Nongboh
Laskein
Lakadong
Raliang
Nongkrem
Mukhla
Ialong
Shangpung
Mukhap
JOWAI
Mawphlang
Sohkymphor
Laitlyngkoi
Sutnga
EAST KHASI HILLS
Jarain
Mustem
KHLIEHRIAT
Shnongrim
Sangbar
Serrarim
Cham Cham
Tuituk
Saipung
Amlarem
Pynurela
Podu
Mynkre
Mopad
Cherrapunji
Thangskai
EAST JAINTIA HILLS
Nongtalang
Dawki
Tamabil
Lumshnong
LEGEND
International Boundary
State Boundary
District Boundary
National Highway
Major Roads
Country Capital
State Capital
District HQ
Other town
Umkiang
N
W
E
S

Rynji Falls

WEST JAINTIA HILLS

VITAL STATISTICS

1. **District Headquarter:** Jowai
2. **Population:** 270,352
3. **Area:** 1,693sq. km.
4. **Population Density:** 160 persons per sq. km.
5. **Literacy:** 63.5%
6. **Sex Ratio:** 974 females per 1000 males

ECONOMIC PROFILES

1. **Agriculture:** Crops like Paddy, maize, jute, cotton, soya-bean etc. Fruits like pineapple, citrus, banana, orange, pears etc.
2. **Industries:** Agro-based, chemical based, Cotton textile, Cane and bamboo, carpentry, blacksmith, Paper products, mineral based, metal based, woolen based etc.
3. **Minerals:** Limestone, coal, clay etc.
4. **Tourism:** Umngot, Krang shuri waterfalls, Syndai caves etc.
5. **Live stocks :** Poultry, cattles, ducks, dogs and bitches etc.

West jaintia hills is an administrative District in the state of Meghalaya in India. The bifurcation of the erstwhile jaintia hills District into east and west jaintia hills District, west jaintia hills came into existence on 31 July 2012. It is bounded on the west by East khasi hills, and on the south by East jaintia hills District, on the north by Assam. The climate of the district is cool round the year. The average temperature of the district ranges a

Scale - 1:0.63 M approx

RI-BHOI

VITAL STATISTICS

1. **District Headquarter:** Nongpoh
2. **Population:** 2,58,840
3. **Area:** 2,378 sq. km.
4. **Population Density:** 123 persons per sq. km.
5. **Literacy:** 77.22%
6. **Sex Ratio:** 951 females per 1000 males

ECONOMIC PROFILES

1. **Agriculture:** Crops like Paddy, maize, Cotton, jute, jowar etc. Fruits like pineapple, banana, Orange, pears etc.
2. **Industries:** Agro based, chemical based, cane and bamboo, carpentry, blacksmith, Cotton textile, paper products, woolen based, jute based etc.
3. **Minerals:** Limestone, coal, clay, uranium etc.
4. **Tourism:** Umiam lake, Diengiei peak, Nongpoh etc.
5. **Live stocks :** Poultry, cattles like cows, buffaloes, goats, sheep,ducks, Mithun, dogs. Fishing and dairy farming etc.

RI-Bhoi is an administrative district in the state of Meghalaya. The district was upgraded from sub-division level to full fledged district on 4 June 1992. The district is carved from East Khasi Hills, and is bounded on the north by Kamrup district and on the east by Jaintia Hills and Karbi Anglong district of Assam and on the west by West Khasi Hills district. In 1981 RI-Bhoi District became home to the Nongkhyllem wildlife sanctuary.

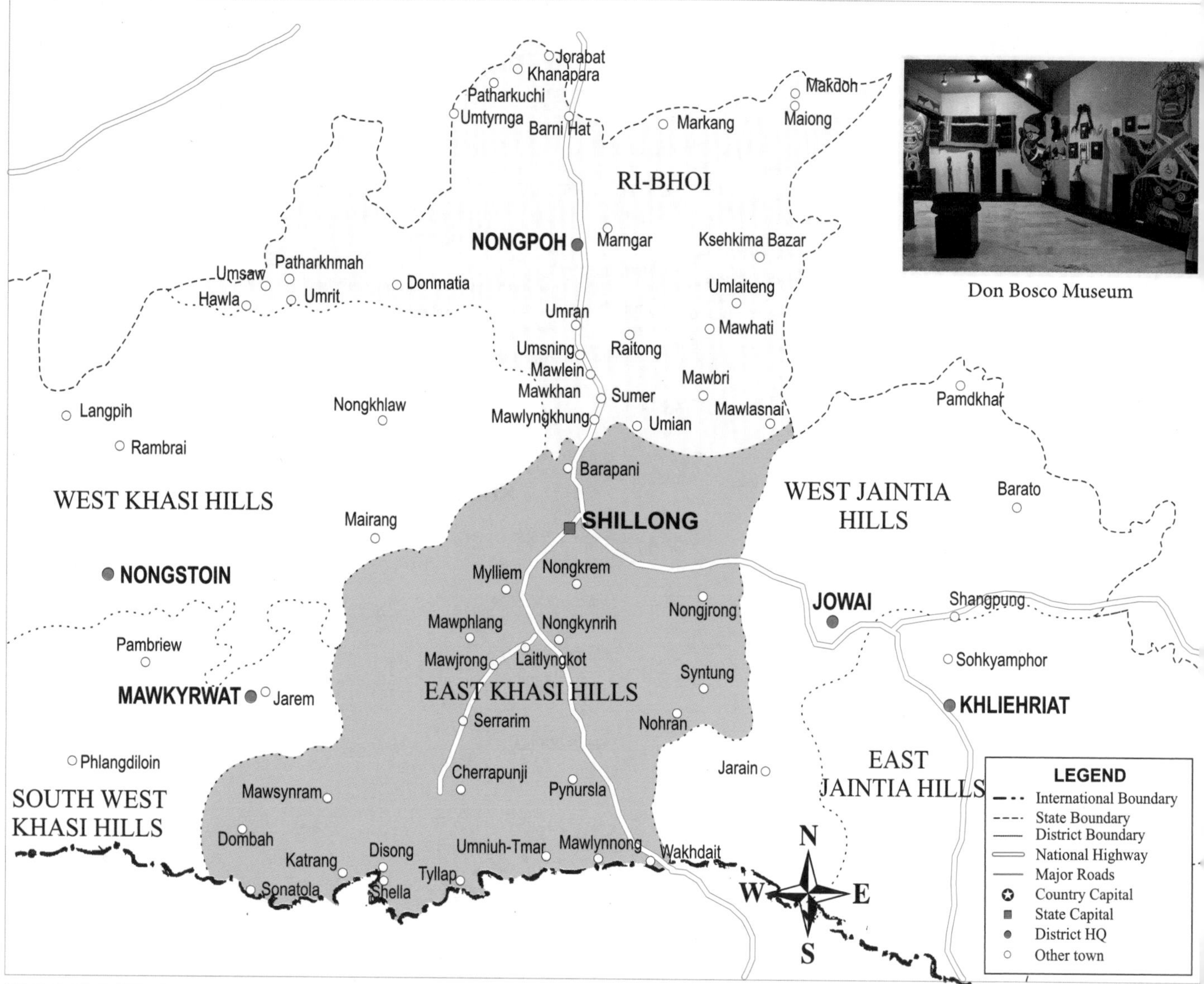

Jorabat
Khanapara
Patharkuchi
Umtyrnga
Barni Hat
Markang
Makdoh
Maiong
RI-BHOI
NONGPOH
Marngar
Ksehkima Bazar
Umsaw
Patharkhmah
Hawla
Umrit
Donmatia
Umlaiteng
Umran
Mawhati
Raitong
Umsning
Mawlein
Mawkhan
Sumer
Mawbri
Mawlynkhung
Umian
Mawlasnai
Pamdkhar
Langpih
Nongkhlaw
Rambrai
Barapani
WEST KHASI HILLS
Mairang
SHILLONG
WEST JAINTIA HILLS
Barato
NONGSTOIN
Mylliem
Nongkrem
Nongjrong
JOWAI
Shangpung
Pambriew
Mawphlang
Nongkynrih
Sohkyamphor
Mawjrong
Laitlyngkot
Syntung
MAWKYRWAT
Jarem
EAST KHASI HILLS
KHLIEHRIAT
Serrarim
Nohran
Phlangdiloin
Jarain
EAST JAINTIA HILLS
Cherrapunji
Pynursla
SOUTH WEST KHASI HILLS
Mawsynram
Dombah
Katrang
Disong
Umniuh-Tmar
Mawlynnong
Wakhdait
Tyllap
Sonatola
Shella
N
W
E
S
LEGEND
International Boundary
State Boundary
District Boundary
National Highway
Major Roads
Country Capital
State Capital
District HQ
Other town

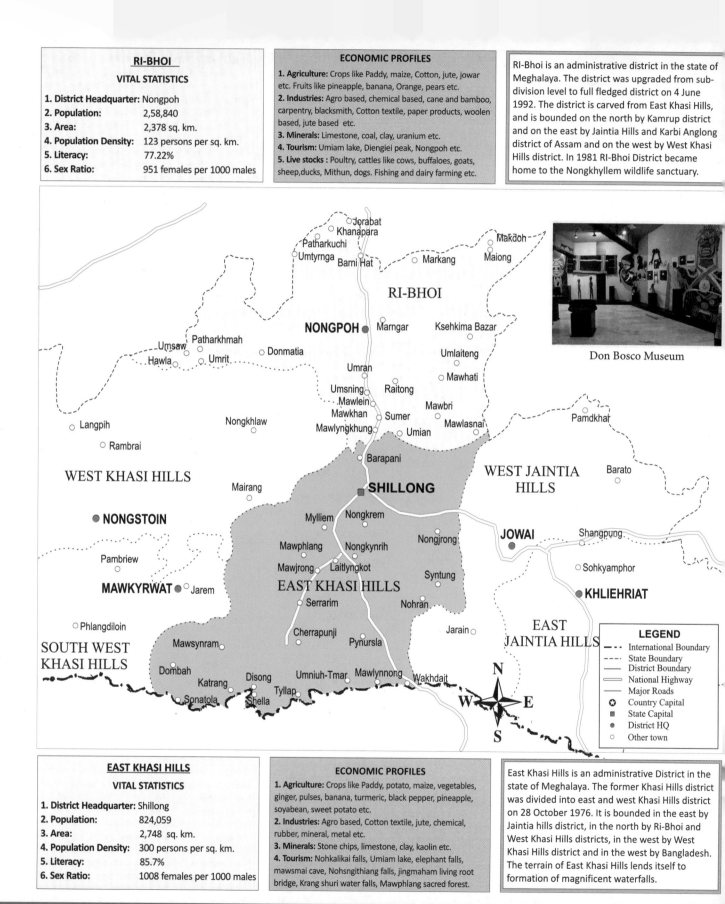

Don Bosco Museum

EAST KHASI HILLS

VITAL STATISTICS

1. **District Headquarter:** Shillong
2. **Population:** 824,059
3. **Area:** 2,748 sq. km.
4. **Population Density:** 300 persons per sq. km.
5. **Literacy:** 85.7%
6. **Sex Ratio:** 1008 females per 1000 males

ECONOMIC PROFILES

1. **Agriculture:** Crops like Paddy, potato, maize, vegetables, ginger, pulses, banana, turmeric, black pepper, pineapple, soyabean, sweet potato etc.
2. **Industries:** Agro based, Cotton textile, jute, chemical, rubber, mineral, metal etc.
3. **Minerals:** Stone chips, limestone, clay, kaolin etc.
4. **Tourism:** Nohkalikai falls, Umiam lake, elephant falls, mawsmai cave, Nohsngithiang falls, jingmaham living root bridge, Krang shuri water falls, Mawphlang sacred forest.

East Khasi Hills is an administrative District in the state of Meghalaya. The former Khasi Hills district was divided into east and west Khasi Hills district on 28 October 1976. It is bounded in the east by Jaintia hills district, in the north by Ri-Bhoi and West Khasi Hills districts, in the west by West Khasi Hills district and in the west by Bangladesh. The terrain of East Khasi Hills lends itself to formation of magnificent waterfalls.

Scale - 1:0.94 M approx

WEST KHASI HILLS

VITAL STATISTICS

1. District Headquarter: Nongstoin
2. Population: 2,94,115
3. Area: 3,911 sq. km.
4. Population Density: 73 persons per sq. km.
5. Literacy: 77.87 %
6. Sex Ratio: 980 females per 1000 males

ECONOMIC PROFILES

1. **Agriculture:** Crops like Rice, maize, soyabean, Millets, pulses, pea, cowpea, sesame, Rapeseed, Tobacco etc. Fruits like pineapple, citrus, banana, papaya etc.
2. **Industries:** Agro-based, Cotton textile, mineral based, metal based, chemical based, carpentry, Cane & bamboo etc.
3. **Minerals:** Stone chips, limestone, lithomargic, karolin etc.
4. **Tourism:** Nongkhnum island and sohtyngkhur village etc.
5. **Live stocks :** Cattle, cross Breed, pigs, buffaloes, goat, sheep, rabbits, poultry, desi, ducks and fisheries etc.

West Khasi hills was carved out of the erstwhile Khasi hills District on 28 October 1976. Because of the considerable variation in altitude, difference in climate condition within the west khasi hills can be expected. The low lying hills and foothills in the north and south may be as low as 50m above sea level, while the central plateau is as high as 1700m above mean sea level.

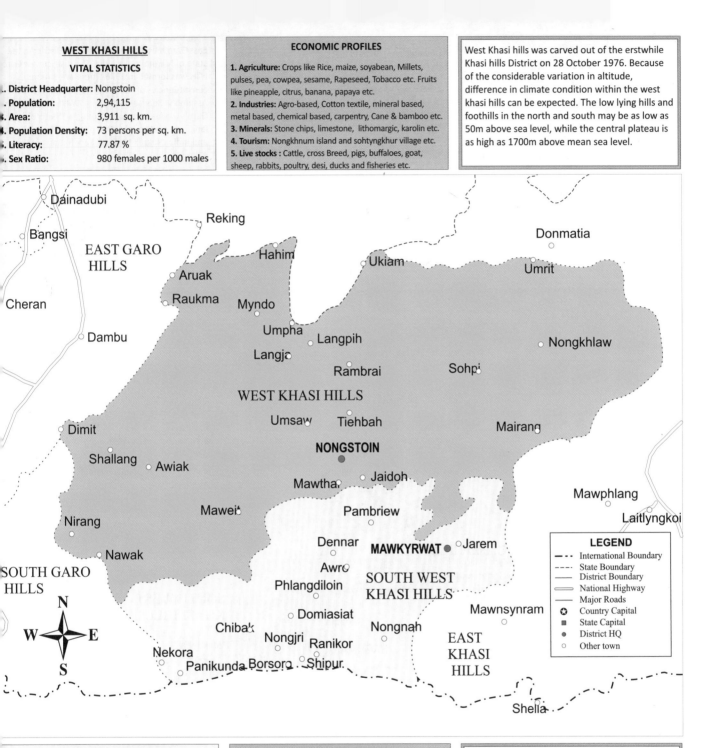

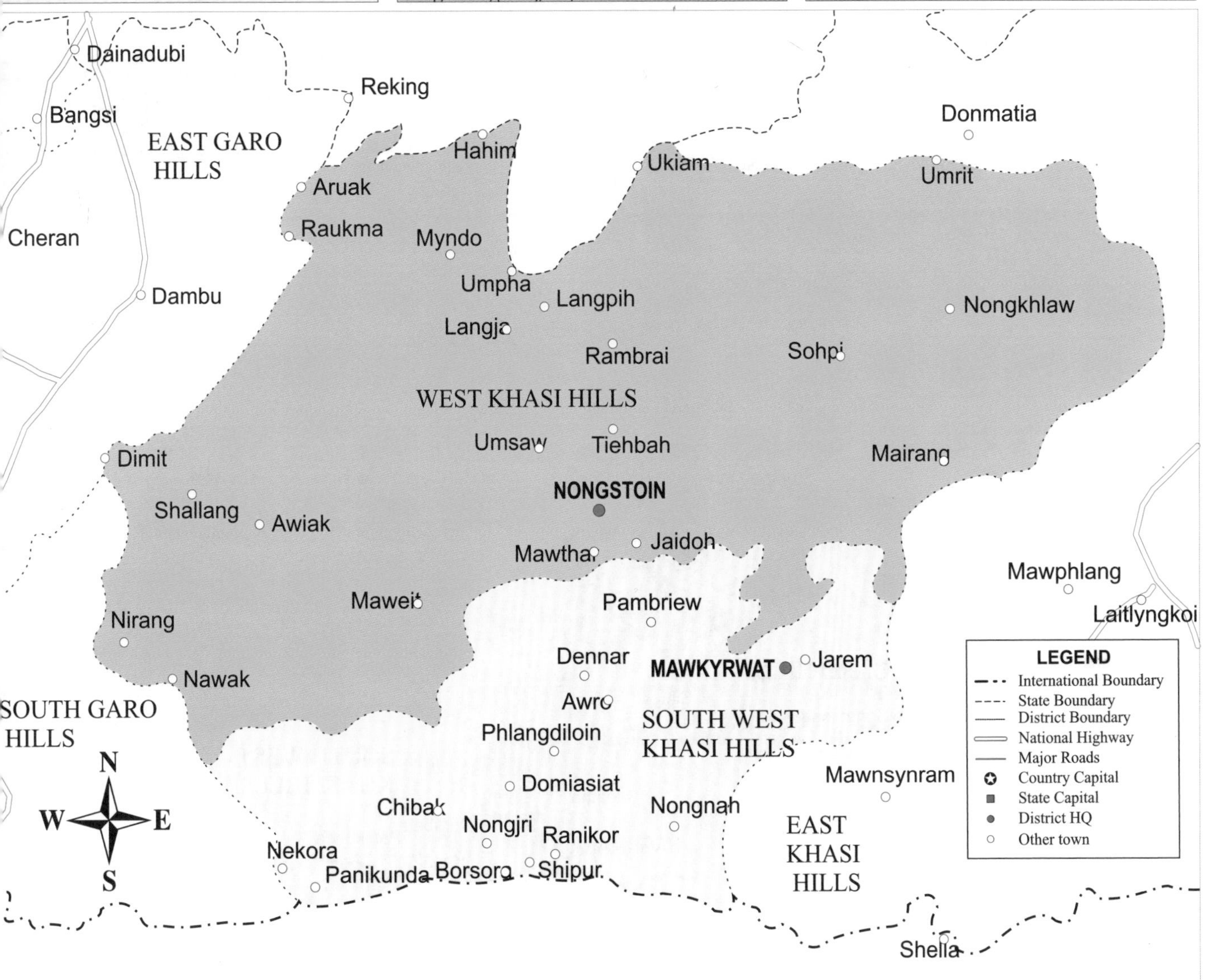
Dainadubi
Reking
Bangsi
EAST GARO HILLS
Donmatia
Hahim
Ukiam
Umrit
Aruak
Raukma
Myndo
Cheran
Umpha
Langpih
Dambu
Nongkhlaw
Langjo
Rambrai
Sohpi
WEST KHASI HILLS
Umsaw
Tiehbah
Mairang
Dimit
NONGSTOIN
Shallang
Awiak
Mawthar
Jaidoh
Mawphlang
Maweit
Pambriew
Laitlyngkoi
Nirang
Dennar
MAWKYRWAT
Jarem
Nawak
Awro
SOUTH WEST KHASI HILLS
SOUTH GARO HILLS
Phlangdiloin
Mawsynram
Domiasiat
N
W
E
S
Chibak
Nongjri
Nongnah
Ranikor
EAST KHASI HILLS
Nekora
Panikunda
Borsora
Shipur
Shella
LEGEND
International Boundary
State Boundary
District Boundary
National Highway
Major Roads
Country Capital
State Capital
District HQ
Other town

SOUTH WEST KHASI HILLS

VITAL STATISTICS

1. District Headquarter: Mawkyrwat
2. Population: 110,152
3. Area: 1,341 sq. km.
4. Population Density: 82 persons per sq. km.
5. Literacy: 76.84 %
6. Sex Ratio: 980 females per 1000 males

ECONOMIC PROFILES

1. **Agriculture:** Crops like Rice, maize, soyabean, Millets, Rabi pulses, pea, cowpea, sesame, rapeseed and tobacco. Fruits like Pineapple, citrus fruits, banana and Papaya etc.
2. **Industries:** Agro based, chemical based, Cotton textile, blacksmith, cane and bamboo, paper products etc.
3. **Minerals:** limestone, uranium, coal, clay etc.
4. **Tourism:** Natural beauty, culture and traditional.
5. **Live stocks :** Cattle like buffaloes, goats, sheep, pigs, rabbits,hens and ducks, yak, horses and donkey etc.

South West Khasi hills is an administrative District in the state of Meghalaya. It was carved out of the West Khasi Hills district on 3 August 2012. It is bounded by on the north west by Khasi Hills district, on the west by South Garo Hills District, on the east by East Khasi Hills district, on the south by International boundary along Bangladesh. The low lying area in the north and south has largely a topical type of climate with hot and humid summer and pleasantly warm winter. The high hills generally enjoy a salubrious climate almost through out the year. The hottest months are May to August and the coldest months are December to February. This district is rich in forest resources. Finest class of timber are abound in the district.

cale - 1:0.61 M approx

EAST AND SOUTH GARO HILLS

EAST GARO HILLS

VITAL STATISTICS

1. **District Headquarter:** Williamnagar
2. **Population:** 1,32,257
3. **Area:** 1,490 sq. km.
4. **Population Density:** 96 persons per sq. km.
5. **Literacy:** 75.51%
6. **Sex Ratio:** 968 females per 1000 males

ECONOMIC PROFILES

1. **Agriculture:** Crops like Ahu rice, Winter rice, small millet, maize, wheat, potato, gram pulses, cotton, jute, sesamum. Fruits like pineapple, citrus and banana, herbs/ aromatics.
2. **Industries:** Agro based, Cotton textile, jute, leather, Chemical, rubber, metal based,mineral based etc.
3. **Minerals:** Coal, limestone and sillimanite etc.
4. **Tourism:** Ta'sek lake, Rong bang falls, Domre falls, Mokma Dare, Naphak or napak, nongchram etc.
5. **Live stocks :** Cattles, cross breed cattle, graded buffaloes, goat, sheep, pig, commercial dairy farms etc.

East Garo hills is an administrative District in the state of Meghalaya in India. The district East Garo Hills was formed in 1976. There are 3 Assembly constituencies of the Meghalaya state legislative Assembly: Songsak, Rongjeng, Williamnagar. East Garo's language include A'Tong, a Tibeto-Burman language spoken by 10000 people in Bangladesh and India. Nokrek National Park has an area of 47km^2.

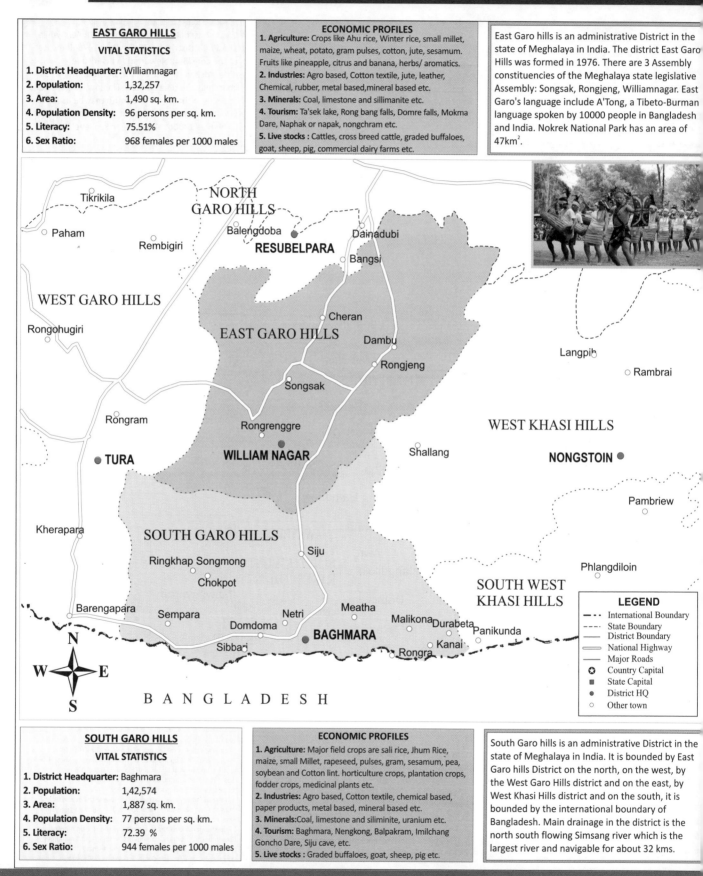

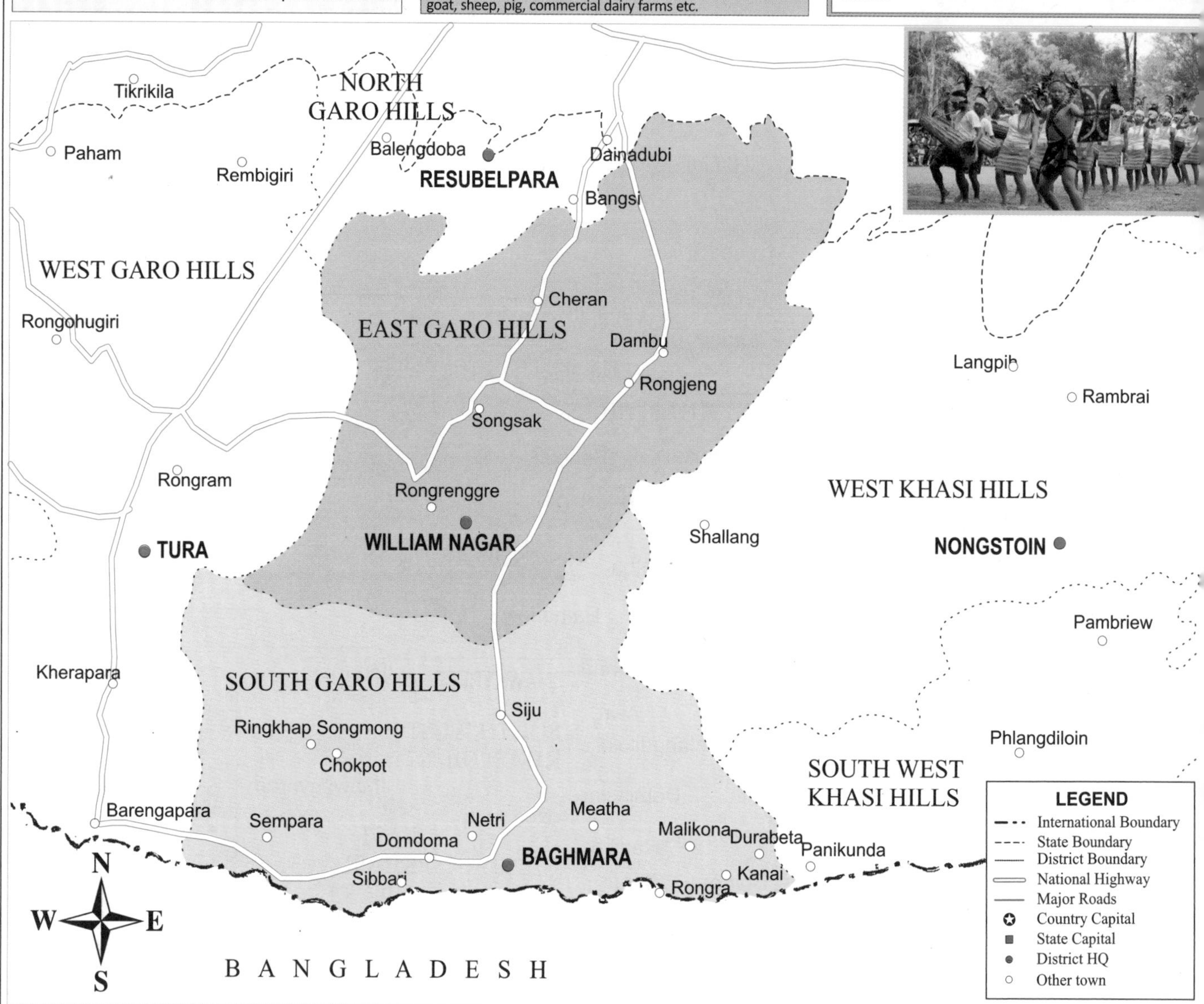
NORTH GARO HILLS
Tikrikila
Paham
Rembigiri
Balengdoba
RESUBELPARA
Dainadubi
Bangsi
WEST GARO HILLS
Cheran
EAST GARO HILLS
Dambu
Rongohugiri
Rongjeng
Langpih
Rambrai
Songsak
Rongram
Rongrenggre
WEST KHASI HILLS
TURA
WILLIAM NAGAR
Shallang
NONGSTOIN
Pambriew
Kherapara
SOUTH GARO HILLS
Siju
Ringkhap Songmong
Chokpot
Phlangdiloin
SOUTH WEST KHASI HILLS
Barengapara
Sempara
Netri
Meatha
Malikona
Durabeta
Panikunda
Domdoma
BAGHMARA
Sibbari
Kanai
Rongra
N
W
E
S
B A N G L A D E S H
LEGEND
International Boundary
State Boundary
District Boundary
National Highway
Major Roads
Country Capital
State Capital
District HQ
Other town

SOUTH GARO HILLS

VITAL STATISTICS

1. **District Headquarter:** Baghmara
2. **Population:** 1,42,574
3. **Area:** 1,887 sq. km.
4. **Population Density:** 77 persons per sq. km.
5. **Literacy:** 72.39 %
6. **Sex Ratio:** 944 females per 1000 males

ECONOMIC PROFILES

1. **Agriculture:** Major field crops are sali rice, Jhum Rice, maize, small Millet, rapeseed, pulses, gram, sesamum, pea, soybean and Cotton lint. horticulture crops, plantation crops, fodder crops, medicinal plants etc.
2. **Industries:** Agro based, Cotton textile, chemical based, paper products, metal based, mineral based etc.
3. **Minerals:**Coal, limestone and siliminite, uranium etc.
4. **Tourism:** Baghmara, Nengkong, Balpakram, Imilchang Goncho Dare, Siju cave, etc.
5. **Live stocks :** Graded buffaloes, goat, sheep, pig etc.

South Garo hills is an administrative District in the state of Meghalaya in India. It is bounded by East Garo hills District on the north, on the west, by the West Garo Hills district and on the east, by West Khasi Hills district and on the south, it is bounded by the international boundary of Bangladesh. Main drainage in the district is the north south flowing Simsang river which is the largest river and navigable for about 32 kms.

Scale - 1:0.69 M approx

NORTH GARO HILLS

VITAL STATISTICS

1. **District Headquarter:** Resubelpara
2. **Population:** 1,18,325
3. **Area:** 1,113 sq. km.
4. **Population Density:** 110 persons per sq. km.
5. **Literacy:** 62%
6. **Sex Ratio:** 973 females per 1000 males

ECONOMIC PROFILES

1. **Agriculture:** Shifting cultivation, Terrace cultivation of Crops like Paddy, wheat, maize, Cotton, sugarcane, etc. Fruits like Pineapple, Banana, Papaya, Vegetables, jack fruits etc.
2. **Industries:** Agro based, chemical based, carpentry, cane and bamboo, Cotton textile, paper products, mineral based, metal based, engineering units, Repairing and servicing etc.
3. **Minerals:** limestone, clay, granite, glass sand and coal etc.
4. **Tourism:** Jolding Wari lake, Resubelpara hotspring etc.
5. **Live stocks :** Poultry, cattles like cows, buffaloes, goats, sheep, ducks, dogs and bitches. Fishing and dairy farming etc.

North Garo Hills was carved out of the erstwhile East Garo Hills district. The climate of the district is tropical. The temperature ranges from 33°C to 4°C. Annual rainfall of the district, recorded is 1908.71 mm. The rainy season in the district starts from the month of May to August. Forest occupies a large part of the geographical area of the state. In North Garo hills district, the life of the tribal population is linked with forest.

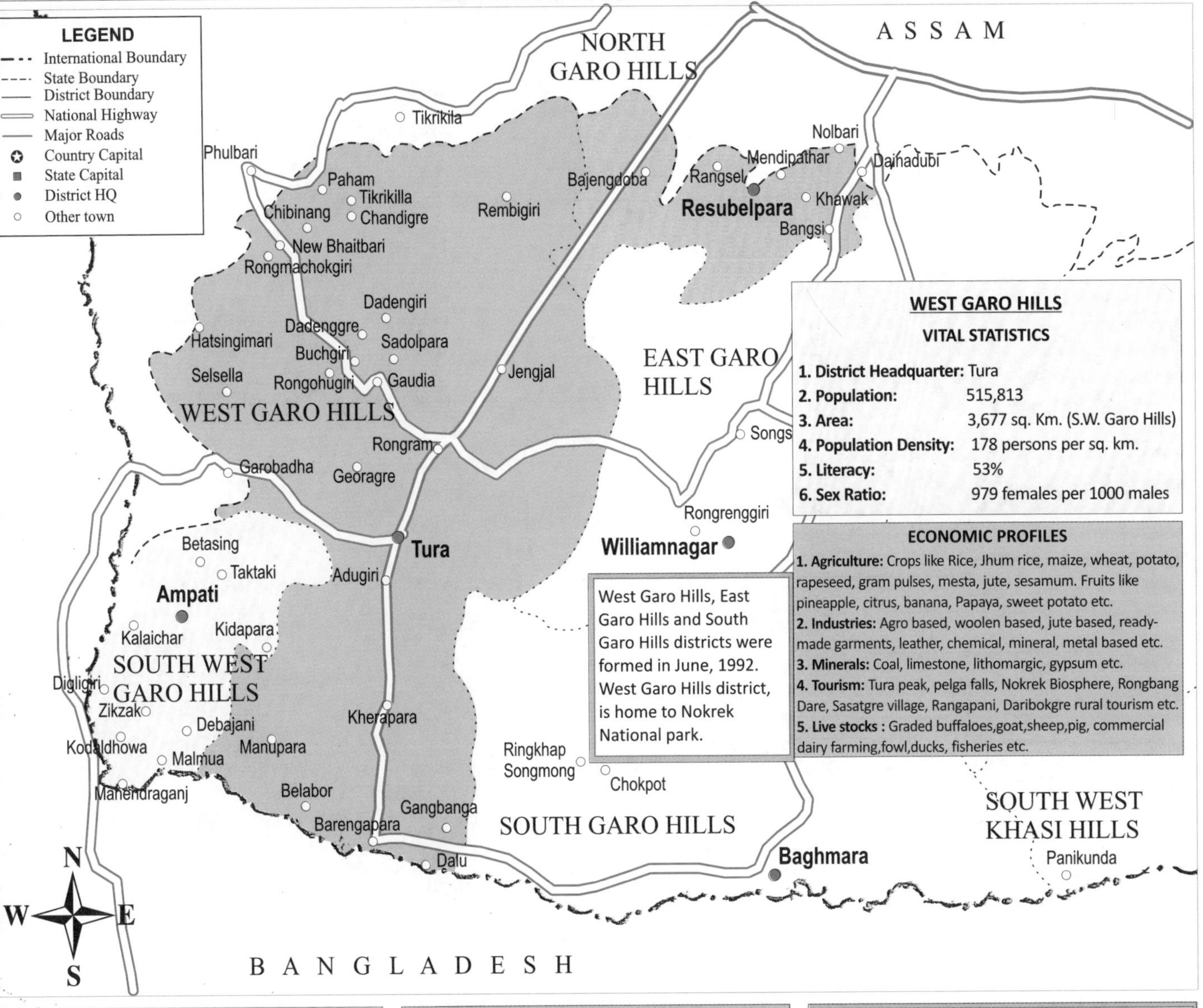

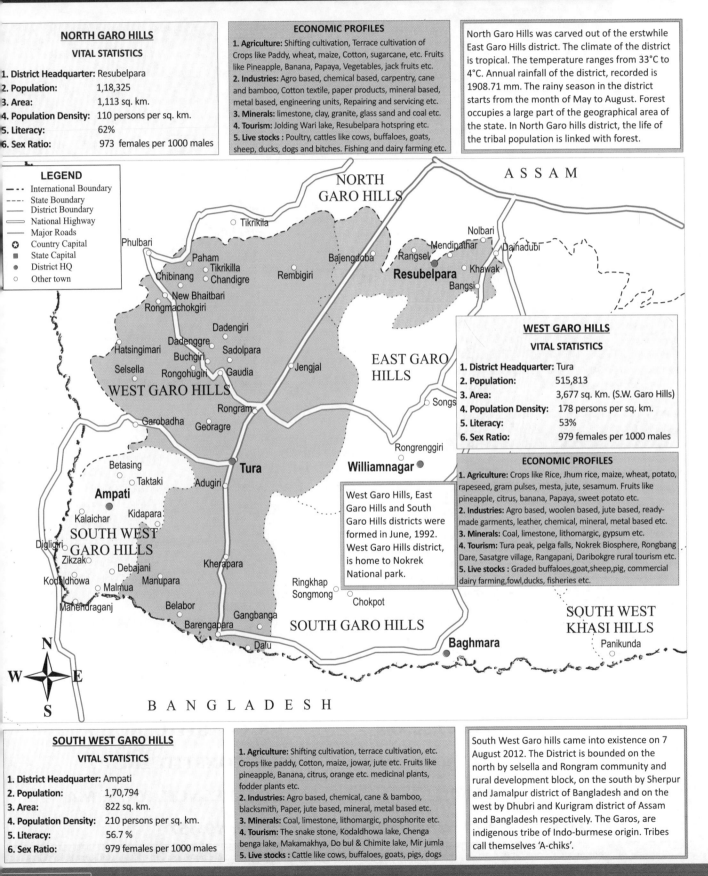

LEGEND
International Boundary
State Boundary
District Boundary
National Highway
Major Roads
Country Capital
State Capital
District HQ
Other town
ASSAM
NORTH GARO HILLS
Tikrikila
Phulbari
Paham
Tikrikilla
Chandigre
Chibinang
New Bhaitbari
Rongmachokgiri
Rembigiri
Bajengdoba
Rangsel
Mendipathar
Nolbari
Dainadubi
Resubelpara
Khawak
Bangsi
Dadengiri
Dadenggre
Hatsingimari
Sadolpara
Buchgiri
Selsella
Rongohugiri
Gaudia
Jengjal
WEST GARO HILLS
EAST GARO HILLS
Songsak
Rongram
Garobadha
Georagre
Rongrenggiri
Betasing
Tura
Williamnagar
Taktaki
Adugiri
Ampati
Kalaichar
Kidapara
SOUTH WEST GARO HILLS
Digligiri
Zikzak
Debajani
Kherapara
Kodaldhowa
Malmua
Manupara
Mahendraganj
Belabor
Gangbanga
Barengapara
Ringkhap
Songmong
Chokpot
SOUTH GARO HILLS
SOUTH WEST KHASI HILLS
Panikunda
Dalu
Baghmara
N
W
E
S
BANGLADESH

WEST GARO HILLS

VITAL STATISTICS

1. **District Headquarter:** Tura
2. **Population:** 515,813
3. **Area:** 3,677 sq. Km. (S.W. Garo Hills)
4. **Population Density:** 178 persons per sq. km.
5. **Literacy:** 53%
6. **Sex Ratio:** 979 females per 1000 males

ECONOMIC PROFILES

1. **Agriculture:** Crops like Rice, Jhum rice, maize, wheat, potato, rapeseed, gram pulses, mesta, jute, sesamum. Fruits like pineapple, citrus, banana, Papaya, sweet potato etc.
2. **Industries:** Agro based, woolen based, jute based, ready-made garments, leather, chemical, mineral, metal based etc.
3. **Minerals:** Coal, limestone, lithomargic, gypsum etc.
4. **Tourism:** Tura peak, pelga falls, Nokrek Biosphere, Rongbang Dare, Sasatgre village, Rangapani, Daribokgre rural tourism etc.
5. **Live stocks :** Graded buffaloes,goat,sheep,pig, commercial dairy farming,fowl,ducks, fisheries etc.

West Garo Hills, East Garo Hills and South Garo Hills districts were formed in June, 1992. West Garo Hills district, is home to Nokrek National park.

SOUTH WEST GARO HILLS

VITAL STATISTICS

1. **District Headquarter:** Ampati
2. **Population:** 1,70,794
3. **Area:** 822 sq. km.
4. **Population Density:** 210 persons per sq. km.
5. **Literacy:** 56.7 %
6. **Sex Ratio:** 979 females per 1000 males

1. **Agriculture:** Shifting cultivation, terrace cultivation, etc. Crops like paddy, Cotton, maize, jowar, jute etc. Fruits like pineapple, Banana, citrus, orange etc. medicinal plants, fodder plants etc.
2. **Industries:** Agro based, chemical, cane & bamboo, blacksmith, Paper, jute based, mineral, metal based etc.
3. **Minerals:** Coal, limestone, lithomargic, phosphorite etc.
4. **Tourism:** The snake stone, Kodaldhowa lake, Chenga benga lake, Makamakhya, Do bul & Chimite lake, Mir jumla
5. **Live stocks :** Cattle like cows, buffaloes, goats, pigs, dogs

South West Garo hills came into existence on 7 August 2012. The District is bounded on the north by selsella and Rongram community and rural development block, on the south by Sherpur and Jamalpur district of Bangladesh and on the west by Dhubri and Kurigram district of Assam and Bangladesh respectively. The Garos, are indigenous tribe of Indo-burmese origin. Tribes call themselves 'A-chiks'.

Scale - 1:0.77 M approx

MIZORAM

Section

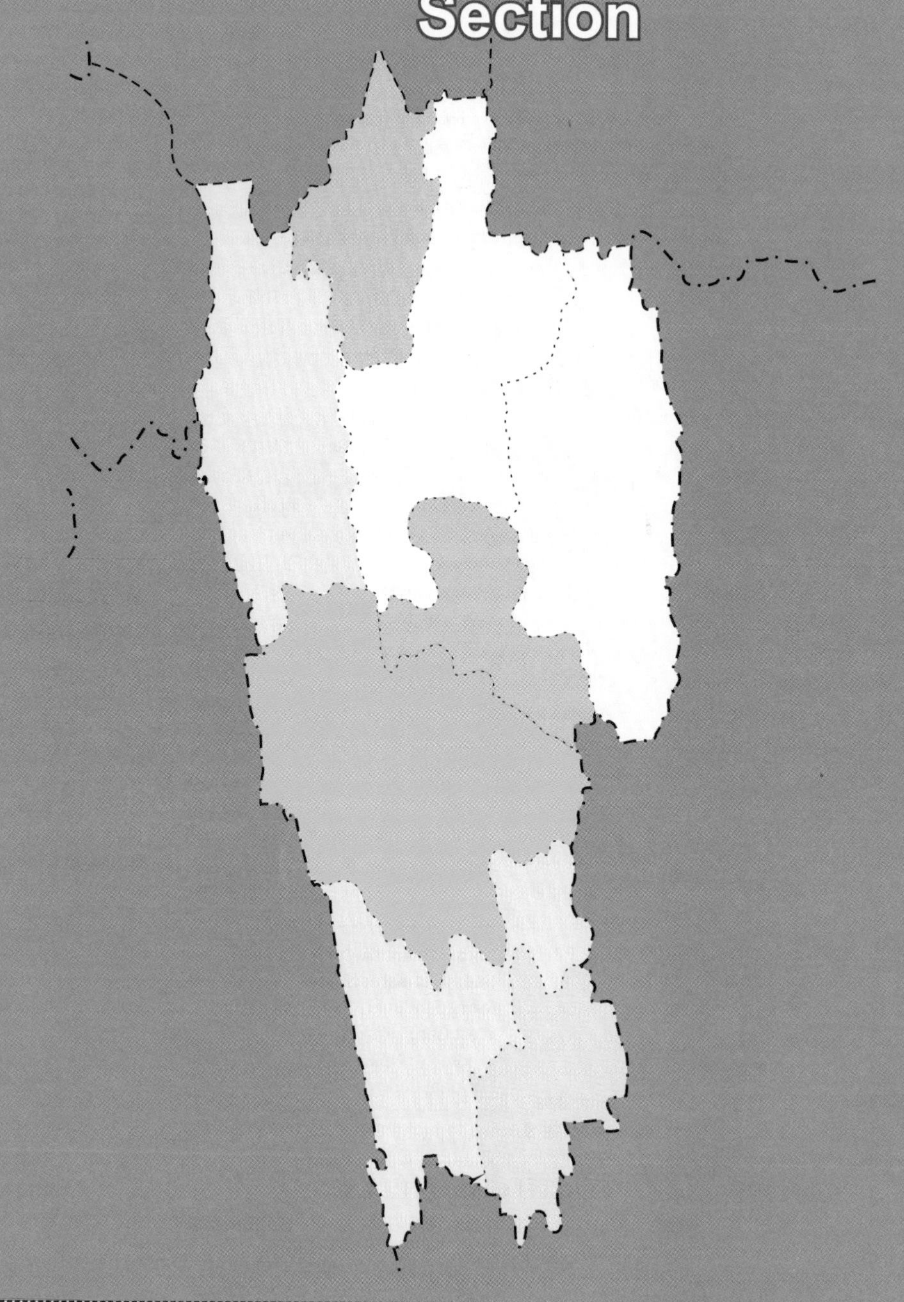

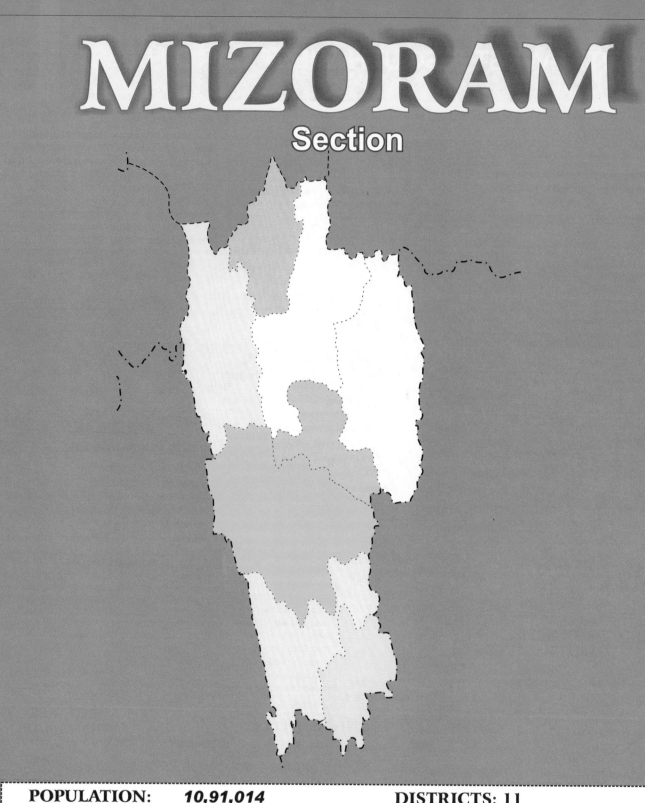

POPULATION:	***10,91,014***	**DISTRICTS: 11**
AREA:	***21,081 sq.km.***	**L.S. CONSTITUENCY: *1***
POP. DENSITY:	***51.7 persons/ Km^2***	**R.S. CONSTITUENCY: *1***
LITERACY:	***91.50%***	**GRAM PANCHAYATS: *N.A***
SEX RATIO:	***971 females/1000 males***	**GSDP: *19,457***

At the time of publishing, government had proposed four new districts namely Sinlung, Sangau, Tlabung & Chawngte for which details are not yet available

VITAL STATISTICS

1. State Bird - Mrs. Hume's pheasant
2. State Animal - Serow
3. State Flower - Vanda
4. State Tree - Indian Rose chestnut
5. Languages - Lushai, Mizo, Bengali, Lakher
6. Primary Rivers - Tlwang, Tlau, Chhimtuipui, Tui-chang, Tuirial
7. Neighbors - Manipur, Assam, Tripura
8. Forest and NPs - Murlen NP, Phawngpui NP, Thoranglang WS, Blue Mts. NP
9. Tribes - Bru (Reang), Chakma, Tanchangya, Chin origin of Northern Arakans.

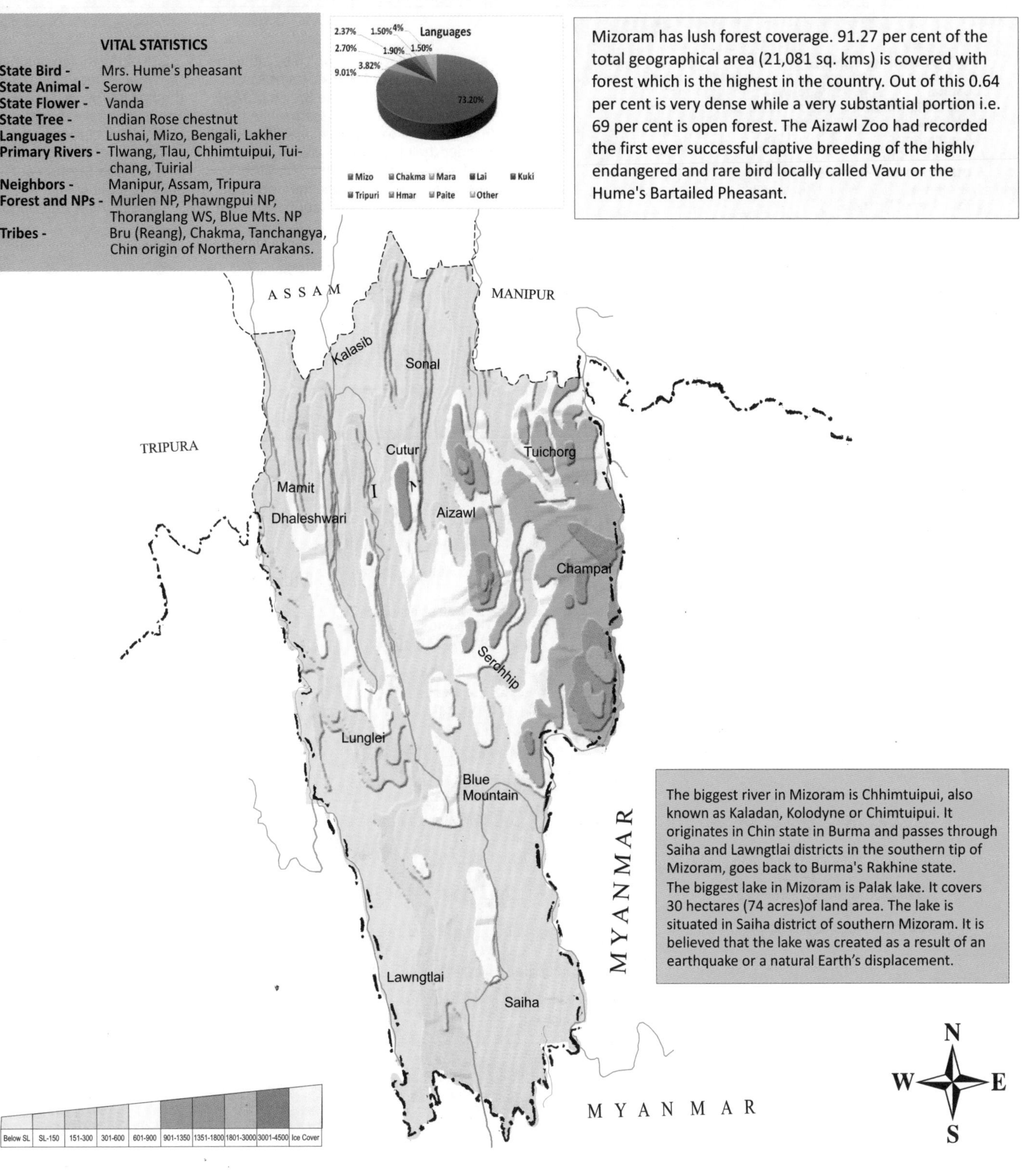

Languages
2.37%
1.50%
4%
1.50%
2.70%
1.90%
9.01%
3.82%
73.20%
Mizo
Chakma
Mara
Lai
Kuki
Tripuri
Hmar
Paite
Other
ASSAM
MANIPUR
TRIPURA
Kalasib
Sonal
Cutur
Tuichorg
Mamit
Dhaleshwari
Aizawl
Champai
Serchhip
Lunglei
Blue Mountain
MYANMAR
Lawngtlai
Saiha
MYANMAR
N
W
E
S
Below SL
SL-150
151-300
301-600
601-900
901-1350
1351-1800
1801-3000
3001-4500
Ice Cover

Mizoram has lush forest coverage. 91.27 per cent of the total geographical area (21,081 sq. kms) is covered with forest which is the highest in the country. Out of this 0.64 per cent is very dense while a very substantial portion i.e. 69 per cent is open forest. The Aizawl Zoo had recorded the first ever successful captive breeding of the highly endangered and rare bird locally called Vavu or the Hume's Bartailed Pheasant.

The biggest river in Mizoram is Chhimtuipui, also known as Kaladan, Kolodyne or Chimtuipui. It originates in Chin state in Burma and passes through Saiha and Lawngtlai districts in the southern tip of Mizoram, goes back to Burma's Rakhine state.
The biggest lake in Mizoram is Palak lake. It covers 30 hectares (74 acres)of land area. The lake is situated in Saiha district of southern Mizoram. It is believed that the lake was created as a result of an earthquake or a natural Earth's displacement.

Scale - 1:0.8 M approx

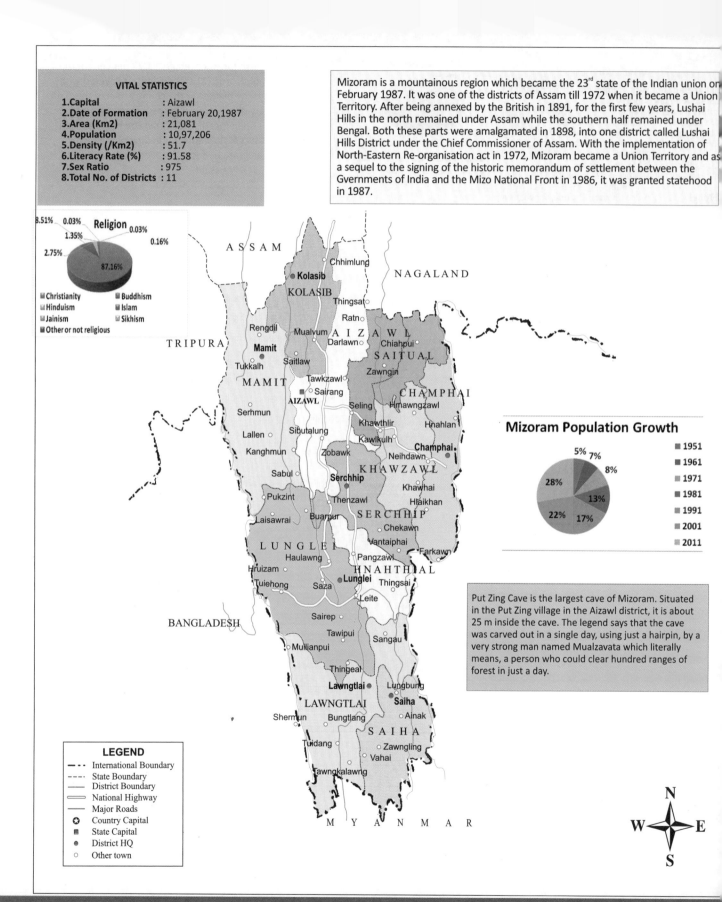

VITAL STATISTICS

1.Capital	: Aizawl
2.Date of Formation	: February 20,1987
3.Area (Km2)	: 21,081
4.Population	: 10,97,206
5.Density (/Km2)	: 51.7
6.Literacy Rate (%)	: 91.58
7.Sex Ratio	: 975
8.Total No. of Districts	: 11

Mizoram is a mountainous region which became the 23rd state of the Indian union on February 1987. It was one of the districts of Assam till 1972 when it became a Union Territory. After being annexed by the British in 1891, for the first few years, Lushai Hills in the north remained under Assam while the southern half remained under Bengal. Both these parts were amalgamated in 1898, into one district called Lushai Hills District under the Chief Commissioner of Assam. With the implementation of North-Eastern Re-organisation act in 1972, Mizoram became a Union Territory and as a sequel to the signing of the historic memorandum of settlement between the Gvernments of India and the Mizo National Front in 1986, it was granted statehood in 1987.

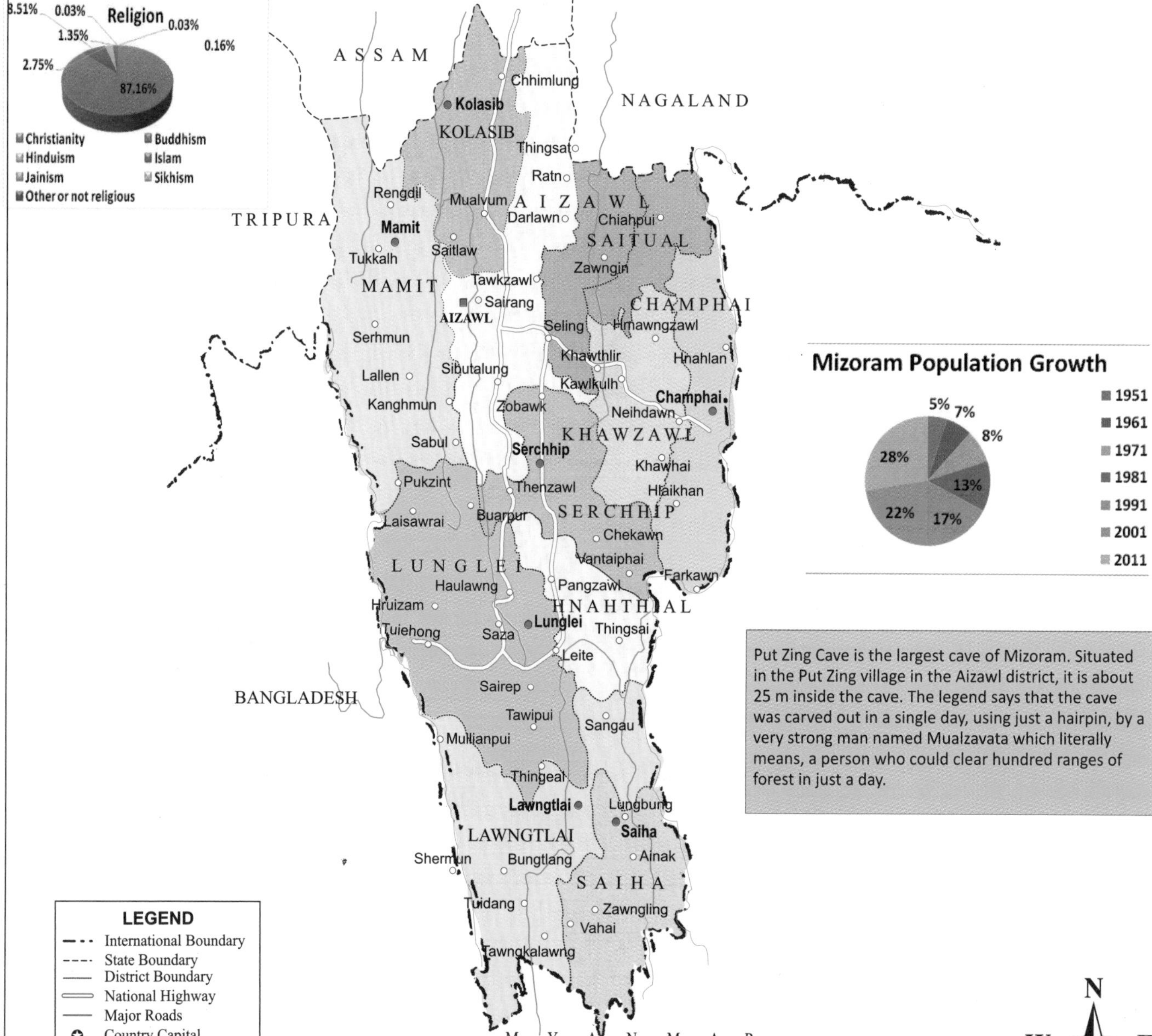
Religion
87.16%
2.75%
1.35%
8.51%
0.03%
0.03%
0.16%
Christianity
Buddhism
Hinduism
Islam
Jainism
Sikhism
Other or not religious
ASSAM
NAGALAND
TRIPURA
BANGLADESH
MYANMAR
Chhimlung
Kolasib
KOLASIB
Thingsat
Ratn
Rengdil
Mualvum
AIZAWL
Darlawn
Chiahpui
SAITUAL
Mamit
Saitlaw
Zawngin
Tukkalh
MAMIT
Tawkzawl
Sairang
AIZAWL
CHAMPHAI
Serhmun
Seling
Hmawngzawl
Khawthlir
Hnahlan
Lallen
Sibutalung
Kawlkulh
Champhai
Kanghmun
Zobawk
Neihdawn
KHAWZAWL
Sabul
Serchhip
Khawhai
Pukzint
Thenzawl
Hraikhan
SERCHHIP
Laisawrai
Buarpur
Chekawn
Vantaiphai
LUNGLEI
Haulawng
Pangzawl
Farkawn
Hruizam
HNAHTHIAL
Tuiehong
Saza
Lunglei
Thingsai
Leite
Sairep
Tawipui
Sangau
Mulianpui
Thingeal
Lawngtlai
Lungbung
Saiha
LAWNGTLAI
Shermun
Bungtlang
Ainak
SAIHA
Tuidang
Zawngling
Vahai
Tawngkalawng
Mizoram Population Growth
5%
7%
8%
13%
17%
22%
28%
1951
1961
1971
1981
1991
2001
2011
Put Zing Cave is the largest cave of Mizoram. Situated in the Put Zing village in the Aizawl district, it is about 25 m inside the cave. The legend says that the cave was carved out in a single day, using just a hairpin, by a very strong man named Mualzavata which literally means, a person who could clear hundred ranges of forest in just a day.
LEGEND
International Boundary
State Boundary
District Boundary
National Highway
Major Roads
Country Capital
State Capital
District HQ
Other town
N
W
E
S

Scale - 1:1.69 M approx

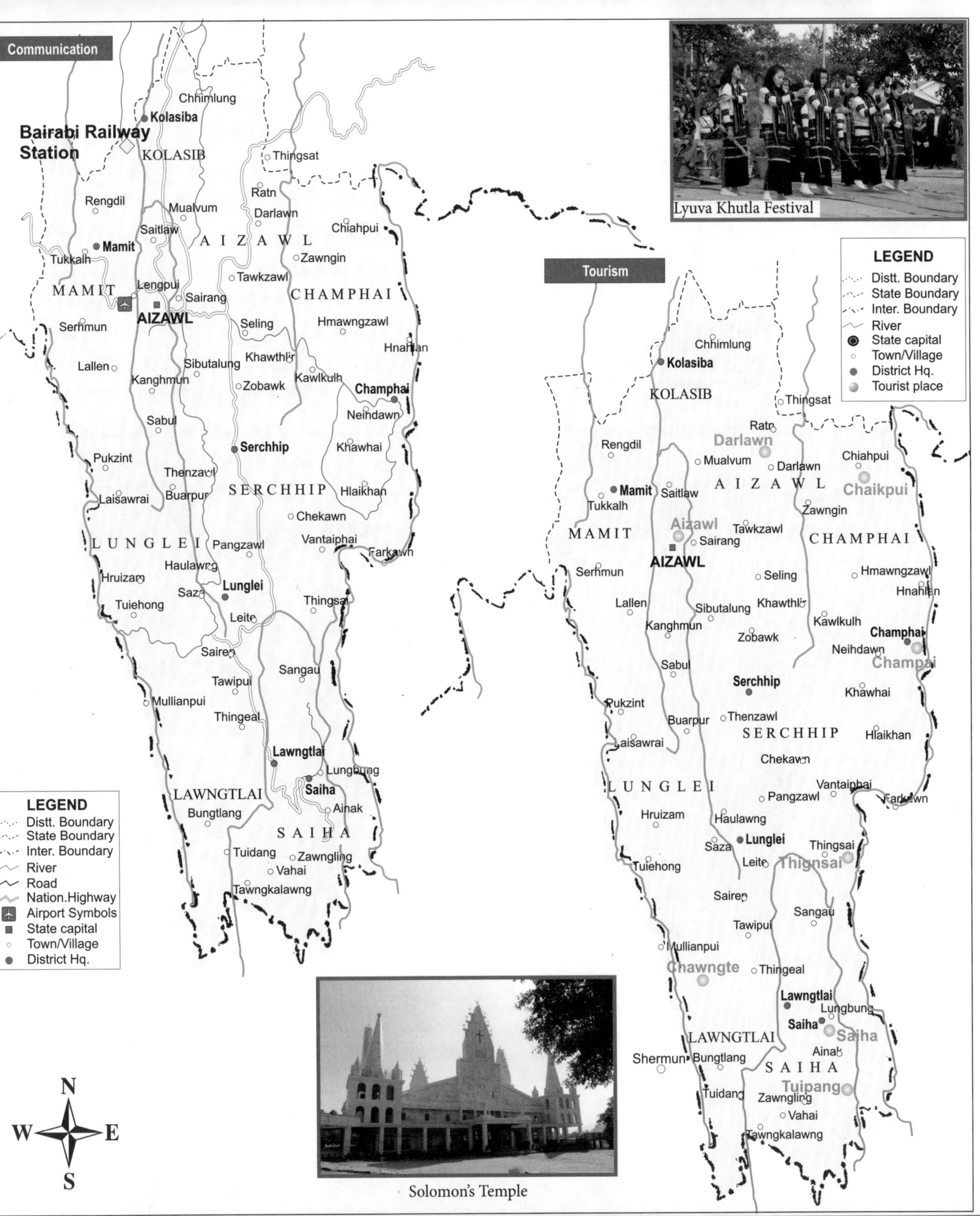
Communication
Chhimlung
Kolasiba
Bairabi Railway Station
KOLASIB
Thingsat
Ratn
Darlawn
Rengdil
Mualvum
Saitlaw
Mamit
A I Z A W L
Chiahpui
Zawngin
Tukkalh
MAMIT
Lengpui
Tawkzawl
C H A M P H A I
Sairang
AIZAWL
Serhmun
Seling
Hmawngzawl
Hnahlan
Khawthlir
Lallen
Sibutalung
Kanghmun
Zobawk
Kawlkulh
Champhai
Neihdawn
Sabul
Serchhip
Khawhai
Pukzint
Thenzawl
Laisawrai
Buarpur
S E R C H H I P
Hlaikhan
Chekawn
L U N G L E I
Pangzawl
Vantaiphai
Farkawn
Haulawng
Hruizam
Saza
Lunglei
Tuiehong
Thingsai
Leite
Sairep
Sangau
Tawipui
Mullianpui
Thingeal
Lawngtlai
Lungbung
Saiha
LAWNGTLAI
Ainak
Bungtlang
S A I H A
Tuidang
Zawngling
Vahai
Tawngkalawng
LEGEND
Distt. Boundary
State Boundary
Inter. Boundary
River
Road
Nation.Highway
Airport Symbols
State capital
Town/Village
District Hq.
N
W
E
S
Tourism
LEGEND
Distt. Boundary
State Boundary
Inter. Boundary
River
State capital
Town/Village
District Hq.
Tourist place
Chhimlung
Kolasiba
KOLASIB
Thingsat
Ratn
Darlawn
Rengdil
Mualvum
Darlawn
Chiahpui
Mamit
Saitlaw
A I Z A W L
Chaikpui
Tukkalh
Zawngin
Aizawl
Sairang
Tawkzawl
MAMIT
C H A M P H A I
AIZAWL
Serhmun
Seling
Hmawngzawl
Hnahlan
Lallen
Sibutalung
Khawthlir
Kanghmun
Kawlkulh
Champhai
Zobawk
Neihdawn
Champai
Sabul
Serchhip
Khawhai
Pukzint
Buarpur
Thenzawl
S E R C H H I P
Hlaikhan
Laisawrai
Chekawn
L U N G L E I
Vantaiphai
Pangzawl
Farkawn
Hruizam
Haulawng
Saza
Lunglei
Thingsai
Tuiehong
Leite
Thignsai
Sairep
Sangau
Tawipui
Mullianpui
Chawngte
Thingeal
Lawngtlai
Lungbung
Saiha
Saiha
LAWNGTLAI
Ainak
Shermun
Bungtlang
S A I H A
Tuipang
Tuidang
Zawngling
Vahai
Tawngkalawng

Lyuva Khutla Festival

Solomon's Temple

Scale - 1:0.72 M approx

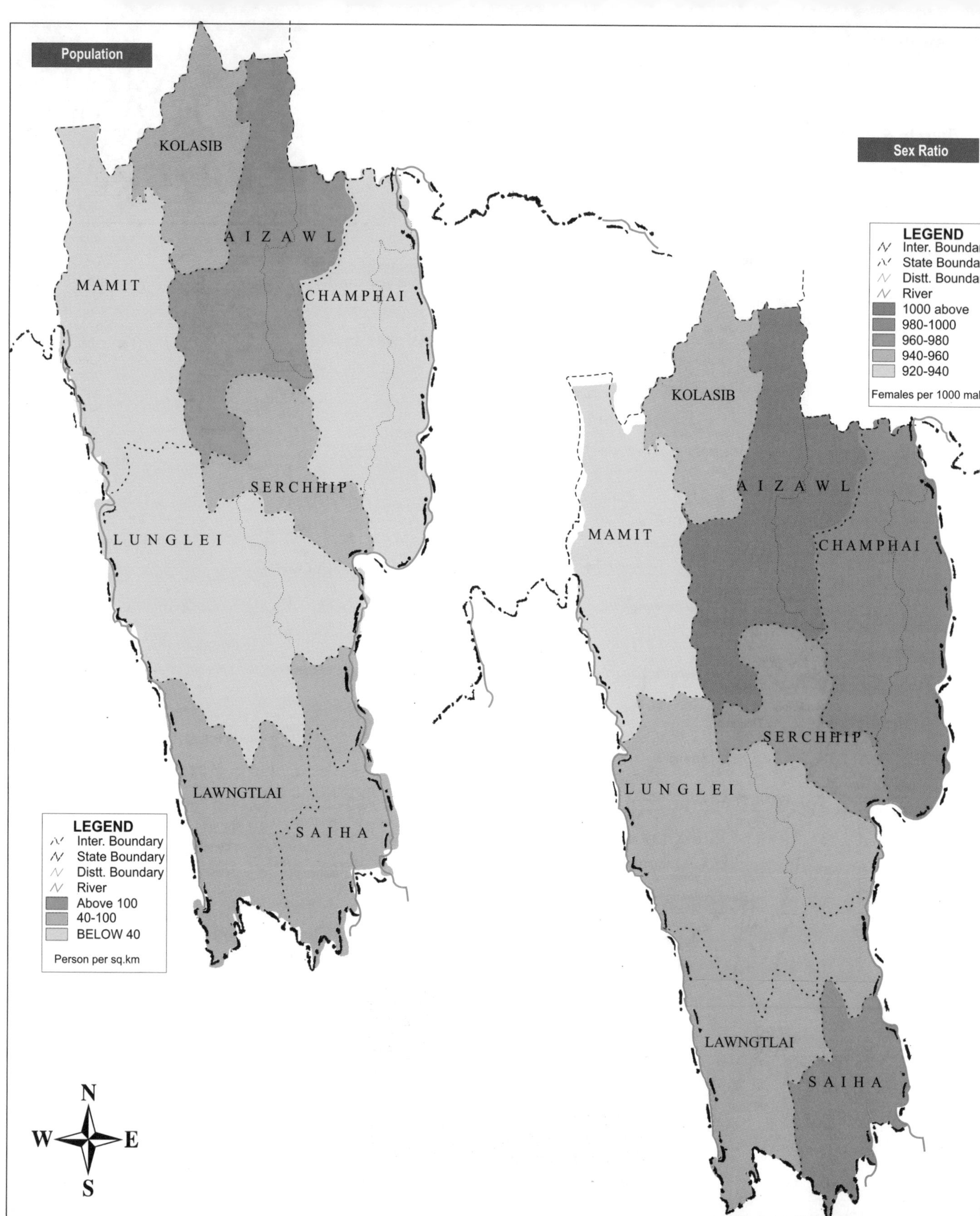
Population
KOLASIB
AIZAWL
MAMIT
CHAMPHAI
SERCHHIP
LUNGLEI
LAWNGTLAI
SAIHA
LEGEND
Inter. Boundary
State Boundary
Distt. Boundary
River
Above 100
40-100
BELOW 40
Person per sq.km
N
W
E
S
Sex Ratio
LEGEND
1000 above
980-1000
960-980
940-960
920-940
KOLASIB
AIZAWL
MAMIT
CHAMPHAI
SERCHHIP
LUNGLEI
LAWNGTLAI
SAIHA

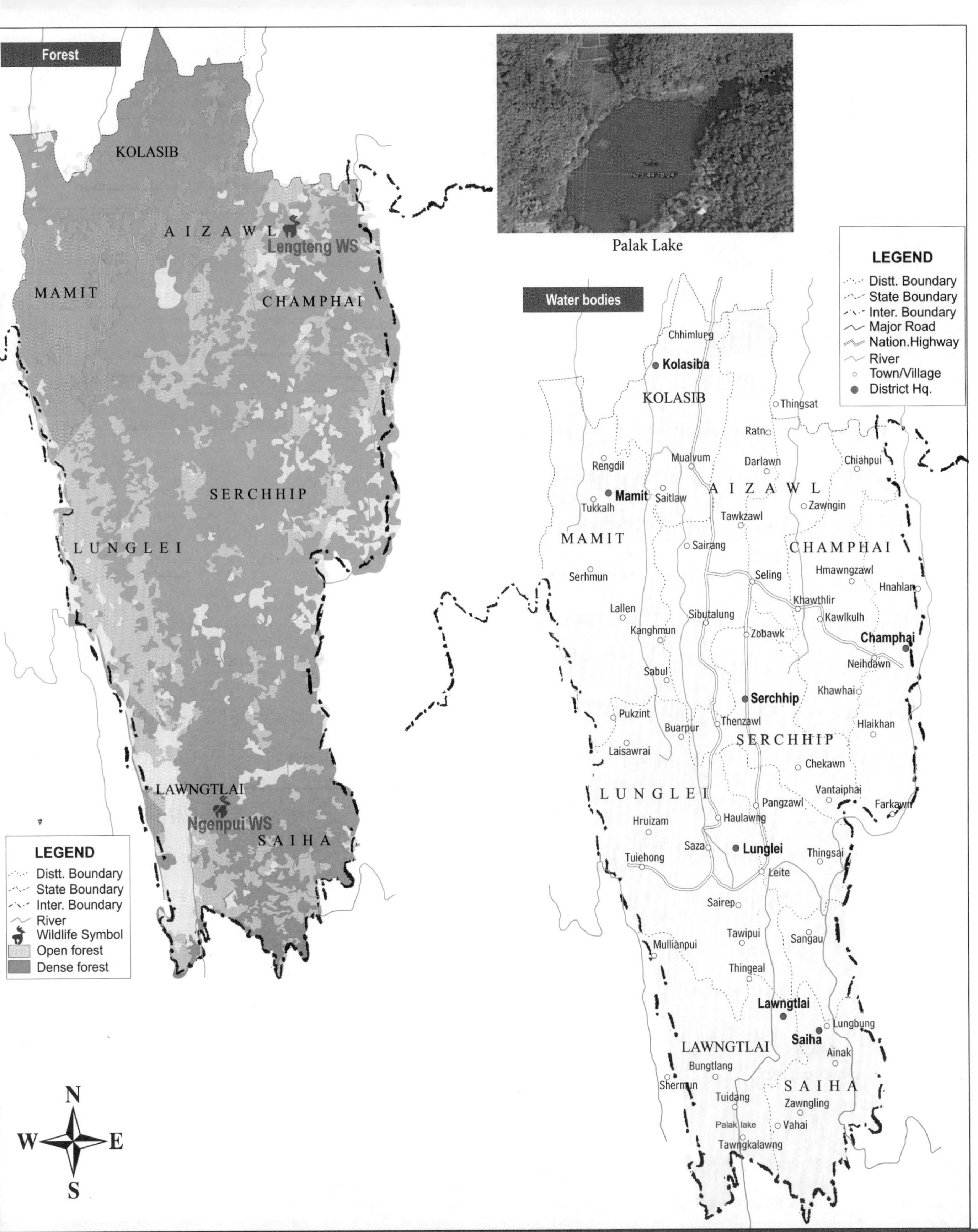
Forest
KOLASIB
AIZAWL
Lengteng WS
MAMIT
CHAMPHAI
SERCHHIP
LUNGLEI
LAWNGTLAI
Ngenpui WS
SAIHA
LEGEND
Distt. Boundary
State Boundary
Inter. Boundary
River
Wildlife Symbol
Open forest
Dense forest
N
W
E
S
Palak Lake
Water bodies
LEGEND
Distt. Boundary
State Boundary
Inter. Boundary
Major Road
Nation.Highway
River
Town/Village
District Hq.
Chhimluang
Kolasiba
KOLASIB
Thingsat
Ratnu
Rengdil
Mualvum
Darlawn
Chiahpui
Mamit
Saitlaw
AIZAWL
Zawngin
Tukkalh
Tawkzawl
MAMIT
Sairang
CHAMPHAI
Serhmun
Seling
Hmawngzawl
Hnahlan
Khawthlir
Lallen
Sibutalung
Kawlkulh
Kanghmun
Zobawk
Champhai
Neihdawn
Sabul
Khawhai
Serchhip
Pukzint
Thenzawl
Hlaikhan
Buarpur
SERCHHIP
Laisawrai
Chekawn
Vantaiphai
LUNGLEI
Pangzawl
Farkawn
Hruizam
Haulawng
Saza
Lunglei
Thingsai
Tuiehong
Leite
Sairep
Tawipui
Sangau
Mullianpui
Thingeal
Lawngtlai
Lungbung
Saiha
LAWNGTLAI
Ainak
Bungtlang
Shermun
SAIHA
Tuidang
Zawngling
Palak lake
Vahai
Tawngkalawng

Scale - 1:0.72 M approx

KOLASIB

VITAL STATISTICS

1. **District Headquarter:** Kolasib
2. **Population:** 83,955
3. **Area:** 1,382 sq. km.
4. **Population Density:** 61 persons per sq. km.
5. **Literacy:** 94.52%
6. **Sex Ratio:** 956 females per 1000 males

ECONOMIC PROFILES

1. **Agriculture:** Main crops are paddy, maize, cotton, sugarcane, millets, ginger, etc. Fruits like pineapple, citrus, banana etc.
2. **Industries:** Agro based, chemical, engineering units, cane and bamboo, mineral, metal, leather based, etc.
3. **Minerals:** Coal and Limestone etc.
4. **Tourism:** River Tlawng, Tamdil Lake, Vairengte, The Blue mountain, Dampa sanctuary etc.
5. **Live stocks :** Poultry, cattle like cows, buffaloes, goat, sheep, ducks, dogs and bitches, fishing and dairy farming etc.

Kolasib enjoys moderate climate owing to it's tropical location. It is neither very hot nor too cold throughout the year. It falls under the direct influence of the monsoon season. The average rainfall of the Kolasib district is 2703mm per annum. The forest cover type of Kolasib district is mainly tropical wet evergreen forest and tropical semi evergreen forest associated with Moist Deciduous forests.

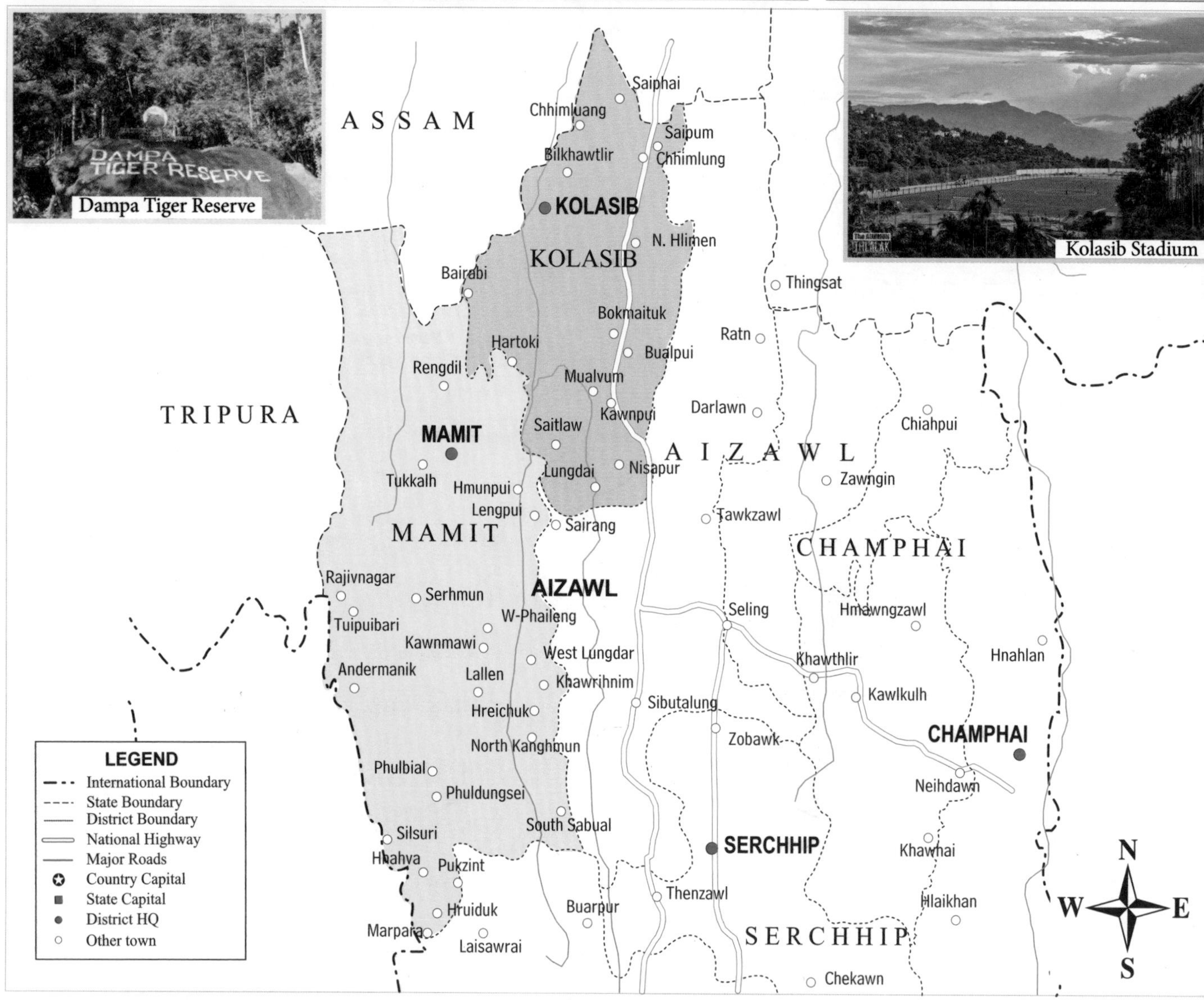

DAMPA TIGER RESERVE
Dampa Tiger Reserve
Kolasib Stadium
ASSAM
TRIPURA
KOLASIB
MAMIT
AIZAWL
CHAMPHAI
SERCHHIP
Saiphai
Chhimluang
Saipum
Chhimlung
Bilkhawtlir
N. Hlimen
Bairabi
Thingsat
Bokmaituk
Ratn
Hartoki
Bualpui
Rengdil
Mualvum
Darlawn
Chiahpui
Kawnpui
Saitlaw
Nisapur
Tukkalh
Lungdai
Zawngin
Hmunpui
Lengpui
Tawkzawl
Sairang
Rajivnagar
Serhmun
Seling
Hmawngzawl
Tuipuibari
W-Phaileng
Kawnmawi
Khawthlir
Hnahlan
Andermanik
West Lungdar
Lallen
Khawrihnim
Kawlkulh
Hreichuk
Sibutalung
North Kanghmun
Zobawk
Phulbial
Neihdawn
Phuldungsei
Silsuri
South Sabual
Hnahva
Pukzint
Khawhai
Thenzawl
Hlaikhan
Hruiduk
Buarpur
Marpara
Laisawrai
Chekawn
LEGEND
International Boundary
State Boundary
District Boundary
National Highway
Major Roads
Country Capital
State Capital
District HQ
Other town
N
W
E
S

MAMIT

VITAL STATISTICS

1. **District Headquarter:** Mamit
2. **Population:** 86,364
3. **Area:** 3,025 sq. km.
4. **Population Density:** 29 persons per sq. km.
5. **Literacy:** 84.93 %
6. **Sex Ratio:** 927 females per 1000 males

ECONOMIC PROFILES

1. **Agriculture:** Crops are paddy, maize, Cotton, sugarcane, ginger, millets, etc. Fruits like pineapple, citrus, banana etc.
2. **Industries:** Agro-based, chemical, Cotton textile, cane and bamboo, carpentry, blacksmith, metal, leather etc.
3. **Minerals:** Coal and limestone etc.
4. **Tourism:** Dampa wildlife sanctuary, Saitlaw, West Phaileng, Kang Mum, Pukzing, Lungkulh etc.
5. **Live stocks :** Poultry, cattle like cows, buffaloes, goat, sheep, ducks, pigs, dogs and bitches, fishing and dairy farming etc.

Mamit district located in the northern part of the state enjoys moderate climate owing to it's tropical location. It is neither hot nor cold throughout the year. The district falls under the direct influence of the south west monsoon. The forest cover type of Mamit District is mainly tropical and evergreen forest associated with Moist Deciduous forest and semi evergreen forest.

Projection: Lambert's Conical Orthomorphic

1000 0 1000 2000

AIZAWL

VITAL STATISTICS

- District Headquarter: Aizawl
- Population: 404,054
- Area: 3,577 sq. km.
- Population Density: 110 persons per sq. km.
- Literacy: 96.64%
- Sex Ratio: 1009 females per 1000 males

ECONOMIC PROFILES

1. **Agriculture:** Jhum cultivation is practiced to grow paddy, maize, jowar, millets, sugarcane, cotton etc. Fruits like pineapple, citrus, banana, orange, jackfruit etc.
2. **Industries:** Agro based, chemicals, cane and bamboo, leather, Cotton textile, woolen, jute based, paper products etc.
3. **Minerals:** Coal and limestone etc.
4. **Tourism:** Tamdil lake, Kv paradise, Khawnglung WLS, Durtlang hills, Vantawng falls etc.
5. **Live stocks :** Poultry, cattle like cows, buffaloes, goat, sheep, ducks, pigs, dogs and bitches, fishing and dairy farming etc.

Aizawl is one of the prominent district of Mizoram. The climate in the district is warm and temperate. When compared with winter, the summers have much more rainfall. This climate is considered to be CWA according to the Koppen-Geiger climate classification. The average annual temperature is 20.6°C in the district. The district comprises of two agriculture sub-divisions namely Aizawl HQ and Darlawn.

Saitual is the new district of Mizoram, Earlier it is one of the city in Aizawl. The average annual temperature is 20.6°C. The major tribes in the district are Chakma, Pawi, Ralte and Kuki tribes. The staple food crop is paddy, maize is secondary. The main industries in the district are Agro based, mineral based, cotton textiles, jute based, bamboo, carpentry etc. The livestock are cattle, cows, buffaloes, goat, dogs etc.

Khawzawl is the new district of Mizoram, which is bifurcated from champhai district in the year 2019. The district has a moderate climate. In winter the temperature varies from 0°C to 20°C and in summer, the temperature varies between 15°C and 30°C. The economy of the district mainly depends on agriculture and border trade. The major tribes in the district are Mizos, Kukis, Hmar, Ralte, etc.

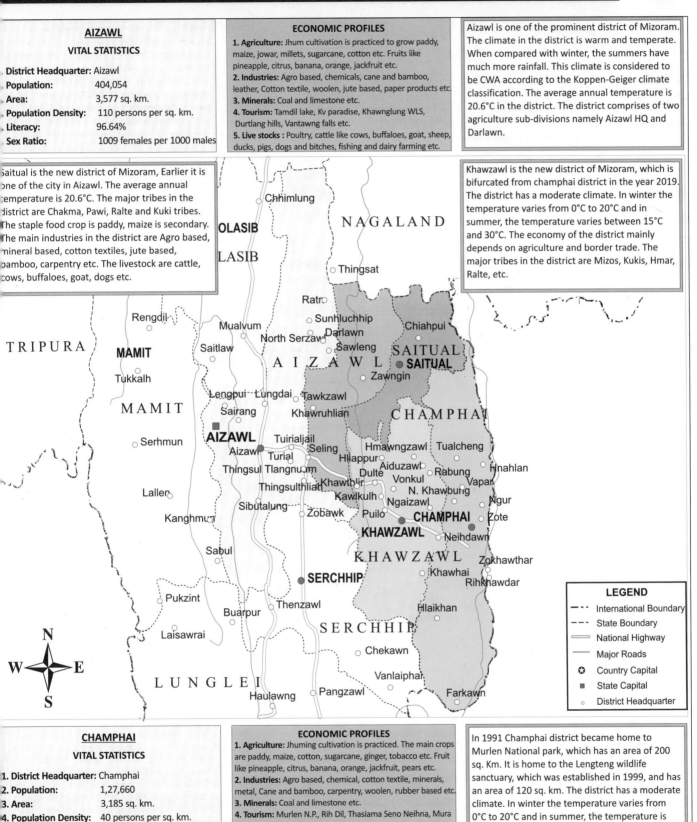

Chhimlung
NAGALAND
OLASIB
LASIB
Thingsat
Ratu
Sunhluchhip
Darlawn
North Serzawl
Sawleng
Chiahpui
Rengdil
Mualvum
TRIPURA
MAMIT
Saitlaw
A I Z A W L
SAITUAL
SAITUAL
Zawngin
Tukkalh
Lengpui
Lungdai
Tawkzawl
MAMIT
Sairang
Khawruhlian
CHAMPHAI
AIZAWL
Serhmun
Aizawl
Tuirialjail
Seling
Turial
Hmawngzawl
Tualcheng
Hliappur
Thingsul Tlangnuam
Aiduzawl
Rabung
Hnahlan
Dulte
Vonkul
Vapar
Khawthlir
N. Khawbung
Lallen
Thingsulthliah
Kawlkulh
Ngaizawl
Ngur
Sibutalung
Zobawk
Puilo
CHAMPHAI
Zote
Kanghmun
KHAWZAWL
Neihdawn
Sabul
KHAWZAWL
Zokhawthar
Khawhai
SERCHHIP
Rihkhawdar
Pukzint
Thenzawl
Hlaikhan
Buarpur
SERCHHIP
Laisawrai
Chekawn
N
W
E
S
Vanlaiphai
L U N G L E I
Haulawng
Pangzawl
Farkawn
LEGEND
International Boundary
State Boundary
National Highway
Major Roads
Country Capital
State Capital
District Headquarter

CHAMPHAI

VITAL STATISTICS

1. District Headquarter: Champhai
2. Population: 1,27,660
3. Area: 3,185 sq. km.
4. Population Density: 40 persons per sq. km.
5. Literacy: 95.91 %
6. Sex Ratio: 984 females per 1000 males

ECONOMIC PROFILES

1. **Agriculture:** Jhuming cultivation is practiced. The main crops are paddy, maize, cotton, sugarcane, ginger, tobacco etc. Fruit like pineapple, citrus, banana, orange, jackfruit, pears etc.
2. **Industries:** Agro based, chemical, cotton textile, minerals, metal, Cane and bamboo, carpentry, woolen, rubber based etc.
3. **Minerals:** Coal and limestone etc.
4. **Tourism:** Murlen N.P., Rih Dil, Thasiama Seno Neihna, Mura puk, Lengteng wildlife sanctuary etc.
5. **Live stocks :** poultry, cattle like cows, buffaloes, goat, sheep, ducks, pigs, dogs and bitches, fishing and dairy farming etc.

In 1991 Champhai district became home to Murlen National park, which has an area of 200 sq. Km. It is home to the Lengteng wildlife sanctuary, which was established in 1999, and has an area of 120 sq. km. The district has a moderate climate. In winter the temperature varies from 0°C to 20°C and in summer, the temperature is varies between 15°C and 30°C.

Scale - 1:1 M approx

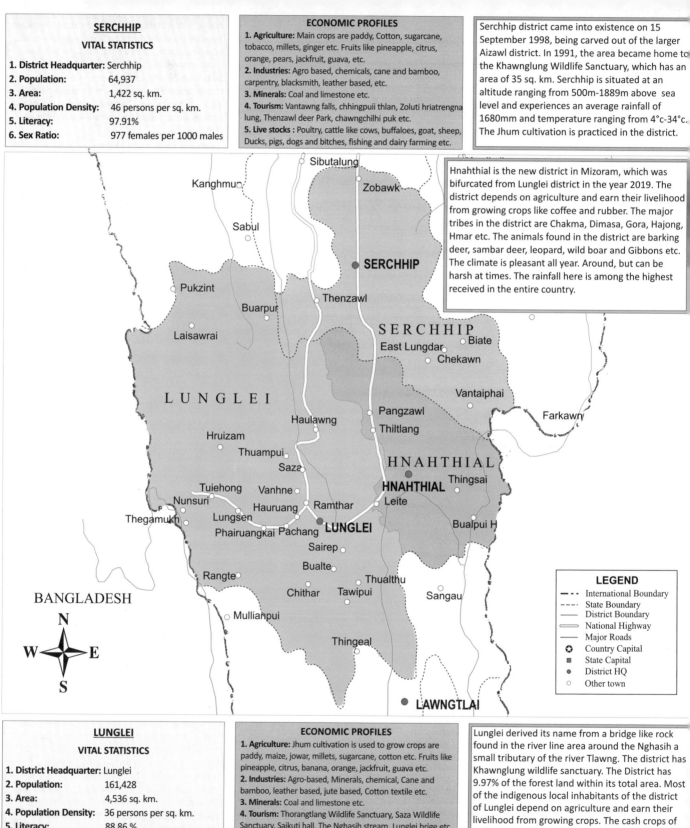

SERCHHIP

VITAL STATISTICS

1. **District Headquarter:** Serchhip
2. **Population:** 64,937
3. **Area:** 1,422 sq. km.
4. **Population Density:** 46 persons per sq. km.
5. **Literacy:** 97.91%
6. **Sex Ratio:** 977 females per 1000 males

ECONOMIC PROFILES

1. **Agriculture:** Main crops are paddy, Cotton, sugarcane, tobacco, millets, ginger etc. Fruits like pineapple, citrus, orange, pears, jackfruit, guava, etc.
2. **Industries:** Agro based, chemicals, cane and bamboo, carpentry, blacksmith, leather based, etc.
3. **Minerals:** Coal and limestone etc.
4. **Tourism:** Vantawng falls, chhingpuii thlan, Zoluti hriatrengna lung, Thenzawl deer Park, chawngchilhi puk etc.
5. **Live stocks :** Poultry, cattle like cows, buffaloes, goat, sheep, Ducks, pigs, dogs and bitches, fishing and dairy farming etc.

Serchhip district came into existence on 15 September 1998, being carved out of the larger Aizawl district. In 1991, the area became home to the Khawnglung Wildlife Sanctuary, which has an area of 35 sq. km. Serchhip is situated at an altitude ranging from 500m-1889m above sea level and experiences an average rainfall of 1680mm and temperature ranging from 4°c-34°c. The Jhum cultivation is practiced in the district.

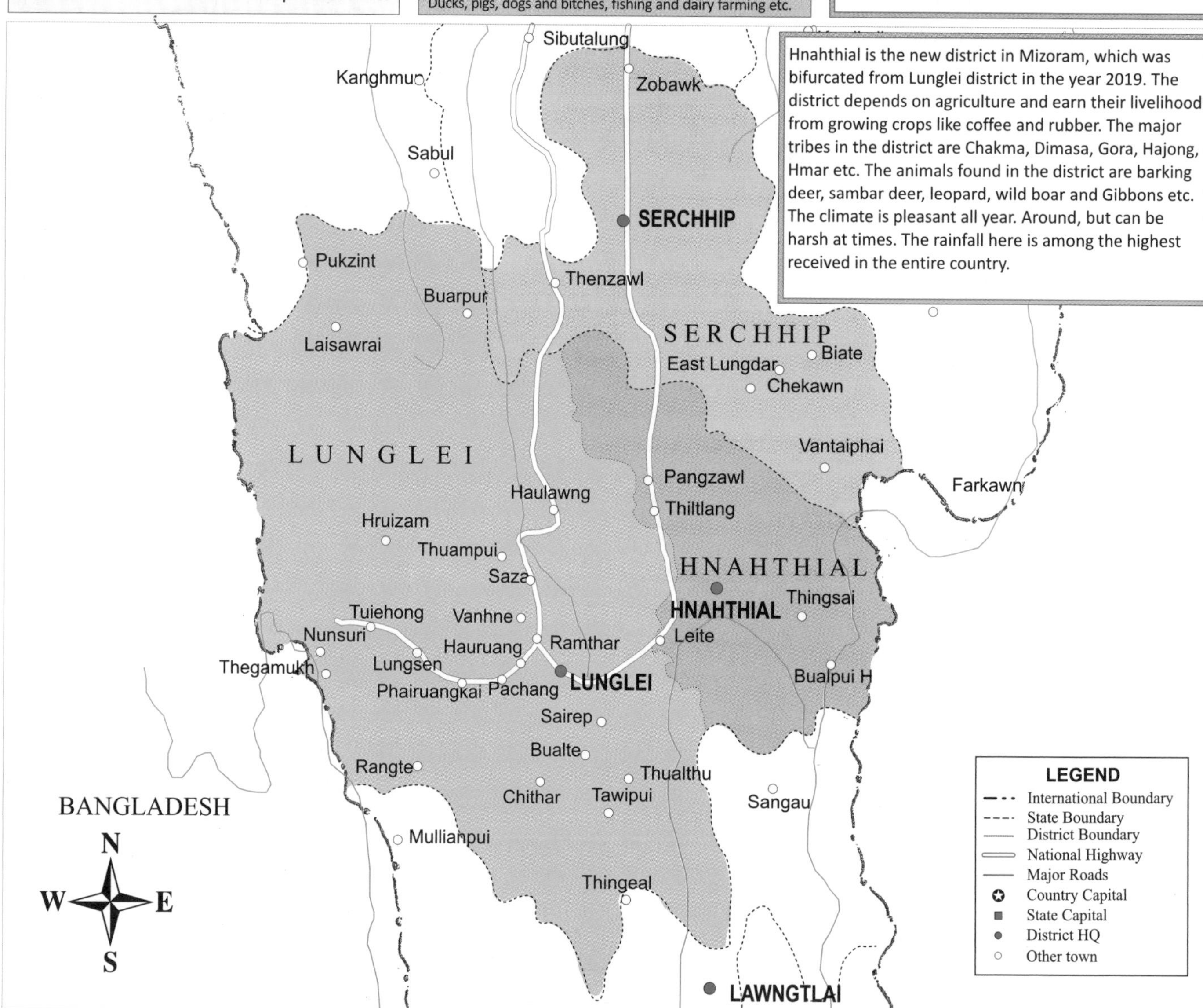

Sibutalung
Kanghmun
Zobawk
Sabul
SERCHHIP
Pukzint
Thenzawl
Buarpui
Laisawrai
SERCHHIP
East Lungdar
Biate
Chekawn
LUNGLEI
Vantaiphai
Pangzawl
Farkawn
Haulawng
Thiltlang
Hruizam
Thuampui
HNAHTHIAL
Saza
HNAHTHIAL
Thingsai
Tuiehong
Vanhne
Nunsuri
Leite
Ramthar
Hauruang
Thegamukh
Lungsen
LUNGLEI
Bualpui H
Phairuangkai
Pachang
Sairep
Bualte
Rangte
Thualthu
Chithar
Tawipui
Sangau
BANGLADESH
Mullianpui
N
W
E
S
Thingeal
LAWNGTLAI
LEGEND
International Boundary
State Boundary
District Boundary
National Highway
Major Roads
Country Capital
State Capital
District HQ
Other town

Hnahthial is the new district in Mizoram, which was bifurcated from Lunglei district in the year 2019. The district depends on agriculture and earn their livelihood from growing crops like coffee and rubber. The major tribes in the district are Chakma, Dimasa, Gora, Hajong, Hmar etc. The animals found in the district are barking deer, sambar deer, leopard, wild boar and Gibbons etc. The climate is pleasant all year. Around, but can be harsh at times. The rainfall here is among the highest received in the entire country.

LUNGLEI

VITAL STATISTICS

1. **District Headquarter:** Lunglei
2. **Population:** 161,428
3. **Area:** 4,536 sq. km.
4. **Population Density:** 36 persons per sq. km.
5. **Literacy:** 88.86 %
6. **Sex Ratio:** 947 females per 1000 males

ECONOMIC PROFILES

1. **Agriculture:** Jhum cultivation is used to grow crops are paddy, maize, jowar, millets, sugarcane, cotton etc. Fruits like pineapple, citrus, banana, orange, jackfruit, guava etc.
2. **Industries:** Agro-based, Minerals, chemical, Cane and bamboo, leather based, jute based, Cotton textile etc.
3. **Minerals:** Coal and limestone etc.
4. **Tourism:** Thorangtlang Wildlife Sanctuary, Saza Wildlife Sanctuary, Saikuti hall, The Nghasih stream, Lunglei brige etc.
5. **Live stocks :** Poultry, cattle like cows, buffaloes, goat, sheep, ducks, pigs, dogs and bitches, fishing and dairy farming etc.

Lunglei derived its name from a bridge like rock found in the river line area around the Nghasih a small tributary of the river Tlawng. The district has Khawnglung wildlife sanctuary. The District has 9.97% of the forest land within its total area. Most of the indigenous local inhabitants of the district of Lunglei depend on agriculture and earn their livelihood from growing crops. The cash crops of coffee and rubber help it to earn it's revenue.

Scale - 1:0.82 M appro

LAWNGTLAI

VITAL STATISTICS

1. District Headquarter:	Lawngtlai
2. Population:	117,894
3. Area:	2,557 sq. km.
4. Population Density:	46 persons per sq. km.
5. Literacy:	65.88%
6. Sex Ratio:	945 females per 1000 males

ECONOMIC PROFILES

1. **Agriculture:** Crops are paddy, maize, cotton, sugarcane, ginger, millets etc. The horticulture crops like pineapple, citrus, orange, banana, jackfruit, guava etc.
2. **Industries:** Agro-based, chemicals, Cane and bamboo, blacksmith, carpentry, Cotton textile etc.
3. **Minerals:** Coal and limestone etc.
4. **Tourism:** Ngengpui WLS, Sinemon WLS, mullianpui, chawngte, uiphum etc.
5. **Live stocks :** Poultry, cattle like cows, buffaloes, goats, sheep, ducks, dogs and bitches, fishing and dairy farming etc.

The inhabitants of Lawngtlai district are Pang, Lai, and Chakma, etc. The main occupation of the people is cultivation and the rural population largely depends on agriculture for their subsistence. The main rivers of the district are Kaladan river, Tuichong river, the Chhimtuipui river etc. The climate of the district has a moderate climate. It is cool in summer and not very cold in winter. The average annual rainfall of the district is about 2558mm. The hottest period is from March to August.

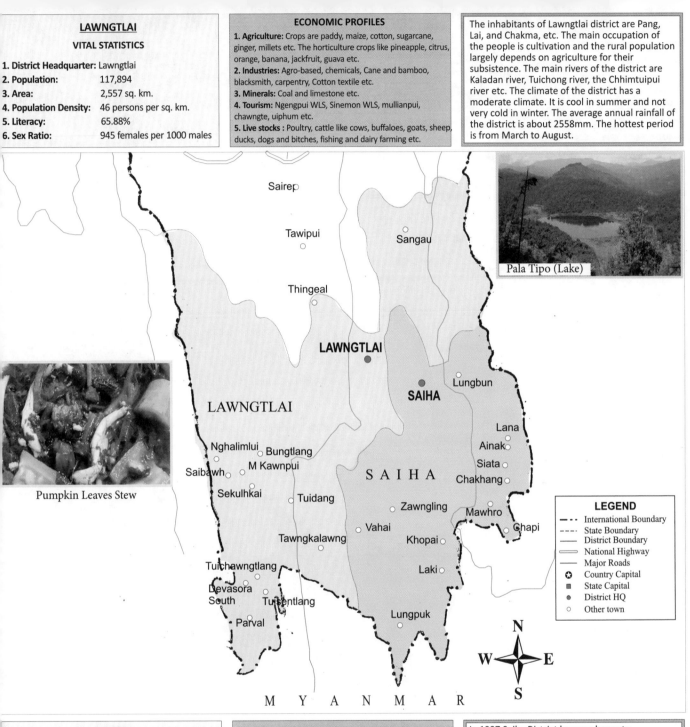

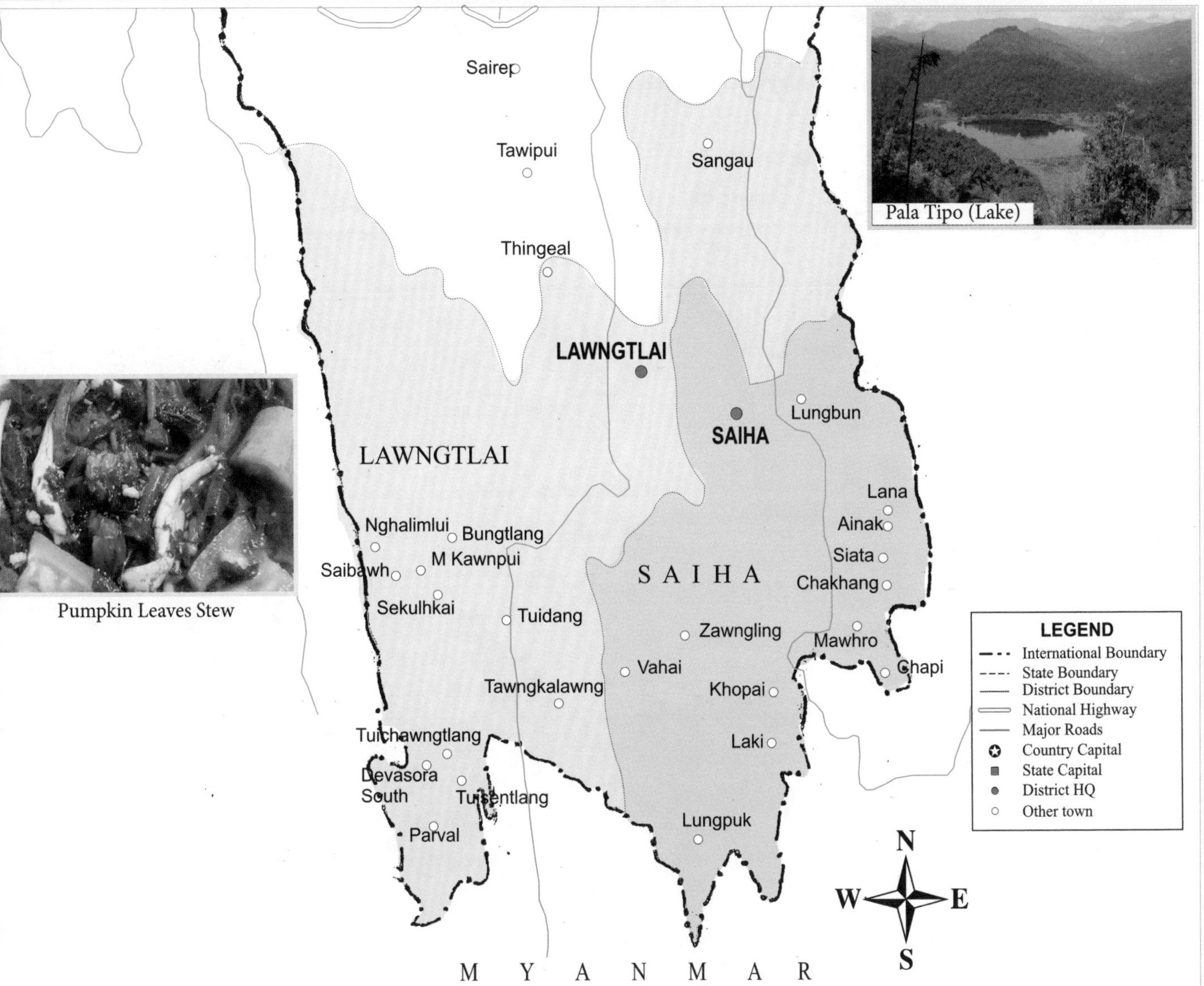

Sairep
Tawipui
Sangau
Thingeal
LAWNGTLAI
SAIHA
Lungbun
LAWNGTLAI
Lana
Ainak
Nghalimlui
Bungtlang
Siata
M Kawnpui
Saibawh
S A I H A
Chakhang
Sekulhkai
Tuidang
Zawngling
Mawhro
Vahai
Chapi
Tawngkalawng
Khopai
Tuichawngtlang
Laki
Devasora South
Tuisentlang
Parval
Lungpuk
M Y A N M A R
N
W
E
S
LEGEND
International Boundary
State Boundary
District Boundary
National Highway
Major Roads
Country Capital
State Capital
District HQ
Other town

Pala Tipo (Lake)

Pumpkin Leaves Stew

SAIHA

VITAL STATISTICS

1. District Headquarter:	Saiha
2. Population:	56,574
3. Area:	1,400 sq. km.
4. Population Density:	40 persons per sq. km.
5. Literacy:	90.01 %
6. Sex Ratio:	979 females per 1000 males

ECONOMIC PROFILES

1. **Agriculture:** Crops are paddy, maize, Cotton, jute, millets, sugarcane etc. Fruits like pineapple, citrus, banana, guava, etc.
2. **Industries:** Agro-based, chemical, engineering units, Cotton textile, minerals, metals, leather based, carpentry etc.
3. **Minerals:** Coal and limestone etc.
4. **Tourism:** Palak wildlife sanctuary, Palak dil etc.
5. **Live stocks :** Poultry, cattle like cows, buffaloes, goats, sheep, ducks, dogs and bitches, fishing and dairy farming etc.

In 1997 Saiha District became home to Phawngpui Blue mountain national park, which is spread over an area of $50km^2$. Climate is classified as warm and temperate. In winter, there is much less rainfall in Saiha than in summer. The temperature here averages 20.5°C and above 2876 mm of precipitation annually. Saiha district is bounded on the north and north-west by Lunglei, on the west by Lawngtlai, and on the south and east by Myanmar.

Scale - 1:0.68 M approx

NAGALAND

Section

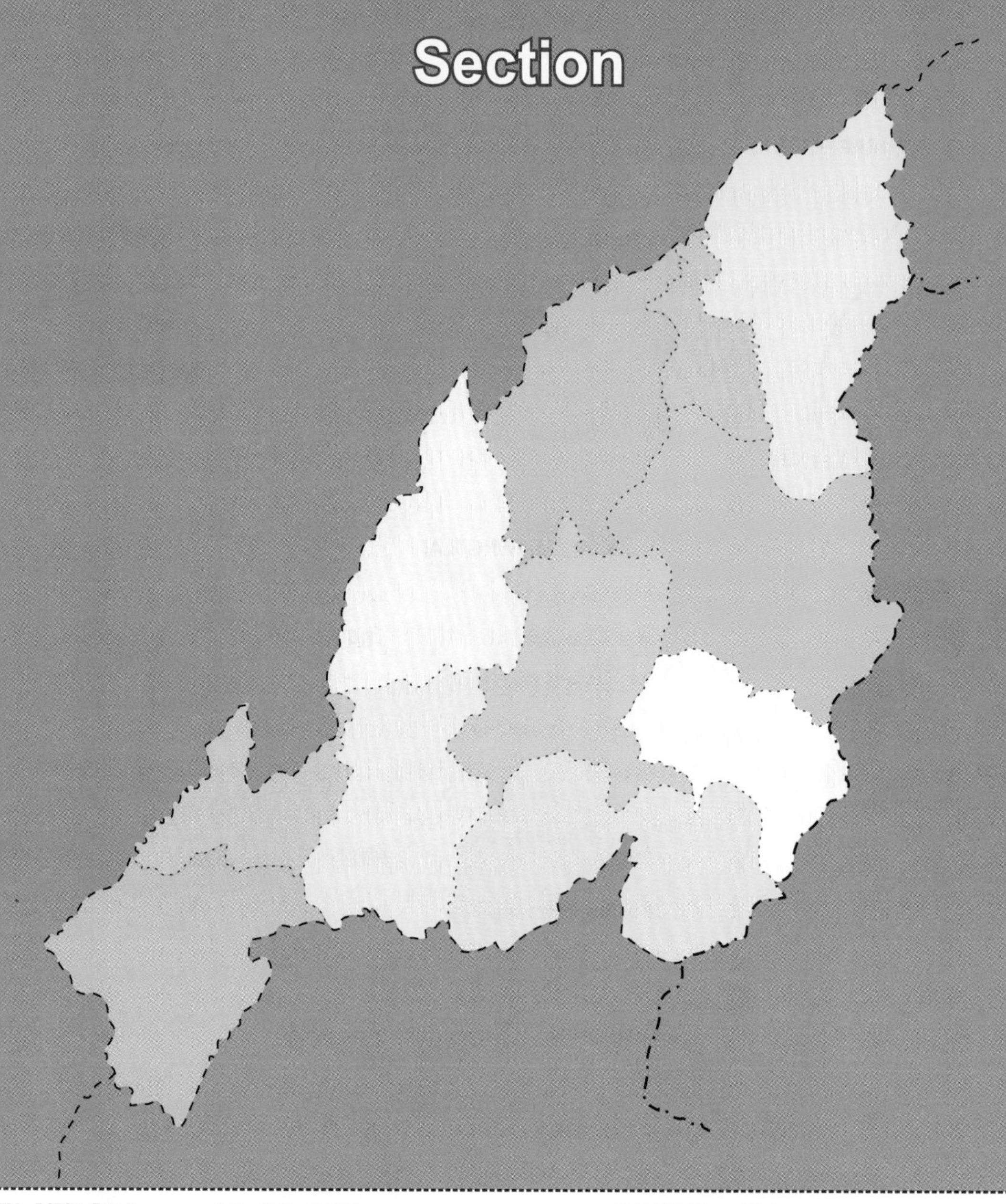

POPULATION:	***19,90,036***	DISTRICTS: ***12***
AREA:	***16,579 sq.km.***	L.S. CONSTITUENCY: ***1***
POP. DENSITY:	***120 persons/ Km^2***	R.S. CONSTITUENCY: ***1***
LITERACY:	***80.11%***	GRAM PANCHAYATS: ***N.A***
SEX RATIO:	***931 females/1000 males***	GSDP: ***24,281***

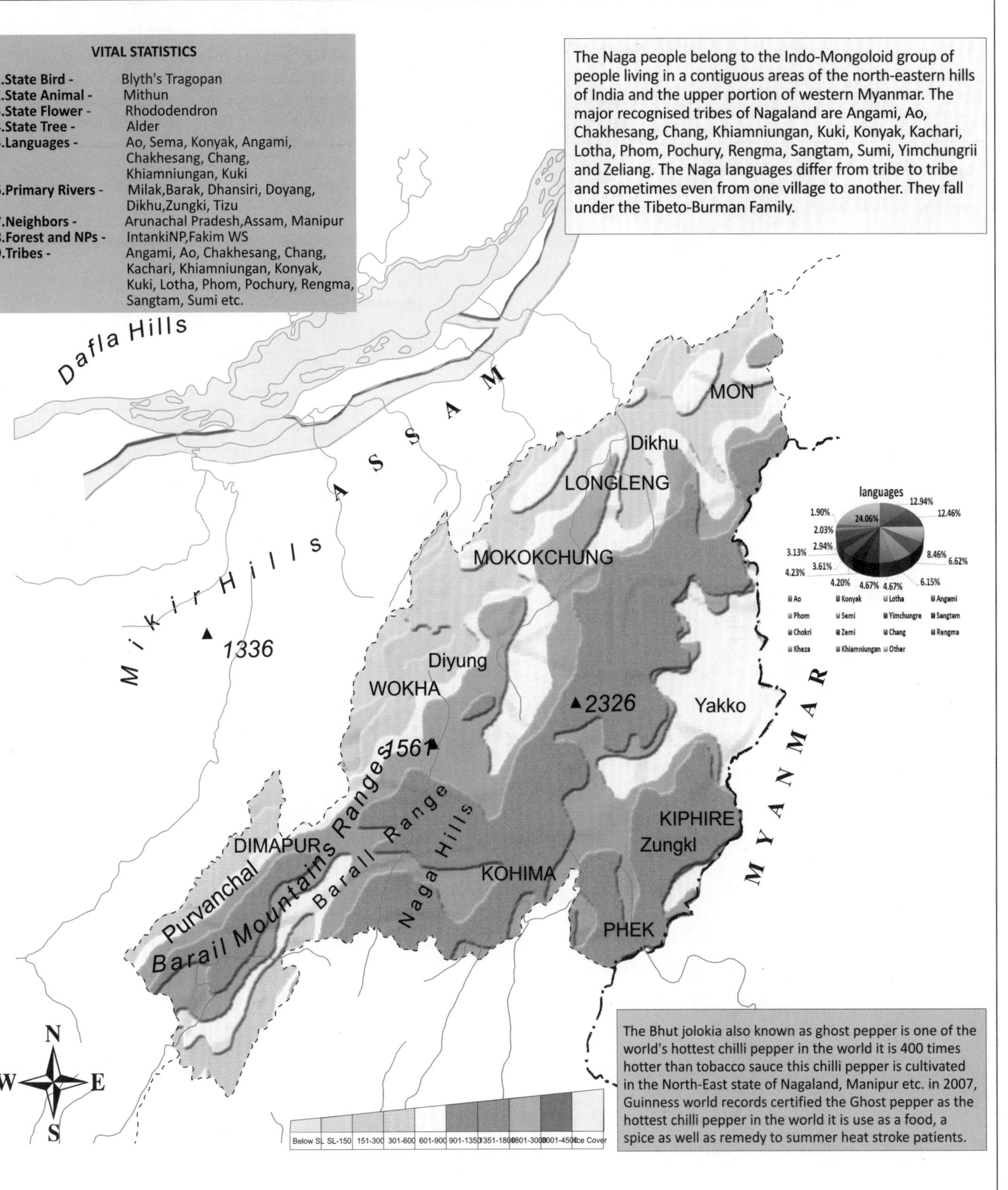
VITAL STATISTICS
1.State Bird - Blyth's Tragopan
2.State Animal - Mithun
3.State Flower - Rhododendron
4.State Tree - Alder
5.Languages - Ao, Sema, Konyak, Angami, Chakhesang, Chang, Khiamniungan, Kuki
6.Primary Rivers - Milak,Barak, Dhansiri, Doyang, Dikhu,Zungki, Tizu
7.Neighbors - Arunachal Pradesh,Assam, Manipur
8.Forest and NPs - IntankiNP,Fakim WS
9.Tribes - Angami, Ao, Chakhesang, Chang, Kachari, Khiamniungan, Konyak, Kuki, Lotha, Phom, Pochury, Rengma, Sangtam, Sumi etc.
The Naga people belong to the Indo-Mongoloid group of people living in a contiguous areas of the north-eastern hills of India and the upper portion of western Myanmar. The major recognised tribes of Nagaland are Angami, Ao, Chakhesang, Chang, Khiamniungan, Kuki, Konyak, Kachari, Lotha, Phom, Pochury, Rengma, Sangtam, Sumi, Yimchungrii and Zeliang. The Naga languages differ from tribe to tribe and sometimes even from one village to another. They fall under the Tibeto-Burman Family.
Dafla Hills
ASSAM
Mikir Hills
1336
MON
Dikhu
LONGLENG
MOKOKCHUNG
Diyung
WOKHA
2326
Yakko
1561
Barail Mountains Ranges
Barail Range
Naga Hills
DIMAPUR
Purvanchal
KOHIMA
KIPHIRE
Zungkl
PHEK
MYANMAR
languages
12.94%
12.46%
1.90%
24.06%
2.03%
2.94%
3.13%
3.61%
8.46%
6.62%
4.23%
4.20%
4.67%
4.67%
6.15%
Ao
Konyak
Lotha
Angami
Phom
Semi
Yimchungre
Sangtam
Chokri
Zemi
Chang
Rengma
Kheza
Khiamniungan
Other
N
W
E
S
Below SL
SL-150
151-300
301-600
601-900
901-1350
1351-1800
1801-3000
3001-4500
Ice Cover
The Bhut jolokia also known as ghost pepper is one of the world's hottest chilli pepper in the world it is 400 times hotter than tobacco sauce this chilli pepper is cultivated in the North-East state of Nagaland, Manipur etc. in 2007, Guinness world records certified the Ghost pepper as the hottest chilli pepper in the world it is use as a food, a spice as well as remedy to summer heat stroke patients.

Scale - 1:1.47 M approx

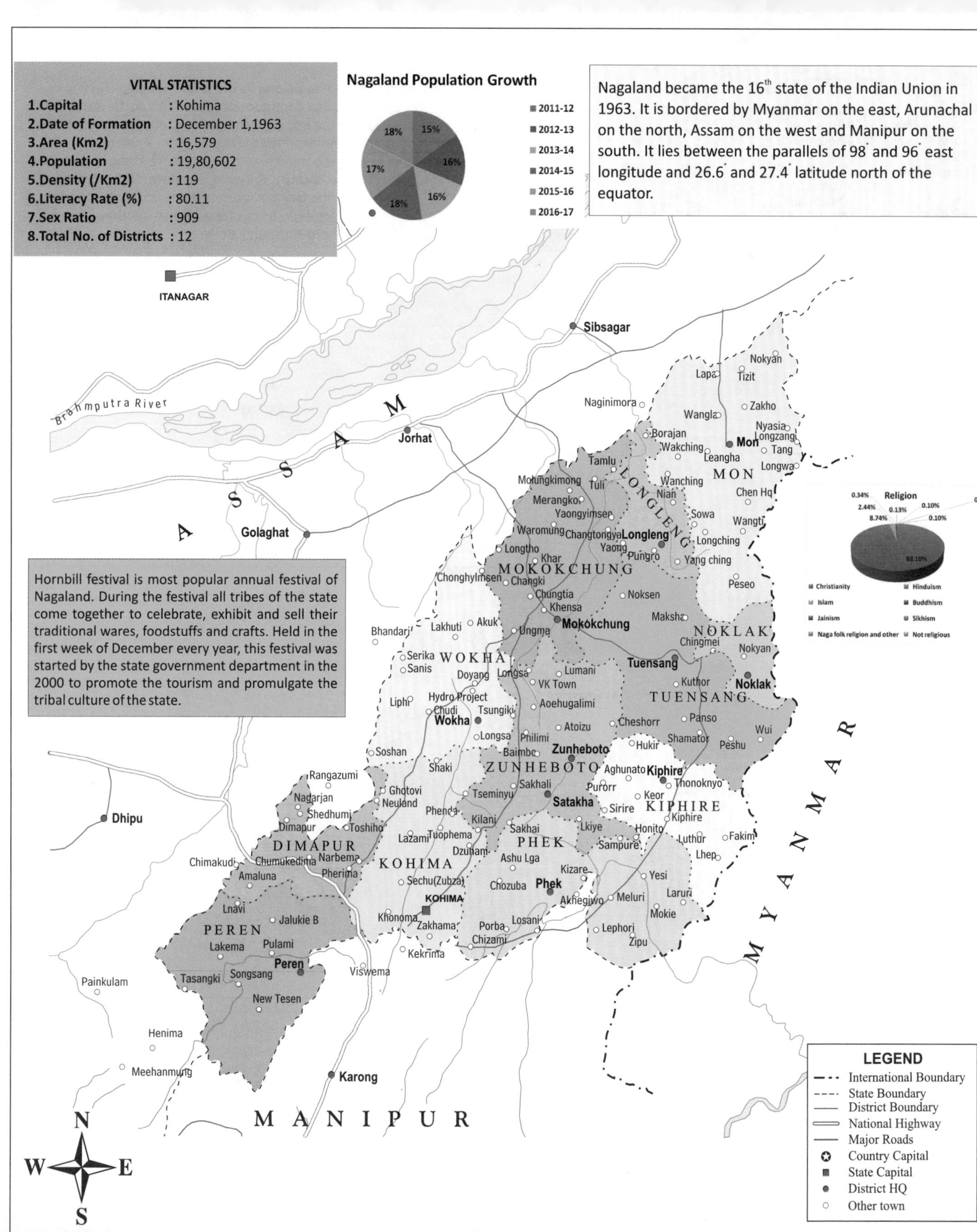
VITAL STATISTICS
1.Capital : Kohima
2.Date of Formation : December 1,1963
3.Area (Km2) : 16,579
4.Population : 19,80,602
5.Density (/Km2) : 119
6.Literacy Rate (%) : 80.11
7.Sex Ratio : 909
8.Total No. of Districts : 12
Nagaland Population Growth
15%
16%
16%
18%
17%
18%
2011-12
2012-13
2013-14
2014-15
2015-16
2016-17
Nagaland became the 16th state of the Indian Union in 1963. It is bordered by Myanmar on the east, Arunachal on the north, Assam on the west and Manipur on the south. It lies between the parallels of 98° and 96° east longitude and 26.6° and 27.4° latitude north of the equator.
Hornbill festival is most popular annual festival of Nagaland. During the festival all tribes of the state come together to celebrate, exhibit and sell their traditional wares, foodstuffs and crafts. Held in the first week of December every year, this festival was started by the state government department in the 2000 to promote the tourism and promulgate the tribal culture of the state.
Religion
0.34%
2.44%
0.13%
0.10%
8.74%
0.10%
88.10%
Christianity
Hinduism
Islam
Buddhism
Jainism
Sikhism
Naga folk religion and other
Not religious
ITANAGAR
Brahmputra River
ASSAM
Sibsagar
Jorhat
Golaghat
Naginimora
Dhipu
MANIPUR
Karong
MYANMAR
MON
Mon
LONGLENG
Longleng
MOKOKCHUNG
Mokokchung
NOKLAK
Noklak
TUENSANG
Tuensang
WOKHA
Wokha
ZUNHEBOTO
Zunheboto
KIPHIRE
Kiphire
PHEK
Phek
KOHIMA
DIMAPUR
PEREN
Peren
LEGEND
International Boundary
State Boundary
District Boundary
National Highway
Major Roads
Country Capital
State Capital
District HQ
Other town
N
W
E
S
Scale - 1:1.47 M approx

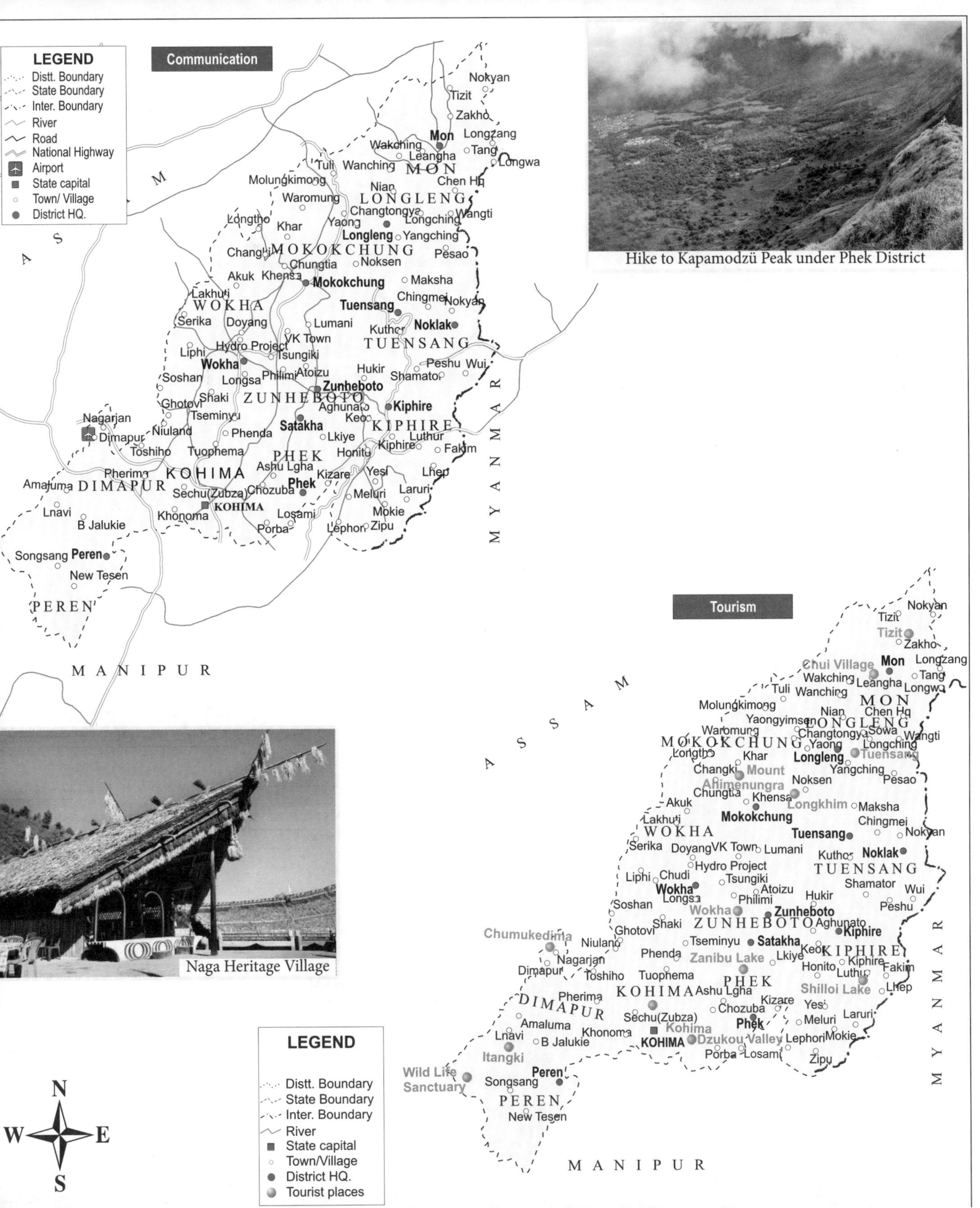
LEGEND
Distt. Boundary
State Boundary
Inter. Boundary
River
Road
National Highway
Airport
State capital
Town/ Village
District HQ.
Communication
A S S A M
M A N I P U R
M Y A N M A R
MON
LONGLENG
MOKOKCHUNG
WOKHA
TUENSANG
ZUNHEBOTO
KIPHIRE
PHEK
KOHIMA
DIMAPUR
PEREN
Nokyan
Tizit
Zakho
Mon
Longzang
Tang
Longwa
Wakching
Leangha
Tuli
Wanching
Chen Hq
Molungkimong
Nian
Waromung
Changtongya
Longching
Wangti
Longtho
Khar
Yaong
Longleng
Yangching
Changki
Pesao
Chungtia
Noksen
Akuk
Khensa
Mokokchung
Maksha
Lakhuti
Chingmei
Nokyan
Tuensang
Serika
Doyang
Lumani
Kuthur
Noklak
VK Town
Hydro Project
Liphi
Tsungiki
Wokha
Peshu
Wui
Soshan
Longsa
Philimi
Atoizu
Hukir
Shamator
Zunheboto
Ghotovi
Shaki
Aghunato
Kiphire
Nagarjan
Tseminyu
Keo
Satakha
Dimapur
Niuland
Phenda
Lkiye
Luthur
Toshiho
Tuophema
Kiphire
Fakim
Honito
Pherima
Ashu Lgha
Lhep
Amaluma
Kizare
Yesi
Phek
Sechu(Zubza)
Chozuba
Laruri
Meluri
Lnavi
Mokie
KOHIMA
Khonoma
Losami
B Jalukie
Porba
Lephori
Zipu
Songsang
Peren
New Tesen
Hike to Kapamodzü Peak under Phek District
Tourism
Tizit
Chui Village
Yaongyimsen
Sowa
Tuensang
Mount
Ahimenungra
Longkhim
Chudi
Wokha
Chumukedima
Zanibu Lake
Shilloi Lake
Kohima
Dzukou Valley
Itangki
Wild Life Sanctuary
Naga Heritage Village
LEGEND
Distt. Boundary
State Boundary
Inter. Boundary
River
State capital
Town/Village
District HQ.
Tourist places
N
W
E
S

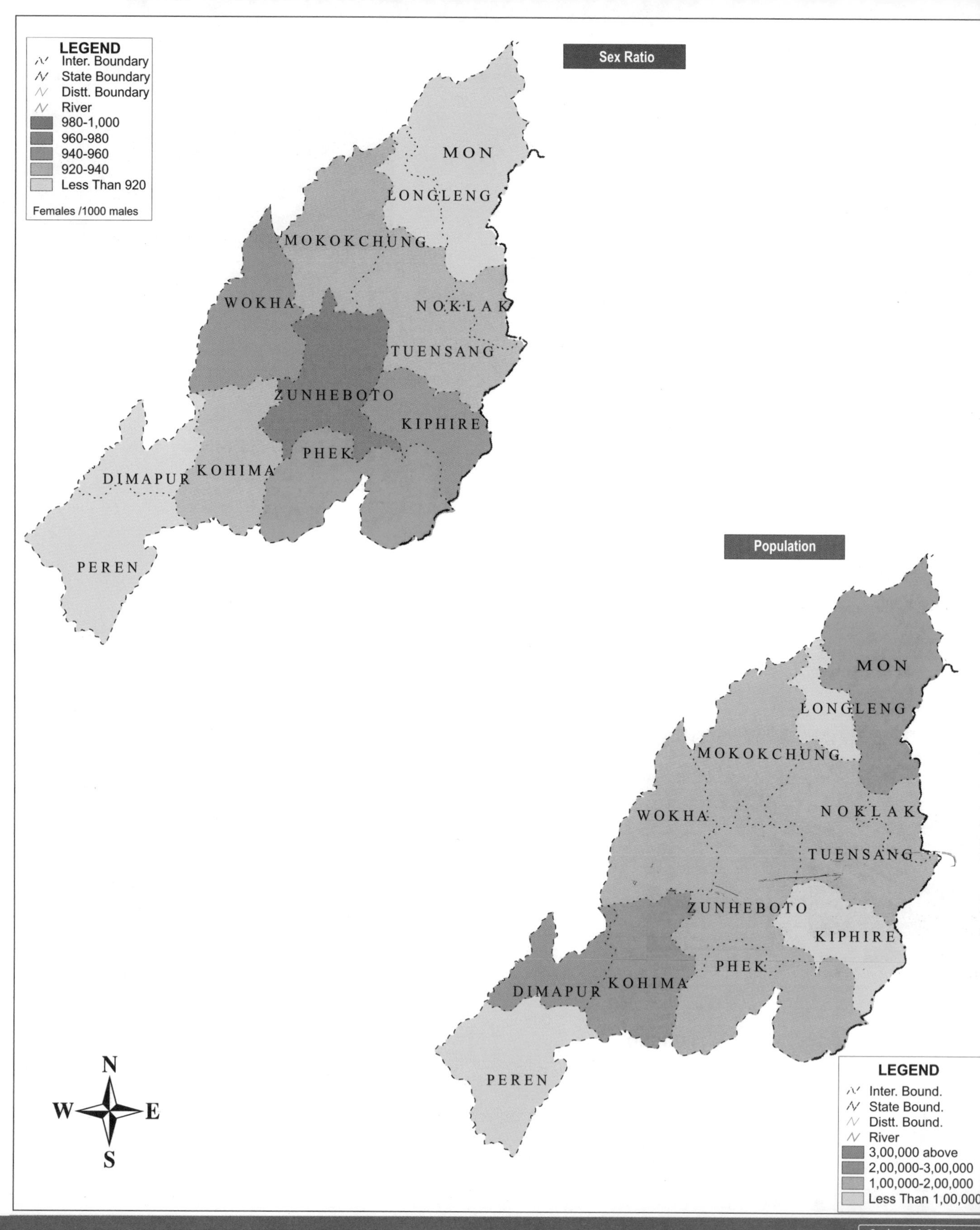
LEGEND
Inter. Boundary
State Boundary
Distt. Boundary
River
980-1,000
960-980
940-960
920-940
Less Than 920
Females /1000 males
Sex Ratio
MON
LONGLENG
MOKOKCHUNG
WOKHA
NOKLAK
TUENSANG
ZUNHEBOTO
KIPHIRE
PHEK
KOHIMA
DIMAPUR
PEREN
Population
MON
LONGLENG
MOKOKCHUNG
WOKHA
NOKLAK
TUENSANG
ZUNHEBOTO
KIPHIRE
PHEK
KOHIMA
DIMAPUR
PEREN
N
W
E
S
LEGEND
Inter. Bound.
State Bound.
Distt. Bound.
River
3,00,000 above
2,00,000-3,00,000
1,00,000-2,00,000
Less Than 1,00,000

Scale - 1:1.8 M approx

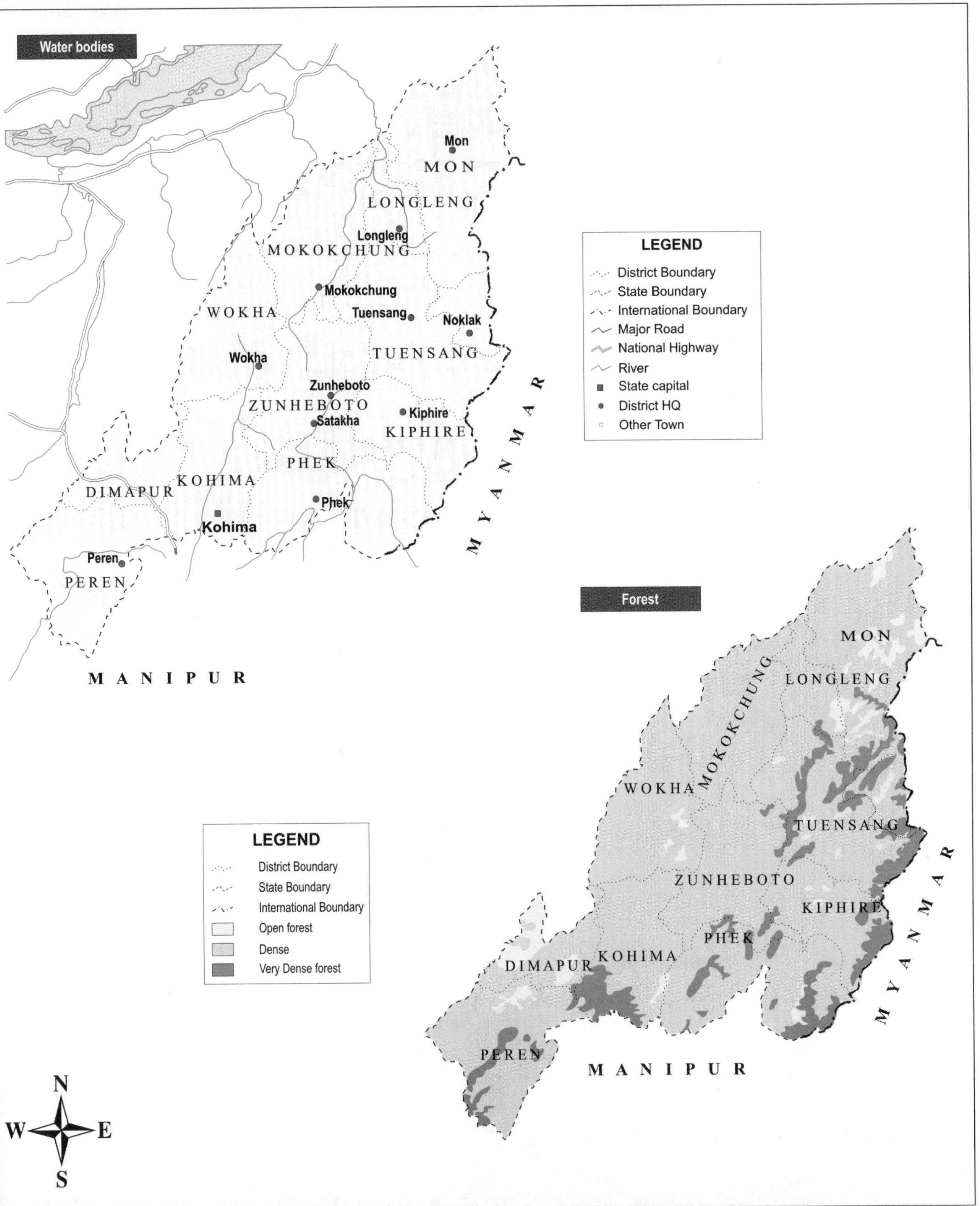
Water bodies
Mon
MON
LONGLENG
Longleng
MOKOKCHUNG
Mokokchung
WOKHA
Tuensang
Noklak
Wokha
TUENSANG
Zunheboto
ZUNHEBOTO
Satakha
Kiphire
KIPHIRE
PHEK
KOHIMA
DIMAPUR
Phek
Kohima
Peren
PEREN
MANIPUR
MYANMAR
LEGEND
District Boundary
State Boundary
International Boundary
Major Road
National Highway
River
State capital
District HQ
Other Town
Forest
MON
LONGLENG
MOKOKCHUNG
WOKHA
TUENSANG
ZUNHEBOTO
KIPHIRE
PHEK
KOHIMA
DIMAPUR
PEREN
MANIPUR
MYANMAR
LEGEND
District Boundary
State Boundary
International Boundary
Open forest
Dense
Very Dense forest
N
W
E
S

Scale - 1:1.8 M approx

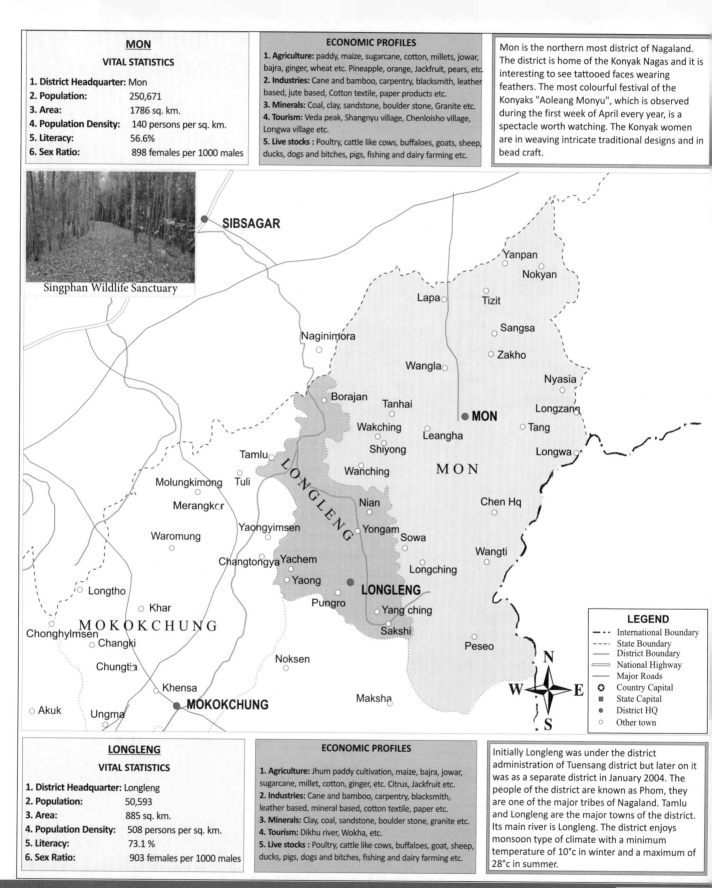

MON

VITAL STATISTICS

1. **District Headquarter:** Mon
2. **Population:** 250,671
3. **Area:** 1786 sq. km.
4. **Population Density:** 140 persons per sq. km.
5. **Literacy:** 56.6%
6. **Sex Ratio:** 898 females per 1000 males

ECONOMIC PROFILES

1. **Agriculture:** paddy, maize, sugarcane, cotton, millets, jowar, bajra, ginger, wheat etc. Pineapple, orange, Jackfruit, pears, etc.
2. **Industries:** Cane and bamboo, carpentry, blacksmith, leather based, jute based, Cotton textile, paper products etc.
3. **Minerals:** Coal, clay, sandstone, boulder stone, Granite etc.
4. **Tourism:** Veda peak, Shangnyu village, Chenloisho village, Longwa village etc.
5. **Live stocks :** Poultry, cattle like cows, buffaloes, goats, sheep, ducks, dogs and bitches, pigs, fishing and dairy farming etc.

Mon is the northern most district of Nagaland. The district is home of the Konyak Nagas and it is interesting to see tattooed faces wearing feathers. The most colourful festival of the Konyaks "Aoleang Monyu", which is observed during the first week of April every year, is a spectacle worth watching. The Konyak women are in weaving intricate traditional designs and in bead craft.

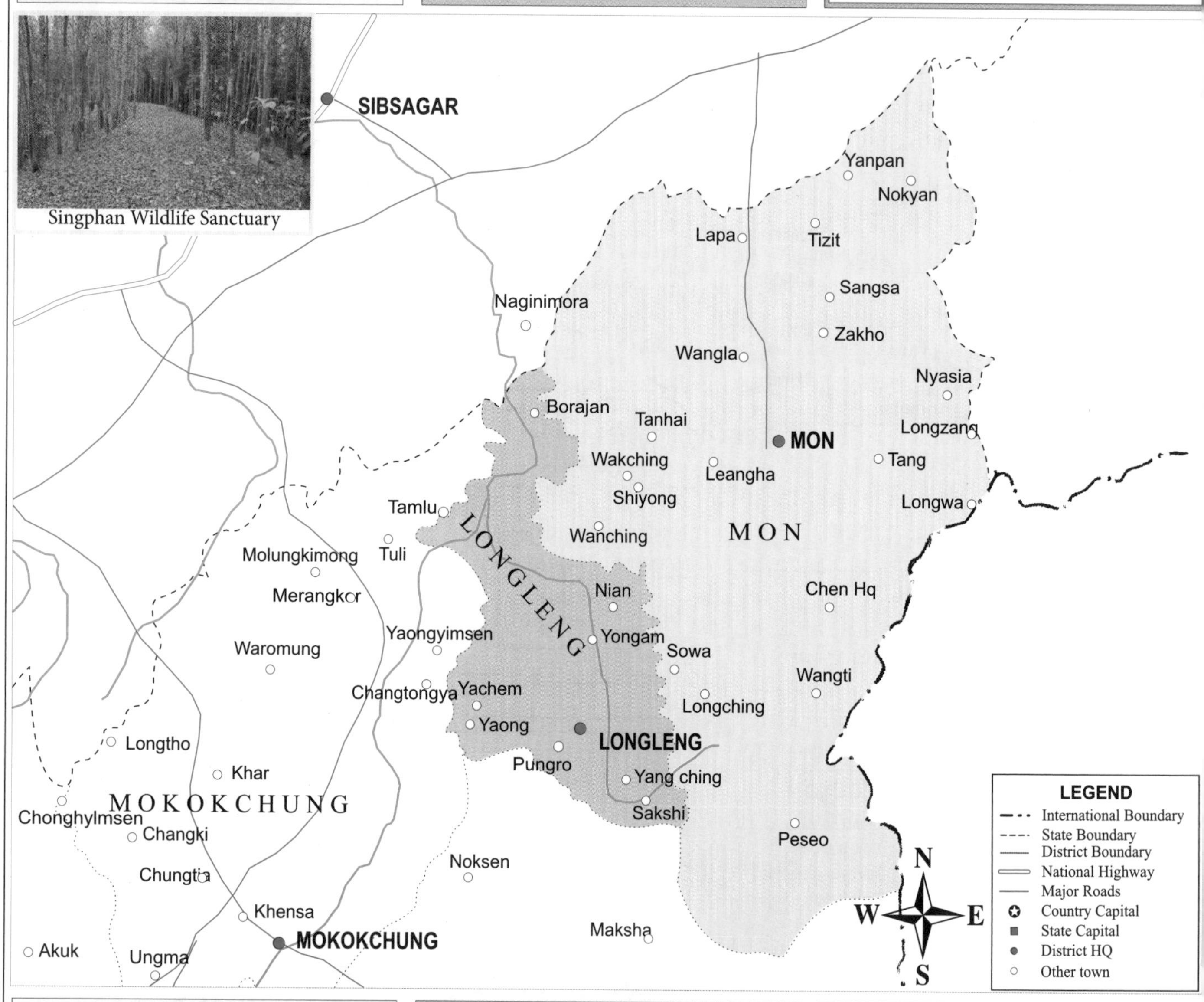

Singphan Wildlife Sanctuary
SIBSAGAR
Yanpan
Nokyan
Lapa
Tizit
Sangsa
Naginimora
Zakho
Wangla
Nyasia
Borajan
Tanhai
Longzang
MON
Wakching
Leangha
Tang
Shiyong
Longwa
Tamlu
Wanching
MON
LONGLENG
Molungkimong
Tuli
Merangkor
Nian
Chen Hq
Yaongyimsen
Yongam
Waromung
Sowa
Wangti
Changtongya
Yachem
Longching
Yaong
Longtho
LONGLENG
Pungro
Khar
Yang ching
MOKOKCHUNG
Sakshi
Chonghylmsen
Changki
Peseo
Noksen
Chungtia
Khensa
Maksha
Akuk
Ungma
MOKOKCHUNG
N
W
E
S
LEGEND
International Boundary
State Boundary
District Boundary
National Highway
Major Roads
Country Capital
State Capital
District HQ
Other town

LONGLENG

VITAL STATISTICS

1. **District Headquarter:** Longleng
2. **Population:** 50,593
3. **Area:** 885 sq. km.
4. **Population Density:** 508 persons per sq. km.
5. **Literacy:** 73.1 %
6. **Sex Ratio:** 903 females per 1000 males

ECONOMIC PROFILES

1. **Agriculture:** Jhum paddy cultivation, maize, bajra, jowar, sugarcane, millet, cotton, ginger, etc. Citrus, Jackfruit etc.
2. **Industries:** Cane and bamboo, carpentry, blacksmith, leather based, mineral based, cotton textile, paper etc.
3. **Minerals:** Clay, coal, sandstone, boulder stone, granite etc.
4. **Tourism:** Dikhu river, Wokha, etc.
5. **Live stocks :** Poultry, cattle like cows, buffaloes, goat, sheep, ducks, pigs, dogs and bitches, fishing and dairy farming etc.

Initially Longleng was under the district administration of Tuensang district but later on it was as a separate district in January 2004. The people of the district are known as Phom, they are one of the major tribes of Nagaland. Tamlu and Longleng are the major towns of the district. Its main river is Longleng. The district enjoys monsoon type of climate with a minimum temperature of 10°c in winter and a maximum of 28°c in summer.

Scale - 1:0.5 M approx

MOKOKCHUNG

VITAL STATISTICS

1. **District Headquarter:** Mokokchung
2. **Population:** 193,171
3. **Area:** 1,615 sq. km.
4. **Population Density:** 120 persons per sq. km.
5. **Literacy:** 91.6%
6. **Sex Ratio:** 925 females per 1000 males

ECONOMIC PROFILES

1. **Agriculture:** Paddy, oilseeds, maize, jowar, bajra, millets, sugarcane, Cotton, wheat, etc. Orange, pineapple, banana etc.
2. **Industries:** Agro-based, cane and bamboo, carpentry, jute.
3. **Minerals:** Crude oil Petroleum, Coal, Sandstone, Clay, Clay.
4. **Tourism:** Longkhum, Ungma village, Langpangkong caves, Molung village, Chuchuyinlang village, caves, Moatsu festival.
5. **Live stocks :** Poultry, cattle like cows, buffaloes, goats, sheep, ducks, dogs and bitches, pigs, fishing and dairy farming etc.

Mokokchung district is mainly occupied by the App Naga tribe who consider it their home and are committed to preserving their culture and tradition. Jungli Ao is the main Language of the Aos followed by Mongsen Ao language and Changki language. The main industrial regions of the district are the Changki valley, Tsurang Valley, lower Milak Tuli region and the Dikhu Chichung valley.

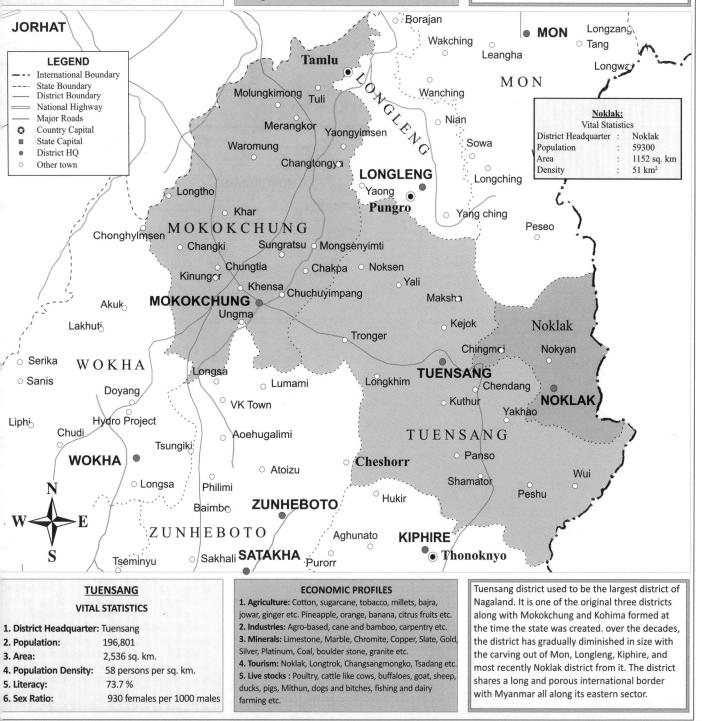

JORHAT
LEGEND
International Boundary
State Boundary
District Boundary
National Highway
Major Roads
Country Capital
State Capital
District HQ
Other town
Borajan
Wakching
MON
Longzang
Tang
Leangha
Longwa
MON
Tamlu
Molungkimong
Tuli
LONGLENG
Wanching
Merangkor
Yaongyimsen
Nian
Waromung
Sowa
Changtongya
LONGLENG
Longching
Yaong
Pungro
Longtho
Khar
Yang ching
MOKOKCHUNG
Chonghylimsen
Changki
Sungratsu
Mongsenyimti
Peseo
Chungtia
Chakpa
Noksen
Kinungor
Khensa
Chuchuyimpang
Yali
Maksha
Akuk
MOKOKCHUNG
Ungma
Lakhuti
Kejok
Noklak
Tronger
Chingmei
Nokyan
Serika
WOKHA
Sanis
Longsa
TUENSANG
Lumami
Longkhim
Chendang
Doyang
NOKLAK
VK Town
Kuthur
Yakhao
Liphi
Hydro Project
Chudi
Aoehugalimi
TUENSANG
Tsungiki
WOKHA
Cheshorr
Panso
Atoizu
Longsa
Shamator
Wui
Philimi
Peshu
Hukir
N
W
E
S
Baimbo
ZUNHEBOTO
ZUNHEBOTO
Aghunato
KIPHIRE
Tseminyu
Sakhali
SATAKHA
Purorr
Thonoknyo
Noklak:
Vital Statistics
District Headquarter : Noklak
Population : 59300
Area : 1152 sq. km
Density : 51 km²

TUENSANG

VITAL STATISTICS

1. **District Headquarter:** Tuensang
2. **Population:** 196,801
3. **Area:** 2,536 sq. km.
4. **Population Density:** 58 persons per sq. km.
5. **Literacy:** 73.7 %
6. **Sex Ratio:** 930 females per 1000 males

ECONOMIC PROFILES

1. **Agriculture:** Cotton, sugarcane, tobacco, millets, bajra, jowar, ginger etc. Pineapple, orange, banana, citrus fruits etc.
2. **Industries:** Agro-based, cane and bamboo, carpentry etc.
3. **Minerals:** Limestone, Marble, Chromite, Copper, Slate, Gold, Silver, Platinum, Coal, boulder stone, granite etc.
4. **Tourism:** Noklak, Longtrok, Changsangmongko, Tsadang etc.
5. **Live stocks :** Poultry, cattle like cows, buffaloes, goat, sheep, ducks, pigs, Mithun, dogs and bitches, fishing and dairy farming etc.

Tuensang district used to be the largest district of Nagaland. It is one of the original three districts along with Mokokchung and Kohima formed at the time the state was created. over the decades, the district has gradually diminished in size with the carving out of Mon, Longleng, Kiphire, and most recently Noklak district from it. The district shares a long and porous international border with Myanmar all along its eastern sector.

Scale - 1:0.7 M approx

WOKHA

VITAL STATISTICS

1. **District Headquarter:** Wokha
2. **Population:** 166,239
3. **Area:** 1,628 sq. km.
4. **Population Density:** 100 persons per sq. km.
5. **Literacy:** 87.7%
6. **Sex Ratio:** 968 females per 1000 males

ECONOMIC PROFILES

1. **Agriculture:** wet rice cultivation, Jhum paddy cultivation, maize, Cotton, sugarcane, tobacco, millets, bajra, jowar etc.
2. **Industries:** Agro-based, cane and bamboo, carpentry, blacksmith, Paper products, Cotton textile etc.
3. **Minerals:** Crude oil of petroleum, hydrocarbon, coal, sandstone, Boulder stone, granite etc.
4. **Tourism:** Doyang hydro project, Doyang river, mount Tiyi, Doyang dam reservoir etc.
5. **Live stocks :** Poultry, cattles, goats, sheep and dairy farming.

Wokha district was created in 1973 when the sub division separated from Mokokchung district. Jhum / shifting cultivation is the main occupation of the farmers due to its topographical terrain. In shifting cultivation, mixed cropping pattern is practiced incorporating cereals, pulses, oilseeds, tuber crops, spices, and condiments using local cultivator, which are organic in nature.

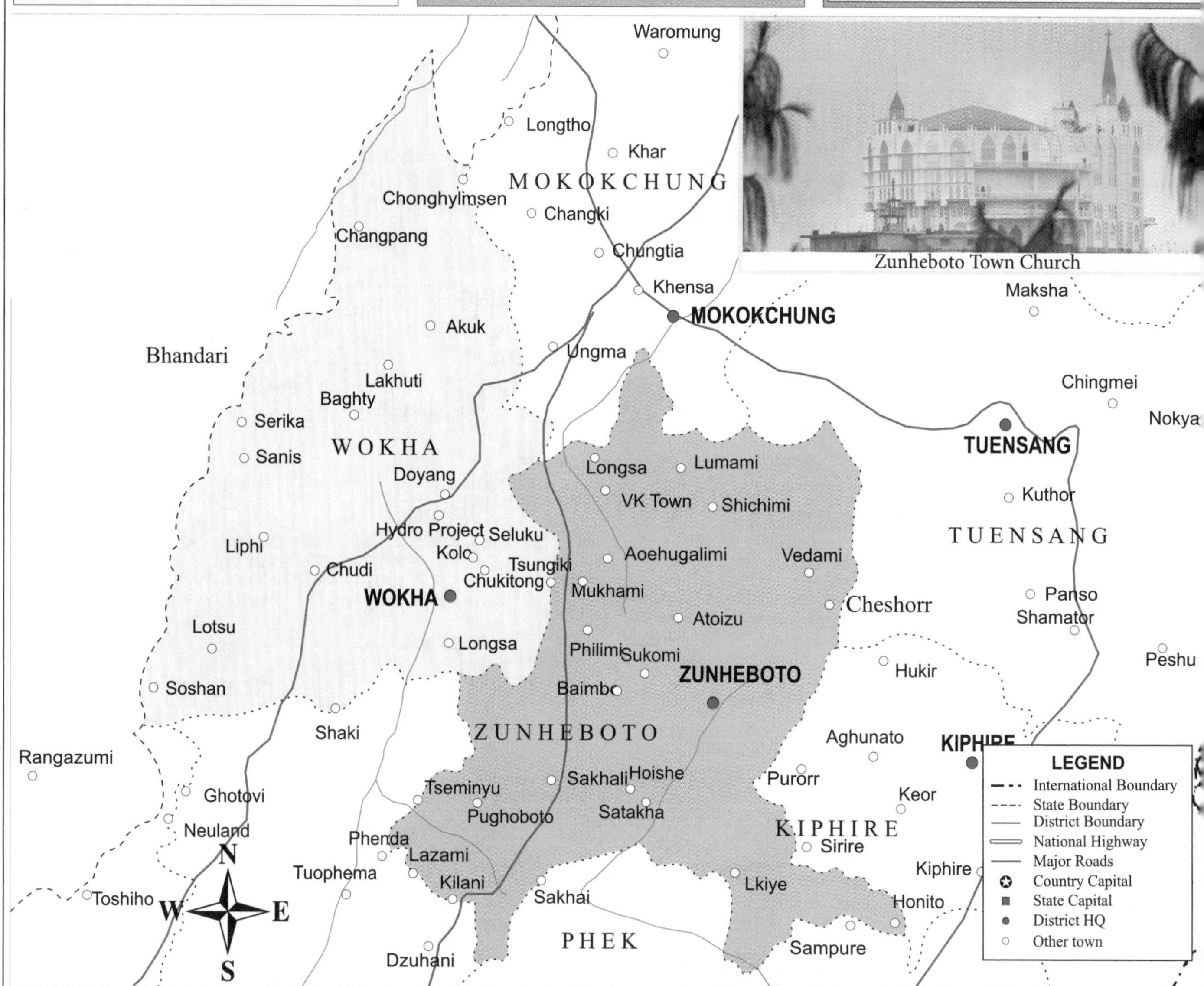

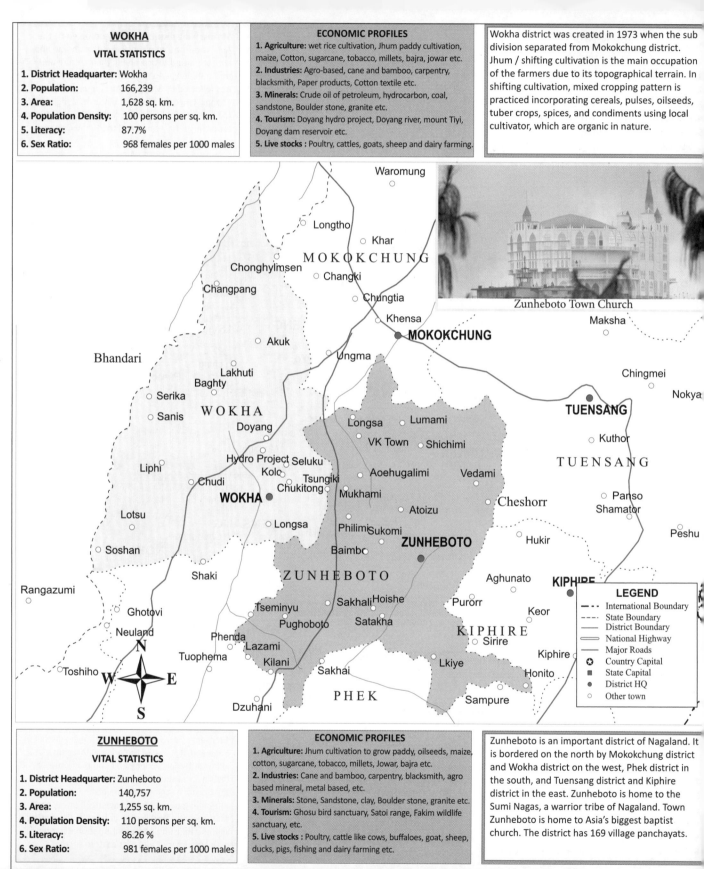

Waromung
Longtho
Khar
MOKOKCHUNG
Chonghylimsen
Changki
Changpang
Chungtia
Khensa
MOKOKCHUNG
Akuk
Bhandari
Ungma
Lakhuti
Baghty
Serika
WOKHA
Sanis
Doyang
Longsa
Lumami
VK Town
Shichimi
Hydro Project
Seluku
Liphi
Kolo
Tsungiki
Aoehugalimi
Vedami
Chudi
Chukitong
Mukhami
WOKHA
Atoizu
Cheshorr
Lotsu
Longsa
Philimi
Sukomi
ZUNHEBOTO
Soshan
Baimbo
Shaki
ZUNHEBOTO
Rangazumi
Ghotovi
Tseminyu
Sakhali
Hoishe
Pughoboto
Satakha
Neuland
Phenda
Lazami
Tuophema
Kilani
Toshiho
Sakhai
Dzuhani
PHEK
Zunheboto Town Church
Maksha
Chingmei
Nokya
TUENSANG
Kuthor
TUENSANG
Panso
Shamator
Peshu
Hukir
Aghunato
KIPHIRE
Purorr
Keor
KIPHIRE
Sirire
Kiphire
Lkiye
Honito
Sampure
N
W
E
S
LEGEND
International Boundary
State Boundary
District Boundary
National Highway
Major Roads
Country Capital
State Capital
District HQ
Other town

ZUNHEBOTO

VITAL STATISTICS

1. **District Headquarter:** Zunheboto
2. **Population:** 140,757
3. **Area:** 1,255 sq. km.
4. **Population Density:** 110 persons per sq. km.
5. **Literacy:** 86.26 %
6. **Sex Ratio:** 981 females per 1000 males

ECONOMIC PROFILES

1. **Agriculture:** Jhum cultivation to grow paddy, oilseeds, maize, cotton, sugarcane, tobacco, millets, Jowar, bajra etc.
2. **Industries:** Cane and bamboo, carpentry, blacksmith, agro based mineral, metal based, etc.
3. **Minerals:** Stone, Sandstone, clay, Boulder stone, granite etc.
4. **Tourism:** Ghosu bird sanctuary, Satoi range, Fakim wildlife sanctuary, etc.
5. **Live stocks :** Poultry, cattle like cows, buffaloes, goat, sheep, ducks, pigs, fishing and dairy farming etc.

Zunheboto is an important district of Nagaland. It is bordered on the north by Mokokchung district and Wokha district on the west, Phek district in the south, and Tuensang district and Kiphire district in the east. Zunheboto is home to the Sumi Nagas, a warrior tribe of Nagaland. Town Zunheboto is home to Asia's biggest baptist church. The district has 169 village panchayats.

Projection: Lambert's Conical Orthomorphic

1000 0 1000 2000 km

KIPHIRE

VITAL STATISTICS

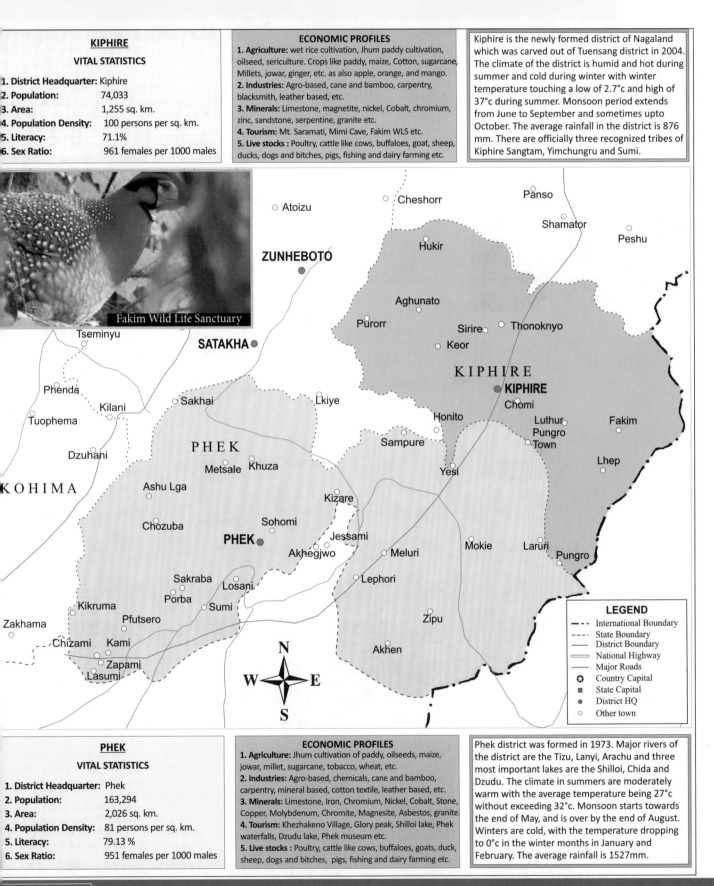

1. **District Headquarter:** Kiphire
2. **Population:** 74,033
3. **Area:** 1,255 sq. km.
4. **Population Density:** 100 persons per sq. km.
5. **Literacy:** 71.1%
6. **Sex Ratio:** 961 females per 1000 males

ECONOMIC PROFILES

1. **Agriculture:** wet rice cultivation, Jhum paddy cultivation, oilseed, sericulture. Crops like paddy, maize, Cotton, sugarcane, Millets, jowar, ginger, etc. as also apple, orange, and mango.
2. **Industries:** Agro-based, cane and bamboo, carpentry, blacksmith, leather based, etc.
3. **Minerals:** Limestone, magnetite, nickel, Cobalt, chromium, zinc, sandstone, serpentine, granite etc.
4. **Tourism:** Mt. Saramati, Mimi Cave, Fakim WLS etc.
5. **Live stocks :** Poultry, cattle like cows, buffaloes, goat, sheep, ducks, dogs and bitches, pigs, fishing and dairy farming etc.

Kiphire is the newly formed district of Nagaland which was carved out of Tuensang district in 2004. The climate of the district is humid and hot during summer and cold during winter with winter temperature touching a low of 2.7°c and high of 37°c during summer. Monsoon period extends from June to September and sometimes upto October. The average rainfall in the district is 876 mm. There are officially three recognized tribes of Kiphire Sangtam, Yimchungru and Sumi.

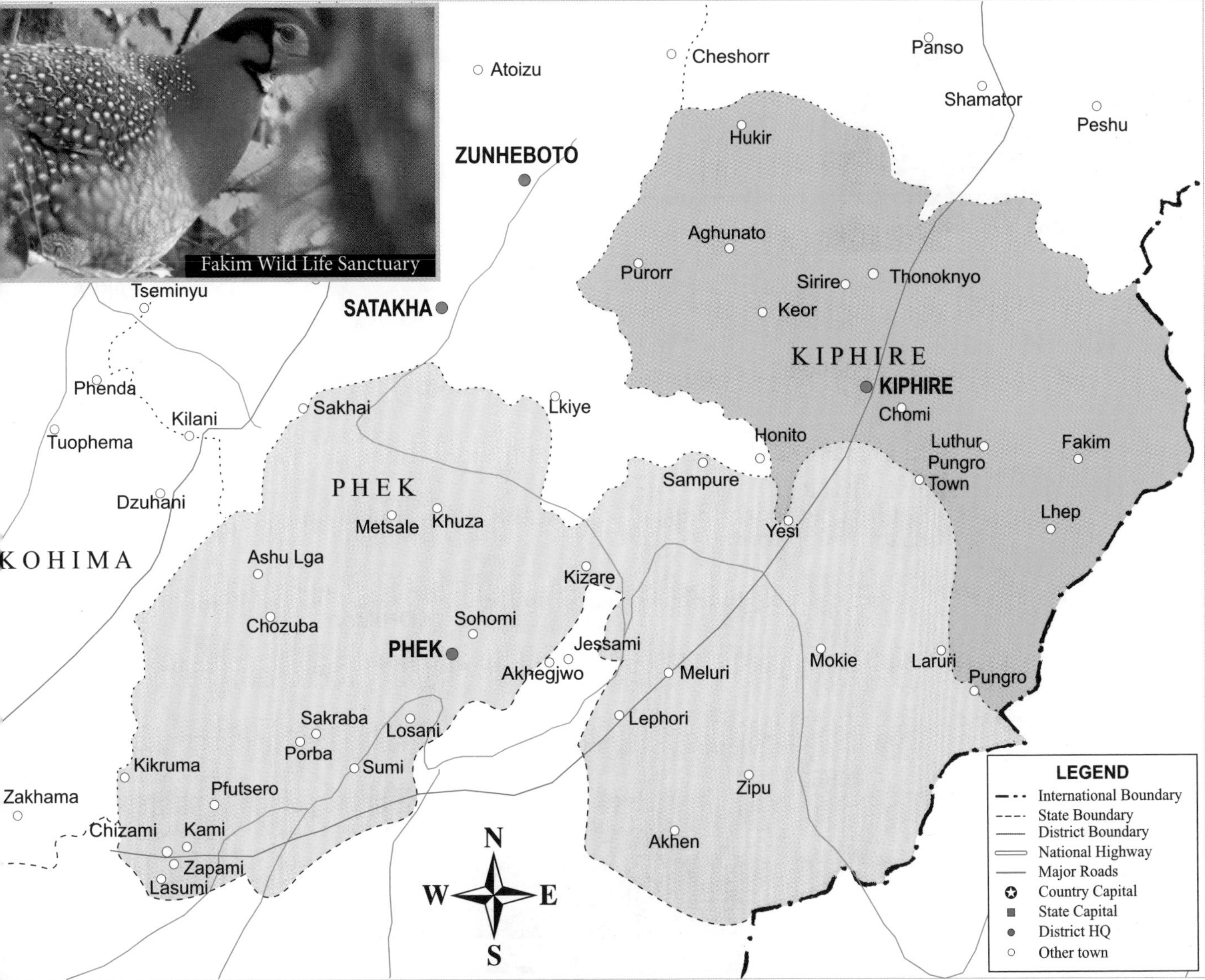

Fakim Wild Life Sanctuary
Atoizu
Cheshorr
Panso
Shamator
Peshu
ZUNHEBOTO
Hukir
Aghunato
Purorr
Sirire
Thonoknyo
Keor
Tseminyu
SATAKHA
KIPHIRE
KIPHIRE
Chomi
Phenda
Sakhai
Lkiye
Kilani
Tuophema
Honito
Luthur
Pungro
Town
Fakim
PHEK
Sampure
Dzuhani
Metsale
Khuza
Yesi
Lhep
KOHIMA
Ashu Lga
Kizare
Chozuba
Sohomi
PHEK
Jessami
Akhegjwo
Meluri
Mokie
Laruri
Pungro
Sakraba
Losani
Lephori
Porba
Kikruma
Sumi
Pfutsero
Zipu
Zakhama
Chizami
Kami
Akhen
Zapami
Lasumi
N
W
E
S
LEGEND
International Boundary
State Boundary
District Boundary
National Highway
Major Roads
Country Capital
State Capital
District HQ
Other town

PHEK

VITAL STATISTICS

1. **District Headquarter:** Phek
2. **Population:** 163,294
3. **Area:** 2,026 sq. km.
4. **Population Density:** 81 persons per sq. km.
5. **Literacy:** 79.13 %
6. **Sex Ratio:** 951 females per 1000 males

ECONOMIC PROFILES

1. **Agriculture:** Jhum cultivation of paddy, oilseeds, maize, jowar, millet, sugarcane, tobacco, wheat, etc.
2. **Industries:** Agro-based, chemicals, cane and bamboo, carpentry, mineral based, cotton textile, leather based, etc.
3. **Minerals:** Limestone, Iron, Chromium, Nickel, Cobalt, Stone, Copper, Molybdenum, Chromite, Magnesite, Asbestos, granite.
4. **Tourism:** Khezhakeno Village, Glory peak, Shilloi lake, Phek waterfalls, Dzudu lake, Phek museum etc.
5. **Live stocks :** Poultry, cattle like cows, buffaloes, goats, duck, sheep, dogs and bitches, pigs, fishing and dairy farming etc.

Phek district was formed in 1973. Major rivers of the district are the Tizu, Lanyi, Arachu and three most important lakes are the Shilloi, Chida and Dzudu. The climate in summers are moderately warm with the average temperature being 27°c without exceeding 32°c. Monsoon starts towards the end of May, and is over by the end of August. Winters are cold, with the temperature dropping to 0°c in the winter months in January and February. The average rainfall is 1527mm.

Scale - 1:0.5 M approx

DIMAPUR

VITAL STATISTICS

1. **District Headquarter:** Dimapur
2. **Population:** 3,78,811
3. **Area:** 927 sq. km.
4. **Population Density:** 409 persons per sq. km.
5. **Literacy:** 84.79%
6. **Sex Ratio:** 937 females per 1000 males

ECONOMIC PROFILES

1. **Agriculture:** Jhum cultivation to grow crops like paddy, maize, ragi, wheat, barley, etc. Fruits like orange, mango etc.
2. **Industries:** Agro-based, Cotton textile, carpentry, Cane and bamboo, paper products etc.
3. **Minerals:** Coal, lignite, petroleum, oil and gas, Uranium and Thorium ores.
4. **Tourism:** The Triple falls, Kachari ruins, Dimapur, Zoological Park, Nagaland center, Rangaphar Forest, Chumukedima etc.
5. **Live stocks :** Poultry, cattle like cows, buffaloes, goat, sheep, ducks, dogs and bitches, pigs, fishing and dairy farming etc.

The name Dimapur is derived from the Kachari language, Di means"water",ma means "large", pur means"city" or city of large water body. The region is under the influence of the monsoon type of climate. Rainfall is moderate and is mostly due to south west monsoon. The temperature during the summer months is hot reaching high of up to 36°c with humidity up to 93% and moderate during the winter.

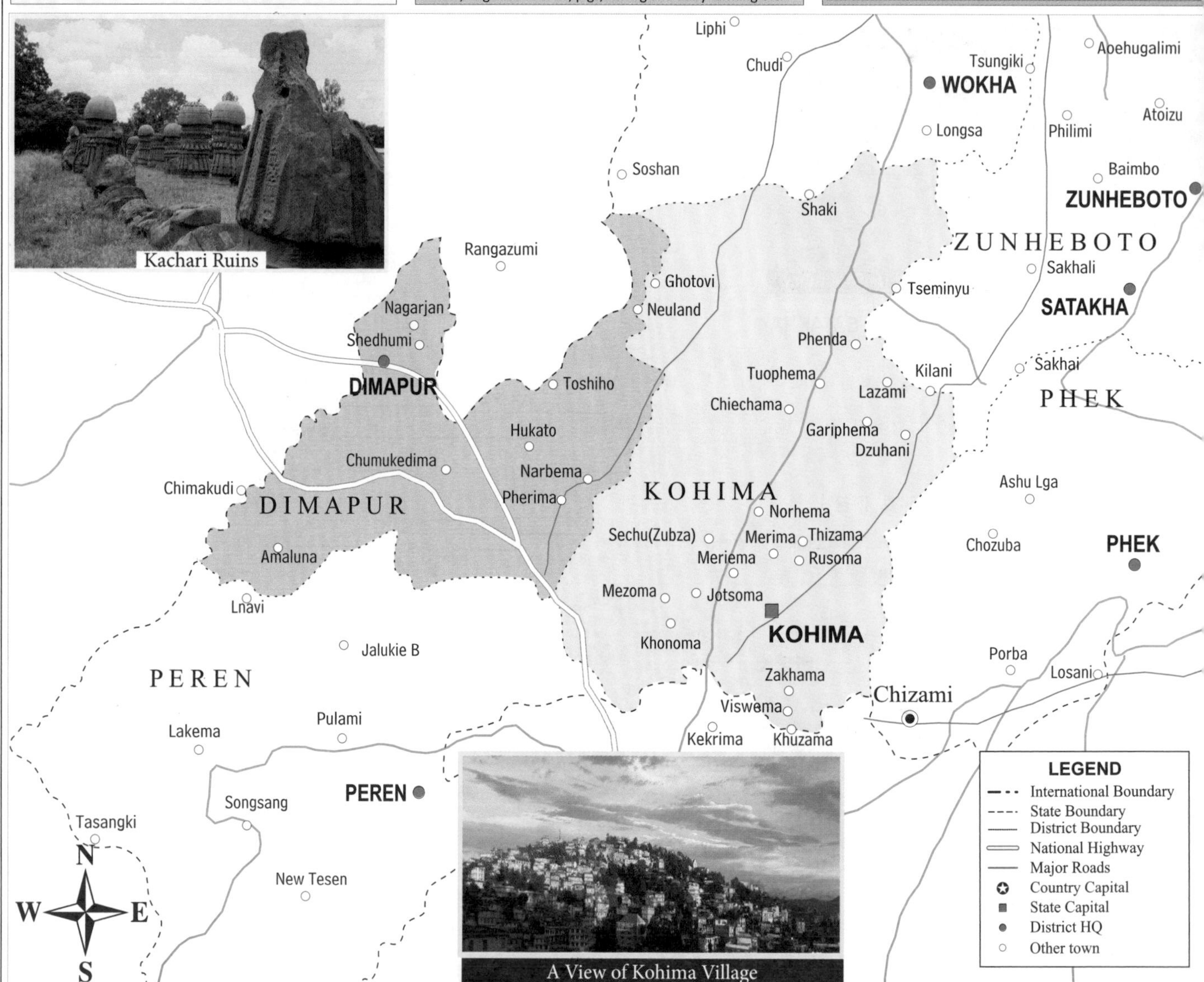

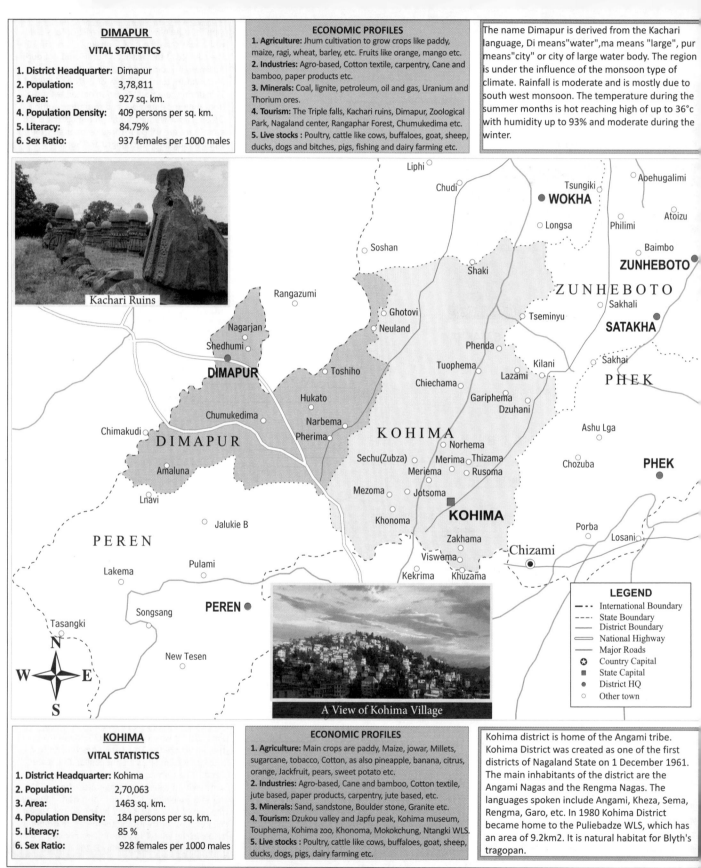

Kachari Ruins
Liphi
Chudi
Tsungiki
WOKHA
Apehugalimi
Longsa
Philimi
Atoizu
Soshan
Baimbo
Shaki
ZUNHEBOTO
Rangazumi
ZUNHEBOTO
Sakhali
Ghotovi
Tseminyu
Neuland
SATAKHA
Nagarjan
Shedhumi
Phenda
DIMAPUR
Toshiho
Tuophema
Kilani
Sakhai
Lazami
PHEK
Chiechama
Hukato
Gariphema
Dzuhani
Chumukedima
Narbema
Ashu Lga
Chimakudi
Pherima
KOHIMA
DIMAPUR
Norhema
Sechu(Zubza)
Merima
Thizama
Chozuba
PHEK
Amaluna
Meriema
Rusoma
Mezoma
Jotsoma
Lnavi
KOHIMA
Khonoma
Jalukie B
Porba
PEREN
Zakhama
Losani
Chizami
Viswema
Lakema
Pulami
Kekrima
Khuzama
PEREN
Songsang
Tasangki
New Tesen
N
W
E
S
LEGEND
International Boundary
State Boundary
District Boundary
National Highway
Major Roads
Country Capital
State Capital
District HQ
Other town
A View of Kohima Village

KOHIMA

VITAL STATISTICS

1. **District Headquarter:** Kohima
2. **Population:** 2,70,063
3. **Area:** 1463 sq. km.
4. **Population Density:** 184 persons per sq. km.
5. **Literacy:** 85 %
6. **Sex Ratio:** 928 females per 1000 males

ECONOMIC PROFILES

1. **Agriculture:** Main crops are paddy, Maize, jowar, Millets, sugarcane, tobacco, Cotton, as also pineapple, banana, citrus, orange, Jackfruit, pears, sweet potato etc.
2. **Industries:** Agro-based, Cane and bamboo, Cotton textile, jute based, paper products, carpentry, jute based, etc.
3. **Minerals:** Sand, sandstone, Boulder stone, Granite etc.
4. **Tourism:** Dzukou valley and Japfu peak, Kohima museum, Touphema, Kohima zoo, Khonoma, Mokokchung, Ntangki WLS.
5. **Live stocks :** Poultry, cattle like cows, buffaloes, goat, sheep, ducks, dogs, pigs, dairy farming etc.

Kohima district is home of the Angami tribe. Kohima District was created as one of the first districts of Nagaland State on 1 December 1961. The main inhabitants of the district are the Angami Nagas and the Rengma Nagas. The languages spoken include Angami, Kheza, Sema, Rengma, Garo, etc. In 1980 Kohima District became home to the Puliebadze WLS, which has an area of 9.2km2. It is natural habitat for Blyth's tragopan.

Projection: Lambert's Conical Orthomorphic

1000 0 1000 2000 km

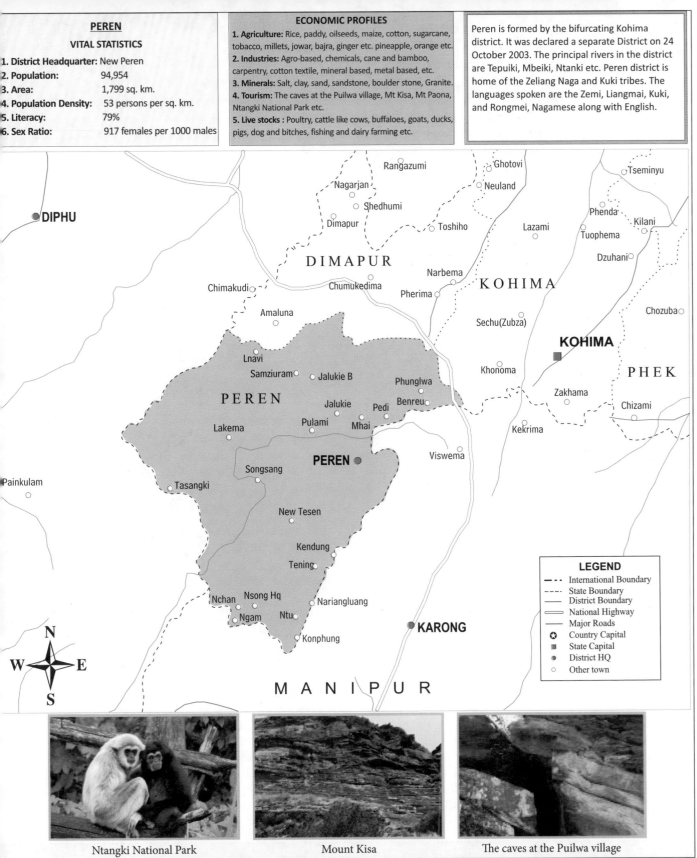

PEREN

VITAL STATISTICS

1. **District Headquarter:** New Peren
2. **Population:** 94,954
3. **Area:** 1,799 sq. km.
4. **Population Density:** 53 persons per sq. km.
5. **Literacy:** 79%
6. **Sex Ratio:** 917 females per 1000 males

ECONOMIC PROFILES

1. **Agriculture:** Rice, paddy, oilseeds, maize, cotton, sugarcane, tobacco, millets, jowar, bajra, ginger etc. pineapple, orange etc.
2. **Industries:** Agro-based, chemicals, cane and bamboo, carpentry, cotton textile, mineral based, metal based, etc.
3. **Minerals:** Salt, clay, sand, sandstone, boulder stone, Granite.
4. **Tourism:** The caves at the Puilwa village, Mt Kisa, Mt Paona, Ntangki National Park etc.
5. **Live stocks :** Poultry, cattle like cows, buffaloes, goats, ducks, pigs, dog and bitches, fishing and dairy farming etc.

Peren is formed by the bifurcating Kohima district. It was declared a separate District on 24 October 2003. The principal rivers in the district are Tepuiki, Mbeiki, Ntanki etc. Peren district is home of the Zeliang Naga and Kuki tribes. The languages spoken are the Zemi, Liangmai, Kuki, and Rongmei, Nagamese along with English.

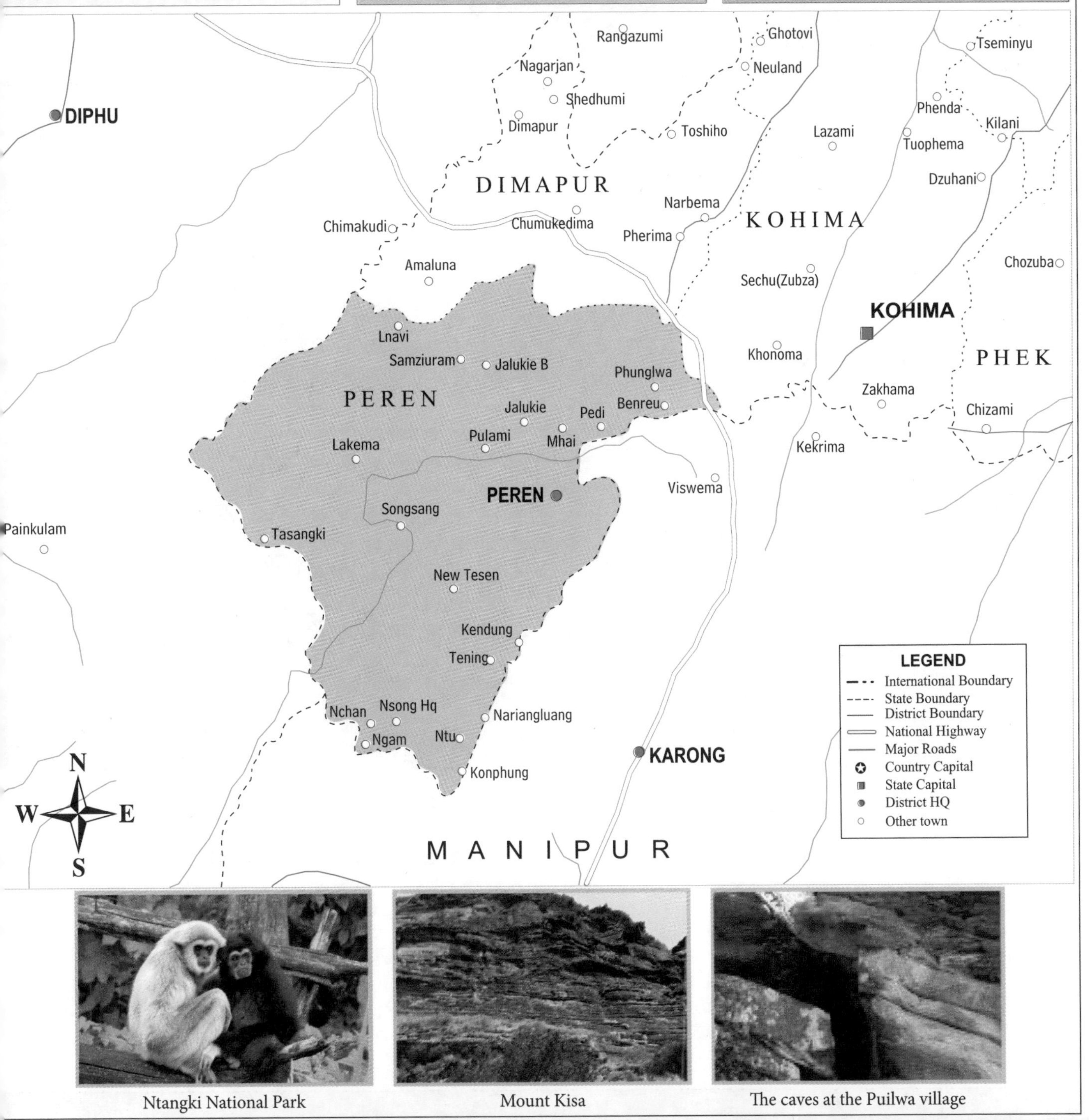

Rangazumi
Ghotovi
Tseminyu
Neuland
Nagarjan
Shedhumi
DIPHU
Dimapur
Toshiho
Lazami
Phenda
Kilani
Tuophema
DIMAPUR
Dzuhani
Narbema
Chimakudi
Chumukedima
KOHIMA
Pherima
Amaluna
Chozuba
Sechu(Zubza)
KOHIMA
Lnavi
Samziuram
Jalukie B
Khonoma
PHEK
Phunglwa
PEREN
Benreu
Zakhama
Jalukie
Pedi
Chizami
Pulami
Mhai
Lakema
Kekrima
Viswema
PEREN
Songsang
Painkulam
Tasangki
New Tesen
Kendung
Tening
Nsong Hq
Nchan
Nariangluang
Ngam
Ntu
KARONG
Konphung
N
W
E
S
MANIPUR
LEGEND
International Boundary
State Boundary
District Boundary
National Highway
Major Roads
Country Capital
State Capital
District HQ
Other town

Ntangki National Park

Mount Kisa

The caves at the Puilwa village

0 1000 2000 km.

Projection: Lambert's Conical Orthomorphic

SIKKIM

Section

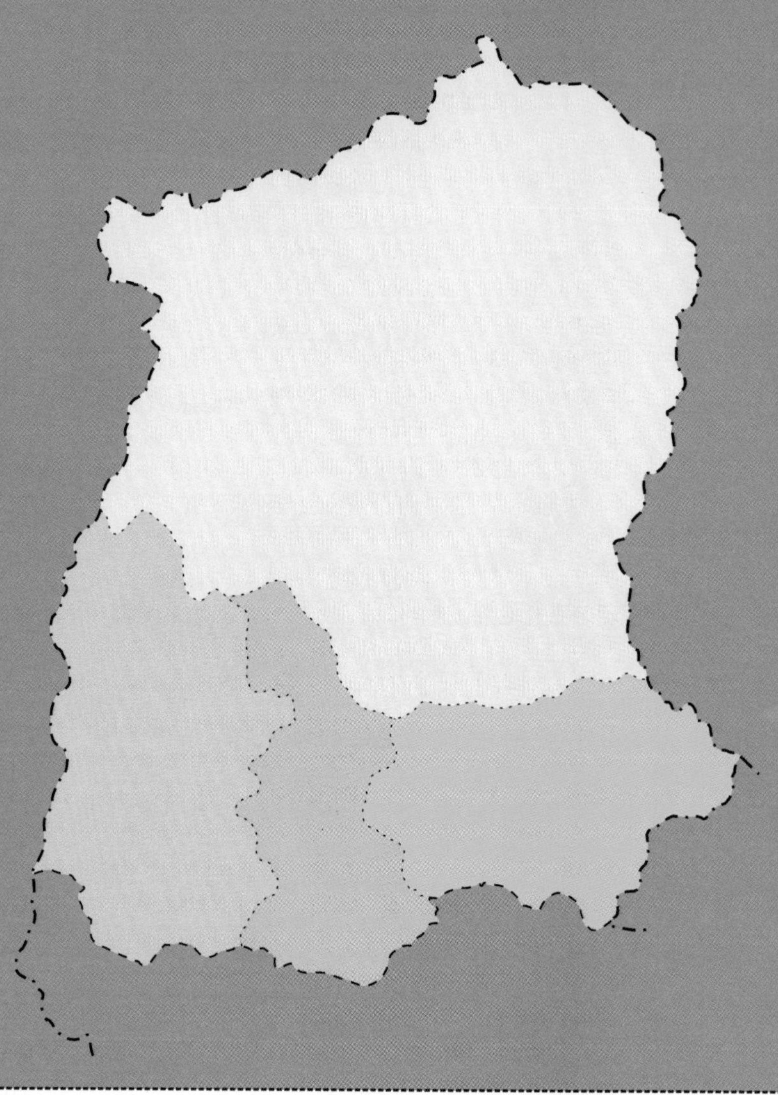

POPULATION:	6,10,577	**DISTRICTS:** ***4***	
AREA:	7096 (sq. kms)	**L.S. CONSTITUENCY:**	1
POP. DENSITY:	86/km^2	**R.S. CONSTITUENCY:**	1
LITERACY:	82.6	**GRAM PANCHAYATS:**	176
SEX RATIO:	890 female/1000 males	**GSDP:**	9,95,654

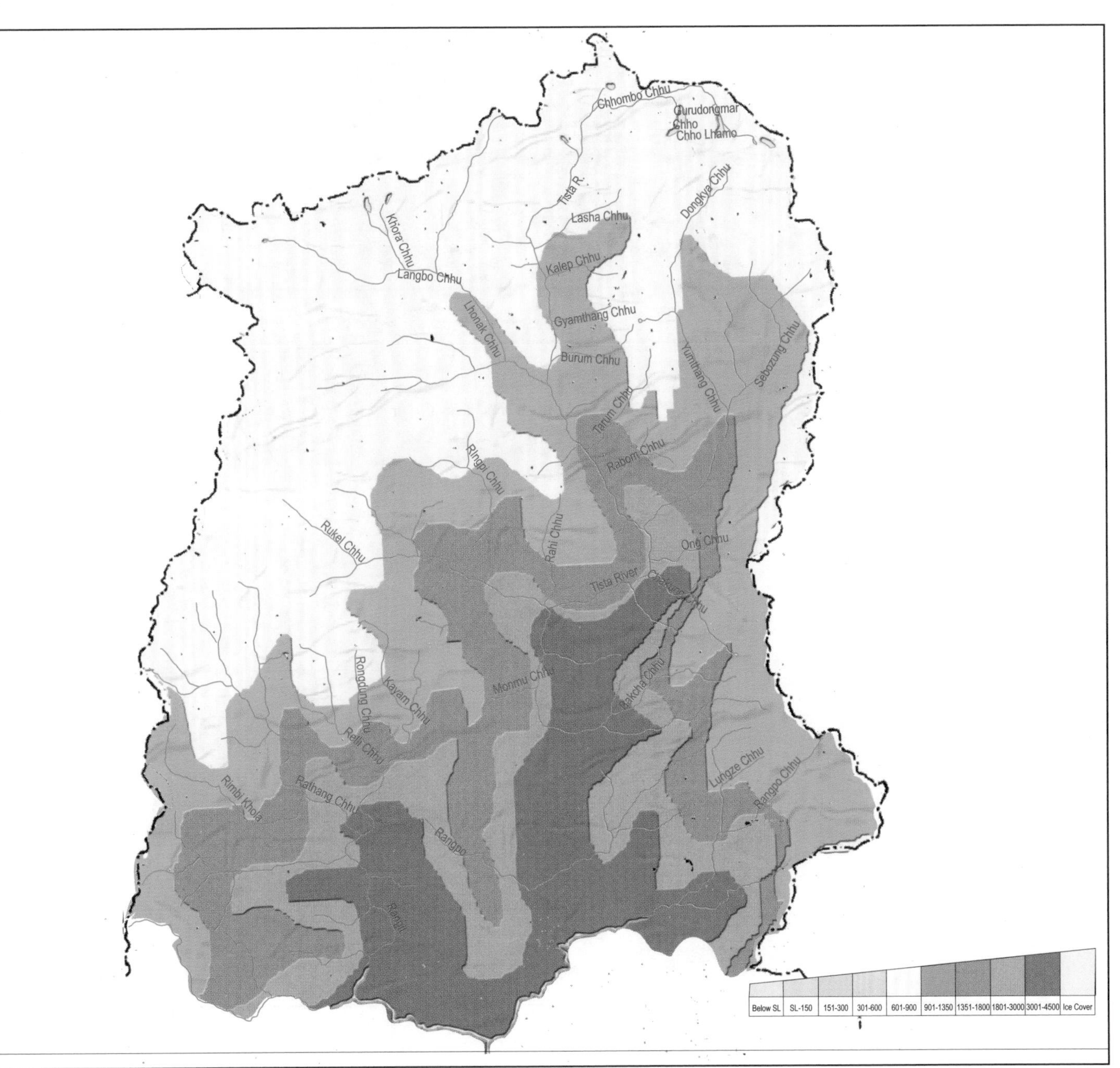
Chhombo Chhu
Gurudongmar
Chho
Chho Lhamo
Tista R.
Lasha Chhu
Dongkya Chhu
Khora Chhu
Langbo Chhu
Kalep Chhu
Lhonak Chhu
Gyamthang Chhu
Burum Chhu
Yumthang Chhu
Sebozung Chhu
Tarum Chhu
Rabom Chhu
Ringpi Chhu
Rukel Chhu
Rani Chhu
Ong Chhu
Tista River
Monmu Chhu
Rongdung Chhu
Kayam Chhu
Relli Chhu
Rakcha Chhu
Lungze Chhu
Rangpo Chhu
Rimbi Khola
Rathang Chhu
Rangpo
Rangit
Below SL
SL-150
151-300
301-600
601-900
901-1350
1351-1800
1801-3000
3001-4500
Ice Cover

Scale - 1 cm = 7.0 kms.

Projection: Lambert's Conical Orthomorphic

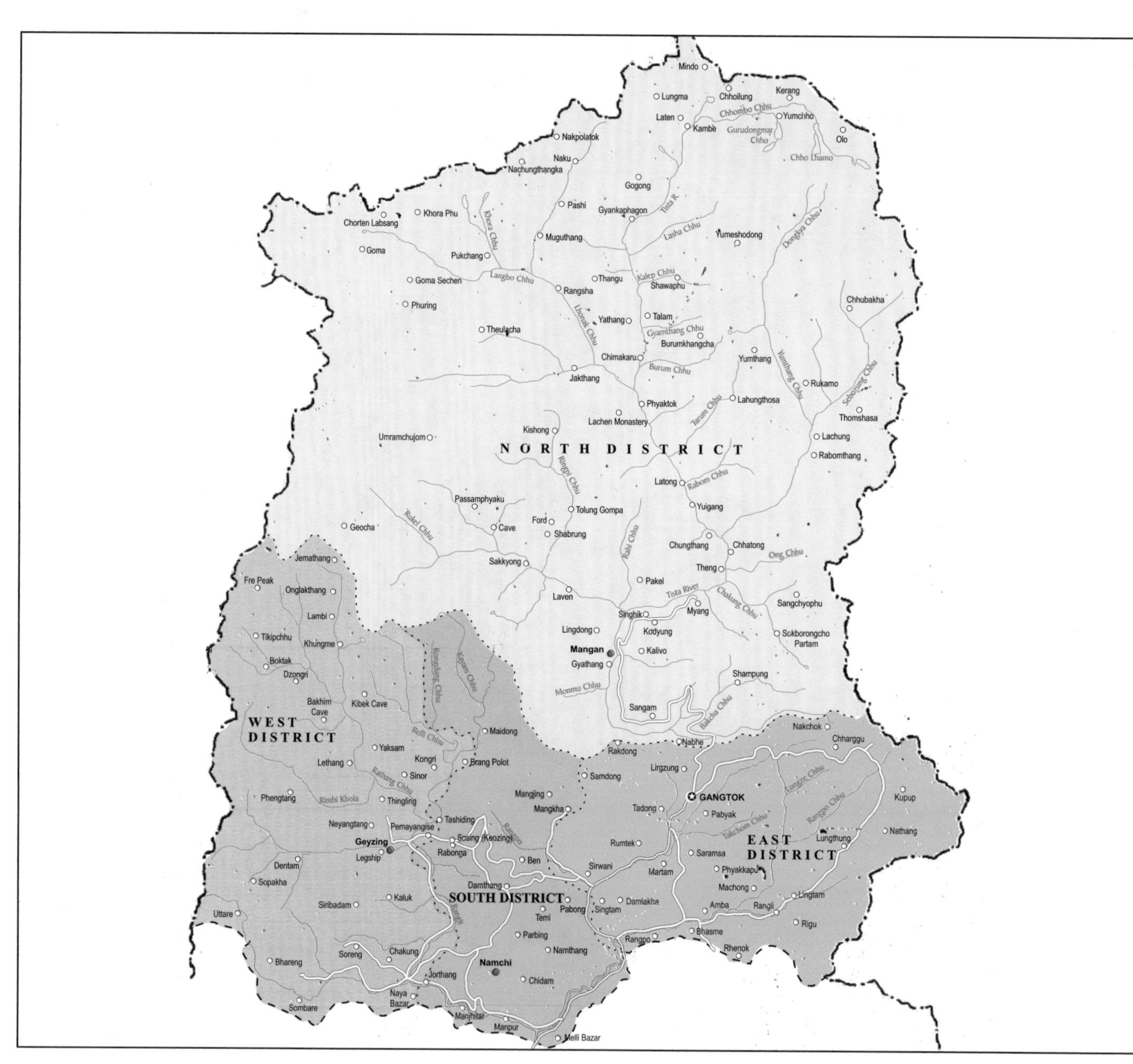

NORTH DISTRICT
WEST DISTRICT
SOUTH DISTRICT
EAST DISTRICT
GANGTOK
Mangan
Geyzing
Namchi
Mindo
Lungma
Chhoilung
Kerang
Laten
Kambe
Yumchho
Olo
Chhombo Chhu
Gurudongmar Chho
Chho Lhamo
Nakpolatok
Naku
Nachungthangka
Gogong
Pashi
Gyankaphagon
Tista R.
Chorten Labsang
Khora Phu
Khora Chhu
Muguthang
Lasha Chhu
Yumeshodong
Dongkya Chhu
Goma
Pukchang
Goma Sechen
Langbo Chhu
Thangu
Kalep Chhu
Shawaphu
Rangsha
Phuring
Chhubakha
Yathang
Talam
Theulacha
Gyamthang Chhu
Burumkhangcha
Chimakaru
Yumthang
Burum Chhu
Jakthang
Yumthang Chhu
Rukamo
Phyaktok
Lahungthosa
Thomshasa
Lachen Monastery
Kishong
Umramchujom
Lachung
Rabomthang
Rabom Chhu
Latong
Ringpi Chhu
Passamphyaku
Yuigang
Tolung Gompa
Ford
Geocha
Rukel Chhu
Cave
Shabrung
Rahi Chhu
Chungthang
Chhatong
Ong Chhu
Theng
Sakkyong
Jemathang
Pakel
Fre Peak
Onglakthang
Laven
Tista River
Chakung Chhu
Sangchyophu
Lambi
Singhik
Myang
Kodyung
Lingdong
Tikipchhu
Khungme
Sokborongcho Partam
Kalivo
Gyathang
Boktak
Dzongri
Monmu Chhu
Shampung
Bakhim Cave
Kibek Cave
Sangam
Rongyang Chhu
Kayam Chhu
Bakcha Chhu
Nakchok
Chharggu
Maidong
Nabhe
Rakdong
Yaksam
Relli Chhu
Kongri
Lethang
Brang Polot
Sinor
Rathang Chhu
Samdong
Lirgzung
Phengtang
Rimbi Khola
Thingling
Mangjing
Mangkha
Pabyak
Kupup
Tadong
Tashiding
Neyangtang
Pemayangtse
Sosing (Keozing)
Rangpo
Rumtek
Takchom Chhu
Nathang
Lungthung
Legship
Rabonga
Ben
Saramsa
Dentam
Sirwani
Martam
Phyakkapu
Sopakha
Damthang
Machong
Lingtam
Kaluk
Damlakha
Siribadam
Singtam
Amba
Rangli
Uttare
Pabong
Temi
Rigu
Rangpo
Parbing
Bhasme
Namthang
Rhenok
Soreng
Chakung
Bhareng
Jorthang
Chidam
Naya Bazar
Sombare
Majhitar
Manpur
Melli Bazar

Projection: Lambert's Conical Orthomorphic | Scale - 1 cm = 7.0 kms.

NORTH DISTRICT
WEST DISTRICT
SOUTH DISTRICT
EAST DISTRICT
Mindo
Chhoilung
Lungma
Kerang
Laten
Kambe
Chhombo Chhu
Yumchho
Gurudongmar Chho
Olo
Chho Lhamo
Nakpolatok
Naku
Nachungthangka
Gogong
Tista R.
Pashi
Gyankaphagon
Khora Phu
Chorten Labsang
Khora Chhu
Lasha Chhu
Yumeshodong
Dongkya Chhu
Muguthang
Goma
Pukchang
Langbo Chhu
Thangu
Kalep Chhu
Shawaphu
Goma Sechen
Rangsha
Chhubakha
Phuring
Lhonak Chhu
Yathang
Talam
Theulacha
Gyamthang Chhu
Burumkhangcha
Chimakaru
Yumthang
Burum Chhu
Yumthang Chhu
Jakthang
Rukamo
Sebozung Chhu
Phyaktok
Tarum Chhu
Lahungthosa
Thomshasa
Kishong
Lachen Monastery
Lachung
Umramchujom
Rabomthang
Ringpi Chhu
Latong
Rabom Chhu
Passamphyaku
Ford
Tolung Gompa
Yuigang
Geocha
Rukel Chhu
Cave
Shabrung
Rahi Chhu
Chungthang
Chhatong
Jemathang
Sakkyong
Ong Chhu
Theng
Fre Peak
Onglakthang
Pakel
Sangchyophu
Laven
Tista River
Chakung Chhu
Singhik
Myang
Lambi
Lingdong
Kodyung
Tikipchhu
Sokborongcho
Khungme
Rongdung Chhu
Kayam Chhu
Mangan
Kalivo
Partam
Boktak
Dzongri
Gyathang
Bakhim
Kibek Cave
Monmu Chhu
Shampung
Cave
Sangam
Bakcha Chhu
Nakchok
Maidong
Relli Chhu
Nabhe
Chharggu
Yaksam
Lethang
Kongri
Brang Polot
Rakdong
Rathang Chhu
Sinor
Samdong
Lirgzung
Lungze Chhu
Mangjing
GANGTOK
Kupup
Phengtang
Rimbi Khola
Thingling
Tashiding
Rangpo
Mangkha
Tadong
Pabyak
Takchom Chhu
Rangpo Chhu
Nathang
Neyangtang
Pemayangise
Rumtek
Lungthung
Geyzing
Sosing (Keozing)
Saramsa
Rabonga
Ben
Phyakkapu
Dentam
Legship
Sirwani
Martam
Sopakha
Damthang
Machong
Singtam
Lingtam
Kaluk
Amba
Rangli
Siribadom
Temi
Pabong
Damlakha
Rangit
Uttare
Rigu
Rangpo
Bhasme
Soreng
Parbing
Rhenok
Chakung
Namthang
Bhareng
Namchi
Jorthang
Chidam
Naya Bazar
Sombare
Manjhitar
Manpur
Melli Bazar

Scale - 1 cm = 5.5 kms.

SENAPATI

VITAL STATISTICS

1. **District Headquarter:** Gangtok
2. **Population:** 283,583
3. **Area:** 954 sq. km.
4. **Population Density:** 290 persons per sq. km.
5. **Literacy:** 84.67%
6. **Sex Ratio:** 872 females per 1000 males

ECONOMIC PROFILES

1.Agriculture: The main crops are paddy, Maize, cereals, millets, sugarcane, Cotton, ginger etc. The horticulture crops are pineapple, orange, banana, citrus, Jackfruit, mango, pears etc.

2.Industries: Agro-based, chemical based, mineral based, metal based, Cotton textile, Cane and bamboo, carpentry, blacksmith, Repairing and servicing, leather based etc.

3.Minerals: Copper, Dolomite, Coal,clay, sandstone, Limestone etc.

4. Tourism: Chengu Lake, Rumtek, Nathu la pass, Hanuman tok

East Sikkim is one of the four administrative Districts of the Indian State of Sikkim.East Sikkim was part of the kingdom of Sikkim for most of its history.In 19th century,the district was under control of bhutanese.After the Anglo Bhutan war, the territory was virtually under the command of British forces.East Sikkim is home to four wildlife sanctuaries: Barsey Rhododendron, fambong lho, pangolakha and kyongnosla Alpine etc.The

Laven
Singhik
Myang
Sangchyophu
Lingdong
Kodyung
Sokborongcho
Partam
Mangan
Kalivo
Gyathang
Shampung
Monmu Chhu
Bakcha Chhu
Sangam
Nakchok
Nabhe
Chharggu
Rakdong
Lirgzung
Samdong
Lungze Chhu
Mangjing
Gangtok
Kupup
Mangkha
Tadong
Pabyak
Rangpo Chhu
Takchom Chhu
Rangpo
Nathang
Lungthung
Rumtek
EAST DISTRICT
Saramsa
Ben
Sirwani
Martam
Phyakkapu
Damthang
Machong
Lingtam
Pabong
Damlakha
Amba
Rangli
Temi
Singtam
Rigu
Parbing
Bhasme
Rangpo
Rhenok
Namthang
Namchi
Chidam
N
W
E
S
Manpur
Melli Bazar

Rumtek Monastery

Changu lake

Scale - 1 cm = 2.98 kms.

SENAPATI

VITAL STATISTICS

1. **District Headquarter:** Geyzing
2. **Population:** 136,299
3. **Area:** 1166 sq. km.
4. **Population Density:** 120 persons per sq. km.
5. **Literacy:** 78.69%
6. **Sex Ratio:** 941 females per 1000 males

ECONOMIC PROFILES

1.Agriculture: The main crops are paddy, wheat, jowar, sugarcane, Cotton, millet, ginger, bajra, etc.The horticulture crops are pineapple, orange, banana, guava, pears, jackfruit, citrus etc.

2.Industries: Agro-based, chemical based, Repairing and servicing, Cane and bamboo, carpentry, blacksmith, engineering units, mineral based, metal based, etc.

3.Minerals:copper, Dolomite, coal, natural gas, Sandstone etc.

West Sikkim is a District of the Indian state of Sikkim. West Sikkim is the site of the ancient state capital Yuksom. In 1977, West Sikkim district became home to khangchendzonga national park, which as an area of 1784 km2. Sikkim climate ranges from subtropical in the South to tundra in the north. Most of the inhabitant regions of Sikkim experience a temperate climate, with temperature seldom exceeding 28°C in summer.

Geocha
Cave
Shabrung
Sakkyong
Jemathang
Fre Peak
Onglakthang
Laven
Lambi
Lingdong
Tikipchhu
Khungme
Mangan
Kalivo
Gyathang
Boktak
Dzongri
Rongdung Chhu
Kayam Chhu
Shampung
Monmu Chhu
Bakhim Cave
Kibek Cave
Sangam
Maidong
Relli Chhu
Bakcha Chhu
WEST DISTRICT
Yaksam
Nabhe
Rakdong
Kongri
Lethang
Brang Polot
Lirgzung
Rathang Chhu
Sinor
Samdong
GANGTOK
Mangjing
Phengtang
Rimbi Khola
Thingling
Mangkha
Tadong
Pabyak
Tashiding
Neyangtang
Pemayangise
Takchom Chhu
Geyzing
Sosing (Keozing)
Rangpo
Rumtek
Legship
Rabonga
Saramsa
Ben
Dentam
Sirwani
Martam
Phyakkapu
Sopakha
Damthang
SOUTH DISTRICT
Kaluk
Damlakha
Siribadam
Pabong
Singtam
Amba
Rangit
Uttare
Temi
Parbing
Bhasme
Rangpo
Rhenok
Namthang
Soreng
Chakung
Bhareng
Namchi
Jorthang
Chidam
Naya Bazar
Sombare
Manjhitar
Manpur
Melli Bazar
N
W
E
S
Rabdentse Ruins
Pelling

Scale - 1 cm = 3.56 kms.

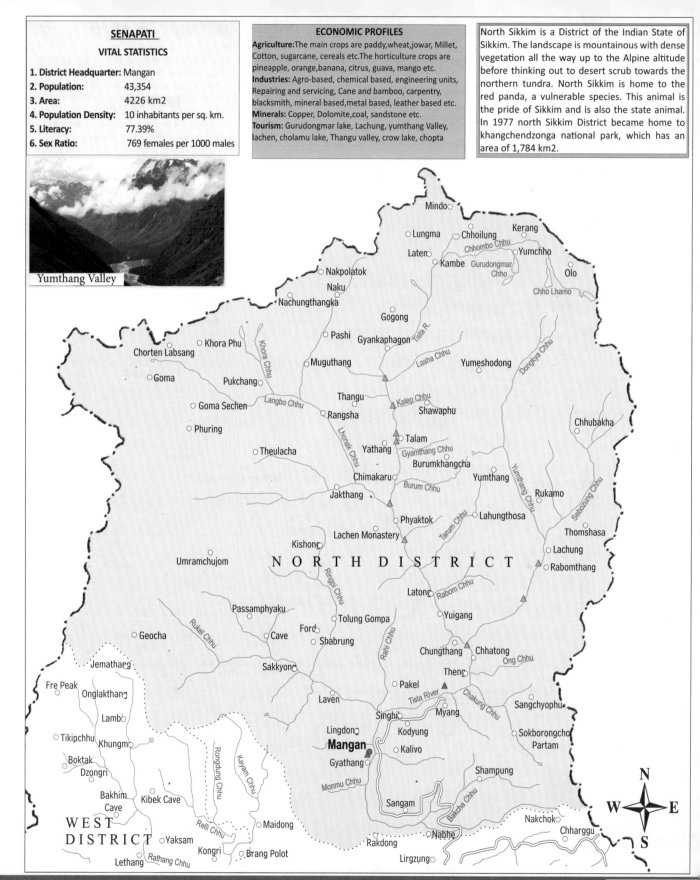

SENAPATI

VITAL STATISTICS

1. District Headquarter: Mangan
2. Population: 43,354
3. Area: 4226 km2
4. Population Density: 10 inhabitants per sq. km.
5. Literacy: 77.39%
6. Sex Ratio: 769 females per 1000 males

ECONOMIC PROFILES

Agriculture: The main crops are paddy,wheat,jowar, Millet, Cotton, sugarcane, cereals etc.The horticulture crops are pineapple, orange,banana, citrus, guava, mango etc.
Industries: Agro-based, chemical based, engineering units, Repairing and servicing, Cane and bamboo, carpentry, blacksmith, mineral based,metal based, leather based etc.
Minerals: Copper, Dolomite,coal, sandstone etc.
Tourism: Gurudongmar lake, Lachung, yumthang Valley, lachen, cholamu lake, Thangu valley, crow lake, chopta

North Sikkim is a District of the Indian State of Sikkim. The landscape is mountainous with dense vegetation all the way up to the Alpine altitude before thinking out to desert scrub towards the northern tundra. North Sikkim is home to the red panda, a vulnerable species. This animal is the pride of Sikkim and is also the state animal. In 1977 north Sikkim District became home to khangchendzonga national park, which has an area of 1,784 km2.

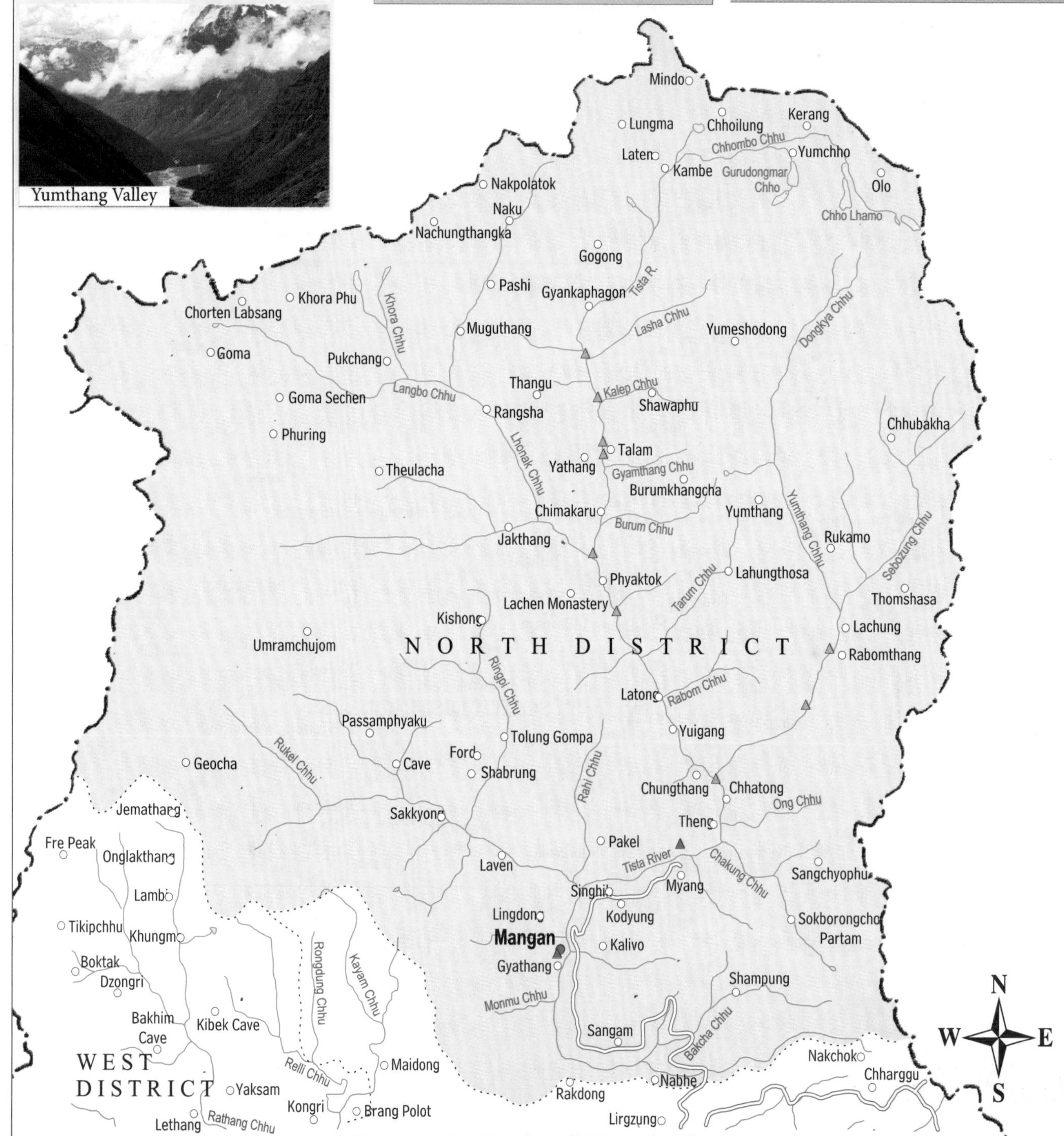
Yumthang Valley
Mindo
Lungma
Chhoilung
Kerang
Chhombo Chhu
Laten
Yumchho
Kambe
Gurudongmar Chho
Olo
Nakpolatok
Naku
Chho Lhamo
Nachungthangka
Gogong
Pashi
Gyankaphagon
Tista R.
Khora Phu
Chorten Labsang
Khora Chhu
Muguthang
Lasha Chhu
Yumeshodong
Dongkya Chhu
Goma
Pukchang
Thangu
Langbo Chhu
Kalep Chhu
Goma Sechen
Rangsha
Shawaphu
Chhubakha
Phuring
Lhonak Chhu
Talam
Theulacha
Yathang
Gyamthang Chhu
Burumkhangcha
Yumthang
Chimakaru
Yumthang Chhu
Burum Chhu
Jakthang
Rukamo
Sebozung Chhu
Lahungthosa
Phyaktok
Tarum Chhu
Thomshasa
Lachen Monastery
Kishong
Lachung
Umramchujom
NORTH DISTRICT
Rabomthang
Ringpi Chhu
Latong
Rabom Chhu
Passamphyaku
Yuigang
Tolung Gompa
Rukel Chhu
Ford
Geocha
Cave
Shabrung
Rahi Chhu
Chungthang
Chhatong
Jemathang
Ong Chhu
Sakkyong
Theng
Fre Peak
Pakel
Onglakthang
Laven
Tista River
Chakung Chhu
Sangchyophu
Lamb
Singhi
Myang
Lingdong
Kodyung
Tikipchhu
Sokborongcho
Khungm
Partam
Mangan
Kalivo
Boktak
Dzongri
Gyathang
Shampung
Rongdung Chhu
Kayam Chhu
Monmu Chhu
N
Bakhim Cave
Kibek Cave
Sangam
W
E
Bakcha Chhu
WEST DISTRICT
Relli Chhu
Maidong
Nakchok
Chharggu
Nabhe
S
Yaksam
Rakdong
Kongri
Brang Polot
Lethang
Rathang Chhu
Lirgzung
Scale - 1 cm = 4.6 kms.

SENAPATI

VITAL STATISTICS

. District Headquarter:	Namchi
. Population:	146,742
. Area:	750 sq. km.
. Population Density:	200 persons per sq. km.
. Literacy:	82.06%
. Sex Ratio:	914 females per 1000 males

ECONOMIC PROFILES

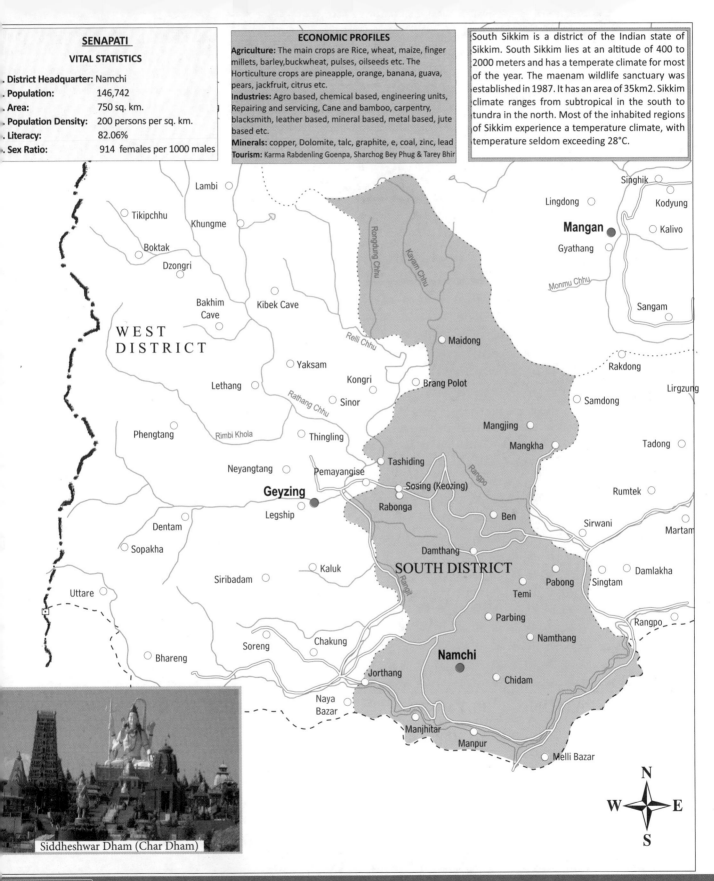

Agriculture: The main crops are Rice, wheat, maize, finger millets, barley,buckwheat, pulses, oilseeds etc. The Horticulture crops are pineapple, orange, banana, guava, pears, jackfruit, citrus etc.

Industries: Agro based, chemical based, engineering units, Repairing and servicing, Cane and bamboo, carpentry, blacksmith, leather based, mineral based, metal based, jute based etc.

Minerals: copper, Dolomite, talc, graphite, e, coal, zinc, lead

Tourism: Karma Rabdenling Goenpa, Sharchog Bey Phug & Tarey Bhir

South Sikkim is a district of the Indian state of Sikkim. South Sikkim lies at an altitude of 400 to 2000 meters and has a temperate climate for most of the year. The maenam wildlife sanctuary was established in 1987. It has an area of 35km2. Sikkim climate ranges from subtropical in the south to tundra in the north. Most of the inhabited regions of Sikkim experience a temperature climate, with temperature seldom exceeding 28°C.

Lambi
Tikipchhu
Khungme
Boktak
Dzongri
Bakhim Cave
Kibek Cave
WEST DISTRICT
Rongdung Chhu
Kayam Chhu
Relli Chhu
Maidong
Yaksam
Lethang
Kongri
Brang Polot
Rathang Chhu
Sinor
Phengtang
Rimbi Khola
Thingling
Tashiding
Neyangtang
Pemayangise
Geyzing
Sosing (Keozing)
Rabonga
Rangpo
Legship
Dentam
Sopakha
Ben
Damthang
SOUTH DISTRICT
Kaluk
Siribadam
Rangit
Uttare
Temi
Pabong
Parbing
Namthang
Soreng
Chakung
Bhareng
Namchi
Jorthang
Chidam
Naya Bazar
Manjhitar
Manpur
Melli Bazar
Singhik
Kodyung
Lingdong
Mangan
Kalivo
Gyathang
Monmu Chhu
Sangam
Rakdong
Lirgzung
Samdong
Mangjing
Mangkha
Tadong
Rumtek
Sirwani
Martam
Singtam
Damlakha
Rangpo
N
W
E
S

Siddheshwar Dham (Char Dham)

Scale - 1 cm = 3.1 kms.

TRIPURA

Section

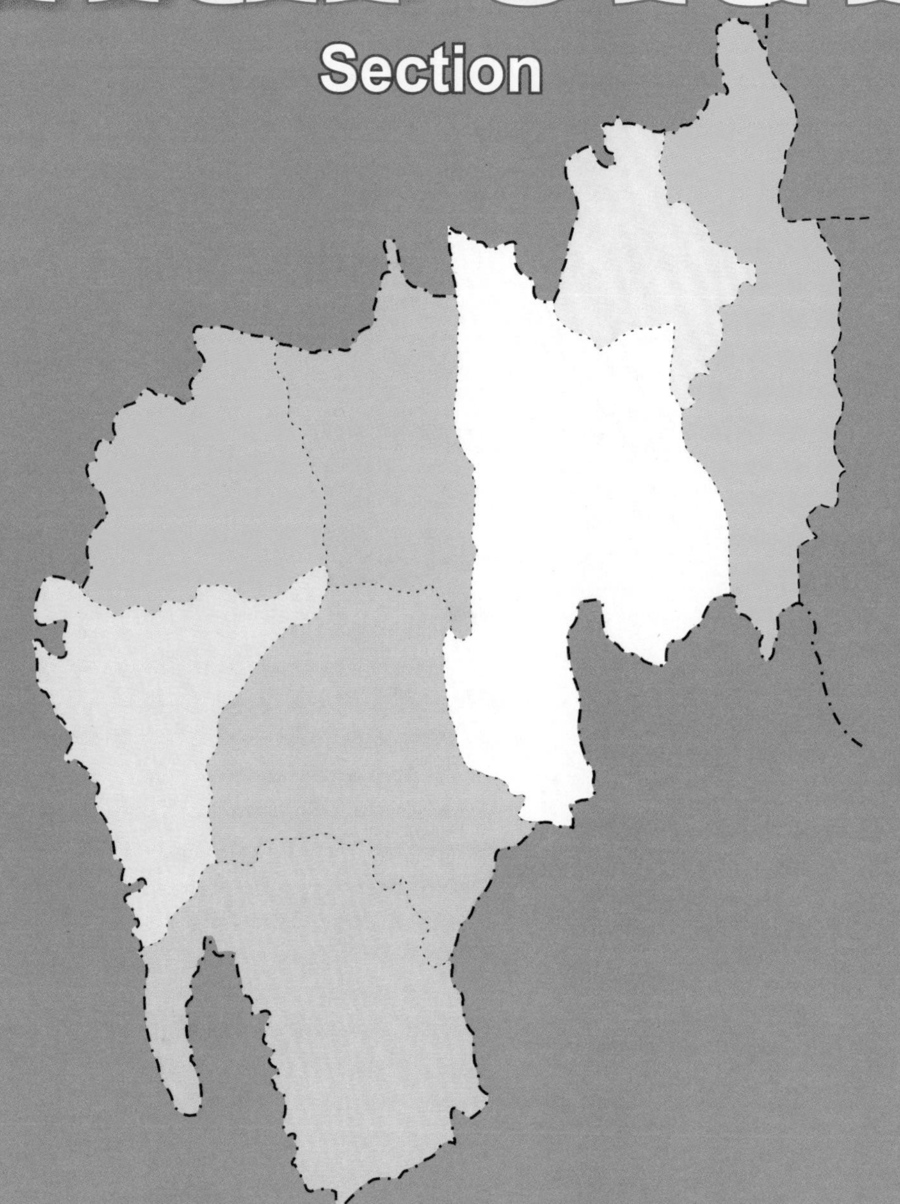

POPULATION:	*36,71,032*	DISTRICTS: *8*
AREA:	*10,486 sq.km.*	L.S. CONSTITUENCY: *2*
POP. DENSITY:	*350 persons/ Km^2*	R.S. CONSTITUENCY: *1*
LITERACY:	*87.75%*	GRAM PANCHAYATS: *591*
SEX RATIO:	*961 females/1000 males*	GSDP: *46,133*

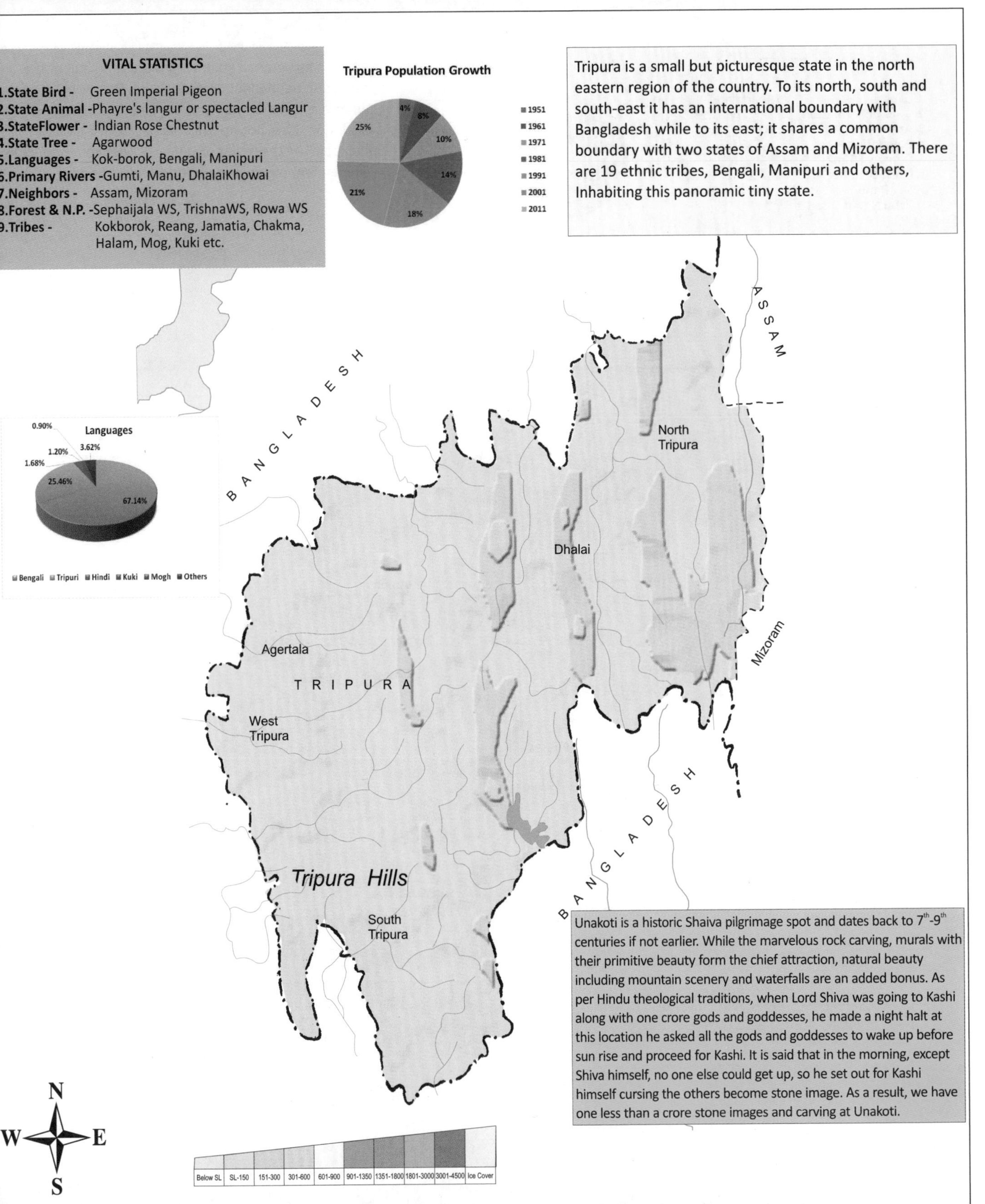
VITAL STATISTICS
1.State Bird - Green Imperial Pigeon
2.State Animal -Phayre's langur or spectacled Langur
3.StateFlower - Indian Rose Chestnut
4.State Tree - Agarwood
5.Languages - Kok-borok, Bengali, Manipuri
6.Primary Rivers -Gumti, Manu, DhalaiKhowai
7.Neighbors - Assam, Mizoram
8.Forest & N.P. -Sephaijala WS, TrishnaWS, Rowa WS
9.Tribes - Kokborok, Reang, Jamatia, Chakma, Halam, Mog, Kuki etc.
Tripura Population Growth
4%
8%
10%
14%
18%
21%
25%
1951
1961
1971
1981
1991
2001
2011
Tripura is a small but picturesque state in the north eastern region of the country. To its north, south and south-east it has an international boundary with Bangladesh while to its east; it shares a common boundary with two states of Assam and Mizoram. There are 19 ethnic tribes, Bengali, Manipuri and others, Inhabiting this panoramic tiny state.
Languages
0.90%
1.20%
3.62%
1.68%
25.46%
67.14%
Bengali
Tripuri
Hindi
Kuki
Mogh
Others
BANGLADESH
ASSAM
North Tripura
Dhalai
Agertala
TRIPURA
West Tripura
Mizoram
BANGLADESH
Tripura Hills
South Tripura
Unakoti is a historic Shaiva pilgrimage spot and dates back to 7th-9th centuries if not earlier. While the marvelous rock carving, murals with their primitive beauty form the chief attraction, natural beauty including mountain scenery and waterfalls are an added bonus. As per Hindu theological traditions, when Lord Shiva was going to Kashi along with one crore gods and goddesses, he made a night halt at this location he asked all the gods and goddesses to wake up before sun rise and proceed for Kashi. It is said that in the morning, except Shiva himself, no one else could get up, so he set out for Kashi himself cursing the others become stone image. As a result, we have one less than a crore stone images and carving at Unakoti.
N
W
E
S
Below SL
SL-150
151-300
301-600
601-900
901-1350
1351-1800
1801-3000
3001-4500
Ice Cover

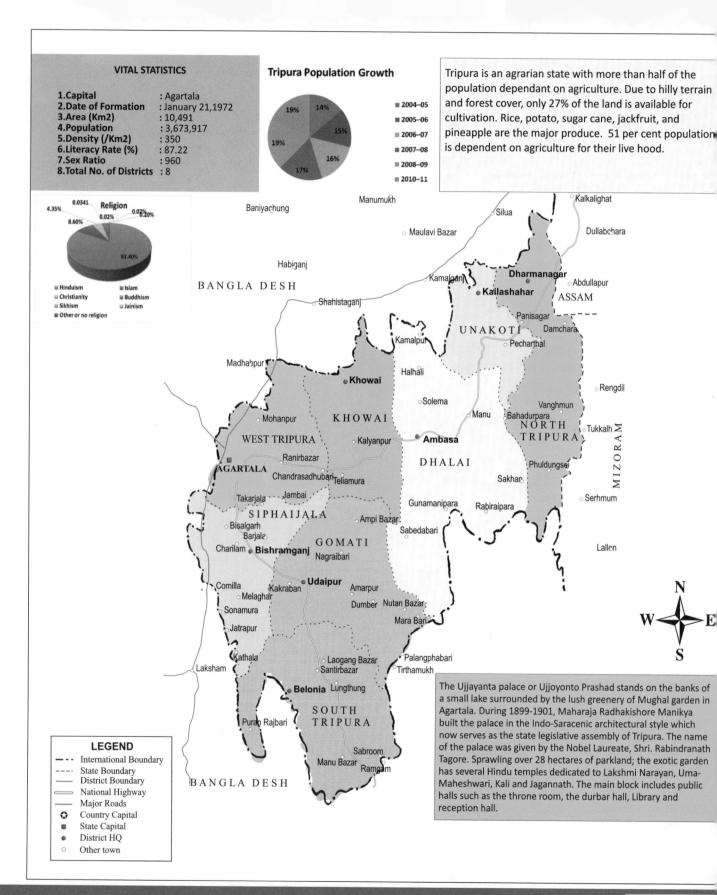

VITAL STATISTICS

1.Capital	: Agartala
2.Date of Formation	: January 21,1972
3.Area (Km2)	: 10,491
4.Population	: 3,673,917
5.Density (/Km2)	: 350
6.Literacy Rate (%)	: 87.22
7.Sex Ratio	: 960
8.Total No. of Districts	: 8

Tripura Population Growth

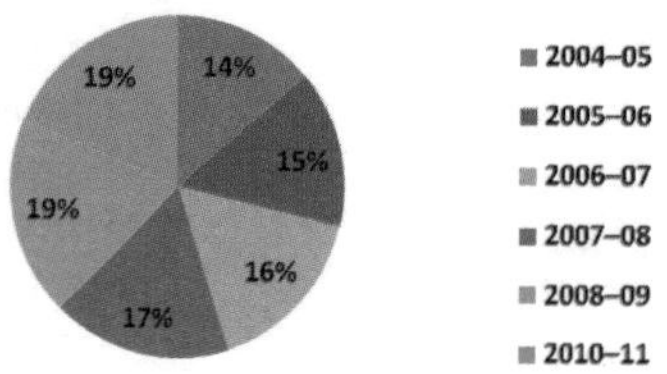

14% 15% 16% 17% 19% 19%

2004–05
2005–06
2006–07
2007–08
2008–09
2010–11

Tripura is an agrarian state with more than half of the population dependant on agriculture. Due to hilly terrain and forest cover, only 27% of the land is available for cultivation. Rice, potato, sugar cane, jackfruit, and pineapple are the major produce. 51 per cent population is dependent on agriculture for their live hood.

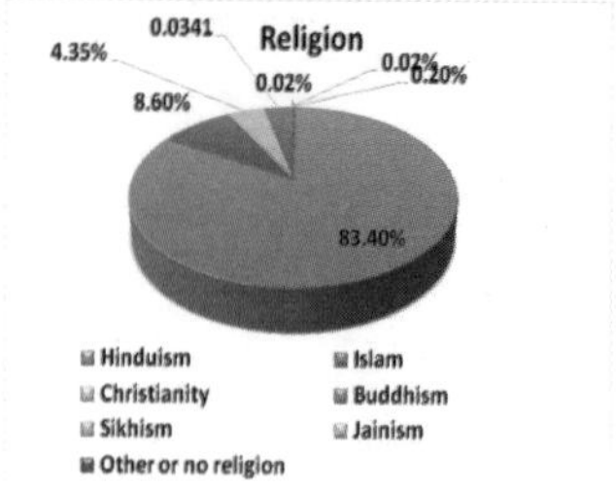

Religion

4.35% 0.0341 0.02% 0.07% 0.20% 8.60% 83.40%

Hinduism
Islam
Christianity
Buddhism
Sikhism
Jainism
Other or no religion

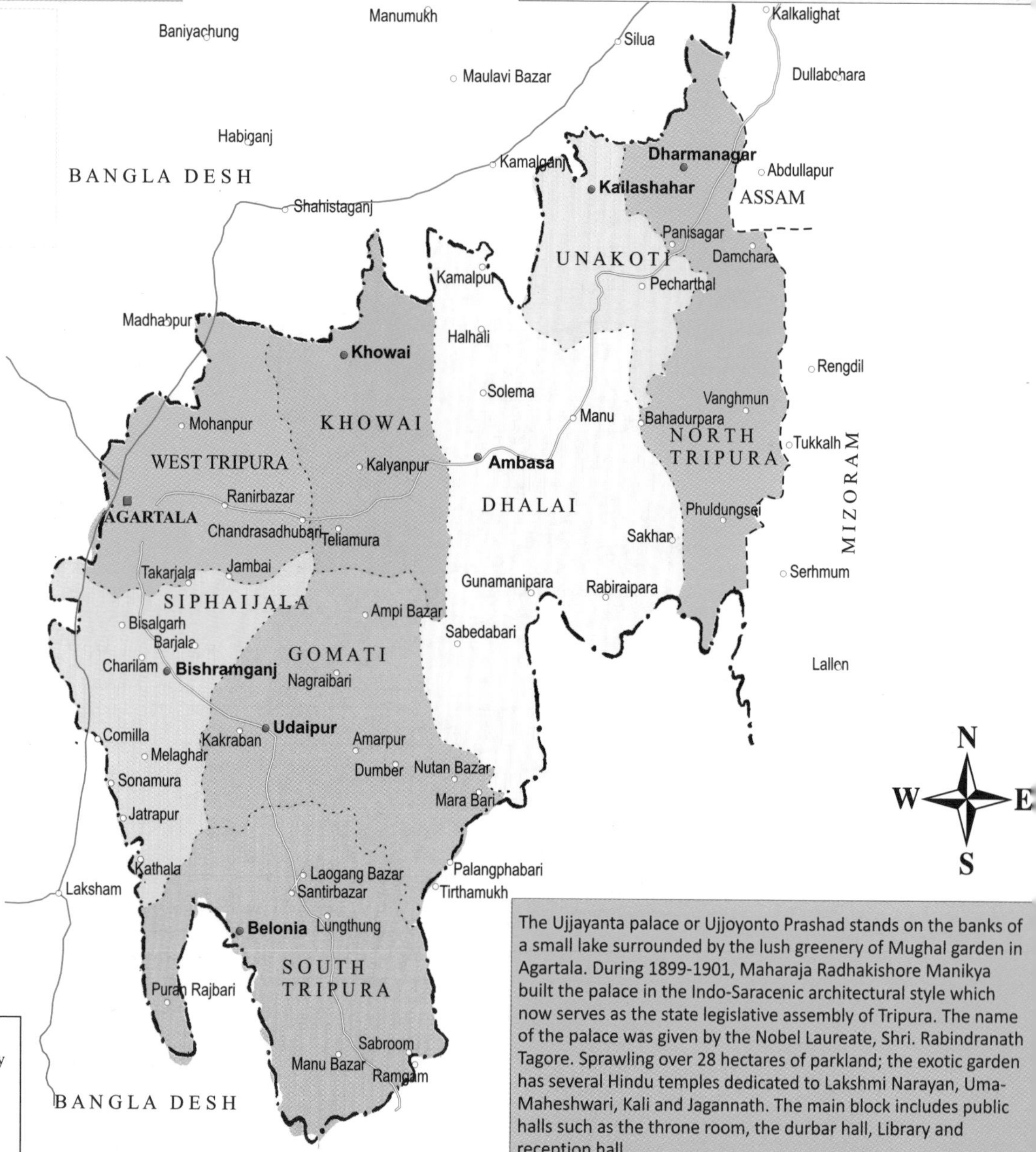

Manumukh
Baniyachung
Silua
Kalkalighat
Maulavi Bazar
Dullabchara
Habiganj
BANGLA DESH
Kamalganj
Dharmanagar
Kailashahar
Abdullapur
ASSAM
Shahistaganj
Panisagar
UNAKOTI
Damchara
Kamalpur
Pecharthal
Madhabpur
Halhali
Khowai
Rengdil
Solema
Vanghmun
Mohanpur
KHOWAI
Manu
Bahadurpara
NORTH TRIPURA
Tukkalh
WEST TRIPURA
Kalyanpur
Ambasa
MIZORAM
Ranirbazar
DHALAI
AGARTALA
Chandrasadhubari
Teliamura
Phuldungsei
Sakhan
Takarjala
Jambai
Gunamanipara
Rabiraipara
Serhmum
SIPHAIJALA
Ampi Bazar
Bisalgarh
Barjala
Sabedabari
Charilam
Bishramganj
GOMATI
Nagraibari
Lallen
Udaipur
Comilla
Kakraban
Amarpur
Melaghar
Sonamura
Dumber
Nutan Bazar
Mara Bari
Jatrapur
Kathala
Laogang Bazar
Palangphabari
Santirbazar
Tirthamukh
Laksham
Belonia
Lungthung
SOUTH TRIPURA
Puran Rajbari
Sabroom
Manu Bazar
Ramgam
BANGLA DESH

N
W E
S

The Ujjayanta palace or Ujjoyonto Prashad stands on the banks of a small lake surrounded by the lush greenery of Mughal garden in Agartala. During 1899-1901, Maharaja Radhakishore Manikya built the palace in the Indo-Saracenic architectural style which now serves as the state legislative assembly of Tripura. The name of the palace was given by the Nobel Laureate, Shri. Rabindranath Tagore. Sprawling over 28 hectares of parkland; the exotic garden has several Hindu temples dedicated to Lakshmi Narayan, Uma-Maheshwari, Kali and Jagannath. The main block includes public halls such as the throne room, the durbar hall, Library and reception hall.

LEGEND

International Boundary
State Boundary
District Boundary
National Highway
Major Roads
Country Capital
State Capital
District HQ
Other town

Scale - 1:1.13 M approx

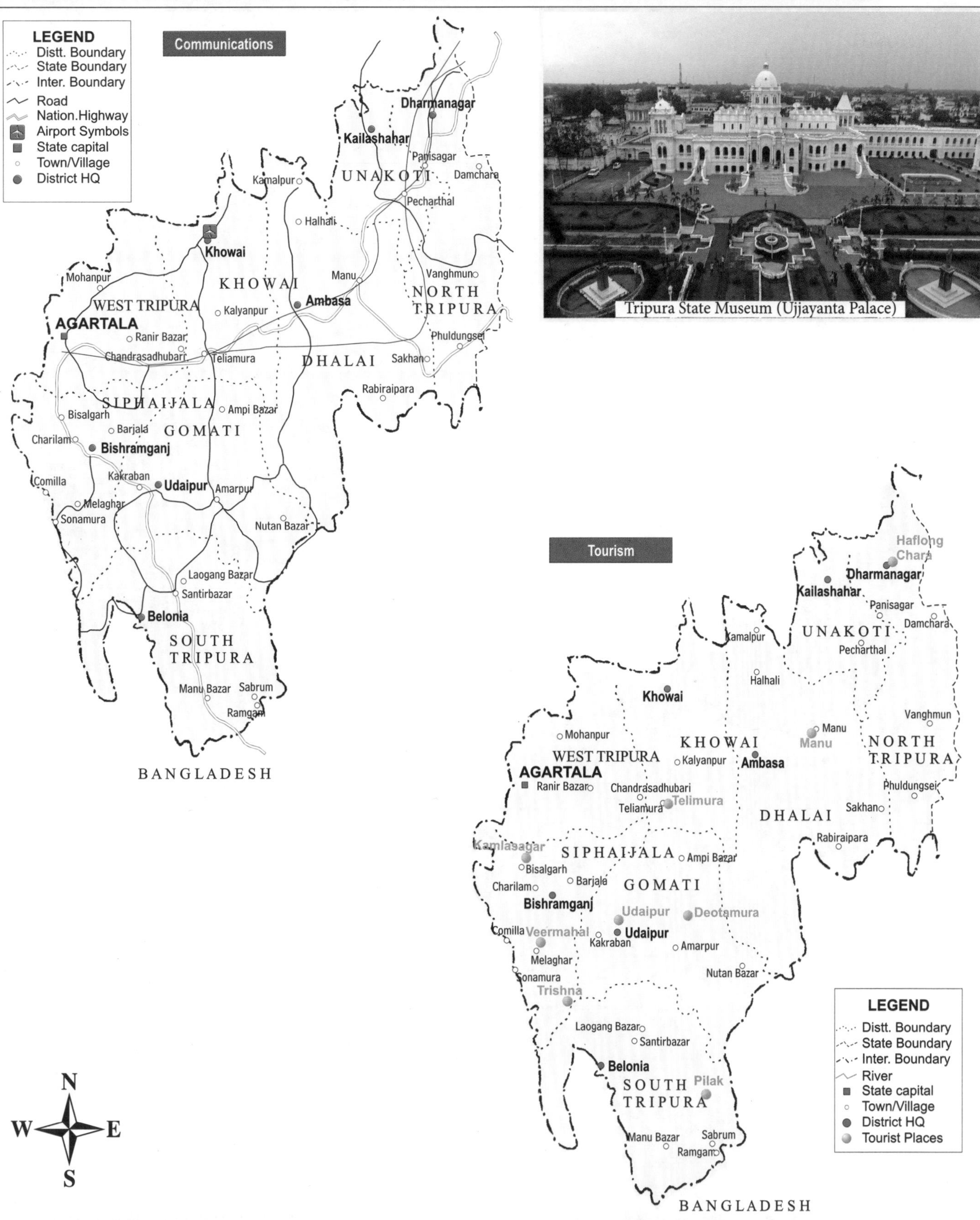
LEGEND
Distt. Boundary
State Boundary
Inter. Boundary
Road
Nation.Highway
Airport Symbols
State capital
Town/Village
District HQ
Communications
Dharmanagar
Kailashahar
Panisagar
UNAKOTI
Damchara
Kamalpur
Pecharthal
Halhali
Khowai
KHOWAI
Manu
Vanghmun
Mohanpur
NORTH
TRIPURA
WEST TRIPURA
Kalyanpur
Ambasa
AGARTALA
Ranir Bazar
Phuldungsei
Chandrasadhubari
Teliamura
DHALAI
Sakhan
Rabiraipara
SIPHAIJALA
Ampi Bazar
Bisalgarh
Barjala
GOMATI
Charilam
Bishramganj
Kakraban
Comilla
Udaipur
Amarpur
Melaghar
Sonamura
Nutan Bazar
Laogang Bazar
Santirbazar
Belonia
SOUTH
TRIPURA
Manu Bazar
Sabrum
Ramgarh
BANGLADESH
N
W
E
S
Tourism
Haflong
Chara
Kamlasagar
Telimura
Udaipur
Deotamura
Veermahal
Trishna
Pilak
Tourist Places
River

Tripura State Museum (Ujjayanta Palace)

SEX RATIO & POPULATION

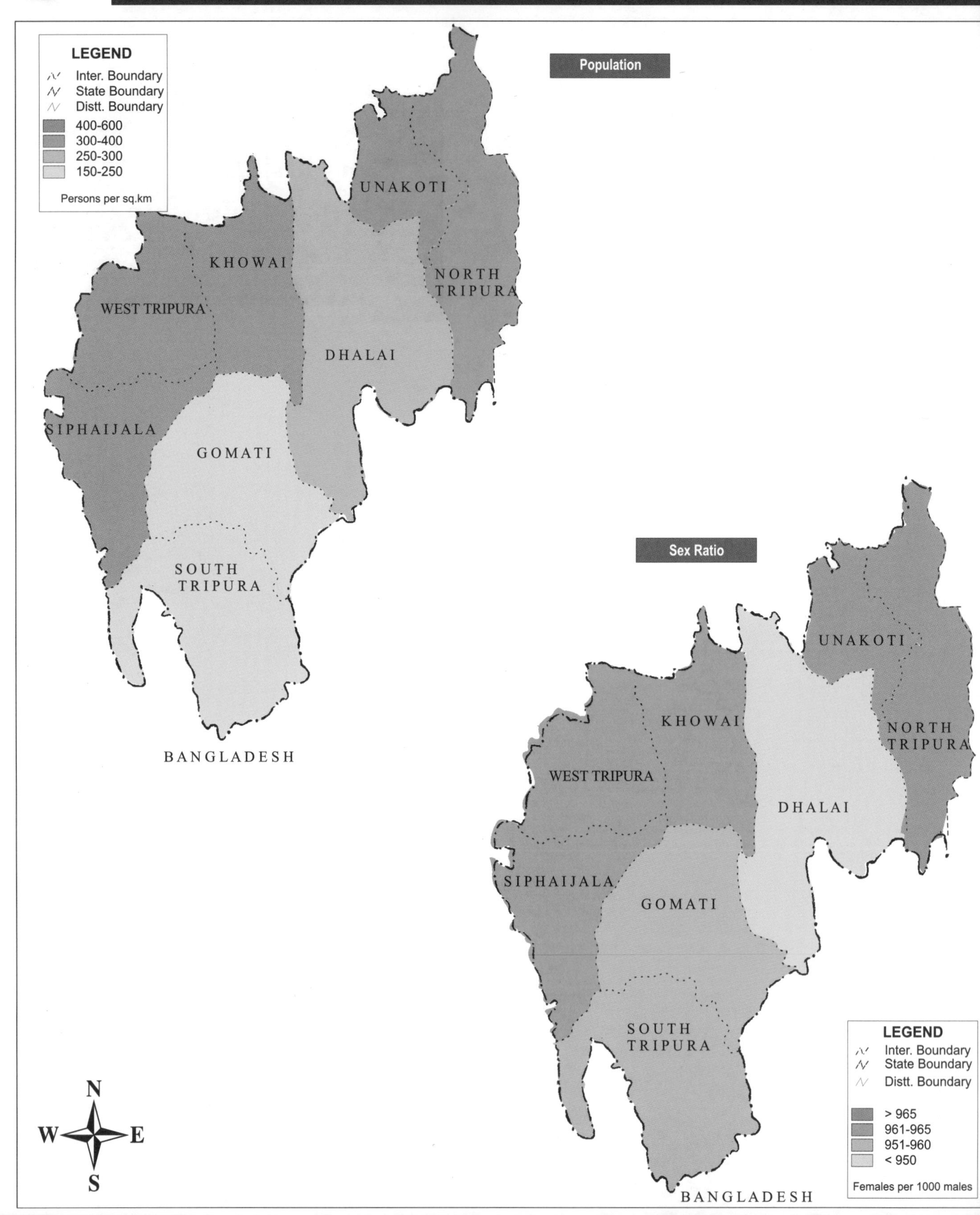
LEGEND
Inter. Boundary
State Boundary
Distt. Boundary
400-600
300-400
250-300
150-250
Persons per sq.km
Population
UNAKOTI
KHOWAI
NORTH TRIPURA
WEST TRIPURA
DHALAI
SIPHAIJALA
GOMATI
SOUTH TRIPURA
BANGLADESH
Sex Ratio
UNAKOTI
KHOWAI
NORTH TRIPURA
WEST TRIPURA
DHALAI
SIPHAIJALA
GOMATI
SOUTH TRIPURA
BANGLADESH
LEGEND
Inter. Boundary
State Boundary
Distt. Boundary
> 965
961-965
951-960
< 950
Females per 1000 males
N
W
E
S

Scale - 1:1.3 M approx

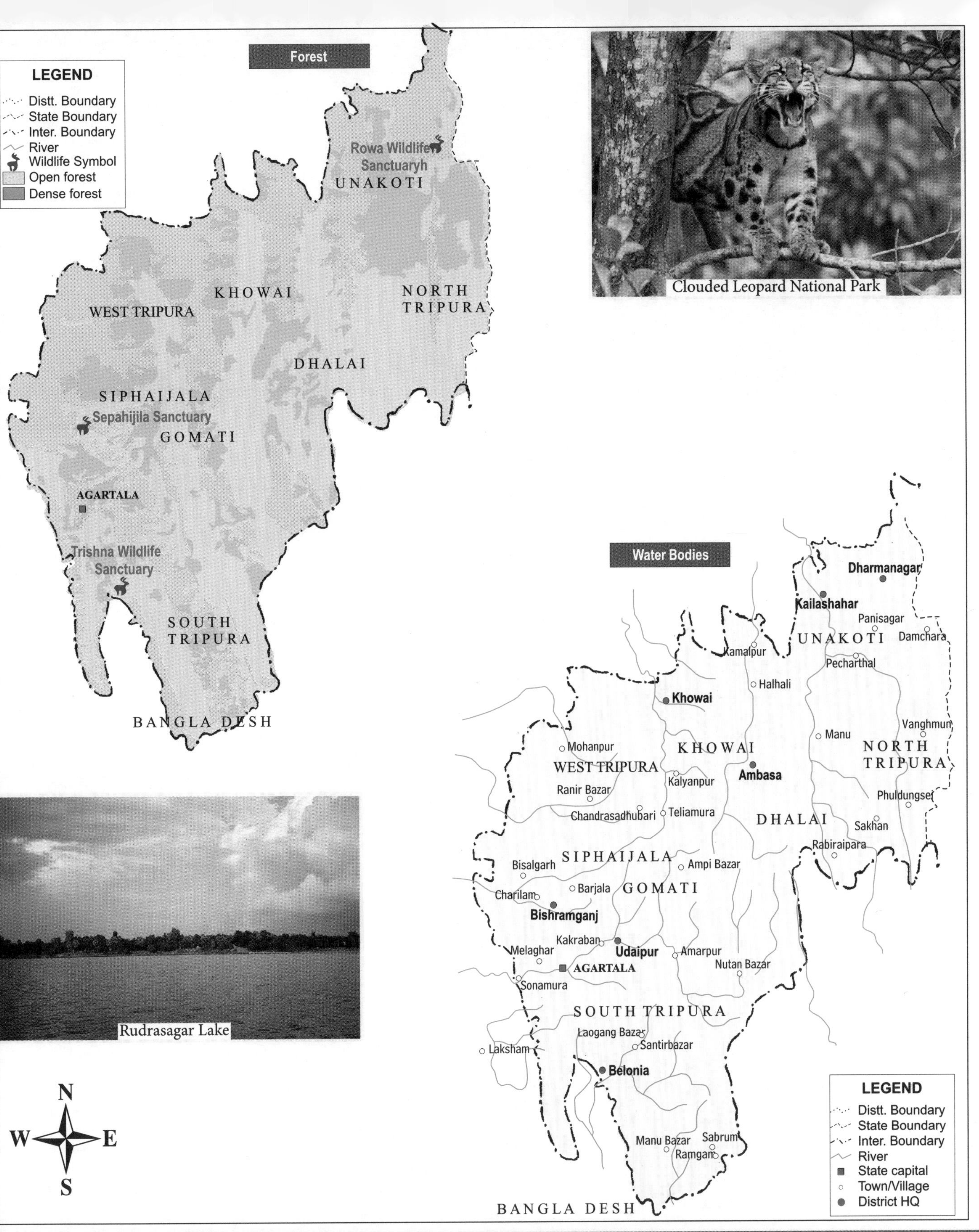

Forest
LEGEND
Distt. Boundary
State Boundary
Inter. Boundary
River
Wildlife Symbol
Open forest
Dense forest
Rowa Wildlife Sanctuaryh
UNAKOTI
KHOWAI
WEST TRIPURA
NORTH TRIPURA
DHALAI
SIPHAIJALA
Sepahijila Sanctuary
GOMATI
AGARTALA
Trishna Wildlife Sanctuary
SOUTH TRIPURA
BANGLA DESH
Water Bodies
Dharmanagar
Kailashahar
Panisagar
Damchara
UNAKOTI
Kamalpur
Pecharthal
Halhali
Khowai
Vanghmun
Manu
Mohanpur
KHOWAI
NORTH TRIPURA
WEST TRIPURA
Ambasa
Kalyanpur
Ranir Bazar
Phuldungsei
Chandrasadhubari
Teliamura
DHALAI
Sakhan
Rabiraipara
Bisalgarh
SIPHAIJALA
Ampi Bazar
Barjala
GOMATI
Charilam
Bishramganj
Kakraban
Udaipur
Amarpur
Melaghar
AGARTALA
Nutan Bazar
Sonamura
SOUTH TRIPURA
Laogang Bazar
Santirbazar
Laksham
Belonia
Manu Bazar
Sabrum
Ramgarh
BANGLA DESH
LEGEND
Distt. Boundary
State Boundary
Inter. Boundary
River
State capital
Town/Village
District HQ
N
W
E
S

Clouded Leopard National Park

Rudrasagar Lake

Scale - 1:1.3 M approx

UNAKOTI & NORTH TRIPURA

UNAKOTI

VITAL STATISTICS

1. **District Headquarter:** Kailashahar
2. **Population:** 2,98,194
3. **Area:** 686 sq. km.
4. **Population Density:** 430 persons per sq. km.
5. **Literacy:** 84.64%
6. **Sex Ratio:** 944 females per 1000 males

ECONOMIC PROFILES

1. **Agriculture:** Wet rice cultivation, Jhum paddy cultivation, oil-seeds production, tea plantation. Crops like maize, cotton, cereals, sugarcane, Jowar, etc.
2. **Industries:** Agro-based, chemical, cane and bamboo etc.
3. **Minerals:** Coal, limestone, sandstone etc.
4. **Tourism:** Maa Bhabatarini mandir, Soteromiar Hawor, Chaturdas Mandir, Buddha Bihar, laxmi Narayan Mandir.
5. **Live stocks :** Poultry, cattle, goats, Sheep, dairy farming etc.

Unakoti district was created on 21 January 2012. The climate of the district is hot and humid during summer with sufficient rainfall between June and October and dry climate during winter. Rainfall is usually high in this district compared to other district in the state. Temperature is generally moderate and mild variations are noticed in various places. The Jhum cultivation and terraced cultivation is practiced in the district.

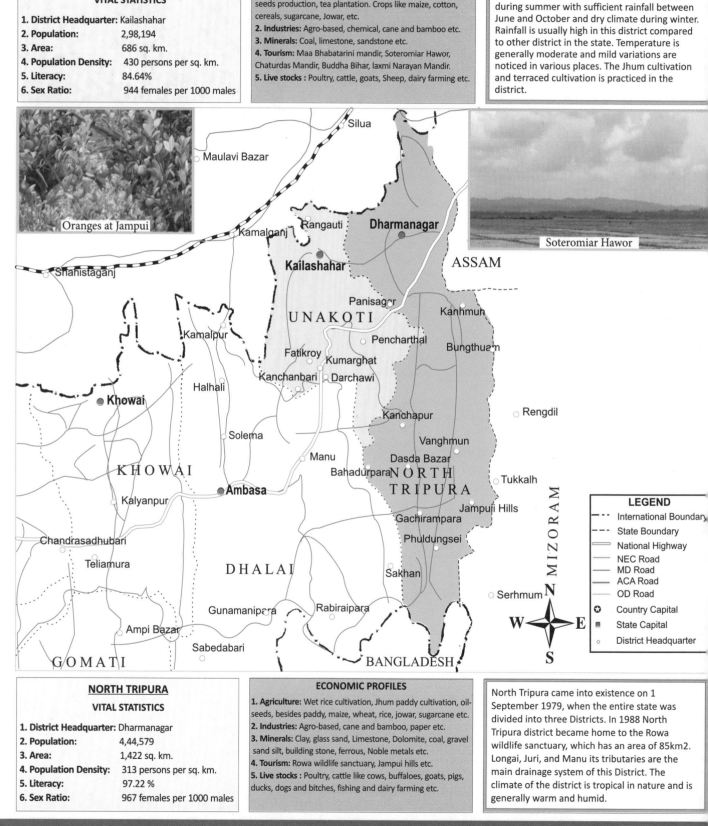

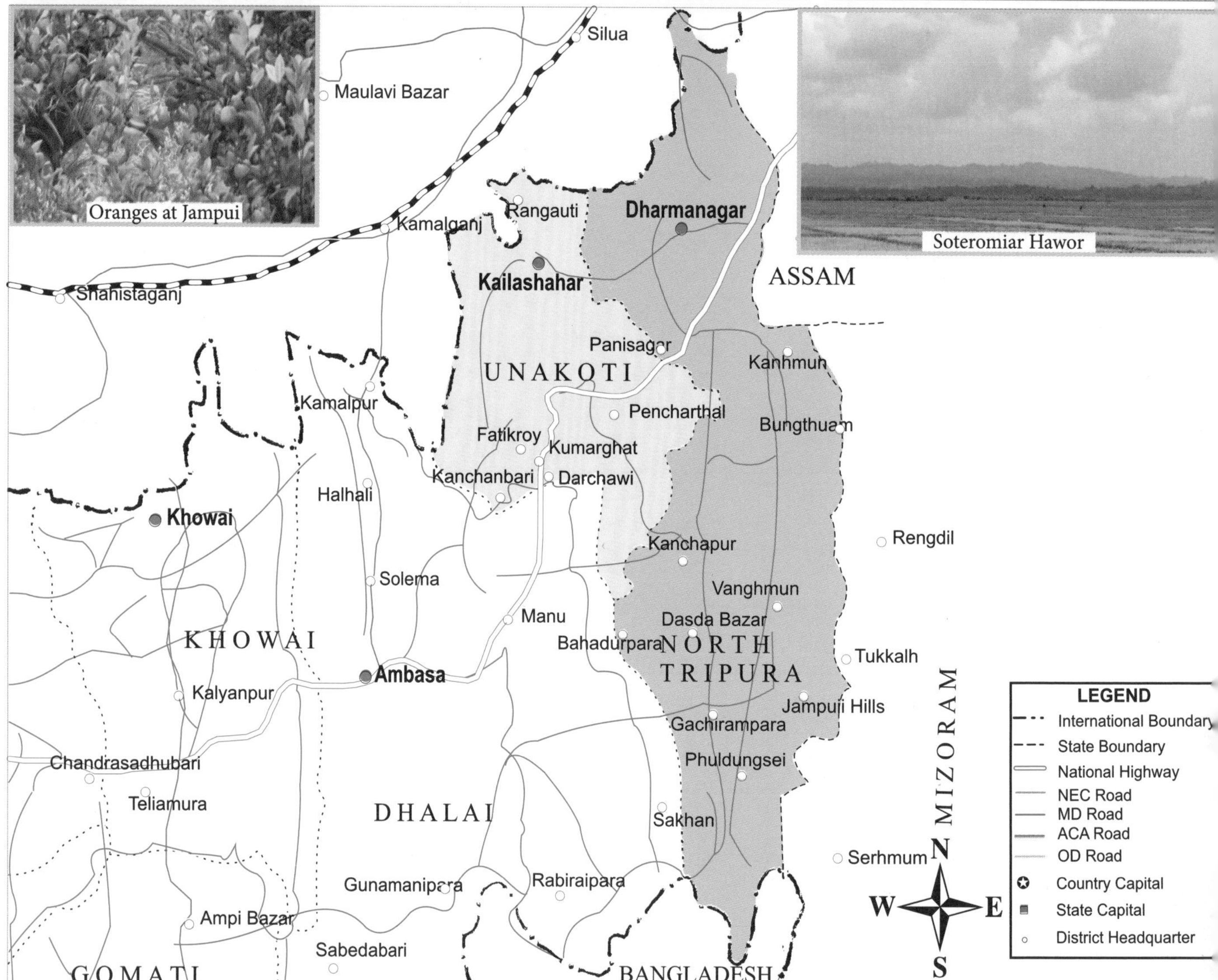
Oranges at Jampui
Soteromiar Hawor
Silua
Maulavi Bazar
Kamalganj
Rangauti
Dharmanagar
Kailashahar
Shahistaganj
ASSAM
Panisagar
UNAKOTI
Kanhmun
Kamalpur
Pencharthal
Bungthuam
Fatikroy
Kumarghat
Kanchanbari
Darchawi
Halhali
Khowai
Rengdil
Kanchapur
Solema
Vanghmun
Manu
Dasda Bazar
Bahadurpara
NORTH TRIPURA
KHOWAI
Tukkalh
Ambasa
Kalyanpur
Jampui Hills
Gachirampara
Chandrasadhubari
Phuldungsei
Teliamura
DHALAI
Sakhan
MIZORAM
Serhmum
Gunamanipara
Rabiraipara
Ampi Bazar
Sabedabari
GOMATI
BANGLADESH
N
W
E
S
LEGEND
International Boundary
State Boundary
National Highway
NEC Road
MD Road
ACA Road
OD Road
Country Capital
State Capital
District Headquarter

NORTH TRIPURA

VITAL STATISTICS

1. **District Headquarter:** Dharmanagar
2. **Population:** 4,44,579
3. **Area:** 1,422 sq. km.
4. **Population Density:** 313 persons per sq. km.
5. **Literacy:** 97.22 %
6. **Sex Ratio:** 967 females per 1000 males

ECONOMIC PROFILES

1. **Agriculture:** Wet rice cultivation, Jhum paddy cultivation, oil-seeds, besides paddy, maize, wheat, rice, jowar, sugarcane etc.
2. **Industries:** Agro-based, cane and bamboo, paper etc.
3. **Minerals:** Clay, glass sand, Limestone, Dolomite, coal, gravel sand silt, building stone, ferrous, Noble metals etc.
4. **Tourism:** Rowa wildlife sanctuary, Jampui hills etc.
5. **Live stocks :** Poultry, cattle like cows, buffaloes, goats, pigs, ducks, dogs and bitches, fishing and dairy farming etc.

North Tripura came into existence on 1 September 1979, when the entire state was divided into three Districts. In 1988 North Tripura district became home to the Rowa wildlife sanctuary, which has an area of 85km2. Longai, Juri, and Manu its tributaries are the main drainage system of this District. The climate of the district is tropical in nature and is generally warm and humid.

Scale - 1:0.7 M approx

KHOWAI

VITAL STATISTICS

District Headquarter: Khowai
Population: 3,27,564
Area: 1,377 sq. km.
Population Density: 240 persons per sq. km.
Literacy: 87.78%
Sex Ratio: 957 females per 1000 males

ECONOMIC PROFILES

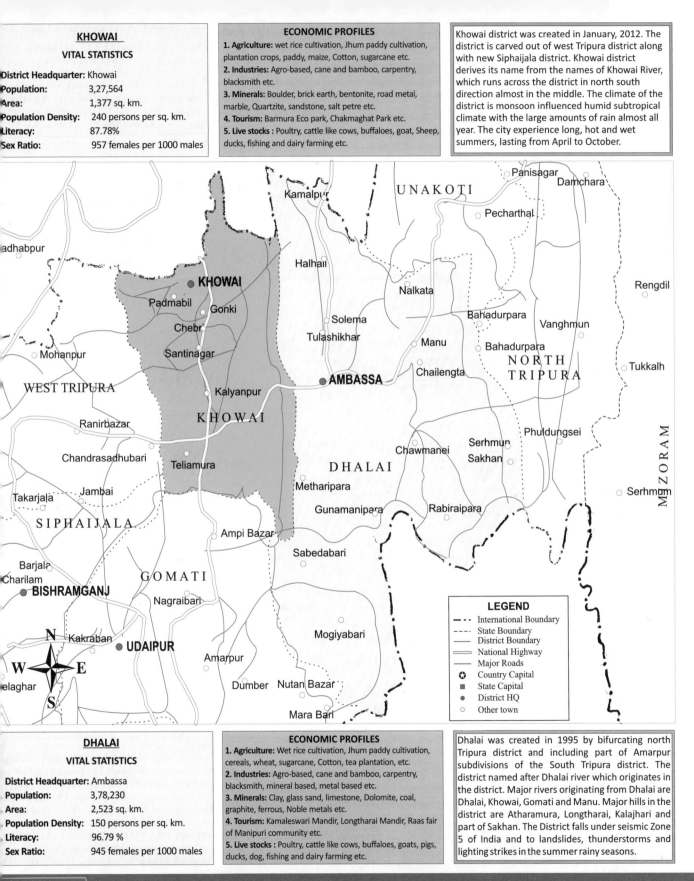

1. **Agriculture:** wet rice cultivation, Jhum paddy cultivation, plantation crops, paddy, maize, Cotton, sugarcane etc.
2. **Industries:** Agro-based, cane and bamboo, carpentry, blacksmith etc.
3. **Minerals:** Boulder, brick earth, bentonite, road metal, marble, Quartzite, sandstone, salt petre etc.
4. **Tourism:** Barmura Eco park, Chakmaghat Park etc.
5. **Live stocks :** Poultry, cattle like cows, buffaloes, goat, Sheep, ducks, fishing and dairy farming etc.

Khowai district was created in January, 2012. The district is carved out of west Tripura district along with new Siphaijala district. Khowai district derives its name from the names of Khowai River, which runs across the district in north south direction almost in the middle. The climate of the district is monsoon influenced humid subtropical climate with the large amounts of rain almost all year. The city experience long, hot and wet summers, lasting from April to October.

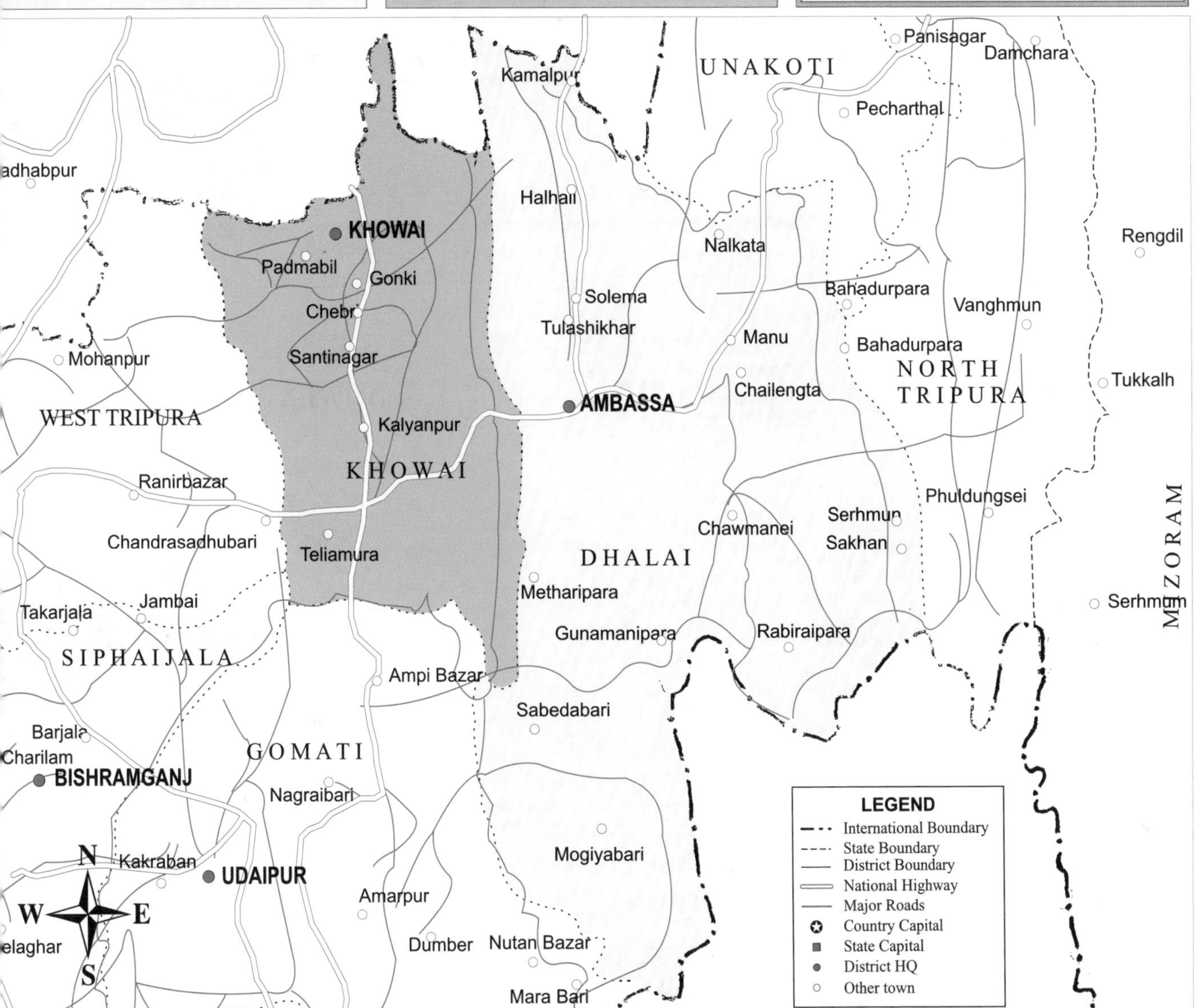
Panisagar
Damchara
UNAKOTI
Kamalpur
Pecharthal
adhabpur
Halhali
Rengdil
KHOWAI
Nalkata
Padmabil
Gonki
Bahadurpara
Solema
Vanghmun
Chebri
Tulashikhar
Manu
Mohanpur
Santinagar
Bahadurpara
NORTH TRIPURA
Tukkalh
Chailengta
AMBASSA
WEST TRIPURA
Kalyanpur
KHOWAI
Ranirbazar
Phuldungsei
Serhmun
Chawmanei
Chandrasadhubari
Sakhan
Teliamura
DHALAI
MIZORAM
Metharipara
Serhmun
Takarjala
Jambai
Gunamanipara
Rabiraipara
SIPHAIJALA
Ampi Bazar
Sabedabari
Barjala
Charilam
GOMATI
BISHRAMGANJ
Nagraibari
Mogiyabari
Kakraban
UDAIPUR
Amarpur
elaghar
Dumber
Nutan Bazar
Mara Bari
N
W
E
S
LEGEND
International Boundary
State Boundary
District Boundary
National Highway
Major Roads
Country Capital
State Capital
District HQ
Other town

DHALAI

VITAL STATISTICS

District Headquarter: Ambassa
Population: 3,78,230
Area: 2,523 sq. km.
Population Density: 150 persons per sq. km.
Literacy: 96.79 %
Sex Ratio: 945 females per 1000 males

ECONOMIC PROFILES

1. **Agriculture:** Wet rice cultivation, Jhum paddy cultivation, cereals, wheat, sugarcane, Cotton, tea plantation, etc.
2. **Industries:** Agro-based, cane and bamboo, carpentry, blacksmith, mineral based, metal based etc.
3. **Minerals:** Clay, glass sand, limestone, Dolomite, coal, graphite, ferrous, Noble metals etc.
4. **Tourism:** Kamaleswari Mandir, Longtharai Mandir, Raas fair of Manipuri community etc.
5. **Live stocks :** Poultry, cattle like cows, buffaloes, goats, pigs, ducks, dog, fishing and dairy farming etc.

Dhalai was created in 1995 by bifurcating north Tripura district and including part of Amarpur subdivisions of the South Tripura district. The district named after Dhalai river which originates in the district. Major rivers originating from Dhalai are Dhalai, Khowai, Gomati and Manu. Major hills in the district are Atharamura, Longtharai, Kalajhari and part of Sakhan. The District falls under seismic Zone 5 of India and to landslides, thunderstorms and lighting strikes in the summer rainy seasons.

cale - 1:0.6 M approx

WEST TRIPURA

VITAL STATISTICS

1. District Headquarter:	Agartala
2. Population:	9,18,200
3. Area:	983 sq. km.
4. Population Density:	934 persons per sq. km.
5. Literacy:	88.91%
6. Sex Ratio:	964 females per 1000 males

ECONOMIC PROFILES

1. Agriculture: Wet rice cultivation, Jhum paddy cultivation, oilseeds production system, tea plantation etc. Crops are paddy, maize, cereals, sugarcane, Cotton etc. Fruits like pineapple, orange, banana, mango, pear, jackfruit etc.

2. Industries: Agro-based, chemical based, blacksmith, cane and bamboo, mineral based, metal based etc.

3. Minerals: Natural gas, glass sand, limestone, clay etc.

4. Tourism: Ujjayantha, Neermahal, Tripura Sundari, Ummaneshwar, Jagannath Temple, Sipahijala WLS, Chittagong hills, etc.

West Tripura is bounded by Bangladesh in th north and west by Khowai district in the east and b Sipahijala district in the south. The climate of th district is tropical in nature and is generally war and humid. The hilly regions enjoy temperatu between 10°c to 35°c. The coldest month of th year are December, January and February.

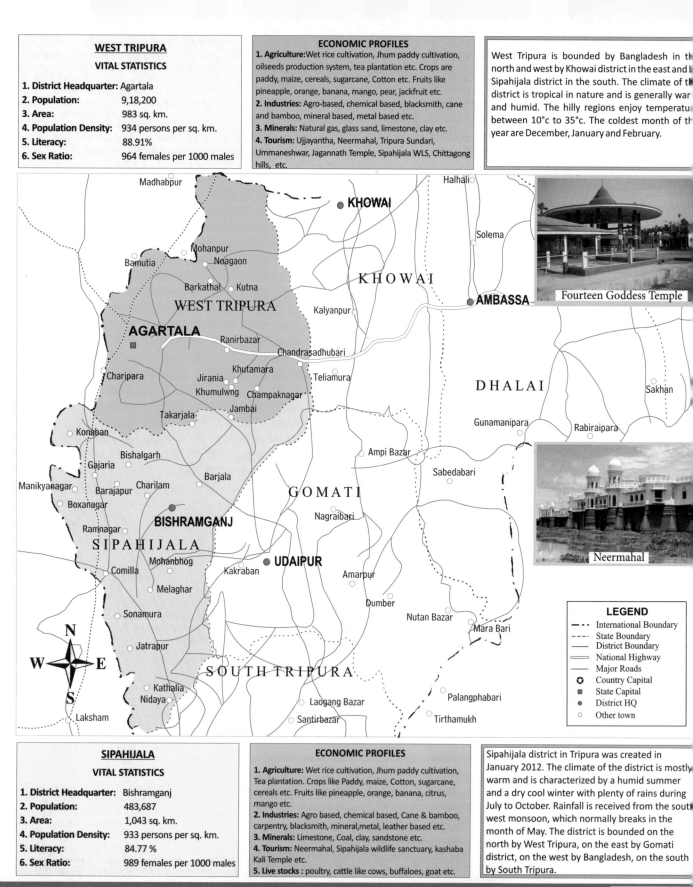

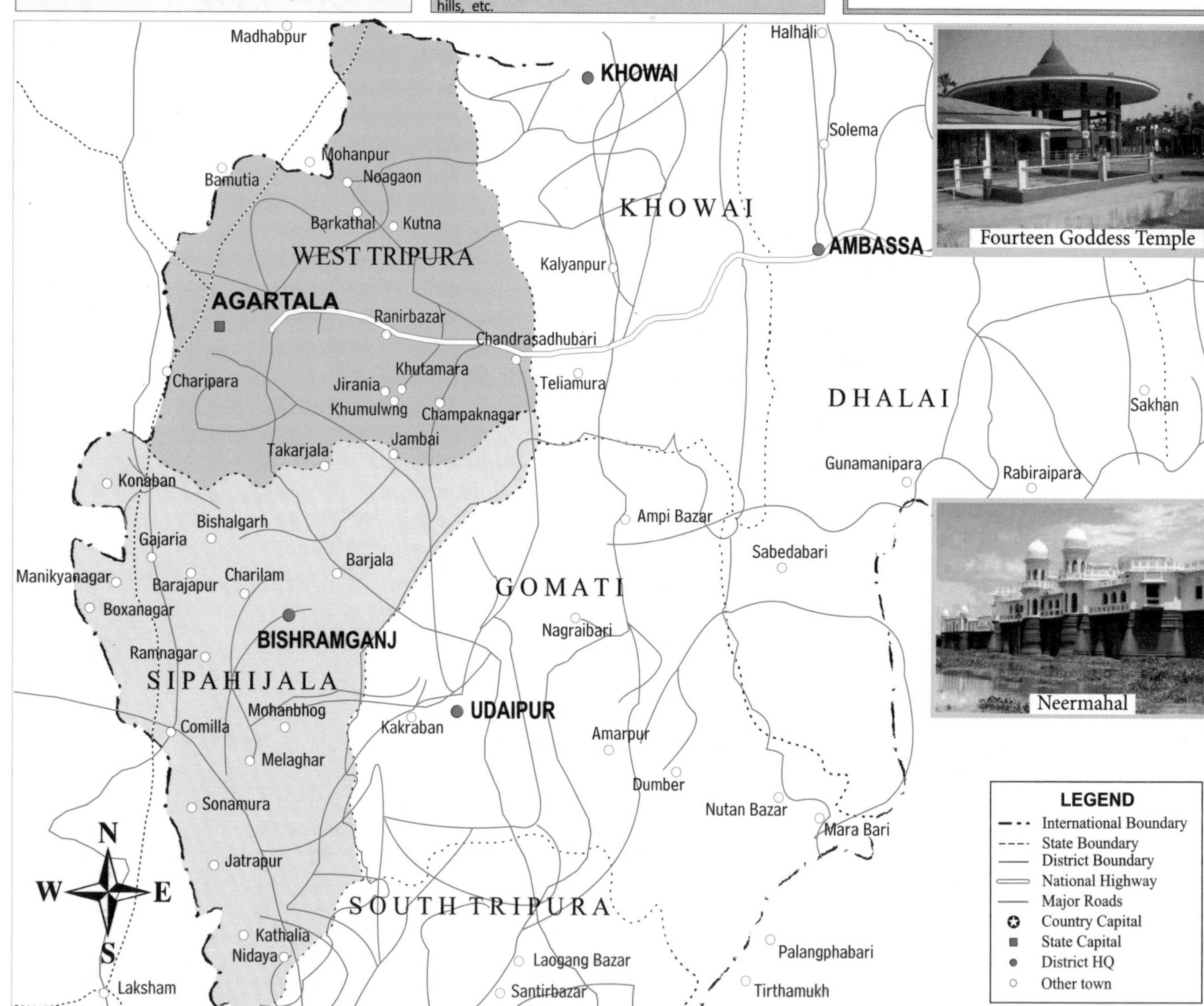

Madhabpur
KHOWAI
Halhali
Solema
Mohanpur
Bamutia
Noagaon
Barkathal
Kutna
KHOWAI
WEST TRIPURA
AMBASSA
Kalyanpur
AGARTALA
Ranirbazar
Chandrasadhubari
Charipara
Khutamara
Jirania
Teliamura
Khumulwng
Champaknagar
DHALAI
Sakhan
Jambai
Takarjala
Gunamanipara
Rabiraipara
Konaban
Bishalgarh
Ampi Bazar
Gajaria
Sabedabari
Barjala
Manikyanagar
Barajapur
Charilam
GOMATI
Boxanagar
Nagraibari
BISHRAMGANJ
Ramnagar
SIPAHIJALA
Mohanbhog
UDAIPUR
Comilla
Kakraban
Amarpur
Melaghar
Dumber
Nutan Bazar
Sonamura
Mara Bari
Jatrapur
N
W
E
S
SOUTH TRIPURA
Kathalia
Nidaya
Palangphabari
Laogang Bazar
Laksham
Santirbazar
Tirthamukh
LEGEND
International Boundary
State Boundary
District Boundary
National Highway
Major Roads
Country Capital
State Capital
District HQ
Other town

Fourteen Goddess Temple

Neermahal

SIPAHIJALA

VITAL STATISTICS

1. District Headquarter:	Bishramganj
2. Population:	483,687
3. Area:	1,043 sq. km.
4. Population Density:	933 persons per sq. km.
5. Literacy:	84.77 %
6. Sex Ratio:	989 females per 1000 males

ECONOMIC PROFILES

1. Agriculture: Wet rice cultivation, Jhum paddy cultivation, Tea plantation. Crops like Paddy, maize, Cotton, sugarcane, cereals etc. Fruits like pineapple, orange, banana, citrus, mango etc.

2. Industries: Agro based, chemical based, Cane & bamboo, carpentry, blacksmith, mineral,metal, leather based etc.

3. Minerals: Limestone, Coal, clay, sandstone etc.

4. Tourism: Neermahal, Sipahijala wildlife sanctuary, kashaba Kali Temple etc.

5. Live stocks : poultry, cattle like cows, buffaloes, goat etc.

Sipahijala district in Tripura was created in January 2012. The climate of the district is mostly warm and is characterized by a humid summer and a dry cool winter with plenty of rains during July to October. Rainfall is received from the sout west monsoon, which normally breaks in the month of May. The district is bounded on the north by West Tripura, on the east by Gomati district, on the west by Bangladesh, on the south by South Tripura.

Scale - 1:0.6 M appr

GOMATI

VITAL STATISTICS

- District Headquarter: Udaipur
- Population: 441,538
- Area: 1,522 sq. km.
- Population Density: 286 persons per sq. km.
- Literacy: 100%
- Sex Ratio: 957 females per 1000 males

ECONOMIC PROFILES

1. **Agriculture:** The main crops are rice, paddy, oilseeds, maize, cereals, sugarcane, Cotton, millets, jowar, bajra etc. The horticulture crops are pineapple, banana, guava, orange, citrus, Jackfruit, etc.
2. **Industries:** Agro-based, chemical based, engineering units, Cane and bamboo, carpentry, blacksmith, mineral, jute, Cotton etc.
3. **Minerals:** limestone, Dolomite, coal, clay, glass sand, gravel sand silt, building Stone, ferrous, Noble metals etc.
4. **Tourism:** Amarpur, Udaipur, etc.
5. **Live stocks :** Poultry, cattle, fishing and dairy farming etc.

Gomati district was created in January 2012 when four new Districts were created in tripura. Climate of the district is mostly warm and is characterized by a humid summer and dry cool winter with plenty of rains during July to October. Rainfall is received from south west monsoon. Average annual rainfall in the district is about 2000mm and temperature varies between a maximum of 35.23°c and minimum of 7.43°c.

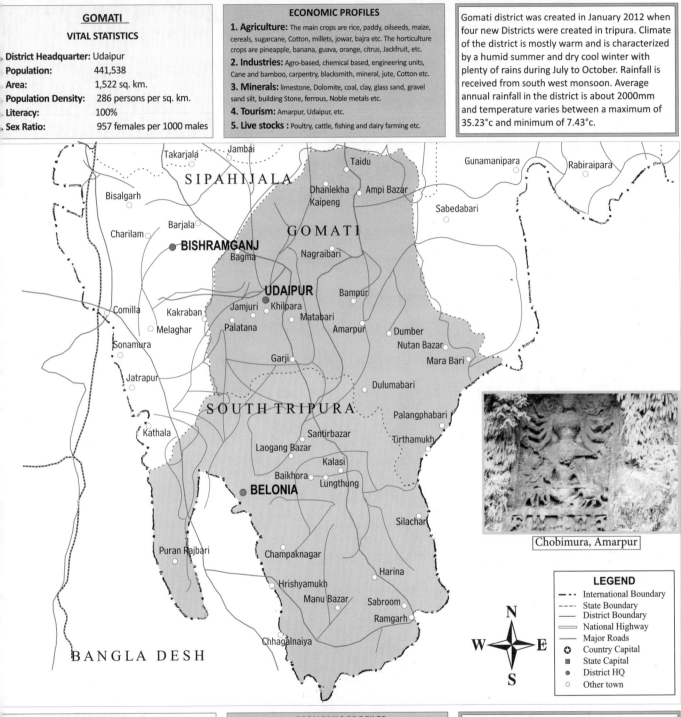

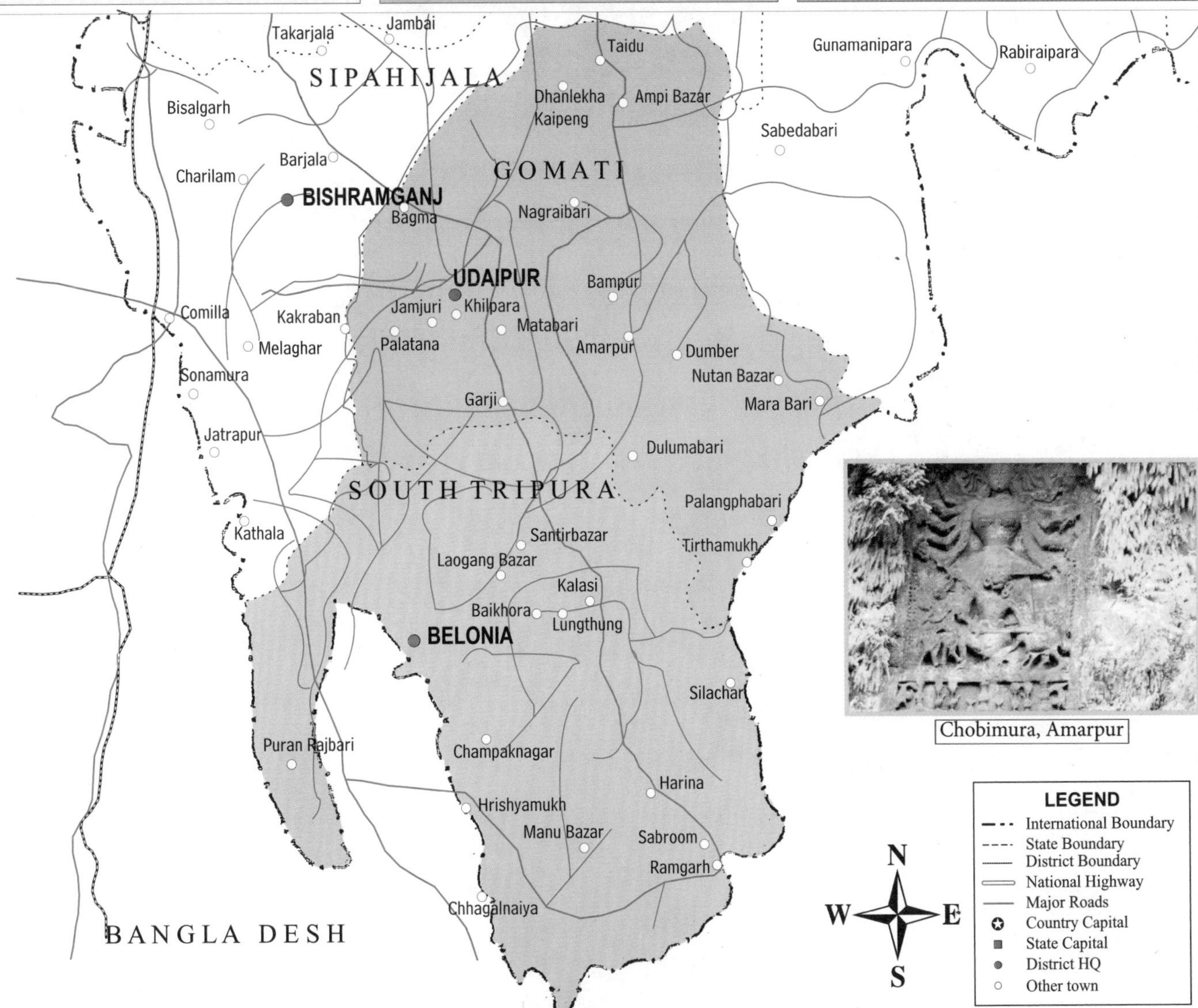

SIPAHIJALA
GOMATI
SOUTH TRIPURA
BANGLA DESH
Takarjala
Jambai
Taidu
Gunamanipara
Rabiraipara
Dhanlekha
Ampi Bazar
Kaipeng
Bisalgarh
Sabedabari
Barjala
Charilam
BISHRAMGANJ
Bagma
Nagraibari
UDAIPUR
Bampur
Jamjuri
Khilpara
Comilla
Kakraban
Matabari
Palatana
Amarpur
Melaghar
Dumber
Sonamura
Nutan Bazar
Garji
Mara Bari
Jatrapur
Dulumabari
Palangphabari
Kathala
Santirbazar
Tirthamukh
Laogang Bazar
Kalasi
Baikhora
Lungthung
BELONIA
Silachar
Puran Rajbari
Champaknagar
Harina
Hrishyamukh
Manu Bazar
Sabroom
Ramgarh
Chhagalnaiya
N
W
E
S
LEGEND
International Boundary
State Boundary
District Boundary
National Highway
Major Roads
Country Capital
State Capital
District HQ
Other town

Chobimura, Amarpur

SOUTH TRIPURA

VITAL STATISTICS

1. District Headquarter: Belonia
2. Population: 4,30,751
3. Area: 2,152 sq. km.
4. Population Density: 200 persons per sq. km.
5. Literacy: 85.41 %
6. Sex Ratio: 957 females per 1000 males

ECONOMIC PROFILES

1. **Agriculture:** The main crops are rice, paddy, oilseeds, tea, maize, sugarcane, Cotton, cereals, ginger, etc. pineapple, orange, guava, banana, jackfruit, citrus, pears, etc.
2. **Industries:** Agro-based, chemical, engineering, carpentry, blacksmith, cane, and bamboo, jute and cotton based fibrous.
3. **Minerals:** Clay, glass sand, limestone, Dolomite, coal, graphite, gravel sand silt, ferrous, Noble metals etc.
4. **Tourism:** Border haat, Butterfly Eco Park, Bharath Bangla Maitree udyan, Dhananjoy and Island eco park Trisha, Kalapania, Pilak.
5. **Live stocks :** Poultry, cattle, fishing and dairy farming etc.

South Tripura district came into existence on 1 September 1970. The district is bounded on the south east west by Bangladesh, on the north by Gomati District. In 1987, south Tripura district became home to the Trishna wildlife sanctuary, which has an area of 195sqkm. It is also home to the Gomati WLS, which was established in 1988 and has an area of 390km2. The climate of the district is tropical in nature and is generally warm and humid.

cale - 1:0.6 M approx

WORLD

Section

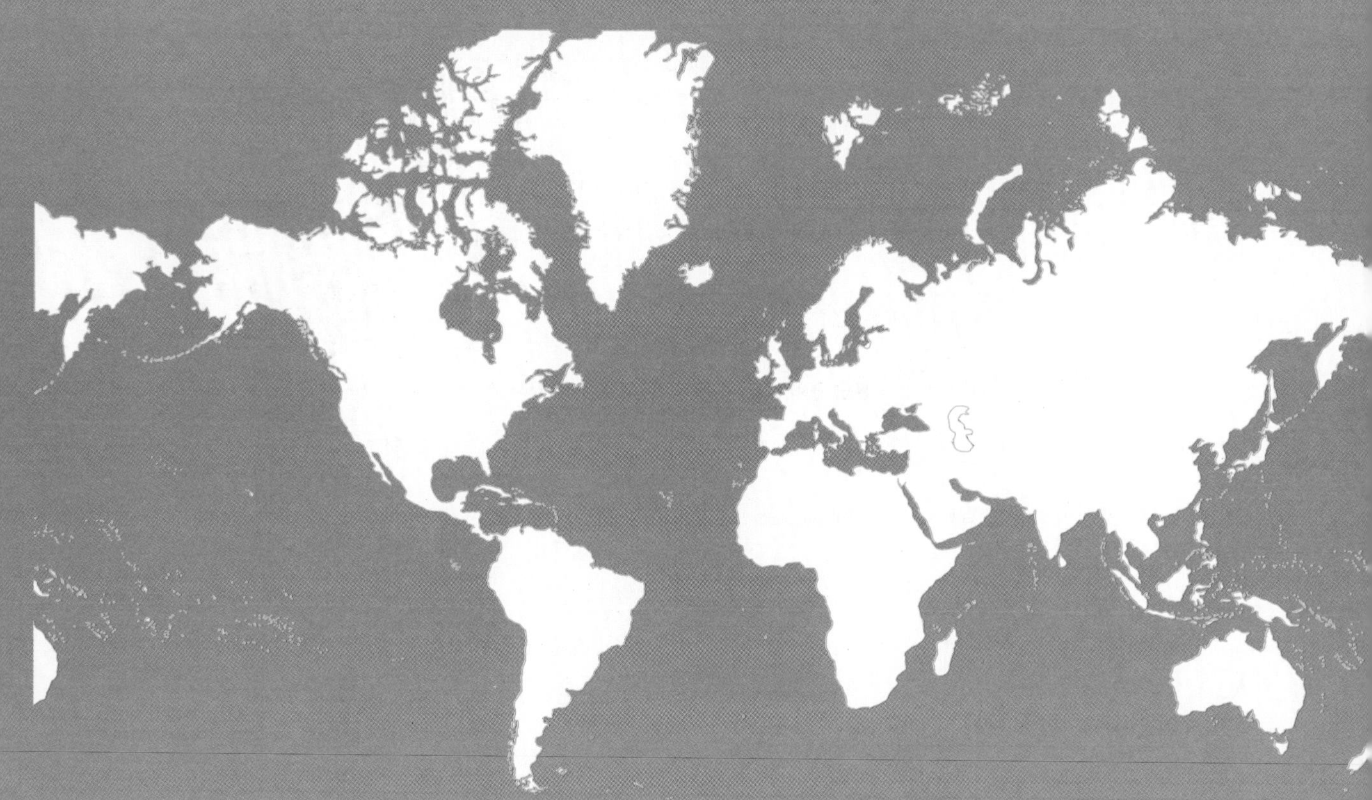

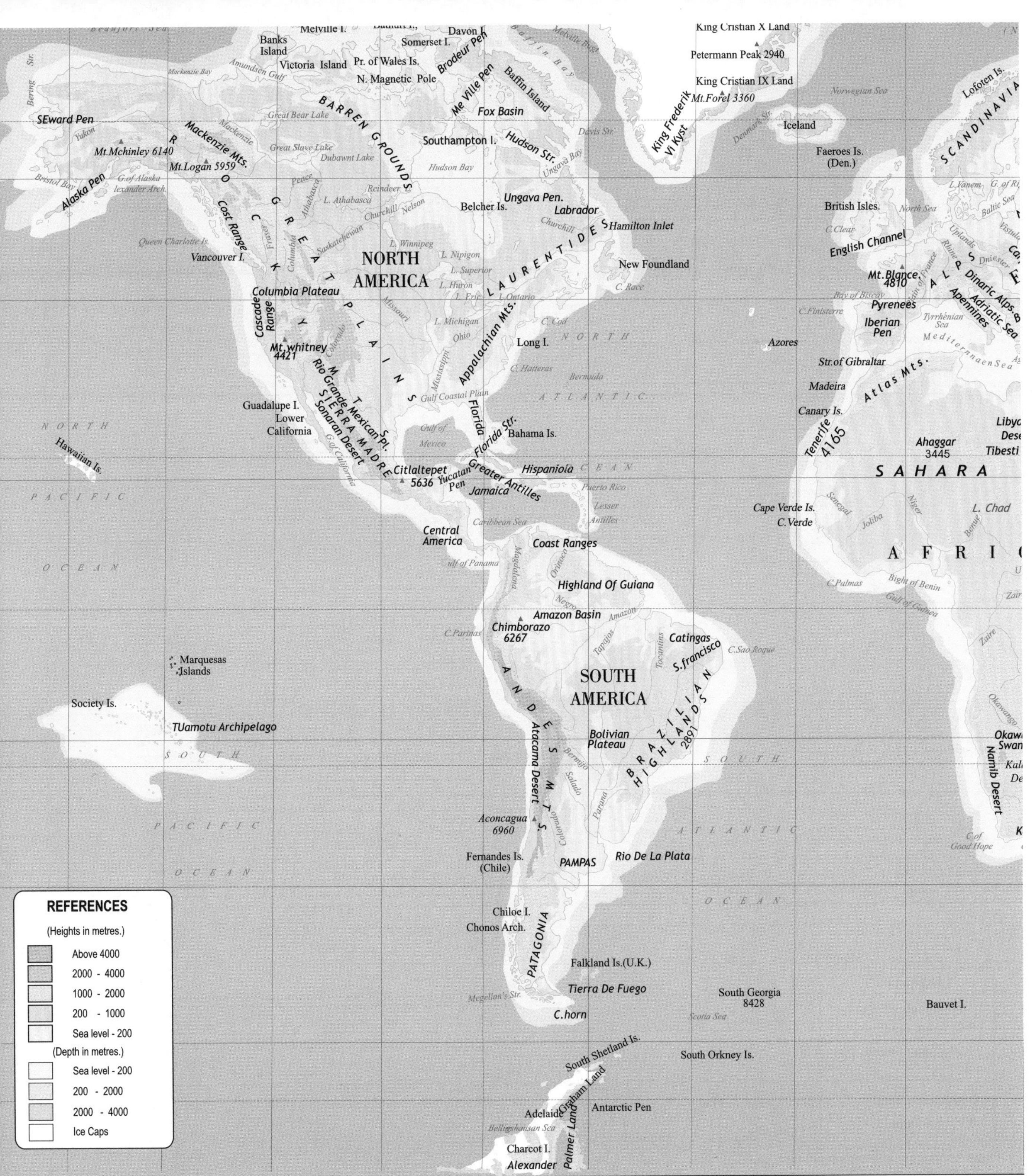

Banks Island
Melville I.
Victoria Island
Pr. of Wales Is.
Somerset I.
Davon I.
N. Magnetic Pole
Brodeur Pen
Amundsen Gulf
Mackenzie Bay
Bering Str.
Baffin Bay
Me Ville Pen
Baffin Island
Fox Basin
King Cristian X Land
Petermann Peak 2940
King Cristian IX Land
Mt.Forel 3360
King Frederik Vi Kyst
Norwegian Sea
Lofoten Is.
SCANDINAVIA
Iceland
Denmark Str.
Davis Str.
SEward Pen
Yukon
Great Bear Lake
BARREN GROUNDS
Mackenzie
Mackenzie Mts.
Mt.Mchinley 6140
Mt.Logan 5959
Great Slave Lake
Dubawnt Lake
Southampton I.
Hudson Str.
Ungava Bay
Hudson Bay
Faeroes Is. (Den.)
Bristol Bay
Alaska Pen
G.of Alaska
Alexander Arch.
Peace
Athabasca
L. Athabasca
Reindeer L.
Churchill
Nelson
Belcher Is.
Ungava Pen.
Labrador
British Isles.
North Sea
Baltic Sea
Queen Charlotte Is.
Cost Range
Fraser
Columbia
Saskatchewan
L. Winnipeg
Churchill
LAURENTIDES
Hamilton Inlet
C.Clear
English Channel
Vancouver I.
GREAT PLAINS
NORTH AMERICA
L. Nipigon
L. Superior
L. Huron
L. Erie
L.Ontario
New Foundland
C. Race
Mt.Blance 4810
ALPS
Dinaric Alps
Adriatic Sea
Apennines
Columbia Plateau
Cascade Range
Missouri
L. Michigan
Ohio
Appalachian Mts.
C. Cod
Bay of Biscay
C.Finisterre
Pyrenees
Iberian Pen
Tyrrhenian Sea
Mediterranaen Sea
Mt.whitney 4421
Colorado
Long I.
NORTH
Azores
Str.of Gibraltar
Atlas Mts.
Rio Grande
SIERRA MADRE
Mississippi
C. Hatteras
Bermuda
Madeira
Sonaran Desert
Gulf Coastal Plain
ATLANTIC
Guadalupe I.
Lower California
Mexican Pl.
Florida
Canary Is.
Tenerife 4165
Libya Desert
NORTH
Hawaiian Is.
G.of California
Gulf of Mexico
Florida Str.
Bahama Is.
Ahaggar 3445
Tibesti
Citlaltepet 5636
Yucatan Pen
Greater Antilles
Hispaniola
OCEAN
SAHARA
PACIFIC
Jamaica
Puerto Rico
Lesser Antilles
Senegal
Niger
Cape Verde Is.
C.Verde
L. Chad
Joliba
Benue
Caribbean Sea
Central America
Coast Ranges
AFRICA
OCEAN
Gulf of Panama
Magdalena
Orinoco
Highland Of Guiana
C.Palmas
Bight of Benin
Gulf of Guinea
Negro
Amazon Basin
Amazon
Chimborazo 6267
C.Parinas
Tapajos
Tocantins
Catingas
S.francisco
C.Sao Roque
Zaire
Marquesas Islands
SOUTH AMERICA
ANDES MTS.
BRAZILIAN HIGHLANDS 2891
Society Is.
Okawango
TUamotu Archipelago
Bolivian Plateau
Okawango Swamp
SOUTH
Atacama Desert
Bermejo
Salado
Parana
SOUTH
Namib Desert
PACIFIC
Aconcagua 6960
Colorado
ATLANTIC
C.of Good Hope
Fernandes Is. (Chile)
PAMPAS
Rio De La Plata
OCEAN
OCEAN
REFERENCES
(Heights in metres.)
Above 4000
2000 - 4000
1000 - 2000
200 - 1000
Sea level - 200
(Depth in metres.)
Sea level - 200
200 - 2000
2000 - 4000
Ice Caps
Chiloe I.
Chonos Arch.
PATAGONIA
Falkland Is.(U.K.)
Tierra De Fuego
Megellan's Str.
South Georgia 8428
C.horn
Scotia Sea
Bauvet I.
South Shetland Is.
South Orkney Is.
Graham Land
Antarctic Pen
Adelaide
Bellingshausan Sea
Palmer Land
Charcot I.
Alexander

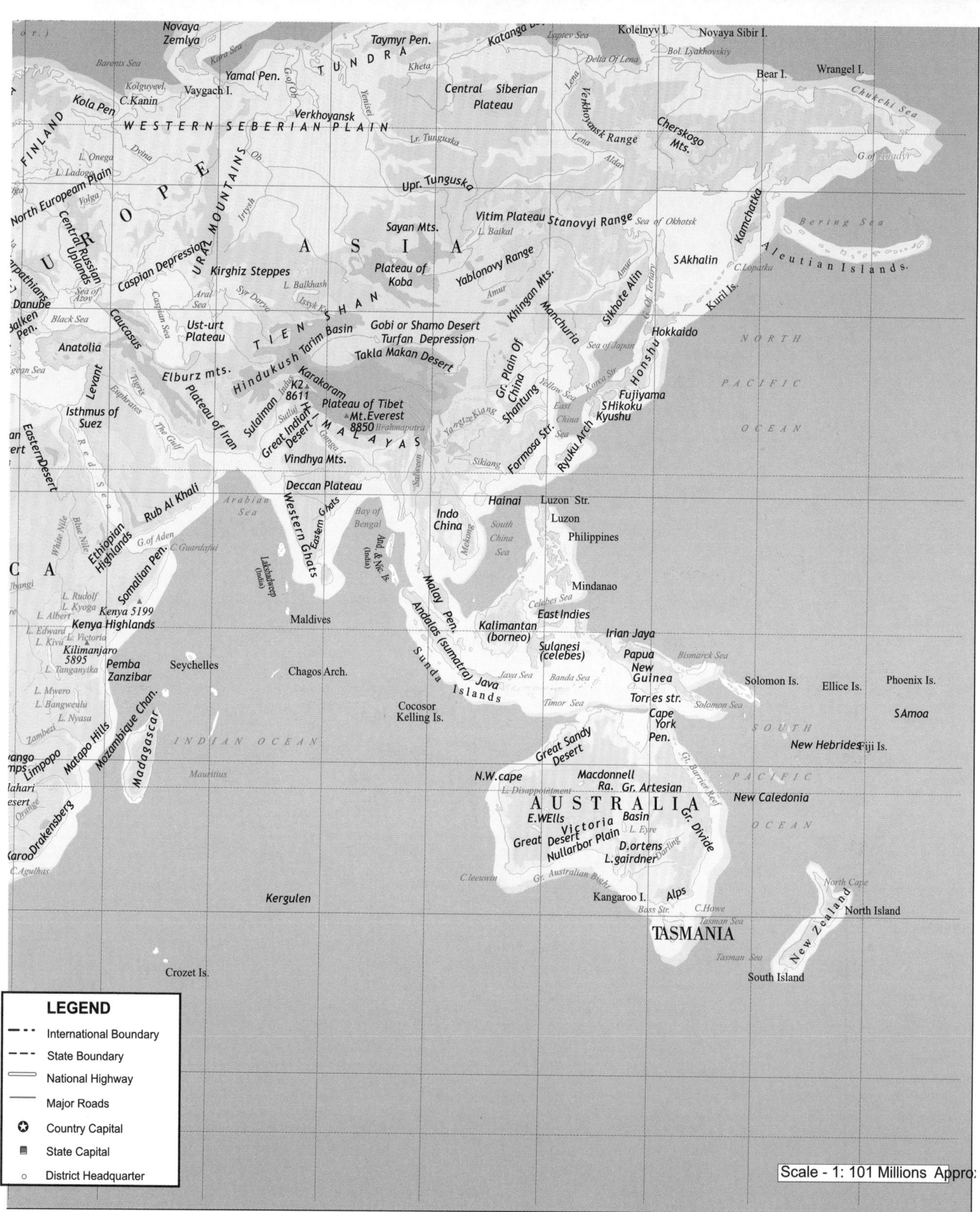
Novaya Zemlya
Taymyr Pen.
Laptev Sea
Kolelnyv I.
Novaya Sibir I.
Bol. Lyakhovskiy
Barents Sea
Kara Sea
TUNDRA
Kheta
Delta Of Lena
Bear I.
Wrangel I.
Kolguyev I.
C.Kanin
Vaygach I.
Yamal Pen.
Central Siberian Plateau
Chukchi Sea
Kola Pen
WESTERN SEBERIAN PLAIN
Verkhoyansk
Lr. Tunguska
Verkhoyansk Range
Cherskogo Mts.
FINLAND
L. Onega
L. Ladoga
Dvina
Ob
Lena
Aldan
EUROPE
North European Plain
Volga
URAL MOUNTAINS
Irtysh
Upr. Tunguska
Central Russian Uplands
Sayan Mts.
Vitim Plateau
L. Baikal
Stanovyi Range
Sea of Okhotsk
Kamchatka
Bering Sea
ASIA
Caspian Depression
Kirghiz Steppes
Plateau of Koba
Yablonovy Range
SAkhalin
C.Lopatka
Aleutian Islands.
Carpathians
Sea of Azov
Aral Sea
Syr Darya
L. Balkhash
Issyk Kul
Amur
Khingan Mts.
Sikhote Alin
Kuril Is.
Danube
Balkan Pen.
Black Sea
Caucasus
Caspian Sea
Ust-urt Plateau
TIEN SHAN
Tarim Basin
Gobi or Shamo Desert
Turfan Depression
Manchuria
Hokkaido
NORTH
Anatolia
Takla Makan Desert
Sea of Japan
Aegean Sea
Levant
Elburz mts.
Hindukush
Karakoram
Gr. Plain Of China
Honshu
PACIFIC
Tigris
Euphrates
K2 8611
Shantung
Yellow Sea
Korea Str.
Fujiyama
Isthmus of Suez
Plateau of Iran
Sulaiman
Indus
Sutlej
Plateau of Tibet
Mt.Everest 8850
Brahmaputra
HIMALAYAS
East China Sea
SHikoku
Kyushu
OCEAN
Eastern Desert
The Gulf
Great Indian Desert
Yangtze Kiang
Ryuku Arch
Formosa Str.
Red Sea
Ganga
Vindhya Mts.
Salween
Siklang
Deccan Plateau
Hainai
Luzon Str.
Rub Al Khali
Arabian Sea
Bay of Bengal
Indo China
Luzon
White Nile
Blue Nile
Ethiopian Highlands
Western Ghats
Eastern Ghats
South China Sea
Mekong
Philippines
G.of Aden
C.Guardafui
And. & Nic. Is (India)
Somalian Pen.
Lakshadweep (India)
Mindanao
L. Rudolf
L. Kyoga
Kenya 5199
Celebes Sea
L. Albert
Kenya Highlands
Malay Pen.
East Indies
L. Edward
L. Victoria
L. Kivu
Maldives
Kalimantan (borneo)
Irian Jaya
Kilimanjaro 5895
Andalas (sumatra)
Sulanesi (celebes)
Papua New Guinea
Bismarck Sea
L. Tanganyika
Pemba
Zanzibar
Seychelles
Chagos Arch.
Sunda Islands
Java
Java Sea
Banda Sea
Solomon Is.
Ellice Is.
Phoenix Is.
L. Mwero
L. Bangweulu
L. Nyasa
Cocosor Kelling Is.
Timor Sea
Torres str.
Solomon Sea
SAmoa
Zambezi
Matapo Hills
Mozambique Chan.
Madagascar
INDIAN OCEAN
Great Sandy Desert
Cape York Pen.
SOUTH
New Hebrides
Fiji Is.
Limpopo
Mauritius
N.W.cape
Macdonnell Ra.
Gr. Artesian
Gr. Barrier Reef
PACIFIC
L. Disappointment
AUSTRALIA
Basin
New Caledonia
Drakensberg
Orange
E.WEIls
Victoria
L. Eyre
Gr. Divide
OCEAN
Great Desert
Nullarbor Plain
D.ortens
Darling
L.gairdner
Karoo
C.Agulhas
C.leeuwin
Gr. Australian Bight
North Cape
Kergulen
Kangaroo I.
Alps
Bass Str.
C.Howe
New Zealand
North Island
Tasman Sea
TASMANIA
Tasman Sea
South Island
Crozet Is.
LEGEND
International Boundary
State Boundary
National Highway
Major Roads
Country Capital
State Capital
District Headquarter
Scale - 1: 101 Millions Appro

ARCTIC OCEAN
GREEN LAND
CANADA
UNITED STATES OF AMERICA
NORTH PACIFIC OCEAN
NORTH ATLANTIC OCEAN
SOUTH PACIFIC OCEAN
SOUTH ATLANTIC OCEAN
Arctic Circle
Tropic of Cancer
Equator
Tropic of Capricorn
ALASKA
MEXICO
BRAZIL
ALGERIA
NIGER
Baffin Bay
Hudson Bay
Labrador Sea
Greenland Sea
NORWEGIAN SEA
BERING SEA
Gulf Of Alaska
Gulf Of Mexico
GUATEMALA
EL SALVADOR
HONDURAS
NICARAGUA
COSTA RICA
PANAMA
ARGENTINA
CHILE
PERU
BOLIVIA
PARAGUAY
URUGUAY
ECUADOR
COLOMBIA
VENEZUELA
FRENCH GUIANA
ICELAND
UNITED KINGDOM
IRELAND
SPAIN
PORTUGAL
FRANCE
MOROCCO
WESTERN SAHARA
MAURITANIA
MALI
NIGERIA
ANGOLA
NAMIBIA

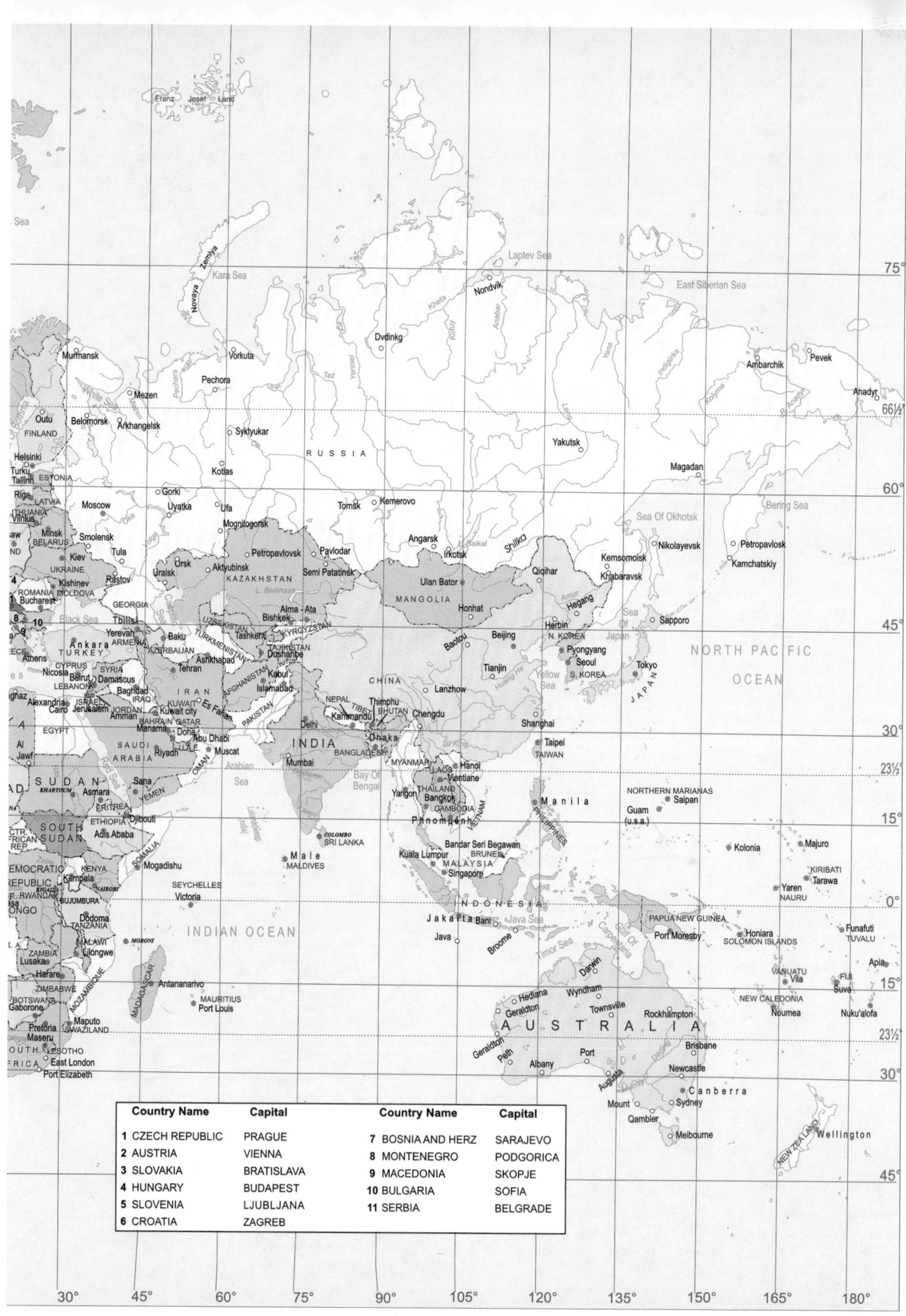

Franz Josef Land
Novaya Zemlya
Kara Sea
Laptev Sea
East Siberian Sea
Nondvik
Dvdinkg
Murmansk
Vorkuta
Pechora
Mezen
White Sea
Belomorsk
Arkhangelsk
Outu
FINLAND
Helsinki
Turku
Tallinn
ESTONIA
Syktyukar
RUSSIA
Kotlas
Yakutsk
Magadan
Ambarchik
Pevek
Anadyr
Gorki
Uyatka
Ufa
Moscow
Tomsk
Kemerovo
Riga
LATVIA
Vilnius
Minsk
BELARUS
Smolensk
Tula
Kiev
UKRAINE
Kishinev
MOLDOVA
ROMANIA
Bucharest
Rastov
Mognitogorsk
Petropavlovsk
Pavlodar
Orsk
Aktyubinsk
Uralsk
KAZAKHSTAN
Semi Patatinsk
Angarsk
Irkotsk
Baikal
Shilka
Ulan Bator
MANGOLIA
Qiqihar
Kemsomoisk
Khabaravsk
Nikolayevsk
Petropavlosk
Kamchatskiy
Sea Of Okhotsk
Bering Sea
GEORGIA
Black Sea
Tbilisi
Yerevan
ARMENIA
Baku
AZERBAIJAN
Ankara
TURKEY
Athens
CYPRUS
Nicosia
SYRIA
Beirut
Damascus
LEBANON
ISRAEL
Jerusalem
JORDAN
Amman
Baghdad
IRAQ
Alexandria
Cairo
EGYPT
Alma - Ata
Bishkek
UZBEKISTAN
KYRGYZSTAN
Tashkent
TURKMENISTAN
TAJIKISTAN
Dushanbe
Ashkhabad
Tehran
IRAN
AFGHANISTAN
Kabul
Islamabad
KUWAIT
Kuwait city
Es Fahan
BAHRAIN
QATAR
Manama
Doha
Abu Dhabi
SAUDI ARABIA
Riyadh
Muscat
OMAN
Hohhot
Herbin
Hegang
Sapporo
Beijing
Baotou
N. KOREA
Pyongyang
Seoul
S. KOREA
Tokyo
JAPAN
NORTH PACIFIC OCEAN
Tianjin
CHINA
Lanzhow
NEPAL
Kathmandu
TIBET
Thimphu
BHUTAN
Chengdu
Shanghai
Delhi
PAKISTAN
INDIA
Dhaka
BANGLADESH
Taipei
TAIWAN
Mumbai
Arabian Sea
Bay Of Bengal
MYANMAR
Hanoi
LAOS
Vientiane
Yangon
THAILAND
Bangkok
CAMBODIA
Phnom Penh
VIETNAM
Manila
PHILIPPINES
NORTHERN MARIANAS
Saipan
Guam (u.s.a.)
SUDAN
Khartoum
Asmara
ERITREA
Sana
YEMEN
ETHIOPIA
Djibouti
Adis Ababa
SOUTH SUDAN
SOMALIA
Mogadishu
KENYA
Kampala
Nairobi
COLOMBO
SRI LANKA
Male
MALDIVES
Bandar Seri Begawan
BRUNEI
Kuala Lumpur
MALAYSIA
Singapore
Kolonia
Majuro
KIRIBATI
Tarawa
Yaren
NAURU
SEYCHELLES
Victoria
INDONESIA
Jakarta
Java Sea
Java
Dodoma
TANZANIA
INDIAN OCEAN
PAPUA NEW GUINEA
Port Moresby
Honiara
SOLOMON ISLANDS
Funafuti
TUVALU
Moroni
MALAWI
Lilongwe
ZAMBIA
Lusaka
Harare
ZIMBABWE
MOZAMBIQUE
MADAGASCAR
Antananarivo
MAURITIUS
Port Louis
Timor Sea
Darwin
Wyndham
Hedlana
Geraldton
Townsville
Rockhampton
AUSTRALIA
Brisbane
VANUATU
Vila
FIJI
Suva
Apia
NEW CALEDONIA
Noumea
Nuku'alofa
BOTSWANA
Gaborone
Pretoria
Maputo
SWAZILAND
Maseru
LESOTHO
East London
Port Elizabeth
Perth
Albany
Port Augusta
Newcastle
Canberra
Sydney
Mount Qambler
Melbourne
NEW ZEALAND
Wellington
75°
66½°
60°
45°
30°
23½°
15°
0°
15°
23½°
30°
45°
30°
45°
60°
75°
90°
105°
120°
135°
150°
165°
180°

Country Name	Capital	Country Name	Capital
1 CZECH REPUBLIC	PRAGUE	7 BOSNIA AND HERZ	SARAJEVO
2 AUSTRIA	VIENNA	8 MONTENEGRO	PODGORICA
3 SLOVAKIA	BRATISLAVA	9 MACEDONIA	SKOPJE
4 HUNGARY	BUDAPEST	10 BULGARIA	SOFIA
5 SLOVENIA	LJUBLJANA	11 SERBIA	BELGRADE
6 CROATIA	ZAGREB		

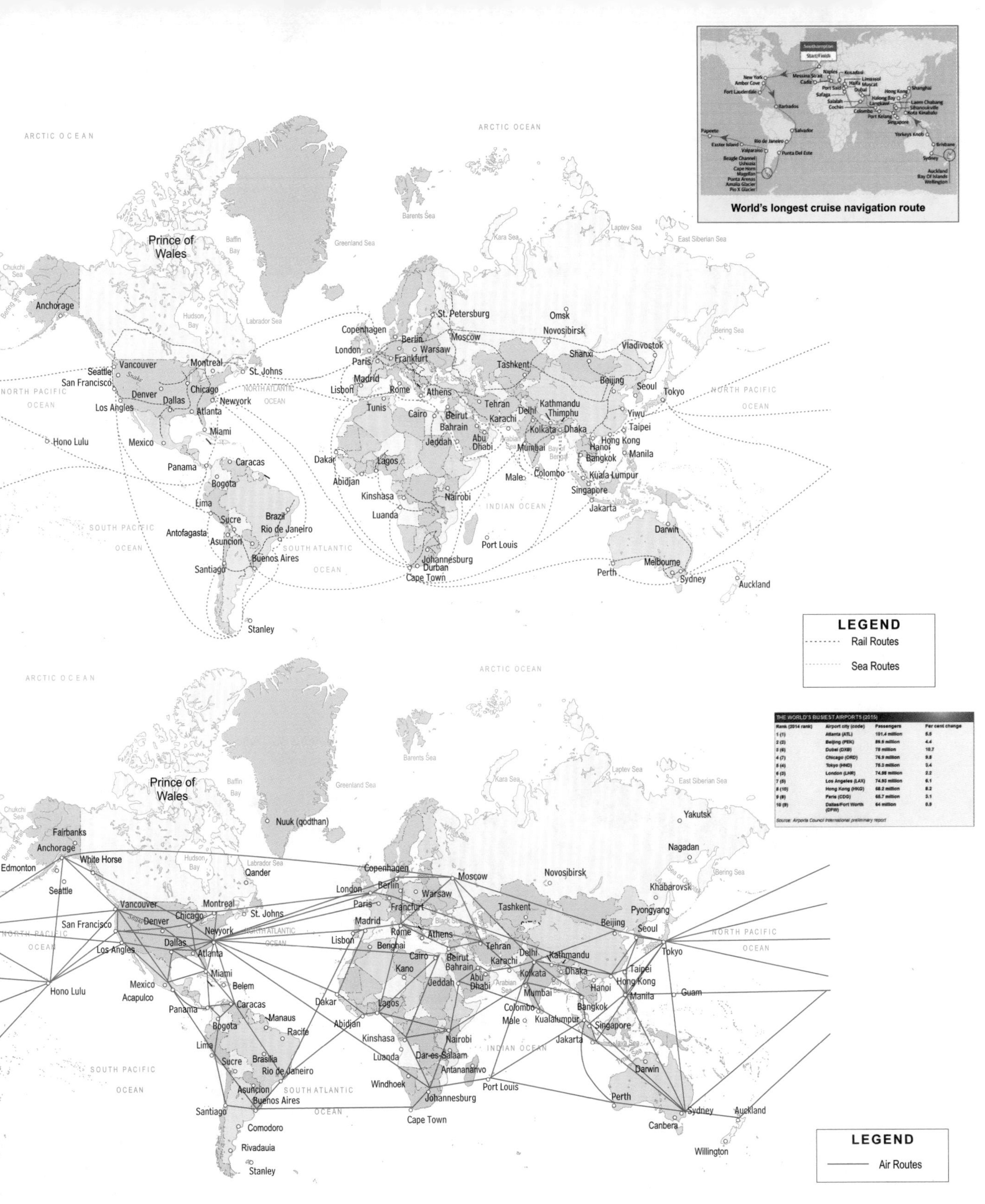

Southampton
Start/Finish
New York
Amber Cove
Fort Lauderdale
Barbados
Naples
Kusadasi
Messina Strait
Cadiz
Limassol
Haifa
Muscat
Port Said
Dubai
Safaga
Salalah
Cochin
Colombo
Langkawi
Port Kelang
Singapore
Halong Bay
Hong Kong
Shanghai
Laem Chabang
Sihanoukville
Kota Kinabalu
Yorkeys Knob
Brisbane
Sydney
Auckland
Bay Of Islands
Wellington
Salvador
Rio de Janeiro
Punta Del Este
Papeete
Easter Island
Valparaiso
Beagle Channel
Ushuaia
Cape Horn
Magellan
Punta Arenas
Amalia Glacier
Pio X Glacier
World's longest cruise navigation route
ARCTIC OCEAN
Prince of Wales
Baffin Bay
Greenland Sea
Barents Sea
Kara Sea
Laptev Sea
East Siberian Sea
Chukchi Sea
Bering Sea
Hudson Bay
Labrador Sea
NORTH PACIFIC OCEAN
NORTH ATLANTIC OCEAN
SOUTH PACIFIC OCEAN
SOUTH ATLANTIC OCEAN
INDIAN OCEAN
Anchorage
Vancouver
Seattle
San Francisco
Los Angles
Denver
Dallas
Chicago
Montreal
St. Johns
Newyork
Atlanta
Miami
Mexico
Hono Lulu
Panama
Caracas
Bogota
Lima
Sucre
Brazil
Rio de Janeiro
Antofagasta
Asuncion
Buenos Aires
Santiago
Stanley
Copenhagen
London
Paris
Berlin
Warsaw
Frankfurt
Madrid
Lisbon
Rome
Athens
Tunis
Cairo
Beirut
Bahrain
Jeddah
Abu Dhabi
Dakar
Lagos
Abidjan
Kinshasa
Nairobi
Luanda
Johannesburg
Durban
Cape Town
Port Louis
St. Petersburg
Moscow
Omsk
Novosibirsk
Tashkent
Tehran
Karachi
Delhi
Kathmandu
Thimphu
Kolkata
Dhaka
Mumbai
Male
Colombo
Shanxi
Vladivostok
Beijing
Seoul
Tokyo
Yiwu
Taipei
Hanoi
Hong Kong
Manila
Bangkok
Kuala Lumpur
Singapore
Jakarta
Darwin
Perth
Melbourne
Sydney
Auckland
LEGEND
Rail Routes
Sea Routes
Fairbanks
Edmonton
White Horse
Qander
Nuuk (qodthan)
Acapulco
Belem
Manaus
Racife
Brasilia
Comodoro
Rivadauia
Benghai
Kano
Dar-es-Salaam
Antananarivo
Windhoek
Kualalumpur
Yakutsk
Nagadan
Khabarovsk
Pyongyang
Guam
Canbera
Willington
LEGEND
Air Routes

THE WORLD'S BUSIEST AIRPORTS (2015)			
Rank (2014 rank)	Airport city (code)	Passengers	Per cent change
1 (1)	Atlanta (ATL)	101.4 million	5.5
2 (2)	Beijing (PEK)	89.9 million	4.4
3 (6)	Dubai (DXB)	78 million	10.7
4 (7)	Chicago (ORD)	76.9 million	9.8
5 (4)	Tokyo (HND)	75.3 million	3.4
6 (3)	London (LHR)	74.98 million	2.2
7 (5)	Los Angeles (LAX)	74.93 million	6.1
8 (10)	Hong Kong (HKG)	68.2 million	8.2
9 (8)	Paris (CDG)	65.7 million	3.1
10 (9)	Dallas/Fort Worth (DFW)	64 million	0.9

Source: Airports Council International preliminary report

0 1000 2000 km.

Projection: Lambert's Conical Orthomorphic

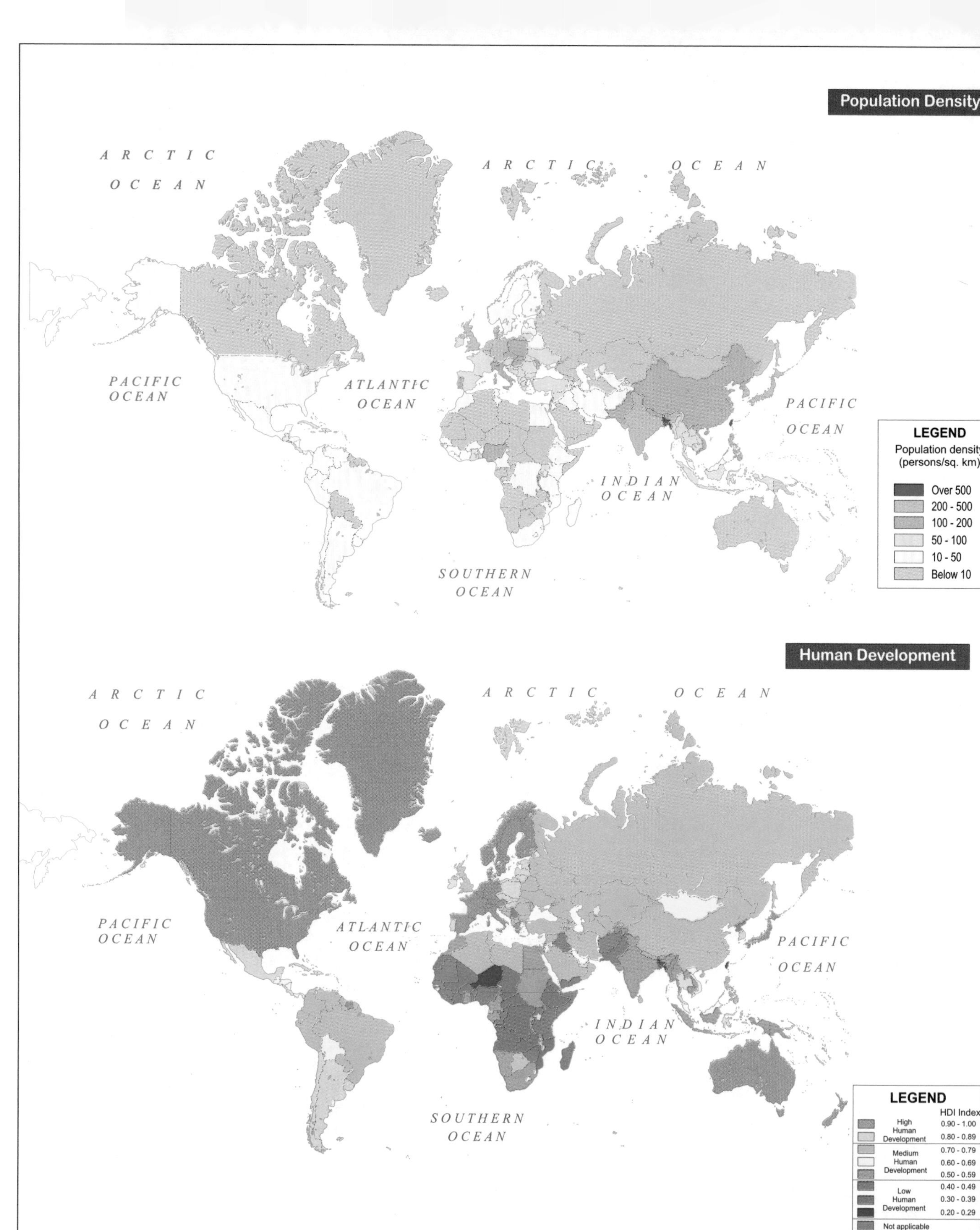
Population Density
ARCTIC OCEAN
ARCTIC OCEAN
PACIFIC OCEAN
ATLANTIC OCEAN
PACIFIC OCEAN
INDIAN OCEAN
SOUTHERN OCEAN
LEGEND
Population density (persons/sq. km)
Over 500
200 - 500
100 - 200
50 - 100
10 - 50
Below 10
Human Development
ARCTIC OCEAN
ARCTIC OCEAN
PACIFIC OCEAN
ATLANTIC OCEAN
PACIFIC OCEAN
INDIAN OCEAN
SOUTHERN OCEAN
LEGEND
HDI Index
High Human Development
0.90 - 1.00
0.80 - 0.89
Medium Human Development
0.70 - 0.79
0.60 - 0.69
0.50 - 0.59
Low Human Development
0.40 - 0.49
0.30 - 0.39
0.20 - 0.29
Not applicable
Projection: Lambert's Conical Orthomorphic
1000 0 1000 2000

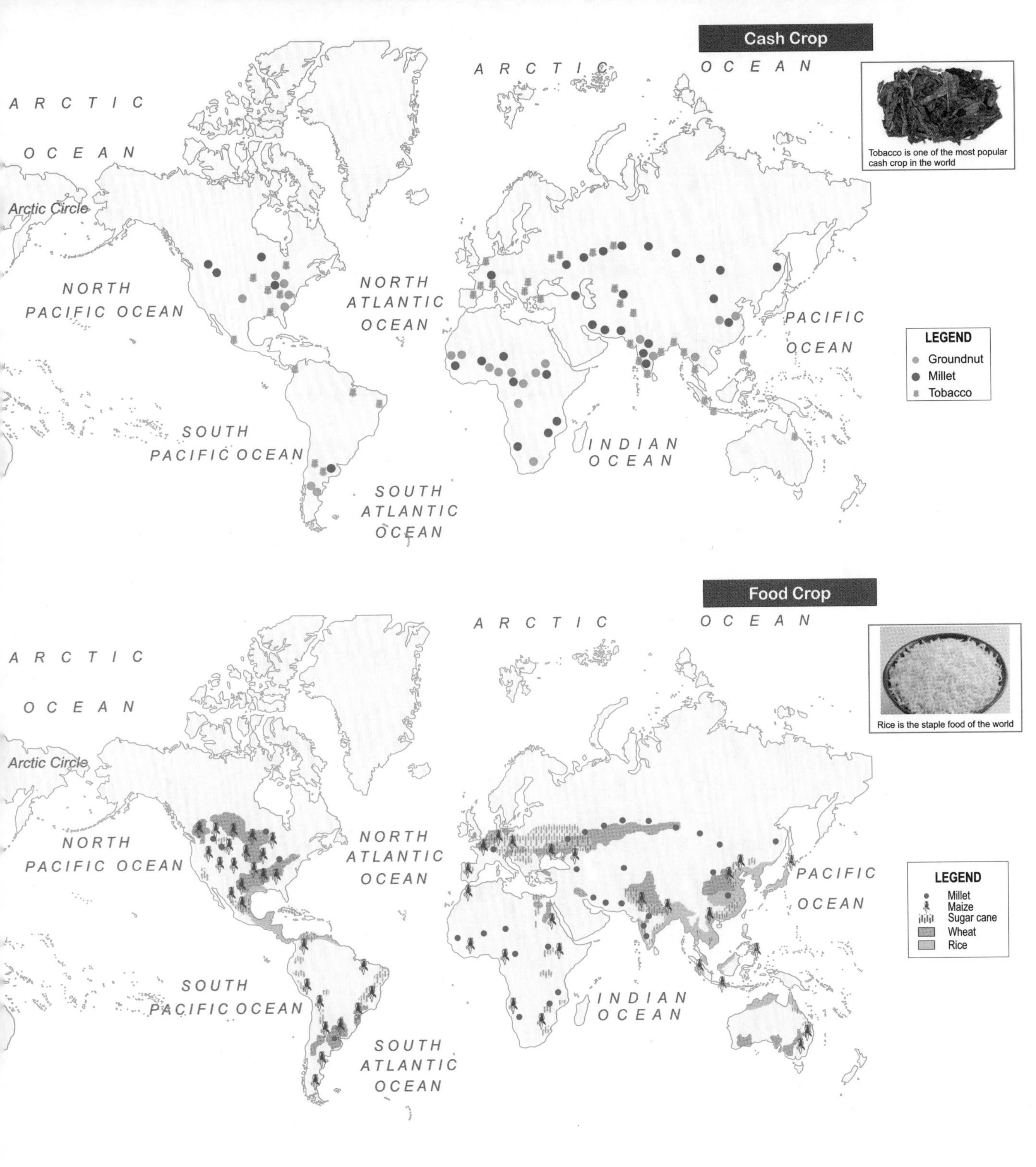
Cash Crop
Tobacco is one of the most popular cash crop in the world
LEGEND
Groundnut
Millet
Tobacco
ARCTIC OCEAN
Arctic Circle
NORTH PACIFIC OCEAN
NORTH ATLANTIC OCEAN
PACIFIC OCEAN
SOUTH PACIFIC OCEAN
SOUTH ATLANTIC OCEAN
INDIAN OCEAN
Food Crop
Rice is the staple food of the world
LEGEND
Millet
Maize
Sugar cane
Wheat
Rice
1000 0 1000 2000 km.

Projection: Lambert's Conical Orthomorphic

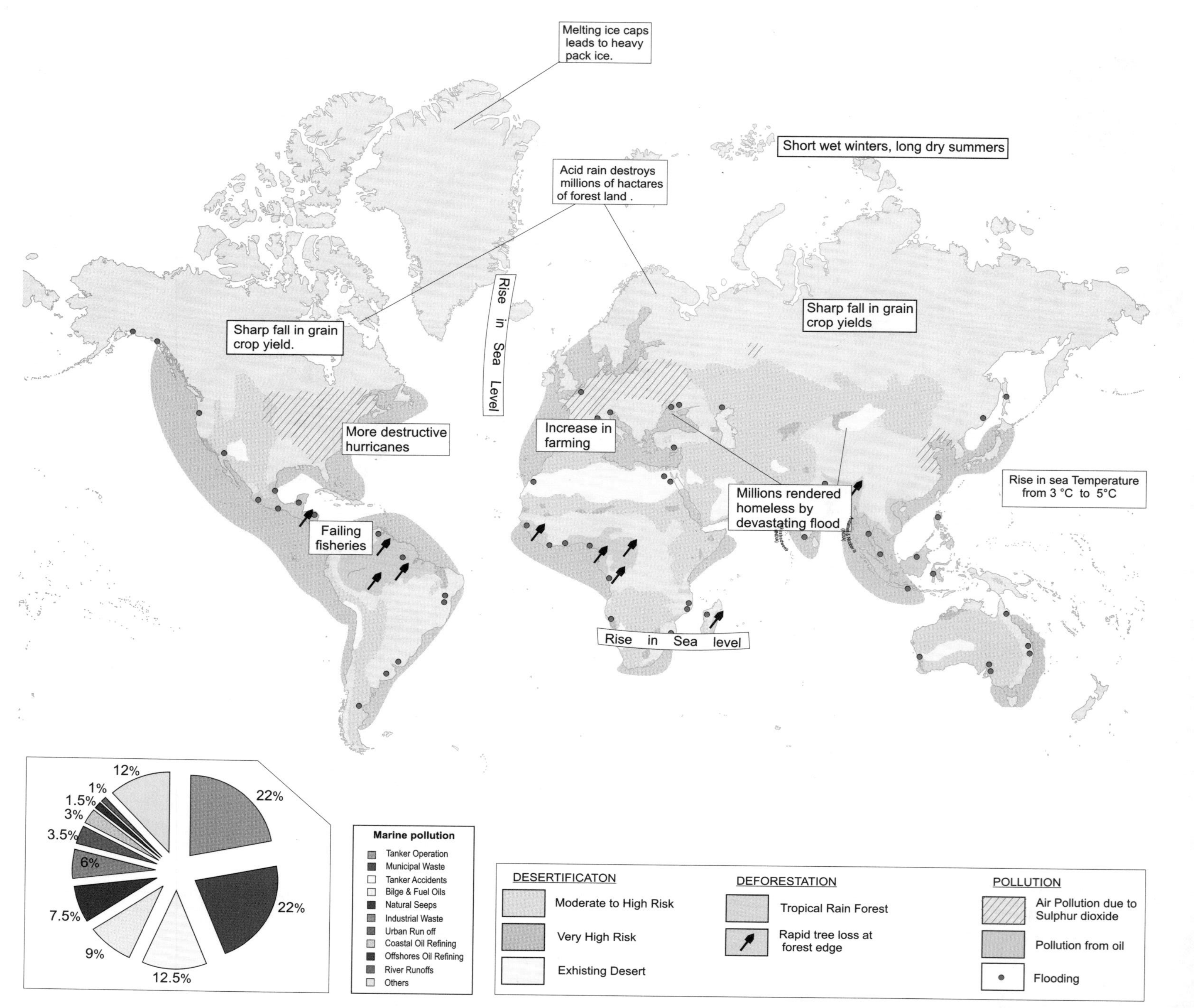
Melting ice caps leads to heavy pack ice.
Short wet winters, long dry summers
Acid rain destroys millions of hactares of forest land .
Sharp fall in grain crop yield.
Rise in Sea Level
Sharp fall in grain crop yields
More destructive hurricanes
Increase in farming
Rise in sea Temperature from 3 °C to 5°C
Millions rendered homeless by devastating flood
Failing fisheries
Rise in Sea level
12%
1%
1.5%
3%
3.5%
6%
7.5%
9%
12.5%
22%
22%
Marine pollution
Tanker Operation
Municipal Waste
Tanker Accidents
Bilge & Fuel Oils
Natural Seeps
Industrial Waste
Urban Run off
Coastal Oil Refining
Offshores Oil Refining
River Runoffs
Others
DESERTIFICATON
Moderate to High Risk
Very High Risk
Exhisting Desert
DEFORESTATION
Tropical Rain Forest
Rapid tree loss at forest edge
POLLUTION
Air Pollution due to Sulphur dioxide
Pollution from oil
Flooding
Projection: Lambert's Conical Orthomorphic
1000 0 1000 2000 km.

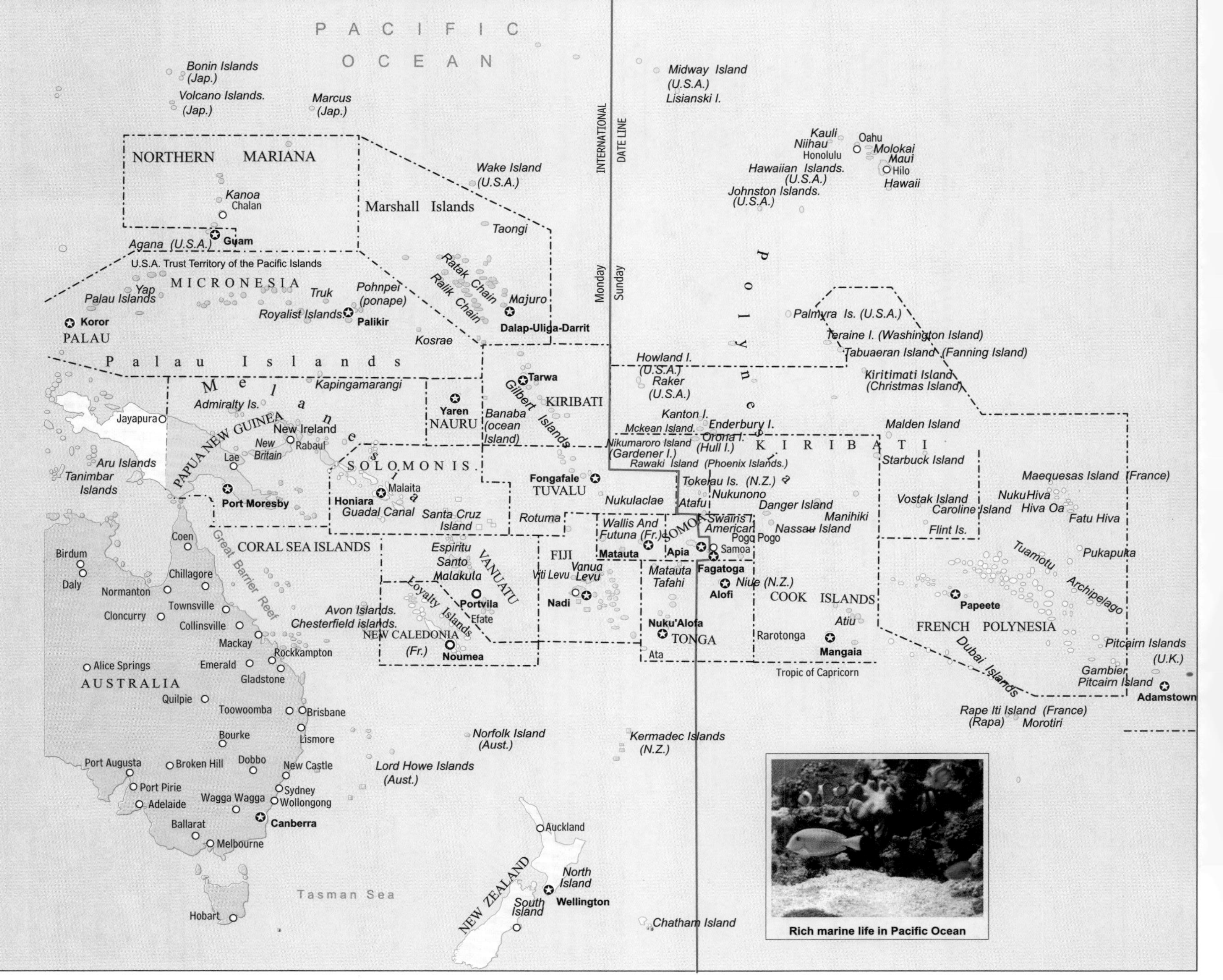
PACIFIC OCEAN
Polynesia
Melanesia
Palau Islands
MICRONESIA
NORTHERN MARIANA
Marshall Islands
KIRIBATI
NAURU
TUVALU
SOLOMON IS.
VANUATU
FIJI
TONGA
SAMOA
COOK ISLANDS
FRENCH POLYNESIA
NEW CALEDONIA (Fr.)
PAPUA NEW GUINEA
AUSTRALIA
NEW ZEALAND
CORAL SEA ISLANDS
PALAU
INTERNATIONAL DATE LINE
Monday
Sunday
Tropic of Capricorn
Great Barrier Reef
Tasman Sea
Bonin Islands (Jap.)
Volcano Islands. (Jap.)
Marcus (Jap.)
Wake Island (U.S.A.)
Midway Island (U.S.A.)
Lisianski I.
Hawaiian Islands. (U.S.A.)
Johnston Islands. (U.S.A.)
Kauli
Niihau
Honolulu
Oahu
Molokai
Maui
Hilo
Hawaii
Palmyra Is. (U.S.A.)
Teraine I. (Washington Island)
Tabuaeran Island (Fanning Island)
Kiritimati Island (Christmas Island)
Malden Island
Starbuck Island
Vostak Island
Caroline Island
Flint Is.
Maequesas Island (France)
NukuHiva
Hiva Oa
Fatu Hiva
Tuamotu Archipelago
Pukapuka
Papeete
Dubai Islands
Pitcairn Islands (U.K.)
Gambier
Pitcairn Island
Adamstown
Rape Iti Island (France) (Rapa)
Morotiri
Rarotonga
Mangaia
Atiu
Manihiki
Nassau Island
Danger Island
Niue (N.Z.)
Alofi
Fagatoga
Apia
Nuku'Alofa
Ata
Kermadec Islands (N.Z.)
Chatham Island
Howland I. (U.S.A.)
Raker (U.S.A.)
Kanton I.
Enderbury I.
Orona I. (Hull I.)
Mckean Island.
Nikumaroro Island (Gardener I.)
Rawaki Island (Phoenix Islands.)
Tokelau Is. (N.Z.)
Nukunono
Atafu
Nukulaclae
Swains I.
American
Pogo Pogo
Samoa
Wallis And Futuna (Fr.)
Matauta
Mataula Tafahi
Vanua Levu
Viti Levu
Nadi
Rotuma
Fongafale
Tarwa
Gilbert Islands
Banaba (ocean Island)
Yaren
Dalap-Uliga-Darrit
Majuro
Taongi
Ratak Chain
Ralik Chain
Kosrae
Pohnpei (ponape)
Palikir
Truk
Royalist Islands
Kapingamarangi
U.S.A. Trust Territory of the Pacific Islands
Guam
Agana (U.S.A.)
Kanoa
Chalan
Yap
Palau Islands
Koror
Admiralty Is.
New Ireland
Rabaul
New Britain
Lae
Port Moresby
Jayapura
Aru Islands
Tanimbar Islands
Malaita
Honiara
Guadal Canal
Santa Cruz Island
Espiritu Santo
Malakula
Portvila
Efate
Loyalty Islands
Noumea
Avon Islands.
Chesterfield islands.
Norfolk Island (Aust.)
Lord Howe Islands (Aust.)
Auckland
North Island
Wellington
South Island
Birdum
Daly
Normanton
Cloncurry
Alice Springs
Coen
Chillagore
Townsville
Collinsville
Mackay
Emerald
Rockkampton
Gladstone
Toowoomba
Brisbane
Lismore
Quilpie
Bourke
Dobbo
New Castle
Sydney
Wollongong
Canberra
Broken Hill
Wagga Wagga
Port Augusta
Port Pirie
Adelaide
Ballarat
Melbourne
Hobart
Rich marine life in Pacific Ocean

0 1000 2000 km.

Projection: Lambert's Conical Orthomorphic

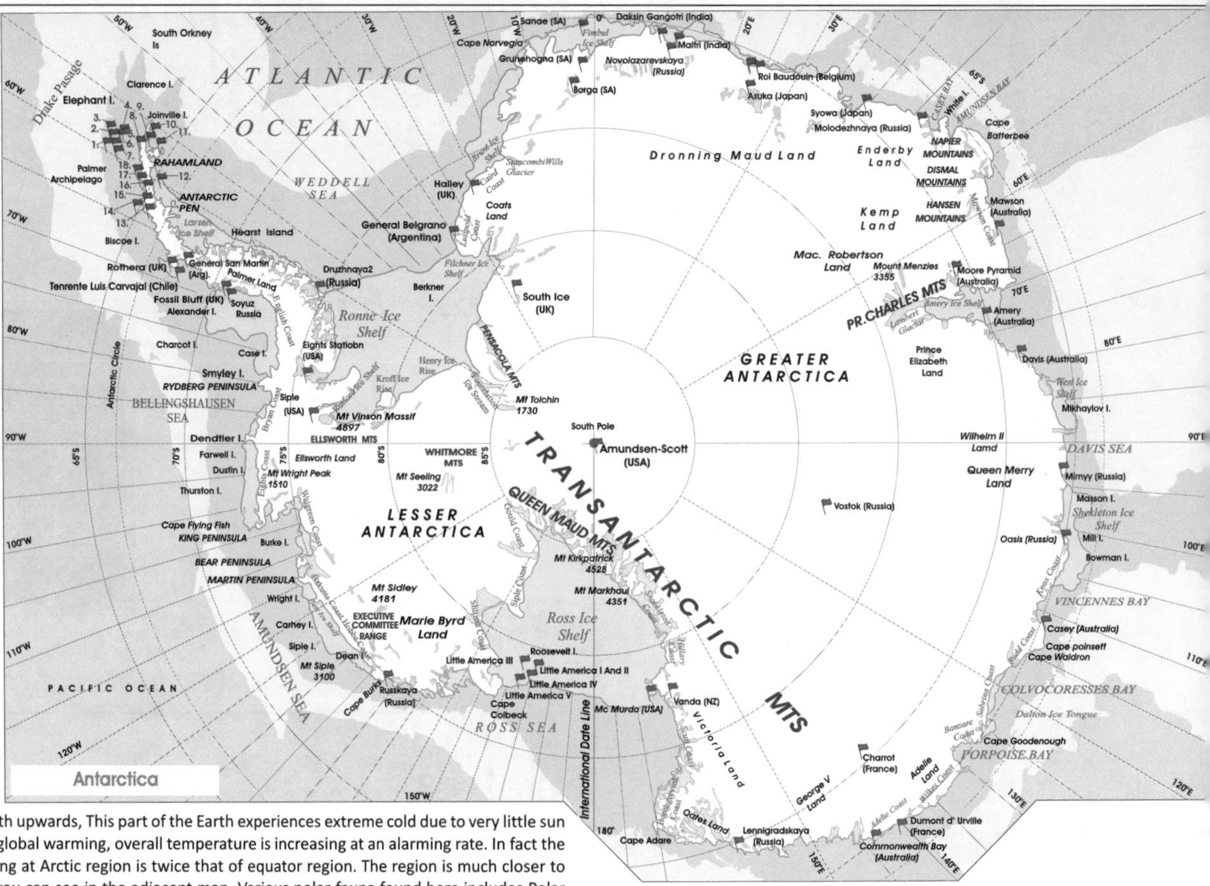

Antarctica

South Orkney Is
ATLANTIC OCEAN
WEDDELL SEA
Drake Passage
Elephant I.
Clarence I.
Joinville I.
Palmer Archipelago
RAHAMLAND
ANTARCTIC PEN
Larsen Ice Shelf
Hearst Island
Biscoe I.
Rothera (UK)
General San Martin (Arg.)
Tenrente Luis Carvajal (Chile)
Fossil Bluff (UK)
Alexander I.
Soyuz Russia
Palmer Land
Druzhnaya2 (Russia)
Halley (UK)
Coats Land
General Belgrano (Argentina)
Berkner I.
Filchner Ice Shelf
Ronne Ice Shelf
South Ice (UK)
Charcot I.
Case I.
Eights Statiobn (USA)
Smyley I.
RYDBERG PENINSULA
BELLINGSHAUSEN SEA
Siple (USA)
Mt Vinson Massif 4897
ELLSWORTH MTS
Dendtler I.
Farwell I.
Dustin I.
Thurston I.
Ellsworth Land
Mt Wright Peak 1510
WHITMORE MTS
Mt Seeling 3022
PENSACOLA MTS
Mt Tolchin 1730
LESSER ANTARCTICA
Cape Flying Fish
KING PENINSULA
Burke I.
BEAR PENINSULA
MARTIN PENINSULA
Wright I.
Carney I.
Siple I.
Dean I.
Mt Sidley 4181
EXECUTIVE COMMITTEE RANGE
Marie Byrd Land
Mt Siple 3100
AMUNDSEN SEA
PACIFIC OCEAN
Cape Burks
Russkaya (Russia)
Little America III
Roosevelt I.
Little America I And II
Little America IV
Little America V
Cape Colbeck
ROSS SEA
Ross Ice Shelf
QUEEN MAUD MTS
Mt Kirkpatrick 4528
Mt Markham 4351
South Pole
Amundsen-Scott (USA)
TRANSANTARCTIC MTS
International Date Line
Mc Murdo (USA)
Vanda (NZ)
Victoria Land
Oates Land
Cape Adare
Lennigradskaya (Russia)
George V Land
Charrot (France)
Adelie Land
Dumont d' Urville (France)
Commonwealth Bay (Australia)
Sanae (SA)
Daksin Gangotri (India)
Maitri (India)
Cape Norvegia
Grunehogna (SA)
Novolazarevskaya (Russia)
Borga (SA)
Roi Baudouin (Belgium)
Asuka (Japan)
Syowa (Japan)
Molodezhnaya (Russia)
Dronning Maud Land
Enderby Land
NAPIER MOUNTAINS
DISMAL MOUNTAINS
HANSEN MOUNTAINS
Kemp Land
Cape Batterbee
Mawson (Australia)
Mac. Robertson Land
Mount Menzies 3355
Moore Pyramid (Australia)
PR. CHARLES MTS
Amery Ice Shelf
Amery (Australia)
Prince Elizabeth Land
Davis (Australia)
GREATER ANTARCTICA
West Ice Shelf
Mikhaylov I.
Wilhelm II Land
DAVIS SEA
Mirnyy (Russia)
Queen Merry Land
Masson I.
Shakleton Ice Shelf
Mill I.
Bowman I.
Vostok (Russia)
Oasis (Russia)
VINCENNES BAY
Casey (Australia)
Cape poinsett
Cape Waldron
COLVOCORESSES BAY
Dalton Ice Tongue
Cape Goodenough
PORPOISE BAY

Situated at 66°33' North upwards, This part of the Earth experiences extreme cold due to very little sun rays. However due to global warming, overall temperature is increasing at an alarming rate. In fact the effect of global warming at Arctic region is twice that of equator region. The region is much closer to human habitation as you can see in the adjacent map. Various polar fauna found here includes Polar bear, seals, puffins etc. Are highly vulnerable and likely to become extinct in a few decades from now.

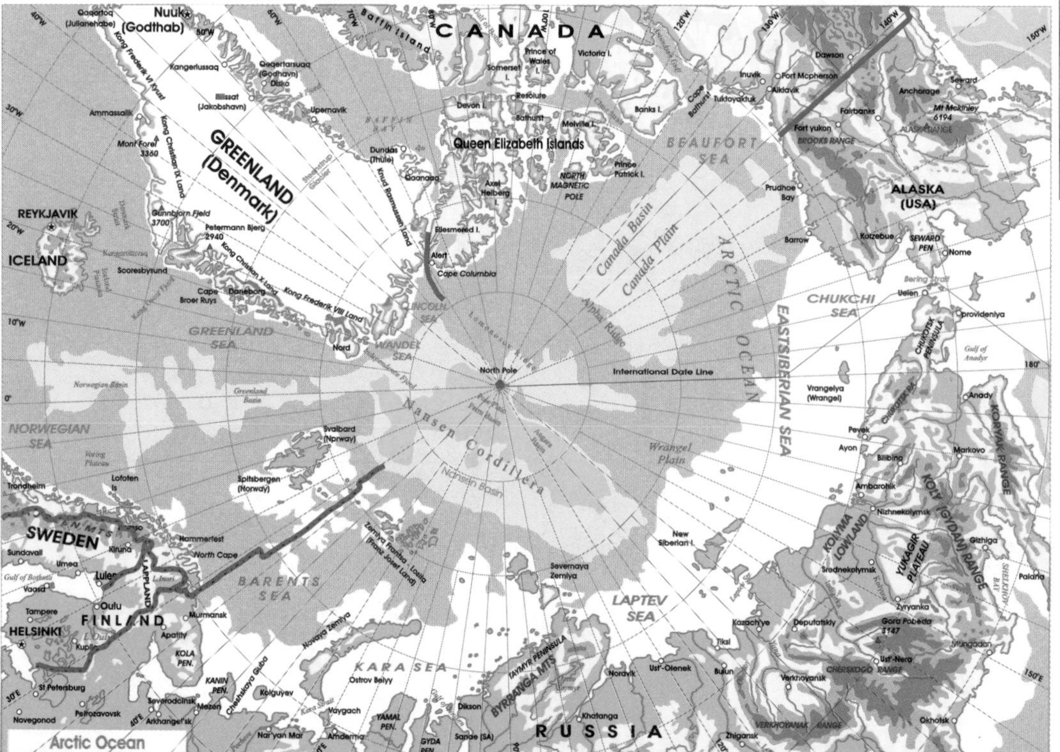

CANADA
Nuuk (Godthab)
Baffin Island
GREENLAND (Denmark)
Queen Elizabeth Islands
BEAUFORT SEA
ALASKA (USA)
REYKJAVIK
ICELAND
GREENLAND SEA
NORWEGIAN SEA
North Pole
International Date Line
ARCTIC OCEAN
CHUKCHI SEA
EASTSIBERIAN SEA
Canada Basin
Canada Plain
Nansen Cordillera
Wrangel Plain
SWEDEN
FINLAND
HELSINKI
BARENTS SEA
KARA SEA
LAPTEV SEA
RUSSIA
Arctic Ocean

As a consequence of global warming, glaciars are melting at an alarming rate.

Antarctica, the southern most contine on Earth is mostly uninhabited. Fe research centers/ bases are setup b various countries to study the origi geology and other geological an meteorological observations. Very litt fauna and practically no vegetation a found. Animals like Polar bears, seal Penguins etc. Are found. Countries hav come together in favour of protecting th region from human abuse such as was disposal, exploration, mining, disturbir its ecology and the likes. It is interesting see how long we can leave it to itself, as

Beautiful sunset preceding dark days ahe

Projection: Lambert's Conical Orthomorphic

1000 0 1000 2000

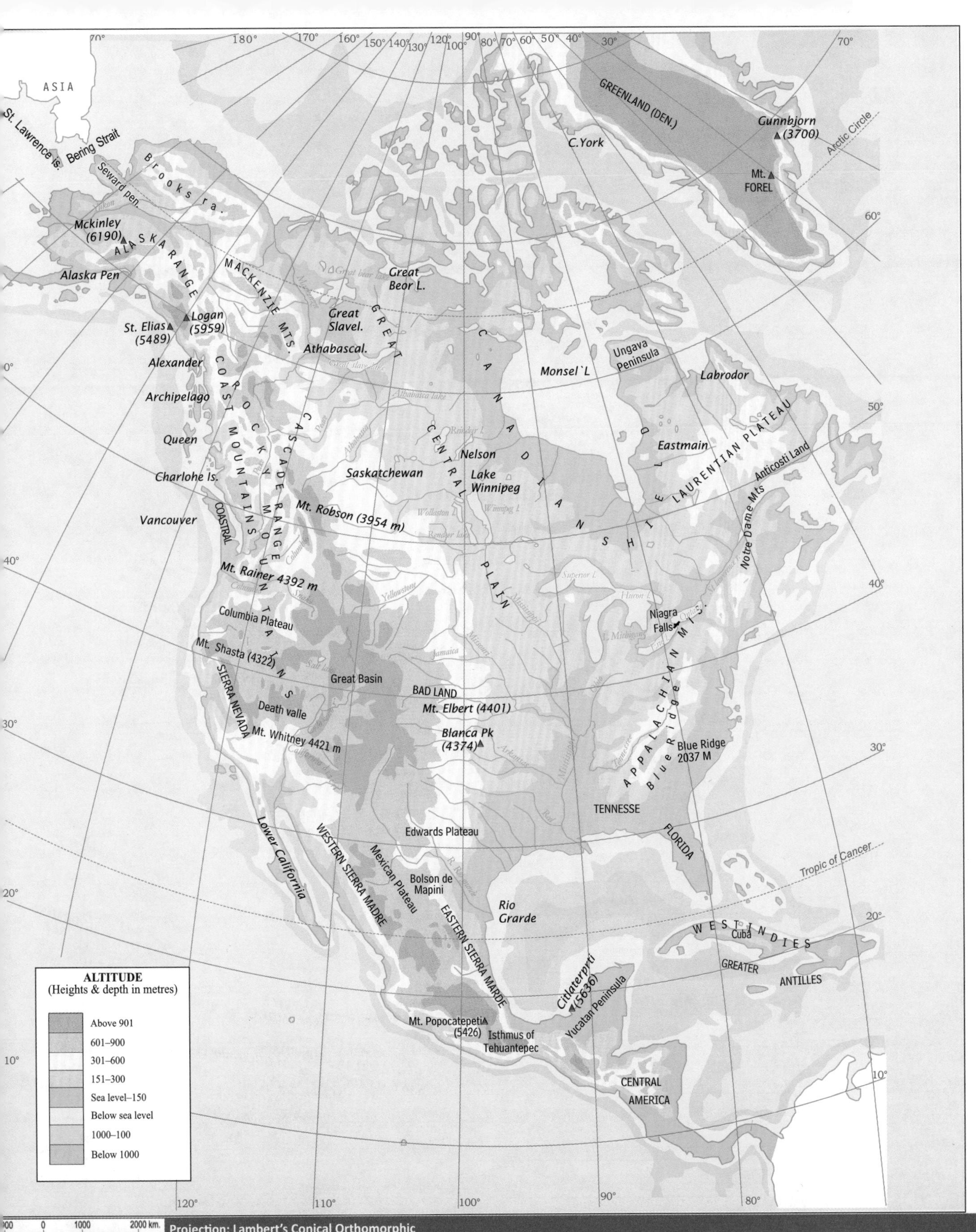
ASIA
St. Lawrence Is.
Bering Strait
Seward pen.
Brooks ra.
Mckinley (6190)
ALASKA RANGE
Alaska Pen
St. Elias (5489)
Logan (5959)
MACKENZIE MTS.
Alexander
Archipelago
Queen
Charlohe Is.
Vancouver
COASTRAL
COAST MOUNTAINS
ROCKY MOUNTAINS
CASCADE RANGE
Great Beor L.
Great Slavel.
Athabascal.
GREAT CENTRAL PLAIN
CANADIAN SHIELD
Saskatchewan
Nelson
Lake Winnipeg
Mt. Robson (3954 m)
Mt. Rainer 4392 m
Columbia Plateau
Mt. Shasta (4322)
SIERRA NEVADA
Death valle
Mt. Whitney 4421 m
Great Basin
BAD LAND
Mt. Elbert (4401)
Blanca Pk (4374)
GREENLAND (DEN.)
C.York
Gunnbjorn (3700)
Mt. FOREL
Arctic Circle
Ungava Peninsula
Monsel`L
Labrodor
Eastmain
LAURENTIAN PLATEAU
Anticosti Land
Notre Dame Mts
Niagra Falls
APPALACHIAN MTS.
Blue Ridge
Blue Ridge 2037 M
TENNESSE
FLORIDA
Tropic of Cancer
Edwards Plateau
Lower California
WESTERN SIERRA MADRE
Mexican Plateau
Bolson de Mapini
EASTERN SIERRA MARDE
Rio Grarde
WEST INDIES
Cuba
GREATER ANTILLES
Citlaterptl (5636)
Yucatan Peninsula
Mt. Popocatepeti (5426)
Isthmus of Tehuantepec
CENTRAL AMERICA
ALTITUDE
(Heights & depth in metres)
Above 901
601–900
301–600
151–300
Sea level–150
Below sea level
1000–100
Below 1000
180°
170°
160°
150°
140°
130°
120°
100°
90°
80°
70°
60°
50°
40°
30°
70°
60°
50°
40°
30°
20°
10°
120°
110°
100°
90°
80°
0
1000
2000 km.
Projection: Lambert's Conical Orthomorphic

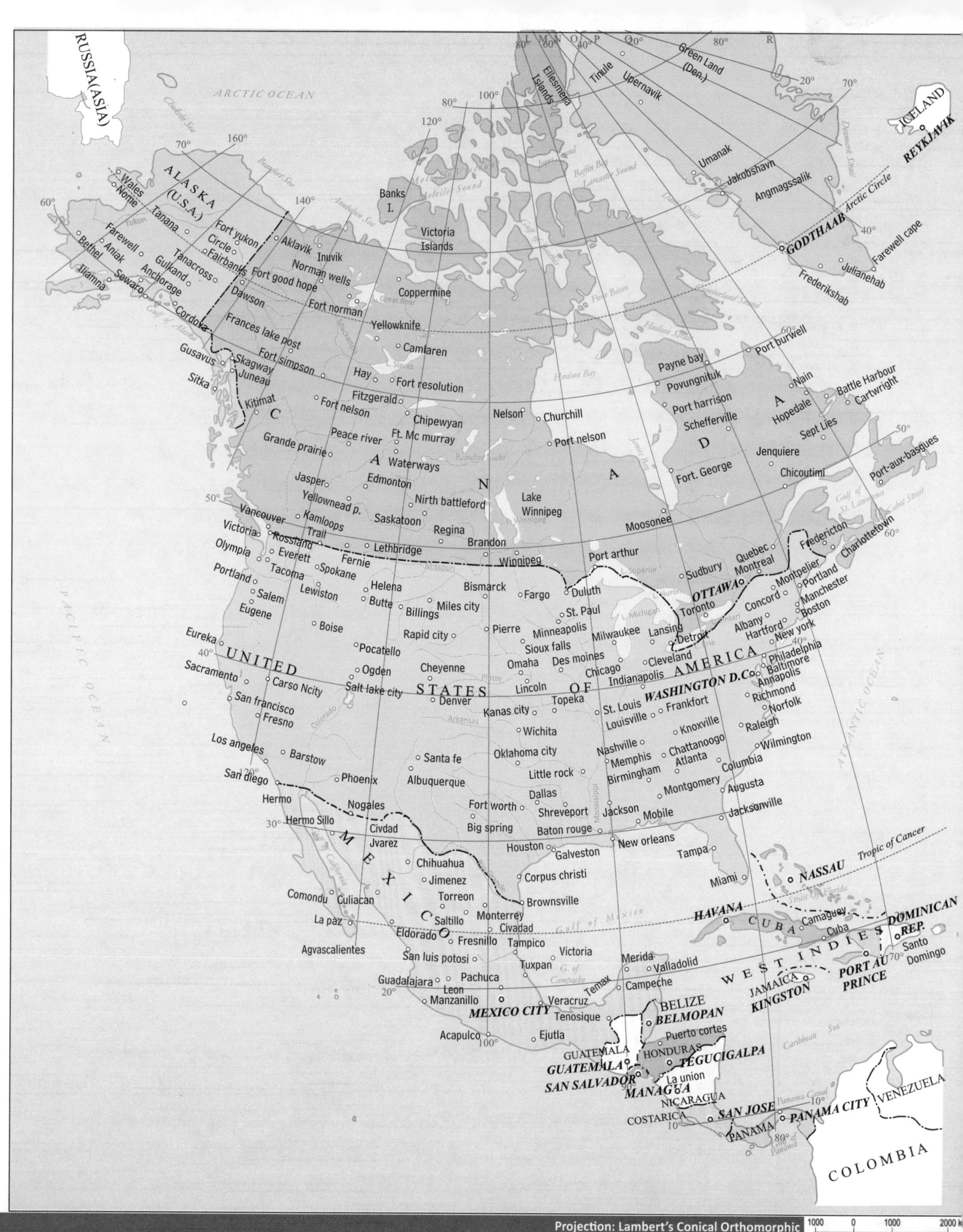
RUSSIA(ASIA)
ARCTIC OCEAN
ALASKA (U.S.A.)
Wales
Nome
Tanana
Fort yukon
Circle
Fairbanks
Tanacross
Gulkand
Anchorage
Farewell
Aniak
Bethel
Iliamna
Sewaro
Cordova
Aklavik
Inuvik
Norman wells
Fort good hope
Dawson
Fort norman
Coppermine
Yellowknife
Frances lake post
Camlaren
Fort simpson
Gusavus
Skagway
Juneau
Sitka
Hay
Fort resolution
Fitzgerald
Fort nelson
Kitimat
Chipewyan
Peace river
Ft. Mc murray
Grande prairie
Waterways
Jasper
Edmonton
Yellowhead p.
Nirth battleford
Vancouver
Kamloops
Saskatoon
Victoria
Trail
Regina
Rossland
Brandon
Lethbridge
Olympia
Everett
Fernie
Winnipeg
Portland
Tacoma
Spokane
Lewiston
Helena
Salem
Butte
Billings
Miles city
Bismarck
Fargo
Eugene
Boise
Rapid city
Pierre
Minneapolis
St. Paul
Duluth
Eureka
Pocatello
Sioux falls
Ogden
Cheyenne
Omaha
Des moines
Sacramento
Carso Ncity
Salt lake city
Lincoln
San francisco
Fresno
Denver
Kanas city
Topeka
Wichita
Los angeles
Barstow
Santa fe
Oklahoma city
San diego
Phoenix
Albuquerque
Little rock
Hermo
Nogales
Dallas
Fort worth
Shreveport
Hermo Sillo
Big spring
Jackson
Civdad
Jvarez
Baton rouge
Houston
Galveston
New orleans
UNITED STATES OF AMERICA
CANADA
Banks I.
Victoria Islands
Ellesmere Islands
Tinule
Upernavik
Green Land (Den.)
Umanak
Jakobshavn
Angmagssalik
GODTHAAB
Arctic Circle
Frederikshab
Julianehab
Farewell cape
ICELAND
REYKJAVIK
Port burwell
Payne bay
Povungnituk
Nain
Battle Harbour
Cartwright
Hopedale
Port harrison
Schefferville
Churchill
Nelson
Port nelson
Sept Lies
Jenquiere
Fort. George
Chicoutimi
Port-aux-basgues
Lake Winnipeg
Moosonee
Fredericton
Charlottetown
Port arthur
Quebec
Sudbury
Montreal
OTTAWA
Montpelier
Portland
Manchester
Concord
Boston
Toronto
Albany
Hartford
New york
Milwaukee
Lansing
Detroit
Cleveland
Chicago
Philadelphia
Baltimore
Annapolis
Indianapolis
WASHINGTON D.C.
Richmond
Norfolk
St. Louis
Frankfort
Louisville
Knoxville
Raleigh
Nashville
Chattanoogo
Wilmington
Memphis
Atlanta
Birmingham
Columbia
Montgomery
Augusta
Mobile
Jacksonville
Tampa
Miami
NASSAU
Tropic of Cancer
HAVANA
CUBA
Camaguey
Cuba
DOMINICAN REP.
Santo Domingo
WEST INDIES
PORT AU PRINCE
JAMAICA
KINGSTON
MEXICO
Chihuahua
Jimenez
Torreon
Corpus christi
Comondu
Culiacan
Saltillo
Monterrey
Brownsville
La paz
Eldorado
Fresnillo
Civdad
Tampico
Agvascalientes
San luis potosi
Victoria
Tuxpan
Merida
Valladolid
Guadalajara
Pachuca
Leon
Manzanillo
MEXICO CITY
Veracruz
Temax
Campeche
Tenosique
BELIZE
BELMOPAN
Puerto cortes
Acapulco
Ejutla
GUATEMALA
HONDURAS
TEGUCIGALPA
SAN SALVADOR
La union
MANAGUA
NICARAGUA
COSTARICA
SAN JOSE
PANAMA
PANAMA CITY
VENEZUELA
COLOMBIA
PACIFIC OCEAN
ATLANTIC OCEAN
Gulf of Mexico
Caribbean Sea
Hudson Bay
Baffin Bay
Projection: Lambert's Conical Orthomorphic
1000 0 1000 2000 km

Mt. Bolivar (5775 m)
Cordillera real
Cordillera occidental
Central Cordillera oriental
Angel's Fall
Mt. Roraima (2810 m)
Guyana Highlands
Selvas
Amazon Basin
Mt. Cotopaxi (5897 m)
Mt. Chimborazo (6267 m)
Serra dos parecis
Serra do roncador
Serra do estrondo
Catinga
Coba huagaruancha
Mt. Huascaran (6768 m)
Andes Mountains
Atacama Desert
Mt. Illampu (6862 m)
Mt. Nevado Sajama (6520 m)
Campos
Brazilian highlands
Mt. Pico da Bandeira (2892 m)
Gran Chaco
Peru chile trench
Mt. Nevado Del Salado (6893 m)
Mt. Pissis (6793 m)
Mt. Cerro Bonete (6872 m)
Mt. Acocagua (6960)
Mt. Cerro Tupungato (6570)
Pampas
Patagonian cordillera
Valdes peninsula
Mt. Cerro San Valentin (4058)
Patagonia
Tierra del fuego
Orinoco
Amazon
Negro
Japura
Purus
Madeira
Tapajos
Xingu
Tocantins
Araguaia
Guapore
Pilcomayo
Parana
Uruguay
Colorado
L. Titicaca
L. Poopo
REFERENCES
(Height & depth in metres)
Above 1301
901—1300
601—900
301—600
151—300
Sea level—150
Below sea level
1000—100
Below 1001
0 1000 2000 km.

Projection: Lambert's Conical Orthomorphic

SOUTH AMERICA - POLITICAL

NICARAGUA
PANAMA
TRINIDAD AND TOBAGO
PORT OF SPAIN
CARACAS
Maturin
Cumana
Barcelona
Santa Marta
Uribia
Cabimas
Maracaibo
Barranquilla
Cartagena
Merido
Montenia
Jurbo
San Cristobal
VENEZUELA
Tucupita
Morawhanna
GEORGETOWN
Bartica
San Pedro
PARAMARIBO
GUYANA
SURINAM
CAYENNE
FR. GUIANA
Linden
Marudi
Dadanawa
Brokopondo
Amapa
Macapa
Dabeiba
Arauca
Puetro
Puetro Ayacucho
Quibdo
BOGOTA
Buenavetura
Neiva
COLOMBIA
Esmeralda
Boa Vista
SanCorles
Cucil
Uaupes
Calamar
Mitu
Guapi
Tumaco
Mocoa
Esmeraldas
Ibarro
Ambato
QUITO
Latacunga
ECUADOR
Guayaguil
Tumbes
Andoas
Iquitos
Lehcia
Santa Fe
Fonta Bao
Moura
Manaus
Faro
Gurupa
Betterra
Baido
Tucurui
Belem (para)
Sao Luis Do Marannao
Parnaiba
Fortaleza(ceara)
Borba
Itaituba
Sobrado
Maraba
Tulora
Piura
Chiclayo
Chachapoyas
Cajamarca
Eirunepe
Manicore
Tres Casas
Rio Brancho
Canudos
Carolina
Teresina
Aracati
Natal
Macau
Jaicos
Joao Pessoa
Paulistana
Sertania
Recife
Remanso
PERU
Trujillo
Santo Antonio
Aripuana
Puerto Maldonado
Cobija
Raiberalta
BRAZIL
Pucdpa
LIMA
Huancayo
Cuzco
Ica
Ayacucha
Trinidad
BOLIVIA
Mato Grosso
Cuiaba
Aruana
Coxin
Barreiras
Propria
Aracaju
Maceio
Salvador (bahia)
Brumado
Ilheus
Puno
Arequipa
Cochabamba
Mollendo
Oruro
Patosi
Santa Cruz
Arica
SUCRE
Anapolis
Goiania
BRASILIA
Janvaria
Iquique
Montes
Villa
Tarija
Fuerte Olimpo
Bahia Negra
Campo Grande
Belo Horizonte
Ribeorao Preto
Vitoria
Calama
PARAGUAY
Pedro Juan Caballero
Concepcion
Campinas
Campos
Cabo Frio
Rio De Janeiro
Antofagasta
Copila
Jujuy
Salta
ASUNCION
Villarrica
Ponta Grossa
Santos
Sao Paulo
Taco Pozo
Tucuman
Pilar
Curitiba
Calama
Copiapo
Resitenci
Encarnacion
Corrients
Chanaral
Catamarca
ARGENTINA
Cruz Alta
Santa Maria
La Serena
La Riajo
Artigas
Porto Alegre
Cordoba
Santa Fe
Salto
Rivera
Vallenar
Parana
Rosario
Rio Grande
URUGUAY
Valparaiso
Mendoza
SANTIAGO
Rio Cuarto
San Luis
Pay Sandu
MONTEVIDEO
BUENOS AIRES
Constitution
CHILE
Talcahuano
Santa Rosa
Tandil
Concepcion
Mar Del Plata
Lebu
Bahia Blanca
Temuco
Nauquen
Tres Arroyos
Valdivia
Carmen De Patagones
Osorno
Ancud
Puerto Monto
Rawson
Dihaiqu
Balmaceda
Comodoro Rivadavia
Puerto Deseado
Medanosa Pt.
San Julian
El Calafate
Rio Gallegos
STANLEY
FALKLAND IS.(U.K.)
Punta Arenas
TIERRA DEL FUEGO
Tierra Del Fuego
Ushuaia
90°
80°
70°
60°
50°
40°
10°
0°
10°
20°
30°
40°
50°
110°
100°
90°
80°
70°
60°
50°
40°
30°
20°
1000
0
1000
2000 km

Projection: Lambert's Conical Orthomorphic

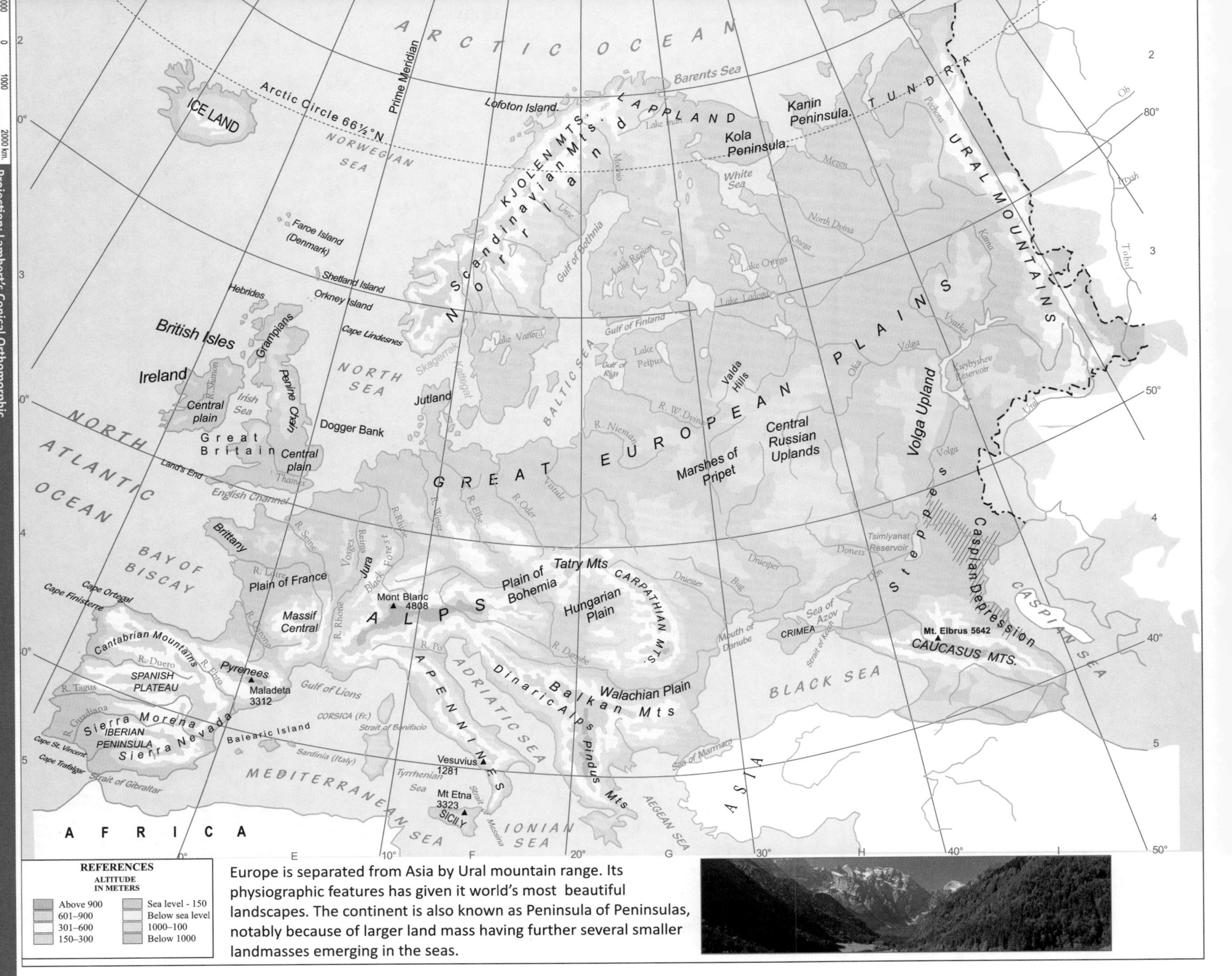
ARCTIC OCEAN
Barents Sea
Arctic Circle 66½°N
Prime Meridian
ICE LAND
NORWEGIAN SEA
Lofoton Island
LAPPLAND
Kola Peninsula
Kanin Peninsula
TUNDRA
URAL MOUNTAINS
KJOLEN MTS.
Scandinavian Mts
Norrland
White Sea
Mezen
North Dvina
Onega
Lake Onega
Lake Ladoga
Gulf of Bothnia
Gulf of Finland
Lake Peipus
Gulf of Riga
BALTIC SEA
Lake Vanern
Skagerrak
Kattegat
Faroe Island (Denmark)
Shetland Island
Orkney Island
Hebrides
Cape Lindesnes
British Isles
Grampians
Ireland
Central plain
Irish Sea
Penine Chain
Great Britain
Central plain
Thames
NORTH SEA
Dogger Bank
Jutland
NORTH ATLANTIC OCEAN
Land's End
English Channel
Brittany
BAY OF BISCAY
Cape Ortegal
Cape Finisterre
Cantabrian Mountains
SPANISH PLATEAU
Sierra Morena
IBERIAN PENINSULA
Sierra Nevada
Cape St. Vincent
Cape Trafalgar
Strait of Gibraltar
Pyrenees
Maladeta 3312
Balearic Island
Gulf of Lions
CORSICA (Fr.)
Strait of Bonifacio
Sardinia (Italy)
Plain of France
Massif Central
Jura
Black Forest
Vosges
Reims
Mont Blanc 4808
ALPS
APENNINES
ADRIATIC SEA
Tyrrhenian Sea
Vesuvius 1281
Mt Etna 3323
SICILY
Strait of Messina
IONIAN SEA
MEDITERRANEAN SEA
AFRICA
GREAT EUROPEAN PLAINS
Plain of Bohemia
Tatry Mts
CARPATHIAN MTS.
Hungarian Plain
Dinaric Alps
Balkan Mts
Walachian Plain
Pindus Mts
AEGEAN SEA
Sea of Marmara
Marshes of Pripet
Valda Hills
Central Russian Uplands
Volga Upland
Kuybyshev Reservoir
Tsimlyanst Reservoir
Steppes
Caspian Depression
CASPIAN SEA
Mt. Elbrus 5642
CAUCASUS MTS.
CRIMEA
Sea of Azov
Strait of Kerch
Mouth of Danube
BLACK SEA
ASIA
Tobol
Irtysh
Ob
Ural
REFERENCES
ALTITUDE IN METERS
Above 900
601–900
301–600
150–300
Sea level - 150
Below sea level
1000–100
Below 1000
2000 km.

Europe is separated from Asia by Ural mountain range. Its physiographic features has given it world's most beautiful landscapes. The continent is also known as Peninsula of Peninsulas, notably because of larger land mass having further several smaller landmasses emerging in the seas.

Projection: Lambert's Conical Orthomorphic

LEGEND
Country capital
Major town
International boundary
ARCTIC OCEAN
ATLANTIC OCEAN
Norwegian Sea
North Sea
Barents Sea
White Sea
Baltic Sea
Gulf of Bothnia
Gulf of Finland
English Channel
Bay of Biscay
Mediterranean Sea
Adriatic Sea
Tyrrhenian Sea
Ionian Sea
Aegean Sea
Black Sea
Sea of Azov
Caspian Sea
Lake Onega
Lake Ladoga
Strait of Gibraltar
Prime Meridian
Arctic Cirde
ICELAND
REYKJAVIK
Keflavik
Husavik
Faroe Islands (Denmark)
TORSHAVN
Shetland Islands (U.K.)
Orkney Is
Hebrides
UNITED KINGDOM
LONDON
Edinburgh
Aberdeen
Glasgow
Leeds
Manchester
Bristol
Southampton
Dover
IRELAND
DUBLIN
Limerick
Cork
NORWAY
OSLO
Bergen
Stauanger
Haugesund
Trondheim
Narvik
Tromso
Harstad
Bodo
Mosjoen
Namsos
Alesund
Flam
Odda
Khristiansand
Frederikshavn
North Cape
Alta
Vadso
SWEDEN
STOCKHOLM
Goteborg
Malmo
Helsingborg
Norrkoping
Gotland
Kiruna
Lulea
Umea
Ostersund
FINLAND
HELSINKI
Turku
Oulu
Vaasa
Tempore
Mikkeli
Kokkola
Inari
Henke
DENMARK
COPENHAGEN
Arhus
Odense
ESTONIA
TALLINN
Haapsalu
Valga
LATVIA
RIGA
LITHUANIA
VILNIUS
Kaliningrad
RUSSIA
BELARUS
MINSK
Brest
Vitebsk
Mogilev
POLAND
WARSAW
Gdansk
Gdynia
Szczecin
Poznam
Wroclaw
Lodz
Krakow
Lublin
Bialystok
GERMANY
BERLIN
Hamburg
Leipzig
Frankfurt
Stuttgart
Munich
NETHERLAND
AMSTERDAM
Rotterdam
BELGIUM
BRUSSELS
LUXEMBOURG CITY
FRANCE
PARIS
Calais
Reims
Caen
Brest
Nantes
Tours
Limoges
Bordeaux
Toulouse
Montpellier
Marseilles
Nice
Lyons
Dijon
Saint-Ebienne
SWITZERLAND
BERN
Genova
LIE
CZECH
PRAGUE
Brno
SLOVAKIA
BRATISLAVA
AUSTRIA
VIENNA
HUNGARY
BUDAPEST
S.L.
CROATIA
B. & H.
SARAJEVO
SERBIA
BELGRADE
MONTENEGRO
PODGORICA
KOSOVO
PRISTINA
MACEDONIA
SKOPJE
ALBANIA
TIRANA
ITALY
ROME
VATICAN CITY
San Marino
Milan
Turin
Genoa
Venice
Foggia
Naples
Salerno
Catanzaro
Reggio
Messina
Palermo
SICILY
Sardinia (Ita)
Cagliari
Corsica (Fr)
Ajaccio
MALTA
VALLETTA
SPAIN
MADRID
La Coruna
Santiago
Vigo
Gijon
Santander
Bilbao
Zaragoza
Lerida
Barcelona
Valencia
Albacete
Murcia
Cartagena
Badajoz
Seville
ANDORRA
ANDORRA LA VELLA
Balearic Islands (Spain)
PORTUGAL
LISBON
Oporto
GIBRALTER (U.K.)
CEUTA (SPAIN)
MELILLA (SPAIN)
MOROCCO
ALGERIA
TUNISIA
AFRICA
ROMANIA
BUCHAREST
Cluj
Timisoara
Galati
Constanta
Lasi
MOLDOVE
CHISINAU
BULGARIA
SOFIA
Plovdiv
Varna
GREECE
ATHENS
Thessaloniki
Larisa
Patrai
Crete Island
TURKEY
ISTANBUL
UKRAINE
KIEV
Chernihiv
Zhytomyr
Lutsk
Chernovtsy
Kharkov
Dnepropetrovsk
Donetsk
Lugansk
Krivoy Rog
Odessa
Simferopol
Sevastopol
Sumy
RUSSIA
MOSCOW
St. Petersburg (Leningrad)
Petrozavodsk
Murmansk
Kelloselko
Arkhangelsk
Mezen
Naryan-Mar
Pachora
Ukhta
Syktyukar
Kotlas
Vologda
Cherepovets
Rybinsk
Kostroma
Ivanovo
Tver
Kaluga
Bryansk
Orel
Kursk
Lipetsk
Tula
Ryazan
Voronezh
Tambov
Penza
Saransk
Nizhni Novgorod (Gorki)
Vyatka (Kirov)
Kazan
Ulyanovsk
Syzran
Togliatti
Samara
Saratov
Volgogtad
Elista
Astrakhan
Rostov
Taganrog
Krasnodar
Stavropol
Maykop
Nalchik
Groznyy
Makhachkala
Sochi
Sukhumi
Batumi
Perm
Berezniki
Izhekvsk
Ufa
Orenburg
Orsk
KAZAKHSTAN
GEORGIA
TBILISI
ARMENIA
AZERBAIJAN
BAKU
Gyandzha
ASIA

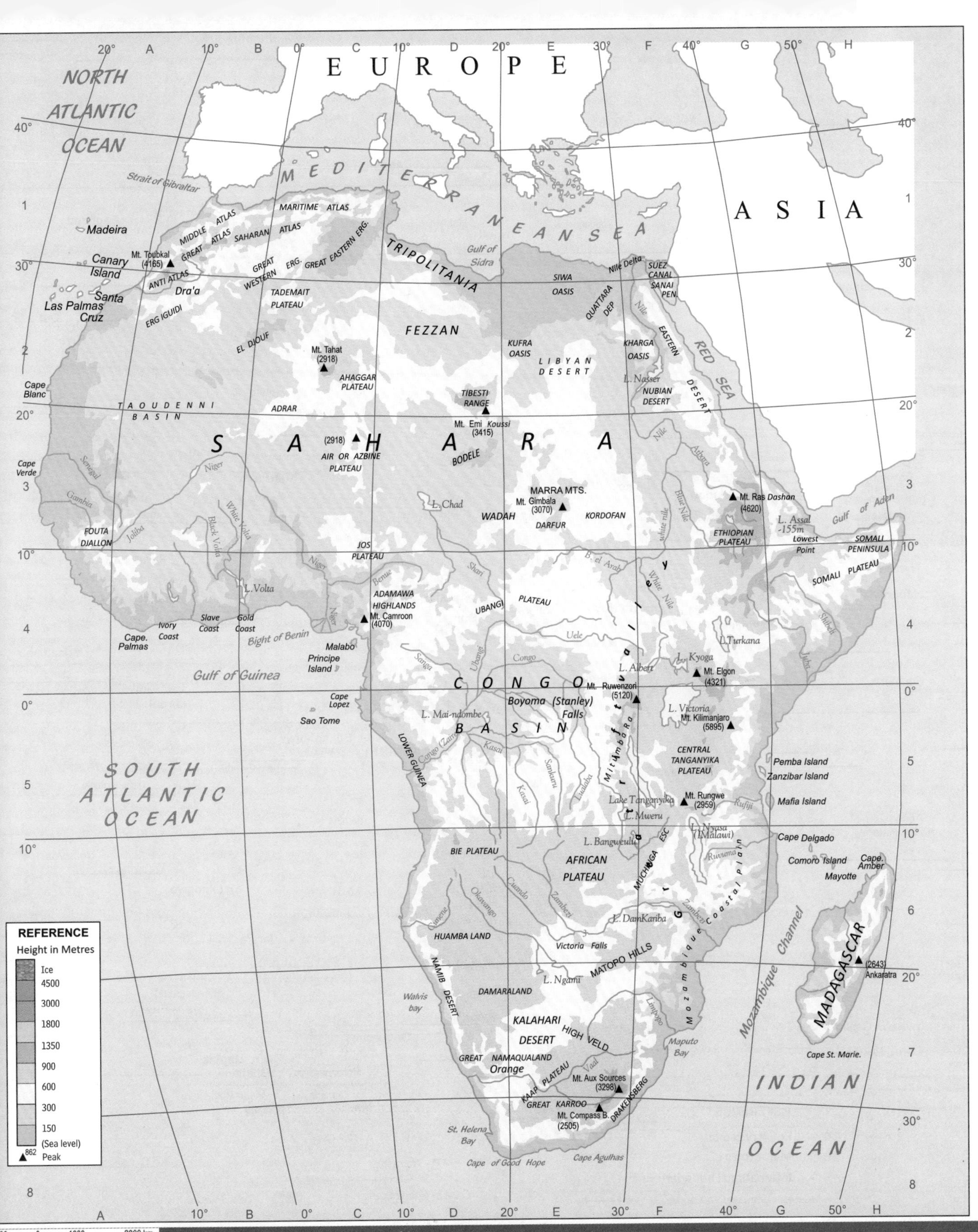
EUROPE
ASIA
NORTH ATLANTIC OCEAN
MEDITERRANEAN SEA
Strait of Gibraltar
Madeira
Canary Island
Las Palmas
Santa Cruz
Mt. Toubkal (4165)
MIDDLE ATLAS
GREAT ATLAS
ANTI ATLAS
SAHARAN ATLAS
MARITIME ATLAS
GREAT WESTERN ERG.
GREAT EASTERN ERG.
Dra'a
ERG IGUIDI
TADEMAIT PLATEAU
TRIPOLITANIA
Gulf of Sidra
FEZZAN
SIWA OASIS
QUATTARA DEP
Nile Delta
SUEZ CANAL
SANAI PEN.
EL DJOUF
Mt. Tahat (2918)
AHAGGAR PLATEAU
KUFRA OASIS
LIBYAN DESERT
KHARGA OASIS
EASTERN DESERT
RED SEA
L. Nasser
NUBIAN DESERT
Cape Blanc
TAOUDENNI BASIN
ADRAR
TIBESTI RANGE
Mt. Emi Koussi (3415)
SAHARA
(2918)
AIR OR AZBINE PLATEAU
BODELE
Cape Verde
Senegal
Niger
Gambia
FOUTA DJALLON
Joliba
Black Volta
White Volta
L. Chad
MARRA MTS.
Mt. Gimbala (3070)
WADAH
DARFUR
KORDOFAN
Mt. Ras Dashan (4620)
ETHIOPIAN PLATEAU
L. Assal -155m Lowest Point
Gulf of Aden
SOMALI PENINSULA
SOMALI PLATEAU
JOS PLATEAU
L. Volta
Benue
Shari
B. el Arab
White Nile
Blue Nile
Atbara
ADAMAWA HIGHLANDS
Mt. Camroon (4070)
UBANGI PLATEAU
Slave Coast
Gold Coast
Ivory Coast
Cape. Palmas
Bight of Benin
Malabo
Principe Island
Gulf of Guinea
Uele
L. Turkana
L. Kyoga
L. Albert
Mt. Elgon (4321)
CONGO BASIN
Mt. Ruwenzori (5120)
Boyoma (Stanley) Falls
Cape Lopez
Sao Tome
L. Mai-ndombe
L. Victoria
Mt. Kilimanjaro (5895)
LOWER GUINEA
Kasai
Sankuru
Lualaba
Mitumba Ra.
Rift Valley
CENTRAL TANGANYIKA PLATEAU
Pemba Island
Zanzibar Island
SOUTH ATLANTIC OCEAN
Lake Tanganyika
L. Mweru
Mt. Rungwe (2959)
Rufiji
Mafia Island
L. Nyasa (Malawi)
Cape Delgado
BIE PLATEAU
L. Bangweulu
AFRICAN PLATEAU
MUCHINGA ESC
Comoro Island
Cape. Amber
Mayotte
Cuando
Okavango
Zambezi
Cunene
L. Dam Kariba
Mozambique Coastal Plain
Mozambique Channel
HUAMBA LAND
Victoria Falls
MATOPO HILLS
(2643) Ankaratra
MADAGASCAR
NAMIB DESERT
L. Ngami
DAMARALAND
Walvis bay
Limpopo
KALAHARI DESERT
HIGH VELD
Maputo Bay
GREAT NAMAQUALAND
Orange
Vaal
Cape St. Marie.
KAAP PLATEAU
Mt. Aux Sources (3298)
DRAKENSBERG
INDIAN OCEAN
GREAT KARROO
Mt. Compass B. (2505)
St. Helena Bay
Cape of Good Hope
Cape Agulhas
REFERENCE
Height in Metres
Ice
4500
3000
1800
1350
900
600
300
150
(Sea level)
862 Peak
1000 0 1000 2000 km.

Projection: Lambert's Conical Orthomorphic

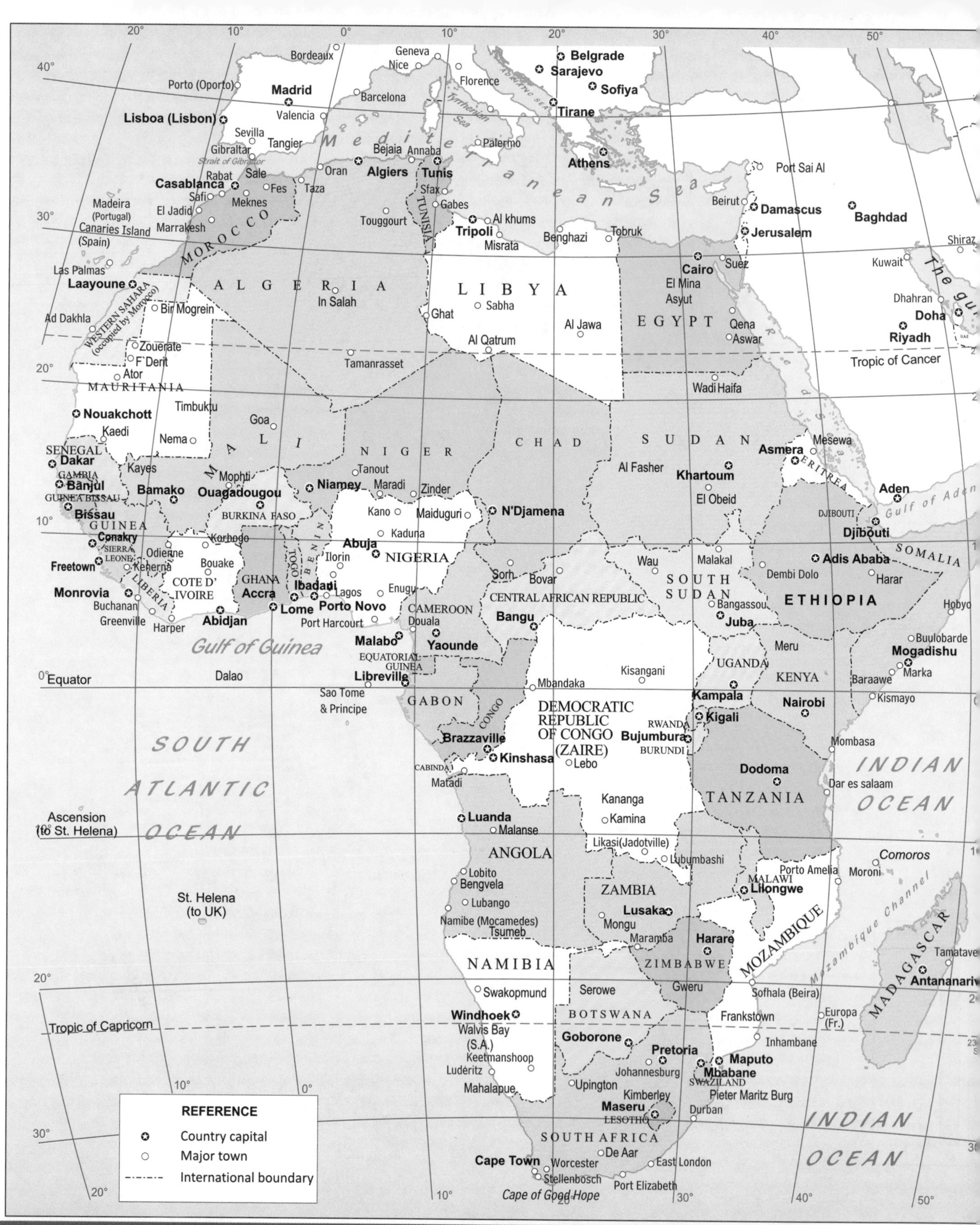

Bordeaux
Geneva
Nice
Florence
Belgrade
Sarajevo
Sofiya
Porto (Oporto)
Madrid
Barcelona
Tirane
Lisboa (Lisbon)
Valencia
Sevilla
Tangier
Gibraltar
Strait of Gibraltor
Mediterranean Sea
Tyrrhenian Sea
Adriatic Sea
Palermo
Bejaia
Annaba
Athens
Rabat
Sale
Oran
Algiers
Tunis
Port Sai Al
Casablanca
Fes
Taza
Sfax
Safi
Meknes
Gabes
Beirut
Damascus
Baghdad
Madeira (Portugal)
El Jadid
Touggourt
Al khums
Canaries Island (Spain)
Marrakesh
Tripoli
Misrata
Benghazi
Tobruk
Jerusalem
Shiraz
MOROCCO
TUNISIA
Las Palmas
Cairo
Suez
Kuwait
Laayoune
ALGERIA
LIBYA
El Mina
Asyut
Dhahran
Doha
In Salah
Sabha
Ad Dakhla
WESTERN SAHARA (occupied by Morocco)
Bir Mogrein
Ghat
Al Jawa
EGYPT
Qena
Aswar
Riyadh
Zouerate
Al Qatrum
F'Derit
Tamanrasset
Tropic of Cancer
Ator
MAURITANIA
Wadi Haifa
Timbuktu
Nouakchott
Goa
Kaedi
Mesewa
SENEGAL
Nema
MALI
NIGER
CHAD
SUDAN
Asmera
Dakar
ERITREA
Kayes
Mophti
Tanout
Al Fasher
Khartoum
GAMBIA
Banjul
Bamako
Ouagadougou
Niamey
Maradi
Zinder
El Obeid
Aden
GUINEA BISSAU
Bissau
BURKINA FASO
Kano
Maiduguri
N'Djamena
Gulf of Aden
DJIBOUTI
GUINEA
Conakry
Korhogo
BENIN
Kaduna
Djibouti
SIERRA LEONE
Odienne
Abuja
Wau
Malakal
Adis Ababa
SOMALIA
Freetown
Kenema
Bouake
TOGO
Ilorin
NIGERIA
Dembi Dolo
Harar
LIBERIA
COTE D' IVOIRE
GHANA
Accra
Ibadan
Lagos
Enugu
Sorh
Bovar
SOUTH SUDAN
Monrovia
CENTRAL AFRICAN REPUBLIC
ETHIOPIA
Hobyo
Buchanan
Lome
Porto Novo
CAMEROON
Bangassou
Greenville
Harper
Abidjan
Port Harcourt
Douala
Bangu
Juba
Gulf of Guinea
Malabo
Yaounde
Buulobarde
Meru
Mogadishu
EQUATORIAL GUINEA
UGANDA
Kisangani
Marka
Equator
Dalao
Libreville
Mbandaka
KENYA
Baraawe
Sao Tome & Principe
GABON
Kampala
Kismayo
CONGO
DEMOCRATIC REPUBLIC OF CONGO (ZAIRE)
Nairobi
Kigali
RWANDA
Bujumbura
BURUNDI
Brazzaville
SOUTH ATLANTIC OCEAN
Kinshasa
Lebo
Mombasa
CABINDA
Dodoma
INDIAN OCEAN
Matadi
Dar es salaam
Kananga
TANZANIA
Ascension (to St. Helena)
Luanda
Kamina
Malanse
Likasi(Jadotville)
ANGOLA
Lubumbashi
Comoros
Lobito
Porto Amelia
Moroni
Bengvela
MALAWI
St. Helena (to UK)
Lubango
ZAMBIA
Lilongwe
Mozambique Channel
Lusaka
Mongu
Namibe (Mocamedes)
Tsumeb
MOZAMBIQUE
Maramba
Harare
MADAGASCAR
Tamatave
NAMIBIA
ZIMBABWE
Antananarivo
Swakopmund
Serowe
Gweru
Sofhala (Beira)
Windhoek
BOTSWANA
Europa (Fr.)
Frankstown
Tropic of Capricorn
Walvis Bay (S.A.)
Goborone
Inhambane
Keetmanshoop
Pretoria
Maputo
Luderitz
Johannesburg
Mbabane
SWAZILAND
Mahalapue
Upington
Pieter Maritz Burg
Kimberley
Maseru
LESOTHO
Durban
REFERENCE
Country capital
Major town
International boundary
SOUTH AFRICA
De Aar
Cape Town
Worcester
East London
Stellenbosch
Port Elizabeth
Cape of Good Hope
20°
10°
0°
30°
40°
50°
1000 0 1000 2000 k

Projection: Lambert's Conical Orthomorphic

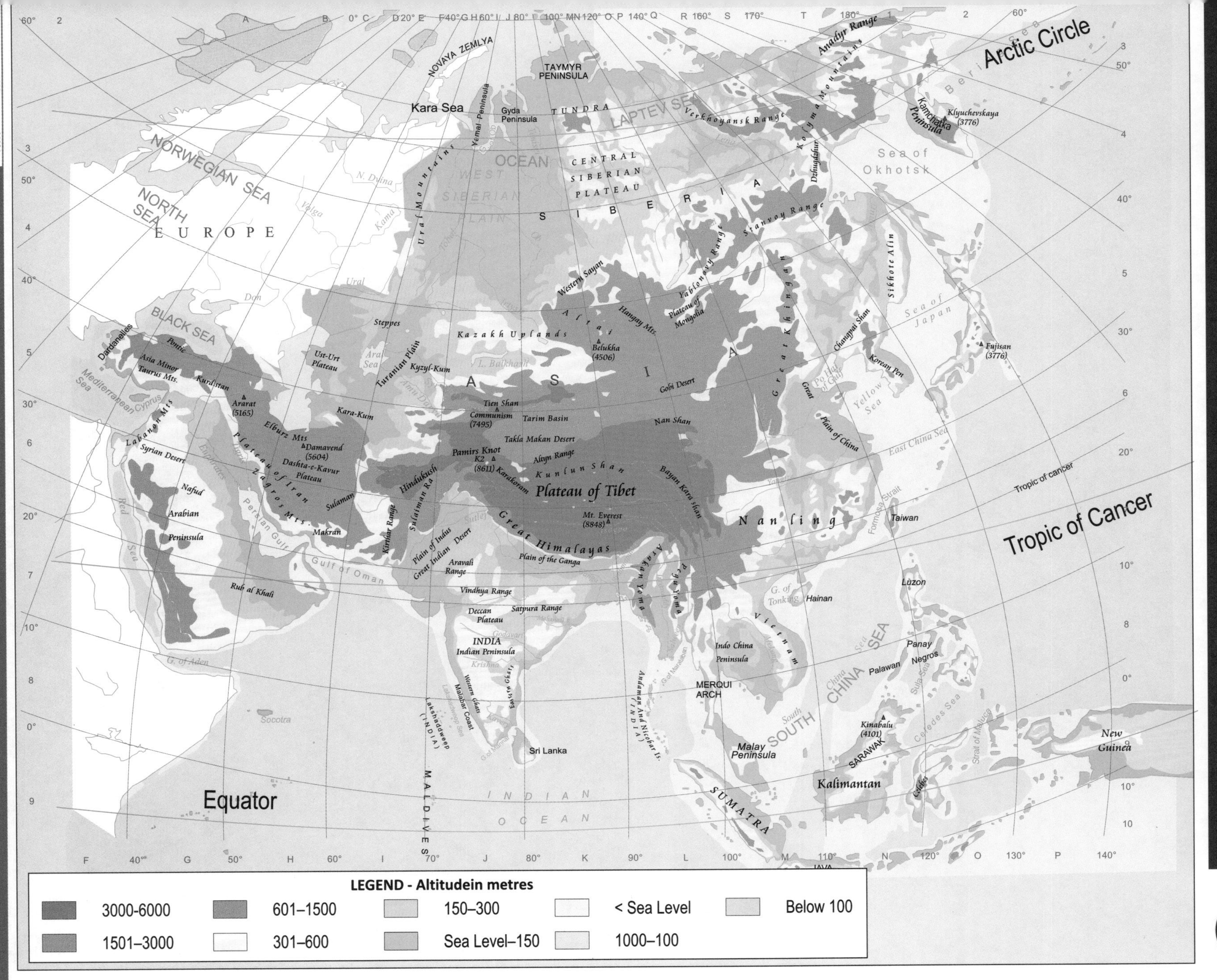
Arctic Circle
Tropic of Cancer
Tropic of cancer
Equator
Kamchatka Peninsula
Klyuchevskaya (3776)
Sea of Okhotsk
Sikhote Alin
Sea of Japan
Fujisan (3776)
Korean Pen
Yellow Sea
East China Sea
Taiwan
Luzon
Panay
Negros
Palawan
Sulu Sea
Celebes Sea
Strait of Moluca
Kinabalu (4101)
SARAWAK
Kalimantan
SOUTH CHINA SEA
Hainan
G. of Tonking
Vietnam
Indo China Peninsula
Malay Peninsula
SUMATRA
MERQUI ARCH
Andaman And Nicobar Is. (INDIA)
Pegu Yoma
Arakan Yoma
Plateau of Tibet
Mt. Everest (8848)
Great Himalayas
Plain of the Ganga
Kunlun Shan
Bayan Kara shan
Nan Shan
Nan ling
Great Khingan
Gobi Desert
Plateau of Mongolia
Yablonovy Range
Hangay Mts.
Belukha (4506)
Altai
Western Sayan
Tarim Basin
Takla Makan Desert
Altyn Range
Tien Shan
Communism (7495)
Pamirs Knot
K2 (8611) Karakoram
Hindukush
Sulaiman Ra
Kirthar Range
Plain of Indus
Great Indian Desert
Aravali Range
Vindhya Range
Satpura Range
Deccan Plateau
INDIA
Indian Peninsula
Eastern Ghats
Western Ghats
Malabar Coast
Sri Lanka
Lakshadweep (INDIA)
MALDIVES
INDIAN OCEAN
Kazakh Uplands
L. Balkhash
Turanian Plain
Kyzyl-Kum
Kara-Kum
Steppes
Ust-Urt Plateau
Aral Sea
Elburz Mts
Damavend (5604)
Dashta-e-Kavur Plateau
Plateau of Iran
Zagros Mts.
Sulaman
Makran
Gulf of Oman
Persian Gulf
Rub al Khali
Arabian Peninsula
Nafud
Syrian Desert
Lebanon Mts
Red Sea
G. of Aden
Socotra
Ararat (5165)
Kurdistan
Asia Minor
Taurus Mts.
Pontic
BLACK SEA
Mediterranean Sea
Dardanelles
Cyprus
EUROPE
NORTH SEA
NORWEGIAN SEA
Ural Mountains
Kara Sea
Yemal Peninsula
NOVAYA ZEMLYA
WEST SIBERIAN PLAIN
OCEAN
Gyda Peninsula
TAYMYR PENINSULA
TUNDRA
CENTRAL SIBERIAN PLATEAU
LAPTEV SEA
SIBERIA
ASIA
Verkhoyansk Range
Stanvoy Range
Kolyma Mountains
Anadyr Range
Dzhugdzhur
Changpai Shan
Great Plain of China
New Guinea
LEGEND - Altitudein metres
3000-6000
601–1500
150–300
< Sea Level
Below 100
1501–3000
301–600
Sea Level–150
1000–100

1000 0 1000 2000 km.

Projection: Lambert's Conical Orthomorphic

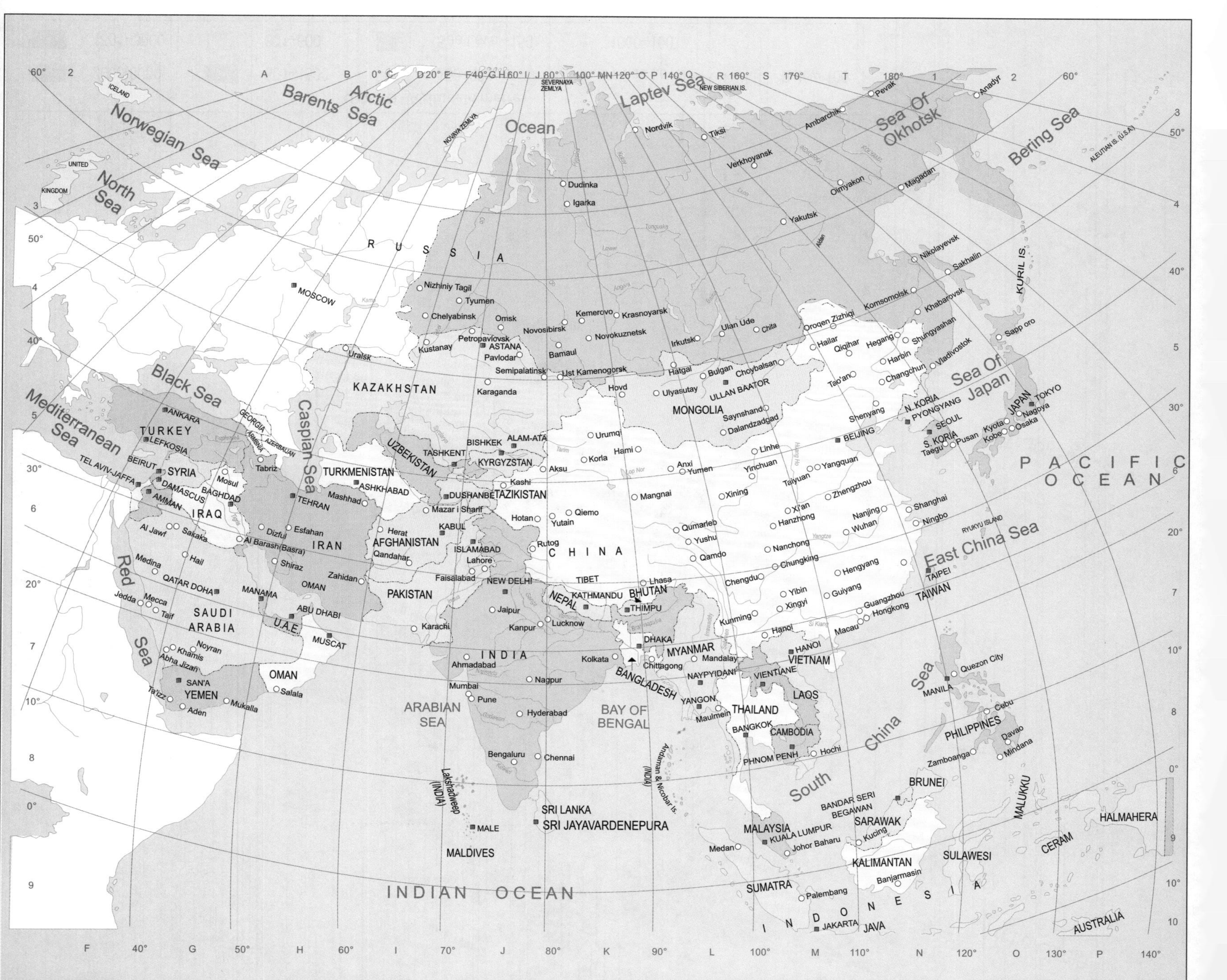
PACIFIC OCEAN
INDIAN OCEAN
Arctic Ocean
Barents Sea
Norwegian Sea
North Sea
Mediterranean Sea
Black Sea
Caspian Sea
Red Sea
ARABIAN SEA
BAY OF BENGAL
South China Sea
East China Sea
Sea Of Japan
Sea Of Okhotsk
Bering Sea
Laptev Sea
RUSSIA
CHINA
INDIA
KAZAKHSTAN
MONGOLIA
IRAN
AFGHANISTAN
PAKISTAN
SAUDI ARABIA
TURKEY
INDONESIA
THAILAND
MYANMAR
BANGLADESH
NEPAL
BHUTAN
SRI LANKA
MALDIVES
PHILIPPINES
JAPAN
VIETNAM
LAOS
CAMBODIA
MALAYSIA
UZBEKISTAN
TURKMENISTAN
KYRGYZSTAN
TAZIKISTAN
IRAQ
SYRIA
YEMEN
OMAN
AUSTRALIA
MOSCOW
BEIJING
NEW DELHI
TOKYO
DHAKA
KATHMANDU
THIMPU
TEHRAN
KABUL
ISLAMABAD
BANGKOK
HANOI
MANILA
JAKARTA

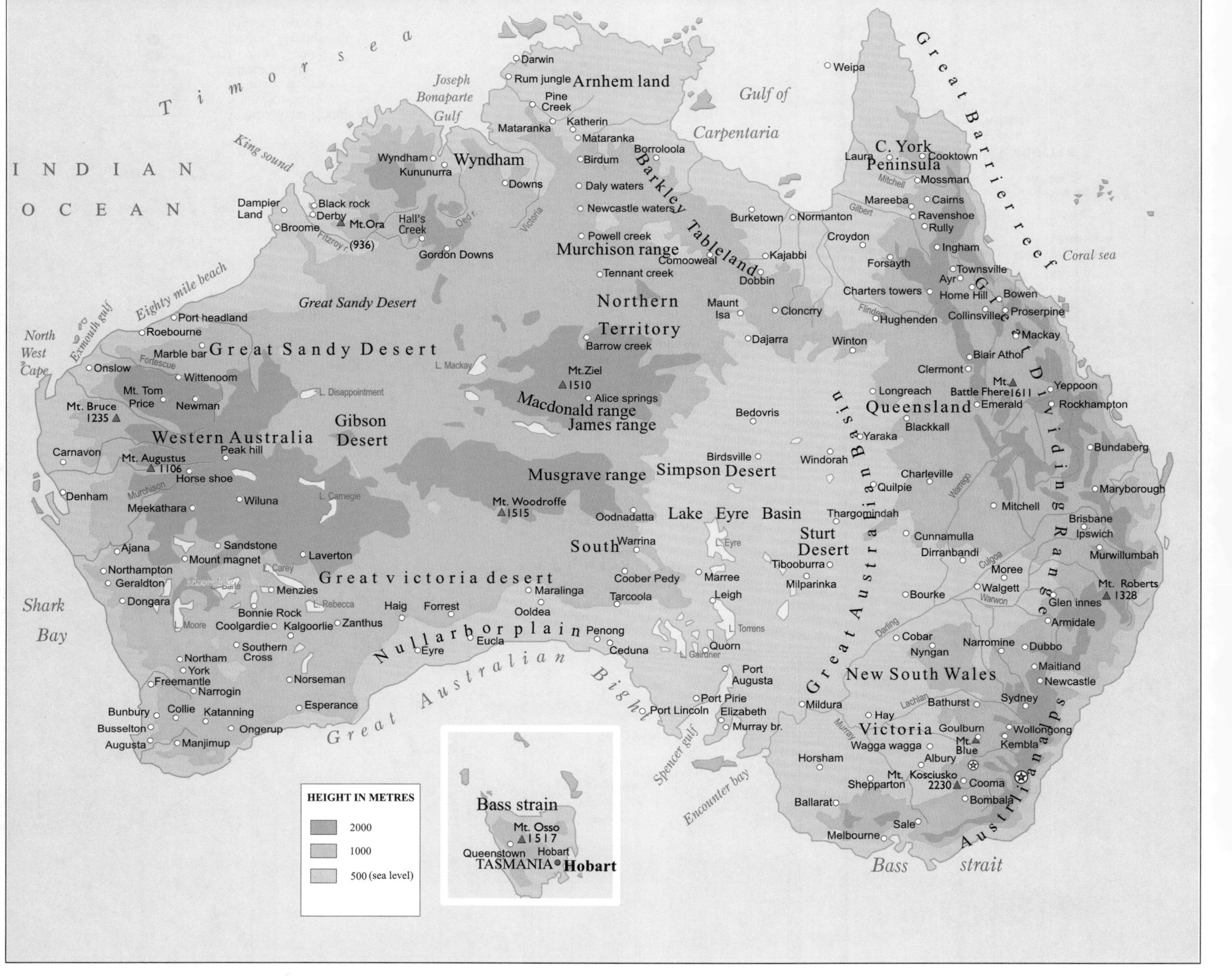

INDIAN OCEAN
Timor sea
Coral sea
Great Barrier reef
Gulf of Carpentaria
Joseph Bonaparte Gulf
King sound
Eighty mile beach
Exmouth gulf
North West Cape
Shark Bay
Great Australian Bight
Spencer gulf
Encounter bay
Bass strait
C. York Peninsula
Arnhem land
Barkley Tableland
Northern Territory
Queensland
New South Wales
Victoria
South Australia
Western Australia
Great Dividing Range
Great Australian Basin
Lake Eyre Basin
Simpson Desert
Sturt Desert
Great Sandy Desert
Gibson Desert
Great victoria desert
Nullarbor plain
Macdonald range
James range
Musgrave range
Murchison range
Australian Alps
Darwin
Rum jungle
Pine Creek
Katherin
Mataranka
Wyndham
Kununurra
Hall's Creek
Gordon Downs
Downs
Derby
Broome
Black rock
Mt.Ora (936)
Dampier Land
Port headland
Roebourne
Onslow
Marble bar
Wittenoom
Mt. Tom Price
Newman
Mt. Bruce 1235
Carnavon
Denham
Mt. Augustus 1106
Peak hill
Horse shoe
Meekathara
Wiluna
Ajana
Northampton
Geraldton
Dongara
Mount magnet
Sandstone
Laverton
Menzies
Bonnie Rock
Coolgardie
Kalgoorlie
Zanthus
Southern Cross
Northam
York
Narrogin
Freemantle
Katanning
Collie
Ongerup
Bunbury
Busselton
Augusta
Manjimup
Norseman
Esperance
Haig
Forrest
Eyre
Eucla
Ooldea
Maralinga
Penong
Ceduna
Tarcoola
Coober Pedy
Oodnadatta
Warrina
Mt. Woodroffe 1515
Mt.Ziel 1510
Alice springs
Barrow creek
Tennant creek
Powell creek
Newcastle waters
Daly waters
Birdum
Borroloola
Comooweal
Maunt Isa
Dobbin
Kajabbi
Burketown
Normanton
Cloncrry
Dajarra
Bedovris
Birdsville
Marree
Leigh
Quorn
Port Augusta
Port Pirie
Port Lincoln
Elizabeth
Murray br.
Mildura
Horsham
Ballarat
Melbourne
Sale
Shepparton
Wagga wagga
Albury
Hay
Goulburn
Mt. Blue
Mt. Kosciusko 2230
Cooma
Bombala
Wollongong
Kembla
Sydney
Newcastle
Maitland
Bathurst
Dubbo
Narromine
Nyngan
Cobar
Bourke
Cunnamulla
Dirranbandi
Moree
Walgett
Armidale
Glen innes
Mt. Roberts 1328
Murwillumbah
Brisbane
Ipswich
Maryborough
Bundaberg
Rockhampton
Yeppoon
Emerald
Mt. Battle Fhere 1611
Mackay
Proserpine
Bowen
Collinsville
Home Hill
Ayr
Townsville
Ingham
Cairns
Mossman
Cooktown
Laura
Mareeba
Ravenshoe
Rully
Forsayth
Croydon
Charters towers
Hughenden
Winton
Longreach
Blackkall
Clermont
Blair Athol
Yaraka
Charleville
Quilpie
Mitchell
Windorah
Thargomindah
Tiboobura
Milparinka
Weipa
Bass strain
Mt. Osso 1517
Queenstown
Hobart
TASMANIA
HEIGHT IN METRES
2000
1000
500 (sea level)
0 1000 2000 km.
Projection: Lambert's Conical Orthomorphic

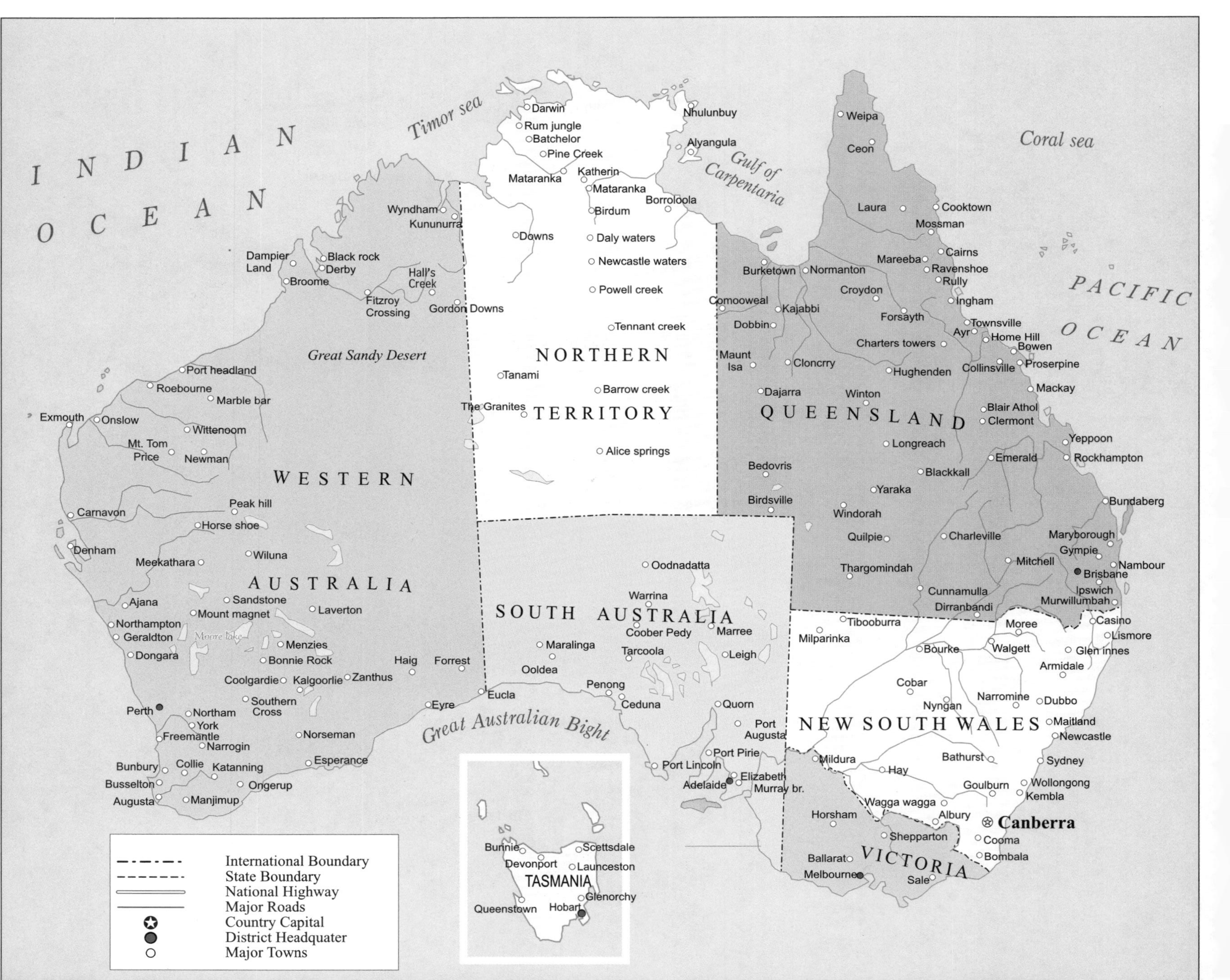

INDIAN OCEAN
Timor sea
Coral sea
PACIFIC OCEAN
Gulf of Carpentaria
Great Australian Bight
Great Sandy Desert
WESTERN AUSTRALIA
NORTHERN TERRITORY
QUEENSLAND
SOUTH AUSTRALIA
NEW SOUTH WALES
VICTORIA
TASMANIA
Canberra
Exmouth
Onslow
Roebourne
Port headland
Marble bar
Wittenoom
Newman
Mt. Tom Price
Carnavon
Denham
Meekathara
Peak hill
Horse shoe
Wiluna
Ajana
Northampton
Geraldton
Dongara
Mount magnet
Sandstone
Perth
Freemantle
Northam
York
Narrogin
Bunbury
Busselton
Augusta
Collie
Katanning
Manjimup
Ongerup
Southern Cross
Coolgardie
Kalgoorlie
Bonnie Rock
Menzies
Laverton
Zanthus
Norseman
Esperance
Haig
Forrest
Eyre
Dampier Land
Broome
Derby
Black rock
Fitzroy Crossing
Hall's Creek
Gordon Downs
Wyndham
Kununurra
Darwin
Rum jungle
Batchelor
Pine Creek
Katherin
Mataranka
Birdum
Downs
Daly waters
Newcastle waters
Powell creek
Tennant creek
Barrow creek
Alice springs
Tanami
The Granites
Borroloola
Nhulunbuy
Alyangula
Weipa
Ceon
Laura
Cooktown
Mossman
Cairns
Mareeba
Ravenshoe
Rully
Ingham
Townsville
Ayr
Home Hill
Bowen
Proserpine
Collinsville
Mackay
Normanton
Croydon
Forsayth
Charters towers
Hughenden
Blair Athol
Clermont
Yeppoon
Rockhampton
Emerald
Longreach
Blackkall
Winton
Cloncry
Kajabbi
Burketown
Comooweal
Dobbin
Maunt Isa
Dajarra
Bedovris
Birdsville
Windorah
Yaraka
Quilpie
Charleville
Thargomindah
Cunnamulla
Dirranbandi
Mitchell
Maryborough
Gympie
Bundaberg
Nambour
Brisbane
Ipswich
Murwillumbah
Casino
Lismore
Glen innes
Armidale
Moree
Walgett
Narromine
Dubbo
Maitland
Newcastle
Sydney
Wollongong
Kembla
Goulburn
Cooma
Bombala
Bathurst
Nyngan
Bourke
Cobar
Tibooburra
Milparinka
Mildura
Hay
Wagga wagga
Albury
Shepparton
Sale
Horsham
Ballarat
Melbourne
Murray br.
Elizabeth
Adelaide
Port Pirie
Port Augusta
Quorn
Leigh
Marree
Oodnadatta
Warrina
Coober Pedy
Tarcoola
Ceduna
Penong
Port Lincoln
Maralinga
Ooldea
Eucla
Scettsdale
Launceston
Glenorchy
Devonport
Burnie
Hobart
Queenstown
International Boundary
State Boundary
National Highway
Major Roads
Country Capital
District Headquater
Major Towns

Projection: Lambert's Conical Orthomorphic

1000 0 1000 2000

A

alborg	57° 2' N	9° 54' E
arhus	56° 8' N	10° 11' E
ba	5° 10' N	7° 19' E
badan	30° 22' N	48° 20' E
bakan	53° 40' N	91° 10' E
BC Islands	12° 15' N	69° 0' W
beokuta	7° 3' N	3° 27' W
berdare Range	0° 15' S	36° 50' E
berdeen	57° 9' N	2° 5' W
bergavenny	51° 49' N	3° 1' W
berystwyth	52° 25' N	4° 5' W
bidjan	5° 26' N	3° 58' W
bu Dhabi	24° 28' N	54° 22' E
buja	9° 5' N	7° 32' E
capulco	16° 51' N	99° 55' W
ccra	5° 35' N	0° 6' W
ccrington	53° 45' N	2° 22' W
chill Island	53° 58' N	10° 1' W
concagua	32° 39' S	70° 0' W
cre	9° 1' S	71° 0' W
d Dammam	26° 20' N	50° 5' E
damawa Highlands	7° 20' N	12° 20' E
dana	3° 0' N	35° 16' E
dare, Cape	71° 0' S	171° 0' E
ddis Ababa	9° 2' N	38° 42' E
delaide	34° 52' S	138° 30' E
delaide Island	67° 15' S	68° 30' W
delie Land	68° 0' S	140° 0' E
den	12° 45' N	45° 0' E
den, Gulf of	12° 30' N	47° 30' E
driatic Sea	43° 0' N	16° 0' E
gean Sea	38° 30' N	14° 57' E
eolian Islands	38° 30' N	14° 57' E
fghanistan	33° 0' N	65° 0' N
frica	10° 0' N	20° 0' E
gra	27° 17' N	77° 58' E
guascalientes	21° 53' N	102° 18' W
hmadabad	23° 0' N	72° 40' E
hvaz	31° 20' N	48° 40' E
ilsa Craig	55° 15' N	5° 6' W
ir	18° 30' N	8° 0' E
irdrie	55° 52' N	3° 57' W
ire	53° 43' N	0° 55' W
ix-en-Provence	43° 32' N	5° 27' E
jaccio	41° 55' N	8° 40' E
kita	39° 45' N	140° 7' E
kosombo Dam	6° 20' N	0° 5' E
kron	41° 5' N	81° 31' W
ksu	41° 5' N	80° 10' E
l Ayn	24° 15' N	55° 45' E
l Aziziyah	32° 30' N	13° 1' E
l Hillah	32° 30' N	13° 1' E
l Hufuf	25° 25' N	49° 45' E
l Jubayl	27° 0' N	49° 50' E
l Kut	32° 30' N	46° 0' E
l Mubarraz	25° 30' N	49° 40' E
labama	33° 0' N	87° 0' W
labama	31° 8' N	87° 57' W
lagoas	9° 0' S	36° 0' W
land Islands	60° 15' N	20° 0' W
laska	64° 0' N	154° 0' W
laska, Gulf of	58° 0' N	145° 0' W
laska Peninsula	56° 0' N	159° 0' W
laska Range	62° 50' N	151° 0' W
Albacete	39° 0' N	1° 50' W
Albania	41° 0' N	20° 0' E
Albany, Australia	35° 1' S	117° 58' E
Albany, U.S.A.	42° 39' N	73° 45' W
Albuquerque	35° 5' N	106° 39' W
Aldabra Islands	9° 22' S	46° 2' E
Aldeburgh	52° 10' N	1° 37' E
Alderney	49° 42' N	2° 11' W
Aleppo	36° 10' N	37° 15' E
Alesund	62° 28' N	6° 12' E
Aleutian Islands	52° 0' N	175° 0' W
Alexander Island	69° 0' S	70° 0' W
Alexandria	31° 13' N	29° 58' E
Algarve	36° 58' N	8° 20' W
Algeria	28° 30' N	2° 0' E
Algiers	36° 42' N	3° 8' E
Alicante	38° 23' N	0° 30' W
Alice Springs	23° 40'	133° 50' E
Allahabad (now Prayagraj)	25° 25' N	81° 58'
Allegheny Mountains	38 o 15' N	80° 10' W
Allen, Bog of	53° 15' N	7° 0' W
Allen, Lough	54° 8' N	8° 4' W
Alloa	56° 7' N	3° 47' W

Alma Ata	43° 15' N	76° 57' E
Almeria	36° 52' N	2° 27' W
Alness	57° 41' N	4° 16' W
Alnwick	55° 24' N	1° 42' W
Alps	46° 30' N	9° 30' E
Altai	46° 40' N	92° 45' E
Altai Altay	47° 48' N	88° 10' E
Altay...Altan Shan	38° 30' N	88° 0' E
Altun Shan Amapa	1° 40' N	52° 0' W
Amarillo...Amarillo	34° 13' N	101° 50' W
Amazonas Amazon	0° 5' S	50° 0' W
Ambon...Amazonas	5° 0' S	65° 0' W
American Ambon	3° 43' S	128° 12' E
American Highlands	73° 0' S	75° 0' E
Amery Ic American Samoa	14° 20' S	170° 0' W
Amery Ice Shelf	69° 30' S	72° 0' E
Amlwch...Amiens	49° 54' N	2° 16' E
Amman...Amalwch	53° 24' N	4° 20' W
Amritsar...Amman	31° 57' N	35° 52' E
Amsterda Amritsar	31° 35' N	74° 57' E
Amudarya Amsterdam	52° 23' N	4° 54' E
Amundsen Amudarya	43° 58' N	59° 34' E
An Najaf... Amundsen Sea	72° 0' S	115° 0' W
An Nasiriya Au Amur	52° 56' N	141° 10' E
Anapolis...An Najaf	32° 3' N	44° 15' E
Anatolia...An Nasiriyah	31° 0' N	46° 15' E
Anchorag Anapolis	16° 15' S	48° 50' W
Ancona...Anatolia	39° 0' N	30° 0' E
Andalucia...Anchorage	61° 13' N	149° 54' W
Andaman lAncona	43° 38' N	13° 30' E
Andaman Andalucia	37° 35' N	5° 0' W
Andaman Islands	12° 30' N	92° 45' E
Andizhan... Andaman Sea	13° 0' N	96° 0' E
Andorra...Andes	10° 0' S	75° 53' W
Andover...Andizhan	41° 10' N72° 15' E	
Aneto, Pic Andorra	42° 30' N	1° 30' E
Angara...Andover	51° 12' N	1° 29' W
Anglesey...Aneto, Pico de	42° 37' N	0° 40' E
Angola...Angara	58° 5' N	94° 20' E
Angoulem Angel Falls	5° 57' N	62° 30' W
Angus...Angers	47° 30' N	0° 35' W
Ankara...Anglesey	53° 17' N	4° 20' W
Annaba...Angola	12° 0' S	18° 0' E
Annan...Angouleme	45° 39' N	0° 10' E
Annan...Angus	56° 46' N	2° 56' W
Annapolis...Ankara	39° 57' N	32° 54' E
Ankara...Annaba	36° 50' N	7° 46' E
Annan	54° 58' N	3° 16' W
Annapolis	38° 59' N	76° 30' W
Annobon	1° 25' S	5° 36' E
Anshan	41° 5' N	122° 58' E
Antalya	36° 52' N	30° 45' E
Antananarivo	18° 55' S	47° 31' E
Antarctic Peninsula	67° 0' S	60° 0' W
Antarctica	90° 0' S	0° 0' W
Antigua & Barbuda	17° 20' N	61° 48' W
Antofagasta	23° 50' S	70° 30' W
Antrim	54° 43' N	6° 14' W
Antrim, Mountains of	55° 3' N	6° 14' W
Antwerp	51° 13' N	4° 25' E
Anvers Island	64° 30' S	63° 40' W
Aomori	40° 45' N	140° 45' E
Aoraki Mount Cook	43° 36' S	170° 9' E
Apennines	44° 30' N	10° 0' E
Apia	13° 50' S	171° 50' W
Appalachian Mountains	38° 0' N	80° 0' W
Appleby-in-Westmorland	54° 35' N	2° 29' W
Aqaba	29° 31' N	35° 0' E
Arabia	25° 0' N	45° 0' E
Arabian Sea	16° 0' N	65° 0' E
Aracaju	10° 55' S	37° 4' W
Aracatuba	21° 10' S	50° 30' W
Araguaia	5° 21' S	48° 41' W
Arak	34° 0' N	49° 40' E
Araks	40° 5' N	48° 29' E
Aral Sea	45° 0' N	58° 20' E
Aran Islands	53° 6' N	9° 38' W
Ararat, Mount	39° 50' N	44° 15' E
Arbroath	56° 34' N	2° 35' W
Arctic Ocean	78° 0' N	160° 0' W
Ardabil	38° 15' N	48° 18' E
Ardnamurchan, Point of	56° 43' N	6° 14' W
Ardrossan	55° 39' N	4° 49' W

Ards Peninsula	54° 33' N	5° 34' W
Arequipa	16° 20' S	71° 30' W
Argentina	35° 0' S	66° 0' W
Argun	53° 20' N	121° 28' E
Argyle, Lake	16° 20' S	128° 40' E
Argyll	56° 10' N	5° 20' W
Argyll & Bute	56° 13' N	5° 28' W
Arica	18° 32' S	70° 20' W
Aripuana	5° 7' S	60° 25' W
Arizona	34° 0' N	112° 0' W
Arkaig, Loch	56° 59' N	5° 10' W
Arkansas	35° 0' N	92° 30' W
Arkansas	33° 47' N	91° 4' W
Arkhangelsk	64° 38' N	40° 36' E
Arklow	52° 48' N	6° 10' W
Armagh	54° 21' N	6° 39' W
Armenia	40° 20' N	45° 0' E
Arnhem	51° 58' N	5° 55' E
Armenia	13° 10' S	134° 30' E
Arnhem	51° 58' N	5° 55' E
Arnhem Land	13° 10' S	134° 30' E
Arran	55° 34' N	5° 12' W
Arranmore	55° 0' N	8° 30' W
Aru Islands	6° 0' S	134° 30' E
Aruba	12° 30' N	70° 0' W
Arusha	3° 20' S	36° 40' E
Arvayheer	46° 15' N	102° 48' E
As Sulaymaniyah, Iraq	35° 35' N	45° 29' E
As Sulaymaniyah, Saudi Arabia	24° 9' N	47° 18' E
Asahikawa	43° 46' N	142° 22' E
Asamankese	5° 50' N	0° 40' W
Ascension Island	7° 57' S	14° 23' W
Ashford	51° 8' N	0° 53' E
Ashington	55° 11' N	1° 33' W
Ashford	37° 58' N	58° 24' E
Ashington	53° 29' N	2° 6' W
Ashkhabad	15° 19' N	38° 55' E
Ashton under Lyne	26° 0' N	93° 0' E
Assam	26° 0' N	93° 0' E
Astana	51° 10' N	71° 30' E
Astrakhan	46° 25' N	48° 5' E
Asuncion	25° 10' S	57° 30' W
Aswan	24° 4' N	32° 57' E
Asyut	27° 11' N	31° 4' E
At Ta' if	21° 5' N	40° 27' E
Atacama Desert	24° 0' S	69° 20' W
Athens	37° 58' N	23° 43' E
Athlone	53° 25' N	7° 56' W
Athy	53° 0' N	7° 0' W
Atlanta	33° 45' N	84° 23' W
Atlantic Ocean	0 0' N	20° 0' W
Atlas Mountains	32° 30' N	5° 0' W
Auckland	36° 52' S	174° 46' E
Augsburg	48° 25' N	10° 52' E
Augusta	44° 19' N	69° 47' W
Austin	30° 17' N	97° 45' W
Australia	23° 0' S	135° 0' E
Australian Capital Territory (A.C.T.)	35° 30' S	149° 0' E
Austria	47° 0' N	14° 0' E
Aviemore	57° 12' N	3° 50' W
Avignon	43° 57' N	4° 50' E
Avon Bristol	51° 29' N	2° 41' W
Avon Dorset	50° 44' N	1° 46' W
Avon Warwickshire	52° 0' N	2° 8' W
Awe, Loch	56° 17' N	5° 16' W
Ayers Rock = Uluru	25° 23' S	131° 5' E
Aylesbury	51° 49' N	0° 49' W
Ayr	55° 28' N	4° 38' W
Azerbaijan	40° 2' ' N	48° 0' E
Azores	38° 0' N	27° 0' W
Azov, Sea of	46° 0' N	36° 30' E

B

Babol	36° 40' N	52° 50' E
Babylon	32° 34' N	44° 22' E
Bacabal	4° 15' S	44° 45' W
Bacau	46° 35' N	26° 55' E
Badajoz	72° 0' N	64° 0' W
Baghdad	33° 20' N	44° 23' E
Bahamas	24° 0' N	75° 0' W
Bahia	12° 0' S	42° 0' W
Bahia Blanca	38° 35' S	62° 13' W
Bahrain	26° 0' N	50° 35' E
Baikal, Lake	53° 0' N	108° 0' E
Baja California	31° 10' N	115° 12' W
Bakersfield	35° 23' N	119° 1' W
Baku	40° 29' N	49° 56' E

Balbriggan	53° 37' N	6° 11' W
Balearic Islands	39° 30' N	3° 0' E
Bali	8° 20' S	115° 0' E
Balikesir	39° 39' N	27° 53' E
Balkan Mountains	43° 15' N	23° 0' E
Balkhash, Lake	46° 0' N	74° 50' E
Ballachulish	56° 41' N	5° 8' W
Ballarat	37° 33' S	143° 50' E
Ballater	57° 3' N	3° 3' W
Ballina	54° 7' N	9° 9' W
Ballinasloe	53° 20' N	8° 13' W
Ballymoney	55° 5' N	6° 23' W
Balmoral	57° 3' N	3° 13' W
Balsas	17° 55' N	102° 10' W
Baltic Sea	57° 0' N	19° 0' E
Baltimore	39° 17' N	76° 36' W
Bam	29° 7' N	58° 14' E
Bamako	12° 34' N	7° 55' W
Banbridge	54° 21' N	6° 16' W
Banbury	52° 4' N	1° 20' W
Banda Aceh	5° 35' N	95° 20' E
Banda Sea	6° 0' S	130° 0' E
Bandar-e Abbas	27° 15' N	56° 15' E
Bandar Seri Begawan	4° 52' N	115° 0' E
Bandeira, Pico da	20° 26' S	41° 47' W
Bandon	51° 44' N	8° 44' W
Bandung . Banff	57° 40' N	2° 33' W
Bangalore	12° 59' N	77° 40' E
Bangka	2° 0' S	105° 50' E
Bangkok	13° 45' N	100° 35' E
Bangladesh	24° 0' N	90° 0' E
Bangor, Northern Ireland	54° 40' N	5° 40' W
Bangor, Wales	53° 14' N	4° 8' W
Bangul	4° 23' N	18° 35' E
Banjarmasin	3° 20' S	114° 35' E
Banjul	13° 28' N	16° 40' W
Bann	54° 30' N	6° 31' W
Bantry	51° 41' N	9° 27' W
Bantry Bay	51° 37' N	9° 44' W
Baoding	38° 50' N	115° 28' E
Baotou	40° 32' N	110° 2' E
Barbados	13° 10' N	59° 30' W
Barcelona, Spain	41° 22' N	2° 10' E
Barcelona, Venezuela	10° 10' N	64° 40' W
Bardsey Island	52° 45' N	4° 47' W
Barents Sea	73° 0' N	39° 0' E
Bari	41° 8' N	16° 51' E
Barkly Tableland	17° 50' S	136° 40' E
Barnsley	53° 34' N	1° 27' W
Barnstaple	51° 5' N	4° 4' W
Barquisimeto	10° 4' N	69° 19' W
Barra	57° 0' N	7° 29' W
Barra Head	56° 47' N	7° 40' W
Barranquilla	11° 0' N	74° 50' W
Barrow	52° 25' N	6° 58' W
Barrow-in-Furness	54° 7' N	3° 14' W
Barry	51° 24' N3° 16' W	
Basel	47° 35' N	7° 35' E
Basildon	51° 34' N	0° 28' E
Basingstoke	51° 15' N	1° 5' W
Basque Country	43° 15' N	1° 20' W
Basra	30° 30' N	47° 50' E
Bass Strait	39° 15' S	146° 30' E
Basseterre	17° 17' N	62° 43' W
Bataques	32° 33' N	115° 4' W
Bath	51° 23' N	2° 22' W
Baton Rouge	30° 27' N	91° 11' W
Batumi	41° 39' N	41° 44' E
Bauchi	10° 22' N	9° 48' E
Bauru	22° 10' S	49° 0' W
Bavaria	48° 50' N	12° 0' E
Bayonne	43° 30' N	1° 28' W
Beachy Head	50° 44' N	0° 15' E
Bear Island, Arctic	74° 30' N	19° 0' E
Bear Island, Ireland	51° 38' N	9° 50' W
Beardmore Glacier	84° 30' S	170° 0' E
Beaufort Sea	72° 0' N	140° 0' W
Beauly	57° 29' N	4° 27' W
Bebington	53° 22' N	3° 0' W
Bedford	52° 8' N	0° 28' W
Beijing	39° 53' N	116° 21' E
Beira	19° 50' S	34° 52' E
Beirut	33° 53' N	35° 31' E
Bejala	36° 42' N	5° 2' E
Belarus	53° 30' N	27° 0' E
Belem	1° 20' S	48° 30' W
Belfast	54° 37' N	5° 56' W

Belfast Lough	54° 40' N	5° 50' W
Belgium	50° 30' N	5° 0' E
Belgrade	44° 50' N	20° 37' E
Belize	17° 0' N	88° 30' W
Belize City	17° 25' N	88° 30' W
Bellingshausen Sea	66° 0' S	80° 0' W
Belmopan	17° 18' N	88° 30' W
Belo Horizonte	19° 55' S	43° 56' W
Belomorsk	64° 35' N	34° 54' E
Ben Cruachan	56° 26' N	5° 8' W
Ben Lawers	56° 32' N	4° 14' W
Ben Macdhui	57° 4' N	3° 40' W
Ben Nevis	56° 48' N	5° 1' W
Benbecula	57° 26' N	7° 21' W
Bendigo	36° 40' S	144° 15' E
Bengal, Bay of	15° 0' N	90° 0' N
Benghazi	32° 11' N	20° 3' E
Benin	10° 0' N	2° 0' E
Benin, Bight of	5° 0' N	3° 0' E
Benue	7° 48' N	6° 46' E
Berezniki	59° 24' N	56° 46' E
Bergen	60° 20' N	5° 20' E
Bering Sea	58° 0' N	171° 0' W
Bering Strait	65° 30' N	169° 0' W
Berkner Island	79° 30' S	50° 0' W
Berlin	52° 31' N	13° 23' E
Bermuda	32° 18' N	64° 45' W
Berne	46° 57' N	7° 28' E
Berwick-upon-Tweed	55° 46' N	2° 0' W
Besancon	47° 15' N	6° 2' E
Beverley	53° 51' N	0° 26' W
Bexhill	50° 51' N	0° 29' E
Bhutan	27° 25' N	90° 30' E
Bialystok	53° 10' N	23° 10' E
Bideford	51° 1' N	4° 13' W
Bie Plateau	12° 0' S	16° 0' E
Bielefeld	52° 1' N	4° 13' W
Bighorn Mountains	44° 25' N	107° 0' W
Bilbao	43° 16' N	2° 56' W
Billingham	54° 36' N	1° 17' W
Bioko	3° 30' N	8° 40' E
Birkenhead	53° 23' N	3° 2' W
Birmingham, U.K.	52° 29' N	1° 52' W
Birmingham, U.S.A.	33° 31' N	86° 48' W
Biscay, Bay of	45° 0' N	2° 0' W
Bishkek	42° 54' N	74° 46' E
Bishop, Auckland	54° 39' E	1° 40' W
Bishop's Storford	51° 52' N	0° 10' E
Bismarck	46° 48' N	100° 47' W
Bismarck Archipelago	2° 30' S	150° 0' E
Bissau	11° 45' N	15° 45' W
Bizerte	37° 15' N	9° 50' E
Black Hills	44° 0' N	103° 45' W
Black Sea	43° 30' N	35° 0' E
Black Volta	8° 41' N	1° 33' W
Blackburn	53° 45' N	2° 29' W
Blackpool	53° 49' N	3° 3' W
Blackwater	52° 4' N	7° 52' W
Blaenau Ffestiniog	53° 0' N	3° 56' W
Blaenau Gwent	51° 48' N	3° 12' W
Blair Atholl	56° 46' N	3° 50' W
Blairgowrie	56° 35' N	3° 21' W
Blanc, Mont	45° 48' N	6° 50' E
Blarney	51° 56' N	8° 33' W
Blida	36° 30' N	2° 49' E
Bloemfontein	29° 6' S	26° 7' E
Bloody Foreland	55° 10' N	8° 17' W
Blue Nile	15° 38' N	32° 31' E
Blue Ridge	36° 40' N	80° 50' W
Blyth	55° 8' N	1° 31' W
Bo Hai	39° 0' N	119° 0' E
Boa Vista	2° 48' N	60° 30' W
Bodmin	50° 28' N	4° 43' W
Bodmin Moor	50° 33' N	4° 36' W
Bodo	67° 17' N	14° 24' E
Boggeragh Mountains	52° 2' N	8° 55' W
Bognor Regis	50° 47' N	0° 40' W
Bogota	4° 34' N	74° 0' W
Bole	44° 55' N	81° 37' E
Bolgatanga	10° 44' N	0° 53' W
Bolivia	17° 6' S	64° 0' W
Bologna	44° 29' N	11° 20' E
Bolton	53° 35' N	2° 26' W
Bolzano	46° 31' N	11° 22' E
Bombay=Mumbai	18° 56' N	72° 50' E
Bonifacio, Strait of	41° 12' N	9° 15' E
Bonn	0° 46' N	7° 6' E
Bordeaux	44° 50' N	0° 36' W
Borneo	1° 0' N	115° 0' E
Bornholm	55° 10' N	15° 0' E

Bosnia-Herzegovina	44° 0' N	18° 0' E
Bosporus	41° 5' N	29° 3' E
Bosten Hu	41° 55' N	87° 40' E
Boston, U.K.	52° 59' N	0° 2' W
Boston, U.S.A.	42° 22' N	71° 3' W
Bothnia, Gulf of	62° 0' N	20° 0' E
Botswana	22° 0' S	24° 0' E
Bougainville Island	6° 0' S	155° 0' E
Boulogne	50° 42' N	1° 36' E
Bourges	47° 9' N	2° 25' E
Bournemouth	50° 43' N	1° 52' W
Bowmore	55° 45' N	6° 17' W
Boyne	53° 43' N	6° 15' W
Bracknell Forest	51° 25' N	0° 44' W
Bradford	53° 47' N	1° 45' W
Braganca	1° 0' S	47° 2' W
Brahmaputra	23° 40' N	90° 35' E
Braintree	51° 53' N	0° 34' E
Branco	1° 20' S	61° 50' W
Brandon Mountain	52° 15' N	10° 15' W
Brasilia	15° 47' N	10° 15' W
Brasov	45° 38' N	25° 35' E
Bratislava	48° 10' N	17° 7' E
Bratsk Reservoir	56° 15' N	101° 45' E
Bray	53° 13' N	6° 7' W
Brazil	12° 0' S	50° 0' W
Brazos	28° 53' N	95° 23' W
Brazzaville	4° 9' S	15° 12' E
Brechin	56° 44' N	2° 39' W
Brecon	51° 57' N	3° 23' W
Beacons	51° 53' N	3° 26' W
Bremen	53° 4' N	8° 47' E
Brentwood	51° 37' N	0° 19' E
Bressay	60° 9' N	1° 6' W
Brest, Belarus	52° 10' N	23° 40' E
Brest, France	48° 24' N	4° 31' W
Bridgend	51° 36' N	3° 36' W
Bridgetown	13° 6' N	59° 37' W
Bridgwater	51° 8' N	2° 59' W
Bridgwater Bay	51° 15' N	3° 15' W
Bridlington	54° 5' N	0° 12' W
Brigg	53° 34' N	0° 28' W
Brighton	50° 49' N	0° 7' W
Brindisi	40° 39' N	17° 55' E
Brisbane	27° 25' S	153° 2' E
Bristol	51° 26' N	2° 35' W
Bristol Channel	51° 18' N	4° 30' W
British Isles	54° 0' N	4° 0' W
Brittany	48° 10' N	3° 0' W
Brno	49° 10' N	16° 35' E
Broad Law	55° 30' N	3° 21' W
Broken Hill	31° 58' S	141° 29' E
Brooks Range	68° 0' N	152° 0' W
Broome	18° 0' S	122° 15' E
Brown Willy	50° 35' N	4° 37' W
Brunel	4° 50' N	115° 0' E
Brunswick	52° 15' N	10° 31' E
Brunt Ice Shelf	75° 30' S	25° 0' W
Brussels	50° 51' N	4° 21' E
Bryansk	53° 13' N	34° 25' E
Bucaramanga	7° 0' N	73° 0' W
Buchan Ness	57° 29' N	1° 46' W
Buckie	57° 41' N	2° 58' W
Buckinghamshire	51° 53' N	0° 55' W
Bucuresti	44° 27' N	26° 10' E
Budapest	47° 29' N	19° 13' E
Bude	50° 49' N	4° 34' W
Buenaventura	3° 53' N	77° 4' W
Buenos Aires	34° 36' S	58° 22' W
Buffalo	42° 53' N	78° 53' W
Bug	46° 59' N	31° 58' E
Builth Wells	52° 9' N	3° 25' W
Bujumbura	3° 16' S	29° 18' E
Bulawayo	20° 7' S	28° 32' E
Bulgaria	42° 35' N	25° 30' E
Bunbury	33° 20' S	115° 35' E
Buncrana	55° 8' N	7° 27' W
Bundaberg	24° 54' S	152° 52' E
Bundoran	54° 28' N	8° 18' W
Buraydah	26° 20' N	43° 59' E
Bure	52° 38' N	1° 43' E
Burgas	42° 33' N	27° 29' E
Burgos	42° 21' N	3° 41' W
Burgundy	47° 0' N	4° 50' E
Burkina Faso	12° 0' N	1° 0' W
Burma	21° 0' N	96° 30' E
Bursa	40° 15' N	29° 5' E
Burton upon Trent	52° 48' N	1° 38' W
Buru	3° 30' S	126° 30' E
Burundi	3° 15' S	30° 0' E

Bury	53° 35' N	2° 17' W
Bury Saint Edmunds	52° 15' N	0° 43' E
Busan	35° 5' N	129° 0' E
Bushehr	28° 55' N	50° 55' E
Bute	55° 48' N	5° 2' W
Buxton	53° 16' N	1° 54' W
Bydgoszcz	53° 10' N	18° 0' E
C		
Cabinda	5° 0' S	12° 30' E
Caceres	39° 26' N	6° 23' W
Cader Idris	52° 42' N	3° 53' W
Cadiz	36° 30' N	6° 20' W
Caen	49° 10' N	0° 22' W
Caernarfon	53° 8' N	4 o16' W
Caerphilly	51° 35' N	3° 13' W
Cagliari	39° 13' N	9° 7' E
Caha Mountains	51° 45' N	9° 40' W
Cahir	52° 22' N	7° 56' W
Cahirciveen	51° 56' N	10° 14' W
Cairn Gorm	57° 7' N	3° 39' W
Cairns	16° 57' S	145° 45' E
Cairo	30° 2' N	31° 13' E
Caithness	58° 25' N	3° 35' W
Calabar	4° 57' N	8° 20' E
Calabria	39° 0' N	16° 30' E
Calais	50° 57' N	1° 56' E
Calcutta=Kolkata	22° 34' N	88° 21' E
Calder	53° 44' N	1° 22' W
Caledonian	57° 29' N	4° 15' W
Canal	51° 0' N	114° 10' W
Calgary	3° 25' N	76° 25' W
California	37° 30' N	119° 30' W
California, Gulf of	27° 0' N	111° 0' W
Callander	56° 15' N	4° 13' W
Cam	52° 21' N	0° 16' E
Camaguey	21° 20' N	77° 55' W
Cambodia	12° 15' N	105° 0' E
Camborne	50° 12' N	5° 19' W
Cambrian Mountains	52° 3' N	3° 57' W
Cambridge	52° 12' N	0° 8' E
Cambridgeshire	52° 25' N	0° 7' W
Cameroon	6° 0' N	12° 30' E
Cameroun, Mount	4° 13' N	9° 10' E
Campbeltown	55° 26' N	5° 36' W
Campeche	19° 51' N	90° 32' W
Campeche, Gulf of	19° 30' N	93° 0' W
Campina Grande	7° 20' S	35° 47' W
Campinas	22° 50' S	47° 0' W
Campo Grande	20° 25' S	54° 40' W
Campos	21° 50' S	41° 20' W
Canada	60° 0' N	100° 0' W
Canadian Shield	53° 0' N	75° 0' W
Canary Islands	28° 30' N	16° 0' W
Canaveral, Cape	35° 15' S	149° 8' E
Canberra	21° 8' N	86° 44' W
Cancun	52° 41' N	2° 1' W
Cannock	43° 0' N	5° 10' W
Cantabrian Mountains	51° 16' N	1° 6' E
Canton= Guangzhou	23° 6' N	113° 13' E
Cape Coast	5° 5' N	1° 15' W
Cape Town	33° 55' S	18° 22' E
Cape Verde Islands	16° 0' N	24° 0' W
Cape York Penins.	12° 0' S	142° 30' E
Capri Caracas	40° 33' N	14° 14' E
Carbon, Lago del	10° 30' N	66° 55' W
Carcassonne	49° 35' S	68° 21' W
Cardiff	43° 13' N	2° 20' E
Cardigan	51° 29' N	3° 10' W
Cardigan Bay	52° 5' N	4° 40' W
Caribbean Sea	52° 30' N	4° 30' W
Carlisle	15° 0' N	75° 0' W
Carlow	52° 50' N	6° 56' W
Carmarthen	51° 52' N	4° 19' W
Carmarthen Bay	51° 40' N	4° 30' W
CarnElge	57° 17' N	5° 8' W
Carnarvon	24° 51' S	113° 42' E
Carpathians	49° 30' N	21° 0' E
Carpentaria, Gulf of	14° 0' S	139° 0' E
Carrauntoohill	52° 0' N	9° 45' W
Carrick-on-Shannon	53° 57' N	8° 7' W
Carrick-on-Suir	52° 21' N	7° 24' W
Carrickfergus	54° 43' N	5° 49' W
Carrickmacross	53° 59' N	6° 43' W
Carrigaline	51° 48' N	8° 23' W
Carron, Loch	57° 22' N	5° 35' W
Carson City	39° 10' N	19° 46' W
Cartagena, Colombia	10° 25' N	75° 33' W
Cartagena, Spain	37° 38' N	0° 59' W
Casablanca	33° 36' N	7° 36' W
Cascade Range	47° 0' N	121° 30' W

Colorado Argentina	39° 50' S	62° 8' W
Colorado N. Amer.	31° 45' N	114° 40'
Colorado Plateau	37° 0' N	111° 0'
Colorado Springs	38° 50' N	104° 49'
Columbia	34° 0' N	81° 2' W
Columbia	46° 15' N	124° 5'
Columbus	39° 58' N	83° 0' W
Colwyn Bay	53° 18' N	3° 44' W
Como, Lake	46° 0' N	9° 11' E
Comorin, Cape	8° 3' N	77° 40' E
Comoros	12° 10' S	44° 15' E
Conakry	9° 29' N	13° 49'
Concepcion	36° 50' S	73° 0' W
Conchos	29° 35' N	104° 25'
Concord	43° 12' N	71° 32'
Congleton	53° 10' N	2° 13' W
Congo	1° 0' S	16° 0' E
Congo	6° 4' S	12° 24' E
Congo, Democratic Republic of the	3° 0' S	23° 0' E
Congo Basin	0° 10' S	24° 30' E
Conn, Lough	54° 3' N	9° 15' W
Connaught	53° 43' N	9° 12' W
Connecticut	41° 30' N	72° 45'
Connemara	53° 29' N	9° 45' W
Consett	54° 51' N	1° 50' W
Constance, Lake	47° 35' N	9° 25' E
Constanta	44° 14' N	28° 38' E
Constantine	36° 25' N	6° 42' E
Conwy	53° 17' N	3° 50' W
Cook Islands	17° 0' S	160° 0' W
Cook Strait	41° 15' S	174° 29'
Cookstown	54° 40' N	6° 43' W
Copenhagen	55° 40' N	12° 26' E
Coquet	55° 20' N	1° 32' W
Coral Sea	15° 0' S	150° 0' E
Corby	52° 30' N	0° 41' W
Cordoba, Argentina	31° 20' S	64° 10'
Cordoba, Spain	37° 50' N	4° 50' W
Corfu	39° 38' N	19° 50' E
Corinth, Gulf of	38° 16' N	22° 30' E
Cork	51° 54' N	8° 29' W
Cornwall	50° 26' N	4° 40' W
Corpus Christi	27° 47' N	97° 24' W
Caspian Sea	43° 0' N	50° 0' E
Castello de la Plana	39° 58' N	0° 3' W
Castile	42° 0' N	5° 0' W
Castle Douglas	54° 56' N	3° 56' W
Castlebar	53° 52' N	9° 18' W
Castleford	53° 43' N	1° 21' W
Castletown Bearhaven	51° 39' N	9° 55' W
Castries	14° 2' N	60° 58' W
Catalonia	41° 40' N	1° 15' E
Catania	37° 30' N	15° 6' E
Caucasus Mountains	42° 50' N	44° 0' E
Cavan	54° 0' N	7° 22' W
Caxias do sul	29° 10' S	51° 10' W
Cayenne	5° 5' N	52° 18' W
Cayman Is.	19° 40' N	80° 30' W
Ceara	5° 0' S	40° 0' W
Cebu	10° 18' N	123° 54' E
Celano	42° 5' N	13° 33' E
Celebes	2° 0' S	120° 0' E
Celebes Sea	3° 0' N	123° 0' E
Central African Republic	7° 0' N	20° 0' E
Central America	12° 0' N	85° 0' W
Central Bedfordshire	52° 5' N	0° 20' W
Ceredigion	52° 16' N	4° 15' W
Ceuta	35° 52' N	5° 18' W
Chad	15° 0' N	17° 15' E
Chad, Lake	13° 30' N	14° 30' E
Chagos Archipelago	6° 0' S	72° 0' E
Changchun	43° 57' N	125° 17' E
Changde	29° 4' N	111° 35' E
Changsha	28° 12' N	113° 0' E
Changzhou	31° 47' N	119° 58' E
Channel Islands	49° 19' N	2° 24' W
Chard	50° 52' N	2° 58' W
Chari	12° 58' N	14° 31' E
Charleston	38° 21' N	81° 38' W
Charleville	26° 24' S	146° 15' E
Charlotte	35° 13' N	80° 50' W
Chartres	48° 29' N	1° 30' E
Chatham	51° 22' N	0° 32' E
Chatham Islands	44° 0' S	176° 40' W
Chattahoochee	30° 54' N	84° 57' W
Chelmsford	51° 44' N	0° 29' E
Corrib, Lough	53° 27' N	9° 16' W
Cashel	52° 30' N	7° 53' W

rrientes, Cape	20° 25' N	105° 42' W
rsica	42° 0' N	9° 0' E
senza	39° 18' N	16° 15' E
smonaut Sea	66° 30' S	40° 0' E
sta Blanca	38° 25' N	0° 10' W
sta del Sol	36° 30' N	4° 30' W
sta Rice	10° 0' N	84° 0' W
tonou	6° 20' N	2° 25' E
topaxi	0° 40' S	78° 30' W
tswold Hills	51° 42' N	2° 10' W
ventry	52° 25' N	1° 28' W
awley	51° 7' N	0° 11' W
ete	35° 15' N	25° 0' E
ewe	53° 6' N	2° 26' W
ianlarich	56° 24' N	4° 37' W
ieff	56° 22' N	3° 50' W
imea	45° 0' N	34° 0' E
oatia	45° 20' N	16° 0' E
omarty	57° 40' N	4° 2' W
omer	52° 56' N	1° 17' E
osby	53° 30' N	3° 3' W
oss Fell	54° 43' N	2° 28' W
ow Head	51° 35' N	10° 9' W
uba	22° 0' N	79° 0' W
ucuta	7° 54' N	72° 31' W
uenca	2° 50' S	79° 9' W
uernavaca	18° 55' N	99° 15' W
uiaba	15° 30' S	56° 0' W
uliacan	24° 50' N	107° 23' W
umberland	37° 9' N	88° 25' W
umberland Plateau	36° 0' N	85° 0' W
umbernauld	55° 57' N	3° 58' W
umbria	54° 42' N	2° 52' W
umbrian Mount.	54° 30' N	3° 0' W
umnock	55° 28' N	4° 17' W
upar	56° 19' N	3° 1' W
uracao	12° 10' N	69° 0' W
uritiba	25° 20' S	49° 10' W
usco	13° 32' S	72° 0' W
wmbran	51° 39' N	3° 2' W
yclades	37° 0' N	24° 30' E
heltenham	51° 54' N	2° 4' W
helyabinsk	55° 10' N	61° 24' E
helyuskin, Cape	77° 30' N	103° 0' E
hemnitz	50° 51' N	12° 54' E
hengdu	30° 38' N	104° 2' E
hennai	13° 8' N	80° 19' E
herbourg	49° 39' N	1° 40' W
herepovets	59° 5' N	37° 55' E
hernigov	51° 28' N	31° 20' E
hernobyl	51° 20' N	30° 15' E
hernovtsy	48° 15' N	25° 52' E
herwell	51° 44' N	1° 14' W
hesapeake Bay	38° 0' N	76° 10' W
heshire East	53° 15' N	2° 15' W
heshire West and Chester	53° 15' N	2° 40' W
hester	53° 12' N	2° 53' W
hesterfield	53° 15' N	1° 25' W
hesterfield Is.	19° 52' S	158° 15'E
heviot, The	55° 29' N	2° 9' W
heviot Hills	55° 20' N	2° 30' W
heyenne	41° 8' N	104° 49' W
hipa	16° 42' N	93° 0' W
hicago	41° 52' N	87° 38' W
hichester	50° 50' N	0° 47' W
hiengmai	18° 47' N	98° 59' E
hifeng	42° 18' N	118° 58' E
hihuahua	28° 38' N	106° 5' W
hile	35° 0' S	72° 0' W
hiloe, Islande	42° 30' S	73° 50' W
hiltern Hills	51° 40' N	0° 53' W
himborazo	1° 29' S	78° 55' W
China	30° 0' N	110° 0' E
China, Great Wall of	38° 30' N	109° 30' E
Chios	38° 27' N	26° 9' E
Chippenham	51° 27' N	2° 6' W
Chita	52° 0' N	113° 35' E
Chittagong	22° 19' N	91° 48' E
Choiseul	7° 0' S	156° 40' E
Chongging	29° 35' N	106° 25' E
Chorley	53° 39' N	2° 38' W
Christchurch	43° 33' S	172° 47' E
Chudskoye, Lake	58° 13' N	27° 30' E
Cienfuegos	22° 10' N	80° 30' W
Cyprus	35° 0' N	33° 0' E
Czech Republic	50° 0' N	15° 0' E
Celtic Sea	50° 9' N	9° 34' W
Cincinnati	39° 9' W	84° 27' W
Cirencester	51° 43' N	1° 57' W
Ciudad Bolivar	8° 5' N	63° 36' W
Ciudad Guayana	8° 0' N	62° 30' W
Ciudad Juarez	31° 44' N	06° 29' W
Ciudad Obregon	27° 29' N	09° 56' W
Clackma-nnanshire	56° 10' N	3° 43' W
Clacton-on-Sea	51° 47' N	1° 11' E
Clare	52° 45' N	9° 0' W
Clare	53° 20' N	9° 2' W
Claremorris	53° 45' N	9° 0' W
Clear, Cape	51° 25' N	9° 32' W
Clear Island	51° 26' N	9° 30' W
Cleethorpes	53° 33' N	0° 3' W
Clermont – Ferrand	45° 46' N	3° 4' E
Cleveland	41° 29' N	81° 41' W
Clew Bay	53° 50' N	9° 49' W
Clifden	53° 29' N	10° 1' W
Clonakilty	51° 37' N	8° 53' W
Cloncurry	20° 40' S	140° 28' E
Clonmel	52° 21' N	7° 42' W
Cluj-Napoca	46° 47' N	23° 38' E
Clwyd	53° 19' N	3° 31' W
Clyde	55° 55' N	4° 30' W
Clyde, Firth of	55° 22' N	5° 1' W
Clydebank	55° 54' N	4° 23' W
Coalville	52° 44' N	1° 23' W
Coast Ranges	39° 0' N	123° 0' W
Coatbridge	55° 52' N	4° 0' W
Coats Land	77° 0' S	25° 0' W
Cobh	51° 51' N	8° 17' W
Cochin	9° 58' N	76° 20' E
Cod, Cape	42° 5' N	70° 10' W
Coimbatore	11° 2' N	76° 59' E
Colchester	51° 54' N	0° 55' E
Coldstream	55° 39' N	6° 34' W
Coleraine	55° 8' N	6° 40' W
Coll	56° 39' N	6° 34' W
Cologne	50° 56' N	6° 57' E
Colombia	3° 45' N	73° 0' W
Colombo	6° 56' N	79° 58' E
Colonsay	56° 5' N	6° 12' W
Colorado	39° 30' N	105° 30' W
D		
Da Nang	16° 4' N	108° 113'E
Dacca	23° 43' N	90° 26' E
Daegu	35° 50' N	128° 37' E
Daejoon	36° 20' N	127° 28' E
Dakar	14° 34' N	17° 29' W
Dakhla	23° 50' N	15° 53' W
Dalian	38° 50' N	121° 40' E
Dallas	32° 47' N	96° 48' W
Damascus	33° 30' N	36° 18' E
Damaturu	11° 45' N	11° 55' E
Dampier	20° 41' S	116° 42' E
Danube	45° 20' N	29° 40' E
Dar es Salaam	6° 50' S	39° 12' E
Dardanelles	40° 17' N	26° 32' E
Darien, Gulf of	9° 0' N	77° 0' W
Darling	34° 4' S	141° 54' E
Darling Range	32° 30' S	116° 20' E
Darlington	54° 32' N	1° 33' W
Darnley, Cape	68° 0' S	69° 0' E
Dart	50° 24' N	3° 39' W
Dartmoor	50° 38' N	3° 57' W
Dartmouth	50° 21' N	3° 36' W
Darwin	12° 25' S	130° 51' E
Dasht-e Kavir	34° 30' N	55° 0' E
Dasht-e Lut	31° 30' N	58° 0' E
Datong	40° 6' N	113° 18' E
Davao	7° 0' N	125° 40' E
Davis Sea	66° 0' S	92° 0' E
Davis Strait	65° 0' N	58° 0' W
DayrazZawr	35° 20' N	40° 5' E
Dayton	39° 45' N	84° 12' W
Dead Sea	31° 30' N	35° 30' E
Deal	51° 13' N	1° 25' E
Death Valley	36° 15' N	116° 50' W
Debrecen	47° 33' N	21° 42' E
Dee, Scotland	18° 0' N	79° 0' E
Dee, Scotland	54° 51' N	4° 3' N
Dee, Wales	53° 22' N	3° 17' W
Delaware	39° 0' N	75° 20' W
Delhi	28° 39' N	77° 13' E
Demavend	35° 56' N	52° 10' E
Denizli	37° 42' N	29° 2' E
Denmark	55° 45' N	10° 0' E
Denmark Strait	66° 0' N	30° 0' W
Denpasar	8° 39' S	115° 13' E
D' Entrecaste-ux Islands	9° 0' S	151° 0' E
Denver	39° 42' N	104° 59' W
Derby	52° 56' N	1° 28' W
Derbyshire	53° 11' N	1° 38' W
Dereham	52° 41' N	0° 57' E
Derg, Lough	53° 0' N	8° 20' W
Derry=Lojndonderry	55° 0' N	7° 20' W
Derwent, Cumbria	54° 39' N	3° 33' W
Derbyshire	52° 57' N	1° 28' W
Derwent North Yorkshire	53° 45' N	0° 58' W
Des Moines	41° 35' N	93° 37' W
Detroit	42° 19' N	83° 12' W
Deveron	57° 41' N	2° 32' W
Devon	50° 50' N	3° 40' W
Dezful	32° 20' N	48° 30' E
Dhahran	26° 10' N	50° 7' E
Dieppe	49° 54' N	1° 4' E
Dijon	47° 20' E	5° 3' E
Dili	8° 39' S	125° 34' E
Dinaric Alps	44° 0' N	16° 30' E
Dingle	52° 9' N	10° 17' W
Dingle Penins.	52° 12' N	10° 5' W
Dingwall	57° 36' N	4° 26' W
Diyarbakir	37° 55' N	40° 18' E
Djerba	33° 48' N	10° 54' E
Djerid, Chott	33° 42' N	8° 30' E
Djibouti	12° 0' N	43° 0' E
Dneprope-trovsk	48° 30' N	35° 0' E
Dnieper	46° 30' N	32° 18' E
Dniester	46° 18' N	30° 17' E
Dodecanese	36° 35' N	27° 0' E
Dodoma	6° 8' S	35° 45' E
Doha	25° 15' N	51° 35' E
Dolgellau	52° 45' N	3° 53' W
Dominica	15° 20' N	61° 20' W
Dominican Republic	19° 0' N	70° 30' W
Don, England	53° 41' N	0° 52' W
Don, Russia	47° 4' N	39° 18' E
Don, Scotland	57° 11' N	2° 5' W
Doncaster	53° 32' N	1° 6' W
Donegal	54° 39' N	8° 5' W
Donegal Bay	54° 31' N	8° 49' W
Donetsk	48° 0' N	37° 45' E
Dongbei	45° 0' N	125° 0' E
Dongting Hu	29° 18' N	112° 45' E
Donostia-San Sebastian	43° 17' N	1° 58' W
Doon	55° 27' N	4° 39' W
Dorchester	50° 42' N	2° 27' W
Dordogne	45° 2' N	0° 36' W
Dornoch	57° 53' N	4° 2' W
Dornoch Firth	57° 51' N	4° 4' W
Dorset	50° 45' N	2° 26' W
Dortmund	51° 30' N	7° 28' E
Douala	4° 0' N	9° 45' E
Douglas	54° 10' N	4° 28' W
Douro	41° 8' N	8° 40' W
Dove	52° 51' N	1° 36' W
Dover, U.K.	51° 7' N	1° 19' E
Dover, U.S.A.	39° 10' N	75° 32' W
Dover, Strait of	51° 0' N	1° 30' E
Down	54° 23' N	6° 2' W
Downpatrick	54° 20' N	5° 43' W
Drake Passage	58° 0' S	68° 0' W
Drakensberg	31° 0' S	28° 0' E
Drammen	59° 42' N	10° 12' E
Drava	45° 33' N	18° 55' E
Dresden	51° 3' N	13° 44' E
Driffield	54° 0' N	0° 26' W
Drogheda	53° 43' N	6° 22' W
Dubai	25° 18' N	55° 20' E
Dubbo	32° 11' S	48° 35' E
Dublin	53° 21' N	6° 15' W
Dubrovnik	42° 39' N	18° 6' E
Dudley	52° 31' N	2° 5' W
Dumbarton	55° 57' N	4° 33' W
Dumfries	55° 4' N	3° 37' W
Dumfries and Galloway	55° 9' N	3° 58' W
Dun Laoghaire	53° 17' N	6° 8' W
Dunabar	56° 0' N	2° 31' W
Dunblane	56° 11' N	3° 58' W
Duncansby Head	58° 38' N	3° 1' W
Dundalk	54° 1' N	6° 24' W
Dundee	56° 28' N	2° 59' W
Dunedin	45° 50' S	170° 33' E
Dunfermline	56° 5' N	3° 27' W
Dungannon	54° 30' N	6° 55' W
Dungarvan	52° 5' N	7° 37' W
Dunkery Beacon	51° 9' N	3° 36' W
Dunnet Head	58° 40' N	3° 21' W
Dunoon	55° 57' N	4° 56' W
Durango	24° 3' N	104° 39' W
Durban	29° 49' S	31° 1' E
Durham	54° 42' N	1° 45' W
Dushanbe	38° 33' N	68° 48' E
Dusseldorf	51° 14' N	6° 47' E
Dyce	57° 13' N	2° 12' W
Dyfl	52° 32' N	4° 3' W
Dzungarian Basin	44° 30' N	86° 0' E
E		
Earn	56° 21' N	3° 18' W
East Antarctica	80° 0' S	90° 0' E
East China Sea	30° 0' N	126° 0' E
East Indies	0° 0' N	120° 0' E
East Kilbride	55° 47' N	4° 11' W
East London	33° 0' S	27° 55' E
East Lothian	55° 58' N	2° 44' W
East Riding of Yorkshire	53° 55' N	0° 30' W
East Siberian Sea	73° 0' N	160° 0' E
East Sussex	50° 56' N	0° 19' E
East Timor	8° 50' S	126° 0' E
Eastbourne	50° 46' N	0° 18' E
Eastern Ghats	14° 0' N	78° 50' E
Eastleigh	50° 58' N	1° 21' W
Ebbw Vale	51° 46' N	3° 12' W
Ebinur Hu	44° 55' N	82° 55' E
Ebro	40° 43' N	0° 54' E
Ecuador	2° 0' S	78° 0' W
Eday	59° 11' N	2° 47' W
Eddystone	50° 11' N	4° 16' W
Eden	54° 47' N	3° 1' W
Edinburgh	55° 57' N	3° 13' W
Edmonton	53° 30' N	113° 30' W
Egadi Islands	37° 55' N	12° 16' E
Egypt	28° 0' N	31° 0' E
Eigg	56° 54' N	6° 10' W
Eilat	29° 30' N	34° 56' E
EileanSiar	57° 30' N	7° 10' W
El Aaiun	27° 9' N	13° 12' W
El Paso	31° 45' N	106° 29' W
El Salvador	13° 50' N	89° 0' W
Elazig	38° 37' N	39° 14' E
Elba	42° 46' N	10° 17' E
Elbe	53° 50' N	9° 0' E
Elbert, Mount	39° 7' N	106° 27' W
Ellesmere Is.		
Ellesmere Port	53° 17' N	2° 54' W
Ellon	57° 22' N	2° 4' W
Ellsworth Land	76° 0' S	89° 0' W
Ellsworth Mt.	78° 30' S	85° 0' W
Ely	52° 24' N	0° 16' E
Empty Quarter= Rub' al Khali	19° 0' N	48° 0' E
Enderby Land	66° 0' S	53° 0' E
England	53° 0' N	2° 0' W
English chnl.	50° 0' N	2° 0' W
Ennis	52° 51' N	8° 59' W
Enniscorthy	52° 30' N	6° 34' W
Enniskillen	54° 21' N	7° 39' W
Enugu	6° 30' N	7° 30' E
Equatorial Guinea	2° 0' N	8° 0' E
Erebus, Mount	77° 35' S	167° 0' E
Erfurt	50° 58' N	11° 2' E
Eriboll, Loch	58° 30' N	4° 42' W
Erie, Lake	42° 15' N	81° 0' W
Eritrea	14° 0' N	38° 30' E
Erne	54° 30' N	8° 16' W
Erne, Lower Lough	54° 28' N	7° 47' W
Erne, Upper Lough	54° 14' N	7° 32' W
Errigal	55° 2' N	8° 6' W
Erzurum	39° 57' N	41° 15' E
Esbjerg	55° 29' N	8° 29' E
Esfahan	32° 39' N	51° 43' E
Esk, England	54° 30' N	0° 37' W
Esk, Scotland	54° 58' N	3° 2' W
Eskisehir	39° 50' N	30° 30' E
Esperance	33° 45' S	121° 55' E
Espirito Santo	20° 0' S	40° 45' W
Espiritu Santo	15° 15' S	166° 50' E
Essen	51° 28' N	7° 2' E
Essequibo	6° 50' N	58° 30' W
Essex	51° 54' N	0° 27' E
Estonia	58° 30' N	25° 30' E
Ethiopia	8° 0' N	40° 0' E
Ethiopian Highlands	10° 0' N	37° 0' E
Etna, Mount	37° 50' N	14° 55' E
Etosha Pan	18° 40' S	16° 30' E
Ettrick Water	55° 31' N	2° 55' W
Euphrates	31° 0' N	47° 25' E
Everest, Mount	28° 5' N	86° 58' E
Everglades The	25° 50' N	81° 0' W

Place	Latitude	Longitude
Evesham	52° 6' N	1° 56' W
Exe	50° 41' N	3° 29' W
Exeter	50° 43' N	3° 31' W
Exmoor	51° 12' N	3° 45' W
Exmouth	50° 37' N	3° 25' W
Eyemouth	55° 52' N	2° 5' W
Eyre, Lake	29° 30' S	37° 26' E
F		
Fair Isle	59° 32' N	1° 38' W
Fairbanks	64° 51' N	147° 43' W
Faisalabad	31° 30' N	73° 5' E
Falkirk	56° 0' N	3° 47' W
Falkland Island	51° 30' S	59° 0' W
Falmouth	50° 9' N	5° 5' W
Far East	40° 0' N	130° 0' E
Fareham	50° 51' N	1° 11' W
Farewell, Cape	59° 48' N	43° 55' W
Farne Islands	53° 38' N	1° 37' W
Faroe Islands	62° 0' N	7° 0' W
Fastnet Rock	51° 22' N	9° 37' W
Fear, Cape	33° 50' N	77° 58' W
Feira de Santana	12° 15' S	38° 57' W
Felixstowe	51° 58' N	1° 23' W
Fens, The	52° 38' N	0° 2' W
Fermanagh	54° 21' N	7° 40' W
Fermoy	52° 9' N	8° 16' W
Ferrara	44° 50' N	11° 35' E
Fes	34° 0' N	° 0' W
Fetlar	60° 36' N	0° 52' W
Fife	56° 16' N	3° 1' W
Fiji	17° 20' S	179° 0' E
Findhorn	57° 38' N	3° 38'W
Finland	63° 0' N	27° 0' E
Finland, Gulf of	60° 0' N	26° 0' E
Fishguard	52° 0' N	4° 58' W
Flamborough Head	54° 7' N	° 5' W
Flannan Islands	58° 9' N	7° 52' W
Flattery, Cape	48° 23' N	124° 29' W
Fleetwood	53° 55' N	3° 1' W
Flensburg	54° 47' N	9° 27' E
Flinders Island	40° 0' S	148° 0' E
Flinders Ranges	31° 30' S	38° 30' E
Florence	43° 46' N	11° 15' E
Flores Sea	6° 30' S	20° 0' E
Florienopolis	27° 30' S	48° 30' W
Florida	28° 0' N	82° 0' W
Florida, Straits of	25° 0' N	80° 0' W
Florida Keys	24° 40' N	81° 0' W
Foggia	41° 27' N	15° 34' E
Folkestone	51° 5' N	1° 12' E
Fongafale	8° 31' S	179° 13' E
Forfar	56° 39' N	2° 53' W
Forres	57° 37' N	3° 37' W
Fort Augustus	57° 9' N	4° 42' W
Fort-de-France	14° 36' N	61° 5' W
Fort Lauderdale	26° 7' N	80° 8' W
Fort William	56° 49' N	5° 7' W
Fort Worth	32° 43' N	97° 19' W
Fortaleza	3° 45' S	38° 35' W
Forth	56° 9' N	3° 50' W
Forth, Firth of	56° 5' N	2° 55' W
Foula	60° 10' N	2° 5' W
Fouta Djallon	11° 20' N	12° 10' W
Foyle, Lough	55° 7' N	7° 4' W
Foz do Iguacu	25° 30' S	54° 30' W
France	47° 0' N	3° 0' E
Frankfurt	38° 12' N	84° 52' W
Franz Josef Land	82° 0' N	55° 0' E
Fraserburgh	57° 42' N	2° 1' W
Fredrikstad	59° 13' N	10° 57' E
Freeport	26° 30' N	78° 47' W
Freetown	8° 30' N	13° 17' W
Freiburg	47° 59' N	7° 51' E
French Guiana	4° 0' N	53° 0' W
Frisian Islands	53° 30' N	6° 0'E
Frome	51° 14' N	2° 19'W
Frome	50° 41' N	2° 6'W
Fuji-San	35° 22' N	138° 44' E
Fukui	36° 5' N	136° 10' E
Fukuoka	33° 39' N	130° 21' E
Fukushima	37° 44' N	140° 28' E
Fushun	41° 50' N	123° 56' E
Fuyu	47° 49' N	124° 27' E
Fuzhou	26° 5' N	119° 16' E
Fyne, Loch	55° 59' N	5° 23'W
G		
Gabon	0° 10' S	10° 0' E
Gaborone	24° 45' S	25° 57' E
Gainsborough	53° 24' N	0° 46' W
Gairdner, Lake	31° 30' S	136° 0' E

Place	Latitude	Longitude
Galapagos, Is.		
Galashiels	55° 37' N	2° 49' W
Galati	45° 27' N	28° 2' E
Galdhopiggen	61° 38' N	8° 18' E
Gallivare	67° 9' N	20° 40' E
Galloway	55° 1' N	4° 29' W
Galloway, Mull of	54° 39' N	4° 52' W
Galtymore	52° 21' N	8° 11' W
Galway	53° 17' N	9° 3' W
Galway Bay	53° 13' N	9° 10' W
Gambia	13° 25' N	16° 0' W
Ganca	40° 45' N	46° 20' E
Ganges	43° 20' N	90° 30' E
Garda, Lake	45° 40' N	10° 41' E
Garissa	0° 25' S	39° 40' E
Garonne	45° 2' N	0° 36' W
Garoua	9° 19' N	13° 21' E
Gateshead	54° 57' N	1° 35' W
Gavle	60° 40' N	17° 9' E
Gaza Strip	31° 29' N	34° 25' E
Gaziantep	37° 6' N	37° 23' E
Gdansk	54° 22' N	18° 40' E
Geneva	46° 12' N	6° 9' E
Geneva, Lake	46° 26' N	6° 30' E
Genoa	44° 25' N	8° 57' E
Genoa, Gulf of	44° 0' N	9° 0' E
George Town	5° 25' N	100° 20' E
Georgetown	6° 50' N	58° 12' W
Georgia	32° 50' N	83° 15' W
Georgia	42° 0' N	43° 0' E
Geraldton	28° 48' S	114° 32' E
Germany	51° 0' N	10° 0' E
Ghana	8° 0' N	1° 0' W
Ghenbt	51° 2' N	3° 42' E
Giants Causeway	55° 16' N	6° 29' W
Gibraltar	36° 7' N	5° 22' W
Gibraltar, Strait of	35° 55' N	5° 40' W
Gibson Desert	24° 0' S	126° 0' E
Gifu	35° 30' N	136° 45' E
Gijon	43° 32' N	5° 42' W
Gillingham	51° 23' N	0° 33' E
Gironde	45° 32' N	1° 7' W
Girvan	55° 14' N	4° 51' W
Gladstone	23° 52' S	151° 16' E
Glama	59° 12' N	10° 57' E
Glasgow	55° 51' N	4° 15' W
Glen Coe	56° 40' N	5° 0' W
Glen Mor	57° 9' N	4° 37' W
Glenrothes	56° 12' N	3° 10' W
Gloucester	51° 53' N	2° 15' W
Gloucestershire	51° 46' N	2° 15' W
Goa	15° 33' N	2° 15' W
Goat Fell	55° 38' N	5° 11' W
Gobi Desert	44° 0' N	110° 0' E
Godavari	16° 25' N	82° 18' E
Goiania	16° 43' S	49° 20' W
Goias	12° 10' S	48° 0' W
Gold Coast	28° 0' S	53° 25' E
Golspie	57° 58' N	3° 59' W
Gomel	52° 28' N	31° 0' E
Good Hope, Cape of	34° 24' S	18° 30' E
Goole	53° 42' N	0° 53' W
Gorey	52° 41' N	6° 18' W
Gosport	50° 48' N	1° 9' W
Gotaland	57° 30' N	14° 30' E
Gothenburg	57° 43' N	11° 59' E
Gotland	57° 30' N	18° 33' E
Gottingen	51° 31' N	9° 55' E
Grampian Mount.	56° 50' N	4° 0' W
Gran Chaco	25° 0' S	61° 0' W
Granada	37° 10' N	3° 35' W
Grand Bahama Is.	26° 40' N	78° 30' W
Grand Canyon	36° 3' N	112° 9' W
Grand Teton	43° 54' N	110° 50' W
Grande, Rio	25° 58' N	97° 9' W
Grantham	52° 55' N	0° 38' W
Grantown-on-Spey	57° 20' N	3° 36' W
Gravesend	51° 26' N	0° 22' E
Graz	47° 4' N	15° 27' E
Great Australian Bright	33° 30' S	130° 0' E
Great Barrier Rf.	18° 0' S	146° 50' E
Great Basin	40° 0' N	117° 0' W
Great Bear Lake	65° 30' N	120° 0' W
Great Britain	54° 0' N	2° 15' W
Great D. Range	23° 0' S	146° 0' E
Great Khinga M.	48° 0' N	121° 0' E
Great Lakes	46° 0' N	84° 0' W
Great Malvern	52° 7' N	2° 18' W
Great Ouse	52° 48' N	0° 21' E
Great Plains	47° 0' N	105° 0' W

Place	Latitude	Longitude
Great Salt Lake	41° 15' N	112° 40' W
Great S. L. Dsrt.	40° 50' N	113° 30' W
Great Sandy Dst.	21° 0' S	124° 0' E
Great Victoria Dst.	29° 30' S	126° 30' E
Great Yarmouth	52° 37' N	1° 44' E
Greater Antilles	17° 40' N	74° 0' W
Greater London	51° 31' N	0° 6' W
Greater Manchtr.	53° 30' N	2° 15' W
Greece	40° 0' N	23° 0' E
Greenland	66° 0' N	45° 0' W
Greenland Sea	73° 0' N	10° 0' W
Greenock	55° 57' N	4° 46' W
Greenwich	51° 29' N	0° 1' E
Grenada	12° 10' N	61° 40' W
Grenoble	45° 12' N	5° 42' E
Gretna Green	55° 1' N	3° 3' W
Greystones	53° 15' N	6° 35' E
Grimsby	53° 34' N	0° 5' W
Groningen	53° 15' N	6° 35' E
Groote Eylandt	14° 0' S	136° 40' E
Guadalajara	20° 40' N	103° 20' W
Guadalcanal	9° 32' S	160° 12' E
Guadalquivir	36° 47' N	6° 22' W
Guadeloupe	16° 15' N	61° 40' W
Guadiana	37° 14' N	7° 22' W
Guam	13° 27' N	144° 45' E
Guangdong	23° 0' N	113° 0' E
Guangzhou	23° 6' N	113° 13' E
Guantanamo	20° 10' N	75° 14' W
Guantanamo Bay	19° 59' N	75° 10' W
Guapore	11° 55' S	65° 4' W
Guatemala	15° 40' N	90° 30' W
Guaviare	4° 3' N	67° 44' W
Guayaquil	2° 15' S	79° 52' W
Guernsey	49° 26' N	2° 35' W
Guiana Highlands	5° 10' N	60° 40' W
Guildford	51° 14' N	0° 34' W
Guinea	10° 20' N	11° 30' W
Guinea, Gulf of	3° 0' N	2° 30' E
Guinea-Bissau	12° 0' N	15° 0' W
Guiyang	26° 32' N	106° 40' E
Gusau	12° 12' N	6° 40' E
Guyana	5° 0' N	59° 0' W
Gwangju	35° 9' N	126° 54' E
Gwynedd	52° 52' N	4° 10' W
Great Slave Lake	61° 23' N	115° 38' W
H		
Hardian's Wall	55° 0' N	2° 30' W
Hague, Cap de la	49° 44' N	1° 56' W
Hague, The	52° 7' N	4° 17' E
HaidaGwaii	53° 20' N	132° 10' W
Haifa	32° 46' N	35° 0' E
Hafll	27° 28' N	41° 45' E
Hailar	49° 10' N	119° 38' E
Hainan	19° 0' N	110° 0' E
Haiphong	20° 47' N	106° 41' E
Haiti	19° 0' N	72° 30' W
Hakodate	41° 45' N	140° 44' E
Halifax, Canada	44° 38' N	63° 55' W
Halifax, U.K.	53° 43' N	1° 52' W
Halle	51° 30' N	11° 56' E
Halmahera	0° 40' N	128° 0' E
Halton	53° 22' N	2° 45' W
Hamadan	34° 52' N	48° 32' E
Hamah	35° 5' N	36° 40' E
Hamamatsu	34° 45' N	37° 45' E
Hamburg	53° 33' N	9° 59' E
Hami	42° 55' N	93° 25' E
Hamilton, Berm.	32° 17' N	64° 47' W
Hamilton, Canada	43° 15' N	79° 50' W
Hamilton, N. Z.	37° 47' S	175° 19' E
Hamilton, U.K.	55° 46' N	4° 2' W
Hammerfast	70° 39' N	23° 41' E
Hampshire	51° 7' N	1° 23' W
Handan	36° 35' N	14° 28' E
Hangzhou	30° 18' N	120° 11' E
Hangzhou Wan	30° 15' N	120° 45' E
Hanoi	21° 5' N	105° 55' E
Hanover	52° 22' N	9° 46' E
Har Us Nuur	48° 0' N	92° 0' E
Harad	24° 22' N	49° 0' E
Harare	17° 43' S	31° 2' E
Harbin	45° 48' N	126° 40' E
Hardanger Fjord	60° 5' N	6° 0' E
Harlow	51° 46' N	0° 8' E
Harris	57° 50' N	6° 55' W
Harrogate	54° 0' N	1° 33' W
Hartford	41° 46' N	72° 41' W
Hartland Point	51° 1' N	4° 32' W
Hartlepool	54° 42' N	1° 13' W

Place	Latitude	Longitude
Harwich	51° 56' N	1° 17' E
Hastings	50° 51' N	0° 58' W
Hatteras, Cape	35° 14' N	75° 32'
Havana	23° 8' N	82° 22'
Havant	50° 51' N	0° 35' E
Haverfordwest	51° 48' N	4° 58' W
Hawaiian Islands	19° 30' N	56° 30'
Hawick	55° 26' N	2° 47' W
Hay-on-Wye	52° 5' N	3° 8' W
Haywards Heath	51° 0' N	0° 5' W
Hebrides	57° 30' N	7° 0' W
Hebrides, Sea of The	57° 5' N	7° 0' W
Hefei	31° 52' N	117° 18
Hegang	47° 20' N	130° 19
Heihe	50° 10' N	127° 30
Helena	46° 36' N	112° 2'
Helensburgh	56° 1' N	4° 43' W
Helmsdale	58° 7' N	3° 39' W
Helsingborg	56° 3' N	12° 42'
Helsinki	60° 10' N	24° 55'
HemelHempst.	51° 44' N	0° 28' W
Hengyang	26° 59' N	112° 22
Herat	34° 20' N	62° 7' E
Hereford	52° 4' N	2° 43' W
Hermosillo	32° 27' N	114° 56'
Herne Bay	51° 21' N	1° 8' E
Herford	51° 48' N	° 4' W
Herfordshire	51° 51' N	0° 5' W
Hexham	54° 58' N	2° 4' W
Heysham	54° 3' N	2° 53' W
High Willhays	50° 40' N	4° 0' W
High Wycombe	51° 37' N	0° 45' W
Highland	57° 17' N	4° 21' W
Hiiumaa	58° 50' N	22° 45'
Himalayas	29° 0' N	84° 0' E
Himeji	34° 50' N	134° 40'
Hinckley	52° 33' N	1° 22' W
Hindu Kush	36° 0' N	71° 0' E
Hiroshima	34° 24' N	132° 30'
Hispaniola	19° 0' N	71° 0' W
Hitachi	36° 36' N	140° 39'
Hitchin	51° 58' N	0° 16' W
Ho Chi Minh City	10° 58' N	106° 40'
Hobart	42° 50' S	147° 21'
Hoggar	23° 0' N	6° 30' E
Hohhot	40° 52' N	111° 40'
Hokkaido	43° 30' N	143° 0' E
Holderness	53° 45' N	0° 5' W
Holguin	20° 50' N	76° 20' W
Holy Is. England	55° 40' N	1° 47' W
Holy Is. Wales	53° 17' N	4° 37' W
Holyhead	53° 18' N	4° 38' W
Homs	34° 40' N	36° 45' E
Honduras	14° 40' N	86° 30' W
Honduras, Gulf	16° 50' N	87° 0' W
Hong Kong	22° 11' N	114° 14'
Honiara	9° 27' S	159° 57'
Honiton	50° 47' N	3° 11' W
Honolulu	21° 19' N	157° 52'
Honshu	36° 0' N	138° 0' E
Hormuz, Strait of	26° 30' N	56° 30' E
Horn, Cape	55° 50' S	67° 30' W
Horsham	51° 4' N	0° 20' W
Hotan	37° 25' N	79° 55' E
Houghton-le-Spring	54° 51' N	1° 28' W
Houston	29° 45' N	95° 21' W
Hove	50° 50' N	0° 10' W
HovsgolNuur	51° 0' N	100° 30'
Howth Head	53° 22' N	6° 4' W
Hoy	58° 50' N	3° 15' W
Huambo	12° 42' S	15° 54' E
Huascaran, Nevado	9° 7' S	77° 37' S
Huddersfield	53° 39' N	1° 47' W
Hudson	40° 42' N	74° 2' W
Hudson Bay	60° 0' N	86° 0' W
Hudson Strait	62° 0' N	70° 0' W
Huelva	37° 18' N	6° 57' W
Hull	53° 44' N	0° 20' W
Humber	53° 42' N	0° 27' W
Hungary	47° 20' N	19° 20' E
Huntingdon	52° 20' N	0° 11' W
Huntly	57° 27' N	2° 47' W
Hurghada	27° 15' N	33° 50' E
Huron, Lake	44° 30' N	82° 40' W
Hwang Ho	37° 55' N	118° 50' E
Hyderabad, India	17° 22' N	78° 29' E
Hyderabad, Pakistan	25° 23' N	68° 24' E
I		
Iasi	47° 10' N	27° 40' E
Ibadan	7° 22' N	3° 58' E

gue	4° 20' N	5° 20' W
rian Pennins.	40° 0' N	5° 0' W
za	38° 54' N	1° 26' E
	2° 55' S	67° 58' W
land	64° 45' N	19° 0' W
aho	45° 0' N	115° 0' W
ane	33° 33' N	5° 7' W
acu Falls	25° 41' S	54° 26' W
acombe	51° 12' N	4° 8' W
eston	52° 58' N	1° 19' W
ley	53° 56' N	1° 48' W
nois	40° 15' N	89° 30' W
rin	8° 30' N	4° 35' E
andra, Lake	67° 30' N	33° 0' E
peratriz	5° 30' S	47° 29' W
ari, Lake	69° 0' N	28° 0' E
cheon	37° 27' N	126° 40' E
dia	20° 0' N	78° 0' E
dian	27° 59' N	80° 34' W
dian Ocean	5° 0' S	75° 0' E
diana	40° 0' N	86° 0' W
dianapolis	39° 46' N	86° 9' W
do-China	15° 0' N	102° 0' E
donesia	5° 0' S	75° 0' E
dore	22° 42' N	75° 53' E
dus	24° 20' N	67° 47' E
shbofin	53° 37' N	10° 13' W
shmore	53° 8' N	9° 45' W
showenPenins..	55° 14' N	7° 15' W
shturk	53° 42' N	10° 7' W
ner Hebrides	57° 0' N	6° 30' W
ner Mongolia	42° 0' N	112° 0' E
nsbruck	47° 16' N	11° 23' E
veraray	56° 14' N	5° 5' W
vercargill	46° 24' S	168° 24' E
vergordon	57° 41' N	4° 10' W
verness	57° 29' N	4° 13' W
verurie	57° 17' N	2° 23' W
na	56° 20' N	6° 25' W
nian Islands	38° 40' N	20° 0' E
nian Sea	37° 30' N	17° 30' E
wa	42° 18' N	93° 30' W
swich	52° 4' N	1° 10' E
aluit	63° 44' N	68° 31' W
uitos	3° 45' S	73° 10' W
aklio	35° 20' N	25° 12' E
an	33° 0' N	53° 0' E
aq	33° 0' N	44° 0' E
bil	36° 15' N	44° 5' E
eland	53° 50' N	7° 52' W
eland's Eye	53° 24' N	6° 4' W
sh Sea	53° 38' N	4° 48' W
kutsk	52° 18' N	104° 20' E
rawaddy	15° 50' N	95° 6' E
tysh	61° 4' N	68° 52' E
vine	55° 37' N	4° 41' W
chia	40° 44' N	13° 57' E
slamabad	33° 40' N	73° 10' E
slay	55° 46' N	6° 10' W
smail Samani Peak	39° 0' N	72° 2' E
smailiya	30° 37' N	32° 18' E
sparta	37° 47' N	30° 30' E
srael	32° 0' N	34° 50' E
stambul	41° 0' N	28° 58' E
abuna	14° 48' S	39° 16' W
aly	42° 0' N	13° 0' E
chen	50° 55' N	1° 22' W
veraghPennins.	51° 52' N	10° 15' W
vory Coast	7° 30' N	5° 0' W
waki	37° 3' N	140° 55' E
zmir	38° 25' N	27° 8' E
zmit	40° 45' N	29° 50' E
abalpur	23° 9' N	79° 58' E
ackson	32° 18' N	90° 12' W
acksonville	30° 20' N	81° 39' W
affna	9° 45' N	80° 2' E
ahrom	28° 30' N	53° 31' E
aipur	27° 0' N	75° 50' E
akarta	6° 9' S	106° 52' E
amaica	18° 10' N	77° 30' W
amshedpur	22° 44' N	86° 12' E
an Mayen	71° 0' N	9° 0' W
apan	36° 0' N	136° 0' E
apan, Sea of	40° 0' N	135° 0' E
apura	3° 8' S	65° 46' W
ava	7° 0' S	110° 0' E
ava Sea	4° 35' S	07° 15' E
edburgh	55° 29' N	2° 33' W
Jedda	21° 29' W	39° 10' E

Jeju-do	33° 29' N	126° 34' E
Jerez de la Frontera	36° 41' N	6° 7' W
Jersey	49° 11' N	2° 7' W
Jerusalem	31° 47' N	35° 10' E
Jiamusi	46° 40' N	130° 26' E
Jilian	43° 44' N	126° 30' E
Jimeta	9° 17' N	12° 28' E
Jinan	36° 38' N	17° 1' E
Jingmen	31° 0' N	112° 10' E
Jinja	0° 25' N	33° 12' E
Jinxi	40° 52' N	120° 50' E
Jixi	45° 20' N	130° 50' E
Joao Pessoa	7° 10' S	34° 52' W
Joensuu	62° 37' N	29° 49' E
Johannesburg	26° 11' S	28° 2' E
John o' Groats	58° 38' N	3° 4' W
Johnstone	55° 49' N	4° 31' W
Jonkoping	57° 45' N	14° 8' E
Jordan	31° 0' N	36° 0' E
Jos Plateau	9° 55' N	9° 0' E
Jotunheimen	61° 35' N	8° 25' E
Juazeiro	9° 30' S	40° 30' W
Juazeiro do Norte	7° 10' S	39° 18' W
Juba	4° 50' N	31° 35' E
Juiz de For a	21° 43' S	43° 19' W
Juneau	58° 18' N	134° 25' W
Jura	56° 0' N	5° 50' W
Jura, Sound of	55° 57' N	5° 45' W
Jurua	2° 37' S	65° 44' W
Juruena	7° 20' S	58° 3' W
Jutland	56° 25' N	9° 30' E
Jyvaskyia	62° 14' N	25° 50' E
K		
K2	35° 58' N	76° 32' E
Kabul	34° 28' N	69° 11' E
Kaduna	10° 30' N	7° 21' E
Kagoshima	31° 35' N	130° 33' E
Kainji Reservoir	10° 1' N	4° 40' E
Kakamega	0° 20' N	34° 46' E
Kalahari	24° 0' S	21° 30' E
Kalgoorlie-Boulder	30° 40' S	121° 22' E
Kaliningrad	54° 42' N	20° 32' E
Kamchatka Peninsula	57° 0' N	160° 0' E
Kampala	0° 20' N	2° 32' E
Kanazawa	36° 30' N	136° 38' E
Kandahar	31° 0' N	65° 0' E
Kanddalaksha	67° 9' N	32° 30' E
Kangaroo Island	35° 45' S	37° 0' E
Kano	12° 2' N	8° 30' E
Kanpur	26° 28' N	80° 20' E
Kansas	38° 30' N	99° 0' W
Kansas City	39° 7' N	94° 38' W
Kansk	56° 20' N	95° 37' E
Kaohsiung	22° 35' N	120° 16' E
Kara Kum	39° 30' N	60° 0' E
Kara Sea	75° 0' N	70° 0' E
Karachi	24° 50' N	67° 0' E
Karaganda	49° 50' N	73° 10' E
Karakoram	35° 30' N	77° 0' E
Karelia	65° 30' N	32° 30' E
Kariba, Lake	16° 40' S	28° 25' E
Karlsruhe	49° 0' N	8° 23' E
Kasai	3° 30' S	16° 10' E
Kashan	34° 5' N	51° 30' E
Kashgar	39° 30' N	76° 2' E
Kashmir	34° 0' N	76° 0' E
Kassel	51° 18' N	9° 26' E
Katmandu	27° 45' N	85° 20' E
Katowice	50° 17' N	19° 5' E
Katrine, Loch	56° 15' N	4° 30' W
Katsina	13° 0' N	7° 32' E
Kattegat	56° 40' N	11° 20' E
Kaunas	54° 54' N	23° 54' E
Kawasaki	35° 31' N	139° 43' E
Kayseri	38° 45' N	35° 30' E
Kazakhastan	50° 0' N	70° 0' E
Kazan	55° 50' N	49° 10' E
Kebnekaise	67° 53' N	18° 33' E
Keighley	53° 52' N	1° 54' W
Keith	57° 32' N	2° 57' W
Kelso	55° 36' N	2° 26' W
Kemi	65° 44' N	24° 34' E
Kemp Land	69° 0' S	55° 0' E
Kendal	54° 20' N	2° 44' W
Kenmare	51° 53' N	9° 36' W
Kennet	51° 27' N	0° 57' W
Kent	51° 12' N	0° 40' E
Kentucky	37° 0' N	84° 0' W
Kenya	1° 0' N	38° 0' E
Kenya, Mount	0° 10' S	37° 18' E

Kerguelen	49° 15' S	69° 10' E
Kericho	0° 22' S	35° 15' E
Kermadec Is.	30° 0' S	178° 15' W
KermadecTrnh.	30° 30' S	176° 0' W
Kerman	30° 15' N	57° 1' E
Kermanshah	34° 23' N	47° 0' E
Kerry	52° 7' N	9° 35' W
Keswick	54° 36' N	3° 8' W
Kettering	52° 24' N	0° 43' W
Khabarovsk	48° 30' N	135° 5' E
Khana, Lake	45° 0' N	132° 24' E
Kharg Island	29° 15' N	50° 28' E
Kharkov	49° 58' N	36° 20' E
Khartoum	15° 31' N	32° 35' E
Khorramabad	33° 30' N	48° 25' E
Kidderminster	52° 24' N	2° 15' W
Kiel	54° 19' N	10° 8' E
Kiel Canal	54° 12' N	9° 32' E
Kielder Reservoir	55° 10' N	2° 29' W
Kiev	50° 30' N	30° 28' E
Kigali	1° 59' S	30° 4' E
Kildare	53° 9' N	6° 55' W
Kilifi	3° 40' S	39° 48' E
Kilimanjaro	3° 7' S	37° 20' E
Kilindini	4° 4' S	39° 40' E
Kilkee	52° 41' N	9° 39' W
Kilkenny	52° 39' N	7° 15' W
Killarney	52° 4' N	9° 30' W
Killiecrankie, Pass	56° 44' N	3° 46' W
Killybegs	54° 38' N	8° 26' W
Kilmarnock	55° 37' N	4° 29' W
Kilrush	52° 38' N	9° 29' W
Kimberley	16° 20' S	127° 0' E
Kimch'aek	40° 40' N	129° 10' E
King Island	39° 50' S	144° 0' E
King's Lynn	52° 45' N	0° 24' E
Kingston	17° 55' N	76° 50' W
Kingston upon Hull	53° 45' N	0° 21' W
Kingston-upon-Thames	51° 24' N	0° 17' W
Kingstown	13° 10' N	61° 10' W
Kingussie	57° 6' N	4° 2' W
Kinross	56° 13' N	3° 25' W
Kinsale	51° 42' N	8° 31' W
Kinshasa	4° 20' S	15° 15' E
Kintyre	55° 30' N	5° 35' W
Kintyre, Mull of	55° 17' N	5° 47' W
Kiribati	3° 0' S	180° 0' E
Kirkcaldy	56° 7' N	3° 9' W
Kirkcudbright	54° 50' N	4° 2' W
Kirkenes	69° 40' N	30° 5' E
Kirkuk	35° 30' N	44° 21' E
Kirkwall	58° 59' N	2° 58' W
Kirov	54° 3' N	34° 20' E
Kiruna	67° 52' N	20° 15' E
Kisangani	0° 35' N	25° 15' E
Kishinev	47° 2' N	28° 50' E
Kisangani	0° 40' S	34° 45' E
Kishinev	0° 3' S	34° 45' E
Kisii	0° 40' S	34° 45' E
Kisumu	0° 3' S	34° 45' E
Kitakyushu	33° 50' N	130° 50' E
Kitale	1° 0' N	35° 0' E
Klaipeda	55° 43' N	21° 10' E
Klyuchevskaya	55° 50' N	160° 30' E
Knock	53° 48' N	8° 55' W
Knockmealdown Mountains	52° 14' N	7° 56' W
Kobe	34° 41' N	135° 13' E
Koblenz	50° 21' N	7° 36' E
Kochi	33° 30' N	133° 35' E
Kokopo	4° 22' S	152° 19' E
Kola Peninsula	67° 30' N	38° 0' E
Kolkata	22° 34' N	88° 21' E
Kolyma Range	63° 0' N	57° 0' E
Kongur Shan	38° 34' N	75° 18' E
Konya	37° 52' N	32° 35' E
Korea Strait	34° 0' N	129° 30' E
Kos	36° 50' N	27° 15' E
Kosciuszko, Mount	36° 27' S	148° 16' E
Kosice	48° 42' N	21° 15' E
Kosovo	42° 30' N	21° 0' E
Kota Kinabalu	6° 0' N	116° 4' E
Kotlas	61° 17' N	46° 43' E
Krakatau	6° 10' S	05° 20' E
Krakow	50° 4' N	19° 57' E
Krasnodar	45° 5' N	39° 0' E
Krasnoyarsk	56° 8' N	93° 0' E
Kristiansand	58° 8' N	8° 1' E
Kristiansund	63° 7' N	7° 45' E
KrivoyRog	47° 51' N	33° 20' E

Kuala Lumpur	3° 9' N	101° 41' E
Kucing	1° 33' N	110° 25' E
Kumamoto	32° 45' N	130° 45' E
Kumasi	6° 41' N	1° 38' W
Kunlun Shan	36° 0' N	86° 30' E
Kunming	25° 1' N	102° 41' E
Kuopio	62° 53' N	27° 35' E
Kurdistan	37° 20' N	43° 30' E
Kure	34° 14' N	132° 32' E
Kuril Islands	45° 0' N	150° 0' E
Kursk	51° 42' N	36° 11' E
Kuwait	29° 30' N	48° 0' E
Kuwait	29° 30' N	47° 30' E
Kyle of Lochalsh	57° 17' N	5° 44' W
Kyoga, Lake	1° 35' N	33° 0' E
Kyoto	35° 0' N	135° 45' E
Kyrgyzstan	42° 0' N	75° 0' E
Kyushu	33° 0' N	131° 0' E
L		
La Coruna	43° 20' N	8° 25' W
La Paz, Bolivia	16° 20' S	68° 10' W
La Paz, Mexico	24° 10' N	110° 18' W
La Perouse Strt.	45° 40' N	142° 0' E
La Plata	35° 0' S	57° 55' W
La Rochelle	46° 10' N	1° 9' W
La Spezia	44° 7' N	9° 50' E
Labradore	53° 20' N	61° 0' W
Ladoga, Lake	61° 15' N	30° 30' E
Lae	6° 40' S	147° 2' E
Lagan	54° 36' N	5° 55' W
Lagos	6° 25' N	3° 27' E
Lahore	31° 32' N	74° 22' E
Lahti	60° 58' N	25° 40' E
Lairg	58° 2' N	4° 24' W
Lake District	54° 30' N	3° 21' W
Lakshadweep Is.	10° 0' N	72° 30' E
Lambert Glacier	71° 0' S	70° 0' E
Lamu	2° 16' S	40° 55' E
Lanark	55° 40' N	3° 47' W
Lancashire	53° 50' N	2° 48' W
Lancaster	54° 3' N	2° 48' W
Land's End	50° 4' N	5° 44' W
Langsing	42° 44' N	84° 33' W
Lanzhou	36° 1' N	03° 52' E
Laois	52° 57' N	7° 27' W
Laos	17° 45' N	05° 0' E
Lapland	68° 7' N	24° 0' E
Laptev Sea	76° 0' N	125° 0' E
Largs	55° 47' N	4° 52' W
Larne	54° 55' N	5° 55' W
Larsen Ice Shelf	67° 0' S	62° 0' W
Las Palmas	28° 7' N	15° 26' W
Las Vegas	36° 10' N	15° 8' W
Latakia	35° 30' N	35° 45' E
Latvia	56° 50' N	24° 0' E
Launceston	41° 24' S	147° 8' E
Lausanne	46° 32' N	6° 38' E
Le Havre	49° 30' N	0° 5' E
Le Mans	48° 0' N	0° 10' E
Lea	51° 31' N	0° 1' E
Lebanon	34° 0' N	36° 0' E
Lee	51° 53' N	8° 56' W
Leeds	53° 48' N	1° 33' W
Leeuwin, Cape	34° 20' S	115° 9' E
Leeward Islands	16° 30' N	63° 30' W
Leicester	52° 38' N	1° 8' W
Leicestershire	52° 41' N	1° 17' W
Leinster	53° 3' N	7° 8' W
Leipzig	51° 18' N	12° 22' E
Leith Hill	51° 11' N	0° 22' W
Leitrim	54° 8' N	8° 0' W
Lena	72° 52' N	126° 40' E
Leon, Mexico	21° 6' N	101° 41' W
Leon, Spain	42° 38' N	5° 34' W
Lerida	41° 37' N	0° 39' E
Lerwick	60° 9' N	1° 9' W
Lesbos	39° 10' N	26° 20' E
Leshan	29° 33' N	103° 41' W
Lesotho	29° 40' S	28° 0' E
Lesser Antilles	15° 0' N	61° 0' W
Letchworth	51° 59' N	0° 13' W
Lethbridge	49° 45' N	112° 45' W
Letterkenny	54° 57' N	7° 45' W
Lewes	50° 52' N	0° 1' E
Lewis	58° 9' N	6° 40' W
Lhasa	29° 25' N	90° 58' E
Liberia	6° 30' N	9° 30' W
Libreville	0° 25' N	9° 26' E
Libya	27° 0' N	17° 0' E
Libyan Desert	25° 0' N	25° 0' E

Place	Latitude	Longitude
Liechtenstein	47° 8' N	9° 35' E
Liepaja	56° 30' N	21° 0' E
Liffey	53° 21' N	6° 13' W
Ligurian Sea	43° 20' N	9° 0' E
Lille	50° 38' N	3° 3' E
Lillehammer	61° 8' N	10° 30' E
Lilongwe	14° 0' S	33° 48' E
Lima	12° 3' S	77° 2' W
Limassol	34° 42' N	33° 1' E
Limerick	52° 40' N	8° 37' W
Limoges	45° 50' N	1° 15' E
Limpopo	25° 5' S	33° 30' E
Linares	38° 10' N	3° 40' W
Lincoin, U.K.	53° 14' N	0° 32' W
Lincoin, U.S.A.	40° 49' N	96° 41' W
Lincoin Sea	84° 0' N	55° 0' W
Lincolnshire	53° 14' N	0° 32' W
LincoinshireWlds.	53° 26' N	0° 13' W
Linhai	28° 50' N	121° 8' E
Linkoping	58° 28' N	15° 36' E
Linyi	35° 5' N	118° 21' E
Linz	48° 18' N	14° 18' E
Lipetsk	52° 37' N	39° 35' E
Lisbon	38° 42' N	9° 8' W
Lisburn	54° 30' N	6° 5' W
Listowel	52° 27' N	9° 29' W
Lithuania	55° 30' N	24° 0' E
Little Minch	57° 35' N	6° 45' W
Little Ouse	52° 22' N	1° 12' E
Little Rock	34° 45' N	92° 17' W
Littlehampton	50° 49' N	0° 32' W
Liupanshui	26° 38' N	104° 48' E
Liuzhou	24° 22' N	109° 22' E
Liverpool	53° 25' N	3° 0' W
Liverpool Bay	53° 30' N	3° 20' W
Livingston	55° 54' N	3° 30' W
Livorno	43° 33' N	10° 19' E
Lizard	49° 58' N	5° 13' W
Ljubljana	46° 4' N	14° 33' E
Llandovery	51° 59' N	3° 48' W
Llandrindod Wells	52° 14' N	3° 22' W
Llandudno	53° 19' N	3° 50' W
Llanelli	51° 41' N	4° 10' W
Llangollen	52° 58' N	3° 11' W
Lleyn Peninsula	52° 51' N	4° 36' W
Lochgilphead	56° 2' N	5° 26' W
Lochy, Loch	57° 0' N	4° 53' W
Lockerbie	55° 7' N	3° 21' W
Lodwar	3° 7' N	35° 36' E
Lodz	51° 45' N	19° 27' E
Lofoten Islands	68° 30' N	13° 59' E
Logan, Mount	60° 34' N	140° 23' W
Loire	47° 16' N	2° 10' W
Lokoja	7° 47' N	6° 45' E
Lome	6° 9' N	1° 20' E
Lomond, Loch	56° 8' N	4° 38' W
London	51° 30' N	0° 3' W
Londonderry	55° 0' N	7° 20' W
Londrina	23° 18' S	51° 10' W
Long, Loch	56° 4' N	4° 50' W
Long Eaton	52° 53' N	1° 15' W
Longford	53° 43' N	7° 49' W
Loop Head	52° 34' N	9° 56' W
Lop Nur	40° 20' N	90° 10' E
Hord Howe Is.	31° 33' S	159° 6' E
Lorient	47° 45' N	3° 23' W
Lorn, Firth of	56° 20' N	5° 40' W
Los Angeles	34° 4' N	118° 15' W
Los Mochis	25° 45' N	108° 57' W
Loughborough	52° 47' N	1° 11' W
Loughrea	53° 12' N	8° 33' W
LouisiadeArchp.	11° 10' S	153° 0' E
Louisiana	30° 50' N	92° 0' W
Louisville	38° 15' N	85° 46' W
Louth, Ireland	53° 56' N	6° 34' W
Louth, U.K.	53° 22' N	0° 1' W
Lowestoft	52° 29' N	1° 45' E
Loyalty Islands	20° 50' S	166° 30' E
Luanda	8° 50' S	13° 15' E
Lubeck	53° 52' N	10° 40' E
Lublin	51° 12' N	22° 38' E
Lubumbashi	11° 40' S	27° 28' E
Luce Bay	54° 45' N	4° 48' W
Lucknow	26° 50' N	81° 0' E
Lugansk	48° 38' N	39° 15' E
Lugnaquillia	52° 58' N	6° 28' W
Lule	65° 35' N	22° 10' E
Lulea	65° 35' N	22° 10' E
Lundy	51° 10' N	4° 41' W
Lune	54° 0' N	2° 51' W

Place	Latitude	Longitude
Lurgan	54° 27' N	6° 20' W
Lusaka	15° 28' S	28° 16' E
Luton	51° 53' N	0° 24' W
Luxembourg	49° 45' N	6° 0' E
Luzhou	28° 52' N	105° 20' E
Lvov	49° 50' N	24° 0' E
Lyme Bay	50° 42' N	2° 53' E
Lyme Regis	50° 43' N	2° 57' W
Lymington	50° 45' N	1° 32' W
Lyons	45° 46' N	4° 50' E
M		
McAllen	26° 12' N	98° 14' W
Macapa	0° 5' N	51° 4' W
Macau	22° 12' N	113° 33' E
Macclesfield	53° 15' N	2° 8' W
MacDonnell Rg.	23° 40' S	133° 0' E
Macduff	57° 40' N	2° 31' W
Macedonia	41° 53' N	21° 40' E
Maceio	9° 40' S	35° 41' W
Macgillycuddy's Reeks	51° 58' N	9° 45' W
Machakos	1° 30' S	37° 15' E
Machu Picchu	13° 8' S	72° 30' W
Mackay	21° 8' S	149° 11' E
Mackenzie	69° 10' N	134° 20' W
Mchinley, Mount	63° 4' N	151° 0' W
Mckinley Sea	82° 0' N	0° 0' W
MacRobertson Land	71° 0' S	64° 0' E
Madagascar	20° 0' S	47° 0' E
Madang	5° 12' S	145° 49' E
Madeira	32° 50' N	17° 0' W
Madeira	3° 22' S	58° 45' W
Madison	43° 4' N	89° 24' W
Madras=Chennai	13° 8' N	80° 19' E
Madre, Laguna	25° 15' N	97° 30' W
Madrid	40° 24' N	3° 42' W
Madural	9° 55' N	78° 10' E
Magadan	59° 38' N	150° 50' E
Magdalena	11° 6' N	74° 51' W
Magdeburg	52° 7' N	11° 38' E
Magellan, Strait	52° 30' S	75° 0' W
Maggiore, Lake	45° 57' N	8° 39' E
Maidenhead	51° 31' N	0° 42' W
Maidstone	51° 16' N	0° 32' E
Maiduguri	12° 0' N	13° 20' E
Maine	45° 20' N	9° 0' W
Mainland, Orkney	58° 59' N	3° 8' W
Mainland, Shetland	60° 15' N	1° 22' W
Majorca	39° 30' N	3° 0' E
Makassar	5° 10' S	119° 20' E
Makgadikgadi Salt Pans	20° 40' S	25° 45' E
Makhachkala	43° 0' N	47° 30' E
Makira	10° 30' S	161° 0' E
Makurdi	7° 43' N	8° 35' E
Malacca, Strait of	3° 0' N	101° 0' E
Malaga	36° 43' N	4° 23' W
Malahide	53° 26' N	6° 9' W
Malaita	9° 0' S	161° 0' E
Malakula	16° 15' S	167° 30' E
Malatya	38° 25' N	38° 20' E
Malawi	11° 55' S	34° 0' E
Malawi, Lake	12° 30' S	34° 30' E
Malay Peninsula	7° 25' N	100° 0' E
Malaysia	5° 0' N	110° 0' E
Maldives	5° 0' N	73° 0' E
Male	4° 10' N	73° 28' E
Mali	17° 0' N	3° 0' W
MalinHeaad	55° 23' N	7° 23' W
Malindi	3° 12' S	40° 5' E
Mallaig	57° 0' N	5° 50' W
Mallow	52° 8' N	8° 39' W
Malmo	55° 36' N	12° 59' E
Malta	35° 55' N	14° 26' E
Malton	54° 8' N	0° 49' W
Mamore	10° 23' S	65° 53' W
Man, Isle of	54° 15' N	4° 30' W
Managua	12° 6' N	86° 20' W
Manama	26° 10' N	50° 30' E
Manaus	3° 0' S	60° 0' W
Manchester	53° 29' N	2° 12' W
Manchurian Plain	47° 0' N	124° 0' E
Mandalay	22° 0' N	96° 4' E
Manila	14° 35' N	120° 58' E
Manisa	38° 38' N	27° 30' E
Manizales	5° 5' N	75° 32' W
Mannheim	49° 29' N	8° 29' E
Mansfield	53° 9' N	1° 11' W
Manzhouli	49° 35' N	117° 25' E
Maputo	25° 58' S	32° 32' E
Mar del Plata	38° 0' S	57° 30' W
Maraba	5° 20' S	49° 5' W

Place	Latitude	Longitude
Maracaibo	10° 40' N	71° 37' W
Maracibo, Lake	9° 40' N	71° 30' W
Maracay	10° 15' N	67° 28' W
Maranhao	5° 0' S	46° 0' W
Marathon	38° 11' N	23° 58' E
Marbella	36° 30' N	4° 57' W
March	52° 33' N	0° 5' E
Maree, Loch	57° 40' N	5° 26' W
Margate	51° 23' N	1° 23' E
Mariana Trench	13° 0' N	145° 0' E
Marie Byrd Land	79° 30' S	125° 0' W
Mariupol	47° 5' N	37° 31' E
Markham, Mount	83° 0' S	164° 0' E
Maroua	10° 40' N	14° 20' E
Marrakesh	31° 9' N	8° 0' W
Marree	29° 39' S	138° 1' E
Marsabit	2° 18' N	38° 0' E
Marseilles	43° 18' N	5° 23' E
Marshall Islands	9° 0' N	171° 0' E
Martinique	14° 40' N	61° 0' W
Maryland	39° 0' N	76° 30' W
Maryport	54° 44' N	3° 28' W
Masai Steppe	4° 30' S	36° 30' E
Maseru	29° 18' S	27° 30' E
Mashhad	36° 20' N	59° 35' E
Mask, Lough	53° 36' N	9° 22' W
Massachusetts	42° 30' N	72° 0' W
Massif Central	44° 55' N	3° 0' E
Matamoros	25° 53' N	97° 30' W
Matanzas	23° 0' N	81° 40' W
Matlock	53° 9' N	1° 33' W
MatoGrosso	14° 0' S	55° 0' W
MatoGrosso, Plateau of	15° 0' S	55° 0' W
MatoGrosso do Sul	18° 0' S	55° 0' W
Matsumoto	36° 15' N	138° 0' E
Matsuyama	33° 45' N	132° 45' E
Maturin	9° 45' N	63° 11' W
Mauna Kea	19° 50' N	55° 28' W
Mauna Loa	19° 30' N	55° 35'W
Mauritania	20° 50' N	10° 0' W
Mauritius	20° 0' S	57° 0' E
Mawsynram	25° 15' N	91° 30' E
Maynooth	53° 23' N	6° 34' W
Mayo	53° 53' N	9° 3' W
Mayotte	12° 50' S	45° 10' E
Mazatlan	23° 13' N	106° 25' W
Mbabane	26° 18' S	31° 6' E
Mbale	1° 8' N	34° 12' E
Mbuji-Mayi	6° 9' S	23° 40' E
Mead, Lake	36° 30' N	114° 44' W
Meath	53° 40' N	6° 67' W
Mecea	21° 30' N	39° 54' E
Medan	3° 40' N	98° 38' E
Medellin	6° 15' N	75° 39' W
Medina	24° 35' N	39° 52' E
Mediterranean Sea	35° 0' N	15° 0' E
Medway	51° 25' N	0° 32' E
Medway	51° 27' N	0° 46' E
Meekatharra	26° 32' S	118° 29' E
Mekong	9° 30' N	108° 16' E
Melanesia	4° 0' S	155° 0' E
Melbourne	37° 48' S	144° 58' E
Melekeok	7° 27' N	134° 38' E
Melilla	35° 21' N	2° 57' W
Melthir, Chott	34° 13' N	6° 30' E
Melton Mowbray	52° 47' N	0° 54' W
Melville Island	11° 30' S	31° 0' E
Memphis	35° 8' N	90° 2' W
Mendip Hills	51° 17' N	2° 40' W
Mendoclno, Cape	40° 26' N	24° 25' W
Mendoza	32° 50' S	68° 52' W
Merida	20° 58' N	89° 37' W
Merida, Cordillera de	9° 0' N	71° 0' W
Merrick	55° 8' N	4° 28' W
Mersey	53° 26' N	3° 1' W
Merseyside	53° 31' N	3° 2' W
Mersin	36° 51' N	34° 36' E
MerthyrTydfil	51° 45' N	3° 22' W
Mesopotamia	33° 30' N	44° 0' E
Messina	38° 11' N	15° 34' E
Messina, Strait of	38° 15'N	15° 35' E
Metz	49° 8' N	6° 10' E
Meuse	50° 45' N	5° 41' E
Mexicall	32° 40' N	115° 30' W
Mexico	19° 24' N	99° 9' W
Mexico	25° 0' N	105° 0' W
Mexico, Gulf of	25° 0' N	90° 0' W
Miami	25° 46' N	80° 11' W
Mianyang	31° 22' N	104° 47' E
Michigan	44° 0' N	85° 0' W

Place	Latitude	Longitude
Michigan, Lake	44° 0' N	87° 0'
Micronesia F. S.	9° 0' N	150° 0'
Middle East	35° 0' N	40° 0'
Middlesbrough	54° 35'N	1° 13'
Midlothian	55° 51' N	3° 35'
Midwest	42° 0' N	90° 0'
Milan	45° 28' N	9° 10'
Mildura	34° 13' S	142° 9'
Milford Haven	51° 42' N	5° 7' W
Milltown Malbay	52° 52' N	9° 24'
Milton Keynes	52° 1' N	0° 44'
Milwaukee	43° 2' N	87° 54'
Milwaykee Deep	19° 50' N	68° 0'
Minas Gerais	18° 50' S	46° 0'
Mindanao	8° 0' N	125° 0'
Minehead	51° 12' N	3° 29'
Minna	9° 37' N	6° 30' E
Minneapolis	44° 57' N	93° 16'
Minnesota	46° 0' N	94° 15'
Minorca	40° 0' N	4° 0' E
Minsk	53° 52' N	27° 30'
Mississippi	33° 0' N	90° 0'
Mississippi	29° 9' N	89° 15'
Mississippi River D	29° 10' N	89° 15'
Missouri	38° 25' N	92° 30'
Missouri	38° 49' N	90° 7'
Missouri, Coteau du	47° 0' N	100° 0'
Mitchell	15° 12' S	141° 35
Miyakonojo	31° 40' N	131° 5'
Miyazaki	31° 56' N	131° 30
Mjosa, Lake	60° 40' N	11° 0' E
Modena	44° 40' N	10° 55'
Mogadishu	2° 2' N	45° 25'
Mogilev	53° 55' N	30° 18'
Moher, Cliffs of	52° 58' N	9° 27'
Mojave Desert	35° 0' N	16° 30'
Mold	53° 9' N	3° 8' W
Moldova	47° 0' N	28° 0' E
Moluccas	1° 0' S	27° 0' E
Mombasa	4° 3' S	39° 40'
Monaco	43° 46' N	7° 23' E
Monaghan	54° 15' N	6° 57'
Mongolia	47° 0' N	103° 0'
Mongolia, Plateau	45° 0' N	105° 0'
Monmouth	51° 48' N	2° 42'
Monrovia	6° 18' N	10° 47'
Montana	47° 0' N	03° 0' E
Montego Bay	18° 28' N	77° 55'
Montenegro	42° 40' N	19° 20'
Monteria	8° 46' N	75° 53'
Monterrey	25° 40' N	100° 19
Montes Claros	16° 30' S	43° 50'
Montevideo	34° 50' S	56° 11'
Montgomery	32° 23' N	86° 19'
Montpelier	44° 16' N	72° 35'
Montpellier	43° 37' N	3° 52' E
Montreal	45° 30' N	73° 33'
Montrose	56° 44' N	2° 27'
Montserrat	16° 40' N	62° 10'
Morar, Loch	56° 57' N	5° 40'
Morava	44° 36' N	21° 4' E
Moray Firth	57° 40' N	3° 52'
Morecambe	54° 5' N	2° 52'
Morecambe Bay	54° 7' N	3° 0' W
Morena, Sierra	38° 20' N	4° 0' W
Morocco	32° 0' N	5° 50'
Morpeth	55° 10' N	1° 41'
Moscow	55° 45' N	37° 37'
Moselle	50° 22' N	7° 36' E
Moshi	3° 22' S	37° 18'
Mossoro	5° 10' S	37° 15'
Mostaganem	35° 54' N	0° 5' E
Mosul	36° 15' N	43° 5' E
Motherwell	55° 47' N	3° 58'
Moulmein	16° 30' N	97° 40'
Mount Gambier	37° 50' S	140° 46'
Mount Isa	20° 42' S	139° 26'
Mourne	54° 52' N	7° 26'
Mourne Mounts.	54° 10' N	6° 0' W
Moville	55° 11' N	7° 3' W
Mozambique	19° 0' S	35° 0' E
Mozambique Ch.	17° 30' S	42° 30'
Mudanjieng	44° 38' N	29° 30'
Muthacen	37° 4' N	3° 20' W
Mull	56° 25' N	5° 56' W
Mullet Peninsula	54° 13' N	10° 2' W
Mullingar	53° 31' N	7° 21' W
Multan	30° 15' N	71° 36' E
Mumbai	18° 56' N	72° 50' E
Munich	48° 8' N	11° 34' E

nster, Germany	51° 58' N	7° 37' E
nster, Ireland	52° 18' N	8° 44'W
rcia	38° 5' N	1° 10'W
rmansk	68° 57' N	33° 10' E
rray	35° 20' S	39° 22' E
rrumbidges	34° 43' S	43° 12' E
scat	23° 37' N	58° 36' E
sgrave Ranges	26° 0' S	132° 0' E
sselburgh	56° 57' N	3° 2' W
z Tag	36° 25' N	87° 25' E
vanza	2° 30' S	32° 58' E
veru, Lake	9° 0' S	28° 40' E
anmar=Burma	21° 0' N	96° 30' E
as	53° 12' N	6° 40' W
fud Desert	28° 15' N	41° 0' E
gano	36° 40' N	138° 10' E
gasaki	32° 47' N	129° 50' E
goya	35° 10' N	136° 50' E
gpur	21° 8' N	79° 10' E
ha	26° 13' N	127° 42' E
irn	57° 35' N	3° 53' W
irobi	1° 17' S	36° 48' E
ivasha	0° 40' S	36° 30' E
kuru	0° 15' S	36° 4' E
mangan	41° 0' N	71° 40' E
mib Desert	22° 30' S	15° 0' E
mibia	22° 0' S	18° 9' E
mpo	38° 52' N	125° 10' E
nchang	28° 42' N	115° 55' E
nchong	30° 43' N	106° 2' E
ncy	48° 42' N	6° 12' E
njing	32° 2' N	118° 47' E
nning	22° 48' N	108° 20' E
ntes	47° 12' N	1° 33' W
nyang	33° 11' N	112° 30' E
ples	40° 50' N	14° 15' E
rvik	68° 28' N	17° 26' E
shville	36° 10' N	86° 47' W
ssau	25° 5' N	77° 20' W
sser, Lake	23° 0' N	32° 30' E
tal	5° 47' S	35° 13' W
tron, Lake	2° 20' S	36° 0' E
uru	1° 0' S	166° 0' E
van	53° 39' N	6° 41' W
xcivan	39° 12' N	45° 15' E
ypyidaw	19° 44' N	96° 12' E
djamena	12° 10' N	15° 0' E
eagh, Lough	54° 37' N	6° 25' W
eath	51° 39' N	3° 48' W
eblina, Pico da	0° 48' N	66° 0' W
ebraska	41° 30' N	99° 30' W
efteyugansk	61° 5' N	72° 42' E
egro	3° 0' S	60° 0' W
eisse	52° 4' N	14° 46' E
elson, N.Z.	41° 18' S	173° 16' E
elson, U.K.	53° 50' N	2° 13' W
ene	52° 49' N	0° 11' E
epal	28° 0' N	84° 30' E
ess, Loch	57° 15' N	4° 32' W
etherlands	52° 0' N	5° 30' E
euquen	38° 55' S	68° 0' W
evada	39° 0' N	117° 0' W
ew Britain	5° 50' S	150° 20' E
ew Caledonia	21° 0' S	165° 0' E
ew Delhi	28° 36' N	77° 11' E
ew England	43° 0' N	71° 0' W
ew Forest	50° 53' N	1° 34' W
ew Georgia Is.	8° 15' S	157° 30' E
ew Guinea	4° 0' S	136° 0' E
ew Hampshire	44° 0' N	71° 30' W
ew Ireland	3° 20' S	151° 50' E
ew Jersey	40° 0' N	74° 30' W
ew Mexico	34° 30' N	106° 0' W
ew Orleans	29° 57' N	90° 4' W
ew Siberian Is.	75° 0' N	142° 0' E
ew South Wales	33° 0' S	146° 0' E
ew York	43° 0' N	75° 0' W
ew Zealand	40° 0' S	176° 0' E
ewark-on-Trent	53° 5' N	0° 48' W
ewbridge	53° 11' N	6° 48' W
ewbury	51° 24' N	1° 20' W
ewcastle, Astr.	33° 0' S	151° 46' E
ewcastle, Ireld.	52° 27' N	9° 3' W
ewcastle-Under-Lyme	53° 1' N	2° 14' W
ewcastle-upon-Tyne	54° 58' N	1° 36' W
ewfoundland	49° 0' N	55° 0' W
ewhaven	50° 47' N	0° 3' E
ewman	23° 18' S	119° 45' E
ewmarket	52° 15' N	0° 25' E

Newport, Engld.	50° 42' N	1° 17' W
Newport, Wales	51° 35' N	3° 0' W
Newquary	50° 25' N	5° 6' W
Newry	54° 11' N	6° 21' W
Newton Abbot	50° 32' N	3° 37' W
Newton Aycliffe	54° 37' N	1° 34' W
Newton Stewart	54° 57' N	4° 30' W
Newton	52° 31' N	3° 19' W
Newtonabbey	54° 40' N	5° 56' W
Newtonards	54° 36' N	5° 42' W
Neyshabur	36° 10' N	58° 50' E
Niagara Falls	43° 7' N	79° 5' W
Niamey	13° 27' N	2° 6' E
Nicaragua	11° 40' N	85° 30' W
Nicaragua, Lake	12° 0' N	85° 30' W
Nice	43° 42' N	7° 14' E
Nicobar Islands	8° 0' N	93° 30' E
Nicosia	35° 10' N	33° 25' E
Nidd	55° 59' N	1° 23' W
Niemen	55° 25' N	21° 10' E
Niger	17° 30' N	10° 0' E
Niger	5° 33' N	6° 33' E
Niger Delta	5° 0' N	6° 0' E
Nigeria	8° 30' N	8° 0' E
Nikolayev	46° 58' N	32° 0' E
Nile	30° 10' N	31° 6' E
Nimes	43° 50' N	4° 23' E
Ningbo	29° 51' N	121° 28' E
Nirth	55° 14' N	3° 33' W
Niue	19° 2' S	169° 54' W
Nizhniy Novgorod	56° 20' N	44° 0' E
Nogales	31° 19' N	110° 56' W
Nore	52° 25' N	6° 58' W
Norfolk, U.K.	52° 39' N	0° 54' E
Norfolk, U.S.A.	36° 50' N	76° 17' W
Norfolk Island	28° 58' S	168° 3' E
Norilsk	69° 20' N	88° 6' E
Normandy	48° 45' N	0° 10' E
Norrkoping	58° 37' N	16° 11' E
Norrland	62° 15' N	15° 45' E
North America	40° 0' N	100° 0' W
North Berwick	56° 4' N	2° 42' W
North Cape	71° 10' N	25° 50' E
North Dakota	47° 30' N	100° 15' W
North Downs	51° 19' N	0° 21' E
North Esk	56° 46' N	2° 24' W
North Foreland	51° 22' N	1° 28' E
North Island	38° 0' S	175° 0' E
North Korea	40° 0' N	127° 0' E
North Magnetic Pole	82° 18' N	113° 24' W
North Minch	58° 5' N	5° 55' W
North Pole	90° 0' N	0° 0' W
North Ronaldsy	59° 22' N	2° 26' W
North Sea	56° 0' N	4° 0' E
North Tyne	55° 0' N	2° 8' W
North Uist	57° 40' N	7° 15' W
North West Cap.	21° 45' S	114° 9' E
North West Hg.	57° 33' N	4° 58' W
North York Mr.	54° 23' N	0° 53' W
North Yorkshire	54° 15' N	1° 25' W
Northallerton	54° 20' N	1° 26' W
Northampton	52° 15' N	0° 53' W
Northampton-Shire	52° 16' N	0° 55' W
Northern Dvina	64° 32' N	40° 30' E
Northern Ireland	54° 45' N	7° 0' W
Nothern Mariana	17° 0' N	145° 0' E
Northern Terroty.	20° 0' S	133° 0' E
Northumberland	55° 12' N	2° 0' W
Norway	63° 0' N	11° 0' E
Norwegian Sea	66° 0' N	1° 0' E
Norwich	52° 38' N	1° 18' E
Noss Head	58° 28' N	3° 3' W
Nottingham	52° 58' N	1° 10' W
Nottinghamshire	53° 10' N	1° 3' W
Nouakchott	18° 9' N	15° 58' W
Noumea	22° 17' S	166° 30' E
Nova Iguacu	22° 45' S	43° 28' W
Nova Scotia	45° 10' N	63° 0' W
Novara	45° 28' N	° 38' E
Novaya Zemlya	75° 0' N	56° 0' E
Novgorod	58° 30' N	31° 25' E
Novokuznetsk	53° 45' N	87° 10' E
Novosibirsk	55° 0' N	83° 5' E
Nubian Desert	21° 30' N	33° 30' E
Nuevo Laredo	27° 30' N	99° 31' W
Nuku'alofa	21° 10' S	175° 12' W
Nukus	42° 27' N	59° 41' E
Nullarbor Plain	31° 10' S	129° 0' E
Nuneaton	52° 32' N	1° 27' W
Nuremberg	49° 27' N	11° 3' E

Nuuk	64° 10' N	51° 35' W
O		
Oates Land	69° 0' S	160° 0' E
Oaxaca	17° 3' N	96° 43' W
Ob	66° 45' N	69° 30' E
Ob, Gulf of	69° 0' N	73° 0' E
Oban	56° 25' N	5° 29' W
Odense	55° 22' N	10° 23' E
Oder	53° 33' N	14° 38' E
Odessa	46° 30' N	30° 45' E
Offaly	53° 15' N	7° 30' W
Ogbomosho	8° 1' N	4° 11' E
Ogooue	1° 0' S	9° 0' E
Ohio	40° 15' N	82° 45' W
Ohio	36° 59' N	89° 8' W
Oita	33° 14' N	131° 36' E
Ojos del Salado, Cerro	27° 0' S	68° 40' W
Okavango Delta	18° 45' S	22° 45' E
Okayama	34° 40' N	133° 54' E
Okhotsk	59° 20' N	143° 10' E
Okhotsk, Sea of	55° 0' N	145° 0' E
Oklahoma	35° 20' N	97° 30' W
Oklahoma City	35° 30' N	97° 30' W
Oland	56° 45' N	16° 38' E
Olbia	40° 55' N	9° 31' E
Oldenburg	53° 9' N	8° 13' E
Oldham	53° 33' N	2° 7' W
Olympia, Greece	37° 39' N	21° 39' E
Olympia, U.S.A.	47° 3' N	122° 53' W
Olympus, Mount	40° 6' N	22° 23' E
Omagh	54° 35' N	7° 15' W
Omaha	41° 17' N	95° 58' W
Oman	23° 0' N	58° 0' E
Oman, Gulf of	24° 30' N	58° 30' E
Omdurman	15° 40' N	32° 28' E
Omsk	55° 0' N	73° 12' E
Onega	63° 58' N	38° 2' E
Onega, Lake	61° 44' N	35° 22' E
Onitsha	6° 6' N	6° 42' E
Ontario, Lake	43° 20' N	78° 0' W
Oporto	41° 8' N	8° 40' W
Oran	35° 45' N	0° 39' W
Orange	28° 41' S	16° 28' E
Orebro	59° 20' N	15° 18' E
Oregon	44° 0' N	121° 0' W
Orense	42° 19' N	7° 55' W
Orinoco	9° 15' N	61° 30' W
Orizaba, Pico de	18° 58' N	97° 15' W
Orkney Islands	59° 0' N	3° 0' W
Orlando	28° 32' N	81° 22' W
Orleans	47° 54' N	1° 52' E
Ormskirk	53° 35' N	2° 54' W
Osaka	34° 42' N	135° 30' E
Osh	40° 37' N	72° 49' E
Oshogbo	7° 48' N	4° 37' E
Oslo	59° 54' N	10° 43' E
Osnabruck	52° 17' N	8° 3' E
Ostersund	63° 10' N	14° 38' E
Oswestry	52° 52' N	3° 3' W
Otranto, Strait of	40° 15' N	18° 40' E
Ottawa	45° 26' N	75° 42' W
Ouagadougou	12° 25' N	1° 30' W
Oubangi	0° 30' S	17° 50' E
Oujda	34° 41' N	1° 55' W
Oulu	65° 1' N	25° 29' E
Oulu, Lake	64° 25' N	27° 15' E
Ouse, East Sussex	50° 47' N	0° 4' E
Ouse North Yorkshire	53° 44' N	0° 55' W
Outer Hebrides	57° 30' N	7° 15' W
Oxford	51° 46' N	1° 15' W
Oxfordshire	51° 48' N	1° 16' W
Oyo	7° 46' N	3° 56' E
Ozark Plateau	37° 20' N	91° 40' W
Ozarks, Lake of the	38° 12' N	92° 38' W
P		
Pacaraima, Sierra	4° 0' N	62° 30' W
Pacific Ocean	10° 0' N	140° 0' W
Padang	1° 0' S	100° 20' E
Padova	45° 25' N	11° 53' E
Pago Pago	14° 16' S	170° 43' S
Paignton	50° 26' N	3° 25' W
Paisley	55° 50' N	4° 25' W
Pakistan	30° 0' N	70° 0' E
Palau	7° 30' N	134° 30' E
Palawan	9° 30' N	118° 30' E
Palembang	3° 0' S	104° 50' E
Palermo	38° 7' N	13° 22' E
Palma de Mallorca	39° 35' N	2° 39' E
Palmas	10° 13' S	48° 16' W
Palmer Land	73° 0' S	63° 0' W

Palmerston North	40° 21' S	175° 39' E
Palmira	3° 32' N	76° 16' W
Pamir	37° 40' N	73° 0' E
Pampass	35° 0' S	3° 0' W
Panama	8° 48' N	79° 55' W
Panama, Gulf of	8° 4' N	79° 20' W
Panama, Isthmus of	9° 0' N	79° 0' W
Panama Canal	9° 10' N	79° 37' W
Pantelleria	36° 50' N	11° 57' E
Panzhihua	26° 33' N	101° 44' E
Papua New Guinea	8° 0' S	145° 0' E
Para	3° 20' S	52° 0' W
Paraguay	23° 0' S	57° 0' W
Paraguay	27° 18' S	58° 38' W
Paraiba	7° 0' S	36° 0' W
Parakou	9° 25' N	2° 40' E
Paramaribo	5° 50' N	55° 10' W
Parana	24° 30' S	51° 0' W
Parana	33° 43' S	59° 15' W
Paris	48° 53' N	2° 20' E
Parma	44° 48' N	10° 20' E
Parnaiba	3° 0' S	41° 50' W
Parrett	51° 12' N	3° 1' W
Passage West	51° 52' N	8° 21' W
Patagonia	45° 0' S	69° 0' W
Patna	25° 35' N	85° 12' E
Patra	38° 14' N	21° 47' E
Pau	43° 19' N	0° 25' W
Peak, The	53° 24' N	1° 52' W
Peari	30° 11' N	89° 32' W
Pecos	29° 42' N	101° 22' W
Peebles	55° 40' N	3° 11' W
Peking=Beijing	39° 53' N	116° 21' E
Peloponnese	37° 10' N	22° 0' E
Pelotas	31° 42' S	52° 23' W
Pembroke	51° 41' N	4° 55' W
Pennines	54° 45' N	2° 27' W
Pennsylvania	40° 45' N	77° 30' W
Penrith	54° 40' N	2° 45' W
Pentland Firth	58° 43' N	3° 10' W
Penza	53° 15' N	45° 5' E
Penzance	50° 7' N	5° 33' W
Pereira	4° 49' N	75° 43' W
Perm	58° 0' N	56° 10' E
Pernambuco	8° 0' S	37° 0' W
Perpignan	42° 42' N	2° 53' E
Persepolis	29° 55' N	52° 50' E
Persian Gulf	27° 0' N	50° 0' E
Perth, Australia	31° 57' S	115° 52' E
Perth, U.K.	56° 24' N	3° 26' W
Peru	4° 0' S	75° 0' W
Perugia	43° 7' N	12° 23' E
Pescara	42° 28' N	14° 13' E
Peterborough	52° 35' N	0° 15' W
Peterhead	57° 31' N	1° 48' W
Peterlee	54° 47' N	1° 20' W
Petrozavodsk	61° 41' N	34° 20' E
Philadelphia	39° 57' N	75° 9' W
Philippines	12° 0' N	123° 0' E
Phnom Penh	11° 33' N	104° 55' E
Phoenix	33° 26' N	112° 4' W
Phoenix Islands	3° 30' S	172° 0' W
Phuket	7° 53' N	98° 24' E
Piacenza	45° 1' N	9° 40' E
Piaui	7° 0' S	43° 0' W
Pierre	44° 22' N	100° 21' W
Pindus Mounts.	40° 0' N	21° 0' E
Pingxiang	27° 43' N	113° 48' E
Pisa	43° 43' N	10° 23' E
Pitlochry	56° 42' N	3° 44' W
Pittsburgh	40° 26' N	79° 58' W
Plata, Rio de ls	34° 45' S	57° 30' W
Ploiesti	44° 57' N	26° 5' E
Plovdiv	42° 8' N	24° 44' E
Plymouth	50° 22' N	4° 10' W
Pizen	49° 45' N	13° 22' E
Po	44° 57' N	12° 4' E
Pobedy Peak	42° 0' N	79° 58' E
Podgorica	42° 30' N	19° 19' E
Pointe-a-Pitre	16° 15' N	61° 32' W
Pointe-Noire	4° 48' S	11° 53' E
Poitiers	46° 35' N	0° 20' E
Poland	52° 0' N	20° 0' E
Polynesia	10° 0' S	162° 0' W
Pompeii	40° 45' N	14° 30' E
Ponta Grossaa	25° 7' S	50° 10' W
Pontchartrain , Lake	30° 5' N	90° 5' W
Pontianak	0° 3' S	109° 15' E
Pontine Mountains	41° 0' N	36° 45' E
Pontypool	51° 42' N	3° 2' W

Pontypridd	51° 36' N	3° 20' W
Poole	50° 43' N	1° 59' W
Poopo, Lake	18° 30' S	67° 35' W
PopocateptlVolcan	19° 2' N	98° 38' W
Pori	61° 29' N	21° 48' E
Port-au-Prince	18° 40' N	72° 20' W
Port Augusta	32° 30' S	137° 50' W
Port Elizabeth	33° 58' S	25° 40' E
Port Harcourt	4° 40' N	7° 10' E
Port Hedland	20° 25' S	118° 35' E
Port Lincoln	34° 42' S	135° 52' E
Port Moresby	9° 24' S	147° 8' E
Port of Spain	10° 40' N	61° 31' W
Port Pirie	33° 10' S	138° 1' E
Port Said	31° 16' N	32° 18' E
Port Talbot	51° 35' N	3° 47' W
Port Vila	17° 45' S	168° 18' E
Portadown	54° 25' N	6° 27' W
Porthmadog	52° 55' N	4° 8' W
Portland, Maine	43° 39' N	70° 16' W
Portland, Oregon	45° 32' N	122° 37' W
Portland Bill	50° 31' N	2° 28' W
Portlaoise	53° 2' N	7° 18' W
Porto-Alegre	30° 5' S	51° 10' W
Porto-Novo	6° 23' N	2° 42' E
Porto Velho	8° 46' S	63° 54' W
Portree	57° 25' N	6° 12' W
Portsmouth	50° 48' N	1° 6' W
Portugal	40° 0' N	8° 0' W
Potomac	38° 0' N	76° 23' W
Potsdam	52° 23' N	13° 3' E
Poulaphouca Reservoir	53° 8' N	6° 30' W
Powys	52° 20' N	3° 20' W
Poznan	52° 25' N	16° 55' E
Prague	50° 4' N	14° 25' E
Preston	53° 46' N	2° 42' W
Pretoria	25° 44' S	28° 12' E
Prince Charles Mts	72° 0' S	67° 0' E
Pripet	51° 20' N	30° 15' E
Prishtine	42° 40' N	21° 13' E
Provence	43° 40' N	5° 46' E
Providence	41° 49' N	71° 24' W
Prydz Bay	69° 0' S	74° 0' E
Pskov	57° 50' N	28° 25' E
Puebla	19° 3' N	98° 12' W
Puerto Barrios	15° 40' N	88° 32' W
Puerto Rico	18° 15' N	66° 45' W
PumlumonFawr	52° 28' N	3° 46' W
Pune	18° 29' N	73° 57' E
Punjab	31° 0' N	76° 0' E
Punta Arenas	53° 10' S	71° 0' W
Purus	3° 42' S	1° 28' W
Putrajaya	2° 55' N	101° 40' E
Putumayo	3° 7' S	67° 58' W
Pwllheli	52° 53' N	4° 25' W
P'yongyang	39° 0' N	125° 30' E
Pyramids	29° 58' N	31° 9' E
Pyrenees	42° 45' N	0° 18' E
Q		
Qaidam Basin	37° 0' N	95° 0' E
Qatar	25° 30' N	51° 15' E
Qazvin	36° 15' N	0° 0' E
Qilian Shan	38° 30' N	96° 0' E
Qingdao	36° 5' N	120° 20' E
Qiqihar	47° 26' N	124° 0' E
Qom	34° 40' N	51° 0' E
Quanzhou	24° 55' N	118° 34' E
Quebec	46° 52' N	71° 13' W
Queen Elizabeth Islands	76° 0' N	95° 0' W
Queen Elibabeth Land	84° 0' S	42° 0' W
Queen Mary Ld.	70° 0' S	95° 0' E
Queen Maud Ld.	72° 30' S	12° 0' E
Queensland	22° 0' S	142° 0' E
Queretaro	20° 36' N	100° 23' W
Quetta	30° 15' N	66° 55' E
Quibdo	5° 42' N	76° 40' W
Quilpie	26° 35' S	44° 11' E
Quimper	48° 0' N	4° 9' W
Quito	0° 15' S	78° 35' W
R		
Rabat	34° 2' N	6° 48' W
Race, Cape	46° 40' N	53° 5' W
Rainier, Mount	46° 52' N	121° 46' W
Rajkot	22° 15' N	70° 56' E
Raleigh	35° 47' N	78° 39' W
Ramsey	54° 20' N	4° 22' W
Rangoon	16° 45' N	96° 20' E
Rannoch, Loch	56° 41' N	4° 20' W
Ra's al Khaymah	25° 50' N	55° 59' E
Rathlin Island	55° 18' N	6° 14' W
Ravenna	44° 25' N	12° 12' E
Reading	51° 27' N	0° 58' W
Recife	8° 0' S	35° 0' W
Red, U.S.A.	31° 1' N	91° 45' W
Red, Vietnam	20° 16' N	106° 34' E
Red Sea	25° 0' N	36° 0' E
Redcar	54° 37' N	1° 4' W
Redditch	52° 18' N	1° 55' W
Redruth	50° 14' N	5° 14' W
Ree, Lough	53° 35' N	8° 0' W
Regensburg	49° 1' N	12° 6' E
Reggio di Cb.	38° 6' N	15° 39' E
Reggio nell' Emilie	44° 43' N	10° 36' E
Reigate	51° 14' N	0° 12' W
Reims	49° 15' N	4° 1' E
Rennell	11° 40' S	60° 10' E
Rennes	48° 7' N	1° 41' W
Reunion	21° 0' S	56° 0' E
Revilla Gigedo Is.	18° 40' N	12° 0' W
Rey Malabo	3° 45' N	8° 50' E
Reykjavik	64° 10' N	21° 57' W
Reynosa	26° 7' N	98° 18' W
Rhine	51° 52' N	6° 2' E
Rhode Island	41° 40' N	71° 30' W
Rhodes	36° 15' N	28° 10' E
Rhodope Mts.	41° 40' N	24° 20' E
Rhondda	51° 39' N	3° 31' W
Rhone	43° 28' N	4° 42' E
Rhum	57° 0' N	6° 20' W
Rhyl	53° 20' N	3° 29' W
Ribble	53° 52' N	2° 25' W
Ribeirao Preto	21° 10' S	47° 50' W
Richmond, U.K.	54° 25' N	1° 43' W
Richmond, U.S.A.	37° 33' N	77° 27' W
Rift Valley	7° 0' N	30° 0' E
Riga	56° 53' N	24° 8' E
Riga, Gulf of	57° 40' N	23° 45' E
Riser-Larsn Sea	67° 30' S	22° 0' E
Rimini	44° 3' N	12° 33' E
Rio Branco	9° 58' S	67° 49' W
Rio de Janeiro	22° 54' S	43° 12' W
Rio G. do Norte	5° 40' S	36° 0' W
Rio G. do Sul	30° 0' S	53° 0' W
Ripon	54° 9' N	1° 31' W
Riviera	44° 0' N	8° 30' E
Riyadh	24° 41' N	6° 42' E
Rochdale	53° 38' N	2° 9' W
Rochester, U.K.	51° 23' N	0° 31' E
Rochester USA	43° 10' N	77° 37' W
Rockhampton	23° 22' S	150° 32' E
Rocky Mnts.	49° 0' N	115° 0' W
Roma	41° 54' N	12° 28' E
Romania	46° 0' N	25° 0' E
Romney Marsh	51° 2' N	0° 54'E
Romsey	51° 0' N	1° 29' W
Rondonia	11° 0' S	63° 0' W
Ronne Ice Shlf	77° 30' S	60° 0' W
Roraima	2° 0' N	61° 30' W
Roraima, Mnt.	5° 10' N	60° 40' W
Rosario	33° 0' S	60° 40' W
Roscommon	53° 38' N	° 11' W
Roscrea	52° 57' N	7° 49' W
Roseau	15° 17' N	61° 24' W
Ross Ice Shelf	80° 0' S	180° 0' E
Ross-on-Wye	51° 54' N	2° 34' W
Ross Sea	74° 0' S	178° 0' E
RosslareHarbr.	52° 15' N	6° 20' W
Rostock	54° 5' N	12° 8' E
Rostov	47° 15' N	39° 45' E
Rother	50° 59' N	0° 45' E
Rotherham	53° 26' N	1° 20' W
Rothesav	55° 50' N	5° 3' W
Rotoua	38° 9' S	176° 16' E
Rotterdam	51° 55' N	4° 30' E
Rouen	49° 27' N	1° 4' E
Rousay	59° 10' N	3° 2' W
Rovaniemi	66° 29' N	25° 41' E
Royal Lmt. Spa	52° 18' N	1° 31' N
Royal Tg. Well.	51° 7' N	0° 16' E
Rub' al Khali	19° 0' N	48° 0' E
Rugby	52° 23' N	1° 16' W
Runcorn	53° 21' N	2° 44' W
Rushden	52° 18' N	0° 35' W
Russia	62° 0' N	105° 0' E
Rutland	52° 38' N	0° 40' W
Rwanda	2° 0' S	30° 0' E
Ryan, Loch	55° 0' N	5° 2' W
Rybinsk Reservoir	58° 30' N	38° 25' E
Ryde	50° 43' N	1° 9' W
Rye	54° 11' N	0° 44' W
Ryukyu Islands	26° 0' N	26° 0' E
S		
Saarbrucken	49° 14' N	6° 59' E
Saaremaa	58° 30' N	22° 30' E
Sabah	6° 0' N	117° 0' E
Sabine	29° 59' N	93° 47' W
Sacrmento	38° 35' N	21° 29' W
Sacramento Mount.	32° 30' N	05° 30' W
Sacramento Valley	39° 30' N	22° 0' W
Sado	38° 0' N	138° 25' E
Sahara	23° 0' N	5° 0' E
Sahel	16° 0' N	5° 0' E
Saimaa, Lake	61° 15' N	28° 15' E
Saint Albans	51° 45' N	0° 19' W
Saint Andrews	56° 20' N	2° 47' W
Saint Austell	50° 20' N	4° 47' W
Saint David's Head	51° 54' N	5° 19' W
Saint-Etienne	45° 27' N	4° 22' E
Saint George's	12° 5' N	61° 43' W
Saint George's Ch.	52° 0' N	6° 0' W
Saint Helena	15° 58' S	5° 42' W
Saint Helens	53° 27' N	2° 44' W
Saint Helens, Mnt.	46° 12' N	122° 12' W
Saint Helier	49° 10' N	2° 7' W
Saint Ives	50° 12' N	5° 30' W
Saint John's Antg.	17° 6' N	61° 51' W
Saint John's Canda	47° 35' N	52° 40' W
Saint Kilda	57° 49' N	8° 34' W
Saint Kitts & Nevis	17° 20' N	62° 40' W
Saint Lawrence	49° 30' N	66° 0' W
Saint Louis	38° 37' N	90° 11' W
Saint Lucia	14° 0' N	60° 57' W
Saint-Malo	48° 39' N	2° 1' W
Saint Mary's	49° 55' N	6° 18' W
Saint-Nazaire	47° 17' N	2° 12' W
Shimonoseki	33° 58' N	130° 50' E
Shiraz	29° 42' N	52° 30' E
Shizuoka	34° 57' N	138° 24' E
Shrewsbury	52° 43' N	2° 45' W
Shropshire	52° 36' N	2° 45' W
Si Kiang	22° 20' N	13° 20' E
Siberia	60° 0' N	00° 0' E
Sichuan	30° 30' N	03° 0' E
Sicily	37° 30' N	14° 30' E
Sidmouth	50° 40' N	3° 15' W
Sidra, Gulf of	31° 40' N	18° 30' E
Siena	43° 19' N	11° 21' E
Sierra Blanca Peak	33° 23' N	105° 49' W
Sierra Leone	9° 0' N	12° 0' W
Sierra Madre	16° 0' N	93° 0' W
Sierra Nevada, Sp.	37° 3' N	3° 15' W
Sierra Nevada, USA	39° 0' N	20° 30' W
SikhoteAlin Range	45° 0' N	36° 0' E
Simpson Desert	25° 0' S	37° 0' E
Sinai	29° 0' N	34° 0' E
Singapore	1° 17' N	03° 51' E
Sinkiang	42° 0' N	86° 0' E
Siracusa	37° 4' N	15° 17' E
Sivas	39° 43' N	36° 58' E
Sjaelland	55° 30' N	11° 30' E
Skagen	57° 43' N	10° 35' E
Skagerrak	57° 30' N	9° 0' E
Skegness	53° 9' N	0° 20' E
Skelleftea	64° 45' N	20° 50' E
Skipton	53° 58' N	2° 3' W
Skopje	42° 1' N	21° 26' E
Skye	57° 15' N	6° 10' W
Slaney	52° 26' N	6° 33' W
Slea Head	52° 6' N	10° 27' W
SlieveDonard	54° 11' N	5° 55' W
Sligo	54° 16' N	8° 28' W
Sligo Bay	54° 18' N	8° 40' W
Slough	51° 30' N	0° 36' W
Slovak Republic	48° 30' N	20° 0' E
Slovenia	45° 58' N	4° 30' E
Smolensk	54° 45' N	32° 5' E
Snaefell	54° 16' N	4° 27' W
Snake	46° 12' N	19° 2' W
Snowdown	53° 4' N	4° 5' W
Saint Neots	52° 14' N	0° 15' W
Saint Paul	44° 56' N	93° 5' W
Saint Peter Port	49° 26' N	2° 33' W
Saint Petersburg Russia	59° 55' N	30° 20' E
Saint Petersburg, U.S.A.	27° 46' N	82° 40' W
Saint Vincent & the Grenadines	13° 0' N	61° 10' W
Saitama	35° 54' N	139° 38' E
Sakai	34° 34' N	135° 27'
Sakhalin	51° 0' N	143° 0'
Salamanca	40° 58' N	5° 39' W
Sale	53° 26' N	2° 19' W
Salerno	40° 41' N	14° 47'
Salford	53° 30' N	2° 18' W
Salisbury	51° 4' N	1° 47' W
Salisbury Plain	51° 14' N	1° 55' W
Salt Lake City	40° 45' N	11° 53'
Saltash	50° 24' N	4° 14' W
Salton Sea	33° 15' N	15° 45'
Salvador	13° 0' S	38° 30'
Salween	16° 31' N	97° 37'
Salzburg	47° 48' N	13° 2' E
Samara	53° 8' N	50° 6' E
Samarkand	39° 40' N	66° 55' E
Samoa	14° 0' S	72° 0' W
Samos	37° 45' N	26° 50' E
Samsun	41° 15' N	36° 22' E
San Andreas Ft.	36° 0' N	21° 0' W
San Antonio	29° 25' N	98° 29'
San Bernardino	34° 7' N	17° 19'
San Blas, Cape	29° 40' N	85° 21'
San Cristobal	7° 46' N	72° 14'
San Diego	32° 42' N	17° 9' W
San Francisco	37° 46' N	22° 23'
San Joaquin Vly.	37° 20' N	21° 0' W
San Jose, ct. Rc.	9° 55' N	84° 2' W
San Jose, USA	37° 20' N	121° 53'
San Juan, Argt.	31° 30' S	68° 30'
San Juan, P. Rio	18° 28' N	66° 7' W
San Lucas, Cabo	22° 52' N	109° 53'
San Luis Potosi	22° 9' N	100° 59'
San Marino	43° 56' N	12° 25' E
San Miguel d T.	26° 50' S	65° 20'
San Pedro Sula	15° 30' N	88° 0' W
San Salvador	13° 40' N	89° 10'
Snowy Mountain	36° 30' S	148° 20'
SobradinhoRsr.	9° 30' S	42° 0' W
Sochi	43° 35' N	39° 40' E
Socotra	12° 30' N	54° 0' E
Sofiya	42° 45' N	23° 20' E
Sogne Fjord	61° 10' N	5° 50' E
Sokoto	13° 2' N	5° 16' E
Solapur	17° 43' N	75° 56' E
Slihull	52° 26' N	1° 47' W
Solomon Islands	6° 0' S	55° 0' E
Solomon Sea	7° 0' S	50° 0' E
Solway Firth	54° 49' N	3° 35' W
Somalia	7° 0' N	47° 0' E
Somerset	51° 9' N	3° 0' W
Songkhla	7° 13' N	00° 37' W
Sonora	29° 20' N	10° 40' W
Sousse	35° 50' N	10° 38' E
South Africa	32° 0' S	23° 0' E
South America	10° 0' S	60° 0' W
South Australia	32° 0' S	139° 0' E
South Carolina	34° 0' N	81° 0' W
South China Sea	10° 0' N	113° 0' E
South Dakota	44° 15' N	100° 0' W
South Downs	50° 52' N	0° 25' W
South East Cape	43° 40' S	146° 50'
South Esk	56° 43' N	2° 31' W
South Georgia	54° 30' S	3° 0' W
South Island	44° 0' S	170° 0' E
South Korea	36° 0' N	128° 0' E
South Magnetic Pole	64° 8' S	138° 8' E
South Orkney Is.	63° 0' S	45° 0' W
South Pole	90° 0' S	0° 0' W
South Ronaldsay	58° 48' N	2° 58' W
South Shetld. Is.	62° 0' S	59° 0' W
South Shields	55° 0' N	1° 25' W
South Sudan	8° 0' N	30° 0' E
South Uist	57° 20' N	7° 15' W
South Yorkshire	53° 27' N	1° 36' W
Southampton	50° 54' N	1° 23' W
Southen-on-Sea	51° 32' N	0° 44' E
Southern Alps	43° 41' S	70° 11' E
South Ocean	62° 0' S	60° 0' E
Southern Uplands	55° 28' N	3° 52' W
Southport	53° 39' N	3° 0' W
Sana	15° 27' N	44° 12' E
Sanaga	3° 35' N	9° 38' E
Sanandaj	35° 18' N	47° 1' E
Sanday	59° 16' N	2° 31' W
Sanliurfa	37° 12' N	38° 50' E
Sanquhar	55° 22' N	3° 54' W
Santa Catarina	27° 25' S	48° 30' W
Santa Clara	22° 20' N	80° 0' W
Santa Cruz	17° 43' S	63° 10' W

Place	Latitude	Longitude
nta Cruz Is.	10° 30' S	66° 0' E
nta Fe. Argnt.	31° 15' S	60° 41' W
nta Fe, U.S.A.	35° 41' N	105° 57' W
ntander	43° 27' N	3° 51' W
ntarem	2° 25' S	54° 42' W
ntiago	33° 26' S	70° 40' W
ntiago de Cp.	42° 52' N	8° 37' W
ntiago de Cub.	20° 0' N	75° 49' W
ntiago de los balleros	19° 30' N	70° 40' W
nto Domingo	18° 30' N	69° 59' W
ntos	24° 0' S	46° 20' W
nya	18° 14' N	109° 29' E
o Francisco	10° 30' S	36° 24' W
o Luis	2° 39' S	44° 15' W
o Paulo	23° 32' S	46° 38' W
o Tome &Prc.	0° 12' N	6° 39' E
one	45° 44' N	4° 50' E
pporo	43° 0' N	41° 21' E
rajevo	43° 52' N	18° 26' E
rasota	27° 20' N	82° 32' W
ratov	51° 30' N	46° 2' E
rawak	2° 0' N	13° 0' E
rdinia	40° 0' N	9° 0' E
rgasso Sea	27° 0' N	72° 0' W
rk	49° 25' N	2° 22' W
sebo	33° 10' N	29° 43' E
ssari	40° 43' N	8° 34' E
udi Arabia	26° 0' N	44° 0' E
vannah	32° 5' N	81° 6' W
vannah	32° 2' N	80° 53' W
afell Pike	54° 27' N	3° 14' W
andinavia	64° 0' N	12° 0' E
arborough	54° 17' N	0° 24' W
ily, Isles of	49° 56' N	6° 22' W
otland	57° 0' N	° 0' W
ain	39° 0' N	4° 0' W
alding	52° 48' N	0° 9' W
arta	37° 5' N	22° 25' E
encer Gulf	34° 0' S	137° 20' E
errin Mountain	54° 50' N	7° 0' W
ey	57° 40' N	3° 6' W
orades	39° 0' N	24° 30' E
ringfield	39° 48' N	89° 39' W
urn Head	53° 35' N	0° 8' E
redinnyyRng.	57° 0' N	60° 0' E
i Lanka	7° 30' N	80° 50' E
inagar	34° 5' N	74° 50' E
affe	56° 27' N	6° 21' W
afford	52° 49' N	2° 7' W
affordshire	52° 53' N	2° 10' W
aines-upon-Thames	51° 26' N	0° 29' W
amford	52° 39' N	0° 29' W
anley	51° 40' S	59° 51' W
anovay Range	55° 0' N	30° 0' E
art Point	50° 13' N	3° 39' W
avanger	58° 57' N	5° 40' E
avropol	45° 5' N	42° 0' E
evenage	51° 55' N	0° 13' W
ewart Island	46° 58' S	67° 54' E
irling	56° 8' N	3° 57' W
ockhalm	59° 19' N	18° 4' E
ockport	53° 25' N	2° 9' W
ockton-on-Tees	54° 35' N	1° 19' W
oke-on-Trent	53° 1' N	2° 11' W
onehaven	56° 59' N	2° 12' W
onehenge	51° 9' N	1° 45' W
ornoway	58° 13' N	6° 23' W
orsjon	63° 9' N	14° 30' E
our, Dorset	50° 43' N	1° 47' W
our, Suffolk	51° 57' N	1° 4' E
ourbridge	52° 28' N	2° 8' W
owmarket	52° 12' N	1° 0' E
rabane	54° 45' N	7° 25' W
ranraer	54° 54' N	5° 1' W
trasbourg	48° 35' N	7° 42' E
traford-upon-Avon	52° 12' N	1° 42' W
trathSpey	57° 9' N	3° 49' W
trathmore	56° 37' N	3° 7' W
tromboli	38° 47' N	15° 13' E
cottish Border	55° 35' N	2° 50' W
cunthorpe	53° 36' N	0° 39' W
eaham	54° 50' N	1° 20' W
eattle	47° 36' N	122° 19' W
eine	49° 26' N	0° 26' E
ekondi-Takd.	4° 58' N	1° 45' W
elkirk.	55° 33' N	2° 50' W
ellafield	54° 25' N	3° 29' W
elsey Bill	50° 43' N	0° 47' W
elvas	6° 30' S	67° 0' W

Place	Latitude	Longitude
Semarang	7° 0' S	110° 26' E
Sendai	38° 15' N	140° 53' E
Senegal	14° 30' N	14° 30' W
Senegal	15° 48' N	16° 32' W
Senkaku Islands	25° 45' N	23° 30' E
Seoul	37° 31' N	26° 58' E
Seram	3° 10' S	29° 0' E
Serbia	43° 20' N	20° 0' E
Serengeti Plain	2° 40' S	35° 0' E
Serglpe	10° 30' S	37° 30' W
Serov	59° 29' N	60° 35' E
Sevastopol	44° 35' N	33° 30' E
Severn	51° 35' N	° 40' W
Sevvernaya Z.	79° 0' N	100° 0' E
Seville	37° 23' N	5° 58' W
Seychelles	5° 0' S	56° 0' E
Sfax	34° 49' N	10° 48' E
Shackleton I. S.	66° 0' S	00° 0' E
Shanghai	31° 15' N	21° 26' E
Shangqiu	34° 26' N	15° 36' E
Shannon	52° 35' N	9° 30' W
Shantou	23° 18' N	16° 40' E
Shaplnsay	59° 3' N	2° 51' W
Sharjah	25° 23' N	55° 26' E
Sharm el Sheikh	27° 53' N	34° 18' E
Shebele	2° 0' N	44° 0' E
Sheerness	51° 26' N	0° 47' E
Sheffield	53° 23' N	1° 28' W
Shenyang	41° 48' N	23° 27' E
Shenzhen	22° 32' N	14° 5' E
Shetland Island	60° 30' N	1° 30' W
Shihezi	44° 15' N	86° 2' E
Shijiazhuang	38° 2' N	14° 28' E
Shikoku	33° 30' N	33° 30' E
Stromeferry	57° 21' N	5° 33' W
Stronsay	59° 7' N	2° 35' W
Stroud	51° 45' N	2° 13' W
Sturt Stony Dst	28° 30' S	141° 0' E
Stuttgart	48° 48' N	9° 11' E
Sucre	19° 0' S	65° 15' W
Sudan	15° 0' N	30° 0' E
Suez	29° 58' N	32° 31' E
Suez Canal	31° 0' N	32° 20' E
Suffolk	52° 16' N	1° 0' E
Suhar	24° 20' N	56° 40' E
Suining	30° 26' N	105° 35' E
Sukhumi	43° 0' N	41° 0' E
SullomVoe	60° 27' N	1° 20' W
Sulu Archipelgo	6° 0' N	121° 0' E
Sulu Sea	8° 0' N	120° 0' E
Sumatra	0° 40' N	100° 20' E
Sumba	9° 45' S	119° 35' E
Sumbawa	8° 26' S	117° 30' E
Sumburgh Hd.	59° 52' N	1° 17' W
Sumy	50° 57' N	34° 50' E
Sunda Islands	5° 0' S	105° 0' E
Sunderland	54° 55' N	1° 23' W
Sundsvall	62° 23' N	17° 17' E
Sungari	47° 45' N	132° 30' E
Superior, Lake	47° 0' N	87° 0' W
Surabaya	7° 17' S	112° 45' E
Surat	21° 12' N	72° 55' E
Surgut	61° 14' N	73° 20' E
Suriname	4° 0' N	56° 0' W
Surrey	51° 15' N	0° 31' W
Sutherland	58° 12' N	4° 50' W
Sutton Coldfld.	52° 35' N	1° 49' W
Sutton in Ashfd.	53° 8' N	1° 16' W
Suva	18° 6' S	178° 30' E
Suzhou	31° 19' N	120° 38' E
Svalbard	78° 0' N	17° 0' E
Svealand	60° 20' N	15° 0' E
Swale	54° 5' N	1° 20' W
Swanage	50° 36' N	1° 58' W
Swansea	51° 37' N	3° 57' W
Swaziland	26° 30' S	1° 30' E
Sweden	57° 0' N	15° 0' E
Swilly, Lough	55° 12' N	7° 33' W
Swindon	51° 34' N	1° 46' W
Switzerland	46° 30' N	8° 0' E
Swords	53° 28' N	6° 13' W
Sydney	33° 52' S	151° 12' E
Syktyvkar	61° 45' N	50° 40' E
Syrdarya	46° 3' N	61° 0' E
Syria	35° 0' N	38° 0' E
Syrian Desert	32° 0' N	40° 0' E
Szczecin	53° 27' N	14° 27' E
T		
Tabriz	38° 7' N	46° 20' E
Tabuk	28° 23' N	36° 36' E

Place	Latitude	Longitude
Tacheng	46° 40' N	82° 58' E
Taff	51° 28' N	3° 11' W
Tagus	38° 40' N	9° 24' W
Tahiti	17° 37' S	49° 27' W
Taichung	24° 9' N	20° 37' E
Taimyr Peninsula	75° 0' N	00° 0' E
Tain	57° 49' N	4° 4' W
Taipei	25° 4' N	121° 29' E
Taiwan	23° 30' N	121° 0' E
Taiyuan	37° 52' N	112° 33' E
Taizhou	28° 40' N	121° 24' E
Tajikistan	38° 30' N	70° 0' E
Takamatsu	34° 20' N	34° 5' E
TaklamakanDesrt.	38° 0' N	83° 0' E
Tallahassee	30° 27' N	84° 17' W
Tallinn	59° 22' N	24° 48' E
Tamale	9° 22' N	0° 50' W
Tamar	50° 27' N	4° 15' W
Tampa	27° 56' N	82° 27' W
Tampere	61° 30' N	23° 50' E
Tampico	22° 13' N	97° 51' W
Tamworth	31° 7' S	50° 58' E
Tana, Kenya	2° 32' S	40° 31' E
Tana, Norway	70° 30' N	28° 14' E
Tana, Lake	13° 5' N	37° 30' E
Tanami, Desert	18° 50' S	32° 0' E
Tanganyika, Lake	6° 40' S	30° 0' E
Tangier	35° 50' N	5° 49' W
Tangshan	39° 38' N	18° 10' E
Tanimbar Islands	7° 30' S	131° 30' E
Tanzania	6° 0' S	34° 0' E
Tapajos	2° 24' S	54° 41' W
Taranto	40° 28' N	17° 14' E
Taranto, Gulf of	40° 8' N	17° 20' E
Taraz	42° 54' N	71° 22' E
Tarim Basin	40° 0' N	84° 0' E
Tarragona	41° 5' N	1° 17' E
Tashkent	41° 20' N	69° 10' E
Tasman Sea	36° 0' S	160° 0' E
Tasmaina	42° 0' S	146° 30' E
Taunton	51° 1' N	3° 5' W
Taurus Mountns.	37° 0' N	32° 30' E
Taw	51° 4' N	3° 5' W
Tay	56° 37' N	3° 38' W
Tay, Firth of	56° 25' N	3° 8' W
Tbilisi	41° 43' N	44° 50' E
Tees	54° 37' N	1° 10' W
Tegucigalpa	14° 5' N	87° 14' W
Tehran	35° 41' N	51° 25' E
Tehuantepec, Gulf of	15° 50' N	95° 12' W
Tehuantepec, Isthmus of	17° 15' N	94° 30' W
Teifi	52° 5' N	4° 41' W
Teign	50° 32' N	3° 32' W
Teignmouth	50° 33' N	3° 31' W
Tel Aviv-Jaffa	32° 4' N	34° 48' E
Teles Pires	7° 21' S	58° 3' W
Telford	52° 40' N	2° 27' W
Tema	5° 41' N	0° 0' W
Teme	52° 11' N	2° 13' W
Temuco	38° 45' S	72° 40' W
Tennant Creek	19° 30' S	134° 15' E
Tennessee	36° 0' N	86° 30' W
Tennessee	37° 4' N	88° 34 ' W
Teofilo Otoni	17° 50' S	41° 30' W
Tresina	5° 9' S	42° 45' W
Terni	42° 34' N	12° 37' E
Test	50° 56' N	1° 29' W
Tetouan	35° 35' N	5° 21' W
Teviot	55° 29' N	2° 38' W
Tewkesbury	51° 59' N	2° 9' W
Texas	31° 40' N	98° 30' W
Thailand	16° 0' N	102° 0' E
Thailand, Gulf of	11° 30' N	101° 0' E
Thame	51° 39' N	1° 9' W
Thames	51° 29' N	1° 9' W
Thames Estuary	51° 29' N	0° 52' E
Thar Desert	28° 0' N	72° 0' E
Thessaloniki	40° 38' N	22° 58' E
Thetford	52° 25' N	0° 45' E
Thika	1° 1' S	37° 5' E
Thimphu	27° 31' N	89° 45' E
Thirsk	54° 14' N	1° 19' W
Three Gorg. Dam	30° 45' N	111° 15' E
Thurrock	51° 31' N	0° 23' E
Thurso	58° 36' N	3° 32' W
Thurston Island	72° 0' S	100° 0' W
Tian Shan	40° 30' N	76° 0' E
Tianjin	39° 7' N	117° 12' E
Tianshui	34° 32' N	105° 40' E

Place	Latitude	Longitude
Tiber	41° 44' N	12° 14' E
Tibesti	21° 0' N	17° 30' E
Tibet	32° 0' N	88° 0' E
Tibet, Plateau of	32° 0' N	86° 0' E
Tierra del Fuego	54° 0' S	67° 45' W
Tigris	31° 0' N	47° 25' E
Tijuana	32° 32' N	117° 1' W
Timbuktu	16° 50' N	3° 0' W
Timisoara	45° 43' N	21° 15' E
Timor	9° 0' S	125° 0' E
Tipperary	52° 28' N	8° 10' W
Tirana	41° 18' N	19° 49' E
Tiree	56° 31' N	6° 55' W
Tiruchirappalli	10° 45' N	78° 45' E
Titicaca, Lake	15° 30' S	69° 30' W
Tiverton	50° 54' N	3° 29' W
Tobermory	56° 38' N	6° 5' W
Tocantins	10° 0' S	48° 0' W
Tocantins	1° 45' S	49° 10' W
Togliatti	53° 32' N	49° 24' E
Togo	8° 30' N	1° 35' E
Tokelau Islands	9° 0' S	71° 45' W
Tokyo	35° 43' N	39° 45' E
Toledo, Spain	39° 50' N	4° 2' W
Toledo, U.S.A.	41° 39' N	83° 33' W
Tombigbee	31° 8' N	87° 57' W
Tomsk	56° 30' N	85° 5' E
Tonbridge	51° 11' N	0° 17' E
Tonga	19° 50' S	74° 30' W
Tonga Trench	18° 0' S	73° 0' W
Tonkin, Gulf of	20° 0' N	08° 0' E
Toowoomba	27° 32' S	151° 56' E
Topeka	39° 3' N	95° 40' W
Torbay	50° 26' N	3° 31' W
Torfaen	51° 43' N	3° 3' W
Toronto	43° 39' N	79° 20' W
Torquay	50° 27' N	3° 32' W
Torrens, Lake	31° 0' S	137° 50' E
Torreon	25° 33' N	103° 26' W
Torres Strait	9° 50' S	142° 20' E
Torridge	51° 0' N	4° 13' W
Torridon, Loch	57° 35' N	5° 50' W
Torshavn	62° 5' N	° 56' W
Tory Island	55° 16' N	8° 14' W
Tottori	35° 30' N	134° 15' E
Toubkal, Djebel	31° 0' N	8° 0' W
Toulon	43° 10' N	5° 55' E
Toulouse	43° 37' N	1° 27' E
Tours	47° 22' N	0° 40' E
Townsville	19° 15' S	146° 45' E
Toyama	36° 40' N	137° 15' E
Trabzon	41° 0' N	39° 45' E
Tralee	52° 16' N	9° 42' W
Tramore	52° 10' N	° 10' W
Transantarctic Mountains	85° 0' S	170° 0' W
Transylvanian Alps	45° 30' N	25° 0' E
Transylv. Lake	52° 54' N	3° 55' W
Trent	53° 41' N	0° 42' W
Trento	46° 4' N	11° 8' E
Trento	40° 14' N	74° 46' W
Trenton	45° 40' N	13° 46' E
Trieste	10° 30' N	61° 20' W
Trinidad &Tob.	29° 45' N	94° 43' W
Trinity	34° 31' N	35° 50' E
Tripoli, Lebanon	32° 49' N	13° 7' E
Tripoli, Libya	37° 6' S	12° 20' W
Trista de Cunha	69° 40' N	18° 56' E
Tromso	63° 36' N	10° 25' E
Trondhelm	55° 33' N	4° 39' W
Troon	51° 18' N	2° 12' W
Trowbridge	39° 57' N	26° 12' E
Troy	48° 19' N	4° 3' E
Troyes	8° 6' S	79° 0' W
Trujillo	50° 16' N	5° 4' W
Truro	2° 59' S	38° 28' E
Tsavo	2° 59' S	38° 28' E
Tucson	32° 13' N	110° 58' W
Tula	54° 13' N	37° 38' E
Tullamore	53° 16' N	7° 31' W
Tulsa	36° 10' N	95° 55' W
Tunis	36° 50' N	10° 11' E
Tunisia	33° 30' N	9° 10' E
Tunrfan	43° 58' N	89° 10' E
Turfan Basin	42° 40' N	89° 25' E
Turin	45° 3' N	7° 40' E
Turkana, Lake	3° 30' N	36° 5' E
Turkey	39° 0' N	36° 0' E
Turkmenbashi	40° 5' N	53° 5' E
Turkmenistan	39° 0' N	59° 0' E

Turks & Caicos Is.	21° 20' N	71° 20' W
Turku	60° 30' N	22° 19' E
Turriff	57° 32' N	2° 27' W
Tuvalu	8° 0' S	78° 0' E
Tuxtla Gutierrez	16° 45' N	93° 7' W
TuzGolu	38° 42' N	33° 18' E
Tver	56° 55' N	35° 59' E
Tweed	55° 45' N	2° 0' W
Tyne	54° 59' N	1° 32' W
Tyne & Wear	55° 6' N	1° 17' W
Tynemouth	55° 1' N	1° 26' W
Tyrone	54° 38' N	7° 11' W
Tyrrhenian Sea	40° 0' N	2° 30' E
Tyumen	57° 11' N	5° 29' E
Tywi	51° 48' N	4° 21' W
U		
Uaupes	0° 2' N	67° 16' W
Uberlandia	19° 0' S	48° 20' W
Ucayali	4° 30' S	73° 30' W
Udine	46° 3' N	13° 14' E
Uganda	2° 0' N	32° 0' E
Ukhta	63° 34' N	53° 41' E
Ukraine	49° 0' N	32° 0' E
Ulan Bator	47° 55' N	06° 53' E
Ulan Ude	51° 45' N	107° 40' E
Ullapool	57° 54' N	5° 9' W
Ullswater	54° 34' N	2° 52' W
Ulm	48° 23' N	9° 58' E
Ulster	54° 35' N	6° 30' W
Uluru	25° 23' S	131° 5' E
Ulverston	54° 13' N	3° 5' W
Ulyanovsk	54° 20' N	48° 25' E
Umea	63° 45' N	20° 20' E
United Arab Emr.	23° 50' N	54° 0' E
United Kingdom	53° 0' N	2° 0' W
United States of America	37° 0' N	96° 0' W
Unst	60° 44' N	0° 53' W
Uppsala	59° 53' N	17° 38' E
Ural	47° 0' N	51° 48' E
Ural Mountains	60° 0' N	59° 0' E
Ure	54° 5' N	1° 20' W
Uramia	37° 40' N	45° 0' E
Urmia, Lake	37° 50' N	45° 30' E
Uruguaiana	29° 50' S	57° 0' W
Uruguay	32° 30' S	56° 30' W
Uruguay	34° 12' S	58° 18' W
Urumqi	43° 45' N	87° 45' E
Usk	51° 33' N	2° 58' W
Ussuri	48° 27' N	35° 0' E
Ust-Ilimsk	58° 3' N	02° 39' E
UstShchugor	64° 16' N	57° 36' E
Ustyurt Plateau	44° 0' N	55° 0' E
Utah	39° 20' N	111° 30' W
Utrecht	52° 5' N	5° 8' E
Utsunomiya	36° 30' N	139° 50' E
UvsNuur	50° 20' N	92° 30' E
Uzbekistan	41° 30' N	65° 0' E
V		
Vaasa	63° 6' N	21° 38' E
Vadodara	22° 20' N	73° 10' E
Vadso	70° 3' N	29° 50' E
Vaduz	47° 8' N	9° 31' E
Valence	44° 57' N	4° 54' E
Valencia, Spain	39° 27' N	0° 23' W
Valencia, Venz.	10° 11' N	68° 0' W
Valencia Island	51° 54' N	10° 22' W
Valladolid	41° 38' N	4° 43' W
Valledupar	10° 29' N	73° 15' W
Valletta	35° 54' N	14° 31' E
Valparaiso	33° 2' S	71° 40' W
Van	38° 30' N	43° 20' E
Van, Lake	38° 30' N	43° 0' E
Vancouver	49° 15' N	123° 7' W
Vaner, Lake	58° 47' N	13° 30' E
Vanuatu	15° 0' S	168° 0' E
Varanasi	25° 22' N	83° 0' E
Vardo	70° 23' N	31° 5' E
Varna	43° 13' N	27° 56' E
Vasteras	59° 37' N	16° 38' E
Vatican City	41° 54' N	12° 27' E
Vatter, Lake	58° 25' N	14° 30' E
Venezuela	8° 0' N	66° 0' W
Venice	45° 27' N	12° 21' E
Veracruz	19° 11' N	96° 8' W
Verkhoyansk	67° 35' N	133° 25' E
Verkhoyansk Rg.	66° 0' N	129° 0' E
Vermont	44° 0' N	73° 0' W
Verona	45° 27' N	10° 59' E
Vesteralen	68° 45' N	15° 0' E
Vesuvius, Mount	40° 49' N	14° 26' E
Vicenza	45° 33' N	11° 33' E
Victoria, Australia	37° 0' S	144° 0' E
Victoria, Canada	48° 30' N	123° 25' W
Victoria, Seychc.	4° 38' S	55° 28' E
Victoria, Lake	1° 0' S	33° 0' E
Victoria Falls	17° 58' S	25° 52' E
Victoria Island	71° 0' N	111° 0' W
Victoria Land	75° 0' S	160° 0' E
Vienna	48° 12' N	16° 22' E
Vientiane	17° 58' N	102° 36' E
Vietnam	19° 0' N	106° 0' E
Vigo	42° 12' N	8° 41' W
Villahermosa	17° 59' N	92° 55' W
Vilnius	54° 38' N	25° 19' E
Vinnitsa	49° 15' N	28° 30' E
Vinson Massif	78° 35' S	85° 25' W
Virgin Islands	18° 30' N	64° 30' W
Virginia	37° 30' N	78° 45' W
Vishakhapatnam	17° 45' N	83° 20' E
Vistula	54° 22' N	18° 55' E
Vitebsk	55° 10' N	30° 15' E
VitiLevu	17° 30' S	177° 30' E
Vitoria	20° 20' S	40° 22' W
Vitoria da Conquista	14° 51' S	40° 51' W
Vladivostok	43° 10' N	131° 53' E
Voi	3° 25' S	38° 32' E
Voiga	46° 0' N	48° 30' E
Volgograd	48° 40' N	44° 25' E
Volta	5° 46' N	0° 41' E
Volta, Lake	7° 30' N	0° 0' W
Vorkuta	67° 48' N	64° 20' E
Voronezh	51° 47' N	33° 28' E
Vyborg	60° 43' N	28° 47' E
Vyrnwy, Lake	52° 48' N	3° 31' W
W		
Wagga Wagga	35° 7' S	147° 24' E
Wakayama	34° 15' N	135° 15' E
Wakefield	53° 41' N	1° 29' W
Wales	52° 19' N	4° 43' W
Wallasey	53° 25' N	3° 2' W
Wallis & Futuna	13° 18' S	176° 10' W
Walney, Isle of	54° 6' N	3° 15' W
Walsall	52° 35' N	1° 58' W
Wanxian	30° 42' N	08° 20' E
Warrego	30° 24' S	45° 21' E
Warrenpoint	54° 6' N	6° 15' W
Warri	5° 30' N	5° 41' E
Warrington	53° 24' N	2° 35' W
Warsaaw	52° 14' N	21° 0' E
Warwick	52° 18' N	1° 35' W
Warwickshire	52° 14' N	1° 38' W
Wash, The	52° 58' N	0° 20' E
Washington,UK	54° 55' N	1° 30' W
Washinton,USA	47° 30' N	20° 30' W
Washington D.C., U.S.A.	38° 53' N	77° 2' W
Washington Mt.	44° 16' N	71° 18' W
Waterford	52° 15' N	7° 8' W
Watford	51° 40' N	0° 24' W
Waveney	52° 35' N	1° 39' E
Wear	54° 55' N	1° 23' W
Weddell Sea	72° 30' S	40° 0' W
Welland	52° 51' N	0° 5' W
Wellingborough	52° 19' N	0° 41' W
Wellington, N.Z	41° 19' S	74° 46' E
Wellington, U.K	50° 58' N	3° 13' W
Wells next sea	52° 57' N	0° 51' E
Welshpool	52° 39' N	3° 8' W
WelwynGrdCty	51° 48' N	0° 12' W
Wensleydale	54° 17' N	° 0' W
Wenzhou	28° 0' N	20° 38' E
Weser	53° 36' N	8° 28' E
West Antarctica	80° 0' S	90° 0' W
West Bank	32° 6' N	35° 13' E
West Bromwich	52° 32' N	1° 59' W
West Lothian	55° 54' N	3° 36' W
West Midlands	52° 26' N	2° 0' W
West Siberian Sea	62° 0' N	75° 0' E
West Sussex	50° 55' N	0° 30' W
West Virginia	38° 45' N	80° 30' W
West Yorkshire	53° 45' N	1° 40' W
Western Australia	25° 0' S	118° 0' E
Western Dvina	57° 4' N	24° 3' E
Wesetern Ghats	14° 0' N	75° 0' E
Western Sahara	25° 0' N	13° 0' W
Westhill	57° 9' N	2° 19' W
Westmeath	53° 33' N	7° 34' W
Weston-super-Mare	51° 21' N	2° 58' W
Westport	53° 48' N	9° 31' W
Westray	59° 18' N	3° 0' W
Wewak	3° 38' S	143° 41' E
Wexford	52° 20' N	6° 25' W
Wey	51° 22' N	0° 27' W
Weymouth	50° 37' N	2° 28' W
Whalesay	60° 22' N	0° 59' W
Wharfe	53° 51' N	1° 9' W
Wharfedale	54° 6' N	2° 1' W
Whernside	54° 14' N	2° 24' W
Whitby	54° 29' N	0° 37' W
White Nile	15° 38' N	32° 31' E
White Sea	66° 30' N	38° 0' E
White Volta	9° 10' N	1° 15' W
Whitehaven	54° 33' N	3° 25' W
Whitley Bay	55° 3' N	1° 27' W
Whitney, Mount	36° 35' N	118° 18' W
Wichita	37° 42' N	97° 20' W
Wick	58° 26' N	3° 5' W
Wicklow	52° 59' N	6° 3' W
Wicklow Mountains	52° 58' N	6° 26' W
Widness	53° 23' N	2° 46' W
Wiesbaden	50° 4' N	8° 14' E
Wigan	53° 33' N	2° 38' W
Wight, Isle of	50° 41' N	1° 17' W
Wigtown	54° 53' N	4° 27' W
Wilkes Land	69° 0' S	120° 0' E
Willemstad	12° 5' N	68° 55' W
Wiltshire	51° 18' N	1° 53' W
Winchester	51° 4' N	1° 18' W
Windermere	54° 23' N	2° 55' W
Windhoek	22° 35' S	17° 4' E
Windrush	51° 43' N	1° 24' W
Windsor	51° 29' N	0° 36' W
Windward Islands	13° 0' N	61° 0' W
Winnipeg	49° 54' N	97° 9' W
Winnipeg, Lake	52° 0' N	97° 0' W
Winsford	53° 12' N	2° 31' W
Wisbech	52° 41' N	0° 9' E
Wisconsin	44° 45' N	89° 30' W
Witham	52° 59' N	0° 2' W
Withernsea	53° 44' N	0° 1' E
Woking	51° 19' N	0° 34' W
Wokingham	51° 25' N	0° 51' W
Wollongong	34° 25' S	50° 54' E
Wolverhampton	52° 35' N	2° 7' W
Worcester	52° 11' N	2° 12' W
Workington	54° 39' N	3° 33' W
Workshop	53° 18' N	1° 7' W
Worthing	50° 49' N	0° 21' W
Wrangel Island	71° 0' N	80° 0' E
Wrath, Cape	58° 38' N	5° 1' W
Wrexham	53° 3' N	3° 0' W
Wroclaw	51° 5' N	17° 5' E
Wuhan	30° 31' N	14° 18'
Wurzburg	49° 46' N	9° 55' E
Wuwei	37° 57' N	02° 34'
Wye	51° 38' N	2° 40' W
Wyndham	15° 33' S	28° 3' E
Wyoming	43° 0' N	10° 30'
X		
Xiamen	24° 25' N	118° 4'
Xian	34° 15' N	109° 0'
Xiangfan	32° 2' N	112° 8'
Xingu	1° 30' S	51° 53'
Xining	36° 34' N	101° 40
Xuzhou	34° 18' N	117° 10
Y		
YablonovyyRng.	53° 0' N	114° 0'
Yakutsk	62° 5' N	129° 50'
Yalta	44° 30' N	34° 10'
Yamoussoukro	6° 49' N	5° 17' W
Yanbual Bahr	24° 0' N	38° 5' E
Yancheng	33° 23' N	120° 8'
Yangtse	31° 48' N	121° 10'
Yanji	42° 59' N	129° 30'
Yantai	37° 34' N	121° 22'
Yaounde	3° 50' N	11° 35' E
Yaqui	27° 37' N	110° 39'
Yare	52° 35' N	1° 38' E
Yaroslavl	57° 35' N	39° 55' E
Yazd	31° 55' N	54° 27' E
Yekateringburg	56° 50' N	60° 30' E
Yell	60° 35' N	1° 5' W
Yellow Sea	35° 0' N	123° 0' E
Yellowknife	62° 27' N	114° 29'
Yellowstone National Park	44° 40' N	110° 30'
Yemen	15° 0' N	44° 0' E
Yenisey	71° 50' N	82° 40' E
Yeovil	50° 57' N	2° 38' W
Yeraven	40° 10' N	44° 31' E
Yinchuan	38° 30' N	106° 15'
Yokkaichi	34° 55' N	136° 38'
Yokohama	35° 27' N	139° 28'
Yongzhou	26° 17' N	111° 37'
York	53° 58' N	1° 6' W
York, Cape	10° 42' S	142° 31'
Yorkshire Wolds	54° 8' N	0° 31' W
Youghal	51° 56' N	7° 52' W
Yu Shan	23° 25' N	20° 52' E
Yucatan	20° 50' N	89° 0' W
Yucatan Chanel.	22° 0' N	86° 30' W
Yukon	62° 32' N	63° 54' W
Yulin	38° 20' N	09° 30' E
Yumen	39° 50' N	97° 30' E
Yuzhno-Sakhalinsk	46° 58' N	42° 45' E
Z		
Zagreb	45° 50' N	15° 58' E
Zagros Mounts.	33° 45' N	48° 5' E
Zambezi	18° 35' S	36° 20' E
Zambia	15° 0' S	28° 0' E
Zamboanga	6° 59' N	122° 3' E
Zanjan	36° 40' N	48° 35' E
Zanzibar	6° 12' S	39° 12' E
Zaporozhye	47° 50' N	35° 10' E
Zaragoza	41° 39' N	0° 53' W
Zaria	11° 0' N	7° 40' E
Zaysan, Lake	48° 0' N	83° 0' E
Zhangjiakou	40° 48' N	114° 55'
Zhangye	38° 50' N	100° 23'
Zhaotong	27° 20' N	103° 44'
Zhengzhou	34° 45' N	113° 34'
Zhezqazghan	47° 44' N	67° 40' E
Zhitomir	50° 20' N	28° 40' E
Zibo	36° 47' N	118° 3' E
Zimbabwe	19° 0' S	30° 0' E
Zonguldak	41° 28' N	31° 50' E
Zurich	47° 22' N	8° 32' E